PENITENTIARIES
OF THE
UNITED STATES

PATTERSON SMITH REPRINT SERIES IN
CRIMINOLOGY, LAW ENFORCEMENT, AND SOCIAL PROBLEMS

A listing of publications in the SERIES *will be found at rear of volume*

PUBLICATION NO. 97: PATTERSON SMITH REPRINT SERIES IN
CRIMINOLOGY, LAW ENFORCEMENT, AND SOCIAL PROBLEMS

REPORT ON THE
PENITENTIARIES
OF THE
UNITED STATES

By
William Crawford

WITH APPENDIX, INDEX AND EIGHTEEN PLATES

Reproduced from the 1835 Edition
With a New Introduction by
NORMAN JOHNSTON

PATTERSON SMITH
Montclair, New Jersey, 1969

Originally published 1835
Copyright ©1969 by
Patterson Smith Publishing Corporation
Montclair, New Jersey

SBN 87585-097-9

Library of Congress Catalog Card Number: 69-16235

Table of Contents

INTRODUCTION   vii

REPORT   3

APPENDIX   [1]

PLATES

Introduction

IDEAS AND INSTITUTIONAL INNOVATIONS OR REFORMS as elements of social change have always had a curious way of passing from country to country, the flow now in one direction, then in another, and at times slowing or stopping and occasionally taking the most circuitous routes. In the history of the treatment of criminals, strong reform movements arose on the Continent and in England in the 18th century, inspiring North American reformers especially in the decades immediately after the American Revolution. By the 1830's European reform forces were in some confusion and turned for a coherent, working philosophy and architecture to the United States. These new ideas became the bases for most of the world's prison systems up until very recent decades. Partly due to the abilities and thoroughness of its author and partly due to the propitious timing, Crawford's report to the British government on United States prisons was destined to play an important role in the development of European prison systems.

To understand Crawford's mission and his subsequent report, it is useful to sketch very briefly the immediate background of the prison reform movements in Britain and in North America.

British Reform

Out of the social ferment of the Enlightenment and the dramatic shifts in power during the Industrial Revolution came increasing concern for the law, both in theory and in practice. Changes in the criminal law, after Beccaria, were effected here and there throughout Europe, but it was in England that the reform of the law and of penal treatment reached its greatest development.[1] Following John Howard's factual and detailed descriptions of British and European prisons and houses of correction, which appeared in successive editions of his *State of the Prisons* (first published in 1777), prison reforms finally gained a large measure of public support. Aside from the wretched physical condi-

[1] For a detailed picture of these reforms see Leon Radzinowicz, *History of English Criminal Law*. Vol. I. *The Movement for Reform: 1750-1833* (New York, 1948).

tions of these early institutions, Howard was struck by the almost complete lack of any real supervision and control over the prisoners. Although prisoners were often put in chains and severely punished for minor infractions of rules, they were also permitted to drink liquor, gamble, and remain in idleness, with males and females, adults and children often unsegregated.

Stimulated by Howard's disclosures and the loss of the American colonies as a dumping ground for convicts, Britain made several efforts to establish a national penitentiary but without success. However as more and more prisoners were sent to jails instead of being subject to execution or transportation overseas, counties and towns began building prisons in the 1780's and 1790's at a furious rate. Some larger county penitentiaries with cells were constructed in Manchester, Gloucester and elsewhere, and for a time, until they became overcrowded, were regarded as model institutions. In 1791 the first general act applying the principles of a projected national penitentiary to county institutions was passed (31 Geo. III, c. 46). The act however was too permissive to enforce the principle of separate accommodations, an arrangement felt necessary in light of the revelations of Howard and others. Although the country became involved in a war with France from 1791 until 1810, and prison reform seemed to slow almost to a halt, the ideas of the reformers survived. Sir James Mackintosh, Sir Samuel Romilly, Sir Robert Peel and others, along with the newly-formed Society for the Improvement of Prison Discipline, carried on a constant struggle. In 1822, Peel became Home Secretary and began a series of reforms, such as his establishment of a national police force, which had far-reaching effects. It was under his administration that after 1823 the idea of individual separation was abandoned in favor of classification of prisoners. For the following ten years local prisons showed steady improvement against a background of increasing attention and controversy over the exact methods which were to be used in treating the offender and arguments as to the sort of architecture which would be most appropriate.

Although a well-worked-out penal philosophy was lacking at this time in Britain, the reformers were quite clear about one matter: the absolute necessity of constant and unremitting surveillance over the prisoners by guards and officials. The evils of unsupervised association in the earlier prisons were widely understood. The assaults, riots, and general dissoluteness which characterized congregate imprisonment were regarded as the most important reasons for the failure of that imprisonment to rehabilitate the prisoners. Individual celling as a solution for the evils of the old system was seldom tried during this period, largely because of the cost and inconvenience. The alternative was thought to be careful and continual observation of the prison exercise yards, workrooms and, in some cases, living quarters of the prisoners. Constant, unseen inspection became the magic formula, the mechanism whereby the prison regimen could be freed of its old abuses, the prisoners protected from corrupting influences, and escapes, riots, and generally unruly behavior prevented. Such surveillance, coupled with a system of either separating prisoners into classes according to their characteristics, or individual celling, was generally regarded as the *sine qua non* of the good jail and prison administration. This was about the extent to which a penal philosophy had developed. The little workhouses, jails, and county prisons erected during this period reflected this preoccupation with surveillance, if nothing else, but seldom permitted even this limited goal to be carried out very efficiently.

Prison Reform in the United States

Prison reform would seem to be a luxury of a settled, economically stable country. But Britain and the Continent in the 19th century were to look to the New World for inspiration to bring new life into their stalemated prison reform movements. In some North American colonies, notably Pennsylvania, where the Quakers were active from its very founding, reform of the criminal law and the prisons came early. However it was in the decades immediately following the Revolution that the influential Quaker establishment in Philadelphia began to make great headway. Establishing the Philadelphia Society for Alleviating the Miseries of Public Prisons (later to become the Pennsylvania Prison Society), they exerted continuous pressure on county and state lawmakers, bringing about the substitution of imprisonment for the death penalty and the creation of a state penitentiary at the famous Walnut Street Jail in Philadelphia. Although physical facilities allowed little scope for experimentation, the Philadelphia reformers were evolving in the 40 years following the Revolution a coherent penal philosophy, with its roots partly in Christian ideas of redemption and earlier use of monastic imprisonment, and partly in ideas imported from the mother country.

One of the reports of the Prison Society summarized such a philosophy, which by 1820 had become almost completely agreed upon:

> It will be admitted that the great objects of punishment are to prevent the commission of crimes, and to reform the criminal. That system of punishment which secures the attainment of these objects in the highest degree will be the most beneficial to the public.
>
> Man, as a social being, derives his chief happiness from his intercourse with his fellows. He eagerly seeks for society, that he may increase his joys, and assuage his sorrows. To be totally cut off from the companions with whom he has been accustomed to associate, and to be secluded from the world, will fill the bosom of any man with dread. Therefore, he whose past life has been such as to render reflection terrible, will endeavour to avoid incurring that punishment, which not only deprives him of liberty and society, but also compels him to commune with his own heart. . . . In the solitude and silence of his room he cannot avoid reflecting on his past life, and is forced to acknowledge that his punishment is a just retribution for his past offences. His conscience is awakened — its whisperings must be heard, and he will probably be aroused to a sense of his situation. Treated with kindness by those who have the charge of him, his evil propensities will be checked and the better feelings of his nature aroused. Instructed in some useful employment, labour will be a source of gratification — habits of industry will thus supplant those of idleness. From the Scriptures and the visits of the ministers of our Holy Religion, he will be taught the value of his immortal soul, and to prepare for the judgment to come. . . . If disposed to do well his path [on release] cannot be crossed by any of his fellow prisoners; to them he is as much as unknown as if he had never entered the walls of the jail; — not having been even subjected to the gaze of visitors, few will know that he has been an inmate of a penitentiary. Should he, however, leave the jail on the expiration of his sentence, not better than when he entered it, he *cannot* be worse. He has been subjected to the influence of no contaminating examples — he has not been the pupil of the expert or daring villain.[2]

This philosophy of treatment had yet by 1820 to be put into practice on a large scale. It is true that a small structure with 16 cells known as the "Penitentiary House" had been erected in the yard of the Walnut Street Jail in Philadelphia, but it is doubtful if it was ever used for other than refractory prisoners. In 1826 a ring-shaped prison was opened as a state penitentiary near Pittsburgh. This structure had the doubtful distinction of surviving less than seven years, being torn down and rebuilt because it had proved so disastrously unworkable from the very beginning.

---

[2] Pennsylvania Prison Society, *Annual Report*, 1833, pp. 8-10.

In 1820 Pennsylvania began building the Eastern State Penitentiary, known as Cherry Hill, in the outskirts of Philadelphia. For this task there was employed a British-born architect, John Haviland, who had been familiar with the small prisons being built in England and Ireland during his apprenticeship years. Those structures tended to consist of a circular governor's house with separate prison wings radiating like wheel spokes. Haviland chose a plan consisting of a central rotunda with seven attached cell wings radiating from it. The success of the Quakers' system of solitary confinement night and day — what came to be known as the Pennsylvania System — relied more heavily than other systems upon the construction and design of the cell itself. Because the prisoner spent his entire sentence there, Haviland gave considerable attention to providing adequate light, warmth, and ventilation, and sufficient space for exercise and work. Innovations in design were made to facilitate communication among the prison staff as well as to improve their surveillance over the prisoners. This was particularly evident in his use of the central rotunda, apparently for the first time, as a sort of communications hub and nerve center for the prison. In Cherry Hill the architect succeeded in combining many technical developments and in so doing set standards of space, plumbing, and ventilation which were seldom to be equalled in prisons during the ensuing 75 years.

From the time it was opened in 1829, the Eastern Penitentiary was a famous and controversial institution. When erected it was the largest and most expensive structure of any kind in America (and the first public building in the country to make large-scale use of hot-water heating and flush toilets). Its dramatic architecture and its regimen of solitary confinement night and day became the subject of endless and bitter arguments. The structure was particularly opposed by the partisans of a penal system developed largely in New York state with the inspiration and blessings of the Boston Prison Discipline Society.

New York began to build a new state prison at Auburn in 1816, but did not start constructing cells until 1821, under the influence of Louis Dwight of the Boston Society.[3] Although New York, like a number of other states, had briefly experimented with the Pennsylvania System, there evolved under Warden Elam Lynds (as well as the Auburn architect and some of the members of the Board of Inspectors)

[3]Ralph S. Herre, "History of Auburn Prison from the Beginning to About 1867" (unpublished Ph.D. dissertation, Penna. State Univ., 1950), p. 50.

a new system which came to be known as the Auburn System. Prisoners slept in tiny solitary cells and worked in congregate shops under the rule of absolute silence during the day. Sing Sing and other prisons were soon operating under this system.

Immediately, a bitter competition developed between the two systems. In reports, speeches, legislative debates, investigations, and newspaper accounts, accusations and claims were hurled back and forth. Charges of cruelty were leveled at the Auburn System. Counter-charges of high rates of insanity and inordinate expense were aimed at the Pennsylvania System. Various state prison systems took sides, as did political opponents in Pennsylvania, Massachusetts, and New York. The controversy undoubtedly sharpened critical judgments of recidivism rates and internal administrative practices. But at the same time, the smoke screen of defensive bitterness obscured issues and delayed objective judgments, postponing for many years the abandonment of the system of solitary confinement in Pennsylvania and probably staving off modifications in the Auburn system in many states where it was strongest.

Crawford and His Report

Europeans were not unmindful of these developments, particularly considering the lack of any successful correctional theory or practice of their own at the time. In Britain under Lord Peel, the famous Gaol Act of 1823 (4 Geo. IV, c. 64) had been passed, consolidating pre-existing statutes and attempting to bring some degree of organization and uniformity to the local institutions, still under the aegis of the county justices, who were now required to make reports to the Home Office from time to time. The Act officially sanctioned the use of classification and abandoned the idea of separate confinement. But reform was slow, and the results of classification were disappointing. The British reformers continued to hear of the Quaker experiments taking place in Pennsylvania and of the modifications in this system made in the New York prisons.[4]

---

[4]Capt. Robert J. Turnbull, *A Visit to the Philadelphia Prison* (London, 1797); Capt. Basil Hall, *Travels in North America in the Years 1827 and 1828* (Edinburgh, 1829); Edward Livingston, *System of Penal Law for the U.S.A.* (Washington, 1828); James Stuart, *Three Years in North America* (Edinburgh, 1833), and many other books of the period carried accounts of these prison experiments, in addition to the reports of the American prison societies which were received in England.

In 1831 the Home Office commissioned Crawford to investigate the prisons of the United States ". . . with a view to ascertain the practicability and expediency of applying the respective systems on which they are governed, or any parts thereof, to the prisons of this country."[5] Crawford (1788-1847), a London wine merchant and philanthropist, had long been interested in social issues such as the abolition of the slave trade and reform of the penal laws. At the time he was selected by the government to make his study, he was secretary of the powerful and active London Prison Discipline Society and edited their annual reports. Not ordinary annual reports, they tended to be publications that were influential and widely regarded in Britain and North America and were known to a small group of Continental reformers as well.

Upon receiving his commission from the government, Crawford traveled extensively in the United States, visiting 14 state penitentiaries and the District of Columbia jail, as well as a number of local jails. He interviewed inmates in their cells, out of earshot of officials. He talked with prison officials and collected detailed information on prisoners' diet, disciplinary measures, vocational instruction and labor, medical care, etc., along with descriptions and plans of the prison structures themselves. In fact his *Report* contains descriptions of some of the smaller state prisons of the time which are virtually unavailable from other sources. Crawford also collected criminal codes for the various states and detailed statistics on commitments and releases. Although thoroughly skeptical of many rosy claims of successes by some state prisons, he dutifully recorded figures on recidivism. For comparative purposes he included data on English prisons, commitments and population.

Crawford's main task was to describe and evaluate the competing American systems. He found the regimen at Cherry Hill, and the Pennsylvania System, to be a superior means of effecting rehabilitation:

> I have uniformly found that the deterring influence is extremely great, and such as I believe belongs to no other system of gaol management; . . . when men are day after day thrown into the society of each other, the irksomeness of imprisonment becomes impaired and its terrors materially diminished. The Eastern Penitentiary imparts no such relief. . . . In the Eastern Penitentiary the separation from the world is certain and complete. So

[5]Crawford, *Report*, p. 3.

strict is the seclusion that I found, on conversing with the prisoners, that they were not aware of the existence of the cholera which had but a few months before prevailed in Philadelphia. . . .

Solitary imprisonment is not only an exemplary punishment but a powerful agent in the reformation of morals. It inevitably tends to arrest the progress of corruption. In the silence of the cell contamination cannot be received or imparted. A sense of degradation cannot be excited by exposure nor reformation checked by false shame. Day after day, with no companions but his thoughts, the convict is compelled to reflect and listen to the reproofs of conscience. He is led to dwell upon past errors, and to cherish whatever better feelings he may at any time have imbibed. These circumstances are in the highest degree calculated to ameliorate the affections and reclaim the heart. The mind becomes open to the best impressions and prepared for the reception of those truths and consolations which Christianity can alone impart.[6]

Addressing himself to the most serious criticism aimed at the Pennsylvania System — that it impaired both the physical and mental health of the inmates — he related that he found no such bad effects. Although he described some abortive attempts to carry out the system in other states, he was convinced that it was a workable one. When he made his final recommendations, however, Crawford admitted that the adoption of the Pennsylvania System throughout British prisons would be too costly because of the necessary construction required, and "reluctantly" concluded that the Auburn System as he observed it at Wethersfield, Connecticut, might be used for some classes of offenders. The others would be subject to solitary confinement. He was not much impressed with Auburn or Sing Sing because of the severe corporal discipline required to enforce silence there. "The whip inflicts immediate pain, but solitude inspires permanent terror."[7]

Crawford included idealized plans supplied to him by Haviland, the architect of the Eastern Penitentiary at Philadelphia and of the New Jersey prison at Trenton, which was just being constructed at the time of his visit. He commented (with questionable accuracy) that the system of solitary confinement was used in the Gloucester Penitentiary 40 years earlier, and "with some trifling difference in arrangements" the plan was the same as the Glasgow Bridewell built five years earlier. Subsequent acts of Crawford suggested that he soon became a firm partisan of both the Pennsylvania System and the architecture which became so closely associated with it.

[6]Crawford, pp. 11-12.
[7]Crawford, p. 19.

Developments Following Crawford's Report

After Crawford's return from America, the Duke of Richmond appointed a parliamentary committee to inquire into the state of the prisons, with the result that new legislation was passed (5 & 6 Will., c. 38) requiring magistrates to lay all new regulations dealing with local prisons before the Secretary of State for the Home Department and providing also for the appointment of five Prison Inspectors. Crawford, Whitworth Russell (who had been chaplain at Millbank), and Joshua Jebb (an engineer) were selected for the important Home District, which included London. It was hoped that these Inspectors, who at that time had the power only to visit prisons and make reports, would bring about a uniformity in practice and theory in the many local institutions. Uniformity was in fact accomplished with some success until these prisons were finally taken over directly by the central government in 1878. The Prison Inspectors strongly supported the philosophy of solitary confinement, and their first reports contained long, carefully-reasoned arguments for this system, as well as numerous plans for prisons of various sizes on the "separate and solitary" system.[8] Except for the smaller structures, these all took the form of either Cherry Hill or Trenton.

By 1838 plans for a contemplated "Model Prison" appeared in the voluminous Inspectors' *Report*. The following year Lord John Russell, Secretary for the Home Department, had legislation introduced into Parliament (2 & 3 Vict., c. 56) which rendered separate confinement legal and gave the central government certain powers over designs of new prisons or alterations of existing ones. The government had recently taken a skeptical attitude towards transportation, and there was a growing demand for the construction of new prisons to implement the experiments in solitary confinement. In 1842 the Model Prison was opened and two years later Reading Prison was completed and modifications and additions made at Preston. In these institutions the new system was begun, although with some opposition. As the Model Prison was at that time a depot for transports, selected first offenders were

---

[8]Great Britain, *Third Report of the Inspectors of Prisons* (1838), Part I, for example, was preceded by over 100 pages devoted to a defense of cellular isolation. The *Second Report* contained 853 pages of material of all sorts, including a number of model plans ranging all the way from a small three-wing prison for 64 to a larger prison with four wings (extremely similar to Trenton) and a six-wing radial plan for 500 prisoners.

subjected to strict cellular isolation followed by penal colony placement.

Until 1848 things seemed to go well under the Pennsylvania regimen, but then came reports of many deaths and cases of insanity, which were blamed by the partisans of the system on the poor physical condition of the prisoners. However, the opponents of the system insisted these were the natural results of unmitigated solitary confinement. Eventually, on the basis of the Penal Servitude Acts of 1853 and 1857, every British prisoner went through a first stage of rigorous cellular confinement with a plank bed, restricted diet, and labor in isolation. That was followed by a stage corresponding to an Auburn-type regimen, and in some cases a later stage of colonization of prisoners, until this practice was halted in 1853. The 18-month period initially set up for isolation was later reduced to 12 and then to nine months, and brisk walking in the open air was added.

When the Model Prison, later known as Pentonville, was opened in London in 1842, it represented in both program and architecture the outgrowth of Crawford's visit to the United States and his *Report*. It also reflected the strong preferences which Sir Joshua Jebb, Crawford's fellow inspector, felt for both the Pennsylvania System and the architectural plans as exemplified in the Philadelphia and Trenton prisons. Pentonville was built upon the Trenton plan, with some modifications made by Jebb after considerable experimentation and study.[9] It was destined to become the most copied prison in the world. In 1842 the King of Prussia, Frederick William IV, paid a visit to the Model Prison with his architect Busse. He was followed shortly by the King of Saxony, Grand Duke Michael of Russia, Prince Alexander of the Netherlands, and commissioners from the governments of France, Prussia, Austria, Holland, Denmark, Sweden, and lesser principalities and states. In each of these countries model prisons were eventually erected, largely patterned after Pentonville. They in turn became the prototypes for further prison building within their countries. Some nations, like Belgium and the Prussian states, virtually rebuilt their entire prison systems along such lines within a few years. In England itself, under the aegis of Jebb and the Prison Inspectors, local prisons were built at a rapid rate in the decade following the opening of the Model Prison.

---

[9]Haviland, the architect, once described Trenton as his prison "most worthy of copying" in a letter written to the French commissioners, Frédéric Demetz and G. Abel Blouet (*Haviland Papers*, Journal No. 3).

When prison construction in England, Scotland, and Ireland stopped around the turn of the century, with two or three notable exceptions all structures above the very smallest were either built, rebuilt or modified to conform to layout principles and cellblock and cell standards established in Pentonville.

Estimates of the actual number of prisons and total cell accommodations in those institutions following the Pentonville design vary considerably.[10] An idea of the pace at which construction proceeded during this period can be drawn, however, from the statement of one of the early chairmen of the Prison Commissioners that within six years after Pentonville was erected, 54 new prisons with a total of 11,000 cells were constructed following its general design.[11] (The majority of these were small by American standards.)

In addition to prisons influenced by the treatment regimen and architecture of Pentonville in Britain and the Continent, colonial systems in India, Egypt, Australia, New Zealand, Canada, and other parts of the world were similarly affected.

Although Crawford's *Report* was not the only source of information for European reformers concerning the new American experiments,[12] its contribution to the shaping of the Model Prison of Pentonville and its importance in its own right make it a work of particular significance to the worldwide transformation of prison systems that took place during the remainder of the nineteenth century.

— NORMAN JOHNSTON

University of Missouri — St. Louis
April, 1969

[10]Great Britain, Colonial Office, *Prison Discipline in the Colonies: Digest and Summary of Information Respecting Prisons in the Colonies* (1867), p. 65, sets the number of prisons modeled after Pentonville in Britain at 145, with over 24,000 cells. The *Second Report of the Surveyor-General of Prisons* (1847), appendix F, gives a list of the prisons which had been erected on this plan "in the last few years," and with the number of cells for each. There were 40 prisons at that early period, with a total of 5,500 cells, and another 22 prisons with an additional 7,000 cells in process of construction.

[11]Edmund F. DuCane, *The Punishment and Prevention of Crime* (London, 1885), p. 56.

[12]See for example Fréderic Demetz & G. Abel Blouet, *Rapports sur les pénitenciers des Etats-Unis* (Paris, 1837); Gustave de Beaumont & Alexis de Tocqueville, *Du système pénitentiaire aux Etats-Unis et son application en France* (Paris, 1833); Nicolaus Heinrich Julius, *Nordamerikas sittliche Zustände. Nach eigenen Anschauungen in den Jahren 1834-1836* (Leipzig, 1839); Oscar I of Sweden, *Om straff och straff-anstalter* (Stockholm, 1840); Mariano Paz Soldán, *Examen de las penitenciarias de los Estados Unidos* (New York, 1853); and Edouard Ducpétiaux, *Des progrés de l'état actuel de la reforme pénitentiaire* (Brussels, 1838).

REPORT

OF

WILLIAM CRAWFORD, Esq.,

ON THE

Penitentiaries of the United States,

ADDRESSED TO

HIS MAJESTY'S PRINCIPAL SECRETARY OF STATE FOR
THE HOME DEPARTMENT.

Presented by His MAJESTY'S COMMAND.

Ordered to be printed 13th March 1835.

(21.)

R E P O R T.

TO LORD VISCOUNT DUNCANNON,

HIS MAJESTY'S PRINCIPAL SECRETARY OF STATE FOR THE HOME DEPARTMENT.

MY LORD,   London, 1st August 1834.

IN obedience to the directions which I received from the Viscount Melbourne, I have visited and inspected the several Penitentiaries of the United States, with a view to ascertain the practicability and expediency of applying the respective systems on which they are governed, or any parts thereof, to the prisons of this country; and I now proceed respectfully to lay before your Lordship the result of my inquiries.

In the United States there are three distinct descriptions of prisons : first, the County Gaols, for the confinement of persons before trial, and of convicts whose sentences do not exceed one, and in some States two years imprisonment. These prisons are under the care of the sheriffs and magistrates of the respective districts. Secondly, the Town Gaols, appropriated to the same descriptions of prisoners committed within local jurisdictions, and subjected to the municipal authorities. Thirdly, the prisons erected at the expense of the State for the confinement of criminals convicted of the higher classes of offences, who are sentenced to various periods, in some cases for life, and in none for less than one year. The latter are indifferently denominated Penitentiaries or State Prisons. They are under the immediate control of a certain number of Inspectors, who are generally paid for their services, and are appointed by, and removable at the pleasure of, the Legislature or Governor of the State. Although the examination of the State Prisons was the main object of my visit to America, I have frequently availed myself of the opportunities which I possessed of inspecting the County and Town gaols. As, however, the exposure of bad prisons formed no part of my mission, I very willingly pass over any lengthened description of these places of confinement. The Americans have, generally speaking, no prisons analogous to the houses of correction in England: hence the county gaols throughout the States contain convicts guilty of the minor crimes of every shade and description. These persons are indiscriminately confined with prisoners of all classes awaiting their trial, of whom a portion may be entirely innocent of the offences with which they are charged, and who are thus subjected, frequently for months, to all the evils which result from idleness and corrupt association. I have visited many miserable places of confinement, but seldom, if ever, witnessed such a combination of wretchedness and depravity as is to be found in some of the county gaols and town prisons of the United States.

Of the twenty-four States which compose the Union, the following have Penitentiaries :

Pennsylvania.	Vermont.	Tennessee.
New York.	Maine.	Ohio.
New Jersey.	Maryland.	Indiana.
Connecticut.	District of Columbia.	Georgia.
Massachusetts.	Virginia.	Illinois.
New Hampshire.	Kentucky.	

I have inspected the whole of these penitentiaries, excepting those of Georgia and Illinois. The penitentiary of the former State, which was some time ago abolished, had been re-established so recently as to afford no inducement to visit it;

and

and I ascertained that at the state prison of the latter there was not a single person in confinement*.

For an Abstract of the principal penal laws of these States, I beg to refer your Lordship to the Appendix to this Report. The offences which, from their general notoriety or frequent occurrence, or from the nature of the penalty attached to their commission, demand the greatest attention, are therein enumerated, with their respective punishments. Amidst a variety of statutes, interfering often one with another, and not always very explicit in themselves, the precision of a legal detail for professional use is not to be expected ; but having examined most of the penal laws, and consulted digests and other more popular works, as well as competent indivi- duals on the spot, I feel confident that the Abstract in the Appendix will be found sufficiently accurate to convey a correct idea of the practical character of the respective criminal codes throughout the penitentiary States. The common law of England is still in force in the United States, except where altered by statute. In Rhode Island the charter of Charles II. still supplies the place of the Constitutions adopted in most of the other States. Disputed points of law are explained and decided by constant reference to the authority of English text-books, and the Reports of deci- sions in the English Courts. The rules of evidence, and the definition of most of the principal crimes, are generally similar to those received in the parent country. A distinction in cases of murder, by recognising different degrees of that crime, prevails in several States. The Pennsylvanian law of 1794, after reciting that the several offences which are included under the general denomination of murder differ so greatly from each other in their atrocity that it is unjust to involve them in the same punishment, enacts, "That all murder which shall be perpetrated by means of poison, or by lying in wait, or by any other kind of wilful, deliberate and premeditated killing, or which shall be committed in the perpetration, or attempt to perpetrate, any arson, rape, robbery or burglary, shall be deemed murder of the first degree ; and all other kinds of murder shall be deemed murder of the second degree." And this is the usual distinction, although slightly varied in different States ; but every State which recognises degrees seems to require, in order to constitute murder in the first degree, either the most deliberate malice, or that it should take place in the commission of a felony, or more frequently one of the principal felonies mentioned in the Pennsylvanian law. The recognition of differ- ent degrees of the same crime is, in some States, extended to several offences, especially where the criminal law has been most systematically arranged, as in New York; but it is somewhat remarkable that in this State there are no degrees of murder. The same effect, however, results from the different degrees of man- slaughter, some of the highest of which comprehend cases which would, by the law of England, amount to murder. The advantages of such an arrangement, inde- pendently of superior system and method, consist in pointing out to the public mind how the same act becomes more dangerous to society, and therefore more highly criminal, according to attendant circumstances ; and also, in many cases, in securing the infliction of a greater penalty for an aggravated offence. To take, for example, the crime of arson in New York : To set fire to an empty house by day is the fourth or lowest degree of arson, and the penalty is imprisonment from two to seven years. If the same should be done by night, it becomes arson of the third degree, and seven years is the shortest term for which the prisoner can be sentenced, and this may be extended to ten years. If the house be not empty, the crime, although committed by day, would be arson of the second degree, and punished with imprisonment for not less than ten years ; and if the offence were committed by night, it would amount to the highest degree of arson, the penalty for which is death. In a similar way the law generally regards the crimes of burglary and robbery as aggravated by the offender being armed, or by the use of violence. In the case of manslaughter, even where degrees are not generally observed, a distinction is fre- quently taken in favour of involuntary manslaughter, committed in doing some un- lawful act, which would not render the offender guilty of murder. The effect of this discrimination is to leave less to the discretion of the court or jury (as the case may be, according to the law of the State,) than must necessarily be done where the
same

same nominal offence comprises every degree of guilt; and so to give less occasion to the greater criminal to calculate upon a lenient punishment. In most of the States a place is assigned in the criminal law for those offences against the morals of society which, in this country, are only liable to the censures of a spiritual court, or form the subject of a civil action.

The criminal law is administered by justices of the peace, circuit judges, and the superior courts. The jurisdiction of justices is confined chiefly to the arresting and taking bail of the accused; the summoning and hearing of witnesses; and securing their subsequent attendance at the time of trial. They receive their appointments in various ways. In several of the States they are elected by the governors, in some cases by the legislature, and in others by the people. The recent alterations which have been made in the mode of appointment have been uniformly in favour of the more popular form of election. There is generally in each county, as in Scotland, a public officer who, in ordinary cases, prefers indictments, and conducts the trial throughout. This, although it will not by any means secure a prosecution wherever it may be required, must certainly render the administration of criminal justice more certain, by diminishing the number of offences which may be committed with impunity from the unwillingness of parties to prosecute. If, indeed, on the commission of an offence, the sufferer determine, from the first, to abstain from proceeding, no prosecution will, in the majority of such cases, be instituted; but if, either irritated by his loss, or impelled by a sense of public duty, he take any step in the affair, the interests of justice cannot easily be defeated by his subsequent conduct. The matter being then in the hands of the public prosecutor, the injured party is merely a witness, and if his testimony be material it is secured; but he is at the same time relieved from all care and consideration as to the manner of conducting the prosecution, the expense attendant upon it, and the means and probability of being reimbursed. The province of the jury is, in some States, of much the same extent as in England, except that they appear less controlled by the judge, even in matters of law; whilst in other States, besides deciding absolutely on the guilt or innocence, of the accused, they determine his punishment if guilty, fixing the amount of the fine, the duration of the imprisonment, and even the number of lashes to be inflicted. How completely uniformity of punishment, one of the most powerful means of rendering it effective, is thus lost sight of, it is needless to observe. Experience shows how difficult it is to preserve an uniform course of punishment wherever the legislature has afforded any latitude for discretion, although this discretion be exercised by men of similar education, habits, studies and employments. But where none of these points of similarity exist in the various tribunals, any approach to uniformity of punishment must be impracticable. The course of legislation in the United States does not at present appear likely to remedy this evil. On the contrary, by a law passed in 1831, the discretionary power in the State of Missouri, which before that time had been exercised by the court, was transferred to the jury. There prevails throughout the penitentiary States a strong feeling in favour of the justice and policy of moderate punishments; but there is a great diversity of opinion as to the extent to which that feeling should be carried. With so many independent legislatures, there is, as might be expected, a wide difference in the degree of punishment awarded to the several crimes. In most of the States, treason, murder and rape, are visited with the extreme vengeance of the law; but in several, capital punishments are extended to arson, burglary with arms, and robbery with violence *. In New Jersey, the crimes of treason, murder, and a second conviction of manslaughter, sodomy, rape, arson, burglary, robbery and forgery, are punished with death. A new code, however, was drawn up for the approval of the legislature, in pursuance of a resolution of the Council and General Assembly passed in February 1833, which, when it becomes law, will deserve the highest rank amongst the criminal statutes of the country. It seems principally framed upon the existing laws, and those of New York, the most systematic and best arranged of any in the United States. Being intended, however, for execution in the new penitentiary, the code partakes also of the Pennsylvanian character, and like the

---

* The legislature of Rhode Island retains the penalty of death for seven offences; and although the laws of this State were revised in 1822, mutilation and other severe and ignominious punishments were retained. Forgery is visited with all or any of the following punishments: pillory, where the offender is cropped by having a piece of each of his ears cut off; being branded with a letter C; imprisoned for a term not exceeding six years; or fined a sum not exceeding 4,000 dollars.

the laws of that State abolishes the punishment of death in every case but that of murder*.   In imitation of the practice which already exists in Pennsylvania, the execution of convicts is not in future to take place in public, but only in the presence of certain official persons†.   In Massachusetts the crime of passing counterfeit notes is generally punished by three years' imprisonment, with hard labour, and a fine of 1,000 dollars.   In Connecticut the term of imprisonment is the same, but there is no fine.   In New York and New Hampshire the utmost penalty for the first offence is extended to five, and in Pennsylvania to seven years' imprisonment.   In Maryland this crime is punished by imprisonment from five to ten years ; and in Virginia for a period of not less than ten, nor more than twenty years.   In Kentucky it varies from two to six, and in Ohio from three to twenty years.   But so fully understood is the inefficiency of capital punishment for the mere purpose of protecting property, that in none of the penitentiary States (whatever may be the general character of the laws) is the first offence of forgery, when committed by a free person, punishable by death; although from the nature of the circulating medium, the crime of forging bank notes offers peculiar temptation ; and in but one State (New Jersey, as the law now stands,) is the second conviction of this offence so punished.   In cases where the protection of the law is peculiarly needed, it has been best afforded, not by attempts to crush the offence itself by means of excessive rigour, but by extending prohibition and punishment to all its connexions, and by endeavouring to restrain those acts which facilitate its commission ; accordingly, the penalties of the law reach not only the possessors of forged notes, but all those who shall without authority possess, make, mend, or in any way furnish the paper or apparatus for such forgery.   Besides the ordinary punishments, there is frequently an additional penalty imposed, not only for a repetition of the same crime, but also for committing any offence punished by penitentiary confinement after having been previously convicted of it.   In New York provision is made for the several cases of second offences, varying according as the first or second, or both, may have been felonies or misdemeanors.

The most striking character, however, respecting the laws of the United States, especially to those familiar only with the circumstances and situation of criminals in Great Britain, is the desire shown for making reparation, not only to the State, by payment of a fine, but also to the party injured in cases affecting his property.   In some States, in New York and Tennessee, for instance, the party injured may have execution against the convict for the amount of his loss, when capable of being estimated by damages, which is done by the jury who try the offender.   In others, as Virginia and Missouri, restoration of the property stolen, or its value, forms part of the sentence.   This practice obtains very generally in the cases of stealing slaves or horses ; and in these instances, where restitution is not made, the sum to be paid is usually double or treble the value of the slave or horse.   In Rhode Island, in the case of larceny, the owner is to receive full value as well as his property.   In Connecticut, part of the punishment for forgery committed on a private person is a fine of double the amount of the damage sustained, to be paid to the injured party.   The convict is generally made liable to the State for the costs of his own prosecution ; but his property, if more than sufficient for this purpose, is not forfeited : indeed, the law in some instances specially provides for the administration of the estates of convicts during their imprisonment.   That the fullest reparation should be made by the offender to the injured party is in the
highest

* The county of Middlesex contains a larger amount of population than the whole State of Pennsylvania, and is settled in the comparatively contracted space of 280 square miles, immense numbers being congregated together, under circumstances the most favourable to the commission of crime ; and yet, although several offences are capital by the law of England, not a single execution has taken place in London and Middlesex during the twelve months in which the present sheriffs (now about to retire) have filled the office.   During the same period one execution has occurred in Pennsylvania, where murder alone is capital, and the population, chiefly agricultural, is scattered over a surface of 46,000 square miles, and in a situation in which there exist no peculiar inducements to violate the law.   By the census of 1830, the population of Pennsylvania amounted to 1,348,233 souls ; that of London and Middlesex was, by the census of 1831, 1,358,541.   To this is to be added the number of inhabitants in those parts of the metropolis and its suburbs which are beyond the jurisdiction of the sheriffs, and south of the Thames, (from among whom no execution has taken place during this period;) and the whole population may be estimated at considerably above a million and a half.   The fact of there not having occurred a single execution within twelve months, in a population so remarkable for its character and extent, is perhaps unparalleled in the history of society.
† *Vide* Appendix, " Pennsylvania."

highest degree desirable, if it can be effected without, on the one hand, excluding a material, or, on the other, admitting an interested witness. But the principal object of such punishments, viz. the increased certainty of their infliction, in consequence of the additional inducement to prosecute, would not be much promoted in a community where the pecuniary circumstances of the criminals must, in the great majority of cases, render this part of the law little else than nominal. To secure the costs and fines where the prisoner has no property, laws have in some States been passed, authorizing the court to transfer the convict to any party as a hired servant for a certain time, or to make him work out the amount in prison, by allowing him a certain sum per diem for his labour. In others he may be detained for costs, or liberated upon giving his note of hand, or continue liable to be apprehended in future should he obtain the means of payment.

But whatever may be the character of the criminal codes or the discipline of the prisons, there exists a power which is constantly at work to impair the efficiency of the law, and undermine the best effects of punishment. The evil to which I advert is the frequent exercise of the privilege of pardon; a power only to be used for the purpose of preventing the law from being carried into effect, contrary to its true spirit, but never to restrain or counteract its obvious operations. Circumstances may arise calculated to excite considerable doubt of the guilt of a party, if not to disprove it altogether. An offence may occur, the punishment of which, according to the letter of the law, would be wholly repugnant to its spirit, arising either from oversight in the legislature, or the peculiar circumstances of the case. In such instances the power of pardoning is required for the protection of innocence, either absolute or comparative; but in all others the remission of punishment by pardon cannot fail to act as a direct incentive to crime. Whenever an offender hears of a pardon being granted for any delinquency which bears but a distant resemblance to his own, although in fifty other such cases the full punishment may be carried into effect, he immediately regards the circumstance not merely as another added to the many chances of escape on which he has relied, but as that resource which, on the failure of all others, will extricate him from his difficulties. He sees no reason why he should be less fortunate than his associate. It is true, that the same principle of calculation ought to be applied to each of the fifty cases in which the punishment is carried into effect; but that this is not the manner in which criminals are prone to reckon is obvious from the history of mankind. All men estimate too highly the chances in their favour, and this propensity is greatly increased by a life of hazard and danger. That offences may be committed with impunity is with the criminal a favourite theory, and he eagerly seizes and applies to himself every instance that can tend to support it. But if one pardon in fifty operates thus injuriously, what must inevitably be the effect when the proportion amounts to one in four? This has been the average rate of pardons in the State of New York during the last ten years. The present rate, however, though quite sufficient to be highly prejudicial, falls far short of the above proportion. A sense of the evils attending the system is now gaining ground, but the obstacles to its abolition are very great. In each State the power of pardon is vested in the governor. Although he may be induced by a sense of duty to resist feelings of private compassion, the importunities of the convict's friends, or the influence of immediate connexions, yet when vast numbers of his constituency, to whom alone he is responsible, from whom he holds his authority, and to whom he looks for its renewal, concur in supporting any of those specious claims to leniency which few cases fail altogether to possess; when petitions are presented numerously signed, and apparently in the cause of mercy, a governor will rarely be found of sufficient firmness to resist the importunity. Should the first application fail, the convict's friends have only to renew their endeavours: perseverance will obtain an increased number of petitioners. The expiration of a part of the term of imprisonment renders the object more easily attainable; while a good account of the prisoner's conduct during confinement, which, with such expectations, he will take care to procure, will be used to prove him the more deserving. Thus each repetition of efforts in favour of pardon is made with additional advantage, and the only limit to these applications is, the duration of the imprisonment. The longer, therefore, the term for which the convict is sentenced, and consequently the more aggravated his crime, the greater are the probabilities of his obtaining a pardon. It is accordingly found, that of twenty-seven prisoners pardoned at Auburn in one year (1831) eight had been sentenced for life, two for ten years and upwards, four for seven, six for five, three for four, and one for two years; so that of the twenty-seven pardoned, seventeen, or nearly two-thirds had been sentenced to seven years or upwards; while those sentenced to less than five years amounted to but little more than one-seventh.

The merit of having been the foremost of the States to mitigate the severity of the criminal law belongs to Pennsylvania. This important subject interested the legislature so early as in the year 1786, when the penalty of death was abolished the crimes of robbery, burglary and the offences against nature. The punishments for substituted were, however, of a most defective character, and consisted of hard labour, publicly and disgracefully imposed. Ignominy was added to other penalties. The heads of the convicts were shaved. They were distinguished by a peculiar dress, and secured by iron chains and collars. Thus shackled, they were turned into the streets of Philadelphia, where they are described to have conducted themselves so riotously as to render it dangerous for the public to approach them. At night they returned to their prison, where all descriptions of the male convicts were herded together. It was principally owing to the exertions of a highly meritorious society*, formed about this period in Philadelphia, that in 1790 the law for the public employment of convicts was repealed. In the course of that year the gaol in Walnut-street, which had hitherto been used for the confinement of prisoners of war, was appropriated to criminals. The sexes were separated, and the convicts were employed in various occupations. The preamble to the Act for the regulation of this prison attributes the failure of the previous laws for the government of the criminals to the want of restraint within their places of confinement; and a hope is expressed, " that the addition of unremitted solitude to laborious employment, as far as it can be effected, will contribute as much to reform as to deter." To carry this object into effect, sixteen separate cells for male, and fourteen for female convicts, were added to the building. The erection of these cells, and the introduction of trades, excited, shortly afterwards, considerable attention. Visitors, struck by the manufacturing character of the establishment, and the apparent industry of its inmates, hastily assumed that the ends of punishment were at once accomplished; and the Walnut-street prison, great as were its defects, was pronounced to be a model for general imitation. This impression derived strength from the circumstance that shortly after these arrangements had been made, the number of commitments became lessened; a fact which was unhesitatingly ascribed to the discipline of the gaol. But what was the nature of that discipline? In the main body of the prison criminals of every shade of guilt were associated; nor could conversation be restrained while they were at work. The newly erected cells, from which it has been inferred that solitary confinement was enforced, were only six feet by eight, and eight feet high; they were badly ventilated, and so defectively arranged that the convicts in the adjoining cells could communicate with ease. There was no seclusion; and I have been assured, by those who have carefully investigated the subject, that neither labour nor employment of any kind was performed in those cells. They were appropriated to the punishment of the refractory only; a statement which is confirmed by the fact of there being in the floor of each cell an iron staple, to which are attached three short chains, for the secure confinement of as many convicts; and there is no reason to believe that this penitentiary was, at any period of its history, less deserving the censures which its own friends have of late unsparingly bestowed upon it. The progressive advance of population in the State was attended with an increase of crime. The district from which convicts were liable to be committed to the penitentiary was extended, until at length it became so over-crowded that the free use of the pardoning power was indispensable, in order to make room for new commitments. In fact, until the erection of the Eastern Penitentiary, in 1829, nearly forty years after the appropriation of the Walnut-street prison, the state of Pennsylvania could not be said to possess a single place of confinement which had the most ordinary pretensions to excellence. That there was a diminution of crime in Philadelphia in the three years immediately following the appropriation of the Walnut-street penitentiary, cannot be denied; but this circumstance may be more correctly ascribed to other causes than to the effect of imprisonment. During the period in question
the

* " The Society for alleviating the Miseries of Public Prisons." The pious and venerable Bishop White, who has long presided over the Episcopalian Church of the United States, was the first chairman of this society; a station which he continues to adorn, although approaching his ninetieth year, with that judgment and benevolence which have rendered his honourable life eminently serviceable to the cause of religion and virtue.

the country had become comparatively settled, and numbers who had for some time after the close of the war been thrown upon the public had found industrious occupations in distant States. The abolition of the degrading practice of employing criminals in the public streets must also have had a sensible effect in improving the morals of the community if the following testimony of a most respectable eyewitness be not greatly overcharged. " The directions of the law of 1786," says an able writer of that day, " were soon found to be productive of the greatest evils, and had a very opposite effect from what was contemplated by the framers of the law. The disorders in society, the robberies, burglaries, breaches of prison, alarms in town and country, the drunkenness, profanity and indecencies of the prisoners in the streets, must be in the memory of most. With these disorders the number of the criminals increased to such a degree as to alarm the community with fears that it would be impossible to find a place either large or strong enough to hold them. The severity of the law and the disgraceful manner of executing it led to a proportionate degree of depravity and insensibility, and every spark of morality appeared to be destroyed. The old and hardened offender was daily in the practice of begging, and insulting the inhabitants, collecting crowds of idle boys, and holding with them the most indecent and improper conversation. Thus disgracefully treated, and heated with liquor, the prisoners meditated and executed plans of escape; and when at liberty, their distress, disgrace, and fears, prompted them to violent acts to satisfy the immediate demands of nature. Their attacks upon society were well known to be desperate, and to some they proved fatal."*

In the year 1818 the legislature of Pennsylvania resolved on the establishment of a penitentiary at Pittsburg for the western division of the State †. It was intended to enforce at this prison solitary confinement without labour; but the building, on its completion, was found to be so ill calculated for that object that the design could not be executed. The convicts were it is true confined in separate cells; but they could and did freely communicate with each other. These facilities for corrupt intercourse were greatly promoted by the idleness to which they were subjected. The mischievous effects of this penitentiary became at length so obvious that the legislature, in 1832, resolved on its re-construction on such a plan as would ensure strict solitude during the hours of labour, as well as at night ‡. This new prison is just completed. Undismayed by the failure of their efforts at Pittsburg the legislature determined in 1821 on the erection of another penitentiary in Philadelphia for the eastern division of the State. The progress of this building was, however, for some time arrested by a difference of opinion which prevailed respecting the nature of the discipline to be enforced. A highly respectable party who had deeply interested themselves in the erection of the penitentiary warmly advocated the infliction of solitary imprisonment without labour. Inquiry was deemed necessary and commissioners were appointed to visit other gaols and report on the most eligible plan. These gentlemen recommended that the convicts should be employed in association during the day, and be confined apart at night. Opinions so opposite demanding still further consideration, the legislature determined upon the

---

* Vide " Account of the Alteration and Present State of the Penal Laws of Pennsylvania," by Caleb Lowndes. Philadelphia, 1793.

† Vide Plans, Appendix, " Pennsylvania."

‡ On reference to the two Plans of the penitentiary at Pittsburg, inserted in the Appendix, the inferiority of the *circular* compared with the *radiating* form is strikingly demonstrated. Defects, arising out of the circular plan, are also to be found in several gaols which have of late years been erected in England and Ireland. There are no means of constant inspection, nor facilities of access to the prisoners; the cell-buildings being placed at a considerable distance from the station occupied by the keeper and officers, the power of secretly inspecting the convicts is thereby precluded, as the officers cannot approach the cells without being exposed to the view of the prisoners in crossing the intervening courts, &c.: but in the radiating plan the whole of the interior may be viewed from the central observatory from which the officers can also visit the cells without passing out of the building or being seen by the prisoners. In the circular plan, the cell-doors being placed externally, facility is afforded for communication between the convicts, and they can even hear each other by sounds or noises through the middle wall. The buildings being placed round the circumference, and the cells back to back, the interior is rendered much less airy and salubrious than when each cell can be properly ventilated, as in the radiating plan. The circular building is also less secure as it conceals the boundary-walls from the view of the officers, and thus forms a screen to assist the prisoner in his escape should he succeed in breaking out of his cell; but in the radiating plan the buildings present but a small obstruction to the view from the centre. The converging form of the corridors facilitates the conveyance of sounds to the centre and thereby adds to the general security. Great convenience is likewise found to arise from the central position of the offices and store-rooms, as the daily provisions, materials for work, &c., can be distributed with order and despatch.

the middle course of solitude by day and night, accompanied by labour. The Eastern Penitentiary was accordingly proceeded with; and a part being completed prisoners were admitted into it in July 1829*.

This penitentiary is situated about a mile from the city of Philadelphia. The site occupies about twelve acres. It is built of stone and surrounded by a wall thirty feet in height. Every room is vaulted and fire-proof. At each angle of the boundary wall is a tower for the purpose of overlooking the establishment. In the centre is a circular building, or observatory, from which several corridors radiate : they are under complete inspection. The cells are ranged on each side of the corridors in the wall of which is a small aperture and iron door to each cell : through this aperture the meals of the prisoner are handed to him without his seeing the officer, and he may at all times be thus inspected without his knowledge. Other openings are provided for the purposes of ventilation and warmth. A privy is constructed in each cell in such a manner as to preserve the purity of the atmosphere, and prevent the possibility of communication from cell to cell. Heated air is conducted by flues from stoves under the corridors. In the arched ceiling of each cell is a window for the admission of light. The cells are eleven feet nine inches long, seven feet six inches wide, and sixteen feet high to the top of the arched ceiling. The cells on the ground floor have double doors leading into a yard, eighteen feet by eight feet, in which the convict is allowed to take exercise for an hour daily. The walls of the yard are eleven feet high. Prisoners are not allowed to walk at the same time in adjoining yards; and when in the yards are inspected by a watchman placed for that purpose in the tower of the observatory. At present but three corridors are completed : the others which are now erecting differ in some of their arrangements from those originally built. The new cells below, as well as in the upper floor, have doors opening into the corridors. These cells vary also in their dimensions being three feet longer than the others. The prisoners in the upper cells are not allowed to go at any time into the open air. This rule had been only seven months in operation at the period of my visit. No inconvenience had at that time been found to result from the arrangement. On the admission of a convict he is taken into an office at the entrance of the penitentiary and subjected to the usual course of examination. His person is cleansed and he is clothed in an uniform. He is then blindfolded and conducted to his cell. On his way thither he is for a short time detained in the observatory where he is admonished by the warden as to the necessity of implicit obedience to the regulations. On arriving in his cell the hood is removed, and he is left alone. There he may remain for years, perhaps for life, without seeing any human being but the inspectors, the warden and his officers, and perhaps occasionally one of the official visitors of the prison. For the first day or two the convict is not allowed to have even a Bible, nor is any employment given to him for at least a week, a period during which he is the object of the warden's special observation. The prisoner soon petitions for an occupation. It is not, however, until solitude appears to have effectually subdued him that employment of any kind is introduced into his cell. Under such circumstances labour is regarded as a great alleviation; and such is the industry manifested that with few exceptions has it been necessary to assign tasks†. Several salutary provisions are made by the legislature against the abuse of the power vested in the warden and his officers. The inspectors are required to visit the prison at least twice in the week, and on those occasions to speak to each prisoner and to listen to any complaint that may be made of

oppression

---

* In the Appendix will be found an enlarged description, together with a plan and elevation of this penitentiary, with a section of the cells. The buildings are on the radiating plan. With the exception of this prison, the penitentiary at Pittsburg (as reconstructed), and that at New Jersey (now 'erecting), the state prisons in America are designed on the quadrangular form, the buildings being placed at right angles or in parallel ranges. Such as have not been recently erected are mostly enlarged, with cells on the Auburn plan. The dormitories are small, and in consequence of being placed back to back, or in double rows, appear very defective in light and ventilation. The radiating plan has been long adopted in the construction of the best prisons in England. It was first introduced about the year 1790, in the borough gaol at Liverpool, and afterwards at Bury gaol. About thirty prisons have since that period been built in England, and about half that number in Scotland and Ireland, on a similar principle, but with considerable improvements, in order to secure the means of general inspection into the day-rooms, airing-courts, &c.

† The first prisoner, a negro lad of twenty, who had been brought up on a farm, made a shoe on the fourth day after the commencement of his instruction. The shoe passed with others, and was paid for by the contractor. Second Report of Inspectors, p. 11.

oppression or misconduct. Neither the warden nor any of his assistants are to be present at these interviews, unless their attendance be desired. The physician is required to visit the infirmary daily, and to attend at the penitentiary twice in every week for the purpose of inquiring into the mental as well as bodily state of every prisoner. The official visitors appointed by the legislature are the governor of the State, the speaker and members of the Senate, the speaker and members of the House of Representatives, the secretary of the State, the judges of the Supreme Court, the attorney-general and his deputies, the president and associate judges of all the courts in the State, the mayor and recorder of the cities of Philadelphia, Lancaster and Pittsburg, the commissioners and sheriffs of the several counties, and the acting committee of the " Philadelphia Society " for the Alleviation of the Miseries of Public Prisons." No person but an official visitor can have any communication with a prisoner, unless under special circumstances; nor is a visitor permitted to deliver to or receive from a convict any letter or message, or to supply him with any article, under the penalty of one hundred dollars. Such are the general arrangements of this penitentiary. There are, however, deviations from the rules which I have described in regard to convicts who are employed at trades which cannot be conveniently carried on in a cell. Those who are employed as blacksmiths, carpenters, &c. are allowed to leave their cells and work separately in small shops in which they are locked up, or they are associated in such cases with an artificer not a prisoner; but the greatest care is observed both during the hours of work and when going to and returning from the shops to prevent any one convict from seeing another. This departure from the ordinary regulations, however it may be the means of increasing the number of employments in the prison, will I fear be found susceptible of abuse, and even calculated to promote escapes, at a future period when the penitentiary may not have the benefit of that anxious care and unwearied vigilance which are exercised by the present warden.

Having had the unrestrained privilege of visiting the cells at all times, I have had many opportunities of conversing in private with a considerable number of the prisoners. Aware of the strong feeling which exists of the danger resulting from long periods of solitary confinement thus strictly enforced, my inquiries were carefully directed to the effects which it had produced upon the health, mind, and character of the convict. I have uniformly found that the deterring influence is extremely great, and such as I believe belongs to no other system of gaol management; for although in large bodies, associated together, silence may by strict discipline be in a great measure maintained, prisoners thus debarred from speaking have inevitably recourse to other modes of communication. I do not wish it to be inferred that moral corruption can result from intercourse so limited, yet when men are day after day thrown into the society of each other, the irksomeness of imprisonment becomes impaired and its terrors materially diminished. The Eastern Penitentiary imparts no such relief. Of the convicts with whom I conversed many had been previously confined in the New York and other prisons where corporal punishments were frequent; but these persons have declared that that discipline was less corrective than the restraints of continued solitude. When prisoners are associated it is extremely difficult to cut off all intercourse from without. The arrival of new and the discharge of other convicts form constant channels of communication. In the Eastern Penitentiary the separation from the world is certain and complete. So strict is this seclusion that I found, on conversing with the prisoners, that they were not aware of the existence of the cholera which had but a few months before prevailed in Philadelphia *. The exclusion of all knowledge of their friends is severely felt. But although every allusion to their situation was accompanied by a strong sense of the punishment to which they were subjected, I could perceive no angry or vindictive feelings. I was indeed

---

* To their ignorance of the existence of the cholera may doubtless be ascribed in a great measure their preservation from this disease, not a single convict having been attacked by it during the whole period that it prevailed in the city of Philadelphia, although the hospital for the reception of patients was in the neighbourhood of the prison. The powerful effect of alarm on the bodily system was singularly illustrated at this period at the Massachusetts State Prison. The chaplain having taken occasion one Sunday, from the pulpit, to advert to the awful ravages of the cholera, most of the prisoners who composed his congregation were on retiring to their cells seized with a complaint which it was greatly feared would lead to, but which happily did not terminate in, malignant cholera.

indeed particularly struck by the mild and subdued spirit which seemed to pervade the temper of the convicts, and which is essentially promoted by reflection, solitude, and the absence of corporal punishment. The only offences in the Eastern Penitentiary which the prisoner can commit are idleness and wilful damage to the materials on which he is at work. On such occasions he is punished by the loss of employment, the diminution of his food, or close confinement in a darkened cell. The necessity for correction is extremely rare. There is not a whip nor are there any fire-arms within the walls of the prison *.

Solitary imprisonment is not only an exemplary punishment but a powerful agent in the reformation of morals. It inevitably tends to arrest the progress of corruption. In the silence of the cell contamination cannot be received or imparted. A sense of degradation cannot be excited by exposure nor reformation checked by false shame. Day after day, with no companions but his thoughts, the convict is compelled to reflect and listen to the reproofs of conscience. He is led to dwell upon past errors, and to cherish whatever better feelings he may at any time have imbibed. These circumstances are in the highest degree calculated to ameliorate the affections and reclaim the heart. The mind becomes open to the best impressions and prepared for the reception of those truths and consolations which Christianity can alone impart. Instances have occurred in which prisoners have expressed their gratitude for the moral benefit which they have thus derived. If such effects are not more generally produced in the cells of the Eastern Penitentiary, the circumstance is to be ascribed not to the system but to the manner in which one of its most essential features has been neglected. The law authorizes the appointment of a chaplain or religious teacher but makes no pecuniary provision for his support. It is true that occasions occur, highly honourable to the parties, in which clergymen visit the penitentiary and gratuitously afford their assistance by the performance of divine worship†. These services are gratefully appreciated by the prisoners. In the impressive stillness of the cell even the sound of the human voice is a relief, and few situations can be more favourable to the reception of religious truth. But valuable as are these services, however desultory, their benefits are but partial and temporary, and utterly inadequate as a substitute for a systematic and unremitted course of religious instruction. Convicts unable to read remain uninstructed. These are vital defects which can alone be remedied by the appointment of a resident clergyman who shall not only regularly perform divine service on the Sunday but devote himself daily to the visiting of the prisoners from cell to cell. It is but justice to the inspectors and warden to state that they are alive to the importance of this evil, and that they have repeatedly expressed to the legislature their conviction that while it is permitted to continue, the good effects of solitary imprisonment can never be fully developed. The regulation by which one prisoner is strictly prohibited from seeing another is peculiarly beneficial. It not only forms a material addition to the punishment, promotes security, and cuts off the possibility of all communication, but it extends great advantages to the individual on his discharge. The propensity of convicts, on their liberation, to revive acquaintances formed in prison, is notorious. If any individual so situated be disposed to abandon his criminal habits he is too often assailed by temptations from his late associates, and threatened by exposure. An instance of this kind was related to me of a convict who had manifested great contrition for his past life, and conducted himself so well as to obtain his pardon from the Walnut-street prison. Having been re-committed he was asked why he had returned: he replied, " I intended to behave well, and I went for that purpose into the State of Ohio where I hoped that my former character would be unknown and I might set out anew in life. I got employment and was doing well, when unfortunately I one day met a man who had been a convict here at the same time as myself. I passed him, feigning not to know him: he followed me and said, ' I know and will expose you, so you need not expect to shun me. It is folly to set out to be honest. Come with

* This circumstance shows the Eastern Penitentiary in striking contrast to every other in the United States. It is the general practice to station sentinels either on the walls or in parts commanding inspection. There is a guard-room in each penitentiary.

† Whenever Divine Service is performed the clergyman stands at the head of the corridor; a small aperture in the cell, which is usually closed by a door, is then opened, and the prisoner sitting near it hears very distinctly without seeing or being seen by the opposite prisoner. To prevent the possibility of communication, a curtain is passed down the centre of the corridor.

with me and drink, and we will talk over old affairs.' I could not escape from him : my spirits sunk in despair, and I went with him. The result you know." The seclusion of the Eastern Penitentiary removes this formidable obstacle to reformation. The convict, on leaving his cell, re-enters the world unknown by any of the former inmates of the prison.

Since the opening of the Eastern Penitentiary not less than four insane persons and one idiot have been in confinement. Considering this circumstance to be of great importance, I felt it my duty to make especial inquiry into the cases of these individuals, and I beg to refer your Lordship to a letter in the Appendix addressed to me by the warden in explanation of the early history and previous habits of these afflicted persons. The statements contained in that letter, and the inquiries which I made upon the spot, together with the opinions expressed in the reports of the physician, leave no room to doubt that the prisoners in question had been subjected to mental disorders before they were admitted, and that the disease was in no respect attributable to any peculiarity in the discipline of the penitentiary. It is the opinion of the physician that the health of the convicts generally is improved by the treatment which they receive, although the average proportion of deaths may appear high while the whole number in confinement continues small. In the last year, however, the proportion was less than one per cent.* The physician remarks that the discipline has the effect of rendering the frame less robust, but at the same time prevents the occurrence of much disease to which persons of the class who generally become the inmates of a prison are usually subjected, either from exposure to weather or the indulgence of vicious habits.

It is expected that the cost of this penitentiary, when completed for the reception of 586 convicts, will amount to 550,000 dollars. A large sum, however, has been unwisely expended in decorations. Under all the disadvantages of a new establishment the earnings of the convicts have not hitherto equalled the amount incurred in their maintenance†. The plan which the inspectors pursue is to purchase the stock, and manufacture on the account of the State, in preference to letting out the labour by contract. On the 1st December last there were 152 males and two females in confinement, principally employed as weavers and shoemakers‡. Some loss is sustained from the former, and the profit on the latter has been but small. In winter the men continue to work in their cells until nine o'clock at night, by lamps. The warden is of opinion that the net profits of a prison in the United States, conducted on the plan of separate confinement, will be greater than that resulting from a penitentiary on the principle of joint labour. In his last report he expresses his conviction that an individual should not be sentenced for any period short of two or even of three years, twelve months not being sufficient to teach a trade, or to eradicate old and fix new habits §.

In regard to the moral effects which have hitherto resulted from the Eastern Penitentiary it is impossible to adduce any strong evidence. The institution has been

---

* The average of deaths during the four years in which the prison has been established is 3 ⅓th per cent. ; viz.

	No. of Prisoners.	Deaths.	Proportion.
In 1830	31	1	3 per cent.
1831	67	4	6 —
1832	91	4	4 ⅓ —
1833	123	1	¾ —

† The daily ration is as follows :—

Morning : 1 lb. bread (two-thirds rye, one-third Indian meal) ; 1 pint of coffee. Noon : 1 pint of soup ; ¾ lb. of beef, without bone, (of which the soup is made) ; and potatoes. Evening : Mush (a preparation of Indian meal), and a gill of molasses. There is no restriction in the quantity of potatoes and mush.

‡ The following are the numbers employed at the several trades :—

Weaving	38	Wheelwright	1	Cigar making	1
Warping, dyeing, winding, &c. in the cotton department	21	Tinman	1	Woolpickers	9
		Stonecutter	1	Washing clothes	2
		Cook	1	Without employment	9
Shoemaking	52	Quilting bed covers	1		
Carpenters	5	Apothecary	1	Total	154
Cabinetmaker	1	Making and mending clothes	5		
Blacksmiths	5				

§ The first year is occupied in teaching the prisoner, at a loss to the State.

a man who had been sentenced to pass seventy days in one of these miserable pits hung himself after four days' imprisonment. Another condemned to sixty days also committed suicide on the twenty-fourth day. It became necessary to remove four others, who were unable to endure this cruelty, from the cell to the hospital repeatedly before the expiration of their sentence. It is said that similar experiments have been made in Virginia, and that various diseases, terminating in death, were the result. The cells in which the prisoners were confined have been since disused: they are, in fact, dungeons, being on the basement story, and so dark as to require a lamp in visiting them. In damp weather the water stands in drops on the walls. The cells were not warmed at any season of the year. A prisoner's feet were actually frozen during his confinement. No fair trial of the effects of solitude could have taken place, as has been alleged, in the penitentiary of New Jersey, the cells being so arranged that the convicts can converse with perfect freedom. From experiments of this character no just conclusions can therefore be derived unfriendly to solitary imprisonment of any kind, especially when accompanied by employment, in large and well-ventilated cells, the arrangements of which have reference to the preservation of the health, regular employment, and improvement of the mind of the offender.

For several years before the erection of the Eastern Penitentiary in Philadelphia the subject of prison discipline had attracted considerable attention in New York. As early as the year 1797, a State Prison had been established at Greenwich, in the suburbs of that city. Various employments were introduced with a view to profit, and sanguine expectations were formed of its success; but these hopes were disappointed. Owing to the want of separation and the absence of strict discipline, the penitentiary inspired no dread and was ruinous in its effects on the morals of its inmates. The increase of population and the crowded state of the establishment determined the legislature in 1816 to build an additional prison at Auburn for the Western Division of the State. There appears to have been nothing worthy of notice in the management of this penitentiary until about the year 1820 when a number of separate sleeping cells were erected. From that period may be dated those subsequent improvements which have conferred on this prison its present character.

The Auburn Penitentiary, with its wings and workshops, occupies four sides of a hollow square, enclosed by a wall 500 feet in length, on each side*. From the central building the wings extend, containing the infirmary and sleeping cells. There are 770 cells, each seven feet long, seven feet high, and three feet and a half wide. They are well adapted for the admission of air, light, and warmth. The cells are unlocked soon after daylight. The prisoners are required immediately to place themselves in order, each having a provision-kid, water-can and night-tub. After depositing these articles, as prescribed by the regulations, they march to the workshops, when the labour of the day begins. At a fixed time they repair in silence, in close file, to the mess-room to breakfast where they sit with their faces in one direction. After an interval of about twenty minutes they return to their work. The same order is observed on proceeding to and returning from dinner. As the hour approaches for retiring in the evening to their cells, they wash. On a signal they again form into line, each according to the number of his cell. The convicts then proceed from the shops into the yard, whence, having taken up their night utensils, they march to their cells. In passing through an apartment adjoining the kitchen, each man takes up the supper prepared for him. On arriving at his cell, he enters it and partly closes the door which is locked by the turnkey. The galleries are occupied by distinct companies, and superintended by different officers. The prisoners eat their supper in their respective cells, after which a prayer is offered up by the chaplain in the area of the gallery. On a signal, they are required to repair to their beds. During the night, turnkeys, with mocassins on their feet, move silently along the galleries. The labour performed in the Auburn Penitentiary is considerable. The following were the trades and occupations at the period of my visit: Stone-cutters, smiths, blacksmiths, carpenters, tool-makers, coopers, cabinet-makers, machinists, turners, saddletree-makers, comb-makers, button-makers, weavers, check-weavers, bed-tick weavers, coverlet weavers, sattinet weavers, tailors, shoemakers. It was formerly the practice to purchase the raw materials, and dispose of the manufactured goods; but such serious losses

arose

---

* *Vide* Plan, Appendix, " New York."

arose from this system, that the legislature was induced to abandon it. The labour is now let out to contractors who furnish the materials, and pay to the State a certain sum per diem for the labour of the convict. The contractors or their agents may be present in the shops, but they must not interfere with the discipline, or speak to any prisoner. Each shop is superintended by an overseer, who gives instruction in the trades. A wooden partition, forming a narrow passage, runs down the side of every workshop. By means of small apertures made in the boards, the operations of the convicts can at all times be conveniently inspected, without exciting their observation.

The discipline by which the government of this penitentiary is maintained may be very briefly described. The convict is prohibited from speaking to any fellow prisoner. He is required to pursue his labour with downcast eyes. If in any case he is detected in looking off his work, in gazing at or attempting to exchange communication with another prisoner, he is flogged by the overseer with a whip (a "cat" or "cow-hide"), in the presence of his associates. The correction is certain and immediate. The quantity of punishment is entirely dependant on the will of the overseer against whose acts there is no appeal. The legislature formerly prohibited more than thirty-nine lashes from being inflicted at one time, unless in the presence of one of the inspectors; but the assistant keepers are now permitted to apply corporal punishment at their pleasure, without previous recourse either to an inspector or the superintendant. All that is required of them on such occasions is to report the name of the prisoner, the nature of the offence, and the number of the lashes which they have inflicted. There is no check upon the accuracy of these reports, nor any protection afforded against the abuse of this authority *. It is owing to no
want

---

* I am aware that the appointment of official Visitors, and the general admission of strangers to the Auburn prison, on the payment of a quarter-dollar, are regarded by many as some security against the infliction of excessive punishments. But this is an error. An assistant keeper may avoid publicity, by ascertaining if there be visitors in the prison, or at least in that part of it in which he attends. Should a stranger be on the premises, the keeper can always postpone the punishment for a few minutes until after the visitor shall have retired. It is indeed scarcely possible for a prisoner to obtain redress for any act of tyranny which the underkeepers may commit. He is not allowed to speak to the inspectors; nor have they any means of hearing his complaints. I refrain from the recital of many circumstances which have been related to me by various convicts, relative to the conduct of the assistant keepers; but in order to convey an idea of the extent to which their power *has been* exercised, I subjoin the following extracts from an official Report made to the Legislature of New York in the year 1827, by a Board of Commissioners appointed to investigate the condition of the Auburn Penitentiary: " Patrick Masteson came to the prison in the summer or fall of 1825, having old sores on his back, as if from a former flogging, respecting which we have no further account. He was, from the beginning, uncommonly unruly and troublesome, and was believed to feign insanity, and was sent from shop to shop as one or another keeper thought he could manage him. The question whether he was really insane excited a good deal of speculation in the prison, and was often a subject of conversation; but in all the former part of his time the most prevailing opinion was that he feigned it. He was whipped repeatedly by order of Mr. Canfield (an assistant keeper); though we regret to say, that a fact so little liable to be forgotten, in so extraordinary a case, is not acknowledged by this officer in his examination. Mr. Canfield found him, on a certain occasion, with the marks of blows on his head, from some of which the blood ran on to his face; but these were found not to be severe, and soon got well. When he was stripped to be washed, his shirt was found sticking to his old sores. After, about this time, his countenance showed signs of derangement; and as soon as it came to be believed that he had not his right mind, he was removed from the shops, and not further punished; and Mr. Powers, when he came into office, solicited his pardon, and obtained it, on the ground of his mental derangement." The commissioners add, " It would seem also (although there is some confusion in the testimony), that this unfortunate man is the person whom Dr. Tuttle compelled to drink some of the contents of a spit-box. Some witnesses understood that it was ordered because Masteson had himself done the same thing to show himself insane. The case of Masteson is understood to be one of those which have been publicly alluded to, as in effect a murder committed in the prison, he having afterwards, as was suggested, but not proved, died in Onondaga Gaol (where he is said to have been committed for a larceny), in consequence of these punishments." . . . . " It appears from the testimony of David Buck, that about January 1826, a prisoner employed in carrying in wood took up a crabbed stick, and asked the guard, David Stoddard, whether he should carry in that stick; for which Stoddard made him kneel down, and whipped him, and afterwards alleged, as a reason, that the prisoner knew he ought to carry in the stick, and had no right to speak to him." . . . . " In the fall of 1825 Charles Wood, then assistant keeper, and since discharged, being in the coopers' shop to relieve Mr. Burr, saw one Beeman, a convict, making gestures, and, as Wood said, laughing; for which Wood gave him six or eight blows with a stick, considering the convict as making sport. Mr. Burr, the regular head of the shop, testifies, that on inquiry he became satisfied that Beeman was only making a gesture for a tool. and he was grieved at the punishment, as Beeman was a well-disposed convict." . . . . " Dr. Tuttle, in answer to the second interrogatory, stated that cases of punishment, so severe as to require hospital treatment, were very common, perhaps every month, and that he considered them as abuses, from the severity of the punishment and the absence of the inspectors." . . . . " We have further to report, that in May 1825 John Hask, one of the present assistant keepers, knocked down

want of exertion on the part of the worthy chaplain that the religious services at this penitentiary are extremely limited. The moral improvement of the convicts has never been adequately appreciated. For some time after the present plans were in operation there was no chaplain, and religious instruction was considered unfavourable to the maintenance of discipline. At present a school is held on Sunday morning for about two hours for the purpose of teaching a select number of the most ignorant to read. Divine service is then performed before all the prisoners after which they are confined in their cells for the remainder of the day. In the afternoon the chaplain visits a few of the cells, this being the only part of the week in which he can confer individually with the prisoners. If such private interviews with the prisoners on week-days be not formally prohibited (which I believe to be the case), the practice of holding them is certainly not encouraged, nor does it prevail. The chaplain assured me that having as many as 680 convicts under his charge he could not, with every exertion, complete the task of visiting them, going from cell to cell, under a period of three months. Is it reasonable to suppose that services thus restricted can make any deep impression upon hardened characters such as are the inmates of this prison?

Those who are acquainted with the history and present state of prison discipline in Europe will at once perceive that the plan adopted for the government of the Auburn Penitentiary is that which has been, with a few periods of intermission, for many years pursued at the Maison de Force at Ghent *. The descriptions given of that celebrated establishment in the works of Mr. Howard and Mr. Buxton strictly apply to the Auburn Penitentiary. The prison has throughout a very imposing appearance. Whatever opinion may be formed of its ultimate influence upon the character of the convict, nothing can be more complete than the vigour and promptitude

---

one Clark, a convict, for not coming soon enough out of his cell, and kicked him after he was down. Clark was a convict who had recently come from the New York Prison." Among the cases investigated by the commissioners was that of a female prisoner, named Rachael Welsh. This woman became pregnant in the prison by one of the convicts, who contrived secretly to obtain access to her apartment. It appears that her conduct to the officers was most violent; and for this she was subjected to the treatment which the commissioners thus describe: " On the 27th July Rachael was whipped. No competent witness was present; and therefore the only account of it to be gained is from the confession of Cobb, (one of the assistant keepers), from her appearance and symptoms afterwards, and from Cobb's testimony before us." Cobb's account of the transaction was as follows: " Mr. Parks told me to flog her. I then took a cow-skin, and went into a room, telling the two blacks to watch, and if she came at me with any dangerous weapon, to defend me. She then went and sat down upon the bed, (appearing to me to be somewhat frightened), and told me if I whipped her to death she would not move. Her convict frock was open and large, so as to leave her shoulders bare, (it being warm weather), and I struck her about three or four blows on the shoulders, (and I think not more), and on the naked skin, and then stopped and admonished her as to her conduct." On receiving from her some abusive language, he says, " I then gave her three or four more strokes with the cow-skin. She sat firm, and seemed determined to brave it out, swearing that she would not submit. I ceased again; and observing that the blows left marks upon her shoulders, and fearing I might break the skin, and as she continued to rave, I struck her a few blows above her knees and in front as she sat. She seemed less violent, but did not altogether submit, and I reported the case immediately to Mr. Parks and the doctor." The woman's own account of the transaction to Dr. Tuttle is thus stated by him: " She described her struggles and resistance as all that she was capable of exercising. She said that she was held down by two big negroes, and whipped almost to death. She told me this on the 28th July, and has repeatedly told me so since. She has been uniform in her statements." In addition to this, Dr. Tuttle's statement of Cobb's confession is, " that he had her held by two negro convicts while he whipped her." " I found her," says Dr. Tuttle, " lying in bed, almost unable to move; examined her back, which was black and blue, with some degree of redness from her shoulders to the calves of her legs; from her neck to below her shoulders, or towards the small of her back, should call it black and blue. The strokes extended in part round her sides, and were less frequent below, say three or four inches apart; skin broken in some places, as I think. There appeared to be a general debility." Her symptoms became highly inflammatory. She was bled six times, and was for some days considered in a dangerous state. It appears, however, that she recovered, or partially so, for a time at least, from the effect of this chastisement. Shortly after her delivery she died, under a succession of the most distressing sufferings. Dr. Tuttle testifies, that, " in his opinion, as a professional man, the whipping which Rachael Welsh received on the 27th July was the cause of her death;" and he assigns his reasons for this opinion, which however is contested by others. On this subject the commissioners remark, that, " as it is strictly a professional question, and one on which physicians have already disagreed, we suppose it would be most discreet in us not to offer to the legislature any opinions of our own upon it."

On one point, however, the reprehensible conduct of Cobb, I should have thought that there could have been no difference of opinion. The most aggravated provocation, on the part of a female, cannot justify the infliction of a blow, nor are there any circumstances to extenuate the brutal treatment which Welsh experienced at the hands of Cobb; and yet, notwithstanding his own confession, and the additional proofs in evidence of the outrageous acts of violence committed on the person of a pregnant woman, the Inspectors did not think proper to remove him from his office.

* I regret to state that the strict discipline of this prison has not of late been maintained.

promptitude with which its several regulations are carried into execution. Silence
is unquestionably a moral agent of great value in the government of prisons. It
operates as a restraint, and is extremely favourable to habits of obedience, thought-
fulness, and industry. Yet the effects of the Auburn Penitentiary, notwithstanding
the order and regularity with which its discipline is enforced, have, I am persuaded,
been greatly over-rated. Its advocates maintain that the mental seclusion at
Auburn is complete, and that the main objects of solitude are in fact accomplished.
But, vigilant as are the precautions taken to prevent communication, the prisoners
do hold intercourse by signs and whispers. For this there are at times opportunities,
both in the workshops and when marching in close files. That such is the fact
I have been assured by those who have been the inmates of this penitentiary.
This intercourse, however slight and occasional, materially contributes to destroy
that feeling of loneliness which is the greatest of all moral punishments, and
which absolute and unremitted seclusion cannot fail to inspire. It is stated in an
official report to the legislature, that " even under the admirable discipline of
Auburn we (the commissioners) have seen, within a few weeks past, notes written
on pieces of leather, tending to insurrection. So far as they can safely venture,
they (the prisoners) will be found talking, laughing, singing, whistling, altercating
and quarrelling with each other, and with the officers. They will idle away their
time in gazing at spectators, and waste or destroy the stock they work upon." " If,"
add the commissioners, " instead of being repressed by a blow, the usual irregularities
of prisoners were to be reported for investigation, we are satisfied that endless liti-
gations before the inspectors would ensue, requiring thereby their constant attention
at the prison *." In the permanent good effects which this discipline is alleged to
produce, I have no faith. It is true that the dominion of the lash produces instan-
taneous and unqualified submission, but this obedience is but of a temporary nature.
It imparts no valuable feeling and presents no motive that is calculated to deter
eventually from the commission of crime and amend the moral character. In the
year 1828, the superintendent of this penitentiary published a work in which he
gave a list of 160 convicts, four-fifths of whom were stated on their liberation to
have become honest and respectable. On my visit to the penitentiary at Sing Sing
I was informed that thirty of these persons were then in that prison, and I was
assured that an additional number of twenty had also been there since the appearance of that publication. But even were its effects on the diminution of crime
apparent, the means by which the discipline is enforced are repugnant to humane
feeling and the spirit of an enlightened age. In the repeated conversations which
I have held in private with convicts who have been thus governed by the terror of the
whip, I have invariably found that this treatment produced strong feelings of
degradation and revenge. The lash is opposed to those moral and religious means
which experience has proved most efficacious in the recovery of the human character; and I feel assured that the idea of its adoption as an ordinary instrument of
discipline would not be entertained, much less would the practice be tolerated,
in the prisons of Great Britain. In judging of the comparative merits of the
two systems it will be seen that the discipline of Auburn is of a physical, that of
Philadelphia of a moral character. The whip inflicts immediate pain, but solitude
inspires permanent terror. The former degrades while it humiliates; the latter
subdues, but it does not debase. At Auburn the convict is uniformly treated with
harshness, at Philadelphia with civility: the one contributes to harden, the other
to soften the affections. Auburn stimulates vindictive feelings; Philadelphia induces habitual submission. The Auburn prisoner, when liberated, conscious that
he is known to past associates, and that the public eye has gazed upon him, sees an
accuser in every man he meets. The Philadelphia convict quits his cell, secure
from recognition and exempt from reproach.

In the year 1825 the legislature of the State of New York determined on the
abolition of the prison at Greenwich, and the erection of another penitentiary in
its stead, to be conducted on the plan pursued at Auburn. This penitentiary was
established at Sing Sing, on the east bank of the Hudson River, thirty-two miles
from the city of New York. The building was commenced by a party of convicts
from Auburn, with materials raised from a marble quarry contiguous to the site.
The prison, which is about 600 feet in length, and 40 feet in breadth, contains
1,000

---

* Report of the Commissioners appointed to visit the Auburn Prison to the Senate, January 1827,
p. 19.

1,000 separate sleeping cells.   There is also a number of large work rooms.   It was a favourite opinion with those who constructed this penitentiary that reliance should be placed for security on the vigilance of sentinels rather than on architectural arrangements.   They considered that it was less objectionable to shoot a convict than resort to the ordinary means by which escape would be prevented.   Hence this prison has no surrounding walls *.   The abundance of marble in the quarries at Sing Sing, and the belief that the convicts would be profitably employed in preparing it for sale at New York, occasioned the selection of this spot.   The quarries, however, have not fully answered the expectations which were formed of them, and recourse has therefore been had to the introduction of trades.   A great number are employed as locksmiths, blacksmiths, coopers, shoemakers, weavers, and hatters. Notwithstanding every effort has been made to render the labour productive, the profits have not, until the last year, equalled the expenditure.   The penitentiary at Sing Sing resembles that at Auburn in most of its arrangements.   Anxious to divest this Report of any detail not essential to the clear understanding of the main features of the two systems prevalent in America, I beg to refer your Lordship to the Appendix for a full description of the Sing Sing Penitentiary.   It will be seen that there are certain deviations from the plan adopted at Auburn.   Instead of repairing to the mess-room for their meals, the prisoners march for that purpose to their separate cells.   Their labour is in certain cases let out to contractors, while other employments are carried on and the articles sold for the benefit of the state. Strangers are not allowed to visit the prison without special permission, while at Auburn and most of the other penitentiaries the public are admitted on the payment of a quarter-dollar.   Slight and inadequate as is the check at Auburn against the abuse of an overseer's power, there is positively none whatever at Sing Sing.   The overseers who superintend the workshops are responsible to no one for, nor are they even required to report, any punishment which they may think proper to inflict.   The prisoners are entirely at the mercy of those placed immediately over them, and unless all credit be denied to the statements of the discharged convicts whom I have met with in the penitentiaries of other States, and who have without concert concurred in the relation of particular circumstances, it is impossible not to believe that the power thus arbitrarily invested in the hands of the under keepers at Sing Sing is at times greatly abused, and that a system of extreme and unjustifiable severity prevails throughout this prison.   I ought to add that the limited portion of time which the chaplain is allowed to devote to the personal improvement of the prisoners renders the religious instruction communicated scarcely more than nominal.   In September last there were 833 in confinement, and yet at Sing Sing, as well as at Auburn, the chaplain has not, except on Sundays, any private intercourse with a prisoner during the day.

   In proof of the efficacy of imprisonment at Auburn and Sing Sing, great stress has been laid on the comparative number of re-convictions which have occurred before and after the introduction of the Ghent system.   No doubt can possibly exist that the plan now enforced produces more terror than that formerly in use ; and it is even probable that the fear of the lash may in some instances have driven the discharged convict to other States for the commission of crime.   That the number of re-commitments is less than formerly may, however, be quite true without the present discipline being materially effective, either for the purposes of correction or reformation.   It is notorious that the New York penitentiaries were in a most wretched state.   Any comparison, therefore, derived from such a standard is but of little value.   Other circumstances, too, not now in operation, contributed formerly in a peculiar manner to increase the chances of impunity, and the number of re-commitments.   Among these were the extraordinary extent to which the pardoning power was abused, the short periods to which prisoners were sentenced, and the absence of those facilities for cheap and expeditious travelling to other States which now enable the felon, on his liberation, to pursue his career where he is unknown. It should also be observed, that the " re-convictions" recorded at an American penitentiary do not include the re-commitment of its discharged prisoners to any other prison, even where such facts are known.   Unless, therefore, the prisoner returns to the identical prison from which he was discharged, it is assumed that he has abstained from crime, although the case may be that within a week of his liberation

                                                                                                          he

---

* *Vide* Plan, Appendix, " New York."

he was committed to the penitentiary of a neighbouring State, no inquiry on that head being instituted. Under these circumstances nothing can be more calculated to mislead than such a test of the effects of Imprisonment.

The legislature has placed the general supervision of the penitentiaries in the hands of a certain number of inspectors. Their powers, which however are more nominal than real, differ in the several States and are defined in the descriptions given of the several penitentiaries in the Appendix. The keeper, or agent, has nothing whatever to do with the management of finance and accounts*. The clerk, on whom these duties devolve, is appointed by the governor of the State or the inspectors, and is entirely independent of the agent. The food supplied to the convicts is generally excellent in quality, and the allowance ample. As the prisoners are committed for long periods, and compelled to work hard during their confinement, it is considered essential that they should be daily supplied with animal food. In most of the penitentiaries, although there is a fixed and uniform ration, an additional quantity is supplied at the request of any individual. At Sing Sing, as well as at Philadelphia, a certain number are known to require more than the ordinary allowance, and this circumstance is duly considered when the rations are apportioned. At Sing Sing about sixty extra rations are commonly issued†. At Auburn, where the prisoners dine together, such as require an additional quantity make a sign to that effect. The health of the prisoners is generally good. The average deaths at Auburn in the last three years has been $1\frac{9}{10}$ per cent., and at Sing Sing $3\frac{5}{8}$ per cent.‡ The female prisoners in the State of New York are not subjected to the same discipline as the male convicts. Those committed within the eastern division of the State are sent to Bellevue, a prison under the superintendence of the municipal authorities of New York. The situation of the women in this place is truly deplorable,

---

* It has been stated in more than one publication, that the office of keeper of an American penitentiary is held by persons higher in rank than those who occupy similar situations in other countries. If this observation be intended to imply that such officers are superior in character, talents and acquirements, to those of other nations, I think it but right to say that this remark does not apply to England. On the appointment of a prison governor in England, the qualifications of the respective candidates are subjected to the scrutinizing investigation of a large body of disinterested and independent magistrates in whom the election rests. This is not the practice in the United States where the office is generally bestowed by the governor of the State, or by the inspectors of the prison, and the election is almost universally influenced by political opinions and party feelings. An individual so chosen may be very competent to discharge the trust confided to him, but as there is no security for this in the mode of election, the reverse not unfrequently occurs. Nor does the evil of allowing politics to interfere with such appointments end here. It often happens that a keeper has no sooner acquired a knowledge of his duties, than by the removal of the governor of the State or the prison inspectors, and the predominance of a different party than that by whose influence the keeper was appointed, he is immediately dismissed from his situation, however creditably he may be engaged in the discharge of its duties.

It has been alleged, as a proof of the superiority of this class of public officers in America, that individuals are to be found in the government of the penitentiaries who were formerly members of the State legislatures, local judges, and officers in the militia. This is unquestionably true ; but the mere statement of such a fact, unaccompanied by explanation, is calculated to deceive those who are apt to be misled by names, and are not acquainted with the peculiar structure of American society.

† The following are the daily rations :—

At Auburn :—10 ounces wheat flour ; 10 ounces Indian meal ; 14 ounces beef or 10 ounces pork ; half gill of molasses ; rye coffee, sweetened with molasses—per man.

$2\frac{1}{2}$ bushels potatoes, or $\frac{5}{8}$ bushel of beans ; 4 quarts salt ; $\frac{1}{2}$ ounce pepper—for every 100 rations.

At Sing Sing :—8 ounces inspected rye flour ; 12 ounces sifted Indian meal ; 16 ounces prime beef, or shin beef without bone, or 12 ounces pork ; half gill of molasses—per man.

4 quarts rye in the grain ; 2 quarts vinegar ; 2 ounces pepper ; 3 bushels potatoes—for every 100 rations during ten months in the year.

40 pounds rice, for every 100 rations during two months ; viz. from 15 June to 15 August.

The weight of this daily ration for each individual is 6 pounds 9 ounces.

‡	—	—	Number of Prisoners.	Number of Deaths.	Proportion per Cent.	Average per Cent.
Auburn	- -	1831	633	15	$2\frac{3}{8}$	
		1832	664	12	$1\frac{7}{8}$	$1\frac{9}{10}$
		1833	681	11	$1\frac{1}{4}$	
Sing Sing	- -	1831	875	28	$3\frac{1}{4}$	
		1832	906	42 (cholera 103)	$4\frac{1}{2}$	$3\frac{5}{8}$
		1833	821	25	$3\frac{1}{8}$	

deplorable, all being confined in one room. No attempt is made to introduce among them any order or discipline. The inspectors justly observe, that here " the old, the young, all colours and conditions, are indiscriminately confined toge- ther; the adept in crime is the companion of the novice in guilt. If virtuous sen- timents linger about the new convict sent to Bellevue, they are sure to be obli- terated by the infamy of the character and conduct of those with whom they are associated *." The female convicts at Auburn are under the direction of a matron; but the space allotted for this department is so contracted as to render any really beneficial arrangement impracticable.

The other penitentiaries in the United States are fully described in the Ap- pendix. That at Wethersfield, in Connecticut, merits the most particular attention †. It is conducted on the plan of association; the discipline adopted at Auburn being enforced as strictly as it can be, without the use of corporal punishment. The penalties for disobedience to the regulations are, as in England, solitude in a darkened cell, and a diminution of the allowance of food. This prison is extremely well managed, and affords the best example which I have seen of governing pri- soners in large bodies without the use of the lash. Although the discipline may not inspire those feelings of terror which are, in that case, produced, it imposes very considerable restraint. That the warden should be able to dispense with the use of the whip arises not only from his own judicious management, but in some measure from the comparatively small number in his custody. A strong opinion prevails in the United States that a discipline, which strictly imposes silence, and prohibits a prisoner from looking off his work, cannot be enforced without corporal punishment. All doubt on this subject has, in my opinion, been removed by the government of the Wethersfield Penitentiary. Great credit is due to Mr. Pilsbury (the father of the present excellent warden), by whom the system of management was established. It should, however, be considered, that the lower classes in Con- necticut, in common with those of the other New England States, are better educated than in those of other parts of the Union. Great attention is also paid to the moral and religious instruction of the prisoners, the whole time and attention of the excellent chaplain being directed to their improvement. He has the privi- lege, in the exercise of which he is indefatigable, of taking an individual aside, and of conferring with him in private at any time during the day. These circum- stances have materially contributed to soften the character of the convicts at Wethersfield, and to render them more manageable than in States where the mind of the criminal has been less instructed, and his habits have become more deeply formed. The remarks respecting Wethersfield apply also, in a great measure, to the penitentiary at Charlestown, in the State of Massachusetts ‡, where considerable attention is likewise paid to religious instruction. The valuable qualities and exem- plary devotedness of the benevolent chaplain of this penitentiary cannot fail to render his services a blessing to those who are the objects of his care. Although corporal punishment is not entirely dispensed with at this prison, the occasions of its infliction are but rare. The warden only has the power to inflict personal correction, nor is it in any case applied without a deliberate investigation into the nature of the offence. The power is limited to ten stripes, and ten days' solitary confinement. The particulars are recorded and submitted to the inspectors, who visit in a body once a month, and individually once a week. A convict can at any time have a private interview with the inspectors, or either of them. No officer is allowed to raise his hand against a convict except in self-defence. The management of this prison reflects much credit on those who have the superintendence of it.

The state prisons for New Hampshire, Maine, and Vermont, are small; and have nothing connected with their management which requires particular notice §. Silence is not strictly maintained, and their discipline is not calculated to make any bene- ficial impressions on the mind of the convict. The State of New Jersey is, greatly to its honour, constructing a penitentiary ‖, on the excellent plan of that at Philadelphia. The Maryland state prison is remarkable for nothing more than for the profits arising from its manufactures ¶. Here, as well as at Sing Sing, the prisoners are liable to be flogged for a breach of the regulations, and at the

pleasure

---

* Report of the Inspectors to the legislature of New York.
† *Vide* Plan, Appendix, " Connecticut."   ‡ *Vide* Plan, Appendix, " Massachusetts."
§ *Vide* Plans, Appendix, " New Hampshire," " Maine," and " Vermont."
‖ *Vide* Plan, Appendix, " New Jersey."
¶ *Vide* Plan, Appendix, " Maryland."

pleasure of the under-keepers who are not required previously to report the offence to the warden. Silence is not strictly observed, and there is consequently a great want of order and discipline throughout the whole establishment. An extensive plan of escape was lately formed, the execution of which had been nearly attended with serious consequences. No chaplain is attached to this penitentiary. For whatever religious instruction the prisoners receive they are indebted to the voluntary labours of benevolent persons resident in Baltimore. I am of opinion that imprisonment in the Maryland Penitentiary is very far from having any tendency to diminish crime.—The management of the Virginia Penitentiary is in some respects different from that of the other State Prisons *. The distinction consists in a certain portion of the sentence being passed in solitude. By a law made in 1833, the solitary confinement of convicts is to constitute one twelfth part of their sentence, and to be inflicted at intervals not exceeding one month. This solitude is unaccompanied by employment of any kind. Some interesting particulars respecting the result of this discipline will be found in the account of this prison inserted in the Appendix. The solitude described ought more properly to be termed separation. Prisoners in adjoining cells can communicate, and having no occupation, they of course endeavour to seek relief in mutual intercourse. The situation of the cells is far too cheerful, there being in each a window looking into a yard in which are the workshops. There is not any chaplain, nor any regular course of moral or religious instruction. Imprisonment in this penitentiary cannot produce the desired ends of punishment.—The Kentucky State prison is much smaller than that of Maryland, and very successful in its pecuniary results †. The warden contracts for the support of the establishment, and agrees to pay over to the State one half of the profits. Not more than ninety persons are usually in confinement, and yet there are not less than twenty-two descriptions of trades which the warden himself teaches and superintends. Although the workshops exhibit scenes of industry, the moral effects of the imprisonment are by no means satisfactory. It has no tendency to deter, and affords no means of reclaiming the offender. Religious instruction is here also neglected. From the smallness of the town in which the prison is situated, those means, imperfect as they are, which are to be found in larger places, do not exist for obtaining even the occasional services of a clergyman.—The Tennessee Penitentiary is but recently established, and is conducted upon the plan of that of Kentucky. Various occupations have been introduced which promise profitable results. Corporal punishment has been hitherto prohibited, but the warden has represented to the legislature the necessity of his having the power to inflict it. There is no attempt to communicate religious instruction in this prison, the discipline of which can have no beneficial effect upon the moral character.—The Ohio Penitentiary is a very wretched and contaminating place of confinement, an account of which I pass over the more readily as a new State prison is now building upon the plan of that at Wethersfield ‡.—The prisoners in the Penitentiary for the State of Indiana are farmed out upon the plan pursued in Kentucky. Although inspectors are nominated by the legislature, they reside at such a distance that their appointment is little more than nominal. The prisoners are employed at those trades which are most likely to produce profit. They are also occasionally taken out in parties and worked as labourers in the streets of Jeffersonville; guards being placed over them. The rifle and the whip are very prominent agents in the management of this penitentiary; and my impression is, that the power of inflicting punishment is at times abused. There is not the slightest attempt to improve the moral condition of the prisoners. At the period of my visit they were shut up nightly, and during the whole of the Sunday, four in a cell, the dimensions of which were about six feet by nine feet, and eight feet high. It is scarcely possible that any one can be confined in the penitentiary of Indiana, for however short a period, without being brutalized by the savage character of the discipline to which he is subjected §.

The

---

* *Vide* Plan, Appendix, " Virginia."   † *Vide* Plan, Appendix, " Kentucky."

‡ *Vide* Plan, Appendix, " Ohio."

§ There is far more injury resulting from confinement in the county gaols of any one of the States than benefit arising from its penitentiary. In the Slave States, particularly, the county gaols are truly deplorable. It is the practice to commit a slave to the common gaol whenever it suits the convenience of the owner. Slaves apprehended in endeavouring to escape are also here imprisoned until claimed, or sold to pay the charges incurred by their re-capture and maintenance. In addition to these classes are to be found, with scarcely any means of separation, persons committed for trial, and convicts sentenced for minor offences—men, women and children. From the number and various descriptions of the prisoners,

The whole of these prisons are conducted upon a plan of associated labour, There is, however, a great variety in their respective modes of management. The marked preference which has been given throughout the penitentiary States to the system adopted at Auburn has arisen from obvious causes. The improvements of that prison were in operation some years before the Philadelphia Penitentiary was constructed. Had, however, the merits of the latter been earlier known, the great expense attending a plan of solitary confinement would alone have been sufficient to render it generally unpopular. To this obstacle must be added the opinion prevalent throughout the United States, but which the able and experienced warden of the Philadelphia Penitentiary with great reason contests, that solitary labour cannot be rendered so profitable as when the prisoners are associated. This object, which is regarded as one of primary importance, has effected a striking change of sentiment in respect to the duration of sentences. A few years since, the ordinary terms of imprisonment were thought inconveniently long, and hundreds were pardoned to make room for new commitments. In certain of the States a sentence of even two years is considered as insufficient to render a prisoner's labour profitable, and hence it is not improbable that the present periods will ere long be extended. It is remarkable that this change of opinion has been produced without reference to the degree of punishment due to specific crimes, but with a view to pecuniary results. The profitable labour of the prisoners is in fact the popular feature in the management of the American penitentiaries; and I am inclined to think that the great desire which exists to rid the community of the burthen of supporting criminals has occasioned in most of the States the establishment of penitentiaries; while, throughout the whole country, this feeling has evidently given a great impulse to the progress of prison discipline. There are, unquestionably, in every State those whose interest in these institutions springs from far higher motives; but, with the exception of New England and Pennsylvania, I have generally found that the public approbation in reference to prisons has been measured not by their permanent effects on the moral character of the liberated convict, but by the profits of the establishment. The productive employment of prisoners is certainly an object of considerable importance, and every exertion should be made for its accomplishment consistently with the great moral purposes of a gaol. I am, however, of opinion, that to attain this result too large a sacrifice is made in some of the penitentiaries of the United States. Various trades are introduced and beneficial arrangements neglected solely with a view to profit. The objects of punishment have been thus lost sight of. The gloom of the penitentiary has been dispelled, and the attention of the convict distracted, by the continued bustle and varied occupations of the manufactory. It is one thing to render a convict a skilful mechanic, and another to induce him to become an honest man; and the interests of society are injured instead of benefited,

---

and the extremely limited space allowed them, these places of confinement exhibit scenes of great wretchedness and oppression. Occasionally the number of slaves in custody far exceeds all other classes of prisoners. Of eighty-eight prisoners whom I found in the gaol at Baltimore seventy-two were slaves, committed not for any offence, but merely for security until they could be sold. They consisted of individuals of all ages, from the old man of seventy to the infant at the breast. Here they were exposed to view previous to sale.

The county gaol for the district of Columbia is situated in the city of Washington. Its interior is divided by a passage which runs through the middle. On each side are eight cells, each eight feet by ten. In these sixteen cells there have been as many as eighty prisoners in confinement *. The cells are opposite, and, there being a small aperture in the doors, conversation can be maintained with the greatest ease. At the period of my visit the prisoners were very clamorous, and resembled more the appearance of wild beasts than of human beings. The cells were extremely close and offensive, and the turnkey who attended me said, " You may wipe down the sweat off the walls in summer." The prisoners are not allowed to take excercise in the open air. It has occurred that parties whose attendance as witnesses has been secured in default of bail by imprisonment in this gaol, have been confined in the same cell with those against whom they were required to give evidence. In 1832, not less than 463 debtors and 194 criminals passed through this wretched place. Of the latter, one hundred and forty-nine were men, twenty-four females, and twenty-one boys. In addition to these numbers, there had been in custody during that period thirty-two free-coloured men, seven free-coloured women, one hundred and twenty-eight runaway slaves; and for safe custody until they could be sold, sixty-five male slaves, forty-three female slaves, and six slave children. A re-captured slave must be advertised within twenty-days of his commitment: he is afterwards usually kept sixty days to afford a reasonable time for his owner to appear. Should there be no claimant, the slave is advertised for sale thirty days, when he is sold in the public market-place to defray the expenses incurred by his imprisonment. Irons are used as a punishment, but the lash more frequently in the case of slaves.

---

* Speech of Mr. Thompson in the House of Representatives, January 1826.

fited, when for the sake of profit the penalties of the law are weakened, and the moral effects of imprisonment suppressed. In forming a comparison between the productive employment of prisoners in the houses of correction in England and the penitentiaries of the United States, it ought always to be borne in mind that the difference in the circumstances of the two countries is so great as to render it impossible that criminal institutions of the same nature should produce similar results. This difference arises, first, from the dense population of England compared with that of America, and the demand for labour which prevails in the several States; and secondly, the long periods for which prisoners are sentenced to the American penitentiaries, the punishment of transportation being unknown. In England the short duration of imprisonment materially increases the difficulty which otherwise exists of making convicts skilful workmen, and of rendering prison labour profitable. In appreciating also the relative effects of punishment it should further be remembered that in the United States there are not the same powerful temptations to crime as in England. An American has in this respect a great advantage over an English convict on his liberation. Hence a recommitment in the one country implies a deeper shade of criminality than in the other. Besides, the facilities for travelling enable the discharged convict to effect a favourable settlement without much danger of his previous habits becoming known. No man need commit crime in the United States from the want of employment.

It is extremely difficult to ascertain the actual amount of crime in any part of the United States owing to the absence of official information on this subject. The authorities of the several States are so entirely independent of each other, as well as of the general government, that there is no approach to centralization for the attainment of criminal statistics. Although, as a matter of courtesy, each State generally transmits a copy of its laws to the library of Congress, there is no collection, in any place, of the legislative proceedings of the different States. In some cases the sheriffs take with them their books on retiring from office, and it is therefore difficult to procure any complete information as to the number of commitments, even during the past year, to the county gaols; and a work of no ordinary labour to obtain the numbers even for the current year, as in most of the States it would be necessary for this purpose to visit the several counties. Many of the statements inserted in the Appendix are original documents, framed for the purposes of this inquiry from the prison registers and criminal calendars to which I had access. These tables have been constructed with much care, but it is necessary that considerable caution should be used in drawing from them general conclusions. They comprise the higher classes only of offenders, and form no criterion by which to judge of the extent and progressive increase or diminution of crime generally throughout any particular State. On reference, for instance, to the commitments to the New York penitentiaries, the numbers in the last two years will appear to have been on the decrease, while the examination of several of the county returns proves that crimes short of state prison offences have gradually increased during that period. Neither can a judgment be correctly formed from these accounts of the relative proportion of crime in the different States. It is well known that the population of New England ranks far superior to any other part of the Union in morals and intelligence. Education is universal, the laws are ably administered, the police is well regulated, and pauperism is limited; and yet the Returns in the Appendix tend to shew that there is more crime in proportion to the population in the most enlightened of these States, viz. Connecticut and Massachusetts, than in Pennsylvania, part of which is but recently settled, or in the more western States, which are comparatively uncivilized. The false impression which these statements are in this respect calculated to convey, is in a great measure to be ascribed to the fact that in New England few crimes pass undetected and escape punishment; but this is far from being the case in other parts of the Union. As the traveller proceeds towards the western and southern States he will find that the numbers in the penitentiary must not be taken as the extent of even the higher classes of offences. In many counties of even New York and Pennsylvania, and still more in those of other States, offences pass unprosecuted which in New England would scarcely fail to incur punishment. In a newly-formed and scattered population, such is the value of labour that the interests of the community would often materially suffer by the incarceration of its members. The prosecution of an offender is attended with the loss of valuable time: hence there is a disposition to overlook crimes which are not of the most flagitious character, and which do not awaken a strong sense of insecurity to person as well as to property. This feeling of repugnance to prosecute for offences is carried so far in the western States that no inference could be more unsafe than to judge of the extent of crime from the returns of commitments to the penitentiaries in those districts. The state of Illinois presents an illustration in point. Its population at the last census amounted to 157,000 souls, consisting of natives of various countries, differing not less in morals than in manners. Crimes are of course matters of frequent occurrence, and yet I was informed during my stay in America that there was not a single prisoner in the penitentiary convicted of any serious offence. The discrepancies between the number of commitments and the actual extent of crime, in the more western as well as the southern States, merit peculiar attention. There exists in those parts of the country a great recklessness of human life. Personal insult is resented by the immediate gratification of revenge. A custom prevails of carrying pocket pistols, or of wearing a dirk in the bosom, while scarcely any of the labouring classes are without a large clasped knife, which, opening with a spring, becomes a truly formidable weapon. Hence assaults of the most desperate character in the public streets frequently occur, and death to the parties often ensues. Prosecutions, however, arising out of these acts of violence, are by no means common. These offences pass in many instances, in a legal sense, entirely unnoticed. An appeal to a court of justice in such cases would not be sanctioned by public opinion; and even if the offender were brought before a jury they would enter into a consideration of the provocation given by the parties, and discountenance by their verdict the practice of rendering such acts amenable to the ordinary course of criminal justice *.

It is impossible, on examining the prisons to which these Tables refer, not to be struck with the great proportion of crime which the coloured bears to the white population. The causes are too obvious. The force of public opinion has in a remarkable degree contributed to retard the education and moral improvement of the coloured race. Hence these oppressed people form, of course, the most degraded class of the community. This prejudice appears to me to be, if possible, stronger in the free than in the slave States. A law has recently passed, even in Connecticut, discouraging the instruction of coloured children introduced from other States; and in the course of the last year a lady, who had with this view established a school for such children, was prosecuted and committed to prison†. From a feeling which is unknown in Europe, a coloured person, although residing in the most enlightened of the States, is prevented from attaining that position in society to which his natural intelligence, aided by the benefits of education, would inevitably raise him. Under such circumstances the only wonder is, that there should not be more crime among a population so numerous, and so disadvantageously situated.

Few circumstances connected with this subject impress a visitor more forcibly than the small number of females to be found in the penitentiaries of the United States. In America, the white woman fills a station superior to that in any other country. This fact arises principally from the circumstance that the most menial occupations are generally performed by coloured females; and even of this despised yet pitiable class, greatly as they are exposed to temptation from the walks of life in which they are compelled to move, there are few commitments compared with the population at large. I fear, however, that the criminal calendars do not convey a correct idea

of

---

* The following fact, in illustration of these remarks, was related to me by a most respectable clergyman of the State in which the circumstance occurred. A gentleman residing in Alabama received a slight personal affront, which, having been privately offered, he was disposed to pass unnoticed. The affair, however, became known, and it was suggested to him that he must resent the insult or withdraw from society. On receiving this intimation he immediately repaired, armed with a brace of pistols, to a neighbouring town, the residence of his opponent, and shot him as he was walking in the public streets. This was of course a matter of notoriety, yet no legal proceedings were adopted. The gentleman, on his return home, was then received into the circle of his acquaintance. They said that the satisfaction which he had taken was, it was true, somewhat late; but that this circumstance would be overlooked in consideration of his having promptly acted on the suggestion which had been made to him. I should add, that the newspapers of the Southern and Western States make frequent mention of assaults of this murderous character (ª), confirmatory of the condition of society which this anecdote implies. I have related it in different States, and repeatedly heard its main features corroborated by similar narratives. On referring however to the Tables of Commitments in those parts of the country, it will appear that the number of prisoners convicted of crimes of this nature is remarkably small.

† The Act declares that "attempts have been made to establish literary institutions in this State, for the instruction of coloured persons belonging to other states and countries, which would tend to the great increase of the coloured population of the State, and thereby to the injury of the people: Therefore it is enacted, that no person shall set up or establish in this State any school, academy, or literary institution, for the instruction or education of coloured persons who are not inhabitants of this State; or instruct or teach in any school, academy, or literary institution, or harbour or board for the purpose of attending or being taught or instructed in any such school, any coloured person not an inhabitant of any town in this State, without the consent in writing first obtained of the majority of the civil authority and select men of the town where such school is situated." Prior to the passing of this law a school for such children had been formed by Miss Crandall, of Canterbury, (Conn.) and for continuing her establishment without the licence required by the statute, she was prosecuted. On conviction, Miss Crandall appealed to a superior court, but before the constitutionality of this act of the legislature of Connecticut could be decided by the competent tribunal, her school was broken up by popular violence.

(ª) These occurrences are usually termed " shooting a man down."

of the extent of crime among the female population : at least I have been assured that from the general sense which exists of the value of female services, particularly in those parts of the country which have been but recently settled, there prevails a strong indisposition to prosecute, especially if the offender be not a woman of colour. Magistrates are also reluctant to commit women from the circumstance of there not being any suitable prisons for their reception. With the exception of Pennsylvania and Connecticut, there is not a single State in which the treatment of female prisoners is not entirely neglected.

In considering the expediency of adapting the prison discipline enforced in the United States to the treatment of criminals in Great Britain, it may be desirable briefly to notice the history of the penitentiary system in England.

More than half a century has elapsed since Mr. Howard suggested the expediency of subjecting criminals to a more severe discipline than that ordinarily enforced in houses of correction. In conformity with this idea an Act for the establishment of penitentiary houses was passed in the year 1776, the provisions of which were framed by that eminent man, in conjunction with Sir William Blackstone and Mr. Eden. The spirit and objects of the Act are expressed in the preamble to the 19 Geo. 3, c. 74 which declares that " if many offenders, convicted of crimes for which transportation has been usually inflicted, were ordered to solitary imprisonment, accompanied by well-regulated labour and religious instruction, it might be the means, under Providence, not only of deterring others from the commission of the like crimes, but also of reforming the individuals, and inuring them to habits of industry :" and Sir William Blackstone states the principal objects of the measure to be, " by sobriety, cleanliness and medical assistance, by a regular series of labour, by solitary confinement during the intervals of work, and by due religious instruction, to preserve and amend the health of the unhappy offenders, to inure them to habits of industry, to guard them from pernicious company, to accustom them to serious reflection, and to teach them both the principles and practice of every Christian and moral duty*." It is to be regretted that the commissioners nominated in this Act could not agree upon a site for the erection of the proposed penitentiary. This difficulty, however, was removed on the appointment of others, and plans had actually been prepared when the Government determined on the expediency of transporting convicts to New South Wales in preference to the establishment of a national penitentiary. But although the idea was for a time suspended,
the

---

* There never was a greater delusion than the opinion which has for many years prevailed in England in favour of the superiority of the criminal institutions of Pennsylvania. This error has doubtless arisen from confounding the mitigation of the penal law, which at an early period honourably distinguished the legislature of this State, with improvements in prison discipline, in the progress of which New York preceded it, and in which Pennsylvania has been considerably behind England. Assertions have nevertheless been made by writers upon this subject, that the solitary imprisonment of criminals originated in Pennsylvania. A mere reference to dates will show the fallacy of this opinion ; and also prove that so far from either the suggestion or the example of this practice having first occurred in Pennsylvania, that State has been indebted to England for the advantage of both.

The first public allusion in Pennsylvania to the solitary confinement of criminals is to be found in an Address issued in 1787 by " The Philadelphia Society for alleviating the Miseries of Public Prisons." Referring to the recent law which sentenced criminals to hard labour, " publicly and disgracefully imposed," the committee suggest that as the good intended by the measure had not fully answered, " punishments by more private or even solitary labour, would more successfully tend to reclaim." Eleven years, however, prior to the date of this Address, which, it will be observed, emanates from an association of private individuals, and contains by no means a strong recommendation of solitary confinement, the statute of the 19 Geo. 3, c. 74, containing the passage above recited, was enacted by the British Parliament. The same sentiments were reiterated in an Act passed six years afterwards, for the erection of the penitentiary at Gloucester. This prison contained seventy-one cells strictly solitary, without any means of exchanging communication, and in which convicts were confined at hard labour. It was opened in the early part of 1791, prior, I believe, to the erection of the sixteen cells for men and fourteen cells for women in the Walnut-street prison (which, however, were in no respect solitary, and in which no labour was ever performed); and it is a fact worthy of notice, that at the time, or within a few months of the period, when the solitary system at Gloucester was in operation, criminals were actually worked in gangs with iron collars round their necks, and chains upon their persons, in the streets of Philadelphia. It is singular to find, that those who ascribe so much excellence to the Walnut-street prison in its earliest days, and who have seriously designated its management the " ancient Pennsylvania system," should in 1828 have recommended, for the government of the Eastern Penitentiary, a plan entirely different from that which it is alleged was enforced in Walnut-street prison; namely, solitary confinement without labour. In the penal law of 1794 the words " penitentiary houses" occur, the phrase being evidently borrowed from the Act of Parliament passed in England in 1776.

the principle laid down in Mr. Howard's Act was carried into effect by the erection in 1785 of a penitentiary in Gloucester. This was the first trial of a prison conducted on the principle of solitary confinement, and the merit of its application belongs to Sir George Paul and the magistrates of that county *. Three years after the completion of this prison the design of a national penitentiary became again the subject of consideration. An offer had been made by Mr. Jeremy Bentham to erect a prison and contract for the safe custody and maintenance of 1,000 convicts; and an Act, authorizing the Government to accede to his proposal, was passed in the year 1794†. Various difficulties, however, occurred to prevent the execution of this plan; nor was the consideration of it renewed until the year 1810, when, on the motion of Sir Samuel Romilly, a Committee was appointed to inquire into the expediency of proceeding further with the measure. The Report of the Committee was unfavourable to the undertaking on the principle that Mr. Bentham's views of penitentiary discipline were not conformable to those on which the 19 Geo. 3, c. 74, were framed, and that the proposed arrangement was too exceptionable, on general grounds, to be adopted, whatever confidence might be reposed individually in Mr. Bentham. Valuable evidence was, however, taken before this Committee of the beneficial results of the system of solitary confinement enforced at Gloucester; and the Committee reported that the system of penitentiary imprisonment, upon the general principles of the 19 Geo. 3, was calculated to reform offenders, and ought to be pursued; that, instead of the national penitentiary house which had been proposed, a separate prison of that description should be erected in the first instance for London and Middlesex, and that measures should be taken for carrying on the penitentiary system, as soon as might be practicable, in different parts of the country. In compliance with the first part of this recommendation, the 52 Geo. 3, c. 44, was framed for the erection of a penitentiary for 300 males and 300 females; and a clause was inserted by which convicts might be sent to this prison from any part of England until provision could be made for their confinement in penitentiary houses elsewhere. Although further measures for the establishment of district penitentiaries were expressly postponed until a future session, the valuable labours of this Committee were never resumed. The means taken at this time to improve the discipline of the hulks had rendered these establishments somewhat less objectionable. This circumstance, combined with the policy of encouraging the transportation of convicts to a great extent, and above all, the serious expense which the erection of district penitentiary houses would necessarily involve, doubtlessly contributed to induce the Legislature to abandon the consideration of the subject. Instead, therefore, of establishing additional prisons, it was determined to enlarge the penitentiary at Millbank, already in progress, and to confine therein a part of all such transportable convicts as, from peculiar

liar

---

* It is impossible to advert to the labours of this able and useful magistrate without acknowledging the very important services which he has rendered to the improvement of prison discipline. Mr. Howard assuredly did more than any other man to expose the miseries which characterized the prisons of his day; but Sir George Paul was the first to show not only that cruelty was unnecessary, but that salutary correction and moral reformation were practicable, in the treatment of criminals. Owing, in a great measure, to his unwearied exertions, the Gloucester penitentiary was erected. The rules for its management were framed by his hand, and have for many years served as a guide for the regulation of prisons, not only in England but in other countries. These rules are distinguished by a regard for enlightened principles of penal jurisprudence and a spirit of benevolence which reflect the highest honour on his understanding and his heart. With peculiar sagacity he foresaw the evils which would result from any innovation upon that strict and undeviating plan of solitude which he had laid down for penitentiary discipline, and he uniformly protested against the formation of a second class in which prisoners were allowed to associate, and in which the benefits derived from previous solitude were entirely counteracted. He possessed a sound and accurate knowledge of the various laws for the government of gaols, since simplified and consolidated, but which were far from being at that time generally understood. He inculcated, with great earnestness, the importance of maintaining a distinction between gaols and houses of correction, and pointed out the inconsistency of committing prisoners accused of felony to a place of confinement not under the charge of the sheriff, but designed for the punishment of the convicted. The close and anxious attention which he bestowed on the various details connected with the construction, regulation, and expenditure, of the Gloucester prison, rendered it for many years an example for general imitation. Others have evinced their regard for humanity by pursuits less repulsive, and more calculated to win popularity and fame; but of Sir George Paul it is not too much to say, that he was the first practical reformer of the discipline of prisons, and that by his indefatigable labours throughout a long and honourable life he largely contributed to advance the great objects of criminal justice. His memory deserves a distinguished place in the affections of his country, and in the respect and gratitude of mankind at large.

† 34 Geo. 3, c. 84.

liar circumstances, were exempted from being sent abroad. The building was accordingly adapted to the confinement of 600 males and 400 females, and became the general penitentiary for England and Wales.

Although solitary confinement was, at an early period, enforced at Gloucester, its effects were, for the first four years, sensibly weakened by a practice of transferring the prisoner into society, after the first portion of his sentence had been passed in seclusion. The injurious effects of this regulation became at length so apparent that in 1794 it was repealed From that period until the year 1809, when, owing to the vast increase of numbers, individual separation became no longer practicable, each prisoner in the Gloucester Penitentiary was compelled to labour in his cell by day, and was confined in a separate dormitory at night. He had no means of seeing or of communicating with any other prisoner when taking exercise in the open air. After the experience which had been derived from Gloucester in favour of solitude, it is to be regretted that the regulations for the management of the Milbank Penitentiary should not have partaken more of that character. Separation, however, not solitude, seems to have been originally the object of the discipline enforced at this penitentiary. The prisoners were divided into two classes, and the period of their detention into two portions. The first period was passed in a class in which every individual had a distinct cell, where he or she worked and slept; but even in this class the prisoners congregated, at intervals, during the time allotted for working at the mills or water-machines, or while taking exercise in the airing-yards, at which periods it was impossible entirely to prevent intercourse. After remaining in the first class from eighteen months to two years, the prisoners were removed to the second division, where they worked in companies. The intelligent and experienced governor and chaplain of this penitentiary have uniformly borne testimony to the good produced by the discipline of the first class, but declared that on being removed to the second class these beneficial results were speedily counteracted. This evil was so strongly represented to the late Committee " on Secondary Punishments," that they recommended the abolition of the second class, which is now no longer in existence.

Partial improvements were effected in several of the prisons during the progress of the inquiry which led to the establishment of the Milbank Penitentiary. It was not, however, until the year 1819 that the state of the gaols throughout the kingdom became the subject of Parliamentary investigation. A Committee of the House of Commons was appointed in 1822 to revise and consolidate the various laws relative to places of confinement; and the Act of 4 Geo. 4, c. 64, was the result of their labours. By that law due provision is made for the enforcement of hard labour in the case of persons sentenced to that punishment, and for the employment of all others. A system of classification is required by which debtors, convicted felons, convicted misdemeanants, persons committed on charge of felonies, persons accused of misdemeanors, or for want of sureties, and vagrants, shall be kept apart. Such further classification is also authorized as the magistrates may consider conducive to good order and discipline. Females are, in all cases, to be attended by officers of their own sex; and the keeper and his officers, when visiting the women, must always be accompanied by a female officer. Each prisoner is to be provided with a distinct hammock or cot, in a separate cell, if possible. No one is to be put in irons except in case of urgent and absolute necessity. Provision is required to be made for the instruction of both sexes in reading and writing. Prayers are to be read every morning. Divine service is required to be performed twice every Sunday. The chaplain is required to catechise and instruct all who are willing to be taught, and to distribute such books as he may think proper for instruction; to visit those in solitary confinement, and to keep a journal and report on the moral condition of his charge. Two or more justices are to be appointed as visitors, and one or more are requested personally to visit and inspect each prison, at least three times in each quarter of the year, and oftener if occasion may require, when they shall examine into the conduct as well of the respective officers as of the prisoners, and into the general condition of the establishment. The keeper is required to make a report of the actual state of the prison, quarterly, to present a return of all persons sentenced to hard labour, to specify the manner in which the sentences are carried into effect, the particular species of labour introduced, and the average number of hours in the day at which the prisoners have been employed. A general Return founded on the reports of the visiting justices, the chaplain and keeper, is required to be transmitted annually to one of His Majesty's principal Secretaries of State. This law is applicable to the regulation of county prisons and a certain number only of the gaols belonging to corporate jurisdictions exercising the right of trial in the case of capital offences. In order to ensure the more certain execution of the Act, it became necessary to limit its application to those prisons which admitted of the possibility of introducing the prescribed scale of classification and arrangements for labour. A considerable number of the smaller places of confinement were consequently excluded from the operation of this law. An Act was therefore passed in the following year (5 Geo. 4, c. 85), authorising the magistrates in whose jurisdiction these local gaols were situated, to contract for the custody and maintenance of their prisoners with the justices of their respective counties in the county gaol or house of correction. A modified scale of classification and other plans of a limited nature were also prescribed for the observance of those prisons which notwithstanding the proposed arrangement should remain under independent jurisdictions. These enactments, together with the publication of several works on this subject, about that period, gave a considerable impulse to the improvement of the gaols. To carry the law into effect great expense has been incurred in several counties *. Prisons have been re-constructed and arrangements made to admit of extended classification. Separate sleeping-cells have in many cases been provided, and manufactures of various kinds, as well as hard labour at the treadwheel, been introduced.

That the benefits which were expected to result from these measures have not been realized may be ascribed to various causes independent of the defective character of the prisons and their discipline; causes too powerful to be counteracted by punishments of any description. The population of the country has at times far exceeded the means of employment. The operation of the poor laws has materially contributed to demoralize those whom they were intended simply to relieve. The moral training and religious education of the lower classes have been insufficient to resist the force of those temptations which are inseparable from indigence. Incitements to crime have received an extraordinary impulse from another evil which is spreading its desolating effects with frightful rapidity. The intemperate use of ardent spirits threatens to change the moral character of the labouring population of large towns, and sets at defiance the combined restraints which education, police and prison discipline are calculated to impose on the growth of crime. From these and other causes the number of offences has increased to an extent beyond the power of any penal institutions to arrest. It must also at the same time be admitted, that notwithstanding all that has been done for the improvement of the prisons in England, they yet continue to be in a very defective state. The physical condition of the convict has been greatly ameliorated, but no adequate sense of dread has been imparted to imprisonment, nor have effectual means been employed to promote the moral reformation of the criminal. Favourable exceptions undoubtedly exist. It would be as erroneous to infer that because most of the county gaols and houses of correction require further amendment, there are no good prisons in the kingdom, as that the discipline of the American penitentiaries is generally of a superior character because a few of these establishments are well governed. It is not, however, too much to say that there prevails throughout the prisons in England a lamentable want of system, vigour, and uniformity. Where labour is imposed, its corrective influence is lost from the absence of constant inspection and the means of restraint. Silence, although nominally enjoined, is not scrupulously maintained ; and prisoners are not, as they ought invariably to be, prohibited from looking off their work, and gazing at various objects in the wards and yards. Even regulations good in themselves are often so injudiciously carried into effect as to interfere with and sensibly weaken the effects of punishment. Friends are permitted to visit. Letters are allowed to be received and transmitted, and the penalties of the law are counteracted by lenient measures, well-intentioned, but in their effects highly injurious. In several instances in which the prison has been built for the separate confinement of the inmates at night, the increase of commitments has no longer allowed of this beneficial arrangement; and in many cases the most useful provisions of the law have been partially evaded and in others altogether neglected†. I make these statements respecting the general condition of the prisons in this country advisedly, and with the

---

* *Vide* Statement in the Appendix, " Miscellaneous."

† A more striking instance to this effect cannot be adduced than the principal gaol in the city of London. Notwithstanding the improvements which have been effected in the prisons throughout the kingdom, Newgate has remained a prolific source of corruption, a disgrace to the metropolis, and a national reproach.

the greater confidence, having visited the principal county gaols and houses of correction in England since my return from the United States.

As all knowledge on this subject must be progressive, it is natural to expect that some of the provisions of the present gaol law should require re-consideration. Since the date of that enactment valuable experience has been obtained on various points. The confidence placed in classification has been materially impaired, while advantages have been developed which were not sufficiently appreciated when the prison law was framed. In regard to the adoption of any specific plan for the regulation of the gaols of this kingdom, two systems are presented for consideration. The solitary discipline, as enforced at Glasgow and Philadelphia, and imprisonment in association, in silence, as practised at Wethersfield in Connecticut, and also in a great measure at the Wakefield house of correction for the West Riding of the county of York*. It is most desirable that the untried should be subjected to no restraint that is not necessary to enforce safe custody, maintain order, and prevent contamination. In determining on a system for the treatment of the convicted, three objects should be kept in view, first, the effect which the discipline is calculated to produce in deterring others; secondly, correction; and, thirdly, reformation. So greatly does increasing experience prove the importance of solitude in the management of prisons, that I could not, if circumstances admitted, too strongly advocate its application in Great Britain for every class of offenders as well as for persons before trial, under modifications which would divest the seclusion of its harshest character. I entertain a strong and deliberate conviction that no other system of prison discipline will produce those feelings of alarm and apprehension, as well as of moral reformation, which a prison ought uniformly to inspire. I perceive, however, many difficulties in the way of its being generally practised. The erection of suitable buildings would occasion enormous expense, as in order to adapt the county prisons to this purpose their entire re-construction would in most cases be requisite. Looking practically at the question, I am therefore driven to consider the alternative of adopting the system of association as pursued at Wethersfield; and which, if it do not accomplish all the great ends of prison discipline, will certainly tend to improve the present state and management of the English gaols. Under these circumstances, and regarding what is attainable rather than that which is to be desired, I am reluctantly compelled to confine my recommendation of solitude to certain classes only. The descriptions of prisoners to be selected for this treatment†, as well as the degree and several modes in which this discipline should be carried into effect, form important subjects of inquiry, in the course of which much useful information may be derived from the experience obtained at Glasgow, Philadelphia, and the house of correction for the county of Essex at Springfield‡. For the establishment of this system I am of opinion that every exertion should be made; but that where, from the difficulties to which I have adverted, it cannot be attained, the Wethersfield plan should be strictly enforced. I consider the nature of the imprisonment in that penitentiary to be as efficient as any description of penal confinement can be rendered on the principle of association. The system consists in the most rigid maintenance of silence, giving to each prisoner a separate dormitory, entirely cutting off all intercourse from without, preventing as much as possible any exchange of communications between the convicts, and prohibiting each individual, as far as is practicable, from even looking at a fellow-prisoner during the hours of labour. I am aware that the facility with which this system may be enforced, compared with that of solitary confinement, will tend to favour the plan of association in England as it already has done in the United States. I am by no means disposed to under-rate the real value of the Wethersfield discipline; but lest it should lead eventually to disappointment, I would caution

those

---

* The observance of silence and of the regulation which prohibits the prisoners from looking off their work, is extremely well enforced at this house of correction, under various disadvantages, arising from short periods of commitment, with which the warden at Wethersfield has not to contend. The discipline at Wakefield is maintained by the judicious arrangement of the men in their workshops, and by constant and vigilant inspection. The punishments for a violation of the rules at this prison are, as at Wethersfield, the withholding of employment, solitary confinement in darkness, and a diminished allowance of food.

† Some judgment may be formed of the extent to which it will be necessary to provide solitary cells for certain classes of prisoners, by reference to the numbers thus sentenced in the past year, a statement of which will be found in the Appendix, " Miscellaneous."

‡ This house of correction affords an interesting example of solitude without employment. Offenders committed for periods extending from one to six months, and sentenced to solitude, are confined in a cell, and not on any occasion allowed to see another prisoner.

those by whom it may be adopted not to be too sanguine as to its results. That the enforcement of silence, and of the rule which prohibits a prisoner, when in the workshops, from looking at any other object than the labour on which he is engaged, will be felt as a restraint prevent in a great degree contamination, and improve the order and appearance of the prison, cannot admit of doubt; but I am confident that this species of imprisonment is calculated to effect but little more. Notwithstanding the immediate infliction of corporal punishment (as at Auburn and Sing Sing) convicts when confined together cannot be prevented from communicating to such an extent as to weaken the severest features of imprisonment, and this intercourse must obviously be more frequent when the lash is not used. Long as are the terms for which prisoners are sentenced to Wethersfield, the discipline, I fear, inspires no lasting sense of dread. If, then, with every advantage which these periods of commitment afford, the system fails essentially to deter, how utterly inadequate in this point of view must be its effects in the houses of correction in this kingdom, where the sentences are comparatively short? In no prison can the results of this discipline be more favourably illustrated than at Wethersfield, and yet in travelling through the several States I met with no one who expressed himself more decidedly in favour of solitary confinement, in preference to the system of association which he has himself so ably enforced, than the warden of this penitentiary.

I do not deem it necessary, for the purposes of this Report, to enter into a full description of the nature of the discipline observed at the principal gaols and houses of correction in England. As, however, my instructions require that I should point out the applicability to this country of any parts of the discipline of the American penitentiaries, I feel it necessary, before I offer such suggestions, to bring under your Lordship's notice a brief sketch of the present state of the English prisons*.

There are one hundred and seven county prisons in England and Wales. They are variously appropriated. Sixteen are gaols exclusively. In thirty-nine, the gaol and house of correction are united in the same building and under the same superintendence. The remaining fifty-two, which are denominated houses of correction, are distinct establishments and are situated generally at a distance from the gaol; but of this number only twelve in fact are appropriated to their original purpose, as in not less than forty it is the practice to confine not the convicted only, but persons before trial. This arrangement is most objectionable as many of the buildings in question do not contain the means of separation required by the Gaol Act†. The discipline also in regard to diet, labour, and the means of restraint, to which offenders before and after trial should be subjected, and which is entirely different, cannot be strictly enforced. In prisons of this description the presence of the untried, who are in idleness and have the free use of their airing-yards, materially interrupts the order and regularity which should prevail in a house of correction. The proportion of prisoners employed in gaols is small, labour of any kind not being compulsory on the unconvicted. Of the sixteen gaols under notice seven have no regular means of occupation. At the remaining nine the average proportion of convicts at hard labour is 9¼ per cent.; and at other employments 21½ per cent. In the thirty-nine prisons, where the gaol and house of correction are united, the average proportion at hard labour is 39½ per cent.; and at other occupations 11 per cent. Of the forty houses of correction at which it is the practice to receive prisoners before trial, as well as after conviction, there are four at which no employment is provided. At the remaining thirty-six, the proportion at hard labour is 45 per cent, and at other employments 19 per cent. At the twelve houses of correction which receive convicts only, the proportion at hard labour is 85½ per cent ‡. The nature of the employments varies considerably. In some gaols the prisoners are occupied in cleaning the apartments, or in other work not laborious. In houses of correction where regular employments are carried on, the periods of actual labour vary in duration from seven to ten hours daily in summer, and from five to seven in winter. In these prisons also the occupations are entirely dissimilar. The tread-wheel has been introduced into two county gaols, twenty-nine prisons where the gaol and house of correction are united, and thirty-six houses of correction. This description of labour is found to differ, in its degrees of severity, from 5,000 to 14,000 feet of

ascent

---

* *Vide* Statement in the Appendix, " Miscellaneous."

† Of the gaols included in the Act six only have the required number of classes. Thirteen houses of correction only have the prescribed classification; and but sixteen prisons, where the gaol and house of correction are united, have been rendered in this respect conformable to the statute.

‡ The highest proportions are at Brixton (Surrey), and Northleach (Gloucestershire).

ascent per day in summer, and in winter from 3,600 to 12,500 feet*. In some prisons women are placed on the tread-wheels, while at others females are not only exempt from this labour, but also from any other which can, in point of severity, be compared with it. At several gaols, not producing any amount of earnings† the prisoners have been variously occupied in the domestic service of the establishments, or in painting, whitewashing, &c.; in others the earnings are but trifling. This is particularly the case in regard to the tread-wheel labour provided in most of the houses of correction.

The daily allowances of food differ considerably. At some gaols bread only is furnished, the quantity for each prisoner varying from one and a quarter to two pounds daily; but where additional diet is allowed, meat, soup, potatoes, porridge, cheese, beer, &c., are provided in different proportions. This want of uniformity causes a difference in the weekly cost of from 1 s. 2 d. to 5 s.‡. No distinction is made in some instances in the allowance of food between the convicted and the unconvicted; while in others a larger quantity is furnished before trial although the individual is kept in idleness and has the privilege of receiving extra diet from his friends. It may be urged in support of this practice that the prisoner ought not before trial to be restricted in his food, nor compelled to labour; while in the case of the convict the reduced allowance is a part of the punishment: but this rule is reversed in other prisons, where the lowest diet is furnished before trial§. At a few county gaols there is no allowance of clothing, and generally it is furnished only after conviction. The quantity and description of these articles, as well as of bedding, vary greatly‖. The average cost of maintaining each prisoner throughout England

---

* *Vide* Appendix, " Miscellaneous."

† In thirty-five county prisons the amount of earnings in 1832 was 8,307 *l*. The average number in confinement at one time was 7,104. The following exhibit the highest earnings :—

	Amount of Earnings.	Average Number of Prisoners.
Chester - - - - - -	£.616	119
Knutsford - - - - - -	1,032	265
Shrewsbury - - - - -	780	176
Stafford - - - - - -	576	363
Somerset - - - - - -	628	378
Lancashire County Prisons - - -	2,655	1,989

‡ In the small borough and other corporate gaols the allowances vary in a much greater degree than at the county prisons. At several of the former only 1 lb. of bread per diem is allowed for each prisoner; and where money is given (a most objectionable practice), the value differs from 3 d. to 1 s.

§ Variations of diet before and after conviction :—

	Before Trial.		After Conviction.	
	s.	d.	s.	d.
Nottingham County Gaol - - - - -	3	6	—	
Ditto - Southwell House of Correction - -	-	-	2	11
Lancaster County Gaol - - - - -	2	2½	—	
Ditto - Kirkdale House of Correction - -	-	-	1	6½
Ditto - Manchester - Ditto - - -	-	-	1	7
Ditto - Ditto, females - - - -	-	-	1	1¼
Surrey, Kingston - - - - - -	2	7½	—	
Ditto, Brixton - - - - - - -	-	-	2	4
Cumberland County Gaol - - - - -	2	1	3	3
Hertford - Ditto - - - - - -	1	9	3	6
Huntingdon - Ditto - - - - - -	1	9	3	6
Leicester - Ditto - - - - - -	2	2	3	1
Suffolk; Bury County Gaol - - - -	1	10	3	2
Worcester County Gaol - - - - -	1	9	3	8
Hereford County Gaol - - - - -	3	8	3	8
Warwick County Gaol - - - - -	2	8	2	8
Ditto - Coventry Gaol - - - - -	1	2	1	2
Brecon County Gaol - - - - - -	1	7	1	7
Flint County Gaol - - - - - -	3	-	3	-

‖ At Shrewsbury County Gaol each prisoner is furnished with a complete suit of clothing. which, together with the requisite bedding ,&c., costs 21 s. per annum; but at Durham County Gaol the expense is 4 *l*. The cost is still higher at other prisons.

England and Wales, including food, clothing, and the salaries of officers, (but exclusive of the repairs of buildings), amounts to eighteen pounds per annum, or nearly seven shillings per week *. There is a great difference in the expenditure incurred on account of salaries to the officers of prisons. At the county gaols salaries are much higher in proportion than when the gaol and house of correction are united, although in the latter case a greater degree of vigilance and attention is required. At the houses of correction the allowances are lower than at either of the other descriptions of prisons †.

During the year 1832 the greatest number of sick at one time in the several prisons in England included in the Gaol Act was 1,178, being in the proportion of one to fifteen. The aggregate of cases was one to eight of the commitments ‡. This extent of sickness however is but apparent, and does not imply the prevalence of serious complaints, or even the admission of the patient into an infirmary, the slightest temporary affection being included. Such cases on the commitment of vagrants are of frequent occurrence.—The number of deaths in the prisons in 1832 was 345, being two and a quarter per cent. of the average at one time in confinement, and less than one half per cent. of the whole number in custody in the year. Of the deaths, 156 were occasioned by the cholera: the remainder is less than the number of ordinary deaths in the same prisons during the two preceding years §. There are yet a few prisons which have no separate infirmary. The cruel practice is still continued in some places of retaining lunatics after they have been acquitted on the ground of insanity, instead of sending them to an asylum. In not less than twenty county prisons are to be found persons thus afflicted.—The number in solitary confinement during the year, for various periods, either in pursuance of sentence or as a prison punishment, has been 6,948, being in the proportion of one in fourteen of the whole committed. In twenty-eight prisons this mode of correction has not been adopted.

It will be seen by a Statement inserted in the Appendix that there are about one hundred and sixty separate prisons belonging to corporate and other jurisdictions, which are not included in the beneficial provisions of the Gaol Act ‖. The prisons belonging to about twenty-five of these jurisdictions have, since the passing of the amended Act (5 Geo. 4, c. 85), been enlarged or rebuilt; and some others have been united with county gaols. There is, however, still a considerable number of corporate prisons which remain in a very defective condition. In many places the buildings are altogether inadequate. Several are also without any regulations to

direct

---

* The proportion of this expense incurred for the maintenance of a prisoner is   £. 12   –   –
  And for the salaries of officers   -   -   -   -   -   -   -   -   -   6   –   –

                                                                        £. 18   –   –

At Petworth House of Correction, where the accounts are kept with great accuracy, the average daily cost of each prisoner in the last year was 12 ½ d., including subsistence, clothing, and the salaries of officers. The highest sum paid for the support of prisoners is in Berkshire, where the average cost per head in the two prisons is 29 l. per annum. At Abingdon it amounts to 33 l. The lowest expense in the English counties is in Kent where it does not exceed 13 l. 5 s. At the county gaol for Lincoln the cost is 32 l. per head; while the average of the several prisons in that county is 23 l.

† At Chester County Gaol the salaries amount to 1,103 l., for an average number of 119 prisoners during the year; but at the house of correction at Knutsford, having 265 prisoners, the salaries were only 999 l. At Durham, where the gaol and house of correction are united, and contain 235 prisoners, the expense on this account was 1,107 l. The lowest amount of salaries is in Staffordshire and Devonshire, both of which average 3 l. 15 s. per head. The highest is at Lincoln County Gaol, being 16 l. 10 s. for each prisoner. At houses of correction the general average is at the rate of about 4 l. The sum, however, varies from 3 l. (at Wakefield) to 10 l. (at Ilford).

‡ The proportion of sick varied from one per cent. (at Winchester) to eighty-six per cent. (at Bristol).

§ The greatest mortality was at Lincoln County Gaol where the proportion amounted to one in forty. In the county prisons at Winchester not one death occurred during the year out of 1,164 persons.

‖ The following corporate prisons are included in the Gaol Act: Bristol, Chester, Coventry, Exeter, Gloucester, Kingston-upon-Hull, Leicester, Liverpool, London, Newcastle-upon-Tyne, Norwich, Nottingham, Portsmouth, Southwark, Westminster, Worcester, York. The following places also exercise the right of trial for capital offences, and from their population should have been included in the Gaol Act with the foregoing: Berwick-on-Tweed, Cambridge, Canterbury, Derby, Ely, Hereford, Ipswich, Lichfield, Lincoln, Lynn, Northampton, Oxford, Peterborough, St. Alban's, Southampton, Winchester, Yarmouth. There are also some other places possessing the like privilege but which do not exercise it. In the latter cases capital offenders are usually transferred to the county prisons, the local gaols being entirely inadequate for the scale of classification required by law.

direct their government and discipline; and the rules required to be enforced by the amended Act are consequently in numerous particulars violated or neglected. The gaols belonging to corporate jurisdictions are for the most part of the smaller class. In eight only did the greatest number at any one time during the year exceed forty. In eight others the largest number was between thirty and forty. In fifteen, between twenty and thirty. In twenty, between ten and twenty; and in one hundred and nineteen others, the greatest number did not exceed ten. Of the latter, forty-six are used merely as lock-up houses for temporary confinement, and ten others are employed for the confinement of persons for a short period only, or until they are finally committed to the county gaol. Of these temporary prisons no regular returns have been furnished, but they consist generally of two cells or rooms: in some few instances there is only one room; and there are not any rules established for their management. The principal defects of the other local prisons may be thus enumerated. Sixty-seven are without any prescribed regulations. In forty-seven, there is but one airing yard, and twenty have not any yard or court. In ninety-five, there is not a sufficient number of sleeping cells. At eighty-eight, a clergyman does not attend. In seven, there is not any allowance of food. In ten prisons only (of the larger description) has the tread-wheel labour been introduced, and in but twenty-two others have any means of employment been provided after trial. In many of the small gaols there is no effectual separation of the sexes. In the greater part, the sick cannot be separated; and the insecurity of the buildings in a number of instances renders it necessary that irons should be used, and other improper means of coercion resorted to, to prevent escape.

A large proportion of the prisoners who now fill the county houses of correction consist of persons committed under the Act for the suppression of vagrancy (5 Geo. 4, c. 83) which was passed at the same period as the amended prison law. The number of persons committed under this Act in 1826, the year after the new law came into operation, was 7,092; in 1829, that number had increased to 9,415; and in 1832 to not less than 15,624 *. The usual term for which offenders of this description are sentenced is one month, while for a second or aggravated offence the period is limited to three months. At some houses of correction the number of vagrants exceeds that of the convictions for all other offences. Experience has proved that the commitment of vagrants inspires but little dread. During the period of their confinement, they are supplied with wholesome food as well as bedding, and clothing if requisite; and at the expiration of their sentence are at liberty to go whither they please. They consequently, in numerous instances, soon return to prison, having frequently with this view committed some trifling offence. The amended Gaol Act of 5 Geo. 4, c. 85 has given to visiting justices the power of granting passes to offenders on their discharge to enable them to return to their legal place of settlement, by receiving from the overseers of parishes through which they travel 1 ½ d. per mile for each adult, and 1 d. per mile for each child. This practice is adopted only in a few districts besides the metropolis; the local authorities in most counties being of opinion that the relief thus afforded has a tendency to encourage rather than suppress acts of vagrancy by inducing the idle and vicious to enter a prison for a short time, for the sake of obtaining the pass and allowance on their discharge. The great difficulty consists in being able to make a just discrimination between the destitute who are really deserving of relief and the habitual vagrant. The Act of 59 Geo. 3, c. 12, has authorised the removal of Scotch and Irish paupers at once to their respective places of settlement. Without offering an opinion on the expediency of extending the practice of dispensing occasionally with the previous imprisonment I would remark that where punishment is really merited, the vagrant should be subjected to such a severe although short period of discipline as would have some effect in correcting his habits and restraining him from the further violation of the law †.

The

---

* *Vide* Appendix, " Miscellaneous."

† In consequence of vagrants being often destitute of clothing, and not unfrequently brought into prison in a diseased state, great expense is incurred for their support during confinement. The cost of keeping a vagrant varies from three pence to one shilling per diem; but estimating the average expense to be that of the ordinary gaol allowance, the total cost of maintaining the number committed in 1832 would not amount to a less sum than 15,000 l. In Middlesex alone, the number of vagrants committed in that year to the house of correction in Coldbath-fields was 4,109. The number of Scotch and Irish paupers removed in the year 1831 in England and Wales was 59,571, and at an expense of 22,872 l. There is also another description of vagrants denominated " trampers," who

The Gaol Act does not extend to Scotland. The prisons in that part of the kingdom, with some few exceptions, are most defective; the buildings being generally old, insecure, and unfit for a lengthened period of confinement. There is a lamentable want of separation both by day and by night. It will be seen by reference to a Statement in the Appendix*, that there are about one hundred and thirty prisons in Scotland, the greater part belonging to the royal burghs, but few of which have adequate funds for the support of their gaols. Almost every county comprises several burghs, and each of these local jurisdictions has its prison for debtors and criminals. Some of these gaols are of the smallest description, and most of them from their injudicious construction preclude separation and employment. In several the keeper does not reside; and the regulations, if there be any, are very lax and defective. It is very desirable that many of these burgh gaols should be abolished, or used only as lock-up houses for the temporary confinement of offenders previous to their committal to the county prison. The Parliamentary Committee appointed in 1826 to inquire into the state of the gaols in Scotland, suggested in their Report the necessity of erecting proper places of confinement in certain districts to receive offenders from several adjoining counties. Such prisons might be constructed and regulated with a much greater degree of advantage and economy than if the present gaols were rebuilt; and as the assizes are not held in every county, but only in the circuit towns, those places would form the most convenient situations for new district prisons. It is to be regretted that this desirable measure was not at that period adopted, especially as, in several burghs, gaols have recently been rebuilt without any material improvement in the principle of their construction.

The statute of 7 Geo. 4, c. 74, for the better regulation of the prisons in Ireland, was framed on the basis of the English Gaol Act; but by the new law a power was vested in the Irish Government of appointing two inspectors-general to visit the prisons throughout that part of the kingdom for the purpose of suggesting improvements in their construction and regulation, and of reporting annually on their condition to His Majesty's Government. The grand jury of each county and city are also required to appoint a Board of Superintendence, and a local inspector, whose duty it is to visit the prison at least twice in every week. From the adoption of these measures, great benefits have been derived. Before this enactment the gaols were in a deplorable condition, but various improvements have since been effected. The tread-wheel labour and employments of various kinds have been introduced into several county prisons; and increased attention is paid to moral and religious instruction. To comply with the provisions of the Act it was found necessary to build new gaols in several counties, and to enlarge others. These important measures have been very generally accomplished as will be seen by reference to a Statement inserted in the Appendix†. Many of the small bridewells and prisons belonging to local jurisdictions have been abolished in pursuance to the statute, but there are yet remaining nearly one hundred prisons of this description.

I now proceed to submit to your Lordship the following suggestions, which I feel the more emboldened to offer, as they are the result of observations made in the course of my visits to a considerable number of places of confinement in England as well as in America. I should add that I have found on these several subjects a striking concurrence of sentiment in the minds of many magistrates and intelligent governors of prisons in both countries, whose opinions I have had the opportunity of consulting.

First. That it is expedient to diminish as much as possible the number of persons committed for safe custody only, and with this view to extend the practice of taking bail as widely as is consistent with the public interests. In the commitment of a prisoner for trial, the law merely contemplates a security for his appearance in court to answer the charge alleged against him. If this object can be attained by
the

---

who contrive to evade imprisonment, or having committed an act of vagrancy, are relieved without being placed in confinement. Persons of this class are usually assisted with a small sum of money by the overseer or constable. The allowance varies from four pence to two shillings per head, with occasionally a night's lodging and provisions in the poor-house. The number of persons relieved in this manner in 1832 exceeded 90,000. *Vide* Appendix, " Miscellaneous."

* *Vide* Appendix, " Miscellaneous," Scotland.   † *Vide* Appendix, " Miscellaneous," Ireland.

the intervention of sureties, instead of throwing the accused into a gaol, the ends of justice are answered, the public are relieved from an unnecessary burden, and the individual is protected from the injurious effects of imprisonment. In reference to the higher classes of crime the law has in certain cases declared that bail shall not, except under special circumstances, be taken; not that the detention before trial is intended as a punishment, but because the motive to abscond is too great to be restrained by ordinary obligations. It is, however, very different in many cases of inferior crimes where the motives for non-appearance are much less powerful. Young and minor offenders can never be committed without the risk of great injury to any portion of good character which they may possess; and it frequently happens that courts of judicature shorten the sentence on the ground that the prisoner has already suffered considerably. Thus safe custody interferes with the administration of justice, and a beneficial punishment is abridged for another which is either injurious or of questionable utility.

2dly. That there should be a more frequent delivery of the county gaols than twice in the year. The long intervals which are at present suffered to elapse in England between the assizes are at variance with that enlightened maxim of jurisprudence which presumes every man innocent until proved guilty. The interests of justice are the more deeply concerned than heretofore in extending the number of gaol deliveries throughout the kingdom, inasmuch as an Act has lately passed the legislature for the more frequent trial of offenders in the metropolis. A prisoner may now remain for six months in most of the county gaols before he can be brought to trial, and for an offence perhaps of the most trifling description, while in London he could not at the utmost suffer detention beyond a few weeks. In the case of parties who are eventually acquitted, the cruelty of the existing system is sufficiently apparent, but with regard to those sentenced to short terms of imprisonment it is scarcely less unjust. A large proportion of prisoners are in confinement before trial for a longer period than that to which if guilty they are ultimately sentenced. The total number of persons committed for trial at the assizes and quarter sessions in England and Wales during the last seven years amounted to 131,818. Of this number 49,845, or upwards of one third, were sentenced to periods not exceeding six months*. Many of these persons therefore suffered before conviction a longer imprisonment than that to which they were subsequently adjudged. Although it is occasionally the practice of the bench in passing sentence to make allowance for previous imprisonment, yet such a practice confers in some cases too much power; while the law, not contemplating the anomaly, gives in others too little discretion.

3dly. That provision should be made in every gaol and house of correction for the solitary confinement of certain classes. The nature of this description of prison discipline admits of three degrees. The first of these is solitude for short periods with employment, combined with arrangements tending materially to diminish the wearisomeness of confinement. This mitigated seclusion is well adapted to the situation of the untried. Justice demands that this class of prisoners should be subjected to no suffering or inconvenience that is not indispensable to their safe custody, and the preservation of their morals. For the attainment of the latter object it is essential that they should be confined apart, furnished with light employment, at which they may have the option to work, and be allowed the privilege of books and of receiving visits from their friends, under restrictions to be clearly defined—indulgences by which solitude would become divested of every harsh character. If decent in their habits and innocent of the crime with which they are charged, separation from other prisoners will greatly contribute to their comfort and advantage. If otherwise, it becomes the more necessary that they should be placed in a situation in which they will be prevented from corrupting others. Should, however, the plan of separation be applied to prisoners before trial, it will become absolutely necessary that the gaols should be more frequently delivered than twice in the year, in order to afford space for carrying this arrangement into effect, as well as to obviate the severity of long-continued solitude.—The next modification of solitary confinement is its infliction for short periods, unaccompanied by employment. The enforcement of solitude and silence changes altogether the character of prison labour which is no longer regarded as a penalty, but as an alleviation of the greater punishment. Employment

---

* *Vide* Appendix, " Miscellaneous," Returns of Criminal Commitments.

ment of some kind is indispensable to the maintenance of silence, but the case is different in respect to solitude. The experience derived from several prisons, but more especially from the Glasgow Bridewell and the house of correction at Springfield is decisive as to the fact that, under proper regulations, solitude without labour may be enforced even for a period of some months with safety and advantage. The seclusion in the cases to which I refer is very strict, no one prisoner having the opportunity of seeing another*. It is certain that when solitude is applied for short periods, employment deprives it of that beneficial sense of dread, to inspire which should be the first object of imprisonment. It becomes therefore of importance to inquire to what degree the withholding of employment to persons sentenced to short periods of solitary imprisonment may be expedient.—The last degree of severity consists in solitary confinement for a long term, and for which labour is absolutely indispensable. This description of penitentiary discipline will, if I mistake not, prove the most effectual punishment which has yet been devised for convicts sentenced to be transported, previously to their embarkation.

4thly. That every prisoner should have a separate sleeping-cell. Where this arrangement does not exist, the most mischievous consequences are the result. It is at night that the communications of convicts confined in the same apartment take place with the greatest ease and to the most injurious extent. The crowded night-rooms of a prison are perhaps of all sources of corruption the most contaminating, where every practice prevails that can debase and harden. A separate cell for each individual at night also affords facilities for occasional separation by day. At various houses of correction the different classes take their meals in their cells, and are confined in them when not at work. From estimates which have been formed in the several counties, it appears that taking the greatest number in confinement at one time during the year, the total expense of providing each prisoner with a separate cell would amount to about 300,000 *l*. †

5thly. When the preferable system of solitary confinement is not adopted, silence should be rigidly maintained by day as well as by night. Silence is the nearest approximation to solitude, and is indispensable to the good government of a prison. The untried as well as the convicted should be required to conform to this regulation.

6thly. That in the confinement of prisoners in association, the convict, when employed, should be required to pursue his work with downcast eyes, take his meals alone, be kept apart when not actually engaged at labour, and at all times prohibited from holding any intercourse with another prisoner ‡.

7thly. That for the maintenance of solitary confinement for lengthened periods, as well as of silence, it is necessary that prisoners subjected to either plan of prison discipline, should be habitually employed. I am aware that the introduction of occupations into gaols is in this country attended with serious difficulties. Beset by competition, arising from the superabundance of both capital and labour, and having to contend against the use of machinery and the superiority of skilful workmen, profitable results cannot reasonably be expected. Except indeed in certain districts, where masters are induced to send raw materials, experience has proved that manufactures can be seldom carried on in gaols without loss. The whole amount

---

* Only certain descriptions of prisoners are so confined at Glasgow and Springfield.

† Estimate of the expense of providing separate Sleeping Cells in the County Prisons, &c. in England and Wales, included in Act 4 Geo. 4, c. 64:

Greatest Number of Prisoners at one time in 1832.	Present Number of Cells.	Additional Cells, by dividing Day Rooms, &c.	New Cells wanting.	Estimated Expense.
17,982	10,200	4,180	4,257	£. 267,761

For the Borough and other Corporate Gaols not included in the said Act:

1,746	1,119	418	402	28,108

Total - - - £. 295,869

A Statement, showing the expense which would be incurred by each county in effecting this arrangement is inserted in the Appendix, "Miscellaneous."

‡ The tread-wheel should uniformly be fitted up with separate compartments, as at Bedford, Gloucester, &c.

amount of a prisoner's earnings are insufficient to compensate for the disadvantage at which materials must be purchased, the loss occasioned by teaching the trade, inferior workmanship, and the difficulties attending the disposal of the goods when manufactured. In agricultural districts especially the want of suitable employment is severely felt. In such cases the introduction of a manufacture is a certain and serious loss; besides which, to teach a husbandry servant, committed perhaps but for a few months, to be a weaver, or a day-labourer to be a mechanic, would be a waste of both time and materials. Objections have, I know, been urged against the employment of criminals at any trade, on the ground that the practice tends to diminish the demand for the labour of the honest and industrious; but the same may be said of the introduction of labour into a parish workhouse. Every man, whether convict or pauper, is entitled to his fair share in the productive employment which the country affords; nor does he forfeit the right of earning his subsistence by becoming either the tenant of a poorhouse or a gaol. The law does not doom the criminal to idleness as well as to imprisonment. If the individual were previously engaged in habits of industry his employment during confinement cannot diminish the demand for the labour of others. Should this not have been the case it becomes the duty of society, by the application of such means as may be essential for the purpose, to render the idle industrious, in order to convert him into an honest man. It cannot be denied that were trades in prison general cases might occur, when by the sale of articles at a rate below the market price labourers would be driven, and capital displaced, from some particular branch of industry; but much as this result would be to be lamented, the consequences must be regarded as a sacrifice of the individual to the general good. While, however, the employment of criminals can be justified on the soundest principles, it should uniformly be rendered subservient to other means which may be necessary for the correction of the offender. There are moral as well as financial objections to the indiscriminate conversion of prisons into mere manufactories. It should never be forgotten that a gaol is not a school for the instruction of artisans, but a place of punishment. It has been said that instruction in useful trades is essential to qualify a prisoner, on his liberation, to earn a livelihood; but the short periods to which convicts are sentenced in this country are not sufficient to enable them to learn a mechanical art. If this were even practicable, the advantage would be but slight, owing to the formidable difficulties with which a discharged criminal has to contend, from the want of character and friends, in order to procure employment.

8thly. That provision be made for establishing a more efficient system than at present prevails of communicating religious instruction. As personal reformation to be permanent must be founded upon Christian principles, so no system of prison discipline can be effectual in which religious instruction does not form a prominent part. The prisons of this country have great advantages over those of the United States in the means afforded by the Legislature for imparting religious instruction*; but notwithstanding the liberal remuneration authorized by law there are too many instances in which chaplains, having other professional engagements, do not devote themselves exclusively to the duties of the prison. On the importance of this subject it is impossible too earnestly to dwell. The vice and depravity to be found in every gaol has led to an impression, by far too general, that most criminals are beyond the reach of reformation. Whatever may be the fact, I feel assured that the trial has in few prisons been fairly made. There can be no limits to the sacred influence of religious impressions upon the hearts of even the most guilty, and I cannot doubt that by the employment of measures adequate to the occasion, minds, however hardened, may be raised from degradation, and reclaimed by the power of the Gospel. When the number of prisoners is considerable, the whole time and undivided attention of a chaplain should be devoted to his duties. Whatever necessity prevails in the world at large for moral education and religious instruction is immeasurably increased in a prison by the character and habits of its inmates, and by the disadvantages under which that instruction can ordinarily be conveyed. The situation of a young criminal, on his first entrance into a gaol, might be rendered eminently favourable to good impressions; nor can any human being,

* The salaries allowed by the legislature of New York to the chaplains at Auburn and Sing Sing, the largest penitentiaries in the Union, are 384 dollars per annum each; the former having, at the period of my visit, 683, and the latter 833, prisoners under their charge. The consequence is that these gentlemen are obliged to have recourse to the funds of a charitable institution for an addition to their incomes.

being, however hardened, be so debased by guilt as to justify the withdrawal of the means which are necessary to his moral restoration. Valuable, however, as are the public services of religion, their effects on prisoners are in general but partial and unsatisfactory. The labours of the chaplain should not therefore be confined to the performance of social worship: to this must be added private and individual instruction in the retirement of the cell. In his efforts to convince the misguided and reclaim the impenitent, sound judgment and knowledge of character are not less essential than ardent piety and persevering benevolence. Against the numerous arts which prevail in prisons the chaplain must habitually guard. Every motive to hypocrisy should be removed. A convict should not be allowed to hope for any temporal advantage during confinement from religious professions, nor ought a chaplain to be exposed to deception by having it in his power to procure for a prisoner any species of indulgence or reward.

9thly. That the mere classification of prisoners fails to prevent corrupt intercourse. In the situation of certain descriptions there are such broad lines of distinction that no question can exist as to the necessity of separation. In respect, however, to any elaborate divisions, the practice is attended with so little benefit, and involves so much expense, that the propriety of continuing them is more than doubtful. The shades of difference in the manners and corrupting influence of the ordinary felon and misdemeanant are often slight, and there exists in each class so great a variety of character as to defy every attempt to prevent contamination by the separation of the classes. When prisoners are confined during the day in association, the only effectual modes of restraint are the rigid observance of silence, and the prevention of any exchange of intercourse, and even of looks from one to another.

10thly. That the rigour of imprisonment should be equal, certain and unremitted. The best system of gaol management will be ineffectual, if its salutary terrors are to be impaired by indulgences of any description. Supplies of food beyond the restricted ration, unless on the recommendation of the medical adviser, should on no account be allowed. All letters, as well as visits and messages from friends, should be strictly prohibited, under a penalty. A prisoner should not be allowed any portion of his earnings, the amount of which more frequently depends on his skill than industry. Those who derive the largest portion are often far from being the most meritorious. Although the prospect of pecuniary reward may induce increased exertion, the idea of compensation weakens the sense and abates the severity of punishment. The convict ought to be imperatively required to do that which the law prescribes. There should be no persuasives to obedience in a prison. It is not less unjustifiable to mitigate than to aggravate the penalties of justice.

11thly. That there should be an uniformity in the discipline of prisons throughout the kingdom. Several important clauses of the Gaol Act are so framed as to authorize rather than to require their execution. This circumstance has led to the neglect of many valuable rules. The law has defined the leading principles, but as the magistracy in the respective counties act independently of each other, a great variety of practice prevails in respect to the allowance of a prisoner's food, the modes of his restraint, and the nature of his employment. Very precise rules, as to diet and degrees of labour, cannot perhaps be laid down for general observance; but the treatment of criminals in these important particulars may be approximated, and rendered in a great measure equivalent, if they cannot be reduced to one standard. It is unnecessary to state that while this neglect of uniformity prevails, the prisoner in the gaol of one county will escape with less punishment than in that of another. Nothing can be more vague and indefinite than a sentence of imprisonment and hard labour. A convict is adjudged to both, but neither the discipline of the prison nor the nature of the employment, on which the severity of the sentence principally depends, is in any manner defined; nor is the Court, in many cases, aware of the actual punishment which it awards. Uniformity of discipline is as much required by the interests of justice as by the welfare of the prisoner.

12thly. That the sentence of the law should not be abridged by recommendation for pardon, in consequence of good conduct during imprisonment. It is important that the prisoner should feel that there is no alternative but to submit to the full penalty to which the law has sentenced him. As in no country has the exercise of the pardoning power been so grossly abused as in the United States, so on no point are the governors of the respective penitentiaries more unanimous than in their condemnation of this practice. The experienced warden of the Eastern Penitentiary assured me, that no favourable impression could be made on any prisoner until the

hope

hope of pardon had been entirely eradicated from his mind. The privilege of recommending for pardon prisoners who have conducted themselves well during confinement should be exercised rarely, and with great caution. It is well known that the most consummate rogues often become, on their commitment, the best conducted prisoners. From the recommendation to pardon the worst characters not unfrequently derive the greatest benefit; and while the possibility of obtaining pardon on such a ground exists, there will always be ample encouragement in a prison for every species of hypocritical profession. Were pardons uniformly granted with the strictest impartiality, and dispensed solely as rewards for good conduct, they would still be open to great objection. If an offender at large knows that, in the event of conviction, he can, by strict attention to prison regulations, obtain an abridgment of his sentence, the terrors of the law become diminished; while, during confinement, the hope of liberation excludes other and legitimate motives to obedience. Neither is the reformation of the offender promoted by pardons; but even were this effect produced, they would not be justified by other considerations. To weaken the deterring influence of penal justice in order to reclaim, is to sacrifice the best interests of society at large for a few of the least worthy of its members.

13th. That the gaols under corporate jurisdictions be abolished (with the exception of those employed for temporary purposes only) the magistrates of which have not complied with the provisions required by the 5 Geo. 4, c. 85, and who refuse to avail themselves of the power which the law has given to them of making arrangements for the committal of their prisoners to the county gaols.

14th. That increased attention be paid to the character and ability of the subordinate officers of prisons. Persons appointed to these situations should be selected from a better educated class of society than that from which they are now generally chosen. The management of large bodies of criminals is itself a science, and requires an union of firmness, temper and discretion. The best system of discipline will be of no avail if those to whom is confided the execution of its details be unable to appreciate its merits and enforce its regulations.

15th. The last suggestion which I take the liberty to offer is, that arrangements should be made for enabling the convict on his discharge to earn an honest subsistence. The best system of prison discipline must necessarily be ineffectual if the offender on his liberation be unable to procure employment by which to earn a creditable livelihood. So greatly, however, does the supply of labour exceed the demand throughout England, that serious difficulties are experienced in this respect by thousands who have the advantage of character and connexions, but who are nevertheless compelled to seek a subsistence by emigration to distant lands. How immeasurably are those difficulties increased when the individual is tainted by crime, and therefore shunned by society! It is in vain to look for the means of procuring employment for the discharged convict in this country. In the colonies alone can the remedy be found. If the emigration of liberated criminals to a penal colony were encouraged, an opportunity would be afforded to the best disposed to change their habits and commence a new life. That there is a large class whose depravity would dispose them to reject such a proposal cannot be questioned, and it might form a subject of consideration whether a criminal who had on his discharge from prison refused an offer of emigration, should not on reconviction be subjected to an increased punishment. There are, however, others who would gladly avail themselves of any opportunity by which they could escape from bad connexions, and avoid the numerous temptations which inevitably beset them in this country. Emigration to Australia would be the means of enabling them to maintain themselves by industry, and become, what they never can hope to be by remaining at home, honest and useful members of society. A measure of this nature should, however, be combined with another, by which the emigrant should be compelled on his arrival in the colony to pay the whole or part of the expenses incurred by his removal. Some plan of this kind would be indispensable in order to prevent persons who are anxious to emigrate, but who have not the means of doing so, from committing minor offences in order to avail themselves of the opportunity of being sent out to Australia free of expense.

Agreeably to the instructions which I received on leaving England, I have visited the Houses of Refuge for the support and reformation of young persons in the cities of New York and Philadelphia.

The house of refuge in New York was established by an Act of Incorporation in March 1824. The idea originated with Professor Griscom, a gentleman of great respectability, who at that period resided in the city of New York. Mr. Griscom had lately returned from England the charitable institutions of which had occupied a large share of his attention. He was particularly struck with the beneficial effects arising from the " Refuge for the Destitute" in London, and on his arrival in New York lost no time in making public its meritorious objects, with a view to the establishment of a similar institution in that city. For this purpose he communicated with a Society which had been recently formed, and of which he was a member, for the prevention of pauperism. An address. earnestly recommending the measure, was immediately issued by that Society. Public benevolence spontaneously answered the appeal, and in a few weeks funds were collected to the amount of 15,000 dollars. The " House of Refuge" in New York, as well as that in Philadelphia, to which I shall presently advert, differs in many respects from the " Refuges" which have been formed in England. The legislatures of New York and Pennsylvania have vested the management of these establishments in a certain number of directors, who are elected annually by the subscribers to the respective charities. The directors have power to receive all children apprehended or committed as vagrants, or convicted of criminal offences, who may be considered proper objects in the judgment of the courts of general sessions of the peace, the court of oyer and terminer, the jury before whom any such offenders shall be tried, the police magistrates, or the commissioners of the almshouses and bridewell of the city. The directors have power to place the children, during their minority, at such employments as shall be suitable to their years and capacities, and to bind them out at their discretion (with the consent of the parties) as apprentices or servants. This power ceases in regard to boys at twenty-one, and in the case of girls at eighteen. The directors are authorised to make such regulations, not contrary to law, as they may deem proper, and they are required to present annually to the legislature a report of their proceedings.

The motives which have led to the formation of these institutions are so truly excellent, that it is with great reluctance I venture to express my dissent from the principle on which they differ from those of a similar character in England. The main points of distinction are that in America these establishments are open to vagrant youth of every description, as well as to young persons not only convicted of but simply charged with crime; while in England the " Refuges" are confined to convicts alone. In America, the personal liberty of youth committed to these institutions becomes forfeited until they have attained their majority, without the sentence of a court of judicature, an interval during which they are placed at the entire disposal of the managers of the institutions.

Houses of refuge for the reception of destitute children, like most other charitable asylums, require to be very carefully guarded by such restrictions as will prevent the encouragement of the evil which they are designed to suppress. The same reasons for which foundling hospitals have proved mischievous in England, apply with equal force to other establishments which open their doors indiscriminately to destitute youth, thus weakening the bonds of parental obligation, and affording encouragement to the vicious and depraved to neglect and forsake their offspring. It is true that in a thinly-peopled country, where the pressure of indigence is not felt, and where the services of a young family soon become in a pecuniary sense a source of profit, there can be but few inducements to a parent to forsake his children; and consequently the evils which flow from indiscriminate charity, although they cannot fail in some degree to exist, are not strikingly apparent. The principle of an enactment is, however, not the less unsound which invites the idle and the dissolute to throw upon a public institution the maintenance of their children, which renders a mere act of vagrancy on the part of a youth a qualification for admission into an asylum, in which he shall be supported, educated and taught a trade, and thus derive advantages superior to those which are enjoyed by the offspring of the honest and deserving. " The Refuge in Philadelphia (says its most eloquent advocate) presents no vindictive or
reproachful

reproachful aspect; it threatens no humiliating recollections of the past; it holds out no degrading denunciations for the future; but in the accents of kindness and compassion invites the children of poverty and ignorance, whose wandering and unguided steps are leading them to swift destruction, to come to a home where they will be sheltered from temptation, and led into the ways of usefulness and virtue *." Such an institution is a direct bounty on parental neglect, and operates most unjustly upon those who, disdaining to have recourse to charitable aid, strive to maintain their families by prudent habits and honest industry.

I do not venture to state these objections to the " houses of refuge " in New York and Philadelphia without having had some experience on this subject. Having been for a period of nearly twenty years connected with the management of the " Refuge for the Destitute" in London, I have had abundant opportunities of witnessing the practical operation of the evils to which I advert; and I have no hesitation in saying that if that establishment were conducted upon the principle of indiscriminately admitting vagrant children, it would prove deeply injurious, instead of being as it now is, highly beneficial to society. For several years after the establishment of the London " Refuge" there was in this respect no restriction. Numberless were the applications of parents for the admission of their children, and this, notwithstanding the present regulations, is so much the case that the closest scrutiny is necessary in every instance in which a boy or girl has friends, in order to prevent an abuse of the charity. Investigation has shown that this urgency on the part of parents was to a great extent occasioned by their own laxity of principle and improvidence, and that their main object was the riddance of their children. That a youth placed in such circumstances is an object of great commiseration cannot be denied, but it has become indispensable that the committee should take care that the relief afforded does not by its misapplication contribute to increase the number thus painfully situated, and that the benefits of the institution be imparted to those only who possess unquestionable and legitimate claims on public charity. If the juvenile vagrant have parents, they are bound to maintain him, or to procure from the parish the means of his subsistence. If his vagrant habits be occasioned by destitution, the workhouse is his asylum. But the situation of the friendless juvenile offender on his discharge from prison is in many important respects different. He is not only destitute, but criminal, and bereft of character. Reformation, induced by a course of moral discipline and religious instruction, is indispensable in order to wean him from the indulgence of vicious habits, enable him to obtain employment, and become an honest member of society. The great difference of circumstances arising out of the peculiar state of the population in England and the United States, is perhaps in no case rendered more manifest than in the opposite views with which the managers of these institutions in the respective countries regard the admission of children. In the London establishment numbers are weekly refused admittance, and the greatest vigilance is necessary to exclude children having parents and friends, and who consequently have other means of support, either of their own or such as the law has provided; but in the Refuges of the United States, complaint is constantly made that there are not more applicants. In London great difficulty has been experienced in providing for the inmates on their discharge; but in America such is the demand for labour of every description that no inconvenience whatever is in this respect experienced. " We think," say the managers of the New York Refuge, in their ninth Report, " that we can safely urge that the condition of all children in the habits of vagrancy, or who are abandoned, or have no parents or guardians, or who have drunken parents, would be much improved if they were sent to the Refuge." " That there are many hundreds of such children in this city cannot be doubted, and it is much to be regretted if from any mistaken views of clemency, either on the part of parents or magistrates, they are not sent to this establishment. We regret to say that many suitable objects of this charity are not sent to the Refuge, although it has been our endeavour to divest the house, as far as practicable, of the gloomy character of a prison, as well as the reality of a mechanic's shop and school." " A discerning public seek for children who have been

---

* *Vide* Address delivered by John Serjeant, esq., the president of the House of Refuge in Philadelphia, 1828, p. 12.

been disciplined in the Refuge, and take them from us as fast as we can provide for
them." Were the committee of the " Refuge," or any other charitable institution
in London, to put forth such an invitation to parents to take their children off their
hands, any one of the populous districts of the metropolis would in one week furnish
the asylum with hundreds of applicants.

The power vested by the legislature in certain authorities, and in the managers of the American " houses of refuge," to commit and detain young persons,
is of an extraordinary character. In cities so comparatively limited as those of
New York and Philadelphia there is less danger to be apprehended from its abuse
than in more crowded communities. There are, however, serious objections to the
principle. A youth may be subjected to imprisonment in a " house of refuge " for a
period of several years by the commission of an act which, although a legal trans-
gression, may not carry with it any great degree of moral turpitude. Mendicity
and other offences which constitute vagrancy, although necessary to be suppressed,
should not be punished with a rigor due only to serious crimes. The principles
of justice are immutable and ought not to be violated even in the person of a
youth, and that violation is the less defensible when the party is weak, destitute,
and unprotected. To separate children from their parents by committing them to
a place of confinement where they may be detained for years or even during the
whole period of their minority, for an act of vagrancy, or on the mere accusation of
such an act, and this too on the decision of a police magistrate or the guardians
of the poor, is a stretch of authority not reconcileable with the spirit of English law,
nor likely to be sanctioned by public opinion in this country.

The " house of refuge " at New York is situated about two miles from the city,
within a walled inclosure, 320 feet by 300 feet. Two stone buildings (separated
by a high wooden fence) have been erected; the one for boys, and the other for
girls. The first story of that appropriated to the boys contains four apartments,
used for dining-room, common hall, superintendent's office, tailors' and shoemakers'
shops. The second story contains an infirmary and two rows of dormitories, 132 in
number, each seven feet by three feet and a half, and six feet high. These rooms
are ventilated by openings in the walls. The corridors or passages into which the
cells open are used as school-rooms. The first story of the girls' building is divided
into four rooms, a kitchen, dining-room and two work-rooms. The remainder of
the story is occupied by the apartment of the matron, a committee-room and
a laundry. In the south end of the second story is the chapel. At the north end
the infirmary has been placed. The intermediate space is occupied by two rows of
dormitories, consisting in the whole of sixty eight, for as many girls. The superintendant and the assistant keeper have residences appropriated to them. An
adjoining building is divided into four work-rooms, each forty feet square; and in
another part of the yard are two wooden buildings in which the boys are also
employed. A bakehouse and storehouses are attached to the establishment. A sum
of 8,000 dollars is annually appropriated to the support of this institution from
funds arising from fees paid by passengers in vessels entering New York. A portion of the revenue of the establishment is also derived from the amount received
for the licences of theatres, and from the duties levied on grocers and tavern-
keepers in the State.

Soon after sun-rise the dormitories are opened, and after washing and a short
time being spent in the open air (when the weather permits) the inmates are summoned to morning prayer. School commences generally in summer at half-past
five. Here they remain until seven, when they are dismissed for a few minutes'
relaxation. Half an hour is then allowed for breakfast, after which the children
repair to their workshops until noon. Tasks are allotted by which arrangement the
most industrious are frequently stimulated to shorten the hours of their labour. At
twelve o'clock work is suspended. An hour is allowed for washing and dinner.
At one the boys return to the shops where they remain until five. The labour of
the day then terminates. Half an hour is allowed for washing and recreation.
Supper is then served at the conclusion of which the evening school commences.
Here the business of instruction continues till eight o'clock when religious service
is performed by the superintendant; after which the inmates are marched to their
respective dormitories. Silence is maintained during the night. Such is the usual
routine

routine in the summer months. In winter, the morning school is suspended. The shops are also closed at four o'clock. On Sundays the children are classed according to the nature of their conduct in the preceding week, and badges denoting degrees of merit are awarded. Religious services are performed twice during the Sunday. In the interval which elapses between them a school is held. At the close of the evening service the inmates are allowed to walk about the grounds, under the inspection of the officer. The boys are classed in four divisions, according to their moral conduct. Their employments consist in carpentering, making chairs, cabinet work, making harness, brass nails, tailoring and shoemaking. Their labour is let out to tradesmen who provide the materials, and pay the institution twelve and a half cents (6 d.) per diem for the services of each boy. The sum received for the labour of the boys in the year 1833 amounted to 3,994 dollars. The girls are subjected to nearly the same course of discipline, and are under the care of female officers who are superintended by a matron and a ladies' committee. The girls are employed in making mending and washing the clothes, linen, and bedding belonging to the institution. They also assist in the household work and are generally placed out as domestic servants. There is no part of the establishment which strikes a visitor with so much satisfaction as the degree of attention which is evidently paid to moral and religious education. Besides the earnest and unremitted instructions of a stated chaplain, resident on the premises, the children have the benefit of an excellent library of nearly five hundred volumes, the selection of which reflects great credit on the managers. Religious services are performed by the different clergymen in the city. Those children who have distinguished themselves by good conduct wear generally an honorary badge on the left arm. The punishments consist in flogging with a whip of strings, solitary confinement, either with or without a diminution of food, or in forbidding any one to hold communication with the offender, and in extraordinary cases in wearing an iron fastened to the waist on one side, and to the ancle of the other. Whipping, however, is the chastisement most usually inflicted, and it was at one period extended even to the females. The average length of time during which the boys remain before they are apprenticed is about eighteen months. Of 108 who were indentured in the course of the year 1833, forty-nine were apprenticed as husbandry servants, nineteen to the sea service, and ten to shoemakers; the remaining thirty were appropriated to nineteen trades. Coloured children are not admitted into the institution.

It is estimated by the managers that nine-tenths of those who have been admitted have been reclaimed. On referring, however, to the cases which are included in some of the last annual reports I suspect that the managers have relied for proofs of reformation on the evidence of good behaviour during the detention of the inmates, rather than on their subsequent conduct; for, with the exception of five cases out of twenty adverted to, no term of probation is instanced so long as ten months (the majority are much shorter), a test which from the experience of the London Refuge I have no hesitation to pronounce fallacious. Nor is this the only instance in which the sanguine spirit of benevolence with which the reports of this institution are drawn up, has I fear led the managers to over-rate its success. In a report of the Senate of New York in 1826, it is stated that since the house of Refuge was opened the number of children who have been brought to the bar of the criminal courts in New York has lessened in the proportion of four to one. This statement is republished by the committee; but at the date of that report the institution had not been above a twelvemonth in existence. It is too much to assume, that this disproportion was occasioned by any actual diminution of juvenile offenders, a meaning which the extract from the report is evidently intended to convey; the simple fact being, that instead of committing these delinquents for trial at the bar of the criminal courts, the magistrates sent them at once to the " House of Refuge"*. The New York institution during the ten years of its existence
has

---

* In looking over the reports of the " House of Refuge" in New York it is scarcely possible to avoid noticing the extreme caution with which the managers have refrained from making any allusion to the " Philanthropic Society" or " Refuge for the Destitute" in London; Institutions to which the New York Refuge owes in a great measure its existence, and which have been in beneficial and extensive operation, the one for a period of forty-six and the other for the space of twenty-nine years. This silence

has received within its walls 1,262 children, viz. 968 boys and 294 girls, of which
number

---

silence is evidently occasioned by a morbid anxiety which the reports throughout betray to show
that houses of refuge originated in the United States.   The question as to the nation which is entitled
to the merit of first establishing institutions for the relief and reform of criminal youth is one of very
little interest, nor should I have thought of adverting to it but for the extraordinary pretensions
which have been set up by the managers of the New York Refuge, and which have been reiterated
by others without inquiry.   The nature and extent of those pretensions will be seen by the following
extract from the fourth annual report of the managers.   " It must be satisfactory to those with whom
this charity originated, and to those by whose exertions it has been and is supported, to find that
it is not only approved at home, but that it has attracted the attention of those in other countries
whose minds are bent on the amelioration of the condition of mankind.   If it were possible that any
feelings but those of pure benevolence could mix with the consideration of this subject, we might
feel a pride in the reflection that our young country, which has so lately assumed the rank of an
independent nation, was the first to adopt with any efficacy the penitentiary system of prison discipline, and the first to attempt to prevent the commission of crimes by seeking out the youthful and
unprotected who were in the way of temptation, and by religious and moral instruction, by imparting to them useful knowledge, and by giving them industrious and orderly habits, rescuing them
from vice, and rendering them valuable members of society."[1]
     In order to set this matter right, I subjoin the following extract from the original address of the
" Society for the Prevention of Pauperism in New York," issued in 1824, containing the first proposal
for this identical house of refuge, and in which, as an inducement to its establishment, the committee state, " *But London and Dublin afford examples quite in unison with that which your committee is anxious to see erected in this city.   In London there are several establishments of this
nature*; but the one instituted in the Borough * appears to come nearest in its general system to that
which we recommend.   It originated from the extent of juvenile depredations in the metropolis,
and from a desire to ascertain the cause and arrest the progress of this great and growing evil.   A
large committee is appointed, who meet every fortnight, and sub-committees, with confidential agents,
are employed to investigate the cases of individuals and to register the particulars.   The building
consists, first, of a range of workshops of one floor, upwards of 500 feet in length, under which is a
rope-walk, where every kind of lines, twine and cord are manufactured; secondly, of a separate
inclosure, used as a house of probation or reform for the criminal classes of boys ; thirdly, of a similar
receptacle for the same description of girls; fourthly, of a chapel for religious worship ; fifthly, of an
eating-room, and also an evening school-room; sixthly, of a warehouse for the reception, delivery
and sale of the manufactured articles ; seventhly, of the general kitchen, bakehouse and dormitories;
and, lastly, of the requisite accommodation for the superintendants.   The quality of the food is
proportioned to the gains of the youth or the hardness of their labour.   The boys are bound apprentices for a certain number of years to the master workmen employed within the institution; they
have a particular dress, and a badge, which is left off at a certain period.   The hours of work are
from six in the morning till six in the evening in summer, and from daylight till half-past seven
in the winter.   The school is open four evenings in the week for reading, writing and arithmetic.
The elder boys are allowed to go out one day in the month, and the younger one day in three
months, to return before dark; if any one escapes, and is retaken, he is treated as a refractory
apprentice.   The task assigned is such as can be easily performed; and of the extra labour, one
half is allowed as a reward, a small part being given in money, and the rest placed to his credit to
be paid at the end of his apprenticeship.   Work of almost every trade is done by the boys.   The
girls are employed in making, mending and washing the boys' clothes, and on different kinds of
needlework ; and at the age of about sixteen they are placed out as house servants, receiving a
quarter's gratuity afterwards for good behaviour during a certain period.   There are about 200
boys and girls in this place."   The address continues : " Some modifications of this plan would
be requisite to adapt it to the local circumstances of this city; but on its general character it
exhibits a cheering evidence of the blessings which flow from well-directed efforts to inure young
people to habits of industry, regularity, sobriety, and morality.   One of your committee, who went
through the various wards of this institution, confirms the account which has been given.   The
cheerful animation of the youthful labourers, and the neatness of their manufactured articles, were
in the highest degree encouraging.
     The annual reports of the committee detail at length numerous striking cases of the efficacy of the
refuge[†] in producing an entire change in the character of individual boys and girls, and their
obtaining situations of comfort and respectability."
     The appendix to this address contains a number of these cases, all of which are extracted from
the reports of the London " Society for the Improvement of Prison Discipline, and for the Reformation of Juvenile Offenders," published in 1821 and 1822[‡].   In compliance with the invitation
contained in the address from which the foregoing extract is taken, the House of Refuge in New
York was established.

     From these extracts it will be seen that the State of New York has no better claim to the
invention of " houses of refuge " for the relief and restoration of criminal youth, than to the discovery
of the Ghent system of penitentiary discipline, which had been in successful operation above half a
century before it was adopted at Auburn and Sing Sing.

---

* The Philanthropic Society, St. George's Fields.
† Refuge for the Destitute, in Hoxton.
‡ *Vide* Third Report of the Prison Discipline Society (London), Appendix, p. 181; also Fourth Report,
Appendix, p. 150.

number 1,033 have been indentured, leaving on the 1st January 1834, 229, of whom 186 are boys and forty-three girls. The average period of confinement is stated to be about eighteen months. The health of the establishment has been excellent, five only of the objects having died since its formation. Of 194 committed in the year 1833, 105 could neither read nor write. The average age at which they are admitted is twelve years. Voluntary applications for admission are rare. Attempts to escape are not unfrequent. On one occasion a desperate plan of this kind devised by a lad of nineteen, was nearly executed ; the lives of several of the officers who suppressed the tumult being greatly endangered.

The " House of Refuge" in Philadelphia was established in the year 1827. The Act for its incorporation is similar to that of the New York Institution, and the same powers are extended as well to the judicial authorities as to the board of management *. The sum of 10,000 dollars from the State treasury, and a similar amount from that of the county of Philadelphia were advanced for the erection of the buildings, and 5,000 dollars were granted annually by the county for five years, for the support of the institution. In 1832 the legislature voted a sum of 10,000 dollars for three years. The ground inclosed is a space of 400 feet in length, and 231 in breadth. The main building is ninety-two feet in length by thirty feet in depth. This building contains the keeper's and matron's residence, rooms for the use of the managers, and infirmaries. The wings on each side of the main building extend the whole length of the front. They contain three ranges or stories of cells, each seven feet by four feet. These cells are well lighted and ventilated. In the centre of the ground is a detached building, containing the chapel, under which is the boys' dining-room; adjoining is the kitchen, with the girls' dining-room. There are separate school-rooms for each sex. The workshops are ranged along the boundary wall, in the rear. The establishment was formally opened in November 1828, the building having cost the sum of 38,025 dollars, besides the purchase of the site for 5,500 dollars. The daily course of duties enforced at both institutions is nearly similar. In Philadelphia, however, there is no chaplain. Divine service on Sundays is performed by clergymen resident in the city who officiate at the institution in rotation. The building was at first calculated to contain 172 children in separate dormitories, but the accommodation having been enlarged 279 inmates can now be lodged, educated, and employed; viz. 196 boys and 83 girls. From the opening of the establishment, on the 8th December 1828, to the 1st May 1833, there had been received 538 children of both sexes; viz. 391 males and 147 females. During the preceding year there had been admitted eighty-two males and forty-one females. In this period seventy-two boys had been indentured. Very favourable reports have been received of the apprentices. In May 1833, there remained in the establishment 109 boys and fifty-five girls. The general good habits and cleanliness which prevail in the institution have been eminently conducive to health, only three of the objects having died since its foundation. All the clothing is made within the house. The amount received for the labour of the boys during the year was 2,894 dollars †.

That the extent of crime among the youth of the labouring classes should be at all times considerable in such a metropolis as London, can excite no surprise when its crowded state and unexampled extent are duly considered. With the increase of population the number of juvenile offenders has, however, become so great that more efficient means than any which have been yet employed are absolutely necessary to arrest the evil. From information which has been laid before Parliament there appear to be not less than 8,000 boys in London who subsist by plunder ‡.

Such

---

* In Philadelphia, three of the board of management are chosen by the court of quarter sessions of the county, and two by the mayor of the city.

† There is an asylum at Boston for young persons of vagrant and criminal habits, called the " House of Reformation." At the period of my visit this establishment was, owing to accidental circumstances, seen to so much disadvantage that I refrain from describing it. The children had been but recently removed from the building which they had formerly occupied to a small island in Boston Harbour, and the ordinary regulations had been but partially resumed.
‡ Evidence taken before the Police Committee of the House of Commons, 1816.

Such estimates are generally formed on calculations too vague to inspire much confidence, but still the records of the several prisons afford incontestable evidence of the prevalence of juvenile depravity to a frightful extent. Whether the criminal habits of this large number of the rising generation shall be suffered to extend their baneful influence, or checked by measures calculated at once to deter and reform, are questions of vital interest to the welfare not only of the individuals in question, but of society at large. As a preventive remedy the diffusion of education is of the first importance. By education is meant not the mere acquirement of the elementary arts of reading and writing, but a course of moral training which shall impress religious principles, impart useful knowledge, control the passions, and amend the heart*. The chaplain of Norwich Castle has well remarked that " nothing but actual investigation can render credible the gross ignorance which painfully comes under the observation of a chaplain of a gaol. Even among prisoners who have mechanically learned to read and write, there exists generally speaking a lamentble ignorance of moral and religious duties, and of the awful sanctions of religion ; and of the rest, some know as little as the wildest savage †." My own observation on this subject—the result of an examination of prisons for many years—enables me to confirm with confidence the accuracy of this statement. Dark as may be at times the moral aspect of society, the friends to the education of the poor have no real ground for discouragement. An early inculcation of the great duties of life must essentially contribute to the right performance of them ; and it may therefore be reasonably inferred that the calendars of crime throughout the country would have been of late years much heavier than they have proved, but for the efforts which have been made to extend among the labouring classes the benefits of knowledge. Let, then, all who are engaged in this important work earnestly persevere, and be assured that the dissemination of a system of sound moral and religious instruction forms the most solid foundation of virtuous habits, and the best security against the violation of the laws ‡. —But inestimable as is the value of early education, it does not supersede the necessity of making further exertions to arrest the course of juvenile delinquency. The circumstances by which a large proportion of the youth now under consideration become the inmates of a prison, arise in a great measure from the prevalence of pauperism, and the numerous vices of which it is the source. Nothing tends more powerfully than indigence to weaken the natural affections, and destroy the sense of parental obligation. Of the number of lads who crowd the gaols and infest the streets of the metropolis, the situation of an immense proportion may be traced to the neglect and criminality of their parents.

For

---

* The following statement will convey a correct idea of the state of instruction among the prisoners confined in several gaols : —

	Number of Prisoners.	Number who can Read only.	Number who can Read and Write.	Number who can neither Read nor Write.
Bodmin County Gaol - - - - -	684	198	317	169
Exeter Gaol - - - - -	114	37	48	29
Ditto - House of Correction - - - -	110	37	48	25
Durham County Gaol - - - - -	75	16	26	33
Northampton County Gaol - - - -	480	129	119	232
Wilton House of Correction - - - -	580	196	245	139
Stafford County Gaol - - - -	785	234	303	248
Ditto - House of Correction - - -	886	233	367	286
Horsham County Gaol - - - -	132	36	61	35
Lewes House of Correction - - - -	1,075	207	385	483
Worcester Gaol - - - - -	240	80	79	81

It appears from this statement, that the proportion of prisoners who could read was 28 per cent. of the whole number in confinement, and the proportion of those who could read and write, 37 per cent.; leaving a proportion of 35 per cent. who could neither read nor write.

† Seventh Report of the London Prison Discipline Society, p. 116.

‡ Infant schools are specially adapted to those classes in which vagrant and criminal youth are usually to be found. The habitation of the parent is in too many such instances the scene of riot, drunkenness and licentiousness, a retreat from the officers of justice, and abounding in whatever can corrupt the imagination and deprave the heart. The attendance of a child at an infant school must have a powerful tendency to counteract the injurious influences of the domestic abode, a consideration which cannot fail to strengthen the claims which these institutions, in other respects, have on the support of the enlightened and humane.

For the relief of *destitute* and *vagrant* youth the workhouse is the legitimate asylum. The improvement which, in consequence of a late enactment, is likely to take place in the character of these establishments will, it is hoped, be productive of great advantage to an extensive class of young persons whose deplorable condition gives them strong claims on public commiseration. In the workhouse the friendless boy may be instructed and employed, and after a time encouraged to emigrate to a colony where he can be indentured as an apprentice, and rendered capable of earning his livelihood with the fairest prospects of future settlement. The welfare of *criminal* youth calls for a different remedy. It is the practice in the best regulated gaols in which prisoners are allowed to associate to confine boys apart from the men. The fallacy of classification was never more strikingly exhibited than by this arrangement; for much as lads are exposed to corruption when confined with adults, that contamination is generally still more rapid and certain when boys are placed together. From such associations no virtuous mind can reasonably be expected to escape injury. Most powerfully, then, do they operate on those who are already debased and alive to every evil impression! If a youth on his entrance into a prison evinces any propriety of feeling, he very soon acquires the bold demeanor of the hardened delinquent. In the midst of the most profligate companions, and compelled as he is to hear honesty reprobated, morality ridiculed, and religion despised, there can be no wonder that he should return into the world confirmed in every species of iniquity. Such effects must in a great degree be the result of confinement in almost any gaol conducted on the plan of association. Let a youth be but subjected day after day to the ordinary routine of prison regulations, accustomed to mix in the society and become familiar to the sight, conversation, and habits, of other prisoners; and even presuming, what is scarcely possible, that he escape direct contamination, the mere circumstance of his being placed in such a situation will in ninety and nine cases out of a hundred eventually prove his ruin. In after-life the idea of an association with convicts is no longer fearful to him, and the dread of a gaol has lost its power.

There are four classes of juvenile prisoners: 1st, Boys committed for trial; 2dly, Boys sentenced to terms of imprisonment; 3dly, Boys committed for vagrancy; and, 4thly, Boys sentenced to be transported. For the first two classes I submit that separate cells should be provided in the county gaols and houses of correction. To the salutary discipline to which they would be thus subjected, should be added some means of provision at the expiration of their sentences. Circumstanced as is this country, with a crowded and increasing population, no sensible effect can be experienced from penal institutions unless attention be paid to this important point. A large number of the lads committed to houses of correction are petty pilferers, whose destitution pleads powerfully in extenuation of their crimes. The brief history of the greatest proportion of these children is truly heart-rending. They are the victims of ignorance, depravity, and neglect. Hundreds have been nursed and tutored in crime. On their discharge from prison they are without character or friends. A workhouse is their legal asylum, but they have contracted habits of wandering and an aversion to restraint. They are repeatedly brought before the magistrates, committed for short periods, and on their liberation are soon again in prison. They continue to increase in guilt as they advance in years, until transportation closes their short but miserable career.—To this evil there is happily a remedy in the resources which the penal colonies of Australia present for the disposal of criminal youth. Those resources are almost boundless; and I submit that what has been successfully accomplished by various parishes and charitable institutions, in regard to the apprenticeship of boys in the colonies, might be extended by His Majesty's Government on a scale which would be highly advantageous to the rising generation, and prove no less beneficial to the interests of the colony than to the parent country.—The third class, viz. vagrants, ought to be sent immediately on their apprehension to the workhouse of the parish to which they belong, and should in no case for a mere act of vagrancy be previously committed to prison. The order and restraints of a well-regulated workhouse will be felt by offenders of this description as a penalty far more severe than any imprisonment to which a boy could be subjected for a short period, without incurring great expense. The confinement of " idle and disorderly" boys for a month only in a house of correction is attended by all the evils without any of the benefits of imprisonment.—The fourth class, viz. boys sentenced to be transported, are very numerous. With the view of instructing and reclaiming lads of this description, a hulk for the reception of three hundred boys has been for several years past appropriated at Sheerness, but notwithstanding that much attention has been bestowed on its management, yet so difficult is it to provide in a vessel the requisite means of separation, and so great are the inherent vices of the hulk system, that the benevolent object contemplated by the plan has in a great measure failed. That object can in fact only be attained by the establishment of a penitentiary expressly adapted for boys of this description, conducted on a system of solitary confinement. This imprisonment should invariably be followed by transportation.

I have now laid before your Lordship the result of my inquiries. If, in the absence of facts, I have occasionally substituted opinions I have been compelled to adopt this course by the difficulty of procuring information on which I could satisfactorily rely. Those opinions have been formed from repeated visits to the several penitentiaries, the renewed inspection of every part of these establishments, a familiar acquaintance with the practical operation of the respective plans, an unrestrained communication with the wardens, and in many instances from private conversation with the convicts. In the Appendix will be found many details respecting the regulation and practical operation of the several penitentiaries. On a review of the information which I now submit, it is impossible not to be struck with the great advantage which the United States possess from the extraordinary demand for labour in that country, and the ample means which her unappropriated territory affords of providing for her increasing population. To this favourable position, and the resources of productive industry to which it gives rise, is principally to be attributed whatever degree of success has attended some of her penitentiaries. There is a broad distinction between the policy of this country and that of the United States, in regard to the disposal of their convict population. It is obviously the interest of Great Britain, who has no means of profitably employing her criminals at home, to transfer them to her colonies, where labour is in great demand. In the United States the respective legislatures, having no such necessity, and possessing no similar resource, resort to long periods of imprisonment. The extreme facility with which employments can be introduced into the penitentiaries harmonizes with this policy; and thus prison labour can be rendered not only an important instrument of discipline, but from the duration of confinement becomes occasionally a source of profit. It is the privilege of America not only to derive from Europe Institutions the value of which experience has confirmed; but to be enabled, by the means to which I advert, to carry out the principles on which they are founded to an unlimited extent, engraft amendments, and exhibit their results with great effect. Hence the powerful influence of solitary confinement, which originated at Gloucester and has subsequently been enforced at Glasgow, is strikingly displayed at the Eastern Penitentiary in Philadelphia. The Auburn and Sing Sing prisons as forcibly exemplify whatever benefits result from the system which has been pursued at the Maison de Force at Ghent; while at Wethersfield, and also in some measure at Charlestown, that system is seen under such favourable modifications as to divest it of its most objectionable features. Great merit is unquestionably due to the legislatures of those States which have availed themselves of their local advantages in the management of criminals. The order, system, and energy, which mark the government of the establishments which I have just named are highly creditable to those who are intrusted with their superintendence; and although some parts of their discipline are most objectionable, and others altogether inapplicable to the circumstances of this country, yet an examination of the prisons to which I allude cannot fail to give rise to many useful suggestions on various points of deep interest.

With the exception, however, of these penitentiaries, there is nothing valuable in the discipline of the prisons in America. Defective as is the condition of the gaols in England, they are superior to those of the United States, especially in the observance of order, the space allotted to the untried, the correction of minor offenders, the treatment of females, and the administration of moral and religious instruction.

                                                                    Believing

Believing the diffusion of knowledge to be connected with the prevention of crime, and considering that the improvement of the education of the lower classes is now under the attention of Parliament, I have availed myself of such opportunities as my visit to the United States afforded of collecting information on this subject; and I beg to refer your Lordship to a Statement in the Appendix, containing an account of the public provision made in the several States for the support of " common schools."

I cannot close my Report without expressing my grateful acknowledgments to the several authorities connected with the government of the American Penitentiaries, as well as to many other gentlemen resident in different parts of the United States, with whom I have had the pleasure to communicate on the various subjects involved in this Inquiry, and from whom I have on all occasions received the most polite attention.   My thanks are, in an especial manner, due to Samuel R. Wood, esquire, the warden of the Eastern Penitentiary in Philadelphia, for much interesting information, and for the cordial assistance which he has at all times been ready to afford in furtherance of the objects of my mission.

I have the honour to be,

My Lord,

Your Lordship's most obedient humble servant,

The Viscount Duncannon,   *Wm. Crawford.*
&c.   &c.   &c.

LIST OF APPENDIX.

PENNSYLVANIA.

H VERMONT.

MISCELLANEOUS.

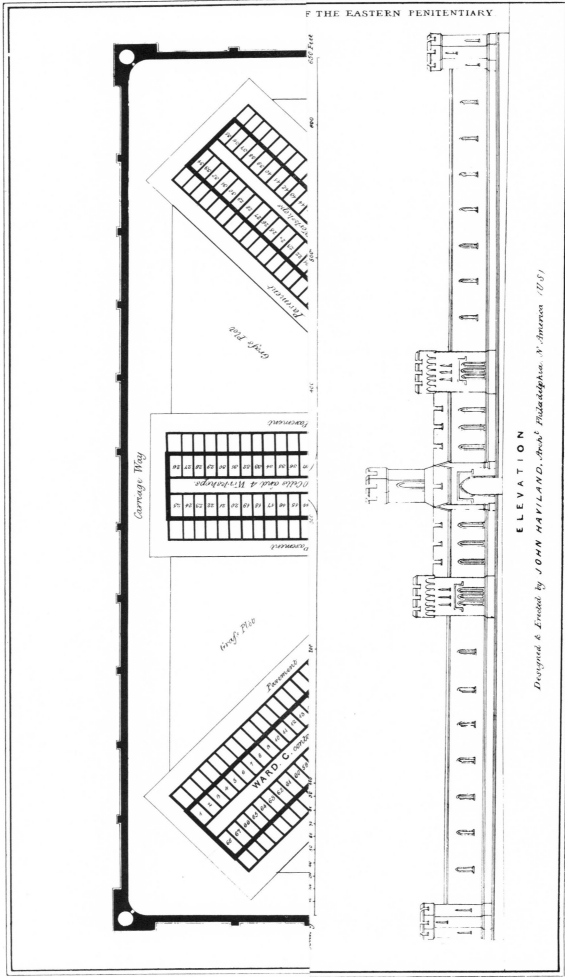

ELEVATION

Designed & Erected by JOHN HAVILAND, Arch't Philadelphia, N. America (US)

to be Printed

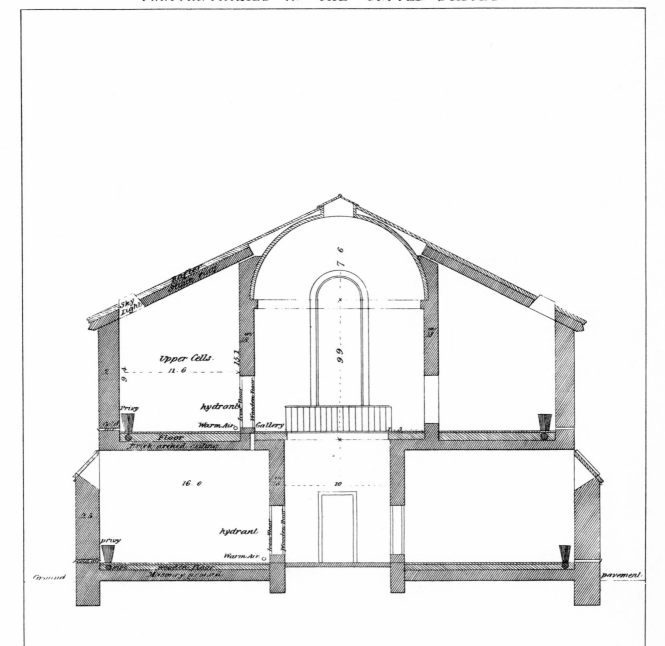

TRANSVERSE SECTION *of the* **CELLS,**

as executed by **J. HAVILAND**, *Arch.t*

in the Eastern, Western, and New Jersey State Penitentiaries.

APPENDIX.

PENNSYLVANIA.

EASTERN PENITENTIARY AT PHILADELPHIA.

THIS prison is situated on an elevated and healthy spot, about two miles from the centre **PENNSYLVANIA.** of the city of Philadelphia. The building was begun in the year 1822, the Act for its erection having passed on the 20th March 1821. It occupies a square plot of ground containing about ten acres, and is one of the largest buildings in the United States. The boundary wall, which extends 670 feet on each side, is thirty feet high, 12 feet thick at the foundation, and diminishes to two feet nine inches at the top. The stone of which the prison is built is granite of a greyish colour. The facade, or entrance front, is in the gothic style of architecture, of a bold and impressive character, possessing the appearance of great strength and solidity.

The accompanying Plan will show the general arrangement of the prison buildings. The design and execution of the work display considerable ingenuity, and are highly creditable to the talented architect, Mr. John Haviland, of Philadelphia. The general arrangement of the prison is on the radiating plan; which possesses many peculiar advantages in respect to superintendence, health and security. By the position of the cell-buildings, forming so many converging lines to the central observatory, an inspector commands from one point a most perfect view to the extremity of the corridors or passages between the cells, as well as over the intervening spaces between the buildings as far as the boundary wall. He may also pass along the corridors under cover, and secretly inspect every cell; and by walking round an elevated gallery on the outside of the central tower, detect any attempt at escape, when the prisoners are admitted into the yards. If, on the other hand, the cells had been placed round the circumference in the circular or polygonal form, they would have screened the prisoner in any attempt to escape by the external wall. The cells would have been very difficult of access, in consequence of their being so far removed from the central station, and the surrounding building would also have obstructed the free circulation of air through the prison. These disadvantages in the circular plan are particularly exemplified in the Pittsburgh Penitentiary, which was originally built on that principle in 1820, but in consequence of its numerous defects has been recently re-constructed on the radiating plan.

On the right of the entrance, in front, are the warden's chambers and the apartments appropriated to the meetings of the inspectors. On the left is the clerk's office and the rooms of the deputy keepers. Over the gateway is the apothecary's apartment, and on the second floor of the left wing is the infirmary, which has a separate entrance by an external door in the rear leading to the staircase; thus providing against the consequences of infectious disease. The entrance buildings occupy a frontage of about 200 feet, and project 10 feet before the boundary wall which appears however to form part of the main edifice; the whole front being pierced with small blank windows, and the upper part surrounded with embattled parapets. At each angle of the boundary wall is a small tower for the purpose of overlooking the establishment. In the centre of the front, over the entrance gateway which is finished with buttresses and pinnacles, rises an octangular tower eighty feet high, containing an alarm bell and a clock. The central building is approached by a paved passage from the entrance. It consists of a circular room or observatory, forty feet in diameter, commanding a view of the corridors leading to the cells, all of which radiate from the centre. Under this room is a large reservoir of water for the supply of the cells, by means of pipes passing under the floors of the corridors. The upper story is used by the turnkeys and for store-rooms. At the top there is a tower, from the external gallery of which the watchman has a complete inspection of the whole prison and grounds, and can also overlook the airing yards attached to the cells.

The buildings occupied by the prisoners consist of seven radiating wings, connected by passages or corridors with the central building. These passages run through the middle of each building, and have a range of cells on each side. Three of the radiating buildings contain each 100 cells, and four others contain 136 cells in each; making, in the whole, 844 separate cells. On the upper story some of the cells are laid two into one, to allow additional space for the prisoner to work in, as well as for air and exercise, the prisoners on the upper story not being permitted to leave their cells at any time to take exercise in the yards. The cells on the ground floor in some of the wings (those which were first erected) have a small airing yard attached to each, 18 feet long and 8 feet wide, surrounded by a wall 12 feet high. These cells are 11 feet 9 inches long, and 7 feet 6 inches wide, arched at the top, and 16 feet 6 inches to the highest part of the ceiling. The cells on the upper floor are 10 feet high. In the four wing-buildings which were last erected the cells on the ground-floor are made 3 feet longer, in consideration of having no yards attached to them. The partition walls between the cells are of stone 18 inches thick. The walls next the corridor,

PENNSYLVANIA. or passage, are the same thickness, and the external walls next the yards are 2 feet 3 inches thick. Under each cell there is a floor of masonry 18 inches in thickness, on which are laid stones 10 inches thick, being the width of the cell, and extending under the partition walls; thus preventing the possibility of escape by excavation. Over this masonry is laid a floor of wood. Each cell is lighted by a small window in the ceiling, about 12 inches long and 4 inches wide, fitted to a cast-iron frame which is fixed in the crown of the arch, the sides of the frame being splayed so as to admit of light sufficient for any purpose.* The cells are well ventilated by means of small openings through the walls into the yards near the floors, and also at the highest point of the ceiling. They are warmed by heated air from large cockle-stoves, the pipes from which pass under the floor of the corridors, the warmth being admitted by cast-iron openings under the doors. The cells first built were entered only from the airing-yard, having a small aperture about 12 inches square next the corridors, through which the keepers can communicate with the prisoners, and furnish them with food. There is also in each cell a small hole by which the keeper can inspect the prisoners, unobserved by them. This arrangement being found inconvenient, the cells which have been since erected have double doors which open into the corridor, the outer one of wood, that inside consisting of bars of iron rivetted across: both are secured by a bar, which passing through the wall is locked on the outside to a staple placed beyond the reach of the prisoner. There are also two doors opening into the airing-yard, one of iron and one of wood; the latter being kept open in hot weather. The fastenings of these doors are simple, yet secure. The cells are very neatly plastered inside, and white-washed. They are supplied with water from the reservoir and the pipes before mentioned. Each cell has a privy in one corner, formed with a cast-iron pan communicating with a large pipe which passes under the floor to the extremity of the cell-building, where the foul water is let off at intervals into a sewer or culvert; the pipe being immediately supplied with fresh water from the reservoir under the central building. Any verbal communication between the prisoners which might take place if the pipes were at any time to remain empty, is thus prevented. By this arrangement, also, the cells are kept free from any unpleasant smell, and there is no occasion for a prisoner at any time to leave his cell.—The total cost of the penitentiary, when completed, is estimated at 560,000 dollars.

When a prisoner is first received he is examined, and his height, complexion, age, &c. are recorded in the usual manner. He is then taken by two assistant keepers into a small building in the yard containing three rooms, in the first of which he undresses, and has his hair cut short: in the next apartment his person is cleansed in a warm bath; and in the third, he is clothed in the prison uniform. He is then blindfolded by having a cap or hood put over his head and face; and in this state he is led between two keepers into the interior of the prison. On his arrival at the central building he is usually met by the warden, who addresses to him a few appropriate words of admonition on the necessity of conforming strictly to the rules of the prison. He is then conducted to the cell assigned to him, where his cap or hood is taken off, and he is left alone. He is subsequently visited only by the warden, the deputy keeper and occasionally by one of the official visitors, during the whole term of his confinement. Finding his solitude become irksome, the prisoner soon petitions for employment. This is granted as a favour, but not until the warden is fully satisfied, by his daily visits, that solitude has produced its effect in subduing the temper, and bringing the prisoner to a proper sense of his situation. Solitude without employment is continued for a few days only, and occasionally at the furthest for a fortnight, at the discretion of the warden. This interval is uniformly alluded to by the prisoners as the most painful part of their sentence. The two leading features of this imprisonment are, 1st, The entire separation of the convicts both by day and night, and seclusion from all others except the officers of the prison and the visitors authorized by the legislature; and, 2d, The deprivation of all intercourse with the world, and of any knowledge respecting their family or friends. Great efforts are used by the advocates of the system to discourage the granting of pardons, in order that the punishment may in all cases be certain, and the board of inspectors have determined to refrain from recommending any prisoner for this purpose to the governor. Among the advantages of this entire seclusion of the prisoners is that of being screened from the public gaze of visitors, an evil common in all the American penitentiaries (with the exception of Sing Sing), where the convicts are viewed as objects of curiosity, not unlike animals in a menagerie. In the solitude to which they are condemned, prisoners cannot corrupt or be corrupted. No punishment is added to that inflicted by the sentence of the law, by floggings, but when any breach of discipline takes place, the offender is corrected, not by the lash, but in such a way as to convince him of his error without degrading him either in the estimation of himself or of his fellow prisoners. This is accomplished in various ways. Experience has shown, that by reducing the quantity of food, placing the offender in a darkened solitary cell for a short time, taking away his bed, or depriving him of work, that the most refractory are soon brought into a state of entire submission. The circumstance of the prisoners not being known in any way by their fellow prisoners is of incalculable advantage on their liberation. On the discharge of criminals from ordinary gaols, the reformation of many who were desirous of doing well has been obstructed by the renewal of acquaintances formed in prison.

On

* As the cells were originally designed to be but one story high, it was intended to light them by conical sky-lights in the roof; but the addition of another story has caused an alteration in the mode of lighting the lower cells. This is now accomplished by means of a sloping sky-light, as shown in the section of the cells. This arrangement has occasioned the lower cells to be constructed three feet longer than those above, in order to obtain light from the ceiling, in preference to windows in the side walls. More light and ventilation are thus afforded, as well as better means of preventing communication through the windows.

On the very important subject of the health of the prisoners, I think it right to give the opinion of the medical attendant in his own words. In his first Report to the Board of Inspectors, dated January 1831, Dr. Bache says :—

" The prisoners thus far have been favoured with a good share of health. Some have acknowledged an improvement in their health, while others have evidently been rendered less robust. These contrary effects are to be explained by adverting to the different conditions in which the prisoners arrive. If, however, the average condition of the health of the prisoners received up to this time be considered, it is the opinion of the physician that it is better than when they arrived. This belief is supported by the condition of the three prisoners that have been discharged. Two of them preserved to the last moment the good state of health in which they were received, and the third was much improved in this respect by his own acknowledgment.

" Several mild cases of intermittent fever have occurred, but in prisoners who had been affected with the disease not long before their arrival. Only two cases of serious indisposition have occurred, and but one death. The fatal case was that of a prisoner of intemperate habits who arrived in a diseased state, having but recently suffered from a severe fit of illness in the Arch-street prison.

" In the questions which have been addressed to the prisoners the physician has directed his inquiries particularly to two points:—namely, the length of their imprisonment before conviction, and their habits in regard to the use of ardent spirits. The imprisonment before conviction has been found to embrace a period, varying from a few days to an entire year. If it be important for the good of society and the sake of the criminal that he should serve out the sentence of the law in separate confinement, it must be equally so for the untried prisoner, on the supposition of his guilt, and for a much stronger reason in case of his innocence. Until this evil be removed, the moral operation of separate confinement on the prisoner after conviction will be lessened in its effects.

" In regard to the other point, the physician has found, that out of 58 prisoners received up to this time, 38, or nearly two-thirds, acknowledge themselves to have been either habitually or occasionally intemperate. This fact shows the close connection which subsists between the vice of drunkenness and the commission of crime.

" The effects of the separate confinement on the mind have been attentively watched. No instance has occurred of the production of mental disease. Its moral effects are encouraging, and are in strong contrast with the contaminating influences arising out of the association of criminals.

" Upon the whole, the physician feels justified to conclude from his experience in this penitentiary that this plan of the separate confinement of criminals, if in some instances injurious to the constitution, is much more favourable to the health and lives of the prisoners, than confinement in prisons on the old plan."

Dr. Bache, in his second Report for the year 1831, observes,

" The health of the prisoners has been generally good, though a few cases of severe indisposition have occurred. The confinement operates differently on different prisoners, increasing the health of some, and lessening that of others ; but the average health of the whole is perhaps as good as when they were received.

" Four deaths have occurred in the course of the year. The following table presents the state of health on admission, and cause of death of each of these prisoners :

No. of the Prisoner.	State of health on admission.	Cause of Death.
33	Good.	Dropsy of the chest.
13	Tolerable.	Epilepsy.
43	Doubtful.	Disease of mesenteric glands.
77	Helpless, from a severe injury to hip and thigh.	Injury to hip and thigh.

" The average number of prisoners in the penitentiary for the year has been 67.4. Four deaths having occurred, gives the mortality for the year at a little less than six per cent. The average number confined in 1830 was 31 ; and there having occurred but one death, the mortality for that year is a little more than three per cent. The average number confined since the opening of the penitentiary has been 44.4. The total number of deaths having been five, gives the average amount of mortality from the commencement, at a little less than five per cent.

" The mortality of the present year, it is perceived, is considerably greater than for the last. The Board, however, will observe, that in 1831, accidental circumstances have increased the number of fatal cases. The physician deemed the health of No. 33 to be good when he arrived ; but dissection revealed the existence of extensive disease of the chest of long standing, which no doubt laid the foundation of the affection of which he died. No. 43 was in bad health when admitted. No. 77 arrived from a neighbouring county in a state of complete helplessness, from a fracture of the neck of the thigh bone, and other serious injuries. His condition was such that he kept his bed from the moment of his reception to the day of his death. He was evidently not in a proper condition to be removed from the county prison, much less to undergo the fatigue of a long journey.

PENNSYLVANIA.   " It is difficult to form an estimate of what will probably be the average mortality among the prisoners in the penitentiary for a series of years, from results deduced from so small a number of prisoners as have yet been received. This difficulty arises from the circumstance that while the number of prisoners is so small a single death bears so large a proportion to the whole number confined as to swell the per-centage of mortality very considerably."

" No particular disease can be said to prevail in the penitentiary, as the result of the mode of confinement or discipline; and no mental affection has been superinduced. The affections which have occurred most frequently have been coughs, rheumatic pains, and diarrhœa."

In his Annual Report for 1832 Dr. Bache states, "that the complaints which have occurred most frequently have been intermittent fever in the spring and autumn; disorders in the bowels in the summer, and catarrhs and rheumatic pains in the winter. But one case of fever of a serious type has occurred."

" No facts have been developed during this year to show that the mode of confinement adopted in the penitentiary, is particularly injurious to health. It has the effect, generally, of rendering the frame less robust; but, at the same time, prevents the operation of numerous causes of disease, to which persons of the class which generally fill our prisons are usually exposed, either from necessity or from the indulgence of vicious habits. The circumstance, indeed, of being withdrawn from the influence of the severer atmospheric vicissitudes, such as wet and cold, which are prolific sources of disease with a large portion of the community, would, of itself, more than compensate for the operation of any unfavourable causes to health, experienced in this prison. But, when it is considered that many of the individuals sent to our prisons have been in previous habits of drunkenness and debauchery, the comparative healthfulness of the confinement and mode of discipline must be apparent."

" The following Table, exhibiting the comparative health on admission and discharge, of the twenty prisoners who have been liberated during this year, fully confirms the views here expressed.

No. of Prisoner.	State of Health when received.	State of Health when discharged.
10	Insane - - - - -	Insane.
12	Good - - - - -	Good.
59	Good - - - - -	Good.
15	Good - - - - -	Good.
18	Subject to asthmatic symptoms	Same as when received.
17	Good - - - - -	Good.
75	Idiotic - - - - -	Idiotic.
63	Good - - - - -	Good.
68	Robust - - - - -	Excellent.
22	Good - - - -	Good.
24	Good - - - - -	Good.
25	Good - - - -	Good.
48	Insane - - - - -	Insane.
3	Good - - - -	Better than on admission.
62	Not good - - - -	Improved.
41	Good - - - - -	Good.
44	Good - - - - -	Good.
93	Not robust - - - -	Better than on admission.
91	Imperfect - - - -	Better.
90	Good - - - - -	Good.

" Four prisoners have died within the year. The state of health of these prisoners on admission, and the cause of death in each case, is shown by the following statement:—"

No. of Prisoner.	State of Health on Admission.	Cause of Death.
112	Predisposed to insanity - -	Mania.
114	Good - - - - -	Hemorrhage.
40	Good - - - - -	Consumption.
49	Insane - - - - -	Suicide.

" Prisoner No. 112 was received on the 16th of February 1832, apparently well. But the appearance of good health proved fallacious; for after the lapse of a month, he began to show symptoms of aberration of mind, and on the 28th of March, less than six weeks after his reception, he was in a state of such violent mental excitement, as to require to be placed in a dark cell. His insanity continued, with but an unimportant abatement in April, until the 26th of May, when he died. These facts prove conclusively, that this prisoner, though apparently well on admission, was strongly predisposed to mania, and on the verge of an attack of that disease."

" Prisoner No. 114 was received on the 22d of March, apparently in good health, and died on the 31st May, after a confinement of ten weeks. The death of No. 40 took place on the
4th

4th of August, after an imprisonment of nearly two years. No peculiar causes can be alleged to have operated on his system in this penitentiary to produce his disease. Consumption is a very prevalent complaint in prisons, and indeed among our population at large; and the prisoners of this penitentiary will necessarily be subject to it, especially if as in the case of the prisoner here referred to they have spent a considerable portion of their lives in other prisons."

" The physician, as well from his personal observation as from the evidence which he heard given before the coroner's inquest, is perfectly satisfied that prisoner No. 49 was labouring under insanity when received into the penitentiary, and that he committed the act of self-destruction under the influence of a paroxysm of that disease."

" Upon the whole, it may be affirmed that the health of the prisoners has been good during this year. The same period has proved destructive of human life in portions of our country from the prevalence of pestilence; but happily, from the isolated condition of our prisoners, and the regularity of their lives, the destructive cause has passed over them without producing disease."

" The deaths which have taken place are not of a character to throw a doubt on the propriety or humanity of the system pursued. Two of them have occurred after very short periods of confinement, while health continues to be enjoyed by a number of prisoners whose periods of imprisonment have been the longest. Without making any deduction for the case of suicide, the mortality of the year has been moderate. Thus, the average number of prisoners in confinement throughout the year has been 91, and the deaths having been 4, gives the mortality at only 4.4 per cent."

Dr. Bache thus reports on the medical state of the establishment during the year 1833 :—
" The health of the prisoners for this year has been better than for any preceding year since the opening of the penitentiary. As heretofore, the diseases which have occurred most frequently have been intermittents in the spring and autumn, bowel complaints in the summer and catarrhs and rheumatic affections in the winter; but the amount of indisposition has been less than could have been reasonably anticipated, considering the number of prisoners which has averaged for this year as high as 123. Upon the whole it may be safely asserted, as the result of more than four years' experience of the operations of this penitentiary, that the peculiar mode of confinement, so far from being injurious to the health of convicts, is generally beneficial, and forms a decided improvement in this particular, over the modes of incarceration pursued in other prisons. One fact, in confirmation of this position, seems fully established ; namely, that the isolated state of the prisoners defends them in a great degree from the invasion of epidemic and contagious diseases. Thus during the prevalence of the Asiatic cholera, while a number of prisons have suffered a mortality more or less severe by that disease, this penitentiary escaped without having had a solitary case within its walls."

" The medical facts derived from the experience of this year are more valuable than those of any former period, inasmuch as they are founded upon the observation of a larger number of prisoners. In order to judge correctly of the influence of the confinement no better way can be adopted than to compare the health, at the time of admission and discharge, of the nineteen prisoners who have been liberated during the year. This comparison which is made in the following table, is drawn up from the entries contained in the medical journal, and exhibits on the whole satisfactory results."

No. of Prisoner.	State of health on admission.	Length of Imprisonment.	State of health on discharge.
115	Good -	One year - - -	Better than on admission.
113	Good -	One year and fifteen days	Excellent.
111	Good -	Thirteen months - -	Excellent.
151	Imperfect	Three and a half months	Improved.
106	Complaining	Eighteen months - -	As good as on admission.
61	Imperfect	Two and a half years -	Slight temporary indisposition.
86	Good -	Twenty-two months -	Better than on admission.
79	Good -	Two years - - -	Good.
134	Good -	One year - - -	Good.
27	Robust -	Three years - - -	Not so strong as on admission.
37	Good -	Three years - - -	Not so strong as on admission.
80	Good -	Two years - - -	Better than on admission.
82	Good -	Two years - - -	Temporary indisposition.
117	Good -	Eighteen months - -	Suffering under mental aberration.
42	Good -	Three years - - -	Affected with inflammation and rheumatism.
98	Good -	Two years - - -	Good.
99	Good -	Two years - - -	Good.
100	Good -	Two years - - -	Better than on admission.
101	Good -	Two years - - -	Improved.

" There were no circumstances in the case of No. 117, which led the physician to believe that his mental disease was produced by causes peculiar to the mode of confinement pursued in this penitentiary."

" But one death has taken place within the year. It occurred in the person of No. 102, and

PENNSYLVANIA. was caused by apoplexy, after a confinement of the prisoner of a little more than eighteen months. This prisoner was received into the penitentiary in an imperfect state of health, the consequence of habitual intemperance. During the whole period of his confinement he frequently exhibited symptoms indicative of a radically diseased and shattered constitution."

" There having occurred but one death in 1833, the mortality for this year is exceedingly low, and is probably less than what the average mortality of this prison will prove to be, when deduced from the observation of a series of years. The average number of prisoners in confinement during the year being 123, a single death gives the mortality for this year at only eight-tenths of one per cent."

" The average number of prisoners in confinement—

In 1830 was	31
1831	67
1832	91
1833	123

" The average number in confinement, therefore, for the whole period of these four years, has been seventy-eight. The deaths during this period having been ten, gives the average mortality, deduced from the experience of four years, at three and two-tenths per cent. per annum."

The tendency of the system to produce mental disease is a subject of such vast importance that I felt it my duty to make every enquiry into the cases of the individuals who had been thus afflicted, in order to ascertain if their lamentable condition could in any degree be ascribed to the peculiar nature of their imprisonment. The information on this point contained in the following letter, addressed to me by the warden of the penitentiary, is so very satisfactory, and was so fully corroborated by other enquiries which I instituted, that no doubt whatever remains on my mind that the parties in question had suffered mental derangement before their committal to this penitentiary. It is proper to observe, that there is no state lunatic asylum in Pennsylvania, and that offenders who are afflicted with disorders of the mind, and who are considered too dangerous to be at large, are consequently sent to the penitentiary for security.

" Philadelphia, first month 20th, 1834.

" In reference to the subject mentioned yesterday, of the cause of the insanity of four and the idiotcy of one of our prisoners, I must refer to the several reports made annually to the Legislature. In addition to what is contained in them I may add that No. 10 appeared very strange on his admission, and told the inspectors, physician, and myself, remarkable tales of his being concerned in killing men, women, and children, in Charleston (South Carolina), who were salted up and sold for pork, and of being concerned with gangs of counterfeiters; that General Jackson was the prime mover of all this, and such a mass of nonsense that we all came to one conclusion that he was either insane, or wished us to think he was so. A two years' residence here induced us to believe that the former was the case. He was sometimes more excited than at others, but went away apparently in very much the same state of mind to that in which he came in. As he talked in the same manner on the day of his admission as on that of his discharge, no one for a moment believed that separate confinement had been the cause of his insanity, *if he was insane*. We knew nothing of him before his reception, and have never heard of him since he left the doors of the penitentiary."

" There was something odd and singular in No. 48 when he arrived here, but this was attributed more to a want of education and an unbroken irritable temper than to insanity. We were told that he had ascended a chimney in the county prison at Lancaster (where he was convicted), and that he remained there three days without food, until it was supposed that he had made his escape. This feat was considered as an attempt to escape, and not attributed to insanity. He was received here Nov. 29th, 1830. On the 7th of Dec. he was set to work as a cabinet maker, at which trade he said he had served two years. We found, however, that he knew but little. On the 11th he refused to do any work, and said that he had been ordered otherwise by a higher authority than any one here. During this night the watchman found him at prayers. About eight o'clock on the morning of the 12th my attention was called to him. He was sitting with his lamp burning and a bible before him. I directed him to put out the light: this he would not do. Thomas Bradford* and S. W. Crawford† saw him this day, and believed him to be under the influence of religious excitement. On the contrary I thought that he was feigning insanity. He became better, but again worse, and continued so until discharged by pardon. He was placed in the poor-house where he remained in the same state, and died during the prevalence of the cholera in 1832. The crime for which he was convicted was committed in a manner that looked more like the act of an insane man than a thief; and as the period of time between his reception and his showing such decided marks of insanity was so brief (only 12 days), we could not for a moment think that solitary confinement could have produced it. If, however, we could have had a doubt, these doubts would have been set at rest by information given to us during the last summer, when a friend of this young man and his family came here from the State of New York to enquire after him. He told John Bacon,‡ Wm. Hood § and myself, that he was an apprentice to
a cabinet

---

* One of the inspectors.
† A clergyman resident in Philadelphia, who in a spirit of the most disinterested benevolence frequently attends at the penitentiary on Sundays for the performance of divine service.
‡ The treasurer, to whose anxious and persevering exertions the institution is greatly indebted.
§ The secretary to the inspectors.

a cabinet maker, in the interior of New York, that he had for some time shown strong symptoms of derangement, which among other things was evinced by his expressing a belief that the Methodist ministers had conspired to destroy him. Soon after he had declared this he left his friends without their knowledge, and the first intelligence they had of him was that he was in this Establishment. His friend, although sorry for the fate of the young man, could not regret, under all circumstances, that he was dead. We have also understood that his notion about the ministers conspiring to destroy him induced him to fly from Harrisburg, and he always said that he took the horse more for the purpose of speedily getting from them."

" A note appended to tabular statement (A.), in the Fourth Report, explains the case of No. 49. I may say, in addition, that the President Judge of the Court at which this prisoner was convicted, declared to me that he had no doubt of this man's insanity when arraigned for the crime of arson ; that on this ground he refused to try him, and sent him to the poor-house where the fatal act for which he was sent here was committed. The Judge added, that it was only to have him in a situation where he could not repeat the act, that he had been induced to allow the trial to take place for the murder, to sentence him here to this penitentiary. Had it not been for the fixed opinion which prevailed of the insanity of this prisoner, there is no doubt he would have been hung, as the man he killed was one of the most respectable in the county, and the prisoner confessed the deed. I never saw the slightest alteration in him from the day he arrived until his decease, and no one doubted his insanity who knew him. He was not violent. He worked daily and industriously. He was never sick, nor took a dose of medicine. An angry word was not spoken to him."

" The case of No. 75 was very evident. The officers who brought him told us that he was an idiot, and well known to be such through the county from which he was committed and in which he was born ; that he was a troublesome fellow, fond of fighting, and would also steal, and that having no poor-house in the county, he was sent here to get rid of him. He was one and the same from the hour of his reception to that of his discharge."

" The next case is 112. He was received Feb. 16, 1832. He behaved well, and nothing very striking was observed in his conduct until March 25th, when he conducted himself very much like a lunatic. He continued so for about two days: he then talked rationally, and said that spells came over him. It was not long however before he had a paroxysm, and after a relapse another followed in which he died. Soon after he came here I received a letter from his brother making particular enquiry as to the state of his mind. This led me to think that all was not right before, and I find, from the very respectable gentleman who was his counsel (a man who stands high in the county in which he lives, and which he has represented in our legislature), that he was fully persuaded that this prisoner (No. 112) committed the various larcenies (for one of which he was convicted) when in a state of derangement ; that his counsel put in this plea on the trial, but as the man then appeared sane, the court and jury would not consider it sufficient for an acquittal. I have since seen several persons who knew the man before his conviction, and all agree that his conduct at times was very strange. As these persons can have no object in making these representations other than to express the truth, and as he had been here only thirty-nine days, I have no doubt, that he had been insane before he came here; and that his imprisonment had no injurious effect on his mind."

" Perhaps there is no one matter in which a correct decision is more difficult for a court and jury, as well as for the warden and physician of a prison, than the particular degree of insanity which should clear a man of crime, or whether it be real or pretended. It is necessary to be cautious not to convict one who is not answerable for his actions, and, at the same time, not to suffer an impostor to go at large."

" We had a German sent to the prison from this city about two months since, who behaved with much violence before his trial, on the day of his conviction, and after his arrival here. The judge suspected him of imposture, and under this impression convicted him. The "German Society" of this city have since ascertained that he was a lunatic in the Baltimore hospital, and had left that establishment in a state of insanity. They have petitioned for his pardon, and I have no doubt that it will be granted."

" Should these explanations not be sufficient, I can produce the certificate of Judge Fox, who sentenced No. 49 ; of Wm. H. Hood and J. Bacon, respecting No. 48 ; of many respectable persons in the county from which No. 71 came, and a certificate from the council and several persons who knew him, all of which prove the correctness of what I have here adduced.

I am, thy sincere friend,

" William Crawford."   *Samuel R. Wood."*

Divine service, whenever performed, is thus conducted :—The clergyman takes his station at the end of one of the corridors. A curtain, suspended from a wire, extends from one extremity to the other, dividing it longitudinally. The wooden doors of the cells are then opened. A temporary screen prevents the convicts from seeing each other, and the deputy keepers are in attendance to prevent any attempt at conversation. Each prisoner, although isolated in his cell, can hear the service distinctly. It is greatly to be lamented that the legislature of Pennsylvania should suffer their principal penitentiary to be deficient on a point so important as religious instruction. There is no regular performance of divine service, nor any instruction in reading. Through an ill-judged parsimony, combined with a feeling of sectarian jealousy, no chaplain has been appointed to this penitentiary; and the duties attached to this important and indispensable office are left to be supplied by such ministers

PENNSYLVANIA.

as may have the power or inclination to offer their gratuitous services. A greater error could not have been committed, for in this penitentiary the best possible opportunity is afforded for the useful labours of a clergyman who shall devote his whole time to the spiritual welfare of the convicts. Of this defect the excellent inspectors of the penitentiary are well aware, and no men can be more anxious to have it removed. In their report to the Legislature in 1832, they observe that—" Moral and religious instruction forms one of the most important features of the system, and will require the faithful, unremitting, and undivided time of a chaplain, or religious instructor, whose duty it shall be to pass from cell to cell; to visit every prisoner frequently during the week; to remain with him a considerable time, teaching him his duty to his Creator, his country and himself; duties which, with the exercises of the sabbath, will require his residence in the penitentiary, or in its immediate neighbourhood. The whole time of any one clergyman will certainly be required as soon as all the convicts of the Eastern district shall be confined within these walls."

The daily allowance of food for each convict is a pint of coffee and a pound of bread (two-thirds rye and one-third Indian meal) for breakfast; a pint of soup, three quarters of a pound of beef (without bone), from which the soup is made, and potatoes for dinner; mush (a preparation from Indian meal) and about a gill of molasses for supper. The prisoners are not restricted in the quantity of potatoes or mush.

The clothing consists in summer of a short jacket, cotton trowsers, and shoes: woollen clothing, stockings and caps are furnished in winter. The bedding is a straw or corn-husk mattress, sheets, with a check counterpane in summer; in winter, blankets are added. The bedstead can be turned up against the wall during the day, thus affording more room in which the prisoner can work. Each cell is furnished with a bible, a tin cup, and a tin pan in which the convict receives his food, and which he is required to keep clean.

The warden, in his last report, has stated his conviction that no great benefit will result to any prisoner whose sentence does not extend to two years or more. One year is not in his judgment sufficient to teach a trade, eradicate old and fix new habits. He entertains no apprehension of the health of the prisoner suffering from long sentences, as experience has shown that those who have been the longest in confinement continue to enjoy good health. For some time after a prisoner commences learning a trade he occasions a loss to the Establishment, as the greater part of the first year is spent before he can acquire any proficiency. The instruction imparted in the second year will perfect him, and repay for the time lost. The inspectors acknowledge that it is extremely difficult to instruct prisoners in any branch of trade, in which they will not be surpassed by the superior skill and efforts of free labourers. In the weaving department a loss has been sustained, and in the shoemaking the profit has been very trifling.*

The first prisoner was admitted on the 25th October 1829. The whole number received up to the 1st January 1834 has been 212. At that date there were in confinement 152 males and 2 females. They were employed at trades and occupations in the following proportions:—

Weaving, 38; warping, dyeing, spooling, winding, &c., in the cotton department, 21; shoemaking, 52; carpenters, 5; cabinet-maker, 1; blacksmiths, 5; wheelwright, 1; tinman, 1; stonecutter, 1; cook, 1; quilting bed-covers, 1; apothecary's assistant, 1; cigarmaker, 1; making and mending clothes, 5; woolpickers, 9; washing clothes, 2; unoccupied, 9. Total 154.

Only seven of the shoemakers, and ten of the weavers, understood their trades on admission.

The

---

* Manufactures from December 1, 1832, to December 31, 1833.

	DR.	CR.
Weaving:		
Stock as valued, Nov. 30, 1832 - - - -	$ 10,521 52	
Materials, &c., since purchased - - - -	7,459 08	
Allowed convicts for labour - - - -	3,670 82	
Wages paid superintendent, dyeing department -	282 50	
Wages paid, spooling, &c. - - - - -	77 39	
	22,011 31	
By sales - - - - - - - -	14,039 08	
By stock, as valued Dec. 31, 1833 - - -	6,635 98	
	20,675 06	
By balance, loss on this account - - - - - -		1,336 25
Cordwaining:		
Stock as valued, Nov. 30, 1832 - - - -	405 26	
Materials, &c., purchased since - - - -	5,333 73	
Allowed convicts for labour - - - -	2,241 58	
	7,981 57	
By sales - - - - - - - -	7,596 85	
By stock as valued Dec. 31, 1833 - - -	1,538 23	
	9,135 08	
To balance, for gain on this account -	1,154 51	
Loss on weaving - - - - - -	1,336 25	
Gain on cordwaining - - - - -	1,154 51	
Total loss on manufactures - - - - -	$ 181 74	

The following are the principal provisions of the law for the regulation of the penitentiary:—

The management is vested in a Board of Inspectors, consisting of five " taxable " citizens of Pennsylvania, to be appointed by the Judges of the Supreme Court, who shall serve for two years, and until successors shall be appointed. The Inspectors are required to meet once a month. They shall appoint semi-annually a warden, a physician, and clerk to the Institution, and fix their salaries as well as those of the under-keepers. They shall serve without any pecuniary compensation. They shall visit the penitentiary at least twice in every week to see that the duties of the several officers are performed. They have power to make such rules for the government of the prison as may not be inconsistent with the principles of solitary confinement set forth by the Act for the establishment of the penitentiary. They shall attend to the religious instruction of the prisoners, and procure a suitable person for this object, provided his services be gratuitous. They shall direct the manner in which all raw materials for manufacture, provisions, and other supplies for the prison, shall be purchased. They are to require accurate accounts to be kept of receipts and disbursements. On the 1st January in every year, the inspectors are required to make a report to the Legislature on the state of the penitentiary. This Report shall contain the number of prisoners in confinement, their age, sex, place of nativity, term of commitment, and term of imprisonment during the year, noticing also those who have escaped or died, or been pardoned or discharged, designating the offence for which the commitment was made, and whether for a first or repeated offence, and when, in what court, and by whose order. The inspectors are required on these occasions to make such observations as to the efficiency of solitary confinement as may have resulted from their experience, and give such information as they may deem expedient for making the penitentiary effectual for the punishment and reformation of offenders.

In their weekly visits the inspectors are required to speak to each prisoner, unaccompanied by the warden or any of his officers, and to listen to any complaints that may be made of oppression or ill conduct of the persons employed in the establishment. They are authorized to examine into the truth of the alleged statement, and to act on the result, should the complaint be well-founded. The warden is required to reside in the penitentiary, to visit every cell and apartment, and see every prisoner under his care at least once in every day. He shall keep a journal, in which shall be entered the reception, discharge, death, pardon, or escape, of any prisoner ; the complaints that have been made, or punishments inflicted for any breach of prison discipline : the visits of the inspector and physician, and all other occurrences requiring notice. The appointment of the under-keepers, and all servants of the establishment, rests with the warden. He can dismiss them whenever he thinks proper, and is directed to do so when the inspectors desire their discharge. It is the duty of the warden to report all infractions of rules to the inspectors ; and, with the approbation of one of them, he may punish the offender. The warden cannot be absent from the penitentiary for a night without permission in writing from two of the inspectors.

The under-keepers (or overseers, as they are designated in the Act) are required to inspect the condition of each prisoner at least three times in every day, to see that his meals are regularly delivered according to the prison allowance, and to superintend the work of the prisoners. They must give immediate notice whenever any convict shall complain of such illness as to require medical aid. Each overseer shall have a certain number of prisoners assigned to his care. He is to make a daily report to the warden of the health and conduct of the prisoners, and a like report to the inspectors, when required. No overseer shall be present when the warden or the inspectors visit the prisoners under his particular care, unless he be required to attend by the inspectors or warden. All orders to the overseers must be given through or by the warden. No overseer shall receive from any one confined in the penitentiary, or from any one on behalf of such prisoner, any emolument or reward whatever, or the promise of any, either for services or supplies, or as a gratuity, under the penalty of one hundred dollars, and imprisonment for thirty days in the county gaol. No overseer who has been discharged can be again employed.

The physician shall visit every prisoner in the penitentiary twice in every week, and oftener if the state of his health requires it, and shall report once in every month to the inspectors. He must attend immediately on notice from the warden that a prisoner is sick. He is to examine every prisoner who shall be brought into the penitentiary before he be confined in his cell. Whenever, in the opinion of the physician, any convict in the penitentiary is so ill as to require removal, the warden shall direct such removal to the infirmary, where the prisoner shall be kept until the physician shall certify that he may return to his cell without injury to his health. The physician is required to visit the patients in the infirmary at least once every day, and to give such directions for the health and cleanliness of the prisoners, and when necessary for the alteration of their diet, as he may deem expedient, provided that they be not contrary to the provisions of the law, or inconsistent with the safe custody of the prisoner. The directions so given, whether complied with or not, shall be entered in the journal of the warden, and in his own. The physician shall inquire into the mental as well as bodily state of every prisoner ; and when he shall have reason to believe that the mind or body is materially affected by the discipline, treatment, or diet, he shall inform the warden thereof, and enter his observations in a journal which he is required to keep. This entry shall be an authority to the warden for altering the discipline, treatment, or diet, of any prisoner until the next meeting of the inspectors who shall inquire into the case, and make orders accordingly. In his journal, the physician shall record the state of every prisoner's health, whether he be in the infirmary or not, together with such remarks as may be deemed important. This journal shall be open to the inspectors and warden, and laid before the inspectors at their monthly meeting.

No prisoner shall, unless at his own desire, be discharged while labouring under a dangerous disease, although entitled to his liberation.

The infirmary shall have a suitable partition between every bed, and no two patients shall occupy the same bed; and the physician and his attendants are required to take every precaution in their power to prevent all intercourse between the convicts while in the infirmary.

No person who is not an official visitor of the prison, or who has not a written permission according to such rules as the inspectors may adopt, shall be allowed to visit it. The official visitors are the Governor, Speaker and Members of the Senate, the Speaker and Members of the House of Representatives, the Secretary of the State, the Judges of the Supreme Court, the Attorney-general and his Deputies, the President and Associate Judges in all the Courts of the State; the Mayor and Recorder of the cities of Philadelphia, Lancaster and Pittsburg; the Commissioners and Sheriffs of the several Counties, and the Acting Committee of the " Philadelphia Society for the alleviation of the miseries of public prisons." None but the official visitors can have any communication with the convicts, nor shall any visitor be permitted to deliver to or receive from any of the convicts any letter or message, or to supply them with any article of any kind, under the penalty of one hundred dollars. Any visitor who shall discover an abuse or infraction of the prison rules, is required immediately to make the same known to the board of inspectors.

On the discharge of a convict, his clothes shall be restored to him, together with other property of any kind that might have been taken from him on his admission. When a prisoner is to be liberated, the warden is to obtain from him, as far as is practicable, his former history; what means of literary moral or religious instruction he enjoyed; what were his early temptations to crime and general habits, and in what part of the country he proposes to fix his residence. This information shall be recorded. If the inspectors and warden have been satisfied with the morality, industry, and order, of the prisoner's conduct, they shall be authorized to give him a certificate to that effect, and shall furnish the discharged convict with four dollars, if destitute.

I conclude this account of the Philadelphia penitentiary by stating that I availed myself freely of the privilege which was in the handsomest manner granted to me by the inspectors and warden, of communicating at all times, and in private, with the prisoners in their cells. Many of these persons had been four years in confinement. I could not perceive, either in their appearance or conversation, any indication that the solitude to which they had been subjected for this long period had injured their health or impaired their understanding. Although generally serious, they were not depressed, and several talked with a cheerfulness which I did not expect to find in men thus situated. In one case only did I meet with any exhibition of angry feeling. They universally concurred in the conviction that solitude was of all punishments the most fearful, and declared that if ever they were liberated they should never be found again within those walls. Most of them, at the same time, acknowledged that the correction was beneficial, and that it would be their own fault if they were not improved by the opportunity for reflection which was thus afforded to them. Several contrasted the superiority of the system, in a moral point of view, over that in which prisoners are allowed to associate. Each cell is provided with a bible and religious tracts; but in other respects the moral and religious instruction of the prisoner is so greatly neglected, that the reformatory effects of which the system is capable, cannot be developed. Two facts, however, of great importance may be collected from even the short-timed and limited experience derived from this penitentiary, viz. 1st, That the discipline of strict solitude for long periods is regarded with a dread which is inspired by no other species of prison management; and 2d, that it can be enforced with perfect safety both to the health and mind of the offender.

Of the seventy-seven prisoners received into the penitentiary in 1833, fifty-five were white and twenty-two coloured. Fourteen are under twenty; thirty-four from twenty to thirty; twenty from thirty to forty; seven from forty to fifty; one from fifty to sixty, and one from seventy to eighty years of age. Thirty-seven are natives of Pennsylvania; five of New York; four of New Jersey; four of Delaware; six of Maryland; three of Connecticut; two of Massachusetts; one of Vermont; one of Mississipi; two of England; eight of Ireland; one of Scotland; one of Denmark, and one of Germany. On their first conviction there were sixty-one; on their second, nine; on their third, five; and on their sixth, two. One only had been before in the penitentiary. Of the whole number received into this penitentiary from the opening, viz. two hundred and nineteen, forty-two could neither read nor write; fifty-nine could read, but not write, and one hundred and eighteen could read and write. Of the latter class, one had been educated at an university, one had a good English education and is a tolerable Latin and French scholar; one understands English, Dutch and Hebrew; besides these, there are not more than seven who have had a good education, and not more than two others who could read and write tolerably, leaving ninety-eight who could read or write indifferently; many of these, as well as most of those who could read only, were not able to read a sentence without spelling many of the words. It is not only in their elementary education that these persons had been neglected in their youth, but also in not having been taught any trade or occupation to qualify them for useful citizens. On an investigation of this point, the warden has ascertained, that of the whole number only thirty were regularly bound and served out their apprenticeship; sixteen remained during their minority with their parents; thirty-eight were apprenticed, but left their masters under various pretences; most of them ran away, and gave as a reason the severity with which they were treated, the want of food, clothing, &c.; two of them declare that their masters first taught them to steal; eight were slaves until twenty-one or twenty-eight years of age, and one hundred and twenty-one never were apprenticed, but lived in an unsettled way during their minority.

PENNSYLVANIA.

Of the previous habits of the prisoners, the warden's inquiries lead to the conclusion that twenty may be considered habitual drunkards ; that forty-nine were frequently intoxicated, and eighty-four occasionally so: fifty-six have stated that they rarely drank ardent spirits. Of twelve who have been convicted of murder of the second degree, eight were at the time under the influence of liquor, and one was deranged. Of ten who had been guilty of man-slaughter, seven acknowledged that they were intoxicated.

The following tabular statements will show the number of convicts received into the penitentiary since its commencement to the year 1833 ; also the offences of which they have been guilty, the periods for which they have been sentenced, the number discharged by the expiration of their sentence and by pardon, as also the number of deaths which have occurred during that period.

NUMBER of CONVICTS received into the PENNSYLVANIA STATE PRISON at PHILADELPHIA, denominated the EASTERN PENITENTIARY, from its commencement to November 21, 1833.

CRIMES.	1829.	1830.	1831.	1832.	1833.
Burglary	1	17	8	6	14
Horse Stealing	5	10	12	9	15
Highway Robbery	2	–	–	–	–
Passing and selling Counterfeit Money	1	2	2	2	5
Forgery	–	6	6	2	2
Manslaughter	–	2	4	2	2
Murder	–	7	1	–	2
Robbery	–	4	2	1	4
Robbing U. S. Mail	–	1	–	–	–
Rape	–	1	–	1	–
Arson	–	–	2	1	–
Assault to commit Rape	–	–	1	–	–
Ditto - ditto - Murder	–	–	1	–	–
Larceny	–	–	10	6	23
Perjury	–	–	1	1	–
Sodomy	–	–	–	1	–
Subornation of Perjury	–	–	–	1	–
TOTAL - 209	9	50	50	33	67
Recommittals - None *-	–	–	–	–	–
Pardons	1	1	3	–	2
Deaths	–	1	4	4	1

White men, 153 ;—Coloured men, 52 ;—Coloured women; 4 ;—Total, 209.

AGES OF PRISONERS.		NATIVES OF	
Under 20 years of age - 24	1st Conviction - 156	United States - 172	
20 to 30 - 102	2d ditto - 25	Ireland - 19	
		England - 10	
30 to 40 - 51	3d ditto - 16	Scotland - 1	
		France - 2	
40 to 50 - 20	4th ditto - 6	Denmark - 1	
50 to 60 - 8	5th ditto - 2	Holland - 1	
60 to 70 - 3		Germany - 1	
	6th ditto - 4	Switzerland - 1	
70 to 80 - 1		Netherlands - 1	
TOTAL - 209	TOTAL - 209	TOTAL - 209	

* Since the date of this Return, a prisoner who had been previously in confinement in this Penitentiary has been re-committed.

b 2

STATEMENT of Particulars respecting the CONVICTS received into the EASTERN PENITENTIARY, from its commencement in 1829 to 1833.

No.	Age.	Sex.	Place of Nativity.	When sentenced.	Time.	Offence.	At what Court sentenced.	Times convicted.	When discharged.	How discharged.
1	18	male	Harrisburgh, Pa.	Oct. 22, 1829	2 years	Burglary	‡ O. T. Delaware co.	First	Oct. 22, 1831	Time out.
2	20	male	Chester county, Pa.	Nov. 7 –	1 year	Horse stealing	‖ Q. S. Chester	First	Nov. 7, 1830	Time out.
3	28	male	Fayetteville, N.C.	Nov. 21 –	11 years	Highway robbery	O. T. Philadelphia	Third	July 6, 1832	Pardoned.
4	18	male	Philadelphia	Nov. 21 –	8 years	Highway robbery	O. T. Philadelphia	Fourth.		
5	42	male	Franklin co. Pa.	Nov. 11 –	2 years	Horse stealing	Q. S. Cumberland	Third	Nov. 11, 1831	Time out.
6	22	male	City of New York	Nov. 17 –	2 years	Horse stealing	O. T. Lancaster	First	Nov. 17 –	Time out.
7	18	male	Perry co. Pa.	Nov. 11 –	1 year	Horse stealing	Q. S. Franklin	First	Nov. 11, 1830	Time out.
8	29	male	Guernsey co. Ohio	Nov. 25 –	2 years	Horse stealing	Q. S. Adams	First	Nov. 25, 1831	Time out.
9	22	male	Armagh, Ireland	Dec. 28 –	1 year	Passing a counterfeit note.	Q. S. Philadelphia	First	Dec. 28, 1830	Time out.
10	31	male	Hartford, Connecticut	Jan. 2, 1830	2 years	Forgery	Mayor's Ct. Philadelphia	First	Jan. 2, 1832	Time out.
11	48	male	Virginia	Dec. 30, 1829	1 year	Horse stealing	O. T. Schuylkill	Fourth	Jan. 21, 1831	Time out.
12	19	male	Lancashire, England	Jan. 5, 1830	2 years	Forging a check	Mayor's Ct. Philadelphia	First	Jan. 5, 1832	Time out.
13	26	male	Trenton, New Jersey	Jan. 5 –	2 years	Forgery	Mayor's Ct. Philadelphia	Sixth	May 17, 1831	Died.
14	21	male	Herkimer, New York	Jan. 4 –	1 year	Forgery	Q. S. Columbia	First	Jan. 21, 1831	Time out.
15	26	male	Carlisle, Pa.	Jan. 15 –	2 years	Manslaughter	O. T. Cumberland	First	Jan. 15, 1832	Time out.
16	20	male	Charleston, S.C.	Jan. 19 –	15 months	Horse stealing	Q. S. Lancaster	Third	Apr. 19, 1831	Time out.
7	30	male	Queen's Anne's co. Md.	Feb. 8 –	2 years	Burglary	O. T. Chester	First	Feb. 8, 1832	Time out.
8	55	male	Near Carlisle, Pa.	Feb. 2 –	2 years	Burglary	Q. S. Lycoming	First	Feb. 2 –	Time out.
9	40	male	Bucks co. Pa.	Mar. 12 –	1 year	Passing a counterfeit note.	Q. S. Philadelphia	First	Nov. 29, 1830	Died.
0	28	male	County Down, Ireland	Apr. 24 –	12 years	Murder	O. T. Philadelphia	First.		
1	21	male	Strasburgh, France	Apr. 24 –	12 years	Murder	O. T. Philadelphia	First.		
22	32	male	Near Albany, New York	Apr. 24 –	2 years	Burglary	O. T. Philadelphia	Third	Apr. 24, 1832	Time out.
23	31	male	Northampton co. Pa.	Apr. 14 –	1 year	Forgery	Q. S. Montgomery	Second	Apr. 15, 1831	Time out.
24	23	male	Chester co. Pa.	May 7 –	2 years	Burglary	O. T. Chester	First	May 7, 1832	Time out.
25	18	male	Wilmington, Del.	May 7 –	2 years	Burglary	O. T. Chester	First	May 7 –	Time out.
26	34	male	Smyrna, Del.	July 31 –	1 year	Forgery	Q. S. Philadelphia	First	Aug. 1, 1831	Time out.
27	28	male	Tyrone co. Ireland	Aug. 5 –	3 years	Horse stealing	Q. S. Perry	Second.		
28	41	male	Philadelphia	Aug. 21 –	4 years	Murder	O. T. Montgomery	First.		
29	23	male	Nashville, Tennessee	Aug. 17 –	5 years	Burglary	O. T. Montgomery	Third.		
30	21	male	New Jersey	Aug. 17 –	10 years	Burglary	O. T. Montgomery	First.		
31	24	male	Cumberland co. N.J.	Aug. 17 –	10 years	Burglary	O. T. Montgomery	First.		
32	22	male	Yardleyville, Pa.	Aug. 17 –	9 years	Burglary	O. T. Montgomery	First.		
33	28	male	Near Kingston, E.Jersey	Aug. 17 –	9 years	Burglary	O. T. Montgomery	First	Mar. 6, 1831	Died.
34	53	male	Chalons, France	Aug. 12 –	12 years	Murder	O. T. Berks	First.		
35	70	male	W. Greenwich, R. Island	Aug. 10 –	8 years	Murder	O. T. Luzerne	First.		
36	31	male	Co. Donnegal, Ireland	Aug. 17 –	4 years	Horse stealing	O. T. Northampton	Second.		
37	28	male	Philadelphia	Aug. 23 –	3 years	Burglary	O. T. Northampton	Third.		
38	19	male	Utica, New York	Aug. 17 –	1 year	Horse stealing	Q. S. Northumberland	First	Aug. 17, 1831	Time out.
39	20	male	Northumberland co. Pa.	Aug. 17 –	1 year	Horse stealing	Q. S. Northumberland	First	Aug. 17 –	Time out.
40	28	male	Adams co. Pa.	Aug. 25 –	3 years	Burglary	O. T. Adams	Third	Aug. 4, 1832	Died.
41	20	male	Philadelphia	Sept. 27 –	2 years	Horse stealing	Q. S. Philadelphia	First	Sept. 27 –	Time out.
42	31	male	Ireland	Sept. 30 –	3 years	Passing forged notes	Q. S. Philadelphia	Second.		
43	35	male	Sussex co. Del.	Oct. 6 –	3 years	Horse stealing	Q. S. Philadelphia	First	Aug. 20, 1831	Died.
44	41	male	Lancaster co. Penn.	Oct. 4 –	2 years	Horse stealing	O. T. Lancaster	First	Oct. 4, 1832	Time out.
45	43	male	Sassafras, Maryland	Oct. 9 –	13 months	Robbery	O. T. Lancaster	First	Nov. 9, 1831	Time out.
46	49	male	Hartford co. Maryland	Nov. 8 –	4 years	Burglary	O. T. Berks	Second.		
47	26	male	Lucerne co. Pa.	Nov. 19 –	8 years	Murder	O. T. Lancaster	First.		
48	19	male	Smithfield, Madison co. N.Y.	Nov. 17 –	2 years	Horse stealing	O. T. Lancaster	First	Mar. 8, 1832	Pardoned.
49	25	male	Chester co. Pa.	Nov. 19 –	12 years	Murder	O. T. Montgomery	First	Sept. 3, 1832	Suicide.*
50	36	male	County Down, Ireland	Dec. 4 –	7 years	Robbery	O. T. Philadelphia	Second.		
51	41	male	Reading, Connecticut	Dec. 4 –	5 years	Robbery	O. T. Philadelphia	Fourth.		
52	37	male	Philadelphia	Dec. 4 –	5 years	Robbery	O. T. Philadelphia	Fourth.		
53	21	male	Philadelphia	Dec. 4 –	5 years	Burglary	O. T. Philadelphia	Sixth.		
54	34	male	Ireland	Dec. 4 –	5 years	Manslaughter	O. T. Philadelphia	First.		
55	20	male	Montgomery co. Md.	Dec. 4 –	5 years	Burglary	O. T. Philadelphia	First.		
56	30	male	Philadelphia	Oct. 25 –	10 years	Robbing U.S.Mail†	Circuit Court, U. S.	Fifth.		
57	54	male	MilesTown, near Philada.	Dec. 20 –	5 years	Burglary	O. T. Philadelphia	First.		
58	40	male	Camden, New Jersey	Dec. 14 –	12 years	Rape	O. T. Bucks	First.		
59	27	male	Ulster co. N.Y.	Jan. 8, 1831	1 year	Passing counterfeit coin.	Q. S. Luzerne co.	First	Jan. 8, 1832	Time out.
60	28	male	Northumberland co. Pa.	Jan. 7 –	1 year	Forgery	Q. S. Columbia	First	Apr. 4, 1831	Pardoned.
61	47	male	Sunbury, Pa.	Jan. 17 –	2½ years	Horse stealing	O. T. Dauphin	First.		
62	31	male	Lancaster co. Pa.	Jan. 25 –	4 years	Forgery	O. T. Lancaster	First	Aug. 6, 1832	Pardoned.
63	21	male	Philadelphia	Jan. 19 –	13 months	Horse stealing	O. T. Lancaster	First	Feb. 19, 1832	Time out.
64	24	male	Southern States	Jan. 19 –	4 years	Burglary	O. T. Lancaster	First.		
65	30	male	Orange co. N.Y.	Mar. 16 –	4 years	Forgery	Q. S. Philadelphia	Third.		
66	21	male	Philadelphia	Mar. 16 –	4 years	Forgery	Q. S. Philadelphia	First.		
67	38	male	Ireland	Apr. 5 –	3 years	Horse stealing	Q. S. York	First.		
68	22	male	Luzerne county	Apr. 8 –	1 year	Horse stealing	Q. S. Luzerne	First	Apr. 8, 1832	Time out.
69	30	male	Connecticut	Apr. 30 –	6 years	Burglary	O. T. Philadelphia	Second.		
70	27	male	Delaware	Apr. 30 –	6 years	Burglary	O. T. Philadelphia	Fourth.		
71	26	male	New Jersey	Apr. 30 –	6 years	Burglary	O. T. Philadelphia	Third.		
72	28	male	Philadelphia	Apr. 30 –	6 years	Burglary	O. T. Philadelphia	Second.		
73	21	female	Delaware	Apr. 30 –	3 years	Manslaughter	O. T. Philadelphia	Third.		
74	20	female	Philadelphia	Ap. 30 –	6 years	Manslaughter	O. T. Philadelphia	Second.		

* No. 49. It was believed that this man committed arson in Montgomery county. He was arrested and about to be put on his trial, but the Court were so well satisfied of his insanity, that they refused to try him, and sent him to the Poor-house for safe keeping. After being confined there for some time he made his escape. He was pursued and overtaken by the Superintendent, when a conflict ensued which terminated in the death of the Superintendent. For this offence he was tried, found guilty of murder in the second degree, and sent here for 12 years. From the day of his reception to his death, he showed strong and decided symptoms of derangement; not more latterly than at first. It is believed that he would not have been convicted of this last offence, but to enable the court to confine him in a place of security.

† Received at the particular request of the United States Marshal, and to be removed if his cell should be required for a State Prisoner.
‡ Oyer and Terminer.
‖ Quarter Sessions.

STATEMENT of Convicts received into the EASTERN PENITENTIARY, from 1829 to 1833—*continued*.

No.	Age.	Sex.	Place of Nativity.	When sentenced.	Time.	Offence.	At what Court sentenced.	Times convicted.	When discharged.	How discharged.
75	19	male	Bradford co. Pa. -	May 14, 1831	1 year	Horse stealing -	Q. S. Bradford -	First -	Feb. 10, 1832	Pardoned.
76	18	male	London - - -	June 23 —	3 years	Forgery -	Mayor's ct. Philadelphia	First.		
77	53	male	Delaware - -	Apr. 19 —	4 years	Horse stealing -	O. T. Lancaster -	First -	Oct. 18, 1831	Died.
78	31	male	Holland - - -	July 9 —	4 years	Forgery -	Mayor's ct. Philadelphia	First.		
79	21	male	Philadelphia -	Aug. 6 —	2 years	Passing counterfeit coin.	O. T. Berks - -	First.		
80	18	male	Berks co. Pa. - -	Aug. 6 —	2 years	Burglary -	O. T. Berks - -	First.		
81	25	male	Berks co. Pa. -	Aug. 6 —	4 years	Arson -	O. T. Berks - -	First.		
82	24	male	New York - -	Aug. 9 —	2 years	Horse stealing -	Mayor's court, Lancaster	First.		
83	30	male	Bucks co. Pa. -	Aug. 16 —	4 years	Robbery -	O. T. Lancaster -	Third.		
84	23	male	England - -	Aug. 19 —	4 years	Horse stealing -	Q. S. Northumberland	First.		
85	25	male	England - -	Aug. 19 —	4 years	Horse stealing -	Q. S. Northumberland	First.		
86	46	male	York co. Pa. -	Apr. 21 —	15 months	Horse stealing -	Q. S. Lancaster -	First.		
87	21	male	Bucks co. Pa. -	Sept. 12 —	3 years	Horse stealing -	Q. S. Bucks -	First.		
88	29	male	Chester co. Pa. -	Sept. 28 —	7 years	Intent to commit rape.	Q. S. Philadelphia -	First.		
89	52	male	England - - -	Oct. 4 —	7 years	Assault and battery with intent to murder.	Mayor's ct. Philadelphia	First.		
90	25	male	Ireland - - -	Oct. 5 —	14 months	Larceny -	Mayor's ct. Philadelphia	First -	Dec. 5, 1832	Time out.
91	24	male	Delaware - - -	Oct. 24 —	13 months	Larceny -	Mayor's ct. Philadelphia	First -	Nov. 24, 1832	Time out.
92	24	male	England - - -	Nov. 1 —	3½ years	Horse stealing -	Q. S. Schuylkill -	First.		
93	60	male	Montgomery co. Pa. -	Nov. 17 —	1 year	Perjury -	Q. S. Columbia -	First -	Nov. 17, 1832	Time out.
94	26	male	Virginia - - -	Nov. 17 —	2 years	Larceny -	Q. S. Cumberland -	Second.		
95	21	male	New Jersey - -	Nov. 17 —	3 years	Larceny -	Mayor's ct. Lancaster -	First.		
96	20	male	Delaware - -	Nov. 17 —	3 years	Larceny -	Mayor's ct. Lancaster -	First.		
97	26	male	Bucks co. Pa. -	Nov. 24 —	4 years	Arson -	O. T. Montgomery -	First.		
98	39	male	London - -	Nov. 30 —	2 years	Burglary -	O. T. Delaware -	Fourth.		
99	15	male	Philadelphia -	Dec. 10 —	2 years	Burglary -	O. T. Philadelphia -	First.		
100	24	fem.	Delaware - - -	Dec. 10 —	2 years	Manslaughter -	O. T. Philadelphia -	First.		
101	29	fem.	Delaware - - -	Dec. 10 —	2 years	Manslaughter -	O. T. Philadelphia -	First.		
102	42	male	Lancaster co. Pa. -	Nov. 23 —	12 years	Murder -	O. T. Lancaster -	First.	- - -	Died.
103	38	male	Maryland - -	Nov. 26 —	3 years	Robbery -	O. T. Dauphin - -	First.		
104	21	male	Philadelphia -	Dec. 20 —	2½ years	Larceny -	Mayor's ct. Philadelphia	First.		
105	18	male	Philadelphia -	Dec. 21 —	3 years	Larceny -	Mayor's ct. Philadelphia	First.		
106	40	male	Ireland - - -	Dec. 27 —	18 months	Larceny -	Mayor's ct. Philadelphia	First.		
107	34	male	New Jersey -	Dec. 29 —	3 years	Larceny -	Mayor's ct. Philadelphia	First.		
108	29	male	Bucks co. Pa. -	Dec. 29 —	3 years	Larceny -	Mayor's ct. Philadelphia	First.		
109	23	male	Maryland - -	Jan. 5, 1832	2 years	Larceny -	Mayor's ct. Philadelphia	Second.		
110	32	male	Pennsylvania -	Jan. 12 —	3 years	Burglary -	O. T. Cumberland -	Fifth.		
111	27	male	New York - -	Jan. 28 —	2 years	Perjury -	Q. S. Wayne - -	First.		
112	27	male	New York - -	Jan. 28 —	2 years	Larceny -	Q. S. Wayne -	First -	May 26, 1832	Died.*
113	36	male	New Jersey - -	Mar. 8 —	1 yr. & 15 ds	Horse stealing -	Q. S. Philadelphia -	First.		
114	36	male	Delaware - -	Mar. 20 —	3 years	Horse stealing -	Mayor's ct. Philadelphia	First.	May 31, 1832	Died.
115	27	male	Pennsylvania -	Mar. 14 —	1 year	Horse stealing -	Q. S. Philadelphia -	First.		
116	26	male	New Jersey - -	Mar. 19 —	2 yrs. & 2 ds.	Larceny -	Q. S. Philadelphia -	First.		
117	21	male	Ireland - -	Mar. 26 —	18 months	Larceny -	Mayor's ct. Philadelphia	First.		
118	27	male	New Jersey - -	Apr. 18 —	4 years	Robbery -	O. T. Philadelphia -	Second.		
119	33	male	France - -	Apr. 17 —	2 years	Burglary -	O. T. Philadelphia -	First.		
120	20	male	New Jersey - -	Apr. 17 —	3 years	Burglary -	O. T. Philadelphia -	First.		
121	22	male	Maryland - -	Apr. 2 —	3 years	Rape -	O. T. Franklin county	First.		
122	51	male	Pennsylvania -	May 2 —	3 years	Passing counterfeit money.	Q. S. Lehigh county -	First.		
123	50	male	Switzerland -	May 2 —	2 years	Passing counterfeit money.	Q. S. Lehigh county -	First.		
124	30	male	Pennsylvania -	May 4 —	2 years	Manslaughter -	O. T. Lehigh county -	First.		
125	22	male	New Jersey - -	May 1 —	6 years	Manslaughter -	O. T. Bucks county -	First.		
126	27	male	Pennsylvania -	Dec. 4, 1830	5 years	Burglary -	O. T. Philadelphia -	Second.		
127	34	male	New York - -	June 18, 1832	6 years	Forgery -	Q. S. Philadelphia -	Second.		
128	69	male	Ireland - -	June 18 —	3 years	Horse stealing -	Mayor's ct. Philadelphia	First.		
129	48	male	Philadelphia -	June 16 —	3 years	Forgery -	Mayor's ct. Philadelphia	Second.		
130	21	male	Maryland - -	June 20 —	2 years	Larceny -	Mayor's ct. Philadelphia	First.		
131	23	male	Pennsylvania -	Aug. 3 —	4 years	Burglary -	O. T. Chester county -	First.		
132	16	male	Delaware - -	Aug. 27 —	5 years	Arson -	O. T. Delaware -	First.		
133	40	male	New York - -	Aug. 23 —	2 years	Subornation of Perjury.	Q. S. Pike county -	First.		
134	22	male	Pennsylvania -	Aug. 16 —	1 year	Horse stealing -	Q. S. Franklin county	First.		
135	18	male	Pennsylvania -	Aug. 21 —	2 years	Burglary -	O. T. Lancaster county	First.		
136	27	male	New York - -	Sept. 11 —	4 years	Horse stealing -	Q. S. Bucks county -	Second.		
137	18	male	New Jersey - -	Nov. 3 —	2 years	Burglary -	O. T. Chester -	First.		
138	32	male	New Jersey - -	Nov. 3 —	2 years	Burglary -	O. T. Chester -	First.		
139	33	male	Pennsylvania -	Nov. 20 —	3 years	Horse stealing -	O. T. Lancaster -	First.		
140	27	male	Pennsylvania -	Nov. 20 —	2 years	Horse stealing -	O. T. Lancaster -	First.		
141	23	male	Pennsylvania -	Nov. 19 —	2 years	Larceny -	Q. S. Northampton co.	First.		
142	27	male	England - -	Dec. 19 —	3 years	Horse stealing -	Q. S. Philadelphia co.	First.		
143	21	male	Philadelphia -	Dec. 10, 1832	2 years	Larceny -	Mayor's ct. Philadelphia	First.		
144	26	male	Pennsylvania -	Jan. 5, 1833	3 years	Horse stealing -	Mayor's ct. Philadelphia	Second.		
145	40	male	Pennsylvania -	Jan. 12 —	5 years	Felony -	Mayor's ct. Philadelphia	First. .		
146	27	male	Massachusetts -	Jan. 19 —	2½ years	Burglary -	O. & T. Philad. county	Second.		
147	28	male	Pennsylvania -	Jan. 19 —	3 years	Burglary -	O. & T. Philad. county	Sixth.		
148	19	male	Pennsylvania -	Jan. 19 —	3 years	Burglary -	O. & T. Philad. county	First.		
149	38	male	Pennsylvania -	Jan. 18, 1833	4 years -	Passing counterfeit money.	Q. S. Cumberland -	First.		
150	24	male	Maryland - -	Jan. 17 —	1 year -	Horse stealing -	Q. S. Franklin - -	First.		

* No. 112. The singular conduct of this man in committing the acts for which he was convicted gave strong grounds to believe that there was a decided aberration of mind.' The very respectable counsel who defended him on trial, put in a plea of insanity; and this gentleman has declared since the prisoner's death that he has no doubt but that he was subject to fits of insanity, and that he was in that state of mind when the acts were committed. About one week after his arrival here, he had one of these fits, which lasted nearly a week; he then became composed, and remained so for some time; he had several repetitions of these fits previous to his death.

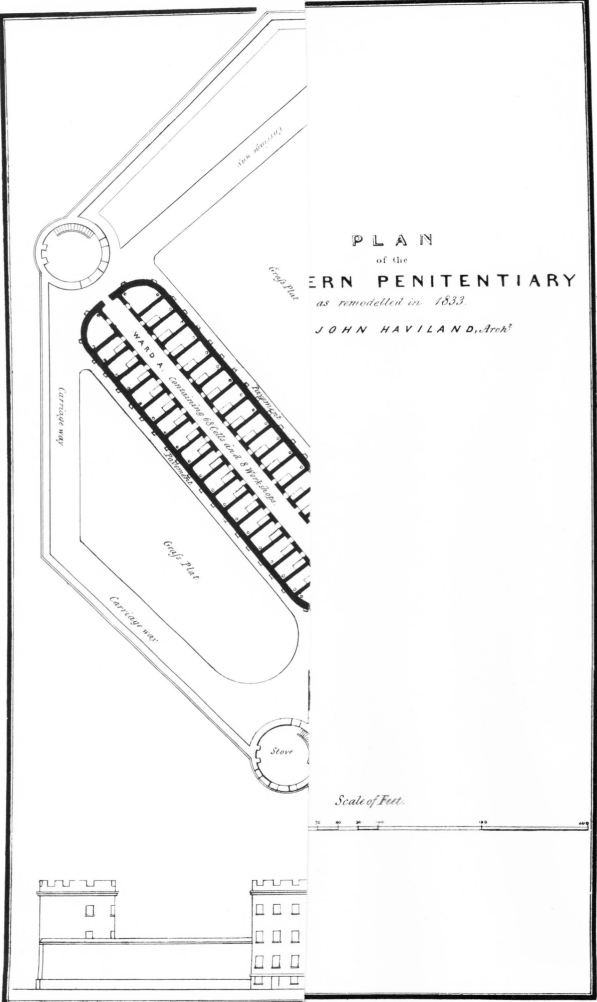

Standidge & Lemon, Lithr.

PLAN
of the
ERN PENITENTIARY
as remodelled in 1833.

JOHN HAVILAND, Arch.

Scale of Feet.

WESTERN PENITENTIARY AT PITTSBURG.

THIS prison was first erected about the year 1820, but on account of the evils which were found to arise from the defective arrangement of the cell-buildings, the greater part of the prison has been recently pulled down and re-constructed on the plan of the solitary cells in the Eastern Penitentiary. The ground inclosed by the boundary wall is in form of an octagon, about 400 feet in diameter. The front, extending 180 feet in length, is occupied by the dwelling-houses and offices of the warden or keeper and his deputy. At the external angles of this building are two large circular towers (containing store-rooms, &c.) which together with the officers' houses are four stories high, and present a handsome elevation being finished in the castellated style of Gothic architecture. A circular tower is also placed at the angle of the boundary wall on each side, for the purpose of overlooking the prison-yards.

The accompanying plans show the construction of the prison in its original form and also the improvements recently adopted. The cells of the prisoners, according to the former design, were built in a double range, being placed back to back (as at Auburn), but in the form of a circle the diameter of which was 320 feet; part of the cells facing the boundary wall, and the other part fronting the large internal area, which was subdivided into nine yards or courts. The cells, forming the circumference of the circle, were each about nine feet long, and seven feet wide. In the front of each cell was a small yard, six feet wide, having a doorway in front, and also an opening on each side, so as to form a continued passage or corridor round each front of the building: into this passage the doors of the cells opened at a short distance from each other. These cells were intended for the purposes of constant solitary confinement, and the prisoners were not permitted to enter the central courts unless their health suffered materially from close imprisonment. The women's cells occupied that part of the circle nearest the entrance (comprising 22 cells), being separated by a wall from the other part of the central court. The kitchen and bakehouse were attached to the women's ward. The cell-buildings were designed to be only one story high; and the plan comprised 194 separate cells on the ground-floor.

This penitentiary was completed and opened for the reception of convicts in 1827. It cost the large sum of 186,000 dollars. Each prisoner was shut up day and night in a separate cell, without being provided with any description of labour or employment. It was, however, soon discovered that the solitude, although intended to be perfect and absolute, was not so in fact; and that, from the bad arrangement and construction of the building, the prisoners could easily communicate from cell to cell. The confinement was thus rendered highly injurious from the absence of all occupation, and the constant facilities which were presented of mutual corruption. The health of the convicts became greatly impaired by close confinement in cells of such limited dimensions, and when admission into the courts for the purpose of air and exercise became indispensable, the advantages of solitude were entirely superseded. The arrangement of the cells was also very unfavourable for the purpose of inspection, as they presented an extensive double frontage, both of which were entirely out of view from the keeper's house. To preserve any degree of order among the prisoners it was necessary that one or more officers should constantly walk round each side of the circle.*

In 1830, the inspectors of the prison made a report to the Legislature on the inconvenience and difficulties arising out of the construction of the cells, observing, that it was unfortunate that the building should have been erected before the system for its government had been prescribed. There is, perhaps, no trade or occupation at which a convict could have worked in any of the cells. Each cell was a kind of vault, about seven feet by nine in the clear; there was not sufficient light, the only supply being admitted through the narrow gratings of a heavy iron door, hung on stone jambs three feet thick, after passing through an outer door and across a vestibule six feet wide. "Constant confinement in the cells," say the inspectors, "is incompatible with the health of the convicts, and we have found it necessary to permit two or three to be out alternately, which gives an opportunity of intercourse that greatly diminishes the benefit of solitary confinement."

An Act of the Legislature was passed in 1832, authorizing the demolition of these cells and the construction of others similar to those in the Eastern Penitentiary, in which the same system of discipline might be established.

The new cell buildings, which are now in progress of erection agreeably to the accompanying plan, were designed by Mr. John Haviland, the able architect of the Eastern Penitentiary. It will be seen that the entrance building is retained in its original position, but an addition is made in the rear, comprising a semi-circular observatory, with a kitchen, bakehouse, and other necessary offices, on each side. From the new observatory, as a central station, three long buildings radiate towards the rear, dividing the ground into equal spaces. The radiating buildings contain the prisoners' cells, ranged on each side of a corridor or passage, twelve feet wide, which runs down the centre of each building. These corridors, with the entrances to the cells, are under complete inspection from the central observatory. Each cell is fourteen feet long, and eight feet wide, fitted up with a privy, water-cistern, sky-light, &c. as at the Eastern Penitentiary. The cells being intended for the constant solitary confinement of the convicts no yards are provided. The buildings are to be two stories high. The cells on the upper floor will be entered from a narrow gallery, suspended along the sides of the corridor, which is open to the roof. The wing building which is just completed contains 108 commodious cells, which are well ventilated and have sufficient light.

* For a description of the advantages of the radiating over the circular form of building, as exemplified in the Philadelphia and Pittsburg Penitentiaries, *vide* note in the Report page 9.

PENNSYLVANIA. light. The buildings are constructed of free-stone, and in a manner which reflects great credit on the skill and judgment of the architect. The cells on the lower story are rather longer than those above, in order to obtain space for the horizontal sky-light; but in both ranges they are considered sufficiently capacious to admit of the employment of the convicts at any ordinary mechanical employment. The buildings are roofed in with solid slabs of stone which extend across from one side wall to the other, and are secured down by strong iron bolts, in such a manner as to render it impossible to escape. This plan is considered preferable to the arched roofs of the Eastern Penitentiary, both as to durability and security.

The amount expended in the erection of the new cell-building, and other works, has been,—

For building materials - - - - - - -	$ 22,680 24
Labour, superintendance, &c. - - - - -	13,444 62
General expenses - - - - - - - -	2,225 41
Total - - -	$ 38,350 27

Several of the prisoners have been employed in the erection of the new buildings. A daily account of their labour has been kept, and credit given for the labour to the particular county from whence they came. In this way, many of the convicts have been enabled to pay the expenses of their maintenance.

It is proposed to complete the structure by erecting the side radiating wings which will contain 152 cells. The sum necessary to carry this desirable object into effect is estimated at 50,000 dollars.

On my visit to the old penitentiary, ninety prisoners were in confinement. They are never assembled for the purpose of divine worship. The state makes no provision for the performance of religious services to the prisoners. A seminary is in the neighbourhood, and several of the students are stated to visit the penitentiary occasionally, for the purpose of affording instruction. It is intended that the discipline of the new prison shall be similar to that of the Eastern Penitentiary.

NUMBER of Convicts received into the Western Penitentiary of Pennsylvania at Pittsburg, from 1826 to 1833 inclusive.

CRIMES.	Totals.	1826.	1827.	1828.	1829.	1830.	1831.	1832.	1833.
Larceny - - -	194	9	14	28	36	22	18	29	38
Horse-stealing - -	25	1	5	5	—	1	3	3	7
Concealing the birth of a child - - -	3	—	1	—	1	—	—	1	—
Murder - - -	17	—	2	1	—	3	1	1	9
Receiving stolen goods	4	—	2	—	1	—	—	1	—
Rape - - -	6	—	2	1	—	2	—	—	1
Bigamy - - -	5	—	1	—	—	2	2	—	—
Malicious mischief -	1	—	1	—	—	—	—	—	—
Passing counterfeit money - -	8	—	1	2	—	—	1	2	2
Perjury - - -	3	—	—	1	1	1	—	—	—
Forging and counterfeiting coin - -	4	—	—	2	—	1	1	—	—
Manslaughter - -	8	—	—	1	1	1	3	—	2
Burglary - - -	12	—	—	1	—	2	5	3	1
Assault, with intent to kill	7	—	—	1	2	—	2	1	1
Subornation of Perjury	1	—	—	—	1	—	—	—	—
Assault, with intent to rape - - -	7	—	—	—	—	3	3	—	1
Embezzling and stealing from U. S. Mail	3	—	—	—	—	1	—	—	2
Horse-stealing - -	3	—	—	—	—	1	1	—	1
Arson - - -	3	—	—	—	—	—	2	1	—
Kidnapping - -	1	—	—	—	—	—	1	—	—
Forgery - - -	1	—	—	—	—	—	1	—	—
Robbery - - -	1	—	—	—	—	—	1	—	—
Buggery - - -	1	—	—	—	—	—	—	1	—
Conspiracy - -	3	—	—	—	—	—	—	3	—
Fraud - - -	2	—	—	—	—	—	—	1	1
Accessory to Rape -	1	—	—	—	—	—	—	—	1
Totals -	324	10	29	43	43	40	45	47	67
Of the above there were									
Pardoned - - -	60	3	5	8	7	7	7	9	14
Reconvicted - -	20	1	2	—	2	1	2	5	7
Coloured persons -	52	1	5	5	11	9	5	7	9
Females - - -	20	1	2	2	4	3	3	1	4
Natives of England -	8	—	—	1	—	1	1	1	4
,, Scotland -	1	—	—	—	1	—	—	—	—
,, Ireland -	48	—	5	9	5	7	6	3	13

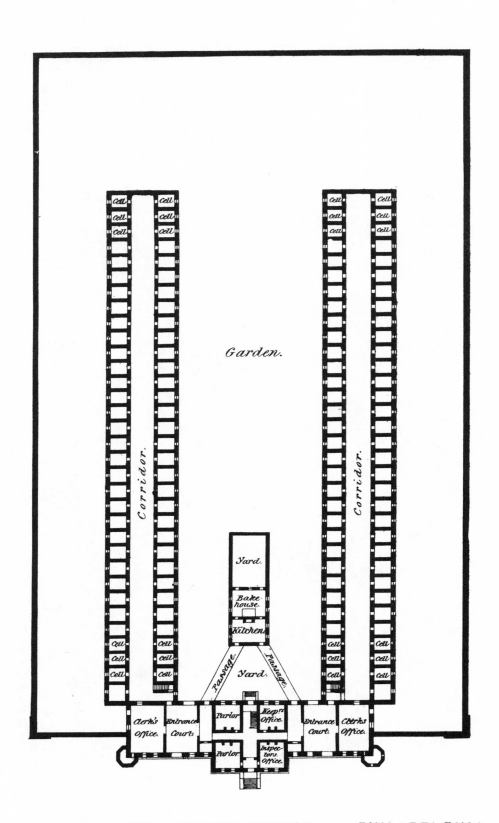

PLAN OF THE NEW COUNTY PRISON FOR PHILADELPHIA.

Scale 0 10 20 30 40 50 60 70 80 90 100   150   200   300 Feet

NEW COUNTY PRISON, PHILADELPHIA.   PENNSYLVANIA.

IN consequence of the many evils arising from the defective construction of the old gaols in Walnut-street and Arch-street, a new county prison has been erected in the city of Philadelphia, on the plan of solitary confinement. It is intended that this prison should receive all persons now committed to the Walnut-street prison for less than one year; and also those usually confined in Arch-street prison before trial, or as witnesses, &c. An Act for this purpose was passed on 30th March 1831, by which three commissioners were appointed to carry the measure into effect. The new prison for the city and county of Philadelphia is to be governed according to such regulations as may be framed by the inspectors, such rules being approved by the courts of common pleas and quarter sessions of the county, and the mayor's court of the city. Convicted prisoners, sentenced for short periods under one year are to be confined separately at hard labour; and are to be fed, clothed and treated as nearly as may be practicable in the same manner as is provided by law in relation to persons confined in the Eastern State Penitentiary.

The demolition of the old gaols is to take place as soon as the new prison is completed. The corner stone was laid on the 2d of April 1832, and the buildings have since rapidly proceeded. The situation appears to be remarkably healthy. The plot of ground is a parallelogram, 310 feet in front, and 525 feet in depth, inclosed by a substantial boundary wall. The buildings are composed of a very durable stone, well adapted to the construction of a prison. The style of architecture is that of the castellated gothic, and has been extremely well designed by Mr. Thomas Walter, of Philadelphia. The façade or entrance front is bold and impressive. It comprises a central building, 52 feet in length, which recedes 50 feet from the line of the street or road. This building is three stories high above the basement: the upper angles are surmounted by circular towers supported on large corbels, and crowned with a projecting parapet, which is also continued along the front between the towers, at the height of 50 feet. The wings on each side of the central building recede 10 feet, and are each 50 feet in length, surmounted by a parapet pierced with embrasures. In each wing there is a spacious entrance or gateway, 17 feet high and 10 feet wide. The gates are of oak, and the upper part secured by a massive portcullis of wrought iron. The wings are ornamented with a tier of slip windows in the upper story: those below are narrow, with pointed arches. Each extremity of the wings is finished with a massive octagonal tower. Beyond these towers the boundary wall recedes 15 feet. The extreme angles are terminated with bastions, 20 feet high, 15 feet wide at the bottom and 13 feet at top.

The central building is intended for the residence of the keeper and his family, and also for offices for the use of the inspectors. In the rear of the keeper's house is a court-yard about 40 feet deep. Beyond, in a detached building, is the kitchen and bakehouse for the service of the establishment. Each of the wings in front contains a large paved court or entrance lobby, and also a clerk's office.

The cells are built in two distinct ranges which extend at right angles from the termination of the front building towards the rear; the length of each range of cell building being about 380 feet, and the breadth 54 feet. A corridor or passage 20 feet wide runs down the centre of each building, and the cells are placed on each side with doors into the corridor, which is open the whole height of the building (three stories), and is lighted by vertical windows in the roof. The cells on the two upper stories are entered from galleries along the sides of the corridors, supported on iron brackets. The dimensions of each cell are 13 feet by nine feet, and nine feet high. Each cell has a slip window in the external wall, four and a half feet long, but only four inches wide, the thickness of the wall being bevelled each way. The glass is pressed or ground, to prevent the prisoners seeing out of the cell. The casings of the cell-doors are of cast iron. The internal doors are of wrought-iron gratings. The doors next the corridors are of wood, having a small aperture in each by which the interior of the cell may at any time be inspected without the officer being observed by the prisoner. These doors are so constructed that they may all be open at the same time without the prisoners seeing each other across the corridors. This arrangement is very convenient for the performance of divine service in the corridor within the hearing of all the prisoners in the cells. The cell-doors may all be seen at the same time from a window in the clerk's office which looks down the centre of each corridor. In each cell there is a separate flue for ventilation, also one for the admission of warm air from the furnace, and an aperture for the entrance of cold air. Each cell is furnished with a water-closet and sink, on the same principle as those at the Eastern Penitentiary.

The prison when completed is intended to contain 408 separate cells. The arrangement of the building, in two distinct wings or divisions, with separate offices, entrances, &c. has been made for the purpose of confining the untried in one wing, and those who are convicted and sentenced for short terms in the other. By these means the solitude of the prison is not at any time liable to be interrupted by the visits of counsel, or the relatives of the untried. There is a considerable space between the cell buildings and the boundary wall round the prison, but it is not intended to separate the ground in the rear with any intervening divisions; and consequently the prisoners will not be allowed to pass out of their respective cells for the purpose of taking air and exercise.

OFFENCES.	PUNISHMENTS.
Accessaries before the fact,—(*see* the various offences.)	
(In cases of felony) { After the fact, in receiving stolen goods, &c. or harbouring the felon.	- - Restoration of property; fine to the same amount; and imprisonment at hard labour not exceeding three years.
In other offences - - - -	Fine, and imprisonment at hard labour not exceeding two years.
Adultery - - - - - - - - -	Fine not exceeding 50 *l.* and imprisonment from 3 to 12 months.
Arson - - - - - Burning any house, outhouse, &c. church, barn, haystack, &c. maliciously, or being accessary thereto before the fact, first offence.	Solitary confinement at labour from 1 to 10 years.
Second offence - - - -	- - The same, not exceeding 15 years.
Bastardy - - Concealing death of bastard child, first offence.	- - Imprisonment in county gaol or solitary confinement at labour, not exceeding 5 years, or fine and imprisonment.
Second offence - - - -	Imprisonment for life.
Bigamy - - - Including second husband or wife, if aware of the fact.	Fine, and imprisonment at hard labour not exceeding 2 years.
Blasphemy - - - - - - - -	Fine of 10 *l.* or 3 months' hard labour.
Bribery at an election - - - - - - -	Fine, not exceeding $50, and impriment not exceeding six months.
Burglary, &c. - - - - Breaking, &c. dwelling-house by night to commit a felony, or accessary before the fact, first offence.	Solitary confinement at labour, from 2 to 10 years.
Second offence - - - -	- - The same, not exceeding 15 years.
Breaking state-house, or public building, by night, with like intent.	Fine and solitary confinement at labour not exceeding 7 years.
Coining - - - See *Forgery*.	
Compounding felony where goods have been stolen - -	A fine of twice the sum agreed for.
Duelling - - - - Fighting a duel, sending or accepting a challenge, posting for not fighting, or printing bills for posting, and refusing to give up authors.	- - Fine of $ 500, imprisonment one year at hard labour, and deprived of rights of citizenship for seven years.
Bearing challenge, or consenting to be second.	- - Fine of $ 500, imprisonment one year at hard labour, and disqualified for holding office.
Having knowledge of a duel, or being present at one.	Fine of $ 50, and imprisonment for nine months.
Forgery - - - - - In general, including coining, altering, embezzling or defacing deeds, &c.; uttering, having forged notes, &c. in possession, making or possessing paper for notes,—first offence.	Solitary confinement at labour, from one to seven years.
Second offence - - - -	Imprisonment not exceeding ten years.
Fornication - - - - - - - - -	Fine and imprisonment at hard labour, not exceeding seven years.
Gaming - - - Keeping certain tables, &c. - -	Fine not exceeding $100, and imprisonment in county gaol, not exceeding one year.
Fighting cocks, or betting on them -	Fine of $ 40, or in default, imprisonment not exceeding 30 days.
Horse-stealing, or accessary before the fact,—first offence -	Solitary confinement at labour, from 1 to 4 years.
Second offence - - - -	- - The same not exceeding 7 years.
Incest - - - - - - - - - -	The same as adultery or fornication (as the case may be).
Kidnapping - - First offence - - - - -	Solitary confinement at labour, from 5 to 12 years.
Second offence - - - -	- - The same for 21 years.
Larceny - - Stealing to the value of 20 *s.* or upwards.	- - Restoration of the goods stolen or their value, fine to the same amount, and hard labour not exceeding 3 years.
Stealing under the value of 20 *s.* -	- - Restoration of the goods stolen or their value, fine to the same amount, and imprisonment at hard labour not exceeding one year.
Receiving stolen goods when principal is not convicted.	- - A misdemeanor; punishment the same as if principal was convicted. (*See* Accessaries after the fact.)

OFFENCES.		PUNISHMENTS.
Maiming - -	Aiding, abetting or counselling thereto,—first offence.	Solitary confinement at labour, from 1 to 7 years.
	Second offence - - - -	- - the same, not exceeding 14 years.
Malicious mischief -	To knockers, sign-boards, &c. - -	Fine and imprisonment, not exceeding 7 years.
Manslaughter - -	First offence - - - - -	Solitary confinement at labour, from 2 to 6 years.
	Second offence - - - -	- - the same from 6 to 12 years.
	Involuntary (committed in some unlawful act, not making it murder.)	A misdemeanor.
Murder* - -	- - First degree,—by poison, lying in wait, or deliberate killing, or in an attempt at arson, rape, robbery or burglary.	Death.
	Second degree, any other kind of murder,)—first offence	Solitary confinement at labour, from 4 to 12 years.
	Second offence - -	- - the same for life.
Perjury, or subornation thereof, first offence - - -		- - Solitary confinement at labour, from 1 to 5 years, and disqualified as a witness.
	Second offence - - - -	- - the same, not exceeding 8 years.
Rape, or accessary before the fact,—first offence - -		Solitary confinement at labour from 2 to 12 years.
	Second offence - - - -	- - the same for life.
Receiving stolen goods. (See Larceny and Accessaries.)		
Robbery, or accessary before the fact,—first offence - -		Solitary confinement at labour, from 1 to 7 years.
	Second offence - - - -	- - the same, not exceeding 12 years.
Sodomy - -	First offence - - - -	Solitary confinement at labour, from 1 to 5 years.
	Second offence - - - -	- - the same, not exceeding 10 years.
Treason - - -	High,—first offence - - -	Solitary confinement at labour from 3 to 6 years.
	Second offence - - - -	Solitary confinement at labour, not exceeding 10 years.
	Petit treason - - - -	As in other kinds of murder.

N. B.—The court determines the precise degree of punishment within the prescribed limits.

* The degree of murder is to be found by the jury. If the prisoner confesses, the court determines it upon the examination of witnesses.

AN ACT TO ABOLISH PUBLIC EXECUTIONS.

Section I.—BE it Enacted by the Senate and House of Representatives of the Common-wealth of Pennsylvania, in General Assembly met, and it is hereby Enacted, by the authority of the same, That whenever hereafter any person shall be condemned to suffer death by hanging for any crime of which he or she shall have been convicted, the said punishment shall be inflicted on him or her within the walls or yard of the gaol of the county in which he or she shall have been convicted; and it shall be the duty of the sheriff or coroner of the said county to attend and be present at such execution, to which he shall invite the presence of a physician, attorney-general or deputy attorney-general of the county, and twelve respectable citizens, who shall be selected by the sheriff; and the said sheriff shall, at the request of the criminal, permit such ministers of the Gospel, not exceeding two, as he or she may name, and any of his or her immediate relatives, to attend and be present at such execution, together with such officers of the prison, and such of the sheriff's deputies as the said sheriff or coroner in his discretion may think it expedient to have present; and it shall only be permitted to the persons above designated to witness the said execution; provided, That no person under age shall be permitted on any account to witness the same.

Section II.—After the execution, the said sheriff or coroner shall make oath or affirmation, in writing, that he proceeded to execute the said criminal within the walls or yard aforesaid, at the time designated by the death-warrant of the Governor, and the same shall be filed in the office of the clerk of the Court of Oyer and Terminer of the aforesaid county, and a copy thereof published in two or more newspapers, one at least of which shall be printed in the county where the execution took place.

> *William Patterson*, Speaker of the House of Representatives.
> *Jacob Kern*, Speaker of the Senate.

Approved. The tenth day of April, One thousand
eight hundred and thirty-four.   *George Wolf.*

PENNSYLVANIA.

NUMBER of CONVICTS committed to the PENNSYLVANIA STATE PRISON (Walnut Street), from its commencement to 1833.

CRIMES	1832	1831	1830	1829	1828	1827	1826	1825	1824	1823	1822	1821	1820	1819	1818	1817	1816	1815	1814	1813	1812	1811	1810	1809	1808	1807	1806	1805	1804	1803	1802	1801	1800	1799	1798	1797	1796	1795	1794	1793	1792	1791	1790	1789	1788	1787
Murder, 1st degree				1		1				1	1	1	1	1	1		1	4			1	1	1		2		1	1	1	1				1		1					2		3	6		3
Ditto, 2d degree				1	1	2	1	3	1	4	3	6	4	5				1	3	4	4	1			1	2	4	1	2	5	2	2		2			5		2							
Manslaughter				1	6		8	1	2	2	2	3	4	2	3	2	3		5	1		4	4		1	2	4	1	4		1	1		1	1	1	1				3					
Burglary				7	1	17	2	14	16	19	11	17	17	20	16	14	4	13	2	12	9	13	11	2	5	20	6	6	5	9	2	2	6	2	5	2	1	4	2	3	7	4	5	22	10	13
Rape					13		8	5		1	2	1	2	1		1	1	2	2					1	2		1	1	1		1	1	1	1	1	1	1	1					5			
Sodomy								1		1	1	1	1				2	1				1	1		1													1								
Arson					3	6	1	6	3	7		1		2	3	7		3	3		3	1		2		1			6	1	1	1			1			1								
Forgery and Counterfeiting	4	5	2	5	7	7	16	22	22	20	23	6	6	6	12	17	22	8	11	8	3	7	10	8	10	6	5	3	6	7	4	1	5	6	6	9	3	10	5	2	4	5	1	1	1	4
Larceny	97	112	220	212	231	239	232	263	216	251	255	238	181	272	234	235	290	266	168	177	170	200	159	147	137	96	144	84	93	82	79	123	81	115	90	81	105	72	71	21	38	58	86	85	68	72
Robbery				4		4	4	2	5	1	4	2	7	5	3	2	2	2	6	1	2	4	3		5	2	1	2			1	1	3				1	4		2	4	2	5	6	3	3
Horse-stealing				3	5	3	5	7	4	15	7	10	7	12	10	7	10	7	1		5	3	4	7		5	5	3	3	3	12	7	5	3	12	15	16	8	7		4	3	2	2	3	
Receiving Stolen Goods							1	1														1				5										3				9						7
Misdemeanour	2	2	8	1	3	1	1	3	3	5	5	3	2	2	5	3	3	6	2		1	2	2	1	3	3	2	2	5			10	2	3			1	4	4	2	2	3	3	4	3	3
Cheating, &c.					10	3				1			3	7	4	5	8	4		1	8	1	1	5	1		1	4	3	2			1	2	1		2	3	3	2			2		8	
Bigamy					1		1						1			1	1			6				1		1		1	1	1		1		1			1	1					1	1		
Assault to Kill	1	2	4	1	2	1	4	2	1	1	2	1		3		1	1						1		11	3	1		3		1		1		1	1	1	1	1	2				3		
Ditto - Rape	1		2				1		1		2			3											3																					
Ditto - Sodomy																																														
Assault and Battery	49	46		1	1	3	1	5	4	4	1	3	2		2	19	50	38	9	26	28	44	24	23	6		5	5		1	1	1	1	3	2			5								3
Disorderly House	1	2			2		2	8		1	4	2	1		5	11	15	17	1	7	28	12	6	8		1	1	2	3	2			2	1	2							1	3	1		
Murder, and Concealing Birth of Child																																				1						1		2	1	
Conspiracy			2	1	1	1		3	2		3	1	3	1	1	5	9	1	3	2	1	4	1		5	1	2	7		1	2			2			2	2	2							
Riot	2	1					1		2	1		5	7			12	2	5	1	4	6	5			1	2		1	1	2					1	1	2									
Perjury		5		1						1	1	1	4		2	1	1		2																											
Adultery							1	2	1	1	3	3	1	6	1	7	8	1	3	2														4												
Other Offences									1								1	2	1	1		1																								
Gaming		46		9				10	1		1	1											8																							
Tippling House																																														
Escape	1	1																																												
Incestuous Marriage																																														
Refractory Apprentice	2	1	1	1																																										
Total	160	224	238	249	285	293	295	358	287	333	329	303	245	353	301	347	433	378	222	252	391	304	236	206	194	149	182	124	140	120	107	151	106	144	122	114	145	116	92	45	65	78	112	141	98	108

NUMBER of COMMITMENTS to the CITY and COUNTY GAOL of PHILADELPHIA for Seven Years, PENNSYLVANIA. distinguishing Offences, Sexes, &c.

CRIMES.	1826.	1827.	1828.	1829.	1830.	1831.	1832.
Felonies and other Offences, punished by fine and imprisonment at hard labour	719	827	775	642	791	816	697
Misdemeanours and other Offences, punished by fine and imprisonment	652	881	991	699	1,102	1,187	1,135
Charged with being idle, disorderly, and disturbers of the peace	948	868	780	730	608	752	954
Convicted as Vagrants; for intoxication, and for profane swearing	1,145	1,369	1,527	946	1,431	1,751	1,729
TOTAL	3,464	3,945	4,073	3,017	3,932	4,506	4,515
Males - - White	1,646	1,995	2,037	1,490	1,872	2,218	2,287
do. - - Black	561	687	690	510	758	850	820
Females - - White	688	704	760	516	618	686	669
do. - - Black	569	559	586	501	684	752	739

NUMBER of PERSONS CONVICTED annually in the CITY and COUNTY of PHILADELPHIA, from 1791 to 1832.

1791 - - -	338	1815 - - -	2,490
1792 - - -	410	1816 - - -	2,675
1793 - - -	438	1817 - - -	1,897
1794 - - -	570	1818 - - -	2,350
1795 - - -	623	1819 - - -	2,396
1796 - - -	651	1820 - - -	2,285
1797 - - -	749	1821 - - -	2,673
1798 - - -	692	1822 - - -	2,805
1799 - - -	763	1823 - - -	2,401
1800 - - -	1,072	1824 - - -	2,036
1801 - - -	1,045	1825 - - -	2,359
1802 - - -	936	1826 - - -	3,464
1803 - - -	1,224	1827 - - -	3,945
1804 - - -	1,318	1828 - - -	4,073
1805 - - -	1,137	1829 - - -	3,017
1806 - - -	1,768	1830 - - -	3,932
1807 - - -	1,807	1831 - - -	4,506
1808 - - -	1,637	1832 - - -	4,515
1809 - - -	1,293		
1810 - - -	1,461		
1811 - - -	1,472		
1812 - - -	1,432		
1813 - - -	1,441	TOTAL -	79,945
1814 - - -	1,849		

NUMBER of PARDONS annually granted in the CITY and COUNTY of PHILADELPHIA, from 1787 to 1832.

1787 - - -	20	1811 - - -	59
1788 - - -	13	1812 - - -	51
1789 - - -	22	1813 - - -	39
1790 - - -	27	1814 - - -	54
1791 - - -	59	1815 - - -	62
1792 - - -	51	1816 - - -	103
1793 - - -	25	1817 - - -	103
1794 - - -	22	1818 - - -	111
1795 - - -	62	1819 - - -	134
1796 - - -	48	1820 - - -	54
1797 - - -	72	1821 - - -	43
1798 - - -	37	1822 - - -	79
1799 - - -	80	1823 - - -	75
1800 - - -	117	1824 - - -	55
1801 - - -	68	1825 - - -	22
1802 - - -	46	1826 - - -	70
1803 - - -	72	1827 - - -	59
1804 - - -	26	1828 - - -	60
1805 - - -	43	1829 - - -	69
1806 - - -	42	1830 - - -	26
1807 - - -	35	1831 - - -	22
1808 - - -	46	1832 - - -	21
1809 - - -	59		
1810 - - -	25	TOTAL -	2,488

PENNSYLVANIA.   NUMBER of PERSONS EXECUTED within the STATE of PENNSYLVANIA, for various Offences, from 1778 to 1833.

No.	COUNTIES.	Date of Warrant.	OFFENCE.	No.	COUNTIES.	Date of Warrant.	OFFENCE.
1	York	1778	Burglary.	49	Bucks	1785	Murder.
2	Bedford	1778	Murder.	50	Franklin	1786	Murder.
3	Philadelphia	1778	Robbery.	51	Franklin	1786	Murder.
4	Philadelphia	1778	Treason.	52	Montgomery	1788	Burglary.
5	Philadelphia	1778	Treason.	53	Philadelphia	1788	Outlawry.
6	Berks	1778	Burglary.	54	Philadelphia	1788	Outlawry.
7	Philadelphia	1778	Burglary.	55	Franklin	1788	Uttering forged coin.
8	Chester	1778	Robbery.				
9	Philadelphia	1778	Not stated.	56	Franklin	1788	Rape.
10	Philadelphia	1778	Not stated.	57	Philadelphia	1789	Robbery.
11	Northampton	1778	Murder.	58	Philadelphia	1789	Murder.
12	Northampton	1779	Murder.	59	Northumberland	1792	Rape.
13	Northampton	1779	Murder.	60	Alleghany	1792	Murder.
14	Philadelphia	1779	Treason.	61	Fayette	1795	Murder.
15	Lancaster	1779	Robbery.	62	Bedford	1795	Murder.
16	Lancaster	1779	Murder.	63	Philadelphia	1797	Murder.
17	Not stated	1779	Robbery.	64	Bucks	1798	Murder.
18	Not stated	1779	Uttering counterfeit money.	65	Dauphin	1798	Murder.
				66	Dauphin	1798	Murder.
19	Not stated	1779	Passing counterfeit money.	67	Cumberland	1799	Murder.
				68	Chester	1806	Murder.
20	Not stated	1779	Murder.	69	Dauphin	1806	Murder.
21	Cumberland	1779	Murder.	70	Dauphin	1806	Murder.
22	Not stated	1779	Counterfeiting.	71	Wayne	1809	Murder.
23	Not stated	1779	Robbery.	72	York	1809	Murder.
24	Lancaster	1779	Burglary.	73	York	1809	Murder.
25	Chester	1780	Burglary.	74	Berks	1809	Murder.
26	Not stated	1780	Burglary.	75	Berks	1812	Murder.
27	Not stated	1780	Burglary.	76	Philadelphia	1816	Murder.
28	Not stated	1780	Burglary.	77	Crawford	1817	Murder.
29	Not stated	1780	High treason.	78	Wayne	1817	Murder
30	Philadelphia	1780	High treason.	79	Adams	1817	Murder.
31	Northampton	1780	High treason.	80	Alleghany	1818	Murder.
32	Not stated	1781	Burglary.	81	Delaware	1818	Murder.
33	Not stated	1781	Arson.	82	Dauphin	1818	Murder.
34	Philadelphia	1781	Burglary.	83	Centre	1818	Murder.
35	Philadelphia	1781	Burglary.	84	Lancaster	1822	Murder.
36	Philadelphia	1781	Robbery.	85	Crawford	1822	Murder.
37	Philadelphia	1781	Robbery.	86	Philadelphia	1823	Murder.
38	Philadelphia	1781	Robbery.	87	Washington	1823	Murder.
39	Lancaster	1781	Rape.	88	Dauphin	1824	Murder.
40	York	1783	Murder.	89	Delaware	1824	Murder.
41	York	1783	Murder.	90	Susquehanna	1824	Murder.
42	Philadelphia	1783	Highway Robbery.	91	Lebanon	1826	Murder.
				92	Wayne	1828	Murder.
43	Philadelphia	1783	Burglary.	93	Washington	1828	Murder.
44	Philadelphia	1783	Burglary.	94	Westmoreland	1830	Murder.
45	Not stated	1783	Not stated.	95	Chester	1830	Murder.
46	Not stated	1783	Not stated.	96	Lancaster	1832	Murder.
47	Not stated	1784	Not stated.	97	Bucks	1832	Murder.
48	Not stated	1784	Robbery.	98	Northampton	1833	Murder.

N. B.—In this official statement five are omitted who were executed in Philadelphia, in October 1789, for breaking gaol, robbery and murder; also two in March 1808, for murder in first degree.

There were also executed in May 1800, in Philadelphia, three persons, convicted before the United States' Circuit Court, of piracy and murder on the high seas.

Also, one convicted by the Circuit Court of the United States, of robbing the mail and putting the life of the driver in jeopardy, and executed in July 1830, in Philadelphia.

NEW YORK.

STATE PRISON AT AUBURN.

THERE are eight " Senate-districts" in the State of New York. The convicts committed from three, including the city of New York, are sent to the Penitentiary at Sing-Sing or Mount Pleasant, while those of the other five districts are confined in Auburn.

The erection of this prison was commenced in 1816. It is well situated, and occupies a plot of ground forming a square, five hundred feet in length each way, inclosed with a boundary wall two thousand feet in extent, thirty feet high, and four feet thick at the base. A small river or creek runs along the south side of the boundary, and sufficient power from this stream is obtained by means of a water-wheel and shaft through the wall to work machinery within the prison. On reference to the accompanying Plan it will be seen that the buildings which surround and intersect the spacious yard in the rear present the appearance of a large manufactory, and for this purpose its position and arrangements are well designed. As a penitentiary the form of construction is defective, inasmuch as there are no means of general inspection from any central point.*

The prison-buildings stand back about eighty feet from the road and form three sides of a square, the front part being about two hundred and eighty feet long. Each of the return wings is two hundred and forty feet long, and forty-five feet in depth. The keeper's house in the centre projects twenty-five feet. A middle passage runs through the keeper's residence, on each side of which are the offices; and in the rear is a large hall or guard room where the assistant keepers assemble, and in which are the entrances to the wing buildings. The keeper's house is four stories high : the basement contains the washing-room and cooking apartments. The front as well as the south wing was built with passages on one side and large rooms on the other : part of these remain, and are now used for the kitchen and female department. About half the south wing is appropriated to the dining-hall and chapel, the partition walls having been taken away and the floors above supported by pillars. The remainder of the south wing is now occupied by a range of sleeping cells recently erected. The opposite wing on the north side comprises a spacious building the interior of which is entirely occupied by a double range of sleeping cells. This part of the prison was erected in 1820, but in consequence of its having been in a great measure destroyed by fire (the floors being at first constructed of wood) the building was not completed until 1825. It is five stories high, being forty-two feet from the lower floor to the ceiling. The cells are placed back to back in the centre of the building, having a passage on each side nine feet wide, which is open from the bottom to the roof. Each cell is seven and a half feet long, three feet eight inches wide, and seven feet high. The floors are of oak plank on brick arches. The external walls are of stone, two and a half feet thick. The middle wall between the two ranges of cells is two feet thick : the partition walls between the cells are one foot thick. The whole of the building is roofed over, and the area or passage is arched at top with brick-work to prevent escapes. This area is lighted by large iron grated windows placed in the outer walls, from which sufficient light is admitted to enable the convicts to read. The doors of the cells are of oak plank, bound together with iron ; the upper part consists of iron grating, to admit light and air, there being no window in the cells. Above the ground the cells are entered by means of a gallery, three feet wide at the level of each floor, along the front. Each cell is ventilated by a pipe two and a half inches in diameter which runs into a flue four inches square, formed in the middle of the wall between the two ranges of cells. These flues terminate at the summit of the roof. Thus a constant current of air is created from the long passages below, which passing through the cells carries off the effluvia. Large ventilators are fixed in the ceiling or roof of the area round the cells, which can be opened or shut at pleasure. The ventilation is, however, defective, and the air-pipes afford the means of communication from one cell to another. Owing to the great number of cells, their position, and small dimensions, they do not require any extraordinary degree of heat in winter. The atmosphere is seldom below 60. The method of warming is simply by stoves placed at the bottom of the area, the flues or pipes from which extend along the passages. The number of separate cells in the north wing and the adjoining part of the building in front is five hundred and fifty. Part of the upper story of this wing is appropriated to the hospital which is not divided into separate apartments.

The new cells at the end of the south wing, containing five stories, were erected in 1832, prior to which this part of the prison was divided into large sleeping rooms. By taking down the side wall of this building additional space has been obtained for an area round the cells. This passage is made thirteen feet wide, thus affording better means of ventilation than on the other side of the prison. There are forty-four cells on each story, making the number in this building two hundred and twenty. The whole number in the prison is seven hundred and seventy. The new cells are paved with limestone, and no wood work is used except in the platform of the galleries. The doors are of iron, grated from top to bottom. They are placed at
the

---

* This remark will in fact apply to all the Penitentiaries in the United States which are not designed on the radiating plan.

the inner edge of the wall next the cell, and removed nearly two feet back, thereby affording room for the keeper or chaplain to stand in the recess, and speak to the convict without being seen or heard by the other prisoners. The doors are also placed at such distances as to render any conversation on the part of the prisoners impossible without being overheard by a watchman in the gallery. Another great advantage in the arrangement is that the locks are placed in front of the pier between each cell. The doors are secured by a latch bar which passes across the thickness of the pier, and is connected with the lock outside which the convict cannot reach. The locks were made in the prison. Large ventilators are placed in the vaulted ceiling over the area, but there is no ventilator in the cells except an aperture in the front wall next the passage.

On each side of the entrance-court is a garden. The guard-house, engine-house, &c. are also in the front yard through which there is an entrance for waggons, &c. The extensive workshops and store-rooms in the rear of the prison are placed round three sides of the boundary wall, and there are also several shops branching off from the others at right angles. The entire length of the range of workshops is nearly two thousand feet. The shops are built of brick, with party walls between each extending above the roofs. In the workshops which surround the yard, a narrow passage (two feet six inches wide) is formed next the wall. This passage serves as a secret way (small apertures being cut in the partition at short distances from each other,) by which the keeper, inspectors and visitors, can view the interior of the shops, without exciting attention or disturbing the business of the establishment. This arrangement, which was introduced in 1828, is valuable, and is in fact the only method by which the keeper or inspectors can secretly detect any act of irregularity. There are two large reservoirs of water in the yard, in front of the workshops. One of them is eighteen feet in diameter, and the other forty-three by sixteen feet. Here the convicts bathe in summer. The erection and enlargement of the prison has cost above three hundred thousand dollars exclusive of the labour of the convicts.

When a prisoner is first received he is shaved, his hair is cut close, and his person well cleansed. He is then clothed in a striped dress. A description of his person, crime, &c. is registered in a book, and he is apprised of the prison regulations. He is then placed at a trade in which he is likely to render himself most useful.

The hours of labour vary according to the season of the year. In summer, work commences at half-past five in the morning and closes at six in the evening. In winter, the hours are so fixed as to obtain the benefit of day light. The prisoners are summoned from their beds at the ringing of a bell by the watchmen on night duty. The officers and guard being assembled, at the end of fifteen minutes from the ringing of the first bell, the assistant keepers proceed to their respective galleries to unlock the cells. Each man brings out with him his night-tub, water-can, and provision-kid. The latter are deposited in the washing-room through which the prisoners pass in their way to the yard, where they empty their night-tubs in the vault, wash them at the pump, and place them in rows. They then enter the workshops and commence labour. Before breakfast they wash at a place prepared for the purpose in the shops. Breakfast takes place at seven or eight o'clock, according to the season, on the ringing of a large bell which is hung in the centre of the interior yard. The convicts form in a line and are marched from the shops across the yard, attended by their respective assistant keepers. On entering the mess-room they face round to their plates and stand in their places until all are assembled, when a signal being given, they instantly sit down to their meals. The places of the convicts at table are so arranged that if any one is absent from accident or design, he is instantly missed. The tables are narrow and the prisoners sit on one side only, and are never placed face to face, in order to avoid the exchange of looks. If a prisoner requires more food than that allotted to him he raises his left hand, and is immediately supplied by waiters. If one man has more food than he can eat he raises his right hand, and the remainder of his allowance is removed to another who may require it. No one is permitted to exchange food with another. As soon as the meal is finished the steward rings a bell, when the prisoners instantly rise and march back to their workshops. This meal occupies from 20 to 30 minutes. The dinner-hour is at 12, when the same time is allowed and similar regulations are observed as at breakfast. A short prayer is repeated by the chaplain previous to the convicts sitting down. In the evening, before quitting labour in the shops the fires are extinguished. The convicts wash and form in line according to the numbers of the cells. After taking up their night-tubs they march to a room adjoining the kitchen where their suppers have been placed for them. The convicts, without losing their step or disturbing the order of their march, proceed to their respective galleries, entering the cells according to their numbers, and partly closing the doors. The assistant keepers then commence locking the cells, and as they enter the key the convict is required to shut the door to prove that he is in his cell. Each gallery is locked by one assistant keeper with two keys differing from each other and from all the rest. The locks are tried a second time after the prisoners lie down. The keys are then deposited in the keeper's hall or guard-room. Immediately after the locking-up, one of the guards inspects the workshops to ascertain that the fires are extinguished: he also goes round the yards to see that all is safe. These precautions are repeated every hour throughout the night. The station for the night-guard is in the hall, within a short distance of the doors leading into the wing-buildings which contain the dormitories. Two assistant keepers and two guards watch alternately. They are required on pain of removal, to report any circumstances that may occur every half hour. As an additional security, the keeper and deputy keeper frequently go round the prison in silence, at different

hours

hours. The assistant-keeper and guard on duty are required to be constantly moving round the galleries, &c. They wear mocassins and consequently move so silently that a prisoner knows not but that the officer may be at the cell door. The space in front of the cells acts as a sounding gallery, and a watchman in the open area below can hear any noise from a distant cell in the upper story although he may be unable to detect the offender. The area round the cells and the guard-room are lighted by lamps.

On Sunday morning the officers and guard are assembled as usual, and the prison is opened at the same hour as on other days. The convicts after emptying their night-buckets march back to the cells, and the doors are latched. One convict is let out from each gallery to distribute clean shirts through the door-grates accompanied by an assistant-keeper. Such of the prisoners as can read are supplied with bibles. The prisoners are marched from their cells to the mess-room to breakfast and back again, where they remain until the time of divine service which takes place at 10 o'clock. Such prisoners, however, as are selected to attend a Sunday school continue at the breakfast table until the other prisoners are marched to their cells, when they are immediately conducted to the chapel. The school which is held but for a short time in the morning consists of about one-fourth of the convicts. It is attended by several young gentlemen, students of a theological semi-nary at Auburn. They are strictly prohibited from holding any conversation with the prisoners except in relation to their studies.* At ten o'clock the officers again assemble, when the convicts are unlocked and marched in silence to the chapel. The prisoners sit facing the minister. Small platforms are erected at the sides and ends of the chapel where the officers sit, and have a perfect view of every prisoner. Divine service is performed according to the Presbyterian form of worship, with the exception of singing. After service, the men are marched back to their cells, and take with them their rations of meat, bread, and vegetables, for the remainder of the day. There is no evening service, but in the afternoon the chaplain visits the prisoners from cell to cell, seeing generally about forty prisoners. This is the only day on which he has this privilege; and as there are 680 prisoners in confinement, the chaplain cannot therefore give a private interview to every prisoner under a period of three months.

In the workshops the convicts are arranged in such a way as not to face each other, and to labour separately as much as possible. In each shop prisoners are selected as attendants, whose business it is to distribute the materials, hand out and grind the tools, and clean the shops, under the direction of the assistant-keeper. All this, however, is done principally by signs, so that the attention of the other convicts is not distracted. Privies are placed in the corners of the shops. Each workshop has a supply of water to which a prisoner can help himself at pleasure. In every mechanical or trade department there is at least one assistant-keeper who attends to the instruction of learners. The assistant-keeper directs the appropriation of all raw materials, keeps a daily account of the work performed by each convict, and regulates his daily task. He also superintends the removal of his men to and from their cells. A prisoner who wilfully or negligently injures his work, tools, wearing apparel, or bedding, is immediately flogged by the assistant-keeper. The prisoners are not allowed to speak to each other on any pretence, except by special direction of the officers. They are not at any time to leave their places without permission. They are never to speak to any person who does not belong to the prison, and must not look off from their work at spectators. They are not to speak even to an officer, except when absolutely necessary relative to their business. For a violation of any of these rules they are immediately flogged A convict's word is never taken even against another convict, and much less against an officer.

Every convict is shaved once a week, and his hair cut short. If his clothes or shoes require change or repair, he is to report the same to the assistant-keeper who sends him at a fixed hour daily, to the clothes-room, where he is furnished by the deputy-keeper with what is requisite. Prisoners in the blacksmith's shop exchange their clothes every Saturday night. Clothing, shoes, and blankets are manufactured in the prison, from materials purchased by the agent: the cotton is purchased in the yarn. The usual dress of the convicts is a coat, vest, and trowsers, made of cotton and wool; a cap of the same materials; cotton shirt; knit woollen socks, and leather shoes. Each prisoner has two or three blankets, made of coarse woollen yarn. The annual expense of clothing and bedding for each prisoner is $5. 87 cents. The daily rations for each man are 10 ounces of pork or 16 ounces of beef, 10 ounces of wheat flour, the wheat ground fine; 12 ounces of Indian meal, and half a gill of molasses; also, for each 100 rations, two quarts of rye-coffee, four quarts of salt, four quarts of vinegar, $1\frac{1}{2}$ ounce of pepper, and $2\frac{1}{2}$ bushels of potatoes. The contract price for each prisoner's food per day is $5\frac{1}{40}$ cents.† Salt pork and salt beef are furnished every other day, and fresh beef once a week. From these provisions the prisoners are supplied in the morning with cold meat, bread, a slice of cold hominy, hot potatoes, and a pint of hot rye-coffee, sweetened with molasses. For dinner they have meat, soup made from the broth thickened with Indian meal, bread, and potatoes. All the cells are swept out daily, and once a week the floors are washed and scrubbed. One man is constantly employed in cleaning the cells, each of which is white washed about once in the month. Sixteen convicts are usually employed in the kitchen and wash-room.

---

* The Sunday School was suspended at the period of my visit, on account of the building in which it was formerly held having been taken down. A new chapel is erecting together with a dining-room, adjoining the new range of cells in the south wing.

† A cent is equivalent to an halfpenny.

The women, the number of whom is generally very small, are confined in the old apartments in the south wing. They are chiefly employed in making the clothing, and work together in the same room. At the period of my visit there were only 26 females in the prison, one of whom was sick. They have recently been placed under the care of a matron. The hours appointed for locking and unlocking their cells are the same as those for the men; and in general the women are under similar regulations, except that they are never subjected to corporal punishment. Silence and obedience are therefore not so strictly enforced as among the male convicts. As an extreme punishment some of the women have been tied down in their rooms. The females are not allowed to go into the open air for exercise at any time. The matron reads prayers daily.

The prisoners are not allowed to write nor receive any letters, or intelligence from or concerning their friends, or on any subject out of the prison. No relative, or friend, is allowed to visit or speak to a convict, except in some extraordinary case which may require a personal interview, and which can only take place in the presence of the keeper or his deputy.

When a convict is discharged he is provided with shoes and suitable clothing, and is usually allowed three dollars in money to enable him to reach his friends. Strangers are permitted to visit the prison on paying 25 cents each, but they are not allowed to pass through the workshops, (except by the secret passage,) hospital, or female department, and are forbidden to speak to any of the convicts.

The general government is vested in a Board of five inspectors who reside in Auburn. They are appointed every two years by the Governor and Senate. They have no compensation, and are forbidden by law to make any contracts for the purchase or sale of any articles with the agent of the prison. They have the power of appointing and removing the agent and keeper, deputy-keeper, and all subordinate officers. The inspectors are required frequently to visit the prison in its various departments. They are authorized to establish from time to time such regulations for its government as they may deem necessary, and according to which the officers are bound, by oath, to discharge their various functions. The inspectors are required to make an annual report to the Legislature on the condition and progress of the Institution, and to make such suggestions for its amendment as they may deem expedient.

The law directs that there shall be one agent and one principal keeper who are to be allowed each a salary of 1,250 dollars. The duties of these offices are, however, at present discharged by a single individual. The keeper is required to give security for the faithful performance of his engagements, to the amount of 25,000 dollars. It is his duty to make all purchases, agreements, and sales, and to manage the financial concerns. He is prohibited from being concerned in any dealings with the prison for his private benefit, but simply to make contracts with other persons for the labour of the convicts; the contractors furnishing the raw materials and disposing of the articles manufactured on their own account. His accounts are annually to be made up on the 30th day of September, and transmitted to the Comptroller of the State. The agent is authorized by law to take charge of the property of any convict at his request, and to repay him, or his legal representatives, on his release. If none appear, the amount is to be applied to the use of the State.

It is required of the keeper to reside in the prison, to superintend and direct the subordinate officers and guards in their various duties, and to be responsible for the entire regulation of the prison. He is obliged once a year (in February) to make a Report to the Secretary of State of the convicts pardoned and discharged in the preceding year, with a statement of their crimes, sentences, and various particulars respecting them. The deputy-keeper exercises a constant superintendance over all the affairs of the prison, excepting its pecuniary concerns. He is responsible to the keeper that his orders, as well as the general regulations, are promptly observed. For this purpose the deputy must always be present at the opening and closing of the cells, in the mess-room while the convicts are at meals, and in the chapel during divine service: he is also expected at other times to be employed in visiting the different parts of the prison, to see that the assistant-keepers are attentive to their duty. He is to report all offences and punishments to the keeper, to superintend the distribution of the clothing, and to be present at the discharge of every convict.

The assistant-keepers are twenty in number. They are required to enforce strictly the general observance of the regulations. They are not to hold any conversation with the convicts, nor even allow them to speak on any subject except on necessary business. Each assistant-keeper must keep a list of the names of the prisoners under his charge, with the respective numbers of the cells occupied by them, and the description of work at which they are employed. If an assistant-keeper punishes a convict for misconduct, he is required within a reasonable time to make a report in writing to the keeper, or his deputy, stating the prisoner's name and offence, and the nature and extent of the punishment inflicted. The assistant-keepers are to correct convicts for every breach of discipline by stripes which are to be inflicted with a raw-hide whip, and applied to the back in such a manner as not to expose the head, face, eyes, or in any way to put the convict's health or limbs in danger. In aggravated cases, a "cat," made of six lashes of small twine, may be applied to the bare back, under the direction of the keeper or deputy. The prisoner is compelled to strip immediately on the commission of an offence, and is flogged before the other prisoners. No superior officer is required to be present on these occasions.

There are ten guards, including the serjeant who commands them. They are all required to be in the guard-house during prison-hours, except those on duty. Besides the rules already mentioned, one of the guards must be constantly placed as a sentinel on the external wall of
the

the prison, to overlook the north yards, and one to overlook the yards on the opposite side. They are relieved every hour.*

The physician is required to attend at the prison every morning at 9 o'clock, and repeat his visit through the day at such times as the condition of any of the prisoners may render it necessary. When a convict becomes sick, he is taken by the assistant-keeper to the hospital, and examined by the physician who orders him to be detained in the hospital, if necessary, and directs suitable medicines to be provided. He is required to keep a register of the deaths which occur, stating the particular circumstances of every case. When a convict dies, a coroner's jury is summoned, consisting of citizens only; the body is kept twenty-four hours, and if not claimed by any relative, the law requires that it shall be delivered for dissection. In case of a prisoner being insane, he is usually placed in the hospital, or confined in a separate cell.

A clerk constantly attends in the prison-office, whose business it is to keep and make out all such accounts and statements relative to the establishment as may be directed by the agent or inspectors.

---

* The keeper has adopted a simple and ingenious method of ascertaining whether the **assistant-**keepers and guards attend to their duty properly during the night. It is by placing at a given time, in a small box inside the door leading to the cell-buildings, a ball, which is to be taken by the assistant-keeper or guard who is watching the cells, and by him deposited in another box at the end of his walk, from whence it is taken by the guard who has the care of the workshops, and by him passed on to the next until it comes back again to the keeper in the hall or guard-room. If it does not arrive in proper time, the keeper is apprised of a neglect of duty somewhere. An inquiry is made into the cause of delay, and it is immediately ascertained whether it is occasioned by accident, neglect or interruption from the convicts.

LIST of CONVICTS remaining in the STATE PRISON, AUBURN, on the 31st day of December 1832.

Convicts in prison 31st December 1831 - - - - - 646 ⎫
Convicts received during the year 1832 - - - - - 192 ⎬ 838

Discharged by expiration of sentence - - - - - - 115 ⎫
— by pardon - - - - - - - 27 ⎬ 155
— by order of the Supreme Court - - - - - 1 ⎪
Died - - - - - - - - - - - - - - 12 ⎭

Remaining in prison 31st December 1832 - - - 683

CRIMES.	OCCUPATION IN PRISON.	REMARKS.
Grand larceny - - - 268	Comb-makers, on contract - - - 29	
Petit larceny, second offence - 82	Coopers - - - ditto - - - 57	First convictions - 633
Burglary - - - 74	Tool-makers - ditto - - - 37	Second convictions 50
Forgery - - - 59	Shoe-makers - ditto - - - 41	
Counterfeiting - - 48	Cotton weavers and spoolers, on contract 86	Total - - 683
Assault and battery to kill - 29	Clock-makers - - - - ditto - 13	
Manslaughter - - 20	Machinists - - - - ditto - 27	
Assault and battery to rape - 15	Blacksmiths - - - - ditto - 8	
Breaking Jail - - 13	Cabinet and chair-makers - ditto - 40	White males - - 592
Perjury - - - 11	Saddle-tree makers - - ditto - 30	White females - - 10
Robbery - - - 9	Check-weavers and spoolers - ditto - 17	Black males - - 66
Rape - - - - 7	Tailors - - - - - ditto - 41	Black females - - 15
Swindling - - - 6	Sattinet-manufacturers - - ditto - 44	
Arson - - - - 6	Stone-cutters custom work - ditto - 38	Total - - 683
Receiving stolen goods - 6	Weavers and spoolers work - ditto - 10	
Bigamy - - - - 7		
Murder - - - - 5	*In employ of the State.*	
Grand larceny and breaking Jail 3	Blacksmiths, &c. - - - - 16	
Sodomy - - - - 3	Carpenters - - - - - 6	
Grand larceny and forgery - 2	Weavers, spoolers and spinners - - 12	
Misdemeanor - - - 2	Tailors and barbers - - - 13	
Poisoning - - - 2	Shoe-makers - - - - - 8	
Incest - - - - 1	Wood-sawyers and labourers - - 26	
Burglary and assault to kill - 1	Soap-boilers and hostler - - 4	
Mail robbery - - - 1	Attendants in the wings - - 6	
Forgery and perjury - - 1	Cooks, washers and waiters - - 28	
— breaking Jail - 1	Cooper - - - - - - 1	
— swindling - - 1	Turner - - - - - - 1	
	Hospital cook and nurse - - 2	
Total - - - 683	— sick - - - - 7	
	Individuals not employed - - - 10	
	Females - - - - - 25	
	Total - - - - 683	

	$	c.
The earnings of the Convicts for the year ending 30th September 1832, which have been charged to Contractors - - - - - - - - - - -	37,951	26
The earnings of Convicts, not employed by Contractors, as charged to individuals, and cash received from Visitors, and for Articles sold, and other incidental sources	3,882	21
The earnings and profits of the Prison for the past year - - -	41,833	47
The Expenditure during the same period, for the general support of the Prison, and which includes all expenses, except those authorized by the Act of the 25th April 1832, for building 220 cells - - - - - - - - - - -	38,305	31
Leaving a balance in favour of the Prison - - - - $	3,528	16

PLAN
of the
STATE PRISON
at
SING-SING
or
Mount Pleasant, New York.

Store-
house.

Work-
shop.

Chapel.

Kitchen
and
Hospital
above.

Range

Range

Keeper's
house.

Scale. 0 10 20 30 40 50 60 70 80 90 100

SING-SING, or MOUNT PLEASANT.

THIS State prison is on the east bank of the River Hudson, near the village of Sing-Sing, about 32 miles from the city of New York. It stands on a quarry of marble which furnishes constant employment for a proportion of the prisoners, who are engaged in raising, cutting and preparing for sale, the several qualities of the material which the quarry affords.

The erection of the prison was commenced in 1825 by a hundred convicts, brought for that purpose from the Auburn Penitentiary, each man having a shackle on one leg. They arrived on the ground on the 12th of May, built a shed to sleep in before night, and in six months completed as much of the prison as would contain 60 convicts. There is at present no complete boundary-wall to the prison, a deficiency which renders an armed guard absolutely necessary; but it has been considered (I think very erroneously) preferable to depend solely on the vigilance of keepers for safe custody, rather than to have recourse to the means of preventing escape by any architectural arrangements. The ground occupied by this prison is a square of 572 feet. At the east end of the square the cell-building occupies the whole space, and contains 1,000 separate sleeping cells, in five stories of 200 each. The cells are each seven feet long, seven feet high and three feet six inches wide. They are placed back to back, as at Auburn, and are surrounded by an area nine feet wide, open to the roof, the whole being enclosed by a wall, three feet in thickness, in which is a window opposite the door of each cell, affording sufficient light for the prisoners to read. The cells are warmed by four stoves placed in the area, and are ventilated by small flues or pipes, three inches in diameter, passing from the back of the cells up to the roof. The doors of the cells are made of iron, the upper half being composed of bars riveted across so as to form openings about two inches square, through which the prisoner and his cell may be inspected by the keepers. The cell-doors are placed on the outer edge of the wall, in order that they may be secured by a long flat iron bar, or slide, which passes over the tops of the doors, and is moved by a lever and cog-wheel fixed against the wall. By this ingenious contrivance, fifty doors are bolted at once by small hooks fixed on the bar, passing through a loop-hole in the top of a long bolt or latch, which fastens the cell-door. This plan of arranging the doors is not, in my opinion, so good as that adopted at Auburn, where they are fixed on the inner edge of the wall, thus forming a recess in which the chaplain may stand to converse privately with a prisoner, without being seen by any one, and without being at the trouble of unlocking the doors. It also removes the prisoner nearly two feet from the outside of the wall, thus increasing the distance between them so much as to prevent their speaking to each other without being heard by the keeper. The locks of the doors being fixed on the outside of the wall are securely out of reach. But there is a still more important advantage, inasmuch as the convicts at Auburn can see but a very short distance from the cell-door along the area or gallery, while those at Sing-Sing can watch the motions of the keeper at a considerable distance, and be fully aware of his approach. Prisoners are also thus brought so near to each other as to be able to converse freely in a low tone of voice. There is a staircase at each end of the building, leading to narrow galleries in front of the cells on the same level as the floors. Every cell is furnished with a wooden bedstead, and three blankets, a tin pint cup and spoon, and a small tin cup for vinegar. A Bible is placed in each cell. The cells on examination appeared to me to be deficient in ventilation: they had a close and offensive smell, probably owing to the low situation in which the building stands, and which prevents as good a circulation of air as might be obtained on a higher spot. The floor is damp in wet weather.

At the south end of the cell-building is the keeper's-house, which is so placed as not to command any view of the prison-yard or workshops. From each end of the cell-building a long range of workshops, two stories high, extends down to the River Hudson, which forms the boundary on the west side, the prison-yard being open to the river for the convenience of loading vessels with the marble prepared by the convicts. In these two ranges of shops the prisoners work at the several trades of shoemakers, tailors, weavers, hatters, blacksmiths, locksmiths and coopers. In the building on the south-side of the yard, and adjoining the cells, is the kitchen, 80 feet by 40 feet, over which is the hospital. Beyond is the chapel, also 80 feet by 40, fitted up with seats for the prisoners on the floor, and also in a gallery up stairs. The stone-cutters' shops occupy the centre of the space in the yard and form three sides of a quadrangle, extending about 500 feet in length and 36 in width.

		Prisoners.	
There were remaining in prison on the 30th September 1831	-	980	
Received during the year to 30th September 1832	-	289	
			1,269
Discharged by expiration of sentence	- - -	133	
Died - - - - - - - -	-	153	
Pardoned - - - - - -	-	28	
Transferred to Auburn Prison - - - -	-	120	
Escaped during the cholera - - - -	-	3	
			437
Remaining in prison 30th September 1832 -	- -	-	832

NEW YORK.   The prisoners were employed as follows :—

Blacksmiths and lockmakers	74
In the manufacturers' shop	74
Shoemakers	60
At railroad, blocks and stone work	156
Stone-cutters	187
In the four quarries	140
Quarrying and carting	20
On prison building	46
Barrow men and waiters	23
In kitchen and hall	29
In hospital and sick	23
TOTAL	832

Remaining in prison 30th September 1832	832	
Received from September 1832 to September 1833	219	
		1,051
Discharged during the same period by expiration of sentence	165	
Died	25	
Pardoned	50	
		240
Remaining in prison 30th September 1833		811

Who were employed as follows :—

In Locksmiths' shops	40
Blacksmiths' shop	56
Coopers' shop	162
Weavers and tailors	56
Shoemakers	99
Hatters	11
Stone shops	174
North and South quarry	76
Masons, stone-cutters and labourers at prison buildings	45
Labourers in cooper's yard and front yard	37
Cooks, bakers and washers	18
Waiters, &c. in prison-hall	15
Waiters, &c. in the hospital	2
Sick and lame in the hospital	20
TOTAL	811

The higher classes of criminals are kept at labour in the shops, and the better behaved and less dangerous convicts work in the quarries. Where one prisoner is punished at the quarries, twelve are punished in the shops. There is no regulated punishment or limited number of stripes for any specific offence, it being the governing principle of this establishment that the mind and will of the prisoner must be completely broken down, whether it be accomplished by ten or by one hundred stripes, by one or by repeated whippings, and until this end be attained, the punishment is continued. The under-keepers are not required to make any report to the warden of the daily punishments inflicted by them. From a power thus unlimited the greatest abuses must inevitably arise.

The daily course of discipline is nearly similar to that pursued at Auburn. The prisoners are aroused at sun-rise, when the chaplain reads a prayer from an elevated spot in the centre of the area on one side of the building: from this station he may, but not without considerable exertion, make himself heard by the prisoners on that side, which contains one-half of the whole number in confinement. The turnkeys proceed to open the doors of the cells, and the prisoners, at a given signal, step out into the gallery (taking with them their tubs, cans and kids), where they form into close line, and march with the lock-step along the passage to the workshops, their eyes being turned towards their keepers.

keepers. On their arrival in the yard, they deposit their cans and kids near the kitchen, and march to the river, where they empty and cleanse their tubs. The prisoners again form into line, and deposit them in the yard at a place appointed. They are then marched to their several shops, or places where their daily occupations are carried on, each shop being under the care of an officer, who, in addition to the performance of other duties, is required to teach and superintend the trades. He is also to enforce the strictest obedience to the rules of the prison, particularly that regulation which enjoins that a prisoner shall be silent, and not look off his work. The prisoners in the shops are placed with their faces in one direction. From twenty to thirty men are usually allotted to the care of one officer.

At eight o'clock in the morning, on the ringing of a bell, work is suspended. The several divisions of prisoners form themselves into close line, under their officers, and at the word of command march back to their cells, where their breakfast is placed ready for them. After breakfast they are marched back to their work until the hour of dinner, when they are again mustered by the assistant-keepers, and conducted to their cells, each man taking up his dinner as he passes the kitchen. By an ingenious contrivance, the meals of the prisoners are placed in cans on a reel or moveable frame, which on the turning of a wheel passes through the wall into the yard, so that each man takes up his can without stopping or altering his pace. Time is not only thus saved, but order and regularity are preserved. The prisoners are locked up during their meals: the time allowed for this meal is one hour, and the assistant-keepers avail themselves of that period to repair to their dinners. On their return the convicts are marched back again to their respective employments until evening, when they are again mustered. Having washed, they form into line according to the number of their cells. As they go through the yard they take up their tubs which are placed in order for the purpose, and again passing by the kitchen they receive their allowance of food for supper (consisting of mush and molasses) which they carry to their cells. The prisoners are then locked up for the night. A prayer is then offered up by the chaplain. At a given time they are directed to undress, and retire to their beds. Officers are stationed in the area to preserve silence. They wear mocassins on their feet, in order to approach the cells without the convicts being aware of their presence. It is stated that this mode of watching is so effectual, that for several years there has not been any case reported of a prisoner talking after he was locked up.

The daily allowance of food allotted to each convict is as follows: sixteen ounces of beef, or twelve ounces of pork, eight ounces of inspected rye-flour, twelve ounces of sifted Indian meal, and half a gill of molasses; and to every one hundred rations, four quarts of rye in the grain, two quarts of vinegar, two ounces of pepper, and three bushels of potatoes for ten months in the year, and for two months (from 15th June to 15th August), forty pounds of rice to every one hundred rations. The weight of the daily food furnished to each convict, when prepared, is six pounds nine ounces. Although this allowance is liberal, complaints have been made that the men do not in all cases receive it; and prisoners have been flogged for taking from each other's cans any meat or potatoes which may have been left at a previous meal. This complaint is rather confirmed by the following extract from the Report of a select committee appointed by the legislature in March 1832:— " Although the committee was assured by the agent that ample provisions were at all times supplied for the prisoners at every meal, the statements of the prisoners not only contradicted that assurance, but added, that they had sometimes had blows inflicted upon them, accompanying a refusal of their request to grant them an additional supply."

Some objections have been made to the manner in which the convicts take their meals in this prison, as no arrangement can thereby be made for the difference of appetite among so large a number, and the various degrees of labour to which they are subjected; a blacksmith, stone-cutter, or other laborious workman, requiring more sustenance than a tailor or shoemaker. It has, therefore, been suggested by the inspectors, in their last annual Report, that the men should dine all together in one large room, as at Auburn, where regulations can be observed for supplying additional food to those who require it. The officers employed in superintending and guarding this prison on the 30th September 1833, were, a warden or agent, a clerk, a deputy-keeper, twenty-one assistant-keepers, and twenty-five guards, including the serjeant of the guard. The salaries of the officers are as follows: keeper and agent, $ 1,750 per annum; deputy-keeper, $ 1,000; clerk, $ 800; physician, $ 500; chaplain, $ 450; assistant-keepers, each, $ 550; guards, each, $ 300. The employment of a greater number of the convicts in different kinds of manufacture has enabled the warden to reduce the number of guards at the quarries, which are more than a quarter of a mile from the prison. The practice of convicts working at such a distance from the prison affords facilities for communication with their friends, through the medium of discharged prisoners. These opportunities not unfrequently occur. I have been assured that by these means the convicts occasionally obtain food, tobacco, and even newspapers, these articles being concealed in or near the quarries where they work. Escapes are rare. A few of the convicts have been wounded in attempting to escape, and one was drowned. Another made several efforts with this view, and being punished with great severity and ignominy, he nearly chopped off his leg, in a state of desperation, in order, he said, to show that he was not likely to repeat the attempt. He died of the injury.

NEW YORK.

The accompanying tables show the number of convictions and crimes since the establishment of this penitentiary; but it is extremely difficult to draw any correct inference from these accounts in respect to the increase or diminution of crime. This circumstance arises from the fact that several material changes have taken place, both in the removal of convicts to Auburn, and from Auburn to Sing-Sing, when either prison has been crowded. An alteration has also been made in the extent of the districts appointed to commit to each penitentiary, as well as in the arrangements which are adopted respecting committals to the New York city prison. The free or restricted use of the pardoning power will probably be also found to have some influence in the increase or diminution of crime; the number of pardons having been in the proportion of one-fourth of the whole number. It is obvious that pardons thus frequently granted must weaken the efficacy of prison discipline. When a convict knows that he has any friends who are supposed to possess an influence with the governor, his mind dwells more on the possible chance of thus obtaining his discharge from prison than on the prosecution of his labour, or in cherishing resolutions to amend his life.

On Sunday morning, a select number of the most ignorant of the prisoners are taught to read for about two hours. Divine service is then performed in the presence of all the prisoners assembled in the chapel, after which the chaplain visits the convicts in their cells. Supposing this practice to be regularly observed, several months must occur before each prisoner can have the benefit of a private interview, and the interval between each visit would be so long as to preclude any hope of advantage to him. The reports of the chaplain from year to year evince his good opinion of the moral effects produced on many of the convicts; but on looking at the whole arrangement and discipline of the prison, I am of opinion, that it is not a place of reformation. Admitting the labours of the chaplain in his pulpit to be such as to awaken serious impressions in the minds of some few, how is he to ascertain amidst so great a number, the parties who may be thus affected, or to follow up the good impressions which may have been produced? The regulations do not admit of his conferring individually with the prisoners during the week. The hours after service on Sundays, or the short time between locking-up and going to bed at night, afford opportunities too short to accomplish much in the way of religious instruction.

The reports of the physician state that the health of the prisoners is generally good. The average number of sick is about three per cent. During the prevalence of the cholera in 1832, the number of convicts who were seriously affected by it was 376, of whom 103 died. The whole number of deaths during the same year was 153. In the preceding year, the number of deaths was 28, and one was drowned in attempting to escape. In the last year (1833) the number of deaths was 25, two of which were by suicide.

The following is a statement of the receipts and expense of the establishment for the last three years, from the period when the present keeper and agent came into office. It will be observed that the past year has in comparison with former periods been extremely favourable to the pecuniary interests of the prison. It is stated in the Annual Report of the Inspectors, that the prison has sustained itself without any aid from the Treasury.

	$	cts.
From 1st November 1830 to 30th September 1831, the total sum expended for the use and benefit of the prison was -	72,334	71
Dining the same period, the sales from the labour of the convicts produced - - - - - - -	38,538	93
Leaving a loss of - - - $.	33,795	78

	$	cts.
From 30th September 1831 to 30th September 1832, the actual expenses of the establishment were - - -	68,051	83
The amount of prisoners' earnings, and materials sold - -	38,767	70
Leaving a loss of - - - $.	29,284	13

During the year 1832 the cholera prevailed in the prison for about fifty days, and occasioned an additional expense of $.1,404. 79 cents., besides the loss of labour from several hundred convicts who were attacked by it.

	$	cts.
From 30th September 1832 to 30th September 1833, the actual expenses of the prison were - - - - -	67,262	74
Amount of prisoners' earnings, and materials sold - -	67,548	65
Leaving a profit to the establishment of - $.	285	91

The actual cost of building the prison, workshops, &c. including the expense of opening quarries, excavating foundations, &c. amounted in January 1832, to 200,105 dollars. But if the labour of the convicts had not been employed in the various works connected with the buildings, it is estimated that the prison would have cost at least 250,000 dollars. This sum is, however, 200,000 dollars less than the total cost of the Auburn Penitentiary.

On

NEW YORK.

Oɴ the moral effects produced by the discipline of the Auburn and Sing Sing penitentiaries, opinion is much divided in the United States.   Its advocates contend that the rigid enforcement of silence, and of the rule which prohibits a prisoner from looking off his work, is felt as a powerful restraint; that contamination is thereby prevented; that separate confinement at night promotes reflection, while personal association during the day deprives the imprisonment of that severity which is ascribed to solitude.   I have already stated in the Report my impressions on this subject; viz. that the prisoners do communicate to such an extent as to deprive the imprisonment of salutary dread; that habit soon reconciles them to their situation; that so long as they can avoid the infliction of the lash the penitentiary imposes little more restraint than that of a well-regulated manufactory; that the punishment of the whip brutalizes, and produces feelings of degradation, anger and revenge; that the arbitrary power invested in the assistant-keepers gives rise to ill-treatment and oppression; and that owing to the large number of prisoners placed under the charge of one chaplain, and the limited periods of instruction to which he is restricted, the moral and religious welfare of the convicts is materially neglected.   As inquiries are not made into the subsequent conduct of discharged prisoners, no judgment can be formed from this test of the efficacy of the imprisonment.   The discipline of Sing Sing is more severe than that of Auburn, inasmuch as at the former the authority of the assistant-keepers is in a great measure uncontrolled.   A committee, appointed by the Legislature in 1832 to inquire into the state of these prisons, examined at Auburn several of the convicts who had been in confinement at Sing Sing. These persons all concurred in the representation of the harsh treatment experienced at this penitentiary.   Among other grounds of complaint, was that of the violent infliction of corporal punishments, generally with the " cat," but frequently by blows on the head and various parts of the body with sticks.   Every assistant-keeper invariably carries a stick; and against the abuse of his power there is no appeal.

NUMBER

NEW YORK.

NUMBER of Prisoners annually committed to the New York State Prison at Greenwich, and subsequently at Sing Sing; distinguishing their Crimes.

CRIMES.	1797	1798	1799	1800	1801	1802	1803	1804	1805	1806	1807	1808	1809	1810	1811	1812	1813	1814	1815	1816	1817	1818	1819	1820	1821	1822	1823	1824	1825	1826	1827	1828	1829	1830	1831	1832	To June 1833.
Grand Larceny	75	38	49	59	39	80	72	61	108	93	88	113	108	101	98	120	149	157	228	319	217	145	110	124	96	107	92	96	80	109	132	94	101	141	133	100	43
Petit Larceny	11	75	44	63	84	86	48	61	47	64	60	13	1	3	—	16	—	1	4	4	22	23	4	9	10	16	9	21	22	29	23	11	20	33	71	47	22
Forgery	22	9	11	6	18	4	3	5	10	9	25	33	44	39	21	9	10	9	15	31	13	6	13	24	20	8	14	14	9	7	6	14	17	29	34	29	4
Burglary	10	5	8	5	6	6	6	2	5	6	5	7	7	3	14	—	5	6	1	15	13	1	12	15	14	11	11	12	8	9	6	4	3	85	56	56	27
Sodomy	—	—	—	—	—	—	—	—	—	—	—	—	—	—	—	—	—	—	1	1	2	1	1	—	—	1	1	1	1	—	1	1	—	—	1	—	1
Murder	—	—	—	1	—	—	—	—	—	—	1	—	—	—	—	1	—	—	—	1	1	3	4	3	6	3	3	6	3	2	1	1	—	—	1	1	—
Perjury	—	—	—	—	2	—	6	—	—	4	2	2	3	4	2	7	8	3	1	20	11	—	4	—	6	—	—	6	—	—	—	—	4	10	5	1	2
Counterfeiting, and passing Counterfeit Money	—	—	1	4	—	—	—	—	3	1	—	—	—	—	9	18	6	16	5	20	14	28	9	23	30	18	5	35	18	10	8	3	6	22	7	8	2
Highway Robbery	1	—	—	4	—	—	—	—	—	—	—	—	1	—	—	—	1	4	3	7	5	2	4	2	6	5	11	8	1	9	2	6	—	3	7	2	5
Assault to commit Rape	—	—	1	4	2	2	3	4	1	1	4	—	—	6	5	2	3	3	9	2	5	2	2	6	4	5	8	5	3	6	4	1	4	9	5	4	4
Ditto with intent to Kill	—	15	—	—	1	1	—	2	1	3	3	1	2	1	3	3	6	3	6	6	6	9	3	2	2	3	4	3	8	3	3	3	2	13	12	6	3
Manslaughter	1	—	—	1	—	—	1	3	1	—	—	1	1	—	3	4	3	—	5	1	—	4	1	4	3	1	8	7	1	4	3	—	2	5	6	3	2
Bigamy	—	2	2	3	—	1	—	3	—	3	—	—	2	—	2	2	—	2	1	1	3	2	2	2	3	1	2	2	1	1	1	—	—	2	4	2	1
Arson	1	—	—	1	1	2	3	3	1	3	1	2	1	—	1	1	1	2	5	5	2	1	3	1	—	—	5	—	3	4	—	—	1	2	1	4	—
Aiding to break Gaol	—	—	1	3	1	1	1	1	1	—	—	2	—	—	1	2	—	2	—	7	—	—	1	1	1	4	—	—	—	1	1	—	—	1	—	1	—
Receiving Stolen Goods	—	—	2	2	1	7	—	3	1	1	—	—	—	—	2	2	1	2	5	5	5	1	4	1	1	—	—	4	4	—	2	—	—	3	8	1	2
Horse-Stealing	—	—	4	7	4	7	14	2	5	5	—	—	—	—	2	2	—	—	1	2	3	—	1	1	1	—	3	2	3	2	—	—	—	1	—	1	—
Rape	—	—	1	1	1	—	1	1	1	2	1	—	—	—	2	1	—	3	1	2	1	—	4	1	5	—	3	—	3	2	—	—	5	—	8	1	2
Swindling and obtaining Goods on false pretences	—	—	—	1	—	—	—	—	2	—	—	—	—	—	1	2	—	1	—	3	1	—	—	3	—	—	—	1	1	—	—	—	—	2	—	3	2
Misdemeanor	—	—	—	—	—	—	—	—	1	3	—	2	—	—	—	—	—	—	—	—	—	—	—	—	—	4	—	—	—	—	—	—	—	—	—	—	—
Fraud	—	—	—	—	—	—	4	—	—	4	—	1	1	7	1	—	—	—	2	1	1	—	5	6	—	4	—	—	—	4	—	—	7	7	—	3	—
Accessory to Murder	—	—	—	—	—	—	—	—	1	—	1	—	1	—	3	—	5	1	3	3	3	2	—	2	—	1	—	1	—	—	—	—	—	—	1	—	—
Breaking Prison	—	—	—	—	—	—	—	—	—	—	—	—	1	—	—	1	—	—	1	1	1	1	1	1	—	—	—	—	—	—	—	—	1	1	—	—	—
Felony	—	—	—	—	—	—	—	—	—	—	—	—	—	—	—	—	—	—	—	—	—	—	—	—	—	—	—	—	—	—	—	—	—	—	—	—	—
Deserting Prison Guard	—	—	—	—	—	—	—	—	—	—	—	—	—	—	—	1	—	—	—	—	—	—	—	—	—	—	—	—	—	—	—	—	—	—	—	1	—
Poison with intent to Kill	—	—	—	—	—	—	—	—	—	—	—	—	—	—	—	—	—	1	—	—	—	—	—	—	—	—	—	—	—	—	—	—	—	—	—	—	—
Robbing a Grave	—	—	—	—	—	—	—	—	—	—	—	—	—	—	—	—	—	—	—	—	—	—	—	—	—	2	—	—	—	—	—	—	—	—	—	—	—
Maiming	—	—	—	—	—	—	—	—	—	—	—	—	—	—	—	1	—	—	—	—	—	—	—	—	1	—	—	—	—	—	—	—	—	—	—	—	—
Child Stealing	1	—	—	—	—	—	—	—	—	—	—	—	—	—	—	—	—	—	—	—	—	—	—	—	—	1	—	—	—	—	1	—	—	—	—	—	—
Sending threatening Letter	—	—	—	—	—	—	—	—	—	—	—	—	—	—	—	1	—	—	—	—	—	—	—	—	—	—	—	—	—	—	—	—	—	—	—	—	—
Extortion and Deceit	—	—	—	—	—	—	—	—	—	—	—	—	—	1	—	—	—	—	—	—	—	—	—	—	—	—	2	—	—	—	—	—	—	—	—	—	—
Bribing Member of Assembly	—	—	—	—	—	—	—	—	—	—	—	—	—	—	—	—	—	—	—	—	1	—	—	—	—	—	—	—	—	—	—	—	—	—	—	—	—
Bestiality	—	—	—	—	—	—	—	—	—	—	—	—	—	—	—	—	—	1	—	—	—	—	—	—	—	—	—	—	—	—	—	—	—	—	—	—	—
Suborbation of Perjury	—	—	—	—	—	—	—	—	—	—	—	—	—	—	—	—	—	—	—	—	—	—	—	—	—	1	—	—	—	—	—	—	—	—	—	—	—
Kidnapping	—	—	—	—	—	—	—	—	—	—	—	—	—	—	—	—	—	—	—	—	—	—	—	—	—	—	—	—	—	—	—	—	—	—	—	—	—
Embezzling Money	—	—	—	—	—	—	—	—	—	—	—	—	—	—	—	—	—	—	—	—	—	—	—	—	—	2	—	—	—	—	—	—	—	—	—	—	2
Total	121	145	120	157	157	190	155	146	190	199	190	176	174	171	167	196	200	212	294	436	317	233	181	231	203	192	190	215	175	200	193	144	167	363	358	270	123

NEW YORK.

Of the foregoing NUMBERS there were in the respective YEARS:—

	To June 1833	1832	1831	1830	1829	1828	1827	1826	1825	1824	1823	1822	1821	1820	1819	1818	1817	1816	1815	1814	1813	1812	1811	1810	1809	1808	1807	1806	1805	1804	1803	1802	1801	1800	1799	1798	1797	Total
Coloured Men	35	45	70	31	32	22	42	47	26	33	34	32	36	45	30	36	34	57	38	23	27	35	22	21	27	35	41	32	46	26	36	49	39	37	20	28	21	–
Coloured Women	–	–	–	–	–	1	8	6	11	4	10	9	6	4	10	7	5	11	16	26	23	16	9	7	11	10	11	16	13	9	16	19	7	10	5	10	3	–
White Women	–	–	–	–	–	–	4	2	3	4	5	9	6	6	6	6	6	10	8	11	8	7	5	2	7	4	8	18	9	9	10	7	14	13	6	5	6	–
Natives of—																																						
England	6	22	22	15	3	13	5	9	3	7	4	11	7	9	8	7	12	28	15	13	8	7	6	4	8	12	11	8	10	6	5	9	11	8	15	10	5	–
Ireland	12	30	43	37	19	13	23	22	15	19	19	22	20	32	20	18	18	50	35	15	11	12	14	7	14	14	19	25	22	28	28	44	30	28	13	24	22	–
Scotland	2	3	3	3	2	2	2	1	1	2	1	1	4	5	1	6	1	6	5	1	2	4	7	1	2	2	4	4	1	5	1	3	2	2	2	3	2	–
France	2	–	–	–	1	1	2	2	1	2	2	1	1	2	2	1	2	3	2	1	2	3	2	1	1	3	2	6	–	1	2	1	3	1	1	3	3	–
Germany	1	–	1	1	2	1	1	1	1	1	–	–	–	1	1	3	3	3	2	1	1	–	1	1	2	1	2	7	4	2	1	4	2	4	2	4	5	–
Nova Scotia	3	1	2	2	1	2	1	1	1	1	1	1	3	2	1	1	2	1	3	3	1	1	2	1	1	1	1	1	1	1	2	1	1	2	1	2	5	–
Canada	1	5	4	3	2	–	–	–	–	2	1	4	3	4	2	6	5	7	5	–	2	–	1	4	4	3	4	2	–	7	1	1	–	–	4	11	4	–
West Indies	–	3	1	1	1	3	2	2	1	1	1	1	7	6	2	5	3	6	3	3	3	3	3	2	5	1	3	2	10	1	2	1	1	9	1	1	–	–
Africa	–	–	–	–	–	–	–	–	–	–	–	–	–	–	–	–	–	3	–	–	2	1	–	–	–	–	–	1	2	–	3	1	2	6	4	2	4	–
Denmark	–	1	–	–	–	1	1	–	–	1	1	–	–	–	1	1	1	1	1	–	–	1	–	1	1	1	–	1	–	1	–	1	1	1	1	–	–	–
East Indies	1	1	–	1	1	1	2	1	1	1	–	1	–	–	1	–	–	2	–	1	–	–	1	1	–	1	1	–	1	1	–	1	1	–	1	–	–	–
Sweden	–	–	–	–	–	1	–	–	–	–	–	–	–	1	–	1	1	–	–	1	–	1	–	1	2	1	–	–	3	2	–	–	1	1	–	–	–	–
Norway	–	1	1	1	–	1	–	–	1	–	2	–	–	–	–	1	2	1	3	1	–	–	–	–	1	1	–	–	1	1	–	1	1	1	–	–	–	–
Spain	1	2	2	–	–	1	–	1	–	–	1	–	–	1	1	1	2	2	1	1	1	1	1	1	1	1	1	4	3	2	–	1	1	1	–	–	–	–
Italy	–	–	–	–	–	–	–	–	–	–	–	–	–	–	–	–	–	2	3	1	–	1	–	1	1	1	–	–	1	1	–	1	–	1	–	–	–	–
Prussia	–	–	–	–	–	1	–	–	–	–	–	–	–	–	–	–	–	–	–	1	1	–	–	–	–	–	–	–	–	–	–	1	1	–	–	–	–	–
Holland	–	–	–	–	–	–	–	–	–	–	1	–	–	–	–	–	–	–	–	1	–	1	–	–	–	–	–	–	–	–	–	–	–	–	–	–	–	–
Portugal	–	–	–	–	–	–	1	–	–	–	–	–	–	–	–	–	–	–	–	1	–	–	–	–	1	–	–	–	–	–	–	–	–	–	–	–	–	–
Otaheite	–	–	–	–	–	–	–	–	–	–	–	–	–	–	–	–	–	–	–	–	–	–	–	–	1	–	–	–	–	–	–	–	–	–	–	–	–	–
Brazil	–	–	–	–	–	–	–	–	–	–	–	–	–	–	–	–	–	1	–	–	1	1	–	–	1	–	–	–	–	–	–	–	–	–	–	–	–	–
Curaçoa	–	–	–	–	–	–	–	–	–	1	1	1	–	–	–	–	–	5	–	–	–	–	–	–	–	–	–	–	–	–	–	–	–	–	–	–	–	–
Russia	1	–	–	1	–	1	–	2	1	–	–	–	–	–	–	–	–	1	1	–	1	–	–	–	1	–	–	–	–	–	–	–	–	–	–	–	–	–
Newfoundland	–	–	–	–	–	–	–	–	–	–	–	–	–	–	–	–	–	–	–	–	–	–	–	–	–	–	–	–	–	–	–	–	–	–	–	–	–	–
South America	–	2	–	1	1	1	–	–	1	1	–	1	–	–	–	–	–	–	–	–	–	–	–	–	–	–	–	–	–	–	–	–	–	–	–	–	–	–
Poland	1	–	–	–	–	–	1	–	–	–	–	–	–	–	–	–	–	–	–	–	–	–	–	–	–	–	–	–	–	–	–	–	–	–	–	–	–	–
Mexico	–	–	–	–	–	–	1	1	1	1	–	–	–	–	–	–	–	–	–	–	–	–	–	–	–	–	–	–	–	–	–	–	–	–	–	–	–	–
TOTAL	28	70	79	65	30	37	37	40	26	37	33	43	43	62	39	50	49	120	74	40	34	31	37	21	41	39	46	61	56	54	53	77	76	64	43	60	51	–

NEW YORK.

NUMBER of Prisoners, before Convicted, who have been confined in the New York State Prison at Greenwich, and subsequently at Sing Sing, from 1798 to 1833.

Year	White Men 2nd Conv.	WM 3rd	WM 4th	White Women 2nd	WW 3rd	WW 4th	WW 5th	WW 6th	Black Men 2nd	BM 3rd	Black Women 2nd	BW 3rd	BW 4th	Total
1798	1	—	—	—	—	—	—	—	1	—	—	—	—	2
1799	1	—	—	—	—	—	—	—	1	—	1	—	—	2
1800	5	—	—	1	—	—	—	—	3	—	—	—	—	9
1801	10	—	—	3	—	—	—	—	4	—	—	—	—	17
1802	18	—	—	1	—	—	—	—	6	1	1	—	—	27
1803	11	2	—	1	—	—	—	—	9	—	1	1	—	25
1804	17	1	—	1	—	—	—	—	3	—	—	—	—	21
1805	18	3	1	—	—	—	—	—	1	1	—	—	—	24
1806	15	2	—	1	—	1	—	—	1	—	2	—	—	21
1807	20	4	—	1	—	—	—	—	5	—	1	—	—	31
1808	12	2	—	—	—	—	—	—	8	2	—	—	—	24
1809	12	2	—	1	—	—	—	—	2	1	1	—	—	19
1810	10	2	—	1	—	—	—	—	3	—	2	—	—	18
1811	8	1	—	1	1	1	—	—	1	—	3	1	—	15
1812	10	2	—	1	—	—	—	—	3	—	2	1	1	18
1813	12	—	—	—	—	1	—	—	2	—	1	1	—	16
1814	15	1	—	1	1	1	—	—	1	1	—	—	—	21
1815	21	2	—	—	—	—	—	—	1	1	—	—	—	23
1816	32	3	—	2	—	—	—	1	3	2	2	1	1	47
1817	23	—	—	2	—	—	—	—	4	—	3	1	—	33
1818	21	—	—	1	—	—	—	—	5	—	—	—	—	27
1819	17	—	—	—	—	—	—	—	2	—	1	—	—	20
1820	12	1	—	—	—	—	—	—	4	—	2	—	—	20
1821	14	1	—	—	—	—	—	—	7	—	1	—	—	23
1822	13	1	—	3	—	—	—	—	2	—	—	—	—	19
1823	8	7	—	1	—	—	—	—	2	—	—	—	—	18
1824	10	2	—	—	—	—	—	—	4	—	—	—	—	16
1825	12	4	1	—	—	—	—	—	1	—	—	—	—	17
1826	16	1	2	—	—	—	—	—	4	1	—	—	—	24
1827	22	3	—	—	—	—	—	—	4	—	1	—	—	30
1828	14	5	—	—	—	—	—	—	2	1	—	—	—	22
1829	6	1	1	—	—	—	—	—	1	1	—	—	—	9
1830	9	6	1	—	—	—	—	—	3	1	—	—	—	20
1831	24	6	1	—	—	—	—	—	7	—	—	—	—	38
1832	15	1	2	—	—	—	—	—	2	—	—	—	—	20
1833 (To June)	8	5	—	—	—	—	—	—	4	1	—	—	—	18

Annual Disposal of Prisoners from 1801 to 1833.

Year	Died	Escaped	Pardoned	Discharged in due course
1801	4	12	21	65
1802	12	1	25	94
1803	26	—	27	109
1804	25	1	48	52
1805	26	—	49	98
1806	37	—	48	89
1807	26	—	107	88
1808	24	—	62	96
1809	23	—	61	36
1810	21	—	130	37
1811	32	—	135	18
1812	32	—	113	10
1813	32	—	134	22
1814	29	—	176	10
1815	29	2	182	17
1816	30	1	293	5
1817	19	1	280	4
1818	38	—	230	15
1819	30	—	147	23
1820	24	—	189	41
1821	21	—	197	11
1822	35	1	98	14
1823	34	—	38	34
1824	30	—	73	51
1825	52	—	92	44
1826	36	—	115	67
1827	29	—	59	52
1828	15	—	89	49
1829	11	—	12	58
1830	15	—	29	63
1831	36	—	33	77
1832	128	1	29	150
1833 (To June)	14	—	26	60

Ages of the Prisoners, from 1822 to 1833.

Year	Under 16 Years of Age	— 20 —	— 30 —
1822	7	20	88
1823	5	23	75
1824	5	26	92
1825	2	18	72
1826	4	30	105
1827	4	37	100
1828	—	30	71
1829	4	24	87
1830	9	38	75
1831	5	48	181
1832	3	37	149
1833 (To June)	—	26	59

Total Number of Prisoners in confinement on the 31st December in each Year.

Year	Total
1797	121
1798	212
1799	225
1800	283
1801	345
1802	404
1803	397
1804	419
1805	436
1806	461
1807	430
1808	424
1809	478
1810	461
1811	447
1812	486
1813	496
1814	494
1815	559
1816	666
1817	669
1818	618
1819	604
1820	580
1821	553
1822	580
1823	608
1824	642
1825	496
1826	491
1827	337
1828	518
1829	584
1830	816
1831	974
1832	832
1833 (To June)	814

NUMBER of PRISONERS, before Convicted, confined in the NEW YORK STATE PRISON at GREENWICH, and subsequently at SING SING.

Date.	First Offence.	Second Offence.	Third Offence.
1803	P. Larceny - 14 / G. Larceny - 11 / **25**	P. Larceny - 15 / G. Larceny - 10 / **25**	
1804	P. Larceny - 11 / G. Larceny - 8 / Forgery - 1 / Horse stealing 1 / **21**	P. Larceny - 10 / G. Larceny - 8 / Horse stealing 1 / Receiving Stolen Goods 2 / **21**	
1805	P. Larceny - 18 / G. Larceny - 5 / Horse stealing 1 / **24**	P. Larceny - 12 / G. Larceny - 11 / Assault and Battery - 1 / **24**	
1806	P. Larceny - 11 / G. Larceny - 8 / Housebreaking 1 / Forgery - 1 / **21**	P. Larceny - 13 / G. Larceny - 7 / Highway Robbery - 1 / **21**	
1807	G. Larceny - 12 / P. Larceny - 14 / Burglary - 1 / Horse stealing 3 / Manslaughter 1 / **31**	P. Larceny - 10 / G. Larceny - 16 / Forgery - 3 / Assault and Battery - 1 / Burglary - 1 / **31**	
1808	G. Larceny - 13 / P. Larceny - 11 / **24**	P. Larceny - 3 / G. Larceny - 18 / Burglary - 2 / Forgery - 1 / **24**	
1809	Burglary - 2 / G. Larceny - 7 / P. Larceny - 8 / Forgery - 1 / Horse stealing 1 / **19**	G. Larceny - 15 / Forgery - 2 / P. Larceny - 1 / Horse stealing 1 / **19**	
1810	P. Larceny - 6 / G. Larceny - 10 / Burglary - 1 / Forgery - 1 / **18**	P. Larceny - 2 / G. Larceny - 12 / Assault and Battery - 1 / Forgery - 1 / Horse-stealing 1 / Breaking Gaol 1 / **18**	G. Larceny 3
1811	G. Larceny - 10 / P. Larceny - 4 / Forgery - 1 / **15**	G. Larceny - 10 / P. Larceny - 3 / Burglary - 2 / **15**	G. Larceny 3
1812	P. Larceny - 5 / G. Larceny - 10 / Forgery - 1 / Horse stealing 1 / Manslaughter 1 / **18**	G. Larceny - 17 / P. Larceny - 1 / **18**	G. Larceny 2 / Forgery - 1 / **3**
1814	Burglary - 1 / Arson - 1 / G. Larceny - 15 / P. Larceny - 2 / Breaking Gaol 1 / Horse stealing 1 / **21**	Perjury - 1 / G. Larceny - 20 / **21**	G. Larceny 4
1815	G. Larceny - 18 / P. Larceny - 3 / Forgery - 2 / **23**	G. Larceny - 20 / Forgery - 1 / Arson - 1 / Burglary - 1 / **23**	G. Larceny 2 / Forgery - 1 / **3**
1816	G. Larceny - 32 / P. Larceny - 5 / Assault and Battery - 1 / Forgery - 5 / Arson - 1 / Burglary - 1 / Horse stealing 1 / Assault to Rape - 1 / **47**	G. Larceny - 37 / P. Larceny - 3 / Forgery - 3 / Burglary - 1 / Robbery - 2 / Counterfeit Money - 1 / **47**	G. Larceny 6 / Burglary 1 / Breaking Gaol - 1 / P. Larceny 1 / **9**
1817	G. Larceny - 26 / Burglary - 1 / Counterfeit Money - 2 / Sodomy - 1 / Forgery - 3 / **33**	G. Larceny - 28 / Breaking Gaol 1 / Counterfeit Money - 2 / Burglary - 1 / Forgery - 1 / **33**	G. Larceny 1
1818	G. Larceny - 22 / Forgery - 2 / Assault and Battery - 1 / Felony - 1 / Burglary - 1 / **27**	G. Larceny - 18 / Assault and Battery - 1 / Rape - 1 / Counterfeit Money - 3 / Forgery - 2 / Burglary - 1 / Horse stealing 1 / **27**	G. Larceny 1 / Counterfeit Money 1 / **2**

RE-CONVICTIONS—*continued.*

Date.	Offence.	Second Offence.	Third Offence.
1819	Burglary - 2 G. Larceny - 15 Forgery - 2 Swindling - 1 —— 20	G. Larceny - 14 Burglary - 3 Robbery - 1 Counterfeit Money - 1 Forgery - 1 —— 20	G. Larceny 1 Counterfeit Money - 1 —— 2
1820	G. Larceny - 13 P. Larceny - 2 Breaking gaol 1 Forgery - 4 —— 20	G. Larceny - 14 P. Larceny - 1 Burglary - 2 Counterfeit Money - 2 Breaking Gaol 1 —— 20	G. Larceny 1
1821	G. Larceny - 21 Arson - 1 Counterfeit Money - 1 —— 23	G. Larceny - 16 P. Larceny - 1 Burglary - 3 Highway Robbery - 1 Counterfeit Money - 2 —— 23	Breaking Gaol - 1
1822	G. Larceny - 15 P. Larceny - 1 Breaking Gaol 1 Counterfeit Money - 1 Forgery - 1 —— 19	G. Larceny - 11 P. Larceny - 4 Burglary - 2 Counterfeit Money - 2 —— 19	G. Larceny 1
1823	G. Larceny - 13 P. Larceny - 1 Forgery - 2 Counterfeit Money - 1 Breaking Gaol 1 —— 18	G. Larceny - 13 P. Larceny - 1 Robbery - 2 Counterfeit Money - 1 Perjury - 1 —— 18	G. Larceny 6 Highway Robbery 1 Burglary 1 —— 8

Date.	First Offence.	Second Offence.	Third Offence.
1824	G. Larceny - 11 Burglary - 2 Robbery - 1 Forgery - 1 Counterfeit Money - 1 —— 16	G. Larceny - 8 P. Larceny - 1 Forgery - 1 Sodomy - 1 Highway Robbery - 2 Counterfeit Money - 2 Assault to Rape - 1 —— 16	Counterfeit Money - 2 Burglary 1 G. Larceny 2 —— 5
1825	G. Larceny - 10 P. Larceny - 1 Burglary - 2 Forgery - 2 Perjury - 1 Breaking Gaol 1 —— 17	G. Larceny - 15 P. Larceny - 2 —— 17	G. Larceny 2 Counterfeit Money - 2 —— 4
1826	G. Larceny - 13 P. Larceny - 2 Horse-stealing 1 Assault and Battery - 1 Forgery - 4 Rape - 1 Breaking Gaol 1 Highway Robbery - 1 —— 24	G. Larceny - 15 Counterfeit Money - 1 Assault to Rape - 2 P. Larceny - 2 Forgery - 1 Rape - 1 Manslaughter 1 Burglary - 1 —— 24	G. Larceny 2 P. Larceny 1 Counterfeit Money - 1 —— 4 Fourth Offence. G. Larceny 12
1827	G. Larceny - 19 Burglary - 2 Robbery - 2 Arson - 1 Forgery - 1 Counterfeit Money - 2 P. Larceny - 3 —— 30	G. Larceny - 23 P. Larceny - 6 Breaking Gaol 1 —— 30	G. Larceny 2 P. Larceny 2 Breaking Gaol - 1 —— 5 Fourth Offence. Counterfeit Money - 1 G. Larceny 2 Breaking Gaol - 3 Petty Larceny - 5 —— 11

NEW YORK.

NUMBER of Deaths and Hospital Cases at the New York State Prison at Sing Sing, from 1828 to 1833.

DATES.	No, of Deaths.	No, of Cases.	The most prevalent Diseases of the Month.			
1828:						
July - - -	—	114 {	Of whom were } 56 Dysentery }	Diarrhœa - 24	Fever - - 8	
August - - -	2	112	- ditto - 51	- ditto - 25	- ditto - 10	
September - - -	3	84	- ditto - 22	- ditto - 24	- ditto - 15	
October - - -	4	48	- ditto - 6	- ditto - 9	- ditto - 7	
November - - -	3	35	- ditto - 8	- ditto - 8	- ditto - 1	
December - - -	1	24	- ditto - 2	- ditto - 8		
1829:						
January - - -	1	24	Pneumonia - 6			
February - - -	1	25	- ditto - 4			
March - - -	1	22	- ditto - 2	Consumption 3	Ophthalmia - 2	
April - - -	1	19	- - -	- ditto - 4		
May - - -	2	19	Diarrhœa - 5	- ditto - 4		
June - - -	1	20	- ditto - 4	- ditto - 3		
July - - -	—	27	- ditto - 3	- ditto - 4	Pneumonia - 2	
August - - -	1	33 {	- ditto - 6 Dysentery - 4 }	} - ditto - 5	Fever - - 3	
September - - -	—	23	- - -	- ditto - 3		
October - - -	—	19				
November - - -	1	15				
December - - -	1	17				
1830:						
January - - -	1	22				
February - - -	1	23				
March - - -	2	22				
April - - -	1	24				
May - - -	1	27				
June - - -	1	38	Diarrhœa - 12			
July - - -	—	53	- ditto - 22	Dysentery - 6		
August - - -	4	52	- ditto - 16			
September - - -	—	88	- ditto - 45	- ditto - 7	Cholera - 19	
October - - -	—	54	- ditto - 8	Influenza - 15		
November - - -	2	24				
December - - -	—	33				
1831:						
January - - -	2	34				
February - - -	1	38				
March - - -	2	42				
April - - -	6	42				
May - - -	2	40	Consumption 6			
June - - -	—	51	Diarrhœa - 13			
July - - -	5	67	- ditto - 17	Consumption 5	Dysentery - 7	
August - - -	2	123	- ditto - 21	Cholera - 22	- ditto - 19	
September - - -	4	107	- ditto - 15	- ditto - 11	- ditto - 18	
October - - -	7	94	- - -	Fever - - 17	- ditto - 15	
November - - -	3	123	Influenza - 64			
December - - -	2	89	- ditto - 25	Typhus Fever, 11		
1832:						
January - - -	2	81	Diarrhœa - 20	- ditto - 17		
February - - -	1	180	- ditto - 93	- ditto - 7	Measles - 34	
March - - -	6	78	- ditto - 23			
April - - -	4	61				
May - - -	1	106	- ditto - 41			
June - - -	4	84	- ditto - 25			
July - - -	66 *	259 *	- ditto - 52	Malig.t Cholera, 174		
August - - -	43 *	239 *	- - -	- ditto - 210		
September - - -	—	138	- ditto - 92	- - -	Dysentery - 15	
October - - -	2	70	- ditto - 25			
November - - -	5	52				
December - - -	1	83	- ditto - 34			
1833:						
January - - -	1	73	- ditto - 17			
February - - -	—	51				
March - - -	1	62				
April - - -	3	65				
May - - -	2	69				
June - - -						

* Mostly Cholera cases.

PUNISHMENTS for the principal OFFENCES in this STATE.

OFFENCES.	PUNISHMENTS.
Abduction. *See* Rape.	
Accessaries in cases of Felony. Before the fact - - - -	Punishment as principals.
After the fact - - - -	- - State prison, not exceeding 5 years, or county gaol not exceeding one year, or fine not exceeding $ 500 ; or both fine and imprisonment.
Arson, &c. - - - - 1st degree.—Setting fire to a dwelling-house, with a human being in it, by night.	Death.
2d degree.—The same by day, or a shop, warehouse, &c. endangering a dwelling-house by night.	State prison, not less than 10 years.
3d degree.—The same by day, or any house not within the first degree, church, public building, ship, barn, &c. by night, or any ship or building, with intent to defraud insurer.	State prison, from 10 to 7 years.
4th degree.—Any building by day, which, if fired by night, would be arson of the 3d degree, or any bridge, haystack, &c. by day or night.	State prison, from 7 to 2 years, or county gaol not exceeding one year.
Assault - - - - - With fire-arms or deadly weapon, with intent to kill, maim, ravish, rob or commit other felony.	State prison, not exceeding 10 years.
Without such weapons - -	- - State prison, not exceeding 5 years, or county gaol not exceeding one year, or fine not exceeding $ 500 ; or both fine and imprisonment.
Attempts, if not expressly punishable : When offence attempted is punishable by death.	State prison, not exceeding 10 years.
When punishable by 4 years or more in state prison, or imprisonment in county gaol, or by fine, or by fine and imprisonment.	Half the heaviest punishment imposed on the offence.
When punishable by less than 4 years in state prison.	County gaol, not more than one year.
Bigamy - - - - - - -	State prison, not exceeding 5 years.
The second husband or wife, if aware of previous marriage.	- - The same, or county gaol not exceeding one year, or fine not exceeding $500 ; or both fine and imprisonment.
Bribery, Embracery, &c. - - Of public officers to obtain their votes, &c. in their official capacity, or taking such bribe by an officer.	State prison, not exceeding 10 years, or fine not exceeding $ 5,000, or both.
Bribing or attempting to bribe jurors, or juror accepting a bribe.	- - State prison, not exceeding 5 years, or county gaol not exceeding one year, or fine not exceeding $ 1,000 ; or both fine and imprisonment.
Attempt to influence jurors, or juror making corrupt agreement, or unfairly drawing names of jurors.	A misdemeanor.*
Burglary - - - - 1st degree.—Breaking, by night, with intent to commit some crime, into a dwelling-house, wherein is some human being, forcibly, or armed, or by means of false keys, picklocks, &c.	State prison, not less than 10 years.
2d degree.—The same by day, or breaking into a dwelling-house by night, but not within the 1st degree, or entering without breaking to commit some crime ; or having entered, committing some crime ; or being in, breaking out through outer door or window ; or entering by night through open outer door, and breaking inner one ; or being lawfully in, breaking inner door by night.	State prison, from 10 to 5 years.

* The punishment for a misdemeanor, when not expressly provided by statute, is imprisonment in the county gaol for a term not exceeding one year, or fine not exceeding $ 250, or both.

PUNISHMENTS for the principal Offences in this State—*continued.*

OFFENCES.		PUNISHMENTS.
Burglary—*continued.*	3d degree.—Breaking and entering building within curtilage of dwelling-house or shop, tent, warehouse, &c. containing valuables, with intent to commit felony; or breaking into dwelling-house by day, under circumstances not within the 1st degree.	State prison, not exceeding 5 years.
Coining. *See* Forgery.		
Compounding - -	Offences punishable with death or state prison.	State prison, not exceeding 5 years, or county gaol not exceeding 1 year.
	Agreeing to compound the same.	State prison, not exceeding 3 years, or county gaol not exceeding 6 months.
	Compounding, or agreeing to compound, misdemeanors.	A misdemeanor, (*see* note p. 39).
Dead Bodies - -	Disinterring or receiving - -	- - State prison, not exceeding 5 years, or county gaol not exceeding one year, or fine not exceeding $500; or both fine and imprisonment.
	Opening graves, with intent to steal bodies or coffins.	- - State prison, not exceeding 2 years, or county gaol not exceeding 6 months, or fine not exceeding $250; or both fine and imprisonment.
Duelling. *See* also Murder.	When death does not ensue - -	State prison, not exceeding 10 years, and disqualified for office.
	Sending, accepting or bearing a challenge; or assisting or being present in any capacity at a duel. (This extends also to parties going into another State for the purpose.)	State prison, not exceeding 7 years.
	Posting, &c. for not fighting -	A misdemeanor, (*see* note, p. 39.)
Embezzlement or receiving property embezzled - -		The same as if the thing embezzled had been stolen.
	By insolvent debtor - - -	A misdemeanor (*see* note, p. 39.)
Escape - - -	Assisting in or attempting to effect the escape of a felon from prison.	State prison, not exceeding 10 years.
	The same of a prisoner not a felon	County gaol, not exceeding one year, or fine not exceeding $500, or both.
	The same of any prisoner criminally charged, from the custody of an officer.	County gaol, not exceeding one year, or fine not exceeding $250, or both.
	Officers refusing to take, or allowing the escape of a prisoner.	- - County gaol, not exceeding one year, or fine not exceeding $1,000, or both, and disqualified for office.
	Prisoner (not confined for life) escaping, or attempting his escape, from State prison.	- - State prison, not exceeding 5 years, after expiration of the term of his imprisonment.
	The same from county gaol -	- - State prison, not exceeding 2 years, or county gaol not exceeding one year, from the expiration of the term of imprisonment.
	Attempting escape from county gaol	County gaol, not exceeding one year.
Extortion. *See* Threats.		
False Personation, Pretences and Tokens. *See* also Swindling.		
	Personating another in marriage, or in judicial proceedings.	State prison, not exceeding 10 years.
	In receiving money - - -	The same as if the money were stolen.
	Producing a false heir (infant) -	State prison, not exceeding 10 years.
	Changing a child - - -	State prison, not exceeding 7 years.

PUNISHMENTS for the principal Offences in this State—*continued.*

OFFENCES.		PUNISHMENTS.
Forgery - -	- - 1st degree.—Of a deed, will, or certificate of a public officer, public security, &c. with intent to defraud.	State prison not less than 10 years.
	2d degree.—Counterfeiting State seals, or those of a body corporate, or altering or destroying wills, conveyances or records, &c. Officer entrusted with the keeping of an instrument giving a false certificate of it, or counterfeiting current coin; or engraving plates for making bank notes or public securities, or possessing them without authority, or possessing impressions of bank notes, &c. to be filled up, or plates for altering notes; or selling, buying, or offering for sale counterfeit notes, checks, &c.	State prison, from 10 to 5 years.
	3d degree.—Fraudulently counterfeiting foreign coin, or forging or altering any process, pleading, &c., pecuniary obligation, &c., by which any person may be defrauded; or making a false entry in the public accounts of the State, or any corporation.	State prison, not exceeding 5 years.
	4th degree—Possessing forged instruments (other than bank notes), or current coin, or fraudulently uttering forged instruments or coin, when *boná fide* taken for value.	State prison, not exceeding 2 years, or county gaol not exceeding 1 year.
	Uttering generally (except in the case last-mentioned.)	The same as for forging the instrument uttered.
	Erasure, alteration by joining parts of several instruments, or destruction.	To be deemed forgery of them.
Incest - - -	- - - - - - -	State prison, not exceeding 10 years.
Kidnapping - -	- - - - - - -	State prison, not exceeding 10 years.
Larceny. *See also* Robbery.		
	Stealing personal property, upwards of $25 (grand larceny).	State prison, not exceeding 5 years.
	If from a dwelling-house, ship, &c. -	May be increased 3 years.
	From the person by night - -	State prison' not exceeding 10 years.
	Stealing records - - - -	- - State prison, not exceeding 5 years, or county gaol not exceeding one year, or fine not exceeding $500; or both fine and imprisoment.
	The same by an officer having the care of them.	State prison, not exceeding 5 years.
	Stealing personal property, $25 or under (petit-larceny).	County gaol, not exceeding 6 months, or fine not exceeding $100, or both.
	Receiving stolen goods (principal need not be convicted).	- - State prison, not exceeding 5 years, or county gaol not exceeding 6 months, or fine not exceeding $250; or both fine and imprisonment.
Maiming, disfiguring, &c.	With express purpose - - -	State prison, not less than 7 years.
Malicious mischief -	Exposing poison for cattle -	- - State prison, not exceeding 3 years, or county gaol, not exceeding one year, or fine not exceeding $250; or both fine and imprisonment.
	Cutting down and destroying trees, carrying away timber, severing and carrying away such property, as if personal, would constitute larceny.	County gaol, not exceeding 6 months, or fine not exceeding $250, or both.

PUNISHMENTS for the principal Offences in this State—*continued.*

OFFENCES.		PUNISHMENTS.
Malicious mischief— *continued.*	Killing or maiming the cattle of another; cruelty to any cattle; destroying mill-banks, embankments, toll-gates, boundary marks, &c.	Misdemeanors, (*see* note, p. 39.)
Manslaughter -	- - 1st degree.—Killing a human being without intending death; by the act or culpable negligence of one engaged in perpetration of, or attempt to perpetrate, an offence less than felony, or assisting a suicide; or killing an unborn child, by such injury to the mother as would be murder if she died.	State prison, for not less than 7 years.
	2d degree.—Administering drugs* to a woman pregnant with a quick child, or using any other means to destroy such child; killing by violence in a passion, and not intending death; or killing unnecessarily in resisting an attempt at felony, or after such attempt has failed.	State prison, from 7 to 4 years.
	3d degree.—Killing in the heat of passion by a dangerous or any weapon, or killing undesignedly by the act or culpable negligence of one committing a trespass; or by a mischievous animal; or by overloading a vessel,† or over-charging the engine of a steam-boat; † by a physician administering medicine when drunk.†	State prison, from 4 to 2 years.
	4th degree.—All other cases of homicide not justifiable or excusable.	- - State prison, 2 years, or county gaol not exceeding one year, or fine not exceeding $1,000; or both fine and imprisonment.
Murder - - -	- - Homicide, when death to some human being is deliberately intended, or by an act regardless of human life, or in the commission of a felony, or in a duel.	Death.
Perjury and subornation of perjury on a trial for felony -		State prison, not less than 10 years.
	In any other case - - - -	State prison, not exceeding 10 years.
	Attempt at subornation - -	State prison, not exceeding 5 years.
Poison. *See* also Malicious mischief.	Administering when death does not ensue.	State prison, not less than 10 years.
	Poisoning food or springs - -	- - State prison, not exceeding 10 years, or county gaol, not exceeding one year, or fine not exceeding $500; or both fine and imprisonment.
	Selling poison without a label -	Fine not exceeding $100.
Rape, abduction, &c.	Including abuse of child under 10 years.	State prison, not less than 10 years.
	By use of drugs - - - -	State prison, not less than 5 years.
	By menace or similar compulsion to marry, or taking away woman for such purpose.	State prison, not less than 10 years.
	Carrying off female under 14 for marriage, concubinage or prostitution.	- - State prison, not exceeding 3 years, or county gaol, not exceeding one year, or fine not exceeding $1,000; or both fine and imprisonment.

* Administering drugs to procure abortion is a misdemeanor, and is punishable by imprisonment in the county gaol for not more than one year, or by fine, not exceeding $500, or both.

† These are misdemeanors when they endanger life, but do not produce death. For punishment, *see* note, p. 39.

NEW YORK

OFFENCES.	PUNISHMENTS.
Rescue. *See* Escape.	
Receiving Stolen Goods. *See* Larceny.	
Robbery - - -1st degree.—Taking property by means of actual, or fear of immediate violence.	State prison, not less than 10 years.
2d degree.—By means of fear of violence not immediate, or to some relative.	State prison, not exceeding 10 years.
Second Offence - After pardon or punishment of a felony:—	
When 2d offence is a felony, punishable in State prison for upwards of 5 years.	State prison, not less than 10 years.
When 2d offence a felony, punishable in State prison for 5 years or under.	State prison, not more than 10 years.
When 2d offence petit-larceny, or an attempt at felony.	State prison, not more than 5 years.
After pardon or punishment of a misdemeanor:—	
When 2d offence a felony, punishable in State prison for life, at discretion of court.	State prison for life.
When 2d offence a felony, punishable in State prison for any term less than life.	State prison, for the longest term imposed upon the offence.
When 2d offence petit-larceny, or an attempt at felony.	State prison, not exceeding 5 years.
Sodomy and Bestiality - - - - - -	State prison, not exceeding 10 years.
Swindling. *See* also False personation. Obtaining property by false tokens or under false pretences.	-- State prison, not exceeding 3 years, or county gaol, not exceeding one year, or fine not exceeding treble the value obtained.
If false token is a promissory note, purporting to be by a bank not in existence.	State prison, not exceeding 7 years.
Fraudulent conveyances, as against parties, and privies thereto.	Misdemeanor, (*see* note, p. 39.)
Threats - - - -- Sending threatening letters to extort money is made an attempt at robbery.	State prison, not exceeding 5 years.
Attempt to extort money by threats.	Misdemeanor, (*see* note, p. 39.)
Treason - - - - - - - - -	Death.

N. B. When a criminal is convicted of several distinct offences, the punishments are to be cumulative.—Felons are the debtors of the parties injured to the amount of their loss, when it can be estimated by damages.—Felons are disqualified as witnesses.—The court determines the precise degree of punishment within the prescribed limits.—The jury may find the offender guilty of any degree of the crime charged, or of any other crime of the same kind, but of less enormity.

Prisoners under 16 years, convicted of a felony, may be sentenced to the House of Refuge, instead of the State Prison.

NEW YORK.

ABSTRACT of Convictions for Criminal Offences in the several Counties of the State of New York, during the Year 1830, according to the Returns made to the Secretary of State.

CRIMES	Albany	Broome	Cattaraugus	Cayuga	Chatauque	Chenango	Clinton	Columbia	Delaware	Dutchess	Erie	Essex	Franklin	Genesee	Herkimer	Kings	Lewis	Livingston	Madison	Monroe	Montgomery	Niagara	Oneida	Onondaga	Ontario	Orange	Oswego	Otsego	Putnam	Queen	Rensselaer	Rockland	Saratoga	St Lawrence	Schoharie	Seneca	Steuben	Suffolk	Sullivan	Tioga	Tompkins	Ulster	Washington	Wayne	West Chester	TOTAL
Forgery	10	-	-	1	1	2	-	2	-	-	2	-	-	2	1	-	1	-	1	2	1	-	1	1	2	2	1	-	-	1	3	-	2	1	-	-	-	-	-	1	1	2	1	1	-	45
Grand Larceny	20	-	-	2	-	-	1	-	-	6	8	1	1	6	-	-	-	4	-	7	2	-	14	3	-	4	2	3	-	2	6	-	2	3	1	1	1	1	1	-	3	3	1	-	-	111
Petty Larceny	27	-	-	2	-	1	1	3	1	7	3	1	1	-	-	4	-	-	2	12	7	1	2	3	2	3	1	-	1	4	8	1	4	1	1	-	1	-	-	-	1	5	-	-	-	108
Disorderly House	2	-	-	-	-	-	-	-	-	-	2	-	-	-	-	-	-	-	-	2	-	-	-	-	-	-	-	-	-	-	9	-	-	-	1	-	-	-	-	-	-	-	-	-	-	17
Assault & Battery	10	-	1	2	1	-	-	6	-	2	5	-	-	1	3	3	1	-	1	6	-	-	4	5	8	1	5	3	-	3	7	1	1	-	1	-	3	1	1	1	5	1	1	-	2	95
Burglary	11	-	-	1	-	-	-	-	-	3	2	-	-	1	1	1	-	-	-	3	3	1	2	2	1	-	-	1	1	1	6	1	6	1	-	-	-	1	-	1	2	1	-	-	2	54
Stolen Goods	3	-	-	-	-	-	-	-	-	-	-	-	-	-	-	1	-	-	-	1	-	-	-	-	-	-	-	-	-	-	-	1	-	-	-	-	-	-	-	-	-	-	-	-	-	5
Perjury	2	1	-	-	-	-	-	-	-	-	-	-	-	-	-	-	-	1	-	-	-	-	-	-	-	-	-	-	-	-	-	-	-	-	-	-	-	-	-	-	-	-	-	-	-	8
Cheating	3	-	1	-	1	1	1	1	-	-	-	-	1	-	-	-	-	-	1	-	1	-	-	-	-	-	-	-	-	-	-	-	-	-	-	-	-	-	-	-	-	-	-	-	-	6
Conspiracy	1	-	-	-	-	-	-	-	-	-	-	-	-	-	-	-	-	-	-	1	-	-	-	-	-	-	-	-	-	1	-	-	-	-	-	-	-	-	-	-	-	-	-	-	1	2
Arson	1	-	-	1	-	-	-	-	-	-	-	-	-	-	-	-	-	-	1	-	-	-	-	-	-	-	2	-	-	-	-	-	-	-	-	-	-	-	-	-	-	-	-	-	1	4
Breaking Gaol	-	-	-	-	-	-	-	-	-	-	-	-	-	-	-	-	-	-	-	-	-	-	-	-	-	-	-	-	-	-	-	-	-	-	-	-	-	-	-	-	-	-	-	-	-	5
Horse-racing	-	-	-	1	-	-	-	-	-	-	-	-	-	-	-	-	-	-	-	-	-	-	-	-	21	-	-	-	-	-	-	-	-	-	-	-	-	-	-	-	-	-	-	-	-	22
Gaming	-	-	-	1	-	-	-	-	-	-	-	-	-	-	-	-	-	-	-	-	-	-	-	-	-	-	-	-	-	-	-	-	-	-	-	-	-	-	-	-	-	-	-	-	-	1
Nuisance	-	-	-	2	-	-	-	-	-	-	-	-	-	-	-	-	-	-	-	1	-	-	-	-	1	-	-	-	-	-	-	-	-	-	-	-	-	-	-	-	-	-	-	-	-	6
Misdemeanor	-	-	-	3	-	-	-	-	-	-	-	-	-	2	-	-	-	-	6	1	-	1	-	-	1	-	-	2	-	-	1	-	-	2	-	-	-	-	-	-	-	-	-	-	-	17
Murder	-	-	-	1	-	-	-	-	-	-	-	-	-	-	-	-	-	-	-	-	-	-	-	-	-	-	-	-	-	-	-	-	-	-	-	-	-	-	-	-	-	-	-	-	-	5
Stealing	-	-	-	-	-	-	-	-	-	-	-	-	-	-	-	-	-	-	-	-	-	-	-	-	-	-	-	-	-	-	-	-	-	-	-	-	-	-	-	-	-	-	-	-	-	2
Counterfeit money	-	-	-	-	1	4	-	1	1	1	-	-	-	-	-	-	-	-	-	1	-	-	-	-	-	-	-	-	-	-	1	-	-	-	-	-	1	-	-	-	-	-	-	1	-	11
Manslaughter	-	-	-	-	-	-	-	-	-	-	-	-	-	-	-	-	-	-	-	-	-	-	-	-	-	-	-	-	-	-	1	-	-	-	-	-	2	-	-	-	-	-	-	-	-	2
Riot	-	-	-	-	-	-	-	-	-	1	1	-	-	-	-	-	-	-	1	4	-	1	5	5	-	-	-	-	-	-	5	-	2	1	1	-	1	-	-	-	-	-	-	-	-	21
Crime	-	-	-	-	-	-	-	-	-	-	-	-	-	-	-	-	-	-	1	-	-	-	-	-	-	-	-	-	-	-	-	-	-	-	-	-	-	-	-	-	-	-	-	-	-	8
Libel	-	-	-	-	-	-	-	-	-	-	-	-	-	-	-	-	-	-	-	-	-	-	-	-	-	-	-	-	-	-	-	-	-	-	-	-	-	-	-	-	1	-	-	-	-	3
Robbery	-	-	-	-	-	-	-	-	-	-	-	-	-	-	-	-	-	-	1	-	1	-	-	-	-	-	-	-	-	-	-	-	-	-	-	-	-	-	-	2	-	-	-	-	1	3
Felony	-	-	-	-	-	-	-	-	-	-	-	-	-	-	-	-	-	-	-	1	-	-	-	-	-	-	-	-	-	-	-	-	-	-	-	-	-	-	-	-	-	-	-	-	-	2
Bigamy	-	-	-	-	-	-	-	-	-	-	-	-	-	-	-	-	-	-	-	-	-	-	-	-	-	-	-	-	-	-	-	-	-	-	-	-	-	-	-	-	-	-	1	-	-	1
TOTAL	90	1	2	17	4	8	3	13	2	20	23	2	3	12	5	9	2	5	15	42	15	4	28	—	37	10	11	9	2	12	47	4	17	9	5	1	9	3	2	5	13	12	3	2	7	564

NEW YORK.

ABSTRACT of Convictions for Criminal Offences in the several Counties of the State of New York, during the Year 1831, according to the Returns made to the Secretary of State.

CRIMES.	Albany	Allegany	Broome	Cattaraugus	Cayuga	Chautauque	Chenango	Clinton	Columbia	Cortland	Delaware	Dutchess	Erie	Essex	Franklin	Genesee	Greene	Herkimer	Jefferson	Kings	Lewis	Livingston	Madison	Monroe	Montgomery	New York	Niagara	Oneida	Onondaga	Ontario	Orange	Orleans	Oswego	Otsego	Putnam	Queens	Rensselaer	Richmond	Rockland	Saratoga	Schenectady	Schoharie	Seneca	St. Lawrence	Steuben	Suffolk	Sullivan	Tioga	Tompkins	Ulster	Warren	Washington	Wayne	Westchester	Yates	TOTAL
Murder	-	-	-	-	-	-	-	-	-	-	-	-	-	-	-	-	-	-	-	-	-	-	-	-	-	1	-	-	-	-	-	-	-	-	-	-	-	-	-	-	-	-	-	-	-	-	-	-	1	-	-	-	-	-	-	2
Arson	-	-	-	-	-	-	-	-	-	-	-	-	1	-	-	-	-	-	-	-	-	-	-	-	-	-	-	-	-	-	1	-	-	-	-	-	-	-	-	-	-	-	-	-	-	-	-	-	-	-	-	-	-	-	-	2
Rape	-	-	-	-	-	-	-	-	2	-	-	-	-	-	-	-	-	-	-	-	-	-	-	-	-	-	-	-	-	-	-	-	-	-	-	-	-	-	-	-	-	-	-	-	-	-	-	-	-	1	-	-	-	-	-	3
Perjury	1	-	1	-	-	-	-	-	-	-	-	-	-	1	-	-	-	-	-	-	-	1	-	-	-	-	1	-	-	-	-	-	-	-	-	1	-	-	-	-	-	-	1	-	-	-	-	-	-	-	-	-	-	-	-	6
Manslaughter	-	-	-	-	-	-	-	-	-	-	-	-	-	-	1	-	-	-	-	-	-	-	1	-	-	2	-	-	-	-	-	-	-	-	-	-	-	-	-	-	-	-	-	-	-	-	-	-	-	-	1	1	-	-	-	6
Bigamy	-	-	-	-	2	-	-	-	-	-	-	-	-	-	-	-	-	-	-	-	-	-	-	1	-	-	-	-	2	-	-	-	-	-	-	-	-	-	-	-	-	-	-	-	-	-	-	-	-	-	-	-	-	-	-	5
Forgery	-	-	-	-	1	-	2	-	-	-	-	-	-	-	1	1	-	-	-	-	-	-	-	1	1	2	-	-	1	1	-	-	-	-	-	-	-	-	-	-	-	-	-	-	-	-	-	-	-	-	-	-	-	2	-	48
Burglary	7	-	1	-	5	1	-	3	3	1	-	2	5	-	1	3	-	2	3	1	-	-	2	1	1	23	-	-	3	3	5	-	1	1	-	-	12	-	-	-	2	1	1	3	-	-	-	2	-	-	-	2	3	-	-	81
Grand Larceny	16	-	1	-	-	1	-	-	-	1	-	5	9	-	-	2	-	-	1	-	-	-	2	5	7	26	3	7	2	2	2	-	-	1	-	-	7	-	1	-	2	-	-	3	-	-	-	-	2	-	-	-	2	-	-	199
Petit Larceny	10	-	-	-	-	-	-	-	-	-	-	3	1	-	-	-	-	-	-	1	-	-	-	6	1	92	-	1	-	-	1	-	-	-	-	2	1	-	1	-	-	-	-	3	1	-	-	-	1	-	-	-	-	-	-	125
Petit Larceny, 2d offence	12	-	-	-	-	-	-	-	-	-	-	-	-	-	-	-	-	-	-	-	-	-	-	-	-	83	-	-	-	-	-	-	-	-	-	-	-	-	-	-	-	-	-	-	-	-	-	-	-	-	-	-	-	-	-	112
Assault to Rape	-	-	-	-	2	-	-	2	6	-	-	-	1	-	-	2	-	-	-	1	-	3	1	8	1	54	-	3	2	1	1	-	1	-	-	-	2	-	-	-	1	2	-	-	2	-	-	-	2	1	-	-	-	-	-	8
Ditto to Kill	1	-	-	-	1	-	-	-	-	-	-	-	1	-	-	-	-	1	-	-	-	1	-	-	1	6	-	1	1	1	-	-	-	-	1	-	1	-	-	-	-	-	-	-	1	-	-	-	-	-	-	1	-	-	-	11
Assault & Battery	2	1	-	1	2	5	-	-	3	-	-	3	3	2	-	6	1	2	2	1	1	3	2	13	-	92	-	-	6	9	1	-	3	-	-	4	7	-	-	-	1	-	2	4	-	-	-	-	3	-	-	-	5	-	-	190
Counterfeiting	-	-	-	-	-	1	-	-	-	-	-	1	2	-	-	-	-	1	1	-	-	-	-	1	-	-	5	1	-	-	-	-	-	-	-	-	-	-	-	-	-	-	-	-	1	-	-	-	-	-	-	-	5	1	-	15
Conspiracy	9	-	-	-	-	-	-	-	-	-	-	-	-	-	-	-	-	-	-	-	-	-	4	2	-	-	-	-	-	-	-	-	-	-	-	-	-	-	-	-	-	-	-	-	1	-	-	-	-	-	-	-	-	-	-	13
Riot, Assault & Battery	-	-	-	-	-	-	-	-	3	-	-	-	-	-	-	-	-	-	-	3	-	1	-	-	-	14	-	-	-	4	-	-	-	-	-	-	-	-	-	-	-	-	-	-	-	-	-	-	-	-	-	-	-	-	-	18
Riot	-	-	-	-	-	-	-	-	-	-	-	-	-	-	-	3	-	2	-	-	-	-	-	-	-	-	-	-	-	-	-	-	-	-	-	-	-	-	-	-	-	-	-	-	-	-	-	-	-	-	-	-	-	-	-	8
Breaking Gaol	-	-	-	-	-	-	-	-	-	-	-	-	-	-	-	1	-	-	-	-	-	-	-	-	-	-	-	-	-	-	-	-	-	-	-	-	-	-	-	-	-	-	-	-	-	-	-	-	-	-	-	-	-	-	-	7
Swindling	2	-	-	-	-	1	-	-	-	-	-	-	-	-	-	-	-	-	-	-	-	-	1	-	-	4	-	-	-	-	-	-	-	-	-	-	-	-	-	-	-	-	-	-	-	-	-	-	-	-	-	-	-	-	-	12
Keeping Disorderly House	-	-	-	-	-	-	-	-	-	-	-	-	-	-	-	-	-	-	-	-	-	-	-	2	-	9	-	-	1	-	-	-	-	-	-	-	-	-	-	-	-	1	-	-	-	-	-	-	-	-	-	-	-	-	-	14
Rec.t Stolen Goods	-	-	-	-	1	-	-	-	-	-	-	1	-	-	-	-	-	-	-	-	-	-	-	1	-	7	-	-	-	-	-	-	-	-	-	-	-	-	-	-	-	-	-	1	-	-	-	-	-	-	-	-	-	-	-	12
Misdemeanor	-	-	-	-	3	-	-	-	1	-	1	-	-	2	-	1	-	1	-	-	-	-	1	2	-	4	2	-	-	3	-	-	-	-	-	-	1	-	-	-	-	1	-	-	-	-	-	-	-	-	-	-	-	-	-	23
Robbery	-	-	-	-	-	-	1	-	-	-	1	-	1	-	-	-	-	-	-	-	-	1	2	-	-	8	-	-	-	-	-	-	-	-	-	-	-	-	-	-	-	-	-	1	-	-	-	-	-	-	-	-	-	-	-	12
Trespass	1	-	-	-	-	-	-	-	-	-	1	-	-	-	-	-	-	-	1	-	-	-	-	-	-	-	-	-	-	-	-	-	-	-	-	-	-	-	-	-	-	-	-	-	-	-	-	-	1	-	-	-	-	-	-	10
Offence agst Nature	-	-	-	-	-	-	-	-	-	-	-	-	-	-	-	-	-	-	-	-	-	-	1	-	-	-	-	-	-	-	-	-	-	-	-	-	-	-	-	-	-	-	-	-	-	-	-	-	-	-	-	-	-	-	-	1
Nuisance	-	-	-	-	-	-	-	-	-	-	-	-	-	-	-	2	-	-	-	-	-	-	-	-	-	1	-	-	-	1	-	-	-	-	-	-	-	-	-	-	-	-	-	-	-	-	-	-	-	-	-	-	-	-	-	3
Kidnapping	-	-	-	-	-	-	-	-	-	-	-	-	-	-	-	-	-	-	1	-	-	-	-	-	-	-	-	-	-	-	-	-	-	-	-	-	-	-	-	-	-	-	-	-	-	-	-	-	-	-	-	-	-	-	-	1
Total	69	1	3	1	17	9	3	5	18	2	3	15	25	5	3	21	1	10	8	7	1	10	17	43	12	427	11	15	18	26	11	1	6	6	1	7	39	1	2	1	7	5	4	15	6	1	!	2	2	6	3	5	10	4	1	947

NEW YORK.

ABSTRACT of Convictions for Criminal Offences in the several Counties of the State of New York, during the Year 1832, according to the Returns made to the Secretary of State.

CRIMES.	TOTAL	Yates	Westchester	Wayne	Washington	Warren	Ulster	Tompkins	Tioga	Sullivan	Suffolk	Steuben	St. Lawrence	Seneca	Schoharie	Schenectady	Saratoga	Rockland	Richmond	Rensselaer	Queens	Putnam	Otsego	Oswego	Orleans	Orange	Ontario	Onondaga	Oneida	Niagara	New York	Montgomery	Monroe	Madison	Livingston	Lewis	Kings	Jefferson	Herkimer	Greene	Genesee	Franklin	Essex	Erie	Dutchess	Delaware	Cortland	Columbia	Clinton	Chenango	Chautauque	Cayuga	Cattaraugus	Broome	Allegany	Albany
Murder	1	-	2	-	-	-	-	-	-	-	-	-	-	-	-	-	-	-	-	-	-	-	-	-	-	-	-	-	-	-	-	-	-	-	-	-	-	-	-	-	-	-	-	-	-	-	-	-	-	-	-	-	-	-	-	-
Arson	8	-	-	-	-	-	-	-	-	-	-	-	-	1	2	-	-	-	-	-	-	-	-	-	-	-	-	-	-	-	-	-	1	-	-	-	-	1	-	-	-	-	-	-	-	1	-	-	-	-	-	-	-	-	-	-
Rape	4	-	-	-	-	-	-	-	-	-	-	-	-	-	-	-	-	-	-	-	-	-	-	-	-	-	-	-	-	-	-	-	-	-	-	-	-	-	-	-	-	-	-	-	-	1	-	-	-	2	-	-	-	1	-	-
Perjury	6	-	-	-	-	-	-	1	-	-	-	-	-	-	-	-	1	-	-	-	-	-	1	-	-	-	1	-	-	-	-	1	-	-	-	-	-	-	-	-	-	-	-	-	1	-	-	-	-	-	-	-	-	-	-	-
Manslaughter	5	-	-	-	-	-	-	-	-	-	-	-	-	-	-	-	-	-	-	-	-	-	-	-	-	-	1	-	-	-	-	-	-	-	-	-	-	1	-	-	-	2	-	-	-	-	-	-	-	-	-	-	-	-	-	1
Bigamy	4	-	-	-	-	-	-	-	-	-	-	-	-	-	-	-	-	-	-	-	-	-	-	-	-	-	-	-	-	-	-	-	-	-	-	-	-	-	-	-	2	-	-	-	-	-	-	-	-	2	-	-	-	-	-	-
Forgery	45	-	-	-	2	-	-	1	-	-	-	-	1	1	1	-	2	-	-	4	-	-	1	1	-	-	-	3	6	-	13	1	2	-	-	-	-	-	-	2	-	1	2	-	-	-	-	-	1	-	-	1	-	-	-	2
Burglary	73	-	-	-	1	-	-	1	1	-	-	-	1	-	1	1	2	-	-	5	-	-	-	-	-	-	-	-	-	-	29	1	1	-	-	-	5	-	-	1	-	-	-	1	-	-	-	-	-	-	-	-	-	-	-	3
Grand Larceny	192	-	-	-	-	-	-	3	-	2	-	-	2	-	1	2	2	1	-	9	1	-	3	-	-	-	1	5	9	-	96	3	4	-	-	-	-	4	2	-	-	1	-	-	5	4	-	4	-	-	3	4	-	-	1	12
Petit Larceny	115	-	-	1	-	-	-	2	-	-	-	-	-	-	-	2	-	1	-	-	1	2	-	-	1	-	-	3	1	1	66	-	5	1	1	-	2	5	5	-	-	-	-	-	-	-	-	2	-	-	2	3	-	-	-	9
Petit Larceny, 2d offence	96	-	-	-	-	-	-	-	-	-	-	-	1	-	-	3	1	-	1	3	-	-	-	-	-	-	-	1	3	-	55	3	5	-	-	-	-	-	-	-	-	-	-	-	2	-	-	-	1	1	-	-	-	-	-	8
Assault, to Rape	2	-	-	-	-	-	-	-	-	-	-	-	-	-	-	-	-	-	-	-	-	-	-	2	-	-	-	-	-	-	-	-	-	-	-	-	-	-	-	-	-	-	-	-	-	-	-	-	-	-	-	-	-	-	-	-
Ditto, to Kill	11	-	-	-	-	-	1	-	-	-	-	-	-	-	-	-	-	-	-	-	3	-	5	-	-	-	-	-	-	-	2	-	-	-	-	-	-	-	-	-	-	-	-	-	-	-	-	-	-	-	-	-	-	-	-	-
Assault & Battery	189	-	-	-	-	-	1	5	1	-	1	-	7	-	-	2	3	-	-	6	-	-	-	2	-	4	-	7	-	2	40	-	9	5	2	-	8	2	2	-	-	-	-	-	5	5	-	1	-	1	1	4	-	-	-	59
Counterfeiting	14	-	-	-	-	-	-	1	-	-	-	-	-	1	-	-	-	-	-	-	-	-	-	-	-	-	-	-	-	-	-	-	1	1	-	-	1	-	-	-	1	-	1	-	-	2	-	-	-	-	-	-	-	-	-	6
Conspiracy	9	-	-	-	-	-	-	-	-	-	-	-	-	-	-	-	-	-	-	-	-	-	-	-	-	-	-	-	-	-	3	-	-	-	-	-	-	-	-	-	-	-	1	-	-	5	-	-	-	-	-	-	-	-	-	-
Riot, and Assault and Battery	70	-	-	-	-	-	-	-	-	-	-	-	2	-	-	3	-	-	-	1	-	-	-	-	-	-	5	3	-	-	4	-	6	-	7	-	-	-	-	-	-	-	-	-	-	-	-	-	-	-	-	-	-	-	-	43
Riot	5	-	-	-	-	-	-	-	-	-	-	-	-	-	-	-	-	-	-	-	-	-	-	-	-	-	-	-	-	-	-	-	5	-	-	-	-	-	-	-	-	-	-	-	-	-	-	-	-	-	-	-	-	-	-	-
Breaking Jail	4	-	-	-	-	-	-	-	-	-	-	-	-	-	-	-	-	-	-	-	-	-	-	-	-	-	-	-	-	-	-	2	-	-	-	-	-	-	-	-	-	-	-	-	-	-	-	-	-	-	-	-	-	-	-	2
Swindling	15	-	-	-	-	-	-	-	-	-	-	-	-	-	-	-	-	-	-	-	-	-	-	-	-	-	-	-	-	-	4	-	-	-	-	-	1	-	-	-	-	-	-	-	-	-	-	-	-	-	-	-	-	-	1	4
Keeping Disorderly House	18	-	-	-	-	-	-	-	-	-	-	-	-	-	-	-	-	-	-	3	-	-	-	-	-	-	-	-	-	-	4	-	2	-	-	-	-	-	-	-	-	-	-	-	-	-	1	-	-	-	-	-	-	-	-	7
Rec'd Stolen Goods	6	-	-	-	-	-	-	-	-	-	-	-	-	-	-	-	-	-	-	-	-	-	-	-	-	-	-	-	-	-	3	-	-	-	-	-	-	-	-	-	-	-	-	-	1	-	-	1	-	-	-	-	-	-	-	1
Misdemeanor	28	-	-	-	-	-	-	-	-	-	-	-	-	-	1	-	-	-	-	-	-	-	-	-	-	-	-	-	-	1	5	-	2	3	7	-	-	-	2	-	-	3	-	-	-	3	-	-	-	-	-	-	-	-	-	3
Robbery	5	-	-	-	-	-	-	-	-	-	-	-	-	-	-	-	-	-	-	3	-	-	-	-	-	-	-	-	-	-	1	-	-	-	-	-	-	-	1	-	-	-	-	-	-	-	-	-	-	-	-	-	-	-	-	-
Trespass	14	-	-	-	-	-	-	-	-	-	-	-	-	-	-	-	-	-	-	-	-	-	1	-	-	-	-	-	-	-	-	-	-	-	-	-	1	-	-	-	-	-	-	-	1	-	-	-	-	-	-	-	1	-	-	-
Nuisance	3	-	-	-	-	-	-	-	-	-	-	-	-	-	-	-	-	-	-	-	-	-	-	-	-	-	-	-	-	-	-	-	-	-	-	-	-	-	-	-	-	-	-	-	-	-	-	-	-	-	-	-	-	-	-	-
Offence ag'st Nature	2	-	-	-	-	-	-	-	-	-	-	-	-	-	-	-	1	-	-	-	-	-	-	-	-	-	-	-	-	-	-	-	-	-	-	-	-	-	-	-	-	-	-	-	-	-	-	-	-	-	-	-	-	-	-	-
Incest	1	-	-	-	-	-	-	-	-	-	-	-	-	-	-	-	-	-	-	-	-	-	-	-	-	-	-	1	-	-	-	-	-	-	-	-	-	-	-	-	-	-	-	-	-	-	-	-	-	-	-	-	-	-	-	-
TOTAL	944	1	2	1	3	2	2	13	2	2	1	1	14	4	6	13	12	2	1	40	5	2	12	6	1	9	11	23	19	5	325	18	43	12	17	1	22	13	13	5	3	13	4	8	15	21	1	9	3	6	6	13	1	1	2	160

NEW YORK.

ABSTRACT of Convictions for Criminal Offences in the several Counties of the State of New York, during the Year 1833, according to the Returns made to the Secretary of State.

CRIMES.	Albany	Allegany	Broome	Cattaraugus	Cayuga	Chatauque	Chenango	Clinton	Columbia	Cortland	Delaware	Dutchess	Erie	Essex	Franklin	Genesee	Greene	Herkimer	Jefferson	Kings	Lewis	Livingston	Madison	Monroe	Montgomery	New York	Niagara	Oneida	Onondaga	Ontario	Orange	Orleans	Oswego	Osego	Putnam	Queens	Rensselaer	Richmond	Rockland	Saratoga	Schenectady	Schoharie	Seneca	St. Lawrence	Steuben	Suffolk	Sullivan	Tioga	Tompkins	Ulster	Warren	Washington	Wayne	West Chester	Yates	TOTAL
Murder	–	–	–	–	–	–	1	–	–	1	–	–	–	–	–	–	–	–	–	–	–	1	–	–	–	1	–	1	1	–	1	–	–	3	–	–	–	–	–	1	–	–	–	1	–	–	–	–	–	–	1	–	–	–	–	2
Arson	–	–	–	1	–	–	–	–	–	1	–	1	–	–	–	–	–	–	–	–	–	1	–	–	–	1	–	–	1	–	1	1	–	–	–	–	–	–	–	–	–	–	–	1	–	–	–	–	–	–	–	–	–	–	–	9
Rape	–	–	–	–	–	–	–	–	–	–	1	–	–	–	–	–	–	–	–	–	1	–	–	–	–	1	–	1	–	1	1	1	2	–	–	–	–	–	–	–	–	–	–	–	–	–	–	–	–	–	–	–	–	–	–	3
Perjury	1	–	–	–	–	–	–	–	–	–	–	–	–	–	–	–	–	–	–	–	1	–	–	–	–	–	–	1	–	–	–	–	–	–	–	–	–	–	–	–	1	–	–	–	–	1	1	–	1	–	1	–	1	–	–	9
Manslaughter	2	1	1	–	–	–	–	–	–	–	–	2	–	–	–	–	–	–	–	–	–	1	–	–	–	3	–	1	–	–	–	–	1	–	–	–	2	–	–	1	–	–	1	1	–	–	–	–	1	–	–	2	1	–	1	7
Bigamy	–	–	–	–	–	1	–	–	–	–	–	–	–	–	–	–	–	1	–	–	–	1	–	–	–	2	–	–	–	–	–	–	–	–	–	–	1	–	–	1	–	–	1	2	1	–	–	2	1	–	–	1	1	–	1	4
Forgery	–	–	1	–	1	1	–	2	2	3	–	2	8	–	3	1	–	1	4	4	–	1	4	5	3	9	2	2	6	4	4	1	1	1	–	4	2	–	–	1	–	2	1	2	–	3	1	2	1	–	1	2	1	–	1	40
Burglary	4	2	–	–	2	–	–	1	–	–	1	1	10	–	–	1	–	1	2	1	–	–	1	6	1	16	6	4	1	5	2	1	3	2	1	1	6	–	–	6	3	2	1	2	1	3	–	2	1	–	1	1	1	–	–	64
Grand Larceny	15	2	1	1	2	2	–	1	3	–	1	1	–	–	–	1	–	1	1	1	–	3	1	9	1	82	1	3	1	1	1	1	–	3	1	4	9	–	–	1	1	–	1	1	1	–	1	1	1	–	1	1	1	–	–	179
Petit Larceny	5	–	1	–	1	–	–	1	2	–	1	2	–	–	1	1	1	1	2	–	–	1	1	3	3	90	2	3	1	1	2	–	1	3	1	1	14	–	–	–	1	–	1	2	1	3	1	2	1	–	1	1	1	–	1	157
P.Larceny 2d Offence	10	–	–	–	1	–	–	1	–	–	1	1	–	1	–	1	–	–	1	1	–	1	1	1	1	8	1	1	1	1	1	1	1	2	1	4	9	–	–	1	1	2	1	1	1	–	1	–	1	–	1	1	1	–	–	61
Assault to Rape	–	–	–	–	–	–	–	–	–	–	–	–	–	–	–	–	–	–	–	–	–	–	–	–	–	–	–	–	–	–	–	–	–	–	–	1	–	–	–	–	–	–	–	–	–	–	–	–	–	–	–	–	–	–	–	1
Ditto to Kill	–	–	–	–	–	–	–	–	–	–	–	–	1	–	1	–	1	1	–	–	–	–	1	1	–	3	–	3	–	–	1	1	–	3	1	1	9	–	–	–	–	2	–	1	–	–	1	–	1	–	1	–	–	–	–	9
Assault & Battery	53	1	1	1	4	2	–	1	1	2	13	9	10	1	1	2	3	1	3	2	–	3	2	12	3	112	4	1	1	3	3	1	6	6	1	9	11	–	–	2	4	4	1	2	1	–	1	–	8	–	1	3	–	–	–	304
Counterfeiting	6	–	–	1	1	–	–	1	–	1	1	1	–	–	–	–	–	–	–	5	–	1	1	–	1	–	–	–	1	1	–	–	1	2	–	1	1	–	–	4	1	1	–	2	1	–	–	–	–	–	–	3	–	–	–	21
Riot & Assault and Battery	–	–	–	–	–	–	–	–	–	–	–	–	–	1	–	5	–	–	–	–	–	5	–	1	–	4	–	–	1	–	–	–	–	–	–	–	4	–	–	–	–	–	–	–	–	–	–	–	4	–	–	–	–	–	–	–
Riot	7	–	–	1	–	–	–	–	1	1	–	–	–	1	–	1	1	1	1	1	–	4	–	4	1	–	–	–	3	1	1	1	–	1	–	–	5	–	–	–	–	1	–	1	–	–	–	–	–	–	–	–	–	–	1	29
Breaking Gaol	1	–	–	–	–	–	–	–	–	–	–	–	–	–	–	–	–	–	–	–	–	1	–	–	–	–	–	–	–	–	–	–	–	–	–	–	7	–	–	–	–	–	–	1	–	–	–	–	–	–	–	–	–	–	–	14
Swindling	5	–	–	1	–	–	–	2	–	–	–	2	–	–	–	1	–	2	1	3	–	–	1	3	1	9	–	–	–	–	–	1	–	–	1	–	2	–	–	2	–	1	–	–	–	–	–	–	–	–	–	–	–	–	–	6
Keeping Dis. House	5	–	–	–	1	2	–	1	1	–	–	1	1	–	–	–	–	1	–	6	–	2	–	6	1	2	–	–	–	1	–	1	–	–	–	–	1	–	–	–	1	–	1	4	–	–	–	–	–	–	–	–	–	–	–	30
Recg Stolen Goods	2	–	–	–	–	–	–	–	–	–	–	–	–	–	–	–	–	–	–	–	–	–	–	–	–	14	–	–	22	–	3	–	–	–	–	–	1	–	–	–	–	–	–	1	–	–	–	–	–	–	–	–	–	–	–	27
Misdemeanor	5	–	–	–	1	–	–	1	–	–	–	1	1	1	–	1	–	–	1	–	–	–	1	–	1	1	–	4	–	1	–	–	–	–	–	1	1	–	–	–	–	1	–	4	–	–	–	–	–	–	–	–	–	–	–	20
Robbery	–	–	–	–	1	–	–	–	–	–	–	–	–	–	–	1	–	–	–	–	–	1	1	–	–	4	–	–	–	1	–	–	–	2	–	–	1	–	–	–	–	1	–	–	–	–	–	–	–	–	–	–	–	–	–	65
Trespass	–	–	–	–	–	–	–	–	–	–	–	–	–	–	–	–	–	–	–	–	–	–	–	–	–	–	–	–	–	–	–	1	–	–	–	–	–	–	–	–	–	–	–	–	–	–	–	–	–	–	–	–	–	–	–	9
Offence agt Nature	–	–	–	1	–	2	–	–	–	–	–	–	–	–	–	–	–	–	–	–	–	–	–	–	–	1	–	–	–	–	–	–	–	–	–	–	–	–	–	–	–	–	–	–	–	–	–	–	–	–	–	–	–	–	–	6
Nuisance	3	–	–	–	–	–	–	–	–	–	–	–	–	–	–	–	–	–	–	–	–	–	–	–	–	–	–	–	–	–	–	–	–	2	–	–	–	–	–	–	–	1	–	1	–	–	–	–	–	–	–	–	–	–	2	1
Incest	–	–	–	–	–	2	–	–	–	–	–	–	–	–	–	–	–	–	–	–	–	–	–	–	–	1	–	–	–	–	–	–	–	–	–	2	–	–	–	–	–	–	–	–	–	–	–	–	–	–	–	–	–	–	–	6
Horse-Stealing	–	–	–	–	–	1	–	–	–	1	–	–	–	–	–	–	–	–	–	–	–	–	–	–	–	1	–	–	–	–	–	–	–	–	–	–	1	–	–	–	–	–	–	1	–	–	–	–	–	–	–	–	–	–	–	4
Libel	–	–	–	–	–	–	–	–	–	–	–	–	–	–	–	–	–	–	–	–	–	–	–	–	–	4	–	–	–	–	–	–	–	–	–	–	–	–	–	–	–	–	–	–	–	–	–	–	–	–	–	–	–	–	–	4
Conspiracy	–	–	–	–	–	–	–	–	–	–	–	–	–	–	–	–	–	–	–	–	–	–	–	–	–	–	–	–	–	–	–	–	–	–	–	–	1	–	–	–	–	–	–	–	–	–	–	–	–	–	–	–	–	–	–	1
TOTAL	124	3	3	3	11	8	3	8	11	8	15	22	34	5	5	14	5	5	11	22	1	22	8	49	15	366	17	18	36	16	16	11	13	20	2	14	75	–	–	14	6	11	3	14	2	4	1	4	16	1	1	7	3	1	2	1093

NEW JERSEY.

STATE PRISON AT LAMBERTON, NEAR TRENTON.

THIS Prison was erected in the year 1798. The arrangement of the building is very defective. It is at all times exceedingly difficult, and sometimes quite impossible, to maintain a proper system of discipline. The prisoners are employed at various trades, as coopers, nailers, shoemakers, weavers and stone-sawyers. The shops are very much subdivided. As there is no inspection but by the actual presence of the officers, when they are absent the prisoners neglect their work. The sleeping-rooms are not sufficiently numerous for individual separation at night, and the convicts are usually placed two, three, or four together in the same apartment. These dormitories are so badly constructed that the men can freely communicate through the doors and windows, and they can likewise hold intercourse with persons in the street. Another evil is that the rooms are removed as far as possible from the inspection and control of the officers, the apartment in which they assemble being separated from the passages leading to the cells. From the situation in which the night-watchman is placed, he cannot see any part of the building in which the prisoners are confined, nor ascertain whether the prisoners remain in the night-rooms, without entering them. The guard-room is situated at one corner of the building, and its position is such that it does not command a view either of the yard, the workshops, buildings, or walls of the prison. Here the keeper is employed a considerable time daily with the clerk in transacting the business of the establishment; and while thus occupied, he is of course entirely prevented from observing the conduct of the assistant-keepers, and of the prisoners. The workshops are placed in different parts of the yard without any systematic arrangement. The chapel is separated by several passages from the building in which the prisoners are lodged, so that much time and precaution are required when they attend divine service, in order to prevent mutual intercourse. The hospital is an old room, badly situated, and open to the other prisoners. It is imperfectly ventilated. The cookery is under the central building next the street, removed from the view of the keeper's office, and easily accessible to the prisoners. The position occupied by the guard or sentinel does not enable him to see the interior of the yard, nor does he command a view of the boundary wall. On three sides persons from without can approach the prison without the knowledge of the guard. In this manner, various articles are frequently conveyed to the prisoners who can also conceal themselves from observation in different parts of the buildings and yards. In consequence of these defects, escapes have taken place; as many at different times as one-twelfth part of the whole number; and if to these be added the frequent attempts which have been detected, the whole would furnish a proof of insecurity perhaps without a parallel.

In a late Report to a committee of the Legislature, the keeper has represented that great laxity prevails on the part of his assistants. It appears that an extensive system of traffic between the convicts and the under-keepers has been carried on in articles made in the prison. The keeper states that occurrences which take place in the town are known throughout the penitentiary within twenty-four hours. Separate confinement on an allowance of bread and water is the ordinary punishment. The period not unfrequently extends to 20 or 30 days, and this too in the winter season in cells which are not warmed. The cold is occasionally intense, and the health of the prisoners suffers in consequence so materially as to render them unfit to work. Nearly as much time is spent in enabling them on such occasions to recruit their strength as they have already passed in the cells for punishment. Chains are also used (sometimes with a weight of 56 lbs. attached to them) for the purpose of occasionally confining the prisoner to the place where he is at work. In a Report which was made by a late committee of inquiry it appears that a lad in confinement, 12 or 14 years of age, had, when they visited the prison, an iron neck-yoke placed on him with branches extending 18 or 20 inches. This yoke was used to prevent him from getting through the grates of his apartment. The clerk, who had been there twenty years, furnished the committee with a list of the names of ten prisoners who were supposed to have died in consequence of being severely punished in the cells for disobedience.

It is hardly necessary to state that the moral effects of confinement in this prison, so far from being beneficial, are most mischievous. It is a nursery for the encouragement of crime of every description. Religious instruction is very much neglected.

NEW JERSEY.

	Cents.	Mills.
The average daily cost of each prisoner's food is	4	8
Ditto - - - - Clothing	1	5
Ditto - - - - incidental Expenses	2	9
Ditto - - - - Officers' pay	9	4
Total	18	6

The average daily proportion of food for each prisoner is 1 lb. 4 oz. of bread ; 6 oz. of meat ; 1 gill of molasses, and 1 lb. of potatoes.

By the persevering exertions of a committee of inquiry appointed by the Legislature, a more vigilant system of superintendance has now been established, and many improvements are introduced in the general regulation of the prison. The expenditure also has been considerably reduced.

The average annual loss to the State from the time of the erection of the prison to the year 1832, was 5,304 dollars.

	Dollars.	Cents.
The expenses of the prison from 30th September 1832 to 1st of October 1833, were	5,124	39
Salary of keeper	1,000	–
Ditto of five assistant keepers	2,437	50
Clerk	550	–
Guard	273	75
Medical Attendant	75	–
Total expenditure	9,460	64

Receipts, profits on prisoners' labour, and stock on hand :—

	Dollars.	Cents.		
Weaving	4,450	66		
Cordwaining	1,030	77		
Smithery	664	55½		
Cooperage	92	7		
Stone-sawing	71	2		
Plaster-work	168	55		
Sundries	2,699	38½		
			9,177	01
Loss for the year			283	63

Number of prisoners in confinement on the 1st day of October 1832		128
Received since (in 1833)		47
Total		175
Discharged : By Expiration of sentence	24	
Pardons	22	
To service	1	
Escaped	1	
Died	1	
		49
Number in confinement on 30th September 1833		126

White men, 82 ; coloured men, 39 ; white females, 3 ; coloured females, 2—Total, 126. Americans, 114 ; English, 4 ; Irish, 6 ; Welsh, 1 ; West Indian, 1. Committed for first offence, 112 ; second offence, 8 ; third offence, 5 ; fifth offence, 1.

The prisoners were employed as follows :—In weaving, 29 ; spooling, 14 ; warping, 1 ; carding, 2 ; colouring yarn, 1 ; putting up cloth, 1 ; spinning, 3 ; shoemaking, 11 ; shoe-binding, 1 ; tailoring, 3 ; coopering, 2 ; carpentering, 1 ; smithing, 5 ; sawing stone, 1 ; pounding plaster, 3 ; labourers at New Prison, 26 ; cooking and baking, 4 ; washing, 1 ; sick, 2 ; attending sick, 1 ; employed in yard 3. Four insane men were confined in the cells ; six were infirm, unable to work ; for safe custody, 1—Total, 126.

In February 1833 an Act was passed by the Legislature, authorizing the erection of a new State Penitentiary. This building is to be rendered capable of holding 150 prisoners, on the principle of separate confinement with hard labour ; the plan to be so arranged that 150 cells may be added when requisite. The sum of 30,000 dollars is appropriated towards the erection of the said penitentiary which is to be constructed on the principle of that in Philadelphia.

The prison is now building agreeably to the annexed plan, which was designed by Mr. Haviland, the able architect of the Eastern Penitentiary. The ground inclosed is
contiguous

contiguous to the present prison, and is in the form of a parallelogram, about 500 feet in length and 320 feet in depth. The central part in front is occupied by the dwelling-house and offices of the warden, in the rear of which is a semi-circular observatory, 55 feet in diameter, from which as a centre the five wing-buildings radiate. These buildings contain the prisoners' solitary rooms and galleries. They consist of a range of cells placed on each side of a long corridor or passage 14 feet wide. The buildings are to be two stories high. On the upper story the cells will be entered from an iron gallery on each side, having a staircase next the centre. The cells are each 12 feet by 8 feet. They are to be arranged and fitted up in the same manner as those at the Eastern Penitentiary. Each cell is to contain a small privy, with a constant supply of water. No yards are provided, as it is not intended to let the prisoners out of the cells on any occasion. There is a large triangular piece of ground between each radiating building: good ventilation will, therefore, be insured. The whole will be enclosed with a lofty boundary wall having a guard-tower at each of the four external angles. From the central observatory there will be a complete view of the five corridors or galleries, into which all the prisoners' cells open. The entrance building will contain on the ground floor the apartments of the warden, and those of the inspector, the clerk's office, the general kitchen and bakery, and the rooms for the reception and examination of the prisoners.

The plan is designed to accommodate 300 prisoners; viz. 150 on each floor.

The following is the general estimate of the expense :—

										Dollars.
External wall - - - - - - - - - -										14,000
Front building, containing the culinary, laundry and bathing offices, store-room, keepers' chambers, observatory, reservoir, belfrey, and other rooms, fire proof - - - - - - -										15,000
Culvert, sinks, cast-iron pipes, covered ways, apparatus for cooking, warming and raising water into reservoirs - - - -										13,000

Five radiating blocks of cells :—

											Dollars.
A. containing	-	50 cells	-	-	-	-	-	-	-		18,000
B.	„	- 75	„	-	-	-	-	-	-		27,000
C.	„	- 50	„	-	-	-	-	-	-		18,000
D.	„	- 75	„	-	-	-	-	-	-		27,000
E.	„	- 50	„	-	-	-	-	-	-		18,000
Cells - -		300					Total - - -				150,000

NEW JERSEY.

NUMBER of Convicts committed to New Jersey State Prison at -   -   -

CRIMES.	1799.	1800.	1801.	1802.	1803.	1804.	1805.	1806.	1807.	1808.	1809.	1810.	1811.	1812.	1813.	1814.
Larceny	5	9	20	12	11	23	19	10	15	17	19	19	17	17	19	19
Misdemeanor	4	8	3	7	4	2	4	3	4	4	4	6	1	5	7	3
Arson	3	–	–	–	1	1	–	–	–	–	–	–	–	–	–	–
Assault and Battery with intent to Kill	2	2	5	4	1	4	3	2	3	5	–	1	2	1	3	2
Blasphemy	1	–	–	–	1	–	1	–	–	–	–	–	–	–	–	–
Horse stealing	2	3	6	3	1	1	3	1	2	1	5	2	1	1	–	–
Burglary	1	–	1	–	4	2	1	–	2	–	3	1	2	–	2	1
Felony	1	1	–	–	–	–	–	–	–	–	–	–	–	–	–	–
Burning Barns, &c.	–	1	1	–	–	–	2	1	–	–	1	–	–	–	–	–
Forgery	–	–	1	–	–	2	–	1	–	–	–	2	1	–	–	–
Perjury	–	–	1	1	2	2	1	–	–	–	–	1	–	1	–	–
Manslaughter	–	–	2	1	2	–	–	–	–	–	1	1	–	–	–	–
Sheep stealing	–	–	–	1	–	–	–	–	–	–	–	–	–	–	–	–
Stealing	–	–	–	1	–	4	4	1	4	2	3	–	–	2	–	3
Deceit	–	–	–	1	–	–	–	–	–	–	–	–	–	–	–	–
Breaking Gaol	–	–	–	1	–	–	1	–	2	–	–	–	1	–	–	2
Assault to commit Rape	–	–	–	1	1	1	2	–	4	1	1	1	–	–	–	–
Receiving Stolen Goods	–	–	–	–	–	–	1	–	–	1	–	–	–	1	–	1
Passing Counterfeit Money	–	–	–	1	–	–	–	–	–	–	1	3	–	1	–	–
Polygamy	–	–	–	1	–	–	–	–	–	–	–	–	–	–	–	–
Murder	–	–	–	–	–	1	–	–	–	–	–	1	–	1	–	1
Highway Robbery	–	–	–	–	–	–	1	–	–	–	–	–	–	–	1	1
Breaking open Store	–	–	–	–	–	–	–	1	–	–	–	–	–	–	–	–
Concealing Birth of Child	–	–	–	–	–	–	–	1	–	–	–	–	–	1	–	–
Rape	–	–	–	–	–	–	–	–	1	–	3	1	–	–	1	–
Housebreaking	–	–	–	–	–	–	–	–	–	1	–	–	2	–	–	–
Malicious Mischief	–	–	–	–	–	–	–	–	–	–	1	–	–	–	–	–
Assaulting Constable	–	–	–	–	–	–	–	–	–	–	–	1	–	–	–	–
Poisoning	–	–	–	–	–	–	–	–	–	–	–	–	–	–	1	–
Lewdness	–	–	–	–	–	–	–	–	–	–	–	–	–	–	–	–
TOTALS	19	24	40	33	35	43	43	21	37	32	42	40	27	31	34	33

AGES.	1799.	1800.	1801.	1802.	1803.	1804.	1805.	1806.	1807.	1808.	1809.	1810.	1811.	1812.	1813.	1814.
15 to 20 years old	4	4	1	6	2	5	4	1	6	1	5	5	3	1	5	6
20 to 30 "	5	8	15	7	17	21	22	9	19	17	21	14	15	10	17	18
30 to 40 "	7	6	12	8	9	10	10	1	8	7	10	11	3	9	7	5
40 to 50 "	1	3	6	8	6	4	1	5	4	3	5	5	4	5	4	2
50 to 60 "	2	2	5	2	1	2	3	4	–	4	1	2	2	4	1	2
60 to 70 "	–	1	1	1	–	–	2	1	–	–	–	2	–	2	–	–
70 to 80 "	–	–	–	1	–	1	1	–	–	–	–	1	–	–	–	–
TOTALS	19	24	40	33	35	43	43	21	37	32	42	40	27	31	34	33

PLACES of NATIVITY.	1823.	1824.
United States	36	29
England	–	–
Scotland	1	1
Ireland	1	3
Canada	1	–
Germany	–	–
Denmark	1	–
Unknown	2	–
	42	33

The number of pardons average 25 in a year, principally

- - - LAMBERTON, near TRENTON, from its commencement to 30 June 1833.   NEW JERSEY.

1815.	1816.	1817.	1818.	1819.	1820.	1821.	1822.	1823.	1824.	1825.	1826.	1827.	1828.	1829.	1830.	1831.	1832.	To 30 June 1833.
30	35	44	27	29	19	10	15	11	8	12	15	16	10	16	20	25	22	7
5	7	5	3	8	11	2	10	8	7	6	4	13	13	4	4	7	3	1
—	1	1	—	—	1	—	—	—	—	—	1	—	—	—	2	1	—	—
4	5	2	6	2	5	—	3	7	6	1	3	4	5	4	9	9	6	2
1	1	—	1	—	—	—	—	—	—	—	—	—	—	—	—	—	—	—
—	2	3	—	1	2	3	2	—	—	2	—	1	3	3	2	—	—	—
—	2	3	1	1	2	7	3	3	—	.5	2	4	—	4	1	5	6	7
—	—	—	—	—	—	—	—	—	—	—	—	—	—	—	—	—	—	—
—	—	—	1	1	—	—	1	1	—	1	2	—	1	1	2	2	—	1
—	1	1	—	1	—	—	2	—	1	—	1	1	1	—	2	4	1	1
—	1	—	1	—	—	—	—	—	—	—	—	—	—	—	—	—	—	—
2	2	—	—	1	—	—	—	2	3	—	—	—	—	—	2	2	1	—
—	—	—	—	—	—	—	—	—	—	—	—	—	—	—	—	—	—	—
—	—	—	5	2	1	—	1	—	2	1	2	—	1	—	—	—	—	—
—	—	—	—	—	—	·	—	1	—	—	—	—	—	—	—	—	—	—
—	1	1	1	—	—	—	2	—	—	—	—	1	2	2	—	—	—	1
1	2	—	—	1	1	1	—	—	1	—	1	2	2	1	—	—	2	1
—	—	—	—	—	1	2	—	—	1	—	—	—	—	—	—	1	—	—
—	—	3	3	—	—	3	—	5	1	4	1	—	1	—	5	3	1	1
—	—	—	—	—	—	—	—	1	—	—	—	1	1	—	—	1	—	—
1	1	—	—	1	—	—	1	1	1	—	—	—	—	—	—	—	—	—
—	3	—	2	—	—	—	1	—	—	—	1	—	—	—	—	—	—	—
—	—	—	—	—	—	—	2	—	—	—	1	1	1	—	2	2	2	—
—	—	—	—	—	—	—	—	1	—	—	—	—	—	—	—	—	—	—
—	1	—	—	1	—	—	—	2	1	—	—	1	—	—	3	—	1	1
2	—	—	—	3	4	1	—	—	—	—	—	2	—	—	6	3	—	—
—	—	—	—	—	—	—	—	—	—	—	—	—	—	—	—	1	—	1
—	—	—	—	—	—	—	—	—	—	—	—	—	—	—	1	—	—	1
1	—	—	—	—	—	—	—	—	—	—	—	—	—	—	—	—	—	—
47	**64**	**63**	**51**	**52**	**47**	**29**	**43**	**42**	**33**	**32**	**34**	**46**	**41**	**36**	**61**	**65**	**46**	**24**

1815.	1816.	1817.	1818.	1819.	1820.	1821.	1822.	1823.	1824.	1825.	1826.	1827.	1828.	1829.	1830.	1831.	1832.	To 30 June 1833.
2	2	8	7	8	7	1	3	7	4	3	5	2	2	9	9	8	8	4
21	32	26	26	27	26	17	22	17	16	16	20	20	19	14	34	32	16	11
9	19	17	12	12	7	9	11	10	9	12	7	12	15	6	14	13	11	7
10	4	7	3	2	4	1	4	5	1	1	1	5	1	4	3	10	6	1
5	5	4	2	2	2	1	3	3	1	—	1	2	1	2	1	2	3	1
—	2	1	1	1	1	—	—	—	1	—	—	4	2	1	—	—	—	—
—	—	—	—	—	—	—	—	—	1	—	—	1	1	—	—	—	—	—
47	**64**	**63**	**51**	**52**	**47**	**29**	**43**	**42**	**33**	**32**	**34**	**46**	**41**	**36**	**61**	**65**	**46**	**24**

1825.	1826.	1827.	1828.	1829.	1830.	1831.	1832.
27	28	42	37	30	51	63	39
—	—	1	2	2	2	1	6
—	2	—	—	—	1	—	—
3	2	1	1	4	7	1	1
—	—	—	1	—	—	—	—
1	—	—	—	—	—	—	—
1	—	—	—	—	—	—	—
—	2	2	—	—	—	—	—
32	**34**	**46**	**41**	**36**	**61**	**65**	**46**

owing to the want of room in the prison.

PUNISHMENTS for the principal OFFENCES in this STATE.

OFFENCES.		PUNISHMENTS.
Abduction - -	Or aiding therein - - - . -	Fine and imprisonment at hard labour not exceeding ten years.
	Of a Child under 15 - - -	Fine and imprisonment at hard labour not exceeding five years.
	Taking away child under 15, with intent to marry, &c.	Fine and imprisonment at hard labour not exceeding two years, or either.
Accessaries - -	- - After the fact; concealment of murder, manslaughter, sodomy, rape, arson, burglary, robbery or forgery.	- - Fine not exceeding $ 500, or imprisonment at hard labour not exceeding three years, or both.
Adultery - -	- - - - - - -	Fine not exceeding $ 100, or imprisonment not exceeding six months.
Arson, &c. - -	Burning dwelling-house - -	Fine and imprisonment at hard labour not exceeding fifteen years.
	Second offence - - - -	Death.
	Burning public buildings, mills, out-houses, &c. and accessaries.	Fine and imprisonment at hard labour not exceeding ten years, or either.
	Setting fire to buildings with intent to burn, and accessaries.	Fine and imprisonment at hard labour not exceeding five years, or either.
Assault - - -	and Battery - - . - -	Fine not exceeding $ 100, and imprisonment not exceeding six months.
	With intent to rob - - -	- - Fine not exceeding $ 500, or imprisonment at hard labour not exceeding ten years, or both.
Bastardy, &c. -	Concealing the death of a bastard child.	- - Fine not exceeding $ 200, and imprisonment at hard labour not exceeding one year, either or both.
	Concealing pregnancy, when the child if born would be a bastard, and being delivered of such child in secret.	- - Fine not exceeding $ 100, and confinement in cells of State prison at hard labour not exceeding four months, either or both.
Bigamy - - -	- - - - - - -	Fine and imprisonment at hard labour not exceeding ten years, or either.
Blasphemy - -	- - - - - - -	- - Fine not exceeding $ 200, or imprisonment at hard labour not exceeding one year, or both.
Bribery, Embracery, &c.	Bribing a judge or justice, or judge or justice accepting a bribe.	- - Fine not exceeding $ 800, and imprisonment at hard labour not exceeding five years, or both, and for ever disqualified for holding any office in the State.
	A juror taking an illegal reward -	- - Fine not exceeding $ 600, and confinement in cells of State prison not exceeding two years, with or without hard labour; disqualified as juror.
	Attempts to influence a juror or jury unlawfully or corruptly.	- - Fine not exceeding $ 300, or imprisonment not exceeding one year, with or without hard labour, or both.
Burglary, &c. - -	Breaking dwelling-house by night, with intent to commit a felony.	- - Fine not exceeding $ 500, and imprisonment at hard labour not exceeding ten years, or either.
	Second offence - - - -	Death.
	House-breaking by day, with felonious intent.	- - Fine not exceeding $ 500, or imprisonment at hard labour not exceeding ten years, or both.
	Entering dwelling-house, shop, &c. either by day or night, without breaking, with intent to kill, rob, steal, &c.	- - Fine not exceeding $ 300, or imprisonment at hard labour not exceeding five years, or both.
Coin. See Forgery.		
Compounding, or agreeing to compound.	- - Treason, misprision of treason, murder, robbery, &c. (including nearly all serious offences.)	- - Fine not exceeding $ 300, or imprisonment at hard labour not exceeding twelve months, or both.
Conspiracy - -	To indict any person, or cause him to be indicted.	- - Fine not exceeding $ 500, or imprisonment at hard labour not exceeding two years, or both,
Duelling - -	- - Fighting a duel where death does not ensue, or being a second, or aiding and abetting.	- - Fine not exceeding $ 1,000, and imprisonment at hard labour not exceeding four years, or both.
	Challenging to fight a duel, though no duel be fought, or bearing a challenge, or aiding and abetting, &c.	- - Fine not exceeding $ 500, and imprisonment at hard labour not exceeding two years, or both.
Embezzlement -	- - Servants or apprentices above 14 years of age entrusted with money, goods, &c. by their masters, who shall run away with or embezzle the same.	- - Fine not exceeding $ 100, or imprisonment at hard labour not exceeding two years, or both.

⊙

PUNISHMENTS for the principal Offences in this State—*continued*.

OFFENCES.		PUNISHMENTS.
Escape, &c. - -	Rescuing prisoners, and officers guilty of voluntary escapes in capital cases.	Death.
	Rescuing prisoners in cases not capital, or in any civil cases, or voluntary escape suffered by officer in cases not capital, or negligent escapes in any criminal cases.	- - Fine not exceeding $ 1,000, or imprisonment at hard labour not exceeding three years, or both, and officers disqualified for any office for ever after, in voluntary cases.
	Prisoner, not confined for capital offence, breaking prison.	- - Fine not exceeding $ 1,000, or imprisonment at hard labour not exceeding three years, or both.
	Assisting prisoner in gaol to escape, by supplying any disguise, arms, tools, &c. or assisting prisoner to escape from officer.	- - Fine not exceeding $ 500, and imprisonment at hard labour not exceeding two years, or both.
	Offenders sentenced to hard labour, and escaping.	- - Such additional sentence to hard labour as the court before which they are convicted shall direct.
Extortion - -	By officer - - - - -	- - Fine not exceeding $ 400, or imprisonment with or without hard labour not exceeding two years, or both.
	By threatening letters, &c. -	- - Fine not exceeding $ 300, or imprisonment at hard labour not exceeding nine months, or both.
Forgery, &c. -	General - - - - -	Fine or imprisonment at hard labour not exceeding ten years, or both.
	Second offence - - - -	Death.
	Counterfeiting or knowingly passing counterfeit coin, uttering or possessing with intent to utter forged bank notes, &c., making or having plates for engraving notes, &c.	- - Fine not exceeding $ 2,000, and imprisonment at hard labour not exceeding ten years.
Fornication - -	- - - - - - -	Fine $ 14.
Fraud, Imposture, &c. *See* also Malicious Mischief.	- - Stealing or avoiding records, whereby any judgment is reversed, and those aiding and abetting.	- - Fine not exceeding $ 7,000, and imprisonment at hard labour not exceeding seven years, or both.
	The same, when judgment is not reversed.	- - Fine not exceeding $ 1,000, or imprisonment at hard labour not exceeding four years, or both.
	Acknowledging fines, recoveries, deeds, bail, judgments, &c. in the names of others not privy thereto, or personating others as bail.	- - Fine not exceeding $ 7,000, imprisonment at hard labour not exceeding seven years.
	Using any false tokens, or writing to obtain money or goods with intent to cheat or defraud.	- - Fine not exceeding $ 1,000, or imprisonment at hard labour not exceeding three years.
	Pretending to exercise witchcraft, or by occult science to discover stolen goods, &c.	- - Fine not exceeding $ 50, or imprisonment at hard labour not exceeding three months, or both.
	Religious impostors (receiving divine honours, or uttering denunciations.)	- - Fine not exceeding $ 100, or imprisonment not exceeding six months, or both.
Incest - - -	- - - - - - - -	- - Fine not exceeding $ 500, and solitary imprisonment in cells not exceeding 18 months, or both.
Kidnapping - -	- - - - - - -	- - Fine not exceeding $ 1,000, or imprisonment at hard labour not exceeding five years, or both.
Larceny - - *See* also Embezzlement, Robbery.	Stealing under the value of $ 20 -	- - Fine not exceeding $ 100, or imprisonment at hard labour in county gaol or whipping not exceeding 39 lashes.
	Stealing to the value of $ 20 or upwards.	- - Fine not exceeding $ 500, or imprisonment at hard labour not exceeding ten years, or both.
	Stealing deeds, wills, letters of attorney, &c.	- - Fine not exceeding $ 500, or imprisonment at hard labour not exceeding ten years, or both.
	Lodgers stealing goods from their lodging.	- - Fine not exceeding $ 200, or imprisonment at hard labour not exceeding two years, or both.
	Persons stealing lead from a house, or corn or grass, &c. growing.	- - Fine not exceeding $ 50, or imprisonment at hard labour not exceeding nine months, or both.
	Stealing fruit or vegetables by night	Fine not exceeding $ 50, or imprisonment not exceeding three months, or both.

wn,

wn,

MASSACHUSETTS.

STATE PRISON AT CHARLESTOWN, NEAR BOSTON.

THIS state prison is situated in the western extremity of Charlestown. The walls which are 18 feet high enclose a quadrangular space, about 500 feet in length and 240 feet in width, and are bounded on the northern and western sides by a creek and river. Adjoining the prison on the south side is a commodious wharf. The buildings of the old prison erected in 1805 consist of two wings, with the warden's apartments and guard-room in the centre. In the rear of these buildings is a garden, and a warehouse next the wharf. Along the top of the prison walls is a platform on which several watch-boxes for sentinels are placed at convenient distances. On the west side a basin has been constructed for admitting canal boats, by which stone, wood, &c. are conveyed into the prison through an opening, which is secured by strong gates. Near this dock is a large shed, 130 feet long and 60 feet wide, open to the roof, in which the convicts are employed in cutting and working stone. There are also several workshops occupied by cabinet makers, tailors, shoemakers, brushmakers, coopers and blacksmiths.

The new prison-building is erected on the east side of the quadrangular space, and contains a range of cells, placed back to back (as at Auburn), with an enclosed area. This building is 200 feet long and 46 feet wide. There are four stories, comprising 304 separate cells. They are built of granite. Each story is covered at the top with large flooring stones. The cells have distinct ventilators in the partition wall between the two ranges of cells, communicating with the external air by flues or chimneys at the top. The doors are of wrought iron, with gratings in the upper part. Each cell is seven feet long, seven feet high, and three feet six inches wide. Stone galleries, three feet wide, are placed on a level with the floors of the cells, and supported by cast-iron pillars, with railings to prevent accidents to the convicts as they march along the galleries to and from their cells. The galleries extend on both sides the whole length of the range of cells. The cell-building is warmed by four stoves, placed in the exterior angles of the area below. The new prison is provided at night with lamps which afford light sufficient to see a person on the galleries, staircases, or area, from the outside gallery. By signal bells, a communication is kept up between the watchmen in the area and those in the guard-room. On the western front of the prison is a new building containing the cookery. The food is passed through apertures in the wall to the convicts, who receive it at the porch as they march from labour (in divisions by single files) to their cells, where they eat their meals in solitude. The porch forms a passage into the new prison, between the cookery and chapel. The chapel is conveniently warmed by steam emitted from the boiler in the cookery, which passing through iron tubes is received into a copper reservoir, and thence extended round the walls so as to produce a sufficient degree of heat.

This prison is for the reception of male convicts only. The roll is called at about day-break in winter, and a short time before sunrise in summer. The prisoners are formed into eight divisions, each being limited to 38, the number of cells in each gallery. The first and second divisions being composed of old men and the prisoners last received, are united under the superintendence of one officer, so that seven turnkeys are required to take charge of the whole. The prisoners, on the word of command being given, open their cell doors, take up their utensils, form into single file, and march forward, followed by the other divisions in the same manner; the turnkeys exercising the strictest vigilance in order to prevent any communication between the prisoners. After emptying their night buckets they proceed to their respective workshops. When the breakfast hour arrives, (which varies according to the time of year, from seven to eight) the convicts, having previously washed, repair at the sound of a bell, in files, to the parade ground, where they arrange themselves and return to their cells, taking on their way their rations which have been placed ready for them. The prisoners on entering their cells, nearly close the doors, so that the officer in command of the division, on shutting them, sees the prisoner's face ; and on going round again to ascertain that the doors are fast, he requires each man to pass his finger through the grating. At the end of about twelve minutes from the time of ringing the bell for breakfast, every convict is in his cell. One assistant only is left in charge to preserve silence. Each officer then reports to the deputy-keeper the number of men in his division. In about half an hour from the ringing of the bell, the whole body of convicts again return to the workshops. On their way thither they repair to the chapel to attend prayers. Dinner takes place between twelve and one ; the time allowed is about 25 minutes in winter, and 35 in summer. When the bell rings for quitting work in the evening, the convicts having first washed form into divisions, and on being searched by their respective officers are conducted into chapel to attend service as in the morning. In the mean time one of the overseers inspects the work-rooms to guard against fire. As soon as evening service is ended, the divisions march from chapel, taking with them their suppers, and also their night-buckets, and entering their cells as before. The doors having been closed, and the prisoners inspected in the same manner as at dinner and breakfast, the convicts are now locked up for the night, and committed to the charge of a single sentinel. The evening locking-up occupies about 40 minutes from the time that the prisoners quit work. When in their cells, they are allowed to read until eight o'clock in winter, and nine in summer, as lights are for that purpose kept in the passages. Reading aloud is never permitted. The first watch lasts from locking-up time until midnight; the second until the prisoners are let out in the morning. This is the routine throughout the week.

On Sundays the convicts remain in their cells, except during their attendance at divine service which is performed in the forenoon. They are marched to and from chapel, in the manner already described. A school is previously held for a short time, principally for the instruction of those who cannot read. The average number of scholars during the year 1833, was about 120. Teachers belonging to various congregations in Boston are allowed to attend. Every convict throughout the prison has a bible, and such tracts as the chaplain shall approve. On the return of the prisoners to their cells, the chaplain devotes the remainder of the day to the visiting of a certain number.

At the commencement of the present year there were 250 prisoners in confinement. They were employed as follows :—

Stone-cutters, 82 ; team-hands, 15 ; carpenters, 2 ; tool-grinders, 2 ; blacksmiths, 18 ; cabinet-makers, on contract, 38 ; brush-makers, on contract, 29 ; hatters, on contract, 6 ; firemen, on contract, 5 ; whitesmiths, 3 ; coopers, 3 ; shoemakers, 12 ; tailors, 5 ; employed in washing and baking, 8 ; sawyers and lumpers, 3 ; waiters and messengers, 3 ;* cleaning the prison, 2 ; barbers, 2 ; attendant in the hospital, 1. There were ten patients in the hospital : one prisoner was imbecile. Besides the employments in the shops, all the stone and materials are conveyed from the river by convicts.

In the performance of their various occupations, silence is strictly enjoined, the prisoners not being permitted to speak to each other, to the officers, or to the contractors for whom they are employed, except when necessary. They are not allowed to stand or move two abreast, except when the nature of their labour absolutely requires it. Conversation, except when indispensable, is prohibited among the officers in the presence of the prisoners, and the greatest quiet is imposed upon the messengers in the discharge of their duties.

The yearly allowance of clothing to each prisoner is two pairs of trowsers, two jackets, two pairs of shoes, two pairs of socks, three shirts and two blankets. Each cell is provided with a cot-frame and canvass sacking, a stool, a night-bucket and water-can, a knife and fork, a spoon, a pot for coffee, and a tin vessel to contain the convict's food. Clean linen is distributed weekly. The convicts are shaved twice a week. During the summer the prisoners may bathe once in the course of the week for ten minutes in the canal whither they are marched in single file. The allowance of food for each convict is one pound of beef, or 12 ounces of pork, 10 ounces of rye-meal, 10 ounces of Indian meal, and $\frac{3}{4}$ of a gill of molasses. For every hundred rations, two and a half bushels of potatoes, or other vegetables, (at the discretion of the warden) not exceeding the cost of the potatoes; two quarts of vinegar, four quarts of salt, and two ounces of black pepper ; and two quarts of rye or barley to be made into a warm drink, and supplied night and morning. During six months of the warmest season of the year, beer (in the proportion of four quarts of molasses and twelve ounces of hops,) is served once, twice, or three times a-day, according to the heat of the weather, and in quantities proportioned to the degree of labour at which the prisoners are employed. The diet of those in the hospital is regulated by the physician. Such as are in solitary confinement are kept on bread and water, unless it appears to the physician that their health requires other treatment. The cost of the daily rations is $7\frac{7}{8}$ cents per man.

The most ordinary offences of the convicts are inattention to their work, disobedience of orders, and talking. In cases of misconduct, the offender at the evening muster is left out of the division. The nature of his offence is then reported by the officer to the warden or his deputy, and the prisoner is admonished, or punished by being flogged with a " cat."

A convict is never flogged before other prisoners, nor unless the warden or his deputy be present. The officer who reports the misconduct of a convict is never permitted to flog him. From the 1st to the 9th July (the period of my visit) there were nine punishments, but this was stated to be beyond the average number. Solitary confinement when forming part of a sentence, is enforced for a few days only. In case of any act of insubordination, or open resistance, the officer is authorized to have recourse to force to compel submission, and the sentinels on the walls have orders immediately to use their fire-arms on observing an assault upon any of the officers.

The most defective part of the establishment is the hospital, which is part of the old prison. The imperfect means of inspection and superintendence, arising from its faulty construction, is the constant subject of complaint. Conversation is necessarily allowed. When the patient is in a state of convalescence, he is employed at some light kind of work, but kept carefully from communicating with the other prisoners. He is not allowed to quit the building, except to take the exercise prescribed by the physician, on which occasion he is circumspectly watched.

Visitors are permitted to see the prison upon payment of 25 cents. They may walk in the yard, and as far as the doors of the workshops, but are not allowed to enter the shops

or

---

* Infirm, but well behaved convicts.

or the hospital. No discharged convict is admitted as a visitor, except under peculiar circumstances.* Visitors are excluded on Sundays, except a certain number of school teachers, and such others as have obtained the consent of the warden and chaplain to attend divine service. The money collected by the admission of visitors forms a fund from which the convict is furnished with pecuniary aid on his discharge.

The officers of the prison are three inspectors, a warden, deputy warden, chaplain, surgeon and clerk. There are also nine overseers and ten watchmen. The duty of the inspectors is to visit the prison either singly or together once a week, and to meet at a board once a month to see that the regulations are observed, and to make such other rules as may be necessary for carrying the law into effect. The warden, in whom all the property, stock, implements, &c. is vested, makes the contracts. It is also his duty to ascertain that the accounts are properly prepared for the visits of the inspectors, and to furnish the secretary of the State with an account, half yearly, of receipts and disbursements, and also a general report in detail on the state of the prison. The duty of the deputy warden, besides the general charge which devolves on him in the absence of the warden, is daily to visit and inspect the hospital, cookery, and work-rooms; to attend to the proper use and application of the property and goods belonging to the prison, and to report any inattention on the part of the officers. He has also to keep a particular account of the number of convicts received or discharged, to receive reports from the officers of the men under their charge three times a-day, to admonish such as are disorderly, or order them to be punished; and to instruct in their respective trades those who have been just received. The chaplain is required to devote himself exclusively to the service of the prison. The convicts attend prayers morning and evening throughout the week. The chaplain can at his discretion send for any of the convicts to converse with them in private. He also occasionally communicates with the friends of the convicts on their behalf. All letters written to or by the convicts are submitted to him before delivery. The physician visits the hospital daily, or oftener if occasion require it. The turnkeys superintend the prisoners while at work, and also conduct them to and from their cells. Three of these officers, together with as many watchmen, form the nightly prison guard. Five sentinels keep guard on the walls during the hours of labour. Their attention is specially directed to those convicts who are employed on the wharf and without the walls.

The present board of inspectors was appointed in the year 1828. The following has been the financial result of the operations at this penitentiary since that period:

						$.	Cents.
In the year ending September 30th, 1828, there was a loss of						12,167	07
Ditto	-	ditto	-	1829	- - -	7,599	70
Ditto	-	ditto	-	1830	- - -	6,897	02
Ditto	-	ditto	-	1831	- - -	477	31
Ditto	-	ditto	-	1832 a profit of -	-	4,192	32
Ditto	-	ditto	-	1833 a profit of -	-	6,995	57

This penitentiary is extremely well conducted. The attention which is paid to the moral and religious improvement of the convicts is highly creditable to the State, and to the excellent chaplain to whose care they are confided. The privilege which he enjoys of conferring at all times in private with a prisoner affords him great advantages. The comparatively limited number under his charge enables him to gain a knowledge of the minds of individuals, which the chaplains of such large prisons as Auburn and Sing Sing cannot possibly acquire.

The discipline, generally, is strictly maintained, but not without the infliction of the whip, a punishment which under any circumstances cannot fail to harden, and excite feelings of debasement and revenge. The abuse of this punishment is, however, carefully guarded against. A prisoner can at any time have a private interview with and submit his complaints to an inspector. The misconduct of an offender is not reported in a momentary feeling of anger, but at the close of the day; and in no case is an officer allowed to punish a prisoner against whom he brings a charge. Flogging is never inflicted until the particulars of the case have been fully investigated by the warden, or his deputy, and an opportunity has been afforded to the prisoner of being heard in his defence.

DISBURSEMENTS

* The regulations prohibit the admission of any intoxicated person, or one habited in a "ridiculous costume."

MASSACHUSETTS.

DISBURSEMENTS and INCOME for the Year ending September 30th, 1833.

Dr		$.	Cents.	Cr		$.	Cents.
To cash paid for provisions	-	6,621	84	By stone department, profits	-	19,609	31
Ditto - clothing - - -	-	2,537	92	Ditto labour - - - -	-	10,988	39
Ditto - hospital expenses	-	256	59	Ditto fees of admittance -	-	949	75
Ditto - fuel, repairs, &c.	-	2,601	37	Ditto coopering department	-	647	48
Ditto - officers' salaries	-	13,050	00	Ditto fixtures and tools -	-	333	43
Ditto - prisoners discharged	-	352	25	Ditto sales of sundry merchan-			
Ditto - conveyance of convicts		678	34	dize - - - -	-	185	29
Ditto - peculiar sickness	-	28	55	Ditto profits and loss, for interest		408	78
Balance, being profits	-	6,995	57				
	$.	33,122	43		$.	33,122	43

Balance, being excess of income over expenditure for the year   -   - $. 6,995. 57.

Number of convicts remaining in confinement, 1st October 1832	227
Received during the year ending 30th September 1833 - -	119
	346
Discharged during the year, by expiration of sentence - 79	
Discharged by remission of sentence - - - - 7	
Ditto by order of court - - - - - 4	
Died - - - - - - - - - 6	
	96
In prison 30th September 1833 - - - - - - -	250

AGES of the PRISONERS remaining in Custody.

From 15 to 20 years - - - - - -	19
— 20 to 25 „ - - - - - -	52
— 25 to 30 „ - - - - - -	53
— 30 to 35 „ - - - - - -	39
— 35 to 40 „ - - - - - -	37
— 40 to 50 „ - - - - - -	38
— 50 to 60 „ - - - - - -	9
— 60 to 70 „ - - - - - -	2
— 70 to 80 „ - - - - - -	1
TOTAL - - -	250

SENTENCES.

For 6 months - - - - -	6	For 7 years - - - - -	13
1 year - - - - -	22	8 ditto - - - - -	4
1¼ ditto - - - - -	1	9 ditto - - - - -	1
1½ ditto - - - - -	2	10 ditto - - - - -	10
2 ditto - - - - -	59	11⅔ ditto - - - - -	1
2½ ditto - - - - -	1	13 ditto - - - - -	1
3 ditto - - - - -	27	14 ditto - - - - -	2
3½ ditto - - - - -	4	15 ditto - - - - -	2
4 ditto - - - - -	16	17 ditto - - - - -	1
4½ ditto - - - - -	3	20 ditto - - - - -	1
5 ditto - - - - -	21	For Life - - - - -	40
5½ ditto - - - - -	4		
6 ditto - - - - -	7	TOTAL - - -	250
6½ ditto - - - - -	1		

STATES and COUNTRIES of which the Prisoners are Natives.

Massachusetts - - - -	110	England - - - - - -	11
Maine - - - - -	14	Scotland - - - - - -	8
New Hampshire - - - -	29	Ireland - - - - - -	26
Vermont - - - - -	4	British Provinces in North America -	5
Rhode Island - - - - -	9	France - - - - - -	1
Connecticut - - - - -	5	Belgium - - - - - -	1
New York - - - - -	6	Italy - - - - - -	2
New Jersey - - - - -	1	Naples - - - - - -	1
Pennsylvania - - - - -	5	Sweden - - - - - -	2
Maryland - - - - -	5	West Indies - - - - - -	1
Virginia - - - - - -	1		
Louisania - - - - - -	1	TOTAL - - -	250
District of Colombia - - -	1		
Florida - - - - - -	1		

CRIMES

⊙

CRIMES of which the Prisoners were Convicted.

Larceny - - - - - - -	150	Burglary - - - - -	21
Assault and Larceny - - -	2	Forgery - - - - -	5
Passing, or having counterfeit money -	5	Adultery - - - - -	4
Assault with intent to kill - - -	12	Bestiality - - - - -	1
Felonious Assault - - - -	3	Burning Barns - - - -	2
Assault and Battery - - - -	1	Malicious burning - - - -	1
Murder, sentence commuted - -	3	Cheating - - - - -	2
Poisoning with intent to murder - -	1	Obtaining goods under false pretences	1
Attempt to poison - - - -	1		
Attempt at rape - - - -	6		250
Common and notorious Thieves - -	8		

On the 23d February 1818, an Act was passed by the Legislature, subjecting those convicts to an additional sentence who shall have been discharged from this prison and re-convicted of new offences. The following statement contains the number of commitments, and re-commitments in each year.

Year.	Commitments.	Re-commitments.
1819 - - -	96 - - -	19
1820 - - -	73 - - -	16
1821 - - -	85 - - -	16
1822 - - -	89 - - -	21
1823 - - -	106 - - -	20
1824 - - -	86 - - -	13
1825 - - -	96 - - -	27
1826 - - -	81 - - -	24
1827 - - -	80 - - -	14
1828 - - -	102 - - -	13
1829 - - -	79 - - -	15
1830 - - -	115 - - -	19
1831 - - -	72 - - -	14
1832 - - -	76 - - -	15
1833 - - -	119 - - -	15

Since the 1st of April 1828, 506 convicts have been discharged. Of that number 33 are now again in confinement in this penitentiary.

MASSACHUSETTS.   NUMBER of CONVICTS committed to the MASSACHUSETTS STATE PRISON   -   -

CRIMES.	1806.		1808.	1809.	1810.	1811.	1812.	1813.	1814.
Murder commuted	—	—	—	—	—	—	—	—	—
Manslaughter	1	1	—	—	—	—	—	—	1
Horse stealing	1	2	4	2	—	—	—	1	1
Burglary	2	3	9	—	4	2	1	3	1
Forgery	4	6	5	9	7	5	7	3	5
Having and passing Counterfeit Money	5	4	21	20	18	10	12	6	7
Rape	—	—	—	—	—	—	2	—	—
Assault to commit a Rape	—	—	—	—	—	1	—	—	1
Assault to kill	—	—	—	—	—	—	—	2	—
Assault and Battery	—	7	1	1	2	—	—	1	1
Theft, Stealing and Larceny	25	32	45	64	51	49	48	84	72
Fraud, and conspiracy to defraud	2	—	—	—	—	—	—	3	—
Common and notorious Thief	—	—	—	—	—	—	—	—	—
Burning Barn, Hay, Gaol, &c.	—	—	1	—	—	3	1	—	1
House and Store-breaking	—	—	2	—	2	1	1	3	4
Highway Robbery	—	—	1	—	2	—	—	1	1
Indecent behaviour	—	—	—	—	—	—	—	—	—
Arson	—	—	—	—	—	1	—	—	1
Receiving stolen Goods	—	—	—	—	—	1	1	1	—
Sodomy	—	—	—	—	—	—	1	—	—
Concealing Birth of Child	—	—	—	—	—	—	—	1	—
Shooting Indians	—	—	—	—	—	—	—	—	2
Perjury	—	—	—	—	—	—	—	—	—
Breaking Gaol, and aiding to break ditto	—	—	—	—	—	—	—	—	—
Sheep-stealing	—	—	—	—	—	—	—	—	—
Fornication	—	—	—	—	—	—	—	—	—
Adultery	—	—	—	—	—	—	—	—	—
Polygamy	—	—	—	—	—	—	—	—	—
Maiming Cattle	—	—	—	—	—	1	—	—	—
Swindling	—	—	—	—	—	—	—	—	—
Bestiality	—	—	—	—	—	—	—	—	—
Poisoning	—	—	—	—	—	—	—	—	—
Aiding to rescue a Convict	—	—	—	—	—	—	—	—	—
TOTAL	40	55	89	96	86	74	74	109	98
Of the above numbers there were—									
Coloured People	1	4	14	21	7	4	8	33	23
Pardons granted	—	—	5	4	8	27	22	10	18
Deaths	—	—	—	—	—	—	—	—	—
Second Convictions	—	—	—	—	—	—	—	—	—
Third ditto	—	—	—	—	—	—	—	—	—
Fourth ditto	—	—	—	—	—	—	—	—	—
Fifth ditto	—	—	—	—	—	—	—	—	—
	—	—	—	—	—	—	—	—	—
Ages :—									
Under 15 years of Age	—	—	—	—	—	—	—	—	—
— 15 to 20	—	—	—	—	—	—	—	—	—
— 20 to 30	—	—	—	—	—	—	—	—	—
— 30 to 40	—	—	—	—	—	—	—	—	—
— 40 to 50	—	—	—	—	—	—	—	—	—
— 50 to 60	—	—	—	—	—	—	—	—	—
— 60 to 70	—	—	—	—	—	—	—	—	—
— 70 to 80	—	—	—	—	—	—	—	—	—
TOTAL	—	—	—	—	—	—	—	—	—
Number of Americans	—	—	—	—	—	—	—	—	—
Foreigners	—	—	—	—	—	—	—	—	—

NUMBER of EXECUTIONS.

1801. Murder	- - 1	1815. Murder - - 1	1825. Rape - - 1
1802. Murder	- - 1	1817. Murder - - 1	1826. Murder - - 2
1804. Rape	- - 1	1819. Rape - - 1	1828. Murder - - 1
1806. { Murder - 2 } 3 { Rape - 1 }		1820. Murder - - 1	1829. Murder - - 1
1808. Murder	- - 1	1821. { Highway Robbery 1 } 2 { Arson - 1 }	1830. Murder - - 2
1810. Murder	- - 1		1831. Piracy and Murder 2
1813. Rape	- - 2	1822. { Murder - 1 } 3 { Highway Robbery 2 }	

- - - - at CHARLESTOWN, near BOSTON, from 1806 to 1833.   MASSACHUSETTS.

1815.	1816.	1817.	1818.	1819.	1820.	1821.	1822.	1823.	1824.	1825.	1826.	1827.	1828.	1829.	1830.	1831.	1832.	To June 1833.
–	–	–	–	–	–	–	–	–	–	2	–	–	..	–	–	–	1	–
–	2	–	1	–	–	1	–	–	3	–	–	4	–	1	1	–	–	–
1	–	–	–	2	–	–	–	–	–	1	–	–	–	–	–	–	–	–
2	2	4	9	2	6	1	1	3	2	1	–	2	1*	5	2	2	3	5
4	3	4	7	3	2	2	2	2	7	1	3	1	4	4	3	3	1	–
6	17	13	6	3	5	1	5	11	11	11	8	3	2	5	11	4	5	5
–	–	–	–	–	–	–	–	1	–	–	–	–	–	–	–	–	–	–
3	–	–	2	2	1	1	3	–	–	5	2	2	–	2	1	–	1	–
1	2	3	–	–	2	3	2	–	–	3	4	3	6	1	–	1	–	3
2	–	4	–	2	–	2	–	–	2	1	–	2	1	7	1	–	2	–
82	102	126	114	55	43	65	80	64	72	60	66	63	69	49	86	48	70	36
1	–	–	1	–	1	2	–	–	3	1	–	–	1	–	1	–	–	–
–	–	–	–	–	–	–	–	–	–	–	–	3	5	5	1	1	1	–
1	–	2	–	–	1	–	–	2	–	1	–	–	–	–	2	–	1	–
1	9	–	–	4	1	1	–	2	2	–	–	2	–	–	–	–	–	–
–	–	1	4	1	–	–	–	6	–	–	–	–	–	–	1	–	–	–
–	–	–	1	1	–	–	–	–	–	1	–	–	–	–	–	–	–	–
–	–	1	1	2	–	1	–	–	–	–	–	–	2	–	–	–	–	–
4	–	1	1	–	1	–	1	1	–	1	2	–	1	–	–	1	–	–
–	–	2	–	–	–	–	–	–	–	–	–	–	–	–	–	–	–	–
–	–	–	–	–	–	–	–	–	–	–	–	–	–	–	–	–	–	–
2	–	–	–	1	–	–	~	–	–	–	–	–	1	1	–	–	–	–
–	–	–	1	–	–	–	1	1	–	–	–	–	–	–	–	–	–	–
–	–	–	1	–	–	–	–	–	–	–	–	–	–	–	–	–	–	–
–	–	–	2	–	–	–	–	–	1	1	–	–	–	–	–	–	–	–
–	–	–	–	3	–	–	–	–	–	–	–	2	–	1	1	–	2	2
1	–	–	–	1	–	–	–	–	–	–	–	–	–	–	–	–	–	–
–	–	–	–	1	–	–	–	–	–	1	–	–	–	–	–	–	–	–
–	–	–	–	1	–	–	–	–	–	–	–	–	–	–	–	–	–	2
–	–	–	–	–	c	–	–	–	–	–	–	–	1	–	–	–	–	–
–	–	–	–	–	–	–	–	–	–	1	–	–	–	–	–	–	2	–
111	137	161	151	83	64	80	95	93	102	92	86	87	94	81	111	60	89	53
15	25	29	23	15	13	17	20	16	13	6	11	11	13	8	13	10	9	9
27	30	29	8	11	20	21	11	7	9	4	13	26	12	14	7	14	7	5
–	–	–	4	3	8	11	5	6	5	1	5	2	4	5	5	11	6	5
–	–	–	19	16	12	13	17	15	17	13	16	11	11	10	16	15	8	5
–	–	–	2	3	–	4	1	2	2	6	4	4	2	4	3	1	2	3
–	–	–	4	1	–	2	1	–	–	1	–	–	–	1	–	–	1	–
–	–	–	1	–	–	–	2	–	1	1	1	–	–	–	–	–	–	–
–	–	–	26	20	12	19	21	17	20	21	21	15	13	15	19	16	11	8
–	–	–	4	2	–	–	1	2	2	1	–	–	–	–	–	–	1	–
–	–	–	23	13	6	9	10	21	11	9	5	16	9	6	9	12	11	9
–	–	–	69	36	34	46	45	32	50	38	37	42	44	43	56	25	48	29
–	–	–	34	18	11	16	25	27	29	26	25	16	22	18	21	14	18	14
–	–	–	17	7	6	3	9	8	5	7	12	10	12	6	19	7	8	1
–	–	–	1	3	7	3	4	3	4	9	4	2	5	7	2	–	2	–
–	–	–	2	3	–	3	1	–	1	1	3	1	2	1	4	1	–	–
–	–	–	1	1	–	–	–	–	–	1	–	–	–	–	–	1	1	–
–	–	–	151	83	64	80	95	93	102	92	86	87	94	81	111	60	89	53
–	–	–	129	73	52	60	70	69	78	75	72	67	78	64	94	47	67	–
–	–	–	22	10	12	20	25	24	24	17	14	20	16	17	17	13	22	–

Of the whole number (1,772) discharged from the Massachusetts State Prison, up to 30th September 1828, there returned, on a second conviction, 290. Of these 32 had been pardoned:—

Discharged on expiration of sentence - - - - 1,379
Pardoned - - - - - - - - 366
Escaped - - - - - - - - 17
Discharged by Court - - - - - - - 10

1,772

MASSACHUSETTS.
———

PUNISHMENTS for the principal OFFENCES in this STATE.

OFFENCES.		PUNISHMENTS.
Adultery - -	- - - - - - -	- - To be set upon the gallows with a rope about the neck for one hour; publicly whipped, not exceeding 39 stripes; imprisonment and fine, and bound to good behaviour; all or either.
Arson, &c. - -	Burning dwelling-house in night-time, and accessaries before fact.	Death.
	Ditto, no one lawfully in the house -	Solitary imprisonment not exceeding 30 days, and hard labour for life.
	Burning dwelling-house in day-time, or meeting-house, court-house, &c. in night time.	Solitary imprisonment not exceeding one year, and hard labour for life.
	Burning meeting-house, public building, store, &c. by day, or store, barn, &c. by day or night.	- - Solitary imprisonment not exceeding one year, and hard labour not exceeding 10 years.
	Burning stack of corn, hay, grain, &c. or accessary before the fact.	- - Solitary imprisonment not exceeding six months, and hard labour, not exceeding three years ; or fine not exceeding $ 500, and imprisonment in common gaol, not exceeding one year.
	Concealing or assisting any incendiaries, or accessaries before the fact.	- - Solitary imprisonment not exceeding one month, and hard labour not exceeding five years ; or fine not exceeding $ 1,000, or imprisonment in common gaol not exceeding one year.
Assault - - - *See* also Rape.	and Battery - - - -	Fine not exceeding $ 20, and to find securities for keeping the peace.
	Ditto with dangerous weapon, with intent to murder or rob; or aiding or abetting, &c.	- - Solitary imprisonment not exceeding one year, and hard labour not exceeding 20 years.
	Ditto with intent to maim, disfigure, &c., or aiding therein.	- - Solitary imprisonment not exceeding six months, and confinement at hard labour, or in common gaol not exceeding four years.
Bastardy - -	Concealing death of bastard child -	- - The mother to be set on the gallows for one hour, with a rope round her neck, and bound to good behaviour.
	Concealing pregnancy, and being secretly delivered of a bastard child.	Fine not exceeding 50l. or imprisonment not exceeding three months.
Bigamy - - -	- - - - - - -	Same as Adultery.
Blasphemy - -	- - - - - - -	- - Imprisonment not exceeding one year ; sitting in pillory; whipping, or sitting on the gallows with rope round the neck, or to be bound to good behaviour.
Burglary - -	Breaking by night, with intent to commit felony, into a dwelling-house in which any person lawfully is, when armed with dangerous weapon, or committing any assault, or accessary before the fact.	Death.
	When not armed, accessary before fact, aiding, &c.	- - Solitary imprisonment not exceeding 30 days, and hard labour not exceeding 20 years.
	Ditto accessaries after fact - -	- - Solitary imprisonment not exceeding three months, and hard labour not exceeding three years.
	Breaking and entering shop, warehouse, &c. by night, and stealing therefrom, or being accessary.	- - Solitary imprisonment not exceeding one year, and hard labour not exceeding fifteen years.
	Breaking into house, shop, &c. in day-time, or entering without breaking at night, to commit felony.	- - Solitary imprisonment not exceeding six months, and hard labour not exceeding ten years ; or fine not exceeding $ 500, and imprisonment in common gaol not exceeding three years.
	Entering without breaking by night or being accessary, the occupier being thereby put in fear.	- - Solitary imprisonment not exceeding one year, and hard labour not exceeding ten years.

PUNISHMENTS for the principal Offences in this State—*continued*.

OFFENCES.		PUNISHMENTS.
Coining, &c. *See* Forgery.		
Dead Bodies, &c. -	- - Disinterring or removing, without authority, or being accessary before or after the fact.	- - Solitary confinement not exceeding ten days, and imprisonment at hard labour not exceeding one year, or fine not exceeding $ 2,000, and county gaol not exceeding two years.
Duelling. *See* also Murder.	- - Fighting a duel when death does not ensue, or challenging though no duel be fought, aiding, &c.	- - Solitary imprisonment not exceeding one year, and hard labour not exceeding twenty years; and disqualified for holding office for twenty years.
	Accepting a challenge though no duel ensue, aiding, &c.	- - Imprisonment in common gaol not exceeding one year, and disqualified for office for five years.
Embezzlement. *See* Officer.		
Escape, &c. - -	- - Rescuing or attempting to rescue any convict sentenced to hard labour and solitary confinement, from prison or officer, or furnishing tools, &c. to such convict.	- - Solitary imprisonment not exceeding one year, and hard labour not exceeding ten years.
	Forcible attempt at escape by convict.	The same, in addition to the original sentence.
Forgery, &c. - -	In general, aiding and assisting therein.	- - Solitary imprisonment not exceeding six months, and hard labour from two to ten years.
	Counterfeiting any certificate of public debt or bank bill.	Solitary imprisonment not exceeding one year, and hard labour for life.
	Passing, ditto - - - -	- - Solitary imprisonment not exceeding thirty days, and hard labour not exceeding three years; or fine not exceeding $ 1,000, and bound to good behaviour for two years.
	Second offence after conviction, or conviction at same term of court on three several indictments for same offence.	- - Solitary imprisonment not exceeding one year, and hard labour from two to ten years.
	Bringing into the State, or having in possession with intent to pass, bills or notes, counterfeits of those of any bank in the United States, or of any foreign bank.	- - Solitary imprisonment not exceeding three months, and hard labour not exceeding three years; or fine not exceeding $ 1,000, and imprisonment in common gaol not exceeding one year.
	Making or mending any tool to counterfeit such bills, or having such tool in possession with intent to use,	- - Solitary imprisonment not exceeding three months, and hard labour not exceeding three years; or fine not exceeding $ 500, and imprisonment in common gaol not exceeding one year.
	Counterfeiting gold or silver coin, or assisting or having in possession, with intent to pass, not less than ten pieces.	Solitary imprisonment not exceeding one year, and hard labour for life.
	Bringing into the State or possessing base coin, with intent to pass.	- - Solitary imprisonment not exceeding three months, and hard labour not exceeding three years; or fine not exceeding $ 1,000, and bound to good behaviour for two years.
	Second offence after conviction, or being convicted on three several indictments for same offence.	- - Solitary imprisonment not exceeding one year, and hard labour from two to ten years.
	Making, mending, &c. any tool or instrument for coining, with intent to use or be used.	- - Solitary imprisonment not exceeding three months, and hard labour not exceeding three years; or fine not exceeding $ 500, and imprisonment in common gaol not exceeding one year.
Fornication* - -	If a man - - - - -	- - Fine from 30 s. to 5 l., and if not paid in 24 hours, whipping not exceeding ten stripes.

(*continued*.)

OFFENCES.		PUNISHMENTS.
Fornication— (*continued.*)	If a woman - - - - -	- - Fine from 6 s. to 3 l., and if not paid in 24 hours, imprisonment from one to ten days.
	Second offence - - -	Fine, and imprisonment in lieu thereof, doubled.
Fraud. *See* Ship.		
Larceny. *See* also Robbery and Burglary.	Stealing $5 or under (if conviction before justice of peace.)	- - Fine not exceeding $5, and imprisonment in common gaol not exceeding twenty days, or either.
	Stealing to the value of $100 or under.	- - Solitary imprisonment not exceeding six months, and hard labour not exceeding one year, or fine not exceeding $100, or imprisonment in common gaol not exceeding one year.
	Above $100, or accessaries - -	- - Solitary imprisonment not exceeding one year, and hard labour not exceeding three years.
	Second commission of larceny after conviction before Supreme Judicial Court, or conviction of three distinct larcenies at same time.	- - Solitary imprisonment not exceeding one year, and hard labour from three to fifteen years.
	Stealing from a dwelling-house, shop, &c. by day, or at night from a church, public buildings, &c.	- - Solitary imprisonment not exceeding six months, and hard labour* not exceeding five years, or common gaol not exceeding five years, or fined.
	Receiving stolen goods or concealing a felon.	- - Solitary imprisonment not exceeding six months, and hard labour not exceeding three years, or fine not exceeding $500, and common gaol not exceeding three years; or either of the two last.
	- - Second offence after conviction, or three separate convictions at the same time.	- - Solitary imprisonment not exceeding one year, and hard labour from three to ten years.
Maiming, disfiguring, &c.	With intent so to do, or aiding, &c.	- - Solitary imprisonment not exceeding one year, and hard labour not exceeding ten years.
	Assault with intent to maim, &c. aiding, &c.	- - Solitary imprisonment not exceeding six months, and hard labour not exceeding four years.
Malicious Mischief -	Killing, maiming, or disfiguring cattle	- - Solitary imprisonment not exceeding six months; hard labour not exceeding three years, or fine not exceeding $100, and common gaol not exceeding one year.
	Injuring or destroying turnpike-gates.	Fine, from $5 to $50.
Manslaughter - -	- - - - - - -	- - Solitary imprisonment not exceeding six months, and hard labour not exceeding ten years.
Murder. *See* also Assault.	Or accessary before the fact - -	- - Death;—and body may be ordered for dissection; in case of murder in a duel this is imperative.
	Accessaries after the fact - -	- - Solitary imprisonment not exceeding six months, and hard labour not exceeding ten years.
	Attempt at murder, or accessary before the fact.	- - Solitary imprisonment not exceeding three months, and hard labour in State prison, not less than five years.
Officers. *See* also Escape.	Being disguised, and impeding an officer in the discharge of his duty.	- - Fine from $20 to $500, and imprisonment in common gaol not exceeding one year, and bound to keep the peace for one year.
	Embezzlement by any servant or officer of a corporate bank.	- - Solitary imprisonment not exceeding one year, and hard labour from three to ten years.

* On the first conviction as an accessary after the fact, in any simple larceny, or as a receiver of stolen goods, where the offender shall not be found to be a common receiver, and makes restitution, the hard labour is to be remitted.

PUNISHMENTS for the principal Offences in this State—*continued*.

OFFENCES.		PUNISHMENTS.
Perjury or subornation of Perjury - - - - -		- - Solitary imprisonment not exceeding three months, and hard labour from two to fifteen years.
	Endeavour to incite to perjury -	- - Solitary imprisonment not exceeding two months, and hard labour not exceeding five years. [The oath of a convict guilty of either of the above offences is not admissible.]
Rape - - -	- - Including abuse of a child under ten years, and accessary before the fact.	Death.
	Accessary after the fact - -	- - Solitary imprisonment not exceeding three months, and hard labour not exceeding ten years.
	Attempt at rape, or aiding and abetting.	- - The same, or by fine not exceeding $ 500, or imprisonment in common gaol not exceeding one year.
	Attempt to commit a rape on a child, under ten years of age.	- - Solitary imprisonment not exceeding four months, and hard labour for any term, or for life.
Receiving Stolen Goods. *See* Larceny.		
Riot - - -	- - - - - - -	- - Forfeiture of property or part thereof at discretion of court; 39 stripes at public whipping post, imprisonment from six to twelve months, and 39 stripes every three months.
Robbery - -	- - Committed with dangerous weapon with intent to kill or maim, when an assault is committed ; or without such intent, if the person robbed is struck or wounded with such weapons.	Death.
	Without weapons - - - -	- - Solitary imprisonment not exceeding two years, and imprisonment for life.
Ship, &c. - -	Destroying vessel, to defraud the underwriters.	- - Imprisonment for life, or any term not less than five years, and liable for damages.
Sodomy - - -	- - - - - - -	- - Solitary imprisonment not exceeding one year, and hard labour not exceeding ten years.
Treason - - -	- - - - - - -	Death.

N. B.—The degree of punishment between the prescribed limits is determined by the Court.

The Supreme Court may, and usually does, substitute solitary confinement not exceeding three months, and hard labour not exceeding five years, for whipping, standing in the pillory, sitting on the gallows, or imprisonment in the county gaol.

CONNECTICUT.

STATE PRISON AT WETHERSFIELD.

CONNECTICUT.   THIS penitentiary stands on the south side of a large bay, formed by the Connecticut river, about three miles from the town of Hartford. The principal building, in front, is 250 feet long, 48 feet wide and 36 feet high. It contains 232 cells, viz. 200 for males and 32 for females, besides the warden's apartments, chapel, hospital and offices for the warden and guard. The department appropriated to the women is entirely detached. The sleeping cells are arranged in four stories, and are placed back to back. They are entered from galleries running alone the sides of the building. The cells are each seven feet long, three feet six inches wide, and seven feet high. They are surrounded by an area enclosed by a lofty wall and roofed over in a manner similar to that described in the account of the Auburn prison. The windows in the external walls afford sufficient light to enable the convicts to read in their cells. The ground in the rear, on which the workshops are erected, is about 315 feet long and 200 feet deep. There are two ranges of workrooms for the male prisoners, 160 feet long and 38 feet wide. Each range is divided into three separate apartments. The kitchen is in the rear of the women's ward, to which is attached a yard. The cost of erecting the prison was about 30,000 dollars. The building was finished in 1827: the female department, however, was not arranged on its present plan until the year 1830.

This prison is conducted on the plan of association with labour by day and separation at night; all intercourse between the convicts being strictly prohibited. At the Auburn, Sing Sing and Charlestown penitentiaries, the use of the lash has been deemed indispensable to enforce this discipline; but at the Wethersfield State prison, although corporal punishment is not interdicted by law, it is entirely dispensed with. On the occasion of a convict being reported to have been guilty of a breach of the prison regulations, the complaint is carefully investigated by the warden, and if punishment be considered advisable, the prisoner is confined in solitude in a darkened cell: employment is withheld from him: his allowance of food is diminished; and for every day thus passed in solitude a day is added to the prisoner's sentence. This mode of correction has in no instance failed to subdue the most refractory.

Great attention is paid at this penitentiary to the moral and religious welfare of the convicts. Attendance at prayers is required every morning, and the evening is employed in teaching the most ignorant. A Sunday school has been established by and under the superintendence of the chaplain. After the performance of service on Sundays, he is assiduously engaged in visiting the prisoners from cell to cell.

The regulations of this penitentiary, respecting the locking and unlocking the prisoners, marching them to and from the workshops and cells, the distribution of provisions, &c. are so similar to those which have been previously described as in force at the Charlestown penitentiary, that I refrain from repeating them. I annex the rules which have been adopted for the general government of the prison. In allusion to them the directors remark, that although they are suitable to the exigencies of this penitentiary, but little confidence can be placed in any system of regulations, unless there be a board of inspectors, who shall by frequent examination ascertain that the regulations are observed.

The male prisoners are employed as carpenters, coopers, shoemakers, tailors, smiths, nailmakers and chairmakers. The females are under the care of a matron, and are occupied in cooking, and in washing and mending the clothing of the establishment. For the first six months after the opening of the penitentiary to March 1828, the nett profits arising from the labour of the prisoners amounted to - - -   **$** | 1,017. 16

From March 1828 to March 1829	-	-	3,229. 41
—	1829 to	—	1830	-	-	5,068. 94
—	1830 to	—	1831	-	-	7,824. 02
—	1831 to	—	1832	-	-	8,713. 53

The female department was organised under a matron and her assistant in December 1830. The directors have stated their conviction that no contract can be made for the profitable employment of this part of the establishment, after paying the expense of its support and management. They justly remark " that there are considerations more important than those of a pecuniary nature involved in maintaining this department as it has been established. Previous to the appointment of a matron, the female convicts were confined in a room together, without any person whose duty it was constantly to superintend their conduct. Thus situated, they were most disorderly. They are now reduced to a state of subordination, lodged in separate cells, and are required to labour. A part of the labour of the women is let out on contract to manufacture cigars, at 12½ cents per day." *

The prisoners take their meals in solitude in their cells. Their daily ration consists of 1 lb. of salt beef per day, for four days in the week; 12 oz. pork, 1 lb. salt cod fish, one day; and soup, one day, to be made from beef, mutton or veal; the quantity to be equal in value to an average ration of beef, together with vegetables and rice; also 1¼ lb. bread per day, made of

two

---

* Report of the Directors of the Connecticut Penitentiary, 1832.

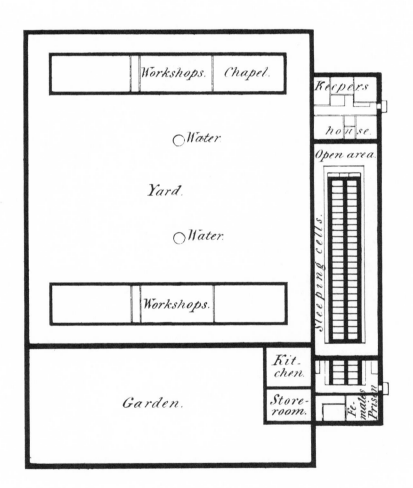

PLAN
of the
STATE PRISON
at
WETHERSFIELD, CONNECTICUT.

Scale, 10 20 30 40 50 60 70 80 90 100   200   300 Feet.

two parts rye and one part common meal. Such is the dietary for each prisoner, besides which there are allowed for every 100 rations five bushels of potatoes, eight quarts of peas or beans, 8 lbs. rice and 20 lbs. Indian meal for porridge. The prisoners are not on any account permitted to be supplied with any description of food besides the prison allowance.

The health of the prisoners is remarkably good, the deaths not averaging more in the last year than about one per cent.

The officers of the penitentiary, besides the matron and her assistants, are three directors, a warden, deputy warden, and an overseer or watchman. The directors visit weekly, in rotation, to examine personally the state of the prison, the treatment of the convicts, and also the accounts. The directors have no immediate authority over the convicts or the funds of the institution.

In order to avoid the temptation to which a prisoner is exposed on his discharge, notice is given to his friends, if he have any, shortly before the expiration of his sentence. The warden, if necessary, supplies him with a sum sufficient to defray his expenses for a short time, to enable him to seek employment.

Much of the success of the penitentiary is owing to the peculiar qualifications of the warden, Mr. Pilsbury. Certain unfounded charges having been brought against him by a late inspector, he was, some time since, induced to retire from the government of the prison. Of these charges he was honourably acquitted. During his secession, the discipline became disordered, and the profits materially diminished: newspapers were surreptitiously introduced, an escape was nearly effected, and a turnkey murdered in the attempt. Mr. Pilsbury was requested again to take the management, and in a few weeks after his reinstatement he succeeded in restoring the prison to its previous order and discipline.

Owing to the entire disuse of corporal punishment, the discipline of this penitentiary is not in every respect so rigidly maintained as in those prisons in which the slightest violation of the rules is followed by the infliction of the lash. The dread of immediate punishment is not visible in the countenances of the convicts, as is the case at Auburn and Sing Sing. Silence is strictly enforced; but the prisoners may be observed to look off their work (although but for a moment) more frequently than at the New York penitentiaries. I think it probable that communications between the convicts, although uniformly punished when detected, takes place to a greater extent than at the prisons to which I refer. On the other hand, the evil arising from this comparative relaxation of discipline is in a great degree compensated by arrangements of a highly valuable character, which render this penitentiary more deserving of attention than perhaps any other (conducted on the principle of association) in the United States. The enlightened feeling which induces, and the vigilance which enables, the warden to dispense with degrading punishments, reflect great credit on his management; while the persevering and judicious labours of the excellent chaplain (who resides in the prison) cannot fail to be most beneficial to the objects of his care. It is impossible to doubt that much good has been effected at this penitentiary in the way of reformation.

PRISON REGULATIONS.

SECTION I.—DUTIES OF THE WARDEN.

1. He shall reside at the prison, and shall visit every cell and apartment, and see every prisoner under his care, at least once every day.

2. He shall not absent himself from the prison for more than a night, without giving notice to one or more of the directors.

3. It shall be his duty to cause the books and accounts to be so kept as clearly to exhibit the state of the convicts, the number employed in each branch of business, and their earnings; the number in the hospital, the expenses of the prison, and all receipts and payments, purchases and sales; and to exhibit the same to the directors at their quarterly meetings, or at any time when required. The quarterly accounts of the warden shall be sworn to by him, and shall specify minutely the persons from whom or to whom monies are received or paid, and for what purpose.

4. It shall be the duty of the warden to make all contracts, purchases, and sales, for and on account of the prison; to oversee and command all the inferior officers in all their various duties, and see that they conform to the law and the rules and regulations prescribed by the directors. He shall see that the prisoners are treated with kindness and humanity, and that no unnecessary severity is practised by the inferior officers; but if the security of the prison shall be in danger, or personal violence should be offered to him or any of the officers or guards, then he or they shall use all lawful means to defend themselves and secure the authors of such outrage. In executing the duties of his office, the warden should never lose sight of the reformation of the prisoners, and should carefully guard himself against personal and passionate resentment. All orders should be given with mildness and dignity, and enforced with promptitude and firmness.

5. It shall be his duty to treat persons visiting the prison with uniform civility and politeness, and to see that they are so treated by the inferior officers.

CONNECTICUT.   6. As it is by law the duty of the directors to see personally to the condition and treatment
of the prisoners, no regulation or order shall be made to prevent prisoners having ready access
to the director who shall be present, nor shall any punishment be inflicted upon them for
speaking to a director. In discharging this part of their duty, the directors will deem it
proper not to suffer a convict to hold any conversation with them in the hearing or presence
of other prisoners.

7. The warden may, with the advice and consent of the directors, in writing, appoint one
person to be a deputy warden, and may with such consent and advice in writing remove him.

Section II.—Of the Deputy Warden.

1. He shall be present at the opening and closing of the prison during the performance of
religious services, and also at all other prison hours.

2. He shall daily visit the hospital, cookery, cells, and see that every part of the institution
is clean and in order.

3. It shall be his duty to exercise, under the direction of the warden, a general inspection
and superintendence over the whole establishment and all its concerns, to see that every subordinate officer strictly performs his appropriate duties, to visit frequently the places of labour
and yards without notice, and see that the convicts are diligent and industrious, and generally
to see that the rules and regulations of the institution are enforced, and that every precaution
is taken for the security of the prison and the prisoners therein confined.

4. He shall attend to the clothing of the convicts, and see that it is whole, properly changed,
and in order.

Section III.—Of the Overseers.

1. There shall be an overseer in each shop, to be appointed by the warden.

2. Each overseer shall, on entering upon his duties, take an accurate account of the various
implements and tools belonging to his department, with the value of the same in money, and
shall lodge a copy of such account under his hand with the warden, and such account shall
be corrected quarterly, by adding such new implements as may have been purchased, or such
as may have been broken, damaged or lost. He shall keep an account of the stock furnished
his department, and of the articles manufactured there and taken therefrom, and also of the
daily and weekly earnings of each convict. He shall see that all the property belonging to
his department shall be carefully preserved, and that the work is well and faithfully done, and
shall consult and promote the interest of the State or the contractor who may employ the
convicts. It is especially enjoined upon each overseer to preserve in his department the
most entire order.

No conversation between prisoners shall be allowed; nor shall any overseer converse with
a prisoner, except to direct him in his labour. If any prisoner is idle, careless or refractory,
he shall be forthwith reported to the warden or deputy warden for punishment. Each overseer shall enter upon his book the name of each sick or complaining prisoner, and shall
before nine o'clock A. M. deliver to the warden or deputy a list of such names, with the date,
which list shall be placed in the hospital.

3. Each overseer shall perform his regular tour of night duty, as he may be directed by
the warden.

Section IV.—Of the Watchmen.

1. It shall be the duty of the several watchmen to perform all such various duties and
services, for the safety and security of the prison, as may be directed by the warden, both by
day and during the night; to be vigilant and active while on post, and to maintain, while off
from duty, and in the guard room, both towards each other and all other persons, a gentle-
manly deportment; to refrain from all those acts which are inconsistent with the strictest
decorum, treating with an uniform politeness and civility all persons who shall visit the prison;
recollecting that the reputation as well as the safety of the institution, depend essentially upon
them, individually as well as collectively. They are to be cautious that they are neat and
cleanly in their own persons, and that the guard room shall at all times exhibit a specimen of
neatness and order; and that their arms are always in repair, and ready for service. No
watchman shall be allowed to hold any conversation with a prisoner, except to direct him in
his labour. Nor shall he receive from or deliver to a prisoner any article or thing, without
the knowledge of the warden or his deputy.

2. It shall be the duty of the warden to designate some person who shall be employed at
the prison, to see, personally, that the various rations ordered by these rules are weighed or
measured for the day, according to the number of prisoners, and delivered to the head cook,
and he shall keep an exact account of all such rations so by him delivered, and shall, under
oath, render the same quarterly to the warden, under his hand, to be laid before the
directors.

3. Each and every person who shall by the warden be appointed to any office in or about
said prison, shall be held as engaged to and attached to the institution; and if in office at
the time a vacancy shall happen in the office of warden, as bound to continue his services at
the

the prison, for at least one month after the death, removal or resignation of the warden, unless sooner discharged by his successor; and in case any such officer shall refuse or neglect to perform his duty, he shall forfeit three months wages, to be recovered by any succeeding warden, and this bye-law shall be considered as one of the terms on which each officer shall contract, and as assented to by him.

Section V.—Of Cleanliness.

1. The hall and cells shall be swept daily, and the sweepings carried outside of the wall. The floor of the hall shall be washed once a fortnight throughout the year. The cells shall also be frequently washed and whitewashed.

2. The beds and bedding shall be taken out of the prison and aired in the yard, once a week in the warm season, and once a fortnight during the rest of the year, when the weather will allow; and each prisoner is to take the utmost care that his cell be kept neat, and that his furniture be not injured; and in default of observing this rule, his bed, bedding, and bedstead are to be taken from him until he will conform.

3. The utmost care is to be taken that the persons of the prisoners are kept clean. For this purpose they shall have suitable accommodation for washing.

4. The night pails shall be kept carefully clean, and their contents carried without the walls, and covered in the manner now practised.

5. No filth, nuisance, or offensive matter, shall be suffered to remain in or about the prison, shops, or yard; but the whole establishment must be made to exhibit throughout a specimen of neatness, good order and cleanliness.

Section VI.—Of the Hospital and Physician.

1. The warden, with the approbation of the directors, shall appoint some proper person to be the physician, who shall receive such compensation as shall be fixed and agreed upon by the directors.

2. The hospital shall be furnished with the necessary beds, bedding, bedsteads, tables and all other necessary utensils, for the comfort and accommodation of the sick, and shall at all times be kept in a state of readiness to receive such patients as are ordered there by the physician.

3. The physician shall direct such supplies, stores, and furniture, as may be necessary in his department; and his order in writing shall authorize the warden to procure the same. He shall record in a book all the orders so given, designating the articles and the time when given. He shall also keep an account of the various articles belonging to his department. He shall also record in the said book his visits, the names of the patients reported as sick or complaining, the names of such as are ordered to the hospital, or as are ordered to their cells on sick diet, or are ordered to their shops. He shall visit the institution every other day through the year, and oftener if it shall be necessary, or if sent for, and shall personally see every patient or prisoner who may, by the respective overseers, be reported as sick or complaining. He shall also enter the names of such as shall be discharged from the hospital, or shall die; the nature of the complaint and the prescription, and shall subjoin such other remarks as he may deem expedient respecting the nature of each case, and the treatment thereof, or in relation to the general health, diet or employment of the prisoners, or cleanliness of the prison, which book shall remain at the prison, and shall be always open to the inspection of the warden and directors.

He may apply to the warden for the assistance of such convicts as may be necessary to nurse and attend upon the sick; and he, as well as the warden, shall endeavour to render the condition of the sick prisoner in all respects as comfortable as his situation will admit. Whenever any prisoner shall not be sufficiently ill to make it necessary that he should be ordered to the hospital, the physician may direct such diet to be prepared for him, from the hospital or prison stores, as he may deem necessary.

4. If it shall so happen that the directions or prescriptions of the physician shall not be complied with, or duly observed, it shall be his duty to enter such failure or omission in his book, with the reason thereof, if he shall be acquainted with the same, to the end that proper measures may be taken to prevent future omissions.

Section VII.—General Regulations.

1. No officer or person connected with the institution shall be permitted to buy from or sell to any convict any article or thing whatever, or make with him any contract or engagement whatsoever, or cause or allow any convict to work for him or his benefit, or grant any favour or indulgence to a convict, except such as the laws allow. Nor shall he receive from any convict, or from any one in behalf of such convict, any emolument, presents, or reward whatever, or the promise of any for services or supplies, or as a gratuity. Nor shall he take or receive to his own use and benefit, or that of his family, any fee, gratuity, or emolument,

CONNECTICUT. from any person committed to his custody, nor from any of their friends or acquaintances, or from any person whomsoever, and every officer offending herein shall be forthwith dismissed.

2. The compensation to each and every officer shall be fixed and settled by the directors before he enters upon the duties of his office, and no officer shall be allowed or permitted to take or receive any other or greater compensation than the sum so fixed; nor shall he take or receive, either from the public property or from the labour or services of the convicts, any perquisite whatever, without the consent of the directors, in writing.

3. Spirituous liquors shall in no case be furnished to the convicts, except on the prescription of the physician. And each and every officer is hereby required wholly to abstain from their use during the period of his employment at this institution, on penalty of being dismissed.

4. No officer, except the warden, shall strike, beat, or punish corporeally any prisoner, except in self defence.

5. In case any officer shall be absent from the prison, except upon the public business of the same, the rateable compensation of such officer shall be stopped during the time of such absence.

6. Each cell shall be furnished with a bible, and the convicts may have such other religious books and attendance as the warden, with the assent of the directors, may think suited to improve their morals and conduct.

7. All sums which shall be received from persons visiting the prison shall be accounted for to the State, and deemed a part of the income of the prison, and such sums shall be included in the quarterly accounts of the warden.

SECTION VIII.—DUTIES OF THE CONVICTS.

1. Every convict shall be industrious, submissive and obedient, and shall labour diligently and in silence.

2. No convict shall secrete, hide, or carry about his person, any instrument or thing with intent to make his escape.

3. No convict shall write or receive a letter to or from any person whatsoever, nor have intercourse with persons without the prison, except by leave of the warden.

4. No convict shall burn, waste, injure or destroy any raw materials or article of public property, nor deface or injure the prison building.

5. Convicts shall always conduct themselves toward the officers with deference and respect; and cleanliness in their persons, dress, and bedding, is required. When they go to their meals or labour, they shall proceed in regular order and in silence, marching in the lock step.

6. No convict shall converse with another prisoner, or leave his work without permission of an officer. He shall not speak to or look at visitors, nor leave the hospital when ordered there, nor shall he make any unnecessary noise in his labour, or do any thing either in the shops or cells which is subversive of the good order of the institution.

The following was the INCOME and EXPENDITURE in the past Year:

INCOME.	Dollars.	Cents.	EXPENDITURE.	Dollars.	Cents.
Smiths' shop - - -	2,138	33	Provisions - - -	3,784	86
Coopers' - ditto - -	535	46	Clothing and Bedding -	889	75
Shoe - - ditto - -	5,142	28	Wages, Subsistence, Fuel, &c.	3,847	30
Nail - - ditto - -	10	71			
Carpenters' ditto - -	4,850	06	Hospital - - -	362	80
Chair - - ditto - -	4,511	54	Repairs and Improvements	272	32
Female department - -	64	26			
Interest received - -	41	67	TOTAL Expenditure - $	9,157	03
Received from visitors -	576	25	BALANCE, being gain to the Institution	8,713	53
TOTAL - - - - $	17,870	56	TOTAL - - -	17,870	56

SUMMARY

SUMMARY of the Numbers of CONVICTS confined in the WETHERSFIELD Penitentiary.   CONNECTICUT.

Number in Confinement March 31, 1831 -	182		
Since received to March 31, 1832 - - -	65	247	
Discharged during the year by expiration of Sentence - - - - - - -	46		
Pardoned - - - - - - -	7		
Died - - - - - - -	2	55	
Total Number in Confinement March 31, 1832 -	- -		192
White Males - - - - - -	143		
Ditto females - - - - -	13	156	
Coloured Males - - - - - -	31		
Ditto - Females - - - - -	5	36	
TOTAL - - -	- -		192

The CRIMES of which the Prisoners had been Convicted.

Murder - - - - -	1	Passing counterfeit money -	10
Rape - - - - -	2	Adultery - - - - -	15
Burglary - - - - -	62	Breaking Prison - -	4
Bigamy - - - -	1	Abuse of Female Child - -	2
Attempt to poison - - -	2	Robbery - - - -	3
Horse stealing - - - -	17	Incest and attempt to kill - -	2
Attempt at rape - - -	10	Perjury - - - -	2
Attempt to kill - - -	28	Theft - - - - -	10
Attempt to murder - - -	3		
Manslaughter - - - -	4	TOTAL - - -	192
Forgery - - - - -	10		

Of which number there were under the age of 20 years - -	18
From 20 to 30 - - -	73
„ 30 to 40 - - -	52
„ 40 to 50 - - -	30
„ 50 to 60 - - -	10
„ 60 to 70 - - -	7
Over 70 years - - - -	2

SENTENCES.

For Life - - - -	17	For 7 years - - -	8
„ 23 years - - -	1	„ 6 „ - - -	10
„ 20 „ - - -	1	„ 5 „ - - -	17
„ 17 „ - - -	1	„ 4 „ - - -	22
„ 16 „ - - -	2	„ 3 „ - - -	43
„ 15 „ - - -	7	„ 2½ „ - - -	2
„ 14 „ - - -	1	„ 2 „ - - -	32
„ 13 „ - - -	1	„ 1⅓ „ - - -	1
„ 12 „ - - -	6	„ 1 „ - - -	4
„ 11 „ - - -	3	„ 9 months - - -	1
„ 10 „ - - -	6		
„ 9 „ - - -	2	TOTAL - - -	192
„ 8 „ - - -	3		

The Places of which the CONVICTS were Natives.

Connecticut - - -	109	Canada - - - -	1
New York - - -	21	Africa - - - -	1
Massachusetts - -	14	England - - -	4
Rhode Island - -	19	Ireland - - -	4
New Jersey - -	4	Scotland - - -	1
New Hampshire - -	3	West Indies - - -	4
Vermont - - -	5		
Maryland - - -	1	TOTAL - - -	192
Pennsylvania - -	1		

CONNECTICUT.

NUMBER of CONVICTS committed to the CONNECTICUT STATE PRISON at NEWGATE, and subsequently to WETHERSFIELD, from 1790 to 30th June 1833.

CRIMES	1790	1791	1792	1793	1794	1795	1796	1797	1798	1799	1800	1801	1802	1803	1804	1805	1806	1807	1808	1809	1810	1811	1812	1813	1814	1815	1816	1817	1818	1819	1820	1821	1822	1823	1824	1825	1826	1827	1828	1829	1830	1831	1832	1833 To June
Horse stealing	4	2	2	4	4	3	2	4	3	3	3	–	4	4	1	3	1	3	1	3	1	2	6	–	6	5	7	4	6	3	4	3	10	2	5	1	5	3	6	11	4	4	7	1
Burglary	7	6	4	4	4	7	1	1	4	4	6	4	7	8	7	7	9	5	6	7	7	5	8	5	9	8	13	20	16	14	18	16	31	22	24	13	14	13	13	37	27	11	25	13
Forgery	–	1	–	–	–	1	–	–	–	–	–	4	–	–	1	1	1	1	4	3	1	1	3	–	3	–	2	2	–	–	4	3	4	4	1	1	4	1	2	1	4	3	5	2
Highway Robbery	–	–	2	–	–	1	–	–	–	–	–	4	–	–	1	–	–	–	1	–	–	–	3	–	3	–	–	2	–	2	–	–	1	–	1	–	4	–	2	–	1	1	5	–
Sodomy	–	–	–	–	–	–	–	–	–	–	–	–	–	–	–	–	–	–	–	–	–	–	–	–	–	–	–	–	–	–	–	–	–	–	–	–	–	–	2	1	1	–	–	–
Passing Counterfeit Money	–	–	–	1	2	–	–	–	2	2	1	2	2	1	–	1	6	1	5	4	6	1	2	1	2	–	–	5	1	1	2	1	3	4	3	–	3	2	4	2	5	5	2	2
High Crime and Misdemeanor	–	–	–	–	–	–	–	–	–	–	–	–	3	–	–	–	1	–	–	1	1	–	1	1	1	–	–	1	1	–	–	1	1	1	2	1	–	2	3	–	5	–	1	–
Assault to Rape	–	–	–	1	1	1	–	1	1	1	1	1	1	1	1	1	1	2	–	1	1	–	1	–	–	–	–	1	–	1	2	–	2	4	2	1	1	2	2	4	5	1	5	2
Assault to Kill	–	–	–	1	–	–	–	–	1	1	–	–	1	–	–	–	–	1	–	1	–	–	1	–	1	–	–	5	1	1	–	–	–	2	–	1	1	1	3	8	4	18	–	–
Burning Barns, &c.	–	–	–	1	1	1	–	1	1	1	1	–	1	–	3	1	–	1	–	1	–	1	–	–	1	4	–	1	–	1	1	1	–	–	–	1	–	2	1	1	3	–	–	–
Arson	–	–	–	–	–	–	–	–	–	–	–	–	–	–	–	–	–	–	–	1	–	–	–	–	–	–	–	–	–	–	–	–	–	–	–	1	–	–	2	2	–	–	–	–
Manslaughter	–	–	–	–	–	–	–	–	–	–	–	–	–	–	–	1	–	–	–	1	2	–	3	–	1	–	–	–	–	1	1	1	1	3	–	1	–	–	1	2	1	–	–	–
Rape commuted	–	–	–	–	–	–	–	–	–	–	–	–	–	–	–	–	–	–	–	–	3	–	–	–	1	–	–	–	–	–	–	–	–	–	1	–	–	1	–	2	1	–	–	–
Impostor	–	–	–	–	–	–	–	–	–	–	–	–	–	–	–	–	–	–	–	1	1	–	1	–	1	–	–	1	–	–	–	1	2	–	1	1	–	–	1	1	1	–	–	–
Attempt to Poison	–	–	–	1	–	–	–	–	–	–	–	–	–	–	–	1	–	–	–	–	–	–	–	–	–	–	–	1	–	1	–	–	–	–	–	–	–	–	–	–	–	–	–	–
Theft and Stealing	–	–	–	1	–	–	–	–	–	–	–	–	–	–	–	–	–	–	–	–	–	1	–	–	–	–	–	–	–	–	–	–	2	5	7	–	2	–	3	9	2	10	6	9
Bigamy	–	–	–	–	–	–	–	–	–	–	–	–	–	–	–	–	–	–	–	–	–	1	–	–	–	–	–	–	–	–	–	–	–	1	3	1	1	–	–	–	–	–	–	1
Housebreaking	–	–	–	–	–	–	–	–	–	–	–	1	–	–	–	1	–	–	1	–	1	1	1	–	–	–	–	1	–	–	–	–	4	1	1	–	–	2	3	9	1	3	4	3
Adultery	–	–	–	–	–	–	–	–	–	–	–	–	–	–	–	–	–	–	–	–	–	–	–	–	–	–	–	–	–	–	–	–	–	–	–	–	–	–	–	–	–	–	–	1
Bestiality	–	–	–	–	–	–	–	–	–	–	–	–	–	–	–	–	–	–	–	–	–	–	–	–	–	–	–	–	–	–	–	–	–	–	–	–	–	2	–	1	1	–	–	–
Murder commuted	–	–	–	–	–	–	–	–	–	–	–	–	–	–	–	–	–	–	–	–	–	–	–	–	–	–	–	–	–	–	–	–	–	–	–	–	–	–	–	2	2	3	4	3
Mail Robbery	–	–	–	–	–	–	–	–	–	–	–	–	–	–	–	–	–	–	–	–	–	–	–	–	–	–	–	1	–	–	–	1	–	–	–	1	1	–	–	1	2	–	–	1
Aiding to break Jail	–	–	–	–	–	–	–	–	–	–	–	–	–	–	–	–	–	–	–	–	–	–	–	–	–	–	–	1	–	–	–	–	–	–	–	–	–	–	–	1	–	1	1	–
Incest	–	–	–	–	–	–	–	–	–	–	–	–	–	–	–	–	–	–	–	–	–	–	–	–	–	–	–	–	–	–	–	–	–	1	1	1	–	–	2	2	–	–	–	–
Breaking Jail	–	–	–	–	–	–	–	–	–	–	–	–	–	–	–	–	–	–	–	–	–	–	–	–	–	–	–	–	–	–	–	2	–	–	–	1	1	1	–	1	–	1	1	–
Perjury*	–	–	–	–	–	–	–	–	–	–	–	–	–	–	–	–	–	–	–	–	–	–	–	–	–	–	–	–	–	–	–	–	–	–	–	–	1	–	–	–	–	1	–	–
Receiving Stolen Goods	–	–	–	–	–	–	–	–	–	–	–	–	–	–	–	–	–	–	–	–	–	–	–	–	–	–	–	–	–	–	–	–	–	–	–	–	–	–	–	–	1	1	1	–
Total	11	9	8	11	10	12	2	7	10	10	11	13	18	14	13	15	18	15	17	20	22	11	26	7	22	18	22	35	23	22	30	26	61	48	50	32	35	33	42	83	63	58	57	32
Of the above number were—																																												
Pardoned	1	1	–	–	–	1	–	–	1	1	1	1	1	1	1	1	1	1	–	1	1	2	1	1	–	1	–	1	1	1	1	–	1	1	2	1	–	1	4	2	2	8	11	7
Coloured People	1	2	2	1	–	2	–	1	1	2	–	3	6	1	–	–	3	2	–	3	7	–	3	3	1	2	–	2	5	4	9	9	17	16	12	6	4	6	5	25	12	9	9	12
Females, White†	–	–	–	–	–	–	–	–	–	–	–	–	–	–	–	–	–	–	–	–	–	–	–	–	–	–	–	–	–	–	–	–	–	–	–	1	2	2	1	7	6	4	2	2
Dito, Coloured	–	–	–	–	–	–	–	–	–	–	–	–	–	–	–	–	–	–	–	–	–	–	–	–	–	–	–	–	–	–	–	–	–	–	–	–	1	1	–	1	1	2	3	1
Deaths	–	–	–	–	–	–	–	–	–	–	–	–	–	–	–	–	–	–	–	–	–	–	–	–	–	–	–	1	–	1	–	–	–	–	2	2	1	–	–	4	4	1	3	–

* Not made a State Prison offence until 1831.

† First committed in 1825.

CONNECTICUT.

COMMITMENTS to the WETHERSFIELD STATE PRISON—*continued*.

	1820.	1821.	1822.	1823.	1824.	1825.	1826.	1827.	1828.	1829.	1830.	1831.	1832.	to June 1833.
AGES.														
From 12 to 15 Years -	–	–	–	–	4	–	–	–	1	–	–	–	–	–
„ 15 to 20 „ -	5	4	12	8	6	6	2	1	13	14	10	6	10	--
„ 20 to 30 „ -	12	14	29	25	24	16	18	15	16	30	25	27	27	–
„ 30 to 40 „ -	4	4	10	7	8	5	5	4	7	17	10	11	8	–
„ 40 to 50 „ -	5	1	3	4	1	1	2	4	3	7	4	3	4	–
„ 50 to 60 „ -	–	1	1	2	4	2	3	1	–	4	2	1	1	–
„ 60 to 70 „ -	-.*	–	1	2	–	–	–	–	1	1	1	2	–	–
„ 70 to 80 „ -	–	–	–	1	–	–	–	–	1	–	–	–	–	–
COUNTRIES.														
England - - -	1	–	4	–	4	1	–	2	–	2	2	2	--	–
Scotland - - -	–	–	–	–	–	–	–	–	1	1	–	–	–	–
Ireland - - -	1	1	4	1	2	–	–	–	3	1	1	2	1	–
West Indies - -	–	–	–	–	1	–	–	–	–	2	1	3	–	–
Corsica - - -	–	–	1	–	1	–	–	–	–	–	–	–	–	–
Portugal - - -	–	–	–	1	–	–	–	–	–	–	–	–	–	–
Russia - - -	–	–	1	–	–	–	–	–	–	–	–	–	–	–
Africa - - -	–	–	1	–	–	–	–	–	–	–	–	–	–	–
Nova Scotia - -	–	–	1	–	–	–	–	–	–	–	–	–	–	–

PUNISHMENTS for the principal Offences in this STATE.

OFFENCES.		PUNISHMENTS.
Adultery - -	If a Man - - - - -	Imprisonment in the penitentiary from two to five years.
	If a Woman - - - - -	Imprisonment in common gaol from two to five years.
Arson, &c. - -	- - Setting fire to any building or vessel, and thereby causing death, or endangering the life of any person.	Death.
	When life is not so endangered -	Imprisonment in the penitentiary not exceeding seven years.
	Burning or destroying any magazine of provision, arms, &c. belonging to the State.	Imprisonment in the penitentiary for life, or any term of years.
	Burning state-house, county-house, court-house, town-house, church, chapel, &c. Burning dwelling-house to defraud insurers, or any vessel, office, store or shop.	Imprisonment in the penitentiary not exceeding seven years.
Assault - - -	With intent to commit rape, murder, or robbery.	Imprisonment in the penitentiary for life, or any term of years.
Bastardy - -	Administering poison with intent to kill or produce miscarriage.	Imprisonment in the penitentiary for life, or any term of years.
	Being secretly delivered of a bastard child.	Fine not exceeding $150, or imprisonment for not more than three months.
	Concealment of the death of a bastard child.	- - The mother to sit on a gallows with a rope about her neck, for an hour, and to be bound to good behaviour, and imprisoned for a term not exceeding one year.
Bigamy - - -	If a Man - - - - -	Imprisonment in penitentiary from two to five years.
	If a Woman - - - - -	Imprisonment in common gaol from two to five years.

CONNECTICUT.

PUNISHMENTS for the principal Offences in this State—*continued.*

OFFENCES.		PUNISHMENTS.
Blasphemy		- - Fine not exceeding $100; and imprisonment in common gaol not exceeding one year, and to be bound to good behaviour.
Bribery		- - Fine not exceeding $1,000; and imprisonment in the common gaol not exceeding two years; and rendered incapable of holding any office in the State.
Burglary, &c.	Breaking and entering with felonious intent a dwelling-house.	Imprisonment in the penitentiary not exceeding three years.
	With violence, or armed with any dangerous weapon.	Imprisonment in the penitentiary for life, or for not less than seven years.
	Breaking and stealing from a building in the day-time.	Imprisonment in the penitentiary not exceeding two years.
Coining. *See* Forgery.		
Dead bodies	Disinterment of deceased persons	- - Fine from $100 to $500, and imprisonment in common gaol from three to twelve months.
Duelling	Accepting or sending a challenge to fight a duel.	- - Fine of $3,000, and to be bound to keep the peace and to good behaviour during life; and disabled from holding office; in default of payment, imprisonment in common gaol for one year.
	Bearing a challenge	- - The same as accepting or sending a challenge, excepting the finding of sureties for good behaviour.
Escape	Effecting escape of prisoners from State prison.	State prison not exceeding six years.
Forgery	On private persons	- - Imprisonment in the penitentiary not exceeding three years; and double the amount of damages to the party injured.
Coin, &c.	- - Counterfeiting public seals, or altering or embezzling any record, will, deed, &c.	Imprisonment in the penitentiary not exceeding seven years.
	Forging public securities	
	Passing counterfeit bills, &c.	
	Possessing counterfeit bills, with intent to fill up, or pass the same.	
	Making plates for counterfeiting bills	Imprisonment in the penitentiary not exceeding three years.
	Possessing plates for forging bank bills	
	Counterfeiting coin	
	Possessing counterfeit coin, with intent to pass.	
Fornication		Fine of seven dollars; or imprisonment in common gaol for one month.
Fraud. *See* Ship.		
Horse stealing		- - Imprisonment in the penitentiary not exceeding two years, and to pay the owner treble the value of the horse.
Incest	If a Man	Imprisonment in the penitentiary from two to five years.
	If a Woman	Common gaol from two to five years.
Kidnapping		Fine of $400, of which half shall go to the prosecutor, and half to the State.
Larceny	Simple theft under $4	- - To pay treble the value of the property stolen, and a fine not exceeding $7; or in default of fine, whipping not exceeding 10 stripes.
See also Horse stealing, Burglary, Robbery.	Simple theft, $4 or upwards	- - The same payment and fine as above, together with whipping not exceeding 10 stripes.
	Receiving and concealing stolen goods	The same punishment as the thief.
	Stealing from the person at a fire	Imprisonment in the penitentiary not exceeding five years.
	Stealing from the person to the amount of $20.	Imprisonment in the penitentiary not exceeding two years.
Maiming	Cutting or maiming any limb of another with intent to disfigure.	Imprisonment for life, or at the discretion of the court.
	Cutting out tongue, or blinding, with malice and lying in wait.	Death.

PUNISHMENTS for the principal Offences in this State—*continued.*

OFFENCES.		PUNISHMENTS.
Malicious Mischief -	Breaking windows, &c. in the night time.	- - Fine not exceeding $100; or imprisonment in common gaol not exceeding six months, or both.
	Destroying turnpike property in the night season.	- - Fine not exceeding $100, and imprisonment in common gaol not exceeding six months.
Manslaughter -	- - - - - - -	- - Fine not exceeding $500, and imprisonment in common gaol or State prison from six months to three years.
Murder - - -	- - - - - - -	Death.
Officer - - -	Resisting, in execution of his duty -	- - Fine not exceeding $34, or imprisonment in common gaol not exceeding two months, or both.
Perjury - - -	Or subornation of perjury -	- - Fine $67, half to the State, and half to the party aggrieved. State prison from six months to two years, and disqualified for giving evidence.
	With intent to take life - -	Death.
Poison. *See* Bastardy.		
Rape - - -	- - - - - - -	Death.
See also Assault.	Abuse of female child under 10 -	Imprisonment in the penitentiary for life, or any term of years.
Receiving stolen Goods. *See* Larceny.		
Riot - - -	- - - - - - -	- - Fine not exceeding $67; or imprisonment in common gaol not exceeding six months, or both.
Robbery - -	- - - - - - -	Imprisonment in penitentiary not exceeding seven years.
	If armed, or using violence - -	Imprisonment in penitentiary for life, or any term of years not less than seven.
	Second Offence after sentence to State prison.	- - Not exceeding double the term to which offender was liable on first conviction.
	Third offence (after such second conviction.)	Imprisonment in the penitentiary for life.
Ship. *See* also Arson	Destroying vessel to defraud insurers	Imprisonment in the penitentiary not exceeding seven years.
Sodomy or Bestiality	- - - - - - -	Imprisonment in the penitentiary for life.
Treason - -	- - - - - - -	Death.
	Misprision of treason - - -	- - Fine not exceeding $1,000, and imprisonment in State prison for not exceeding seven years.

N.B. The Court determines the precise degree of punishment within the limits prescribed by law.

NEW HAMPSHIRE.

STATE PRISON AT CONCORD.

THE space of ground on which this penitentiary has been built is about 260 feet in front and 200 feet in depth, inclosed with a stone wall fourteen feet high, above which are pickets ten feet high. The old part of the prison consists of a long stone building three stories high, containing large rooms in which it has been usual to place several convicts together at night. The new building which has been recently erected was occupied by the prisoners in June 1832. It is at the north end of the keeper's house, but entirely detached from the boundary wall. The external walls are of rough split granite. The interior walls of the cells are of brick. The middle wall between the two ranges of cells is sixteen inches, and the other walls are twelve inches thick. The exterior building is 124 feet long and 38 feet wide. The area round the cells is only eight feet wide. It is well lighted by large windows in the wall. The cells are placed back to back There are forty on each floor, and the building being three stories high, contains altogether 120 cells. Each cell is six feet ten inches long, three feet four inches wide, and six feet six inches high. The door is twenty inches wide, of wrought iron, placed in a recess of ten inches from the outer face of the wall. There is a distinct flue for ventilating each cell. In winter the fire that serves for cooking, supplies warmth to the area round the cells, the heated air being conveyed by pipes. At one end of the new building next the keeper's house is the officers' bed-room, with the chapel over it, from which there is an entrance from the cell gallery. Alarm bells are placed so as to form a communication from the cell-building to the keeper's room. The kitchen is on one side of the new building in the rear: beyond this is a workshop for shoemakers. There is also a long range of detached shops in the prison-yard parallel with the boundary wall. These are occupied by wheel-wrights, cabinet-makers and blacksmiths. In the centre of the yard is a large shed building in which the stone-masons work. Granite is brought by land carriage from a quarry about two miles distant.

This penitentiary had been in operation but a short time before my visit. I was informed that a very favourable change had taken place in the conduct of the prisoners since their removal from the old building. There was an appearance of quiet and good order throughout the establishment; but the discipline, if such it might be called, is far too lax to inspire dread; and indulgences are permitted quite inconsistent with the character of a penitentiary. Prisoners are allowed, under certain restrictions, to receive from their friends visits and articles of food. Imprisonment in this penitentiary cannot have much, if it have any, effect in deterring an offender, while the religious improvement of the prisoners is much neglected.

The following were the number of prisoners employed at the period of my visits: stone-masons, 30; smiths, 12; waggon-makers, wheelwrights and cabinet-makers, 8; shoe-makers, 20; cooks and washers, 4. The articles made in the prison are readily disposed of. Shoes have a better sale than other goods.

There was but one woman in the prison. The keeper stated that the absence of female convicts is not owing to their abstaining from crime so much as to an indisposition which prevails generally throughout the State, and particularly with magistrates, to punish women; arising from the fact of there not being a proper place for their reception.

In summer the prisoners rise at half past four o'clock; and after being marched into the yard proceed to work at their respective occupations until seven o'clock, when they are allowed an hour for breakfast and rest. The time allotted for dinner is from twelve to one o'clock. These meals are taken in solitude. At seven in the evening they return to their cells, in the front of which lights are placed in the winter evenings. Each cell is furnished with a bible. A sermon is usually preached on Sunday, but in consequence of the State not making an adequate allowance to the chaplain, he is obliged to devote most of his time to other duties. There are but few prisoners who cannot read. More than two-thirds attribute their crimes to intemperance. The convicts are of a far less hardened character than those found in other penitentiaries, being for the most part husbandry servants convicted of light offences, who having had some degree of education, and being civilized in their manners, are kept in order without difficulty.

The law of this State forbids flogging, or the infliction of any corporal punishment. The keeper says that the whip irritates and depraves; and he thinks that he could manage a much larger number of convicts without the necessity of having recourse to it. The extent to which a prisoner may be placed in solitary confinement is thirty days; but this punishment is not resorted to above once in the course of a month. There is one convict who is sentenced to an imprisonment of twelve years. He has been employed alone for about twelve months, and being under peculiar circumstances, would be allowed to leave his cell on making an application to that effect. He has, however, never solicited the favor.

The

Plan of the STATE PRISON, at Concord,

NEW HAMPSHIRE.

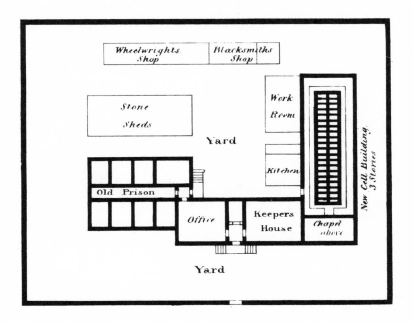

| Wheelwrights Shop | Blacksmiths Shop |

Stone Sheds

Work Room

Yard

Kitchen

Old Prison

Office

Keepers House

Chapel above

New Cell Building. 3 Stories

Yard

Scale.

5 10 20 30 40 50 60 70 80 90 100   150   200   300 Feet

S. Arrowsmith, Litho.

The governor in council is inspector of the prison. There are ten officers and guards, besides the keeper and his deputy. Two guards are always on duty in the area in front of the cells. After each period of locking up at breakfast, dinner, and in the evening, the turnkeys are required to report the number of prisoners, so that they are counted three times a day.

The convicts in this penitentiary are remarkably healthy. But one death has occurred within the last three years. On the discharge of a prisoner he is allowed a suit of clothing, and about three dollars in money. Eleven pardons have been granted in the course of a year, out of an average number of about ninety prisoners. There are two gaol deliveries in the year. About nine counties commit to this penitentiary. The cost of the new building has been 17,600 dollars.

NEW HAMPSHIRE.

The following STATEMENT shows the INCOME and EXPENDITURE of the Prison during the last Year:

INCOME.

	Dollars. cents.	Dollars. cents.	Dollars. cents.
STONE SHOP:			
Property on hand, May 31, 1832 - - - - -	1,589 51		
Since purchased of overseers. - - - - -	1,895 42		
		3,484 93	
Sales of stone, labour on new prison, &c. - - -	3,819 35		
Stock and tools on hand, April 30, 1833 - - -	3,430 98		
		7,250 33	
Making the net gain of the stone shop -	- -	- -	3,765 40
SMITH'S SHOP:			
Stock and tools on hand, May 31, 1832 - - -	3,592 80		
Stock and tools since purchased, wages of overseers, &c.	4,834 78		
		8,427 58	
Sales and amount charged new prison for iron and labour	6,921 55		
Property on hand, April 30, 1833, including two horses and apparatus in machine shop - - - -	3,517 03		
		10,438 58	
Income since May 1832 - - -	- -	- -	2,011 00
SHOE SHOP:			
Property on hand, May 31, 1832 - - - -	2,020 40		
Property since purchased, salary of overseer, &c. -	3,467 31		
		5,487 71	
Amount of sales since May 31, 1832 - - -	4,956 31		
Stock and tools on hand, April 30, 1833 - - -	2,195 70		
		7,152 01	
Balance in favour of Shoe Shop - - -	- -	- -	1,664 30
WHEELWRIGHT'S SHOP:			
Stock and tools on hand, May 31, 1832 - - -	883 69		
Stock and tools since purchased, including stock and tools of cooper's shop (discontinued,) pay of overseer, &c. - - - - - - - -	2,899 30		
		3,782 99	
Sales of last year - - - - - - -	2,713 91		
Property on hand, April 30, 1833 - - - -	2,423 3		
		5,136 94	
Income of last year - - - - - - -			1,353 95
Cash received from visitors, since May 1832 - -			208 73
TOTAL - -			9,003 38

EXPENDITURE:

	Dollars. cents.	Dollars. cents.	Dollars. cents.
Provisions on hand, May 31, 1832 - - - -	1,022 92		
Provisions since purchased - - - - -	2,901 55		
		3,924 47	
Provisions on hand, April 30, 1833 - - - -	- -	997 03	
Amount consumed last year - ' - - -	- -	- -	2,927 44
Carried forward - -	- -	- -	2,927 44

NEW
HAMPSHIRE.

	Dollars. cents.	Dollars. cents.	Dollars. cents.
Brought forward - -	- -	- -	2,927 44
Bedding and clothing on hand, 31 May 1832 - -	416 25		
Bedding and clothing since purchased - - -	1,228 26		
		1,644 51	
Bedding and clothing on hand, April 30, 1833 - -	- -	948 69	
Cost for the last year - - - -	- -	- -	695 82
Expenses for furniture, fuel, books on hand, last year	660 11		
Salary of deputy warden, pay of watchmen, fuel, &c.	2,814 56		
		3,474 67	
Furniture, fuel, books, &c. on hand, 30 April 1833 -	- -	1,924 65	
Consumed of those articles last year - -	- -	- -	1,550 02
Discharged convicts, for clothes and cash furnished on leaving - - - - - - - - -	- -	- -	267 31
Hospital, for pay of physician, medicines, &c. - -	- -	- -	137 60
Repairs on buildings, yard, &c. - - - -	- -	- -	245 06
Interest for balance paid out - - - - -	- -	- -	14 01
Total amount of Expenditure, since May 31, 1832 - - -			5,846 26
Leaving the amount of last year's net gains to the institution $			3,157 12

RECAPITULATION:

	Dollars cents	Dollars cents
Whole amount of property on hand, May 31, 1832 - - -	10,463 34	
Cash on hand same time - - - - - - - -	130 93	
Debts due to the prison, after deducting the amount owed May 31, 1832 - - - - - - - - - - -	13,388 43	
		23,982 70
Amount of property on hand, April 30, 1833 - - - -	15,437 11	
Cash on hand same time - - - - - - - -	435 90	
Balance of debts due to the prison, above the amount owed -	11,266 81	
		27,139 82
Increased amount of last year - - $		3,157 12

Number of convicts in confinement, May 31, 1832 - -	89	
Since committed - - - - - - - - -	14	
		103
Discharged by expiration of sentence - - - -	8	
Pardoned - - - - - - - - - -	7	
Died - - - - - - - - - - -	—	
Escaped - - - - - - - - - -	1	
		16
Number now in confinement - - - -		87
Decrease since May 31, 1832 - - - - - - -		2

SENTENCES of 89 prisoners, confined in June 1833:

For life - - - - - -	5	
13 years - - - - -	1	on four indictments.
12 ,, - - - - -	2	
11 ,, - - - - -	1	
10 ,, - - - - -	7	
8 ,, - - - - -	3	
7 ,, - - - - -	11	
6 ,, - - - - -	8	
5 ,, - - - - -	32	
Under 5 years - - - - -	19	
	89	

NUMBER of CONVICTS committed to the NEW HAMPSHIRE STATE PRISON, at CONCORD, from its commencement to 30 June 1833.

CRIMES.	Nov. 1812.	1813.	1814.	1815.	1816.	1817.	1818.	1819.	1820.	1821.	1822.	1823.	1824.	1825.	1826.	1827.	1828.	1829.	1830.	1831.	1832.	June 1833.
Horse stealing	1	2	3	5	1	—	3	4	1	2	1	3	2	—	1	6	6	—	1	2	1	1
Forgery	—	1	—	—	2	2	2	2	1	1	2	1	1	—	1	1	1	1	1	2	—	—
Larceny	—	1	—	—	1	—	—	—	—	—	—	—	—	—	—	—	—	1	—	—	—	—
Arson	—	—	—	—	—	1	—	—	1	—	1.	—	—	1	—	—	—	—	—	—	—	—
Rape, and Assault to commit Rape	—	—	—	—	—	—	—	—	—	—	—	—	—	—	—	—	1	—	{ Rape 1 }	—	—	—
Assault to kill	—	—	—	—	1	—	2	3	—	1	1	2	1	3	2	1	—	—	1	1	—	—
Counterfeiting Notes or Money	—	—	—	1	3	1	3	—	1	—	—	—	—	—	—	—	—	—	—	1	—	—
Passing counterfeit Money	—	—	—	—	—	1	—	—	2	4	1	6	2	1	2	—	—	—	2	—	1	1
Manslaughter	—	—	—	—	—	1	—	—	1	—	1	—	—	—	—	—	—	—	—	2	1	—
Burglary	—	—	—	—	—	—	1	1	—	1	—	—	—	1	—	—	—	—	—	1	—	—
Felony	—	—	—	—	—	—	—	—	1	—	—	—	—	—	—	—	—	—	—	—	—	—
Perjury	—	—	—	—	—	—	—	1	—	—	—	—	—	1	—	—	—	—	—	—	1	—
House and Store breaking	—	—	—	—	—	—	—	—	—	—	—	—	—	—	—	—	1	—	1	1	—	—
Burning Barn and Shingles	—	—	—	—	—	—	—	—	—	—	—	—	—	—	—	1	1	—	—	1	—	—
Stealing	—	7	11	7	23	23	15	6	10	14	7	14	13	15	7	2	9	7	24	13	15	6
Sheep-stealing	—	—	—	—	1	—	—	—	—	1	1	—	—	—	—	1	1	—	—	—	—	—
Maiming	—	—	—	—	—	—	—	—	—	—	—	—	—	2	—	—	—	—	—	—	—	—
Killing a Ram	—	—	—	—	—	—	—	—	—	—	—	—	—	—	—	—	—	1	—	—	—	—
Highway Robbery	—	—	—	—	—	—	—	—	—	—	—	—	—	—	—	—	—	1	—	—	—	—
TOTAL	1	11	14	13	32	29	26	17	18	23	16	26	19	24	13	12	20	11	31	24	19	8
Coloured People	—	F1	1	—	—	—	—	—	—	—	—	—	—	—	—	—	2	—	—	—	1	—
White Females	—	—	—	—	—	—	—	—	—	—	—	—	—	—	—	—	—	—	—	—	1	—
Pardoned	—	—	—	2	1	2	—	1	2	2	2	5	5	3	4	8	4	8	4	3	5	6
Escaped	—	—	—	4	—	1	—	2	—	—	—	—	3	—	1	—	—	1	—	2	—	—
Died	—	—	—	—	—	1	—	1	1	1	2	1	2	2	1	2	—	1	—	—	1	—
Natives of America	1	11	13	11	29	27	24	16	18	18	15	25	17	19	12	12	16	10	29	23	18	7
Canada	—	—	1	—	—	—	—	—	—	—	—	—	1	—	—	—	—	—	1	—	—	1
England	—	—	—	—	1	1	1	—	—	2	—	—	—	1	1	—	—	—	1	1	1	—
Ireland	—	—	—	2	2	1	1	1	—	2	—	1	—	2	—	—	3	1	—	—	—	—
Scotland	—	—	—	—	—	—	—	—	—	1	—	—	—	1	—	—	1	—	—	—	—	—
France	—	—	—	—	—	—	—	—	—	—	—	—	1	—	—	—	—	—	—	—	—	—
Nova Scotia	—	—	—	—	—	—	—	—	—	—	—	—	—	1	—	—	—	—	—	—	—	—
TOTAL	1	11	14	13	32	29	26	17	18	23	16	26	19	24	13	12	20	11	31	24	19	8
Re-convictions	—	—	—	—	—	—	—	1	—	—	—	1	1	2	1	2	1	—	—	3	5	—
Third Convictions	—	—	—	—	—	—	—	—	—	—	—	—	—	—	—	—	1	—	—	1	—	—
AGES.																						
Under 15 Years	—	—	—	—	(13) 2	(14) 1	—	—	—	—	—	—	—	—	—	—	—	—	(14) 2	—	—	—
15 to 20	—	—	3	2	4	2	2	1	4	1	2	4	3	6	1	2	4	—	4	2	1	3
20 to 30	—	8	7	7	16	17	13	10	7	13	7	12	10	11	5	9	9	9	18	12	15	5
30 to 40	1	1	2	3	6	7	5	4	4	6	3	5	2	3	4	1	5	1	6	5	1	—
40 to 50	—	2	1	—	3	2	3	1	2	—	4	3	2	3	—	—	2	—	1	4	2	—
50 to 60	—	—	1	1	—	—	1	1	1	1	—	1	1	—	2	—	—	—	1	—	—	—
60 to 70	—	—	—	—	1	—	—	—	—	2	—	1	1	1	1	—	—	1	—	—	—	—
70 to 80	—	—	—	—	—	1	—	2	—	—	—	—	—	—	—	—	—	—	—	—	—	—
TOTAL	1	11	14	13	32	29	26	17	18	23	16	26	19	24	13	12	20	11	31	24	19	8

N.B. There has been only two executions in 25 years.

PUNISHMENTS for the principal Offences in this STATE.

OFFENCES.		PUNISHMENTS.
Adultery		- - Confinement in common gaol not exceeding one year, and a fine not exceeding $ 400., and to enter into recognizances for not exceeding five years.
Arson, &c.	Burning dwelling-house, or being accessary before the fact.	Solitary imprisonment not exceeding six months, and hard labour for life.
	Firing public buildings, store, &c.	- - Solitary imprisonment not exceeding six months, and hard labour from two to twenty years.
	Firing corn or hay stacks, lumber, &c.	- - Imprisonment and hard labour from one to three years, or by fine not exceeding $ 1,000. and imprisonment in county gaol not exceeding one year.
Assault -	- - With intent to commit murder, rape, sodomy or robbery.	- - Solitary imprisonment not exceeding six months, and hard labour from one to ten years.
	Common assault and battery -	- - Fine not exceeding $ 10. and recognizances for good behaviour for not exceeding one year.
Bastardy	Concealing the death of a bastard child.	Imprisonment not exceeding two years or fine not exceeding $ 1,000.
Bigamy		- - Imprisonment in common gaol not exceeding two years, or fine not exceeding 400 $., and to give security for good behaviour not exceeding five years.
Blasphemy		- - Fine not exceeding $ 200., and to find security for good behaviour for not exceeding one year.
Burglary, &c. -	Breaking into a house in the night with intent to commit a felony.	Solitary imprisonment not exceeding six months, and hard labour for life.
	Breaking and entering any office, bank, &c. in the night.	Confinement at hard labour from three to ten years.
	Entering in the night without breaking, or in the day with breaking, with intent to commit a felony; or being accessary before the fact.	Confinement at hard labour from two to seven years.
Coining. &c. See *Forgery*.		
Dead Bodies -	Digging up, removing or assisting therein.	- - Fine not exceeding $ 2,000. nor less than $ 500., to be publicly whipped not exceeding 39 stripes, or imprisonment not exceeding two years nor less than one year.
Escape, &c. -	Voluntary, permitted by gaoler -	- - The same punishment as that to which the prisoner is sentenced, whether convicted or before trial.
	Negligence of or permitted by gaoler, or voluntary, if prisoner retaken.	Fine at discretion of court, not exceeding $ 300.
	Assisting a prisoner in escape, furnishing tools, &c., where a prisoner, not committed for a capital offence, escapes.	The same punishment to which the prisoner is sentenced.
	Where the offence is capital.	Imprisonment for life, or any less period.
	If the prisoner does not escape, or if he is re-taken.	Fine not exceeding $ 100.
Forgery -	Of bank-note or public security -	- - Solitary imprisonment not exceeding six months, and hard labour from five to twenty years.
	Passing forged notes, &c. -	- - Solitary imprisonment not exceeding four months, and hard labour from two to five years.
	Bringing into the State or having in possession counterfeit bills, with intent to pass them. Making or having in possession plates, &c., with intent to make counterfeit bank bills, &c.	- - Solitary imprisonment not exceeding four months, and hard labour from two to five years.
	Forgery of records, judicial proceedings, obligations, promissory notes, &c., or knowingly uttering the same.	- - Solitary imprisonment not exceeding six months, and hard labour from three to seven years.
	Counterfeiting coin - -	- - Solitary imprisonment not exceeding six months, and hard labour from four to ten years.

PUNISHMENTS for the principal Offences in this State—*continued.*

OFFENCES.		PUNISHMENTS.
Forgery—*continued.*	Uttering counterfeit coin — Bringing into the State or having counterfeit coin, with intent to pass.	- - Solitary imprisonment not exceeding four months, and hard labour from two to five years.
	Making or possessing any tool for counterfeiting coin, with intent to make false coin.	- - Solitary imprisonment not exceeding four months, and hard labour from two to five years.
Fornication - -	- - - - - - -	Fine of $50. or imprisonment in common gaol not exceeding six months.
Horse Stealing. *See* Larceny.		
Incest - - -	- - - - - - -	- - To be placed on a gallows for an hour, with a rope about the neck; fine not exceeding 100 l., imprisonment not exceeding one year, and bound to good behaviour not exceeding five years; any or all.
Larceny - - *See* also Robbery.	Stealing under $20. - - -	- - Imprisonment in common gaol from one month to one year, and fine not exceeding $100., and to pay treble value to owner of goods with costs.
	Stealing $20. or upwards - -	Imprisonment at hard labour from two to five years.
	Stealing in a dwelling house - -	Imprisonment at hard labour from two to ten years.
	In a shop, vessel, &c. - - -	Imprisonment at hard labour from one to seven years.
	From the person - - -	Ditto from three to seven years.
	Stealing horse, cattle or sheep - -	Ditto from three to seven years.
	Receiving or concealing stolen goods.	The same as the thief.
Maiming, disfiguring &c. - - -	With design so to do, or being accessary before the fact.	- - Solitary imprisonment for not exceeding six months, and hard labour from one to twenty years.
Malicious Mischief -	Killing, maiming, beating or wounding cattle.	Fine not exceeding $100. or imprisonment not exceeding ninety days.
	Killing, maiming or poisoning cattle with intent to injure the owner.	- - Imprisonment at hard labour from one to three years, or fine not exceeding $100., or imprisonment in common gaol not exceeding one year.
Manslaughter -	- - - - - - -	- - Fine not exceeding $1,000., or fine not exceeding $500., and imprisonment in common gaol not exceeding one year, or solitary imprisonment not exceeding six months, and hard labour not less than one year, or for life; one or more of the above.
Murder - - -	- - - - - - -	Death.
Officers, &c. - - *See* also Escape.	Obstructing officers in duty - -	- - Imprisonment in common gaol not exceeding one year, or fine not exceeding $500.
Perjury - - -	Or subornation thereof - -	- - Solitary imprisonment not exceeding four months, and hard labour from two to five years.
Rape - - -	Including abuse of child under 10 years of age.	- - Solitary imprisonment not less than six months, and afterwards imprisonment for life.
Riot - - -	- - - - - - -	- - Fine not exceeding $1,000., and imprisonment in common gaol not exceeding one year.
Robbery - -	With violence from the person, or assisting therein.	- - Solitary imprisonment not exceeding six months, and afterwards hard labour for life.
Do. Second Offence -	- - Committed after conviction, where the punishment of both is imprisonment at hard labour.	- - Imprisonment at hard labour for first offence doubled, and to be marked on the arm.
	A repetition of an offence so punished, after two such convictions.	Imprisonment for life.
Sodomy - - -	- - - - - - -	- - Solitary imprisonment not exceeding six months, and afterwards hard labour from one to ten years.
Treason - - -	- - - - - - -	Death.
	Misprision of treason - - -	- - Imprisonment in common gaol not exceeding seven years, and fine not exceeding $2,000.

N.B. In general, the owner of goods stolen may have execution for the value against either the thief or receiver, and for the costs of prosecution against any convict sentenced to hard labour or solitary confinement.

The degree of punishment within the prescribed limits, is determined by the Court.

VERMONT.

STATE PRISON AT WINDSOR.

VERMONT.

THIS penitentiary is on an eminence on the west bank of the Connecticut River. The original part of the building was erected in 1809. The boundary wall, which is 20 feet high, incloses a plot of ground, about 280 feet long and 200 feet deep. In the centre of the front is the keeper's house, a stone building, 50 feet long and four stories high: adjoining is another stone building, three stories high, 84 feet long and 36 feet wide, containing several large rooms on each side which open into a middle passage: this part of the prison is now principally used for store-rooms and the solitary confinement of refractory prisoners. The upper story is appropriated to the hospital.

In 1830, a double range of sleeping-cells was built on the other side of the keeper's house. The cells are placed back to back (as at Auburn) and are surrounded by an area 11 feet wide. This building is four stories high, and contains 136 cells. Each cell is seven feet long, three feet six inches wide, and six feet nine inches high. The doors are of wood, having an opening in the upper part about nine inches square. The width of the pier or wall between the doors is only two feet six inches. The bedsteads are of wood. A ventilator which is fixed in the ceiling at the back part of each cell goes into a flue and is carried up to the roof.* The cells appeared dirty and smelt offensively close, but they are said to be white-washed once a quarter. A stove is placed in the middle of the area, on each side, with iron pipes passing along the front of the cells. The area is ventilated by windows in the sides and openings in the ceilings. There are three ranges of workshops in the large yard in the rear, one of which is placed against the boundary wall: the others are detached. The kitchen adjoins the new range of cells.

The prisoners can converse together at night in the cells, if not very strictly watched, and there is great difficulty in detecting them. They are locked up in their cells at sun-set, and unlocked at sun-rise. Last winter the prisoners were allowed lights in the cells for an hour and an half, in order that they might read.† The prisoners do not march to and from their cells with the "lock step," as this plan has been considered dangerous and likely to lead to conversation. The prisoners are forbidden to talk together while at their work, but this desirable regulation does not appear to be strictly enforced. The convicts gaze at strangers without restraint. The punishment for a breach of the rules is being shut up in a dark cell. This seldom exceeds 48 hours before it leads to submission. The longest period of confinement in a dark cell has been 35 days. The infliction of the whip is prohibited by law. The number of prisoners at the period of my visit was 118 men and one woman; the latter is constantly employed in sewing. The men work at dyeing yarn, weaving, spinning, tailoring, shoe-making, and as blacksmiths and wheelwrights. They are selected for particular trades according to their age and strength, and as it suits the convenience of the prison. Each convict has an assigned task of work, but if it is finished earlier he must still work until sun-set. The well-behaved are reported in order that they may receive certain indulgences from the keeper. Snuff and tobacco are allowed in moderate quantities. The prisoners are permitted to send and receive letters to and from their friends. They may see visitors by permission of the keeper, for one hour at a time, but not on Sundays.

The manufactured articles, linen, shoes, &c. are sent to an agent at Boston, who finds a ready sale for them. The labour of the prisoners in this penitentiary has, on an average, paid the amount of its expenditure. The daily ration for each convict is 18 ounces of beef or 12 ounces of pork, 10 ounces of rye meal and 10 ounces of Indian meal; also for every 100 rations three bushels of potatoes, two ounces of black pepper, and a suitable quantity of salt. In summer, a pint of beer is allowed in the forenoon and a pint in the afternoon for each man. The supper consists of coffee or burnt-rye. The prisoners take their meals in the cells. The prison generally is very healthy. At this time there was only one prisoner (an idiot) in the hospital.‡

A clergyman attends every evening, when the prisoners are assembled in the open space at the end of the cell-building, where he reads a portion of Scripture and offers up a prayer, before they are locked up for the night. He also preaches a sermon twice on Sundays. The chaplain is appointed by the superintendent, as are also the other officers. The Legislature fix and pay the salaries. There are four assistant keepers and four guards.

No prisoner is committed for less than a year. Counterfeiting is considered to be on the increase; a circumstance which is attributed to Vermont being a border state. Not less than 80 counterfeiters were taken up this summer in Canada.—An execution has not taken place since 1814.

---

* Complaint is made that the rats come down these flues, and devour the provisions of the prisoners.

† Eighteen newspapers were lately found in the prison.

‡ It is the custom in this State for parishes to dispose of their insane paupers to those who will take charge of them on the most advantageous pecuniary terms. If the individual be capable of work a sum will be given for him in proportion to the prospect of making him useful. If otherwise, the parish will pay a sum to any one who will undertake the charge of him.

Plan of the VERMONT STATE PRISON at *WINDSOR*

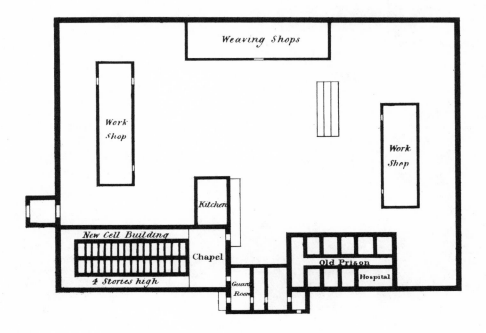

Weaving Shops

Work Shop

Work Shop

Kitchen

New Cell Building

Chapel

Old Prison

4 Stories high

Guard Room

Hospital

Scale

5 10 20 30 40 50 60 70 80 90 100   150   200   300 Feet

NUMBER of Convicts committed to Vermont State Prison at Windsor from 1816 to 30th June 1833.

CRIMES.	1816.	1817.	1818.	1819.	1820.	1821.	1822.	1823.	1824.	1825.	1826.	1827.	1828.	1829.	1830.	1831.	1832.	To June 1833.
Theft or stealing	24	16	14	21	20	16	17	13	16	17	26	18	17	17	25	16	21	9
Horse stealing	7	10	4	5	1	1	7	—	1	8	2	3	4	—	7	3	3	1
Counterfeiting and passing Counterfeit Money	5	4	1	11	11	8	5	3	3	3	3	3	2	4	6	2	3	4
Forgery	3	2	1	2	2	—	1	2	3	—	6	—	2	2	1	5	1	1
Larceny	2	4	—	—	—	—	—	—	—	—	—	—	—	—	—	—	—	—
Burglary	1	2	2	2	4	—	3	4	—	6	—	—	1	2	5	1	3	—
Swindling	1	1	—	—	—	—	—	1	1	1	4	—	1	—	—	1	—	1
Assault with intent to Murder	—	1	1	—	—	—	—	1	1	—	—	1	—	—	—	—	—	1
Aiding to break Gaol or escape of Prisoner	—	2	—	4	—	—	1	1	2	—	1	1	:	1	3	1	3	1
Polygamy	—	—	1	—	1	—	—	1	1	1	1	—	1	1	1	1	1	—
Rape	—	—	1	—	2	1	1	1	2	—	2	1	2	—	1	—	1	2
Assault with intent to commit Rape	—	—	—	4	1	—	—	—	1	1	1	1	—	—	1	—	1	1
Adultery	—	—	1	—	2	2	1	—	2	1	—	—	2	—	—	—	—	—
Highway Robbery	—	—	—	—	—	—	—	—	—	—	—	—	—	1	1	—	1	—
Manslaughter	—	—	—	—	—	—	—	—	1	1	—	—	—	—	—	—	1	—
Arson	—	—	—	—	—	—	—	—	—	—	—	—	—	—	—	—	—	—
Burning	—	—	—	—	—	—	1	—	2	—	—	—	—	1	—	—	1	—
Perjury	—	—	—	—	—	—	—	—	—	—	—	—	—	—	1	—	1	—
Resisting an Officer	—	—	—	—	—	—	—	—	—	1	2	—	—	—	2	—	—	2
Infanticide	—	—	—	—	—	—	—	—	—	—	—	—	—	—	2	—	—	—
TOTAL	43	42	25	45	42	28	36	26	33	37	49	26	31	28	55	28	35	18
AGES — 15 to 20 years of age	10	8	3	2	4	4	3	4	—	3	3	3	3	5	8	1	5	—
20 to 30	24	19	16	26	27	12	20	13	21	18	19	8	12	12	22	12	15	8
30 to 40	6	6	4	11	4	8	5	5	9	12	12	7	11	7	16	9	11	7
40 to 50	3	4	2	4	3	2	6	4	1	3	8	4	4	2	4	4	2	1
50 to 60	—	2	1	2	3	1	1	1	2	—	5	4	1	2	4	2	1	1
60 to 70	—	2	—	—	3	—	1	—	1	(†)1	2	1	2	—	4	1	1	1
70 to 80	—	1	—	—	1	1	1	—	—	—	—	—	—	—	—	—	1	—
TOTAL	43	42	25	45	42	28	36	26	33	37	49	26	31	28	55	28	35	18
Females	—	—	—	1	1	—	1	1	—	1	3	—	1	—	2	—	1	—
Reconvictions	—	—	—	—	7	4	6	4	2	6	6	3	2	3	4	2	7	3
Pardons	9	19	24	25	20	26	16	13	15	16	21	23	19	23	24	22	14	—
COUNTRIES of Foreigners — England	2	1	—	5	3	1	1	4	4	6	6	2	1	—	1	1	1	—
Scotland	—	—	—	—	—	—	—	—	—	—	—	—	—	1	1	—	—	1
Ireland	2	2	1	3	4	2	1	3	3	5	2	5	3	1	2	2	1	1
Canada	1	2	1	1	2	—	2	1	3	2	2	3	2	2	6	1	5	1
Switzerland	1	—	—	1	—	—	—	—	—	1	—	—	—	—	—	—	—	1
Hayti	—	—	—	1	—	—	—	—	—	—	—	—	—	—	—	—	—	—
Italy	—	—	—	1	—	—	—	—	—	—	—	—	—	—	—	—	—	—
Russia	—	—	—	1	—	—	—	—	—	—	—	—	—	—	1	—	—	—
France	—	—	—	1	—	—	—	—	1	—	—	—	—	—	—	—	—	—
Nova Scotia	—	—	—	1	—	—	—	—	1	—	—	—	—	—	—	—	—	—
Germany	—	—	—	—	—	—	—	—	—	—	—	—	—	—	—	—	—	—

593.

l 3

APPENDIX TO CRAWFORD'S REPORT

VERMONT,
PUNISHMENTS for the principal Offences in the STATE.

OFFENCES.		PUNISHMENTS.
Adultery	- - - - - - - - -	- - Confinement in State prison, for not exceeding three years, and fine not exceeding $ 1,000, or either.
Arson - - -	- - Burning the dwelling house of another, or any other building, whereby any person suffers death, or is injured in his or her body, or members.	Death.
	Burning the dwelling house of another, or any other building, or corn, hay or grain, or any vessel.	- - State prison and hard labour not exceeding ten years, and fine not exceeding $ 1,000, or either.
Assault - - -	And Battery - - - -	Fine, or if unable to pay, county gaol not exceeding one year.
	With intent to ravish - - -	- - State prison not exceeding seven years, and fine not exceeding $ 500, or either.
	With intent to murder or rob - -	- - State prison not exceeding ten years, and fine not exceeding $ 1,000, or either.
Bastardy - -	- - Being privately delivered of a bastard child, and such child being found dead, where presumptive evidence shall appear that the child was born alive, and its death procured by the mother.*	- - Hard labour in State prison, for not exceeding three years, and fine not more than $ 200, or either.
Bigamy - - -	- - - - - - - -	The same as adultery.
Blasphemy - -	- - - - - - - -	- - Fine not exceeding $ 200 ; and bound to good behaviour for not exceeding one year.
Burglary, &c. - -	- - Breaking by night into dwelling house, storehouse, workshop, &c. with intent to commit a high crime or misdemeanor.	- - State prison not exceeding fifteen years, and fine not exceeding $ 1,000, or either, and disqualified for giving evidence or verdict.
	Second offence - - - -	State prison for life, or term of years not less than seven.
Coin. *See* also Forgery.	- - Furnishing goods, or lending money to be paid at an advanced rate in base coin.	- - State prison at hard labour not exceeding three years, and fine not exceeding $ 300.
Dead Bodies - -	Digging up, removing or disturbing the remains of the dead.	- - Fine not exceeding $ 1,000, or publicly whipped, not exceeding 39 stripes, or imprisonment not exing one year.
Duelling - -	Fighting a duel, when death ensues -	Death.
	When death does not ensue, or sending, bearing or accepting a challenge.	Fine from $ 50 to $ 1,000, and incapacitated from holding office.
Escape, &c. *See* also Officer.	Breaking gaol - - - -	- - Fine not exceeding $ 300, and confined in State prison for not exceeding three years.
False Pretences -	Obtaining money, goods, &c. by means of.	- - State prison not exceeding five years, and fine not exceeding $ 500, or either.
Forgery - -	- - Counterfeiting or altering bank bills or notes, State or county money orders, or assisting therein engraving bank notes, or possessing plates for such purpose, or altering such forged orders, bills or notes, or possessing them with intent to utter.	- - State prison not exceeding 14 years, and fine not exceeding $ 1,000, or either.

* A woman may be found guilty of this offence on an indictment for murdering her child.

PUNISHMENTS for the principal Offences in this State—*continued.*

OFFENCES.		PUNISHMENTS.
Forgery—*(continued)*	Forging or uttering any other bills, notes, &c. forging or altering record, process, deed, will, &c. or assisting therein.	- - Hard labour in State prison not exceeding ten years, and fine not exceeding $ 1,000, or either, and disqualified as witness or juror.
	Counterfeiting or passing coin, making or mending instruments for coining.	- - State prison not exceeding ten years, and fine not exceeding $ 1,000. or either.
	Counselling or advising in forging or passing base coin.	- - State prison not exceeding five years, and fine not exceeding $ 500, or either.
	Teaching or contracting to teach the art of counterfeiting or debasing metals.	- - State prison not exceeding three years, and fine not exceeding $ 300, or either.
Horse stealing -	- - - - - -	- - Hard labour in State prison not exceeding ten years, and fine not exceeding $ 1,000, or either.
	Second offence - - -	- - State prison not exceeding fifteen years, and fine not exceeding $ 1,000, or either.
Incest - - -	- - - - - -	The same as adultery
Kidnapping - -	- - - - - -	- - Publicly whipped, not exceeding 39 stripes, or fine not exceeding $ 1,000, and hard labour not exceeding seven years.
Larceny - -	Stealing to any amount - -	- - State prison not exceeding seven years, and fine not exceeding $ 500, or either.
	Stealing fruit from any garden, orchard, &c. by night.	Fine not exceeding $ 100.
	Receivers - - -	As thieves.
Maiming, disfiguring, &c.	Cutting out tongue, or putting out eyes, &c.	State prison for life, or not less than seven years.
Manslaughter - -	- - - - - -	- - State prison for life, or not less than seven years, and fine not exceeding $ 1,000, or either.
Murder - - -	- - - - - -	Death.
Officer - - -	Impeding civil or military officer in the discharge of his duties.	- - Fine not exceeding $ 300, and State prison not exceeding three years, or either.
	Defaming judges or magistrates, respecting any sentence passed by them officially.	Fine not exceeding $ 200.
Perjury, or subornation thereof	- - - -	- - State prison not exceeding ten years, and fine not exceeding $ 1,000, or either; and disabled from giving evidence or verdict.
	In a case affecting life, but where life is not taken.	The same as manslaughter.
	Where life is taken - -	Death.
Rape, including abuse of child under 11 years of age - -		- - State prison, and hard labour not exceeding ten years, and fine not exceeding $ 1,000, or either.
Riot - - -	- - - - - -	- - Fine not exceeding $ 100, and imprisonment not exceeding six months, or either
Robbery - -	- - - - - -	The same as burglary.
	Second offence - - -	Same as second conviction for burglary.
Treason - - -	- - - - - -	Death.
	Misprision of treason - -	- - Hard labour in State prison for not exceeding seven years, and fine not exceeding $ 2,000, or either.

N. B.—The court determines the precise degree of punishment within the limits prescribed.

MAINE.

STATE PRISON AT THOMASTON.

THE situation of this prison is extremely healthy, the ground being elevated and at a short distance from a navigable river. In the large space behind the building is a quarry of limestone which furnishes employment to some of the convicts. There is a boundary wall, with a separate entrance for waggons, and a road-way round the interior. A building, 50 feet by 40 feet and two stories high, forms the central part of the prison in front, and is used as the keeper's house, on each side of which is a double range of night-cells of very peculiar construction. These cells or pits (which were originally designed with a view of trying the experiment of solitary confinement) are only one story high, but are sunk below the surface, so that they have no doors, nor is there any passage way to them, the only entrance being from the top of each cell by means of an aperture about two feet square, which is secured by an iron grating. The convicts descend to these dungeons by means of a ladder, which is removed when the convict is in his cell. The dimensions of the cells are eight feet nine inches long, four feet six inches wide, and nine feet eight inches high. There is a small orifice in the external wall of each cell, eight inches long and one inch and a half wide, to admit air, but this is formed with an angle in the wall, in order to prevent the prisoner seeing through the aperture. The cells are consequently dark and gloomy. At the bottom there is a small hole, an inch and a half in diameter, for the purpose of warming the interior by means of heated air from a flue which passes under the floor, and communicates with a furnace. The cells are covered with a roof supported on posts of wood, seven feet high: the sides or enclosures under the roof are formed of large moveable partitions or doors, fixed on rollers. Part of them are kept unclosed during the day, to admit of the circulation of air over the tops of the cells: at night these partitions are closed and secured with fastenings. Next the road or street in front, the part over the cells is secured with iron railed bars, about four inches asunder. The original number of cells was 48. There have been since added 28. Two prisoners are frequently placed in the same cell. The cells are furnished with tubs at night, there being no privies.

The workshops in the rear consist of several detached buildings. There is a stone shed 120 feet long. A new kitchen, dining-hall, and chapel, have been recently erected. Besides working at a stone quarry, some of the prisoners are employed as blacksmiths, waggon-makers, joiners, shoe-makers and tailors. The women are occupied in the wash-house under the care of a female officer. There is no task work, and no portion of the earnings is allowed. It is stated that labour is regarded as a relief rather than as a punishment. No difficulty whatever is experienced in disposing of the articles made in the prison, which obtain the full market price. The prisoners are locked up in the winter at sun-set, and in summer an hour before. Lights are not allowed in the cells. The daily ration for each prisoner is one pound of beef or pork, half a pound of bread, and an allowance of potatoes, as much as is required. Mush and molasses are served for breakfast. The prisoners take their suppers in their cells. The average daily cost of food is 12½ cents per head. Each convict is allowed three quarters of a pound of tobacco monthly. The annual expense of clothing each prisoner is 12 dollars. Religious service is performed on Sunday, in the afternoon. There is also a Sunday-school for an hour and a half, in which the officers act as teachers.

The friends of prisoners are allowed to write to and visit them, except when under punishment, in the presence of the keeper. They may write to their connexions once in three months. When a convict is discharged, he is allowed from two to five dollars. On his liberation he may readily obtain employment if he can work. Besides the warden, there are 14 assistant keepers and guards. The inspectors visit the prison weekly, and make an annual report on its state to the Legislature. The average of deaths is two per cent: the average of sick is only two per cent.

The pits or dungeons in which the prisoners are confined at night, form the worst part of this establishment. The discipline is very relaxed, and the indulgence of allowing prisoners to receive visits and letters from their friends, tends essentially to counteract the ends of imprisonment. The slight degree of attention which is paid to the religious instruction is a great defect. The performance of service once on Sundays only, and the attendance for an hour or two at school once a week, as at other prisons, can be attended with but little, if any benefit.

On the 12th December 1832 there were 91 convicts in the prison who were employed in the following manner, viz.:—

In the smiths' shop, 5; stone-cutters, 38; wheelwrights, 3; shoe-binder, 1; cooks, 2; attending the hospital, 1; cutting wood, 1; shoe-makers, 9; tailors, 7; picking oakum, 15; washers, 2; waiters, 3; invalids, 4:—Total, 91.

PLAN OF THE MAINE STATE PRISON, THOMASTOWN.

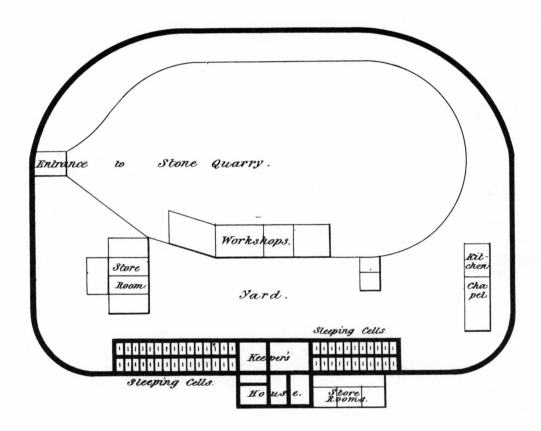

J. Basire, Lincoln

NUMBER of Convicts committed to the Maine State Prison at Thomaston, from 1824 to 1833.

CRIMES.	1824.	1825.	1826.	1827.	1828.	1829.	1830.	1831.	1832.	To 30 June 1833.
Shop and housebreaking	1	3	5	2	6	–	–	–	–	–
Having and passing counterfeit money	3	2	1	2	2	5	1	–	2	1
Larceny	48	47	44	17	35	32	27	36	36	19
Forgery	1	1	1	4	2	3	3	1	2	1
Swindling and obtaining goods under false pretences	–	–	–	–	1	3	–	–	–	–
Adultery	3	8	3	3	3	4	1	1	4	–
Horse stealing	1	–	–	–	1	–	–	–	–	–
Manslaughter	1	2	1	–	4	–	–	–	–	–
Assault to commit rape	2	–	6	2	–	1	2	1	–	–
Murder commuted	–	–	–	–	–	–	1	–	–	–
Killing and maiming cattle	–	–	–	–	–	–	2	–	–	–
Perjury	–	–	–	1	–	–	–	–	–	–
Blasphemy	1	–	–	–	–	–	–	–	–	–
Burning gaol	–	–	–	–	–	–	–	1	–	–
Burglary	–	–	–	–	–	–	–	–	–	2
Assault to kill	–	–	–	3	–	–	–	–	–	1
Receiving stolen goods	–	1	–	–	–	–	–	–	–	–
Arson	1	–	1	–	–	–	–	–	–	–
TOTAL	62	64	62	34	54	48	37	40	44	24
Coloured people	–	–	–	–	–	2	–	1	–	–
Second conviction	–	–	–	–	11	8	3	9	9	4
Natives of United States	62	57	53	30	41	40	32	37	34	11
„ England	–	–	3	1	2	1	1	1	2	6
„ Scotland	–	1	1	–	–	1	–	–	1	–
„ Ireland	–	3	2	2	10	2	3	1	4	4
„ Nova Scotia	–	1	2	1	–	3	1	1	–	1
„ France	–	2	–	–	1	–	–	–	–	1
„ Germany	–	–	1	–	–	–	–	–	–	1
„ New Brunswick	–	–	–	–	–	1	–	–	3	–
TOTAL	62	64	62	34	54	48	37	40	44	24
Ages of the prisoners:										
Under 15 years	4	2	1	–	–	–	–	–	–	–
15 to 20	4	12	9	4	6	7	7	5	2	4
20 to 30	25	30	31	21	29	23	14	19	22	16
30 to 40	21	13	15	3	10	11	10	9	11	2
40 to 50	6	6	4	4	8	3	4	4	4	1
50 to 60	–	1	2	–	1	4	2	2	4	1
60 to 70	2	–	–	2	–	–	–	1	1	–
TOTAL	62	64	62	34	54	48	37	40	44	24

PUNISHMENTS for the principal Offences in this STATE.

OFFENCES.			PUNISHMENTS.
Accessaries - -	- - Either before or after the fact, may be tried before the conviction of the principals.		For the punishments, *see* the several offences.
Adultery - -	Man or woman - - - -		- - Solitary imprisonment not exceeding three months, and hard labour not exceeding five years.
Arson, &c. - -	- - Setting fire to the dwelling-house of another, or other building, with intent to burn dwelling-house by night, or being accessary before the fact.		Death.
	- - To dwelling-house by day, or public buildings, churches, &c.; or stores, barns, &c. by night.		- - Solitary imprisonment not exceeding one year, and hard labour afterwards for life.
	- - Public buildings, churches, barns, &c. by day; or any other building by day or night.		- - Solitary imprisonment not exceeding one year, and hard labour not exceeding ten years.
	- - Corn, hay, fences, timber, &c. -		- - Solitary imprisonment not exceeding six months, and hard labour afterwards, not exceeding three years; or fine not exceeding $500, and imprisonment in common gaol not exceeding one year.
	Accessaries after the fact - -		- - Solitary imprisonment not exceeding one month, and confinement afterwards not exceeding five years; or by fine not exceeding $1,000, and imprisonment in common gaol not exceeding one year.
	Setting fire to woods without leave -		Fine $10, and liable for damage done.
Assault - - -	And Battery - - - -		Fine not exceeding $5.
	With intent, &c. - - - -		*See* several crimes intended.
Bastardy - -	Endeavouring to conceal the death of a bastard child.		- - Solitary imprisonment not exceeding three months, and hard labour not exceeding five years.
	Concealing pregnancy, or being secretly delivered of a bastard.		Fine not exceeding $100, or imprisonment for three months.
Bigamy - -	- - - - - - -		- - Solitary imprisonment not exceeding three months, and hard labour not exceeding five years.
Blasphemy - -	- - - - - - -		- - Solitary imprisonment not exceeding three months, and hard labour not exceeding five years.
Burglary, &c, - -	- - Breaking and entering a dwelling-house by night with intent to commit a felony, and committing an assault, or being armed with a dangerous weapon, any one being in the house; or accessary before the fact.		State prison for life, at hard labour.
	The same not armed, or committing any assault; or accessary before the fact.		- - State prison for a term of years, or for life
	Accessaries to either of the above after the fact.		- - Solitary imprisonment not exceeding three months, and hard labour not exceeding ten years.
	Entering with felonious intent by night, without breaking, or by day, with breaking; or accessary before the fact.		- - Solitary imprisonment not exceeding six months, and hard labour not exceeding three years; or fine not exceeding $500, and imprisonment not exceeding three years.
	Breaking and entering shop, ship, warehouse, office, &c. by night, and committing larceny therein.		- - Solitary imprisonment not exceeding one year, and hard labour not exceeding fifteen years.
	The same in case of a church, public building, store, stable, &c.		- - Solitary imprisonment not exceeding six months, and hard labour not exceeding five years.
	Entering dwelling-house by night without breaking, or by day with breaking, the owner or other person being therein, and put in fear.		- - Solitary imprisonment not exceeding one year, and hard labour not exceeding ten years.
Coining. *See* Forgery.			

PUNISHMENTS for the principal Offences in this State—*continued*.

OFFENCES.		PUNISHMENTS.
Dead Bodies - -	Disinterring, removing, receiving or disposing of.	Imprisonment not exceeding one year, and fine not exceeding $ 1,000.
Duelling, &c. *See* also Murder.	When death does not ensue; fighting a duel, giving a challenge, or acting as second.	- - Punished as a felonious assault, and disqualified from holding office for twenty years.
	Accepting a challenge - - -	- - Imprisonment in common gaol not exceeding one year, and disqualified for office for five years.
Embezzlement -	By officer of a bank - - -	- - Fine not exceeding $ 5,000, or imprisonment not exceeding ten years, or both.
Escape, &c. - -	- - Gaoler voluntarily permitting escape of a prisoner convicted of a capital felony.	Fine not exceeding $ 1,000, and State prison for life at hard labour.
	Where a prisoner is so charged but not convicted.	Fine not exceeding $ 1,000, and State prison from five to fifteen years.
	In other cases of voluntary escape -	The same punishment as the prisoner would suffer, if convicted.
	Negligent escape - - - -	Fine at discretion of the court.
	Rescuing, or attempting to rescue from officer, or from prison, any convict sentenced to solitary confinement, or hard labour; or conveying tools, &c. to him to effect his escape, whether successful or not.	- - Solitary imprisonment not exceeding six months, and hard labour, at the discretion of the court; or by fine not exceeding $ 500, and bound to good behaviour for not exceeding three years.
	Conveying tools, &c. to prisoner, whereby he escapes, when the offence capital.	- - Fine, imprisonment, or sitting on the gallows with rope about the neck, or solitary imprisonment not exceeding three months, and hard labour not exceeding five years; one or more of the above.
False Pretences -	Obtaining goods, money, &c. by means of	Fine from $ 40 to $ 400, or hard labour not exceeding seven years.
Forgery - -	- - Of public records, certificates, &c.; wills, deeds, &c.; private securities, or uttering them as true, or assisting therein.	- - Solitary imprisonment not exceeding six months, and hard labour from two to ten years.
	Of public bills of credit, bank-bills, &c.; or of gold or silver current coin, or assisting therein, or possessing ten or more notes, &c. or pieces of coin, with intent to utter.	Solitary imprisonment not exceeding one year, and hard labour for life.
	Knowingly offering forged notes, bills, &c. (1st offence).	- - Solitary imprisonment not exceeding thirty days, and hard labour not exceeding three years; or fine not exceeding $ 1,000, and binding to good behaviour for two years.
	Second offence, or conviction on three separate indictments in the same term.	- - Solitary imprisonment not exceeding one year, and hard labour from two to ten years.
	Bringing into the State or possessing counterfeit bank-notes, with intent to pass them as true.	- - Solitary imprisonment not exceeding three months, and hard labour not exceeding three years; or fine not exceeding $ 1,000, and common gaol not exceeding one year.
	Engraving or making plates, press, &c. for forging; or possessing plates, with intent to use, or making, mending or possessing, or permitting to be used, any instrument for coining.	- - Solitary imprisonment not exceeding three months, and hard labour not exceeding three years; or fine not exceeding $ 500, and common gaol not exceeding one year.
	Bringing into the State or possessing counterfeit coin, with intent to pass. (1st offence).	- - Solitary imprisonment not exceeding three months, and hard labour not exceeding three years; or fine not exceeding $ 1,000, and bound to good behaviour for two years.
	Second offence, or conviction on three separate indictments in the same term.	- - Solitary imprisonment not exceeding one year, and hard labour from two to ten years.
Fornication - -	- - - - - - -	- - Imprisonment in common gaol from ten to sixty days, or fine from $ 20 to $ 100.

(continued)

MAINE.   PUNISHMENTS for the principal Offences in this State—*continued*.

OFFENCES.		PUNISHMENTS.
Fraud. *See* Swindling, Ships, False Pretences.		
Larceny - - *See* also Burglary and Robbery.	Not exceeding $5, or accessary before or after the fact.	- - Fine not exceeding $5, and imprisonment in common gaol not exceeding twenty days, or both.
	Not exceeding $100, or accessary before the fact.	- - Solitary imprisonment not exceeding six months, and hard labour not exceeding one year; or fine not exceeding $100, and common gaol not exceeding one year.
	Exceeding $100, or accessary before the fact.	- - Solitary imprisonment not exceeding one year, and hard labour not exceeding three years.
	Stealing in a dwelling-house, shop, or office, &c. by day, or accessary before the fact.	- - Solitary imprisonment not exceeding six months, and hard labour not exceeding five years.
	Stealing from the person (not robbery) or accessary before the fact.	- - Solitary imprisonment not exceeding one year, and hard labour not exceeding five years.
	On second conviction for larceny, or on conviction for three distinct offences in the same term, either as principal or accessary before the fact.	- - Solitary imprisonment not exceeding one year, and hard labour from three to fifteen years.
	Assault with violence or dangerous weapon, with intent to steal.	- - Solitary imprisonment not exceeding one year, and hard labour not exceeding ten years.
	Receiving stolen goods, or harbouring thieves or robbers.	- - Solitary imprisonment not exceeding six months, and hard labour * not exceeding three years; or fine not exceeding $500, and imprisonment in common gaol not exceeding three years, or either of them.
	On second conviction of receiving stolen goods, or three separate convictions in one term.	- - Solitary imprisonment not exceeding one year, and hard labour from three to ten years.
Maiming - -	Or disfiguring, or being accessary before the fact.	- - Solitary imprisonment not exceeding one year, and hard labour or common gaol not exceeding ten years.
	Assault with intent to maim, or accessary before the fact.	- - Solitary imprisonment not exceeding six months, and hard labour or common gaol not exceeding four years.
Malicious Mischief.	*See* also Ship, and Arson.	
	Killing, wounding or disfiguring cattle	- - Solitary imprisonment not exceeding six months, and hard labour not exceeding three years; or fine not exceeding $500, and imprisonment in common gaol not exceeding one year.
	Accessaries thereto after the fact -	- - Solitary imprisonment not exceeding one month, and confinement not exceeding five years; or fine not exceeding $1,000, and common gaol not exceeding one year.
Manslaughter -	- - - - - - - -	- - Solitary imprisonment not exceeding six months, and hard labour not exceeding ten years; or fine not exceeding $1,000, and common gaol not exceeding three years.
Murder - - -	- - - - - - - -	- - Death; the bodies given up for dissection or not, at the discretion of the court.†
	Accessary after the fact - - -	- - Solitary confinement not exceeding six months, and hard labour not exceeding ten years.
	Assault with intent to murder, or accessary before the fact.	- - Solitary imprisonment not exceeding one year, and hard labour not exceeding twenty years.

* The sentence of hard labour to be remitted on first conviction of receiving stolen goods, or being accessary thereto, unless the offender is adjudged a common receiver.

† In case of murder committed in a duel this is imperative.

PUNISHMENTS for the principal Offences in this State—*continued.*   MAINE.

OFFENCES.		PUNISHMENTS.
Perjury or subornation thereof - - - - - -		- - Solitary imprisonment not exceeding three months, and hard labour from two to fifteen years.
	Attempt at subornation - - -	- - Solitary imprisonment not exceeding two months, and hard labour not exceeding seven years.
Rape - - -	Including abuse of a child under ten years, or accessary before the fact.	State prison for life.
	Accessary after the fact - - -	- - Solitary imprisonment not exceeding three months, and hard labour not exceeding ten years.
	Assault with intent to commit a rape	- - The same, or fine not exceeding $500, and common gaol not exceeding one year.
	The same on a child under ten years	- - Solitary imprisonment not exceeding four months, and hard labour for a term of years, or for life.
Receiving Stolen Goods. *See* Larceny.		
Rescue. *See* Escape.		
Riot - - -	- - - - - - -	- - Solitary imprisonment not exceeding one year, and hard labour not more than one year ; or fine not exceeding $500 ; or any or all of these punishments.
Robbery - -	- - Assaulting, taking property from the person, at the same time being armed with intent to kill or wound, or being armed and actually striking or wounding, or accessary before the fact.	State prison for life at hard labour.*
	Taking property from the person by force or fear, not being armed, or intending to kill, or accessary before the fact.	Solitary imprisonment not exceeding two years, and hard labour for life.
	Assault with intent to rob, being armed.	- - Solitary imprisonment not exceeding one year, and hard labour not exceeding twenty years.
	Accessaries to robbery after the fact	*See* Larceny.
Second Offences -	- - Prisoner convicted of an offence of which the punishment is solitary confinement or hard labour, after pardon or punishment for an offence similarly punished.	- - Hard labour in State prison for a limited time, or for life, in lieu of the other punishment prescribed by law, if the court thinks fit.
Ship - - -	- - Fitting out ship for the purpose of being lost, or making false invoice, with intent to defraud underwriters.	- - Solitary imprisonment not exceeding three months, and hard labour not exceeding five years, or fine not exceeding $5,000.
	- - Wilfully destroying a vessel, or causing it to be done with intent to injure or defraud.	Imprisonment for life, or a term not less than five years.
Sodomy or Bestiality	- - - - - -	- - Solitary imprisonment not exceeding one year, and hard labour not exceeding ten years.
Swindling. *See* False Pretences.		
Treason - -	- - - - - -	Death.
	Misprision thereof - - -	- - Imprisonment from two to five years, and the offender to forfeit goods and chattels, and profits of lands for his life, to the use of the State.

* This punishment, as well in this case as in that of rape, burglary, and voluntary escape, in capital cases, was substituted for death by Act of 1827 ; by which means the punishment for the minor offence next following is, nominally at least, the more severe of the two, being part of the old law of 1821.

N. B.—The Court determines the precise degree of punishment within the prescribed limits.

Nearly all the above punishments, consisting of solitary imprisonment and subsequent hard labour, were imposed by Acts passed in 1821, before the building of the State prison at Thomaston. By subsequent Acts, the prisoners so sentenced were to be removed to the State prison, and similar punishment was to be inflicted there ; but in 1827 it was enacted, that all punishments by imprisonment in the State prison should be by hard labour, and not by solitary confinement.

By the same Act of 1827, it is enacted, that any female, or any person under 18 years, sentenced to imprisonment, shall be imprisoned in the county gaol, unless the court shall decree otherwise.

MARYLAND.

STATE PRISON AT BALTIMORE.

MARYLAND.   THIS Penitentiary was opened for the reception of criminals in January 1812.* It is built on an eminence in the suburbs of Baltimore, on the north-east side of the city. The walls, which are of stone, 18 feet high, and surmounted by a wooden parapet, inclose a square of four acres. There is also a vacant space without the walls on each side belonging to the prison, so as to insure its being kept detached from other buildings. The cost of the ground and buildings amounted to 196,000 dollars. Within the walls across the entrance court in front is the keeper's house, three stories high, about 60 feet in length, and 55 feet in depth. On each side of this central building is a large wing connected by a corridor or passage, and extending at right angles into the yard in the rear. The upper stories of the central building, each containing four rooms, are occupied by the keeper and his family. The principal story is divided into a clerk's office, where the directors also hold their monthly meetings, a guard-room for the deputy keepers, and store-rooms for the sale of manufactured articles. Until the year 1829 the western wing building was used exclusively for the convicts to sleep in at night. It consists of a spacious hall and large sleeping rooms, 36 in number, of sufficient magnitude to accommodate 10 persons in each. There is also a kitchen and bake-house for the service of the prisoners. The hospital departments are on the upper stories. The female convicts still occupy the principal floor of this building. The basement floor, containing a large hall or passage, is used as the dining-room for the male prisoners.

The eastern wing, which was erected in 1829, contains 320 solitary cells for the male convicts.† The position of the cells is different from that at Auburn, each range being placed against the walls instead of the centre. A passage 15 feet wide separates the two ranges of cells the entire length of the building, and being open from the bottom to the roof, affords a free and unbroken view of each range. The cells are five stories high, built on arches. Above the ground-floor the cells are entered from small galleries at the level of each floor, projecting three feet from the wall. These galleries are supported by iron brackets in the wall, so as to prevent the least obstruction to the sight and to a free current of air. Each cell is eight feet six inches in length, three feet seven inches in width, and seven feet in height. From a glazed window in the external wall, three feet in height and four inches in breadth on the outer face, and twelve inches on the inner surface of the wall, light and air are admitted to each cell. On the eastern side of each story, in the centre of the range of cells, is a room eight feet six inches square occupied by the guard. The galleries are approached by two flights of winding stairs on each side of the north entrance. The cells have iron grated doors,‡ with a bar attached to each, extending to a staple in the wall beyond the reach of the prisoner. The ends of the bars of two doors clasp on one staple, and are fastened together with a common padlock. Each cell contains a cot and sacking bottom, (furnished in the winter season with a mattrass made of waste yarn,) three blankets, and a coverlid of cotton and wool. The cells are heated by means of three large stoves placed at equal distances on the lower floor of the central passage between the ranges of cells: they are lighted by large lamps in the passage. There are no privies in this part of the building, but the convict takes with him into his cell a covered bucket. Each cell is furnished with a can of water every evening. The general privies at the end of the prison yard are built over a sewer which runs into a stream of water in the vicinity.

The

---

* On the opening of the penitentiary, fifty-one convicts were removed to it from the public roads throughout the State, and served the remainder of their sentence.

† The number at present confined in the penitentiary is 310 males and 56 females. The greatest number confined at any one time has been 327 males and 66 females.

‡ In consequence of the doors being hung on the outer face of the wall next the middle passage, the prisoners can talk together from cell to cell, and make signs to those opposite: it is therefore proposed to have a second door to each cell placed on the inside of the wall.

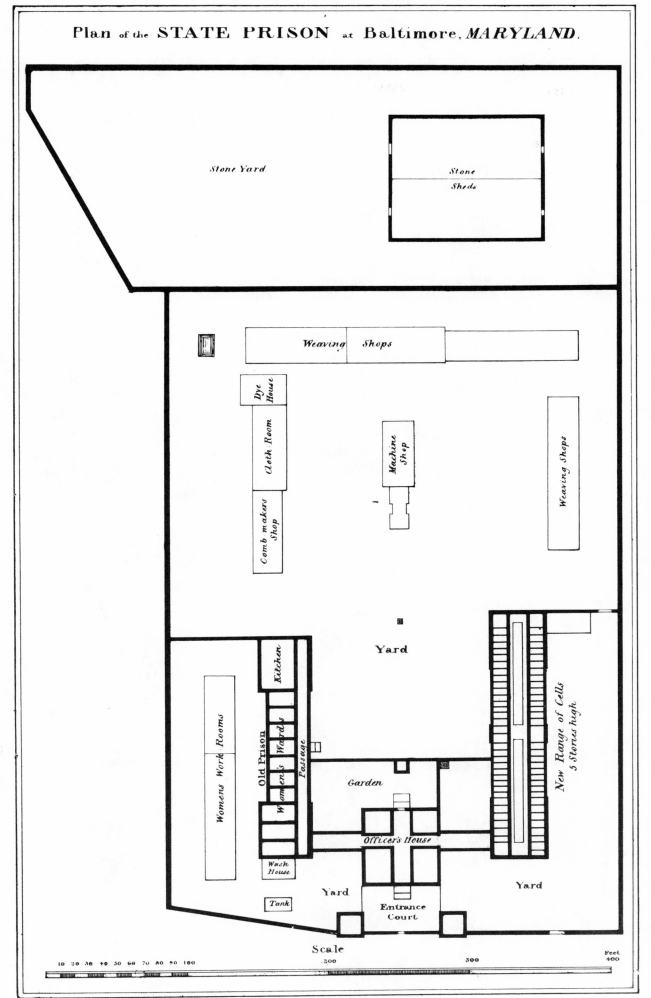

Plan of the STATE PRISON at Baltimore, MARYLAND.

Stone Yard

Stone Sheds

Weaving Shops

Dye House

Cloth Room

Comb makers Shop

Machine Shop

Weaving Shops

Yard

Kitchen

Womens Work Rooms

Old Prison

Women's Wards

Passage

New Range of Cells 5 Stories high

Garden

Officer's House

Wash House

Yard

Yard

Tank

Entrance Court

Scale

10 20 30 40 50 60 70 80 90 100   200   300   Feet 400

The large prison-yard* occupied by the men's workshops, &c., is separated from the central buildings by a brick wall which extends from wing to wing, and incloses a garden in the rear; another wall, extending from the west wing to the boundary wall, separates the men's department from that of the women, who have an airing yard adjoining the wing they occupy. The male convicts are employed in weaving and dyeing, making combs and shoes, and sawing marble. The last occupation is carried on in a space of about 150 feet square, in the centre of the yard, the sides of the square being formed by three long ranges of work-shops occupied by the convicts. There is a space of about 30 feet between the workshops and the outer wall. There is nothing particular to notice in the construction or general arrangements of these workshops, except that the limited space on which they are erected has rendered two stories necessary, a circumstance unfavourable to inspection and strict discipline. The work-rooms are heated by common stoves, and are lighted and ventilated by windows in the sides.

The hours for locking and unlocking the cells are at sunset and sunrise, and it is only between these hours that the convicts are alone. Labour ceases half an hour before sunset. The prisoners are marched to and from their cells and workshops, with the close lock-step in silence, their heads being all turned one way. They take their meals together in a room appropriated for the purpose. For breakfast, which takes place at eight o'clock, half-an-hour is allowed. The same time is set apart for dinner at one o'clock. Supper is prepared imme-diately on the closing of the workshops. At their meals the prisoners sit down and rise up at the ringing of a bell. The tables are arranged in such a manner as to prevent the men facing each other : the seats are divided, and the number assigned to each man is painted on the table opposite. The officers watch the prisoners closely at their meals to prevent communication, and such as are detected in holding intercourse, are flogged.

Immediately on the reception of a prisoner he is obliged to bathe. He is then clothed in the prison dress, and shaved on one side of his head; an operation which is repeated every week until within three months of his discharge, being partly intended as a punish-ment, but chiefly as a mark by which he may be detected in case of escape, and conse-quently as the means of deterring him from making the attempt. He is then placed in a solitary cell until the following day, and having been examined, and not found to be in need of medical aid, he is placed at some suitable employment. All the earnings of a prisoner over and above his daily task are placed to his account, and the amount is paid to him on leaving the prison. The money which a convict can receive in this manner is usually suffi-cient to clothe him respectably, and to supply his immediate wants on his liberation. Should a prisoner from sickness or other cause not have any thing due to him for his overwork at his discharge, he is provided with a decent suit of clothes at the expense of the State, and a few dollars are given to him. The clothes with which he entered are always examined, and if worth preserving, put by for him until the time of his disharge.

There is not any system of instruction, nor is there any chaplain. Service, however, is generally performed on a Sunday morning by some one of the ministers resident in Baltimore. On these occasions the minister takes his station in the middle of the corridor be-tween the cells, in order that all may hear his voice. Most of the white convicts can read and write, but beyond this they have rarely any pretensions to education. A bible is placed in each cell. The friends of convicts are admitted to see them, on obtaining an order from the keeper or one of the directors. A deputy keeper is always present at the interview which takes place at the entrance to the men's yard. This entrance is through a small apartment constructed in the wall about ten feet square, in two sides of which is an iron grated door. At one of these doors stands the prisoner, and at the opposite door his visitor, the deputy keeper being in the space between. Respectable persons not connected with the prisoners are allowed to visit the interior of the penitentiary, accompanied by an officer, who is forbidden to receive any fee. No men are permitted to visit the female convicts but in the company of the matron.

The discipline in this prison, as compared with that at Auburn, Charleston, or Weathersfield, is extremely lax. It retains the degrading punishments, without having the wholesome severity of the New York prisons.. An inquiry into the state of the penitentiary was insti-tuted in 1833, by a committee appointed by the legislature for that purpose. The constant means of communication afforded to prisoners in the hospital, at the pumps, at the privies, at meals, in their work-shops, and even in their cells, are pointed out; and it is acknowledged that the means of communication are not entirely cut off between the males and females. For remedying these evils certain local alterations are proposed, and new regulations suggested for the government of the prison, and a greater severity of discipline is recommended for

carrying

---

* It will be seen by reference to the accompanying plan, that there is a large space of ground in the rear of the prison beyond the square plot already described as being inclosed with the boundary wall. This additional space has recently been inclosed and a large shed-building erected thereon, in which several convicts are employed in hammering granite. The prisoners are here in every respect subject to the general discipline established by the board of directors, the enforcement of which is secured by the presence of a deputy keeper or inspector over every fifty workmen.

MARYLAND.
carrying these objects into effect. The erection of dark solitary cells as places of punishment is recommended, as well as the more frequent and immediate use of the " cat," or whip, to enforce silence. It is also thought advisable to refuse admission to visitors on ordinary occasions, and entirely to exclude the friends of prisoners. The appointment of a regular chaplain is recommended in order that the prisoners may have their moral and religious instruction attended to on Sundays, without quitting their cells. It is not proposed that the convicts should discontinue taking their meals together, but the erection of a more commodious room for the purpose is suggested, in order that discipline may be more strictly enforced. The practice of granting pardons, or indeed of entertaining any application on this subject, is strongly reprobated. The committee object to the prisoner being allowed to communicate at all with any of the directors, and recommend that all communications and requests should be made in writing to the Board. They also propose to prohibit the convicts from doing any work for an officer of the establishment.

No distinction is made in the treatment of coloured from other prisoners. The numbers of each are nearly equal, notwithstanding the difference of numbers between the white and black population, the former being to the latter as six to one. The crimes of the coloured convicts are generally confined to theft. The punishments for offences in the prison are whipping or solitary confinement, or both. The convict in ordinary cases receives five lashes. For serious misconduct he has thirteen, or repeated whippings of thirteen each; but cases deserving this extent of punishment are required to be previously reported to the directors. Solitary confinement seldom extends beyond ten or twelve days; and from the small size and inconvenient character of the cell, its effect upon the mind, health, and morals, of the prisoner is not likely to be very favourable. The prisoners are never chained, shackled, or fettered, unless for attempts to escape : such attempts are sometimes punished by fastening about the neck a small iron yoke, which it is said is so constructed as not to interfere with the prisoner's labour or nightly rest. The only reward is in the case of first offenders, who are not unfrequently pardoned on the ground of good conduct before the expiration of their sentence.

The convicts have three meals daily. The ration of each man is as follows : a loaf, consisting of one quarter of a pound of rye flour; three quarters of a pound of fresh beef boiled or made into soup, or half a pound of pork instead of the beef; a pint of potatoes, peas, beans, or other vegetables, with the proper allowance of salt; one pint of rye coffee, one herring, and one gill of molasses. The prison dress or uniform in winter is made of cotton and wool, with alternate stripes of black and white about an inch wide. In summer the dress is of cotton only. In winter each convict is allowed a pair of pantaloons, a jacket, two shirts, two pair of yarn stockings and one pair of shoes. In summer the allowance is two pair of pantaloons, two shirts (changing once a week) and one pair of shoes.

In the women's yard is a large shop, in which the female convicts are employed in spinning, knitting, binding shoes, making clothing, &c. Some of the women are constantly engaged in washing wool, and also the clothing for the establishment : there is a wash-house with large boilers, tank, &c. attached to the wing building in which they reside.

The hospital for the males is on the fourth or upper story of the west wing. It consists of a room forty-five feet square, furnished with cast iron bedsteads.. A small room adjoining is used for cooking, &c., contiguous to which is the surgeon's apartment. A convict, when sick, is at liberty to apply directly to the physician who is required to visit the prison early every morning. Two convicts perform the office of nurses, prepare and administer the medicines according to the physician's directions, and attend to any alteration in food and clothing which he may order. Convalescent patients are allowed to take air and exercise in a long passage in the west wing which is well ventilated and adapted to the purpose. Contagious diseases seldom appear in the prison. To guard against small pox the physician ascertains on the admission of each convict whether he has been vaccinated; if not, the operation is immediately performed. So great is the apprehension which prevails from this disease, that occasionally when the small-pox has been prevalent in the city, all the convicts have been vaccinated indiscriminately. In any case of insanity which may occur, the patient is not removed to a lunatic asylum. If he fail to recover, the prisoner is continued at any employment suited to his condition, and is retained in custody after the expiration of his sentence if he has no friends to take charge of him, or in case of his being dangerous to society. Except in the case of epidemics, the average number under medical care is about twenty, many of whom are not taken from their employments, and not more than seven or eight are confined to their beds. The annual average of deaths in healthy periods is about one and a half per cent., the majority from consumption. After death the body is examined by the surgeon : it is then buried in the public burial ground.

The women's hospital is on the second floor of the west wing, corresponding in arrangement with that of the men and under similar regulations. The average proportion of Health is the same in both sexes.

The government of this penitentiary is vested in 12 directors, a keeper, 16 deputy keepers, a surgeon and a clerk.

The directors are appointed annually by the governor and council. At the time of their appointment, two are chosen as an executive committee, to attend to the purchase of provisions and materials, also to superintend the sale of manufactures, and to report their proceedings

ceedings monthly to the board of directors. The executive committee attend the institution at least one hour each day. Each member receives annually $ 625 for his services. The other directors act gratuitously. The board meet monthly. They elect all the officers, except the keeper, who, although subject to the control of the board, is appointed by the governor and council. They frame all regulations for the government of the prison, both in respect to its police and the direction of the various manufactures.

Of the 16 deputy keepers, five are superintendents of different manufacturing departments; six are guards and turnkeys; four police officers, whose duty it is constantly to parade the yard and workshops, for the purpose of enforcing attention to the discipline. The remaining deputy keeper acts as a messenger.

The physician has to keep a journal of all the cases under his care, and make a monthly report of them to the board of directors. This officer is appointed annually, and receives a salary of 400 dollars.

The clerk fills a very important and responsible situation in this establishment, having the entire management of the finance and accounts.

This prison is extremely defective, not only in its discipline, but also as regards the moral improvement of its inmates. It is greatly to be regretted that in a penitentiary containing so many convicts there should not be a chaplain. The separation of the convicts by night is almost the only time in which the prisoners do not communicate, for it is impossible to prevent intercourse in the workshops, in the yards, and at their meals. The average number of recommittals is stated to be 15 per cent.

On the first establishment of this penitentiary, a sum was voted by the Legislature, as a capital, for carrying on manufactures. An annual grant of about 8,000 dollars was also made towards the payment of the salaries of officers; the other expenses being defrayed from the profits of the prison. In January 1828 the annual appropriation was discontinued. Since that period the expenses of the institution have ·been paid by the labour of the prisoners. The net gain has always been carried to the increase of the capital, the amount of which is now about $ 75,000. The profits have been as follows:

In 1828	-	-	-	-	-	-	-	$ 10,804 16
1829	-	-	-	-	-	-	-	17,053 89
1830	-	-	-	-	-	-	-	5,046 94
1831	-	-	-	-	-	-	-	3,338 06

In 1832 the profits were insufficient to defray the expenses by the sum of $ 981. 22.

During the year ending 30th November 1833, the aggregate expenditure of the penitentiary was $ 40,479. 19; of this sum, the expenses for the maintenance of the convicts, salaries of officers, &c. amounted to $ 35,081. 83; the remainder was paid into the treasury as instalments and interest on the original capital. The profits of the establishment during the same period amounted to 881 dollars. The diminution has arisen chiefly in the weaving department, at which about two-thirds of the convicts were formerly employed; but this branch has during the last three years sustained severe competition, in consequence of the use of machinery in other manufactories. This circumstance has induced the directors to change the nature of the employments, with a view to more profitable results. The hammering of granite is now carried on to some extent; the labour being let to a contractor, at the rate of 50 cents per day for each convict so employed.

On the 30th November 1832 there were confined in the penitentiary 350 convicts.

Received from 1st December 1832 to 30th November 1833 - -	120
	470

Discharged during the same period:

By expiration of sentence	-	-	-	-	-	-	73	
Escaped	-	-	-	-	-	-	-	2	
Pardoned	-	-	-	-	-	-	-	16	
Died	-	-	-	-	-	-	-	16	
								107

Remaining in confinement 30th November 1833 - - -	363

Of the 120 prisoners received during the year, 58 were sentenced for 2 years; 2 for 3 years; 10 for 4 years; 28 for 5 years; 2 for 6 years; 8 for 7 years; 1 for 9 years; 8 for 10 years; 1 for 14 years; 1 for 15 years; and 1 for 21 years.

MARYLAND.

ABSTRACT of PRISONERS received into the MARYLAND PENITENTIARY, from 1st December 1832, to the 30th November 1833, inclusive.

CRIMES	Whites Males	Whites Females	Blacks Males	Blacks Females	Maryland	Delaware	Virginia	D. Columbia	Pennsylvania	Ohio	New Jersey	Connecticut	Mississippi	Germany	France	Ireland	Scotland	S. America	Baltimore	Harford	Cecil	A. Arundel	Frederick	Washington	P. George's	Q. Anne's	Kent	Dorchester	Caroline	Somerset	U. S. Circuit Court	TOTAL
Stealing	29	4	42	15	70	1	2	2	4	1	1	1	1	-	-	4	2	1	70	-	1	2	2	2	-	3	1	4	3	2	-	90
Felony	-	-	1	-	1	-	-	-	-	-	-	-	-	-	-	-	-	-	1	-	-	-	-	-	-	-	-	-	-	-	-	1
Horse-stealing	2	-	-	1	1	-	1	-	-	-	-	-	-	1	-	-	-	-	1	-	-	-	1	-	-	1	-	-	-	-	-	3
Receiving stolen goods	2	-	-	1	3	-	-	-	-	-	-	-	-	-	-	-	-	-	-	-	-	-	1	-	2	-	-	-	-	-	-	3
Passing counterfeit notes	3	-	-	-	-	-	-	-	3	-	-	-	-	-	-	-	-	-	2	-	-	-	-	-	-	-	-	1	-	-	-	3
Enticing a Slave to run away	-	-	1	-	1	-	-	-	-	-	-	-	-	-	-	-	-	-	1	-	-	-	-	-	-	-	-	-	-	-	-	1
Breaking the condition of a pardon	-	-	-	1	1	-	-	-	-	-	-	-	-	-	-	-	-	-	1	-	-	-	-	-	-	-	-	-	-	-	-	1
Manslaughter	1	-	-	-	1	-	-	-	-	-	-	-	-	-	-	-	-	-	-	-	-	-	-	-	-	-	1	-	-	-	-	1
Murder	-	-	1	-	1	-	-	-	-	-	-	-	-	-	-	-	-	-	1	-	-	-	-	-	-	-	-	-	-	-	-	1
Rape	1	-	2	-	2	-	-	-	-	-	-	-	-	-	1	-	-	-	1	-	-	-	-	-	-	-	-	-	1	1	-	3
Burglary	3	-	3	-	4	1	-	-	-	-	-	-	-	1	-	-	-	-	-	1	-	-	2	-	-	-	-	2	-	1	-	6
Assault and Robbery	-	-	2	-	2	-	-	-	-	-	-	-	-	-	-	-	-	-	-	-	-	-	2	-	-	-	-	-	-	-	-	2
Assault with intent to kill	1	-	-	-	-	1	-	-	-	-	-	-	-	-	-	-	-	-	1	-	-	-	-	-	-	-	-	-	-	-	-	1
Robbing the mail	2	-	-	-	1	-	1	-	-	-	-	-	-	-	-	-	-	-	-	-	-	-	-	-	-	-	-	-	-	-	2	2
Counterfeiting U. S. Coin	1	-	-	-	-	-	-	-	-	-	-	-	-	-	-	1	-	-	-	-	-	-	-	-	-	-	-	-	-	-	1	1
Quackery—Bleeding a man to death	1	-	-	-	1	-	-	-	-	-	-	-	-	-	-	-	-	-	1	-	-	-	-	-	-	-	-	-	-	-	-	1
TOTAL	46	4	52	18	89	3	4	2	7	1	1	1	1	2	1	5	2	1	80	1	1	2	8	2	2	4	2	7	4	4	3	120

Group totals: Whites and Blacks — 120; Americans — 109; Foreigners — 11; Counties where convicted — 120.

NUMBER of CONVICTS committed to the MARYLAND STATE PRISON at BALTIMORE, from its commencement in 1812 to 1832.

CRIMES.	1812.	1813.	1814.	1815.	1816.	1817.	1818.	1819.	1820.	1821.	1822.	1823.	1824.	1825.	1826.	1827.	1828.	1829.	1830.	1831.	1832.	—
Stealing, Larceny and Felony	52	64	73	69	81	111	100	70	65	79	105	90	91	102	62	62	87	98	98	82	92	
Vagrancy	21	66	40	12	19	17	14	1	—	—	—	—	—	—	—	—	—	—	—	—	—	
Receiving stolen Goods	—	3	9	7	2	4	4	1	5	3	4	3	2	2	4	—	2	2	1	3	2	
Horse stealing	2	2	6	5	2	6	4	1	4	9	5	5	2	3	3	2	—	2	4	4	6	
Burglary	6	8	13	9	14	5	4	1	5	—	3	6	2	3	3	1	—	—	1	—	—	
Forgery	1	3	1	—	5	—	—	1	—	1	—	5	2	2	1	2	1	—	—	—	1	
Counterfeiting and passing counterfeit Notes and Coin	1	—	—	—	—	1	3	—	1	—	1	—	2	—	2	—	1	3	—	—	—	
Murder	—	—	2	2	—	—	—	1	1	—	—	1	2	—	1	—	1	—	2	4	4	
Murder in second degree	3	2	1	2	1	3	3	4	4	4	1	1	—	1	4	4	1	1	3	2	2	
Assault, with intent to kill	3	4	3	—	3	1	1	—	2	1	1	2	—	2	—	—	2	2	1	3	2	
Rape	—	—	1	2	2	1	1	—	1	—	—	1	—	—	2	1	—	—	—	—	—	
Assault, with intent to Rape	1	—	1	1	1	2	2	1	2	—	1	—	—	1	—	1	—	1	1	2	2	
Arson	1	2	2	1	1	—	2	1	4	1	—	1	—	—	—	—	1	—	—	1	—	
Cutting off the Ears of a Boy	1	—	—	—	—	—	—	—	—	—	—	—	—	—	—	—	—	—	—	—	—	
Gambling and keeping Gaming Tables	—	2	—	—	1	—	—	—	—	—	—	1	—	—	1	—	—	—	—	—	—	
Insurrection	—	—	3	—	—	1	1	—	—	—	—	—	—	—	—	—	—	—	—	—	—	
Bestiality	—	—	1	—	—	—	—	—	—	—	—	—	—	—	—	—	—	—	—	—	—	
Attempt to Poison	—	—	—	1	—	—	—	—	—	—	—	—	—	—	—	—	—	—	—	—	—	
Assault, with intent to disfigure	—	—	—	—	1	—	—	—	—	—	—	—	—	1	—	—	—	—	—	—	—	
Kidnapping	—	—	—	—	2	4	5	1	3	2	3	1	—	—	—	3	1	—	—	—	2	
Robbery	—	—	—	—	2	—	—	4	—	—	1	1	—	—	—	—	—	—	—	—	1	
Perjury	—	—	—	—	—	—	1	—	1	—	—	—	—	—	1	—	—	—	—	—	—	
Aiding Slaves to escape	—	—	—	—	—	—	—	—	3	2	1	—	—	1	—	—	2	1	1	2	1	
Killing and stabbing Horses	—	—	—	—	—	—	—	—	—	—	—	1	—	1	—	—	—	—	—	—	—	
Bigamy	—	—	—	—	—	—	—	—	—	—	—	—	—	1	—	—	—	—	—	—	—	
Concealing himself in a House	—	—	—	—	—	—	—	—	—	—	—	—	—	1	—	1	—	—	—	—	—	
Grand Larceny	—	—	—	—	—	—	—	—	—	—	—	—	—	—	5	—	—	—	—	—	—	
Assault and Battery	—	—	—	—	—	—	—	—	—	—	—	—	—	—	—	—	—	—	—	1	1	
Ditto, with intent to kill and breaking Gaol	—	—	—	—	—	—	—	—	—	—	—	—	—	—	—	—	—	—	—	2	—	
Ditto, with intent to rob	—	—	—	—	—	—	—	—	—	—	—	—	—	—	—	—	—	1	2	—	—	
Burning a Barn	—	—	—	—	—	—	—	—	—	—	—	—	—	—	—	—	—	1	—	—	—	
Breaking the condition of Pardon	—	—	—	—	—	—	—	—	—	—	—	•	—	—	—	—	—	1	—	—	—	
Breaking and entering a Barn	—	—	—	—	—	—	—	—	—	—	—	—	—	—	—	—	—	—	—	1	—	
TOTAL	92	156	156	111	137	156	145	87	101	102	126	119	103	120	89	78	99	113	117	105	115	

	1812.	1813.	1814.	1815.	1816.	1817.	1818.	1819.	1820.	1821.	1822.	1823.	1824.	1825.	1826.	1827.	1828.	1829.	1830.	1831.	1832.	Total.
Slaves included above*	11	9	14	8	7	8	2	1	—	—	—	—	—	—	—	—	—	—	—	—	—	
White Males	21	40	35	42	57	48	71	54	51	53	71	57	46	37	70	43	32	47	58	43	45	1,021
„ Females	11	39	27	16	19	16	15	3	6	5	7	—	2	5	2	1	—	1	1	1	1	178
Black Males	42	30	53	26	36	65	47	22	31	29	41	48	35	57	12	25	55	52	43	42	51	842
„ Females	18	47	41	27	25	27	12	8	13	15	7	14	20	21	5	9	12	13	15	19	18	386
Under 16 years old	6	6	8	5	3	5	5	4	3	—	—	1	7	6	1	4	4	5	2	4	1	80
„ 16 to 20	11	31	36	28	25	38	19	18	17	17	18	22	23	22	21	20	25	25	27	15	21	479
„ 20 to 30	33	69	60	48	63	66	70	35	49	45	55	58	48	60	38	31	41	51	50	46	49	1,065
„ 30 to 40	25	31	19	19	24	18	23	17	14	24	28	20	15	15	12	9	12	18	19	22	32	416
„ 40 and upwards	17	19	33	11	22	29	28	13	18	16	25	18	10	17	17	14	17	14	19	18	12	387
Foreigners	14	30	29	18	29	19	29	18	23	19	32	13	8	8	15	11	6	5	15	13	13	367
Re-convictions	—	—	3	6	19	24	9	11	14	9	14	20	20	19	14	11	19	18	14	10	16	270
Pardons	7	4	12	9	6	9	19	14	14	23	40	16	23	19	15	15	20	14	15	26	30	350
Deaths	1	2	4	8	16	14	18	11	7	4	5	16	4	7	14	2	4	4	13	24	22	200
Executions	2	—	—	—	4	1	—	—	6	3	—	—	—	1	—	2	1	2	—	2	—	24

* Until the year 1819, convict slaves were sentenced to the penitentiary, or to capital punishment. Their value was determined by the Courts in which they were convicted, and paid to the owner. After the expiration of their sentence they were sold by auction, and the money arising from the sale was applied to the use of the county in which the conviction took place. In 1819 this law was so modified as to require the sale of convict slaves out of the limits of the State, or that they should be hanged if convicted of capital crimes.

The sudden diminution of the number of commitments in 1826 and 1827 was the consequence of a law which was passed in 1826, directing that convict free negroes should be sold beyond the limits of the State. The term for which they should be sold to be the same as that to which the crime would have previously rendered them liable to imprisonment. In 1827 this law was repealed, and free negroes have always since been sentenced to the Penitentiary under the same laws as the whites.

MARYLAND.

PUNISHMENTS for the principal Offences in this STATE.

OFFENCES.		PUNISHMENTS.
Arson, &c. - -	Burning a dwelling-house - -	Death, or confinement in penitentiary from five to twenty years.
	Any mill, distillery, or any out-house not being parcel of a dwelling-house, hay stack, &c. or aiding.	Death, or penitentiary from three to twelve years.
	Any ship or vessel - - -	Penitentiary, from two to twelve years.
	Wilfully burning, or conspiring to burn any court-house, prison, office, &c. or any church, college, &c. or market-house, or aiding therein.	Death, or penitentiary not exceeding fifteen years.
	Wilfully and maliciously burning, or conspiring to burn, any public arsenal, magazine, or military or naval stores, ships, &c.	Death, or penitentiary from three to ten years.
Assault - - -	With intent to rob, murder or rape -	Penitentiary from two to ten years.
Bigamy - -	- - - - - - -	Penitentiary from one to nine years.
Bribery, Embracery, &c.	Giving a bribe to, or acceptance of a bribe, by any judicial officer.	Penitentiary from two to twelve years.
	The same to or by a juror - -	- - Penitentiary from one to six years; disqualified from serving on jury ever after.
Burglary, &c. - -	Or accessary before the fact - -	- - Restoration of property or payment of the value, and penitentiary from three to ten years.
	Breaking a dwelling-house in the day time, or a store-house, &c. in the day or night, with intent to commit felony, or aiding.	Penitentiary from two to ten years.
	Breaking into a shop, &c. and stealing money or goods to the value of 1 dollar and upwards, or being accessary.	- - Restoration or payment of value, and penitentiary, from two to twelve years.
	Under 1 dollar - - - -	- - Restoration or payment of value, and penitentiary from three to twelve months.
	Carrying a picklock, weapon, &c. with intent to break into a house, &c. or feloniously to assault, or being in or about a house with intent to steal.	Penitentiary from three months to two years.
Duelling - -	- - Fighting a duel and killing an antagonist, or wounding him, so that he shall die thereof within twelve months and a day, and aiding and abetting.	Penitentiary from five to eighteen years.
	Challenging or accepting a challenge to a duel.	- - Declared incapable ever after of holding any office, civil or military, in the State.
Forgery, &c. - -	- - Counterfeiting the great seal of the State, or of any court, or of any other public seal, or using the same, or stealing any of them, or being in possession of and wilfully concealing them.	Penitentiary from five to ten years.
	Forging and counterfeiting any gold or silver coin, current in the State, or uttering or aiding therein.	Penitentiary from four to ten years.
	Employing an artist to engrave, or being concerned in engraving, any plate for forging bank notes, or in altering or forging any bank note, or knowingly passing the same, or passing as genuine a note purporting to be of a bank which does not exist.	Penitentiary from five to ten years.
	Passing or uttering counterfeit bills, &c. a second time after conviction, or forging any deed, will, receipt, &c.	Penitentiary from ten to twenty years.
	Forging the Maryland brand on any hogshead or cask of tobacco.	Penitentiary from two to four years.
	Embezzling, rasing, &c. any will, patent, deed, &c. record or parcel thereof, whereby any right may be defeated.	Penitentiary from three to seven years.

PUNISHMENTS for the principal Offences in this State—*continued.*

OFFENCES.		PUNISHMENTS.
Forgery—*continued.*	- - Forging or counterfeiting any commission, patent or pardon, or any treasury money warrant, or being knowingly concerned therein.	Penitentiary from two to ten years.
Gaming - -	- - Keeping gaming tables (except billiard tables) or banks with permission to bet against them, and strolling about and deriving support from horse racing or gaming.	Penitentiary, from three months to two years.
Horse-stealing -	Or accessary before or after the fact	- - Restoration or payment of value, and penitentiary from two to fourteen years.
Insurrection. *See* Riot.		
Kidnapping. *See* Slaves.		
Larceny - - *See* also Burglary, Robbery, and Horse-stealing.	Simple, to the value of $5 and upwards, or accessary before the fact. Stealing a vessel or slave, or being accessary. Stealing under the value of $5 - Receiving stolen goods, &c. - -	Restoration or payment of value, and penitentiary from one to fifteen years. - - Restoration and payment of value, and penitentiary not exceeding twelve years. - - Restoration or payment of value, penitentiary from three months to one year. - - Restoration or payment of value, and penitentiary from three months to ten years.
Maiming, &c. - -	Mayhem, tarring and feathering, or aiding. - - Cutting out tongue, slitting nose, putting out an eye, &c. to maim or disfigure.	Penitentiary, not exceeding ten years. Penitentiary from two to ten years.
Malicious mischief -	- - Maliciously stabbing, killing or destroying any horse, mule, ass, &c. Cutting away, stealing, &c. any buoy in the Chesapeake or Petapsco, legally placed therein, or aiding and abetting.	Penitentiary from one to four years. Penitentiary not exceeding seven years.
Manslaughter - -	- - - - - - -	Penitentiary not exceeding ten years.
Murder - - -	Of the first degree, and aiding - - Of the second degree, and aiding -	Death. Penitentiary from five to eighteen years.
Perjury - - -	Or subornation of perjury - -	Penitentiary from five to ten years.
Rape - - -	Including abuse of female under ten years, or accessary.	Death, or penitentiary from one to twenty-one years.
Receiving stolen goods. *See* Larceny.		
Riots - - -	- - Insurrection by free negroes, mulattos or slaves, and white persons with them. Conspiring to cause such insurrection	Death. Penitentiary from six to twenty years.
Robbery - -	Or accessary before the fact - -	- - Restoration or payment of value, and penitentiary from three to ten years.
Slaves - - - *See* Larceny, Riot, &c.	- - Wilful importation, by any commander of a vessel, from any foreign country, of any felon, convict or slave, or bringing into the State, by any person, by land or water, from any foreign country, any negro or mulatto, with intent to dispose of such negro or mulatto as a slave. Free persons enticing slaves to run away.	Penitentiary from one to five years. Penitentiary not exceeding six years.
Sodomy - -	- - - - - - -	Penitentiary from one to ten years.
Treason - - -	- - - - - - -	- - Death, or confinement at hard labour in the penitentiary from six to twenty years.

N. B.—The convicts sentenced to the penitentiary as aforesaid, may be ordered by the court to solitary confinement, for a term not exceeding one half, nor less than one-twentieth part of the whole term of sentence.

DISTRICT OF COLUMBIA.

PENITENTIARY AT WASHINGTON.

District of
COLUMBIA.

THIS new penitentiary is situated on a point of land projecting into the Potomac river, south of the capitol, and in the direction of Alexandria, from which convicts are sent as well as from Washington. The plot of ground occupied by the buildings and yard is about 300 feet square, inclosed by a wall nearly 20 feet high. There are two watch-towers at the angle of the wall, to command the workshops and yards in the rear of the prison.

The principal building stands back about 60 feet, in a parallel line with the front wall. The entrance court is in the centre, having two lodges at the gates. On one side is the warden's court, and on the other a smaller court occupied by the female prisoners. The range of building is divided by cross walls into different departments. The houses of the warden and deputy-warden occupy the opposite ends of the building, the latter being connected with the female prison. Adjoining the warden's house are the dining-hall and chapel, with the hospital above. The centre is entirely appropriated to the sleeping cells for the male prisoners, which are constructed on the plan of those at Auburn. This part of the building is 120 feet long, 50 feet wide, and 36 feet high. The cells are placed back to back, in a continued range, with an open area on each side, four stories high: the women's cells are on a similar plan. There are 150 cells for male prisoners, and 64 for females.

The principal floor of the warden's house is used for the offices. The rooms in the upper part of the deputy-warden's house are occupied as work-rooms by the women, who have also a detached wash-house in their airing yard. In the rear of the main building are two store-houses for clothing, materials, &c. The large yard behind the prison is about 200 feet in depth. In the centre is a building 100 feet long and 40 feet wide, containing the kitchen or cookery, and provision-room, adjoining to which are the men's work-rooms, two stories high. There is also a bath-house and three privy-sheds in different parts of the yard, and a wharf entrance for landing goods.

The cells of the male prisoners are seven feet eleven inches long, three feet four inches wide, and seven feet eight inches and a half high. Those of the females, seven feet ten inches long, three feet seven inches wide, and seven feet nine inches in height. Each cell is well ventilated by a flue in the back wall, which runs up to the summit of the roof, but does not communicate with any other part. The cells are warmed by stoves in the area, as described at the Sing Sing penitentiary. The space from the cell to the window of the surrounding area, is twelve feet three inches. The windows are large, but the light is imperfect at the back of the cells.

The prisoners work during the day in association and in silence. On their entrance they are employed at such labour as seems best suited to their habits and capacity. They commence work at daylight and are locked up in the cells at sunset; but if they can complete their daily task sooner, they may employ the interval (before sunset) in reading the scriptures and religious tracts. Silence is strictly preserved in the cells at night, watchmen being constantly placed in the passage or area in order to prevent noise. The prisoners are not allowed any portion of their earnings. On their discharge they are furnished with a dress suitable for a labourer, and money sufficient to bear their expenses home.

The warden or agent generally finds a ready market for articles manufactured in the prison, particularly for shoes, which are considered superior in quality to those made in the neighbourhood, and are sold at a cheaper rate.

The punishment for idleness and conversation are being placed in the stocks, and in solitary confinement in the cells (but not in darkness) on bread and water diet, the period not in any case exceeding twenty days, The agent has petitioned for the use of the whip, from a conviction that there would really be less punishment in the prison had he this privilege, as the knowledge that he cannot by law inflict corporal punishment, often induces disorder. The prisoners are under no other restraint during the hours of work than that of maintaining silence, and are not punished for gazing at visitors or at each other.

The

Plan of the **PENITENTIARY** at Washington for the

District of *COLUMBIA*.

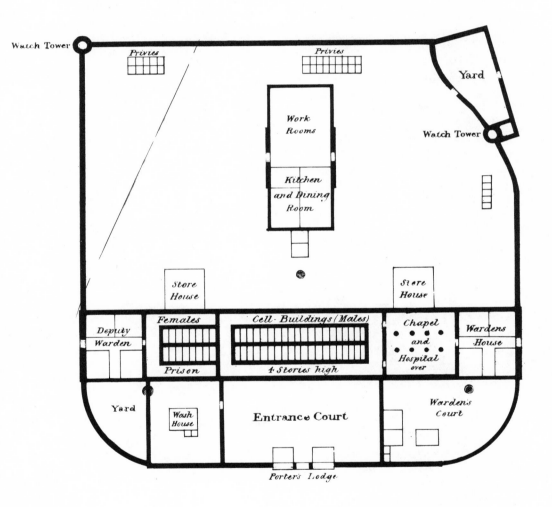

Watch Tower

Privies

Privies

Yard

Work
Rooms

Watch Tower

Kitchen
and Dining
Room

Store
House

Store
House

Deputy
Warden

Females

Cell Buildings (Males)

Chapel
and
Hospital
over

Wardens
House

Prison

4 Stories high

Yard

Wash
House

Entrance Court

Wardens
Court

Porter's Lodge

Scale.

5 10 20 30 40 50 60 70 80 90 100   150   200   300 Feet

The daily ration of each prisoner is twelve ounces of pork or sixteen ounces of beef, ten ounces of wheaten flour (not bolted), or twelve ounces of Indian meal, and half a gill of molasses: in addition to which, for every 100 rations, there are allowed two and a half bushels of potatoes, two quarts of rye, four quarts of salt, four quarts of vinegar, and one and a half ounce of pepper. The cooking is performed by a steam apparatus. The meals are taken in the cells. The hour for breakfast from March to September is seven o'clock, and during the other part of the year eight o'clock. The time allowed for breakfast is forty-five minutes, and for dinner, one hour. When the convicts go to meals, or to or from the shops, they march in silence with the lock-step, accompanied by the officers. The clothing for each convict is a woollen jacket, vest, and pantaloons for the winter, and cotton or linen for summer, with shirts of coarse cotton or linen. He is also allowed a cloth cap and woollen socks. Each bed has a mattress and two blankets.

The officers of the prison are three inspectors, who are chosen annually, a warden, deputy-warden, assistant keeper, three guards, one clerk and a physician. The inspectors visit the prison weekly and see all the convicts, during which time the warden is not to be present unless required by the inspectors.

It is stated that about half the prisoners can read. Each convict has a bible allowed him. A chaplain attends to perform divine service once on Sunday; when a school is held for a short time. When not thus engaged on the Sunday the prisoners are confined to their cells. Prayers are not read every morning and evening by the chaplain. The prisoners are not allowed to be visited by their friends, nor to receive any letters. It is discretionary with the warden to admit strangers into the prison.

At the period of my visit there were forty-six male convicts employed; viz. eight picking oakum, twenty-five shoemakers, two tailors, two carpenters, one plasterer, one painter, one blacksmith, three cooks, and three employed in the prison; also two women, occupied in washing and mending the clothing. This penitentiary has but recently been in operation, and a small number of convicts only have been admitted. The amount received during the year 1832 for articles manufactured and sold, together with book debts and manufactures in store, exceeded the support of the convicts, including the cost of their clothes, bedding and hospital expenses. The convicts have further saved to the State four or five hundred dollars in labour for the completion of the building.

There has been but one death in the establishment since its institution. The prisoners have in general enjoyed good health, with the exception of fevers in the autumn, arising principally from the situation of the prison.

Great disadvantage attends the defective nature of the plan on which this penitentiary has been erected. There are no means of secretly inspecting the convicts, and of ascertaining if the officers are in the discharge of their duties. The men are permitted to look off their work. The discipline is not in other respects sufficiently strict, nor calculated to deter or make any deep impression on the minds of the convicts. The warden is much to his credit warmly interested in the moral welfare of those committed to his charge.

NUMBER and DESCRIPTION of CONVICTS received into the PENITENTIARY for the District of COLUMBIA from the commencement to December 1832.

No.	When received.	Sex and Colour.	Term of Sentence.	Crime.	How employed at Penitentiary.	When and how discharged.
1	April 9th, 1831	White man -	1 year -	Stealing -	Blacksmith's shop.	Released 9th April 1832, by expiration of sentence.
2	June 21st „	ditto - -	1 year -	ditto -	Shoe shop -	Released 21st June 1832, by expiration of sentence.
3	Ditto „	Negro girl -	1 year -	ditto -	Washing, &c.	Released 21st June 1832, by expiration of sentence.
4	Ditto „	ditto - -	1 year -	ditto -	ditto -	Released 21st June 1832, by expiration of sentence.
5	Ditto „	Negro man -	1 year -	ditto -	Labourer -	Released 21st June 1832, by expiration of sentence.
6	Oct. 19th „	White man -	3 years -	ditto -	Shoe shop -	- - Escaped January 12th, 1832, by scaling the prison walls, and subsequently sentenced to the penitentiary, Baltimore.
7	Ditto „	ditto - -	3 years -	ditto -	ditto -	- - Escaped January 12th, 1832, by scaling the prison wall, and subsequently sentenced to the penitentiary, Baltimore.
8	Ditto „	Negro man -	3 years -	ditto -	ditto.	
9	Ditto „	Mulatto woman	1 year -	ditto -	Washing, &c.	Released 19th October, by expiration of sentence.
10	Ditto „	Negro girl -	1 year ‹	ditto -	ditto -	Ditto ditto.
11	Oct. 26th „	Negro man -	1 year -	ditto -	Labourer -	Ditto 26th ditto.
12	Ditto „	ditto - -	3 years -	Horse stealing	Shoe shop -	- - Escaped 25th Sept. 1832, committed to the prison in Frederictown, Md., and died on the very day the officer arrived, of the cholera.
13	Oct. 27th „	White man -	1 year -	Stealing -	Cooking -	Released 27th October 1832, by expiration of sentence.
14	Nov. 5th „	ditto - -	2 years -	Horse stealing	Labouring -	- - Pardoned by the President of the United States, July 28th, 1832.
15	Ditto „	Mulatto man -	2 years –	Stealing -	Shoe shop	
16	Ditto „	Negro man -	2 years -	ditto -	Labourer.	
17	Nov. 19th „	Mulatto man -	2 years -	ditto -	Shoe shop.	
18	Ditto „	White man -	2 years -	ditto -	Cooking	
19	Dec. 13th „	ditto - -	3 years -	ditto -	Shoe shop.	
20	Dec. 15th „	ditto - -	3 years -	Horse stealing	ditto.	
21	Dec. 22d „	ditto - -	2 years -	Stealing -	ditto.	
22	Jan. 7th, 1832	ditto - -	3 years -	ditto -	ditto.	
23	Ditto „	ditto - -	3 years -	ditto -	ditto	- - Escaped May 25th, 1832, by scaling prison wall, and subsequently sentenced to the penitentiary in Philadelphia.
24	May 19th „	ditto - -	4 years -	ditto -	ditto.	
25	Ditto „	ditto - -	2 years -	ditto -	Carpentry.	
26	Ditto „	Negro man -	2 years 6 months	ditto -	Labourer.	
27	Ditto „	White man -	5 years -	ditto -	Shoe shop.	
28	Ditto „	ditto - -	6 years -	ditto -	ditto.	
29	Ditto „	Mulatto man -	2 years 6 months	ditto -	Lathing and Plastering.	

⊙

NUMBER and Description of Convicts received into the Penitentiary for District of Columbia—*continued.*

No.	When received.	Sex and Colour.	Term of Sentence.	Crime.	How employed at Penitentiary.	When and how discharged.
30	May 19th 1832	Mulatto boy -	3 years -	Stealing -	Tailoring.	
31	Ditto ,,	White man -	2 years -	ditto -	Cooking.	
32	May 21st ,,	ditto - -	2 years 6 months	ditto -	Carpentry.	
33	Ditto ,,	Dark Mulatto boy	6 years -	Manslaughter	Shoe shop.	
34	June 30th ,,	White man -	2 years -	Stealing -	Washing, &c.	
35	Ditto ,,	ditto - -	2 years -	Passing counterfeit money	Shoe shop.	
36	July 4th ,,	ditto - -	3 years -	ditto -	ditto -	Pardoned by the President of the United States.
37	Nov. 8th ,,	ditto - -	4 years -	Felony -	ditto.	
38	Ditto ,,	ditto - -	2 years -	Larceny -	Tailoring.	
39	Ditto ,,	Negro man -	3 years -	ditto -	Labouring.	
40	Dec. 7th ,,	White man -	3 years -	ditto -	Shoe shop.	
41	Dec. 15th ,,	ditto - -	2 years -	Felony -	ditto.	
42	Dec. 18th ,,	Negro man -	2 years -	Larceny -	ditto.	

RECAPITULATION :

Shoemaking - - - - - - - - - - 16
Carpentry - - - - - - - - - - 2
Washing - - - - - - - - - - 1
Cooking - - - - - - - - - -
Lathing and plastering - - - - - - - 1
Labourers - - - - - - - - - 3
Tailoring - - - - - - - - - - 2
Discharged by expiration of sentence - - - - - 9
Escaped - - - - - - - - - - 4
Pardoned - - - - - - - - - - 2

Total - - - - - 42

VIRGINIA.

STATE PRISON AT RICHMOND.

VIRGINIA.
———

THIS State Prison is situated on a hill between two deep watercourses or ravines, which meeting together open into a canal on the bank of the James River, and then form a pool, into which all the filth, not only of the prison but also of the western part of the town, is deposited. The pond, which is midway between the prison and the river, is about 200 yards distant from either. In the summer time the water of the pond remains stagnant, and frequently, from the evaporation which then takes place, leaves part of its deposit exposed. The prison was built in 1796. It contains 14 cells or dungeons designed for convicts sentenced to solitary confinement, and 168 cells for separating at night the prisoners who work together in shops during the day. The solitary cells are more calculated to inflict bodily suffering by darkness, cold, and disease, than to leave the prisoner to the natural and beneficial effects of silence and separation. The number of other cells (originally not so numerous as at present) has frequently been found insufficient to accommodate each prisoner separately, but the size being large has readily allowed more than one inmate to each. The dimensions of each cell are twelve feet long, six feet and a half wide, and nine feet high; the ceiling is arched. The dungeons or solitary cells are in the basement story, and in passing along the narrow passage which leads to them it is necessary to use lights. These cells are cold and damp, and an instance has occurred of a prisoner's feet having been frozen while confined therein. In some of the cells a small aperture above the prisoner's head admits a faint light, but in others there is only a small opening in the door communicating with the dark passage.

The sleeping cells are arranged in the form of a crescent, two stories high, and are entered from an external gallery. The cell doors open into the air, and the walls are consequently exposed to wet and cold. In the summer of 1823, the prison buildings suffered very materially from fire. Since that event various improvements have been introduced. The whole space occupied by the prison, being about 300 feet square, was enclosed in the year 1824 by a wall 20 feet in height. At the period of my visit (September 1833) there were 168 cells above ground, which were well lighted and ventilated, each cell having a separate privy and drain; but the pipes connected with them admit of communication from cell to cell when the water is let out. No means have been adopted for heating the cells. Bedsteads are not allowed except in case of sickness. Each cell is furnished with a bible and a slate which the prisoner has an opportunity of using on Sundays throughout the year, and also after he is locked up for the night during the summer months, his cell at that time admitting sufficient light for the purpose. The doors of the cells are of wood, and afford no means of inspection after the prisoner is locked up : this is a great defect, particularly as the means of verbal communication exist between adjoining cells. A watchman is stationed every night in the semicircular gallery in front of the cells, to preserve silence, and as far as in his power to prevent intercourse.

The convicts are let out of their cells as soon as they can see to perform their work in the morning. Breakfast is prepared at eight o'clock in the winter, and at seven in the summer, for which three quarters of an hour is allowed. Dinner takes place at one. An hour is appropriated to this meal and to rest which is allowed afterwards. In their way from the shops the prisoners pass through the mess-rooms, and take their rations to the cells, and on their return to labour, deposit the pans &c. again in the mess-rooms. There is no stated allowance of food, each man being furnished with as much as he requires. The prisoners are locked up for the night at sunset throughout the year. Each convict is furnished with a suitable working-dress which as far as it differs from the ordinary prison clothing is left in the shops. Previously to quitting their cells the prisoners wash themselves, a can of water being always placed in each cell. They are principally employed as harness-makers, shoemakers, tailors, blacksmiths, nail-makers, wheelwrights, coopers, carpenters and weavers. The range of workshops is a detached building in the rear of the cells. The tailoring department had until lately been nearly confined to the supply of the institution. It was in contemplation to execute orders for the public; the bare proposal of which had excited great opposition on the part of persons engaged in that trade in Richmond. The other manufactures are partly on account of the prison, and also in working up materials for contractors, the institution being paid for the labour of the prisoners. The latter plan, which is attended with less risk, is now preferred. Other convicts are employed in domestic and necessary
occupations

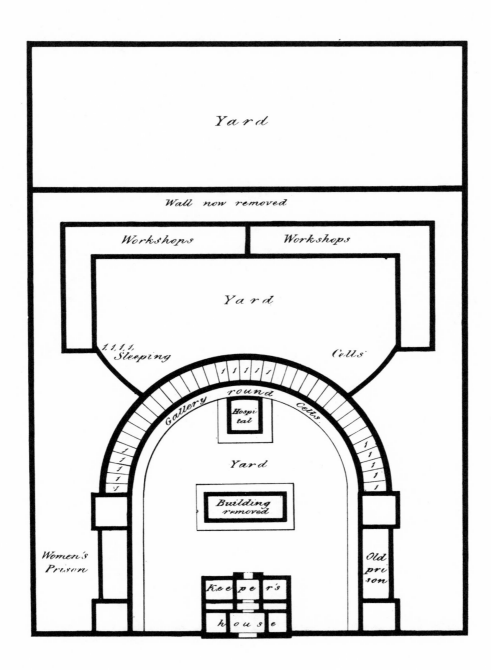

PLAN
of the
STATE PRISON,
at
RICHMOND, VIRGINIA.

Yard

Wall now removed

Workshops   Workshops

Yard

1.1.1.1.
Sleeping   Cells

Gallery round Cells

Hospital

Yard

Building
removed

Women's
Prison

Old
prison

Keeper's

house

SCALE 0 10 20 30 40 50 60 70 80 90 100   200   300 FEET

occupations about the prison. The work is conducted in silence as far as is practicable. Conversation is not allowed between the officers in the presence of the convicts, or between an officer and a convict, except when indispensable.

Independently of the arrangements connected with the labour of the prisoners they are divided into three classes, and distinguished by badges worn as tokens of good conduct. During the first third part of the time of a prisoner's confinement he is kept in the first class; after which, if his behaviour has been good, he is promoted to the second, and for the last third part of his time to the third. For extraordinary good conduct a prisoner is sometimes promoted to a superior class before the ordinary time, and is also similarly degraded for demerit. A prisoner in either of the two lower classes is not allowed to speak with the keeper or superintendent, but must make his communication through the assistant under whom he is placed. Besides the punishment of degradation to an inferior class, the superintendent may inflict solitary confinement by day in the night cells, or confine the prisoner in one of the dungeons, but the latter punishment is now seldom resorted to. The superintendent may also order a diminution in the allowance of food, or may punish the prisoner by whipping; this last is the most usual course adopted. The whippings always take place in private, under the direction of the superintendent, and apart from the other prisoners. They were formerly inflicted in the workshops, but the superintendent found the punishment to have a very pernicious and degrading effect. A day or two before my visit, a black woman had received six lashes for talking to a prisoner through the drain pipes of the cell.

The use of tobacco is permitted, but no smoking of any kind is allowed either by the officers or the prisoners. On the entrance of a convict he is placed in a solitary cell until the surgeon has ascertained that he has no infectious disorder. He is stripped, and clothed in the prison uniform which consists of coarse cloth of different colours. His head is shaved: this is repeated every Saturday during his confinement, except occasionally during the last five weeks of a prisoner's sentence. On a convict's discharge he resumes his own or is otherwise provided with decent clothing, and a small sum of money is given to him to meet his immediate wants. If a convict possesses any property, a trustee is appointed for its administration during his confinement who accounts to the prisoner on his discharge; the trustee being remunerated out of the estate according to the directions of the court by whom he is appointed.

The officers of the prison are a board of five directors, a superintendent, and five assistants, a surgeon, two clerks, a police officer or serjeant, and an agent or storekeeper. The directors are appointed by the Governor of the State, annually, with a salary not exceeding $150 per annum. Their duty is to see the laws of the prison carried into effect. They have, in this respect, some discretionary power, according to circumstances, and they make bye-laws. They also audit the accounts of the superintendent, over whom though not appointed by them they exercise a control.

The superintendent is chosen annually by the two Houses of General Assembly, with a salary of $2,000 per annum. He is removable by the Governor in Council. His office is to enforce the due discharge of the several duties of the subordinate officers, arranging them at his discretion. He is required to receive and examine the convicts on their admission, to allot to each his respective occupation, to divide the whole into wards or classes according to his judgment, and to attend to the moral improvement of the prisoners.

The assistants (two of whom receive a salary of $700 per annum, and three a salary of $600 per annum) have the superintendence of the different classes or divisions of the convicts. They enforce the discipline during the day, examine and lock up the prisoners at night, and also keep an account of the work done and materials used in their respective wards. On the serjeant or police officer devolves the duty of enforcing order when the prisoners are proceeding to or from their work and meals, of delivering out the rations, and of seeing that the cells are kept in proper order. The five assistants, the police officers, and one of the clerks form a guard, four of whom are always on duty at night. The agent or storekeeper is appointed by the General Assembly and may be removed by a majority of the Board of Directors, with the consent of the Governor. His duty is to purchase the materials to be manufactured by the prisoners, to dispose of the articles when made up, and to account to the directors for all the property passing through his hands. He is at present remunerated by a premium of seven per cent. upon all goods sold, and he guarantees the payment of the amount of the sales.

The directors and the superintendent make a report annually of the state of the prison, the number of convicts, and also the receipts, expenditure, &c.; and the Agent furnishes a detailed account of the expenses of his department. Besides these officers there are thirteen prison guards.

The physician visits the prison daily. There was last year a sum of money voted for the improvement of the hospital, of which it stood greatly in need; for without being conducive to health, it was destructive of all discipline, by admitting free intercourse amongst its inmates.

There is no chaplain. At the period of my visit all the white convicts (82 in number) could read, but not one of the coloured prisoners, amounting to 43. On Sundays, they are all, with the exception of those employed in cooking, strictly confined to their cells, and only quit them during the day for their meals, and occasionally for divine service, the time for

VIRGINIA. which, when it does take place, is limited to an hour and a quarter. The performance of
public worship is by no means customary; and the late superintendent expressed his opinion
that the practice, when adopted, tended to increase the number of corporal punishments; the
intercourse and communication which were the result, rendering its infliction more necessary.
For such prisoners as can read, the superintendent selects suitable tracts; with which, in
addition to a bible, every cell is furnished.

Visitors are not admitted into the prison, as their presence has been considered to interfere
with its discipline. The relatives of convicts are not allowed to see them except in case of
sickness. Letters are not permitted to pass oftener than once in three months, and then
only through the medium of the superintendent.

The mortality in this prison has always been very great. In previous years the dungeons
which were in ordinary use were the cause of much suffering and disease. Even since the
discontinuance of the dungeons the health of the prisoners has been affected by the *miasma,*
arising from the deposit of filth in the neighbourhood; and when the violence of cold in the
cells was in some measure alleviated by the erection of the external wall a deficiency in
ventilation was thereby occasioned, making the effects of the *miasma* still more pernicious.
During the years 1831 and 1832, when means had been taken to obviate this defect, the
ravages of the cholera in one year, and its less immediate consequences in the next, made
the degree of mortality greater than ever.

The shortest period for which a convict is now sent to this prison is two years. In the
state of Virginia, as in many others, the imprisonment prescribed by law is composed partly
of solitary confinement, and partly of confinement to hard labour in association with other
prisoners. In most of the States, however, the maximum only being fixed by statute, the
term of solitary confinement has in practice been so much reduced, as to become little
more than nominal. But in Virginia this subject appears to have undergone much consideration, and frequent alterations have been made in the law respecting it. Under the statute
now existing, and by the present practice of the penitentiary, a twelfth part of the time of
imprisonment is to be passed in solitude. The times at which this punishment is inflicted
are for one week in every three months, except during the last year, when the four weeks'
solitude (the maximum allowed at any one period) is inflicted immediately previous to the
prisoners discharge. Although this is the practice adopted by the superintendent of the
penitentiary, as most in accordance with the spirit of the existing law, his own opinion is not
favourable to the adoption of solitary confinement in ordinary cases; considering that it is
injurious to the health of the convict, and calculated to diminish the effect of prison punishments by inflicting on the orderly and obedient a sentence which should be reserved for the
most refractory. He also thinks that it greatly diminishes the profits of the establishment,
by interrupting its manufactures, and thereby depriving it of much valuable labour. With a
superintendent who entertains these opinions, and a law which leaves him at liberty to act in
conformity with them, there seems reason to suppose that the present system of temporary
solitude will not be very long continued, especially when it is found that every alteration of
the law on this subject has approached by degrees nearer to the present one, which admits
of the term of solitude being so reduced as to render it nearly nominal.

An Act passed in 1824 contains the two following rules : " First, so much of the sentence
of every prisoner as prescribes solitary confinement shall be rigidly executed, and no part of
it shall be remitted unless the offender be pardoned, or unless under imperious circumstances
in some special case such remission be recommended by the superintendent, advised by the
surgeon as essential to the prisoner's health, approved by the Board of Directors, and authorized
by the Executive." " Secondly, every convict hereafter brought to the penitentiary shall, within
ten days after his commitment, or as soon as is found practicable, be confined in a dark and
solitary cell, and continued therein on low and coarse diet without interruption for the period
of six months, unless such period exceed the time for which he was sentenced to solitary
confinement, or he be sooner discharged by law. The residue of the sentence for solitary confinement shall be executed at convenient intervals, at the discretion of the Board of Directors,
but in portions of time not less than a fortnight each, and so distributed that they shall fall as
nearly as may be at regular intervals from each other."

By an Act of 1826 it is required that the period of solitary confinement soon after
entering the prison shall be three months only instead of six, and that three months of continued solitary confinement shall also be inflicted immediately preceding the discharge of
the prisoner.

In 1827 a power was given to the superintendent, with the approbation of the physician,
of removing any prisoner from solitude if his health should require it, without obtaining the
authority of the Board of Directors and the Executive as before provided, but in this case
the convict must again return to solitude, and complete the term so interrupted.

In 1829 an Act decreed that every convict should be confined in his solitary cell at convenient intervals of time, reserving to be inflicted, immediately preceding his discharge, three
months of his sentence of solitary confinement, but that it should be the duty of the superintendent to remove any convict from the cell, if in his opinion and the opinion of the
physician, the state of such convict's health should require it.

In the year 1833 the law now in force was passed, viz. that the solitary confinement of convicts in the penitentiary, constituting a part of the sentence of the court, should not exceed one-twelfth part of the whole term of imprisonment, and that it should be inflicted at intervals not exceeding one month of solitude at a time. It should be borne in mind that this solitude is unaccompanied by employment of any description. To the beneficial effects of the law, as it stood before the last alteration, the late superintendent, Mr. Parsons, (with whom I had an interview), who held the office for many years, bears strong testimony. He stated that from 1826 to the end of 1831 (the time of his retiring from office) the prisoners always endured three months' solitude immediately before the expiration of their sentences. This was rigidly enforced, and not one person so confined was during that time recommitted; although before this system was in action five or six prisoners often returned in the course of a year. So important did he consider this part of the sentence, that he would never allow any pecuniary consideration arising from the loss of a convict's labour to interfere with it. He mentioned to me that on one occasion there were three prisoners whose labour was valued at a dollar and a half per day, and the work on which they were engaged was much wanted, but he would on no account admit of a precedent for disturbing the system of solitude immediately before the prisoner's discharge. He was of opinion that this system was not seriously prejudicial to the prisoner's health. At one time he had a prisoner in strict solitude without labour for nine months. The cell in which he was confined was eight and a half feet long, six and a half feet wide, and in height ten feet from the floor to the top of the arched ceiling, or on an average about eight feet high. This vaulted cell contained two windows, three feet by two and a half feet, with venetian blinds which the prisoner could open and shut at pleasure. The officers visited him twice a day with food. When released from his solitary cell this man's health had not suffered. This rigid confinement had been enforced in consequence of an attempt to escape.

In cases of solitary confinement the prisoner is still allowed the use of his bible and slate. The opportunity of writing is felt as a great alleviation. About two per cent. of the number of those who are placed in solitude without employment are found to be lazy and sleep away their time. The cells can be darkened to any degree that may be found requisite.

The recent interference of the legislature with a system apparently so successful may be sufficiently accounted for by considering how much attention is paid to the profitable employment of prisoners, and the sacrifices in this point of view which the late superintendent found himself obliged to make in order to carry his system into effect. The severity of the law as to the period of solitary confinement on the convict's first imprisonment has been mitigated without any prejudicial result, and if the term of solitude just before his discharge, when his labour would be much more valuable, could be similarly shortened, the State would obviously derive pecuniary advantage.

Both male and female convicts are received into this penitentiary, but the females are not subject to the same regulations as the men, either in their general government or as it regards solitary confinement. The latter punishment is said to have been found too severe for them; the death of one female having been attributed to the severity of the discipline. This, however, is denied by the late superintendent.

SUPERINTENDENT'S GENERAL STATEMENT.

THE PENITENTIARY in account with the Commonwealth of VIRGINIA.

Dr.

	Dollars.	c.	Dollars.	c.
1833 : October 1.—To amount of raw materials on hand this day, as per inventory - - - - - -	8,447	63		
Ditto on which labour has been expended - - -	2,159	42		
Articles of contingency - - - - - -	2,130	89		
Machinery, tools and fixtures - - 4,860 98				
Tools, &c. reduced in value by the board of directors - 260 82				
Ditto of last inventory, worn out 70 25				
Five timber sheds, &c. - - 210 00	541	07		
	4,319	91		
			17,057	85
Amount of manufactured articles - - - - - - -			5,235	34
Carried forward - - - - - - - $.			22,293	19

o 3

	Dollars.	c.
To Amount brought forward - - - -		
1833 : Sept. 30th.—To amount for reduction in price of goods made by the	22,293	19
board of directors - - - - - - - -	289	44
To amount for raw materials purchased and delivered at the penitentiary by the general agent - - - - - - -	16,917	59
To amount for rations furnished prisoners and transports - - -	2,850	22
To compensation allowed the board of directors, paid out of the treasury - - - - - - - - -	672	00
To amount for salaries of the superintendent and other officers of the institution, including the physician - - - - -	6,790	85
To amount for contingent expenses of the penitentiary, including extra expenses incurred on account of the cholera - 1,268 93		
To amount paid discharged convicts - - - - 540 70		
	1,809	63
To balance in favour of manufacturing operations - - -	1,967	86
TOTAL - - - $.	53,590	78

Cr.

	Dollars.	c.
1833 : Sept. 30th.—By amount of sales made at the penitentiary - - - - - - - - 2,837 29		
Ditto for accounts and job work - - - - 9,772 03		
Ditto manufactures, ditto, ditto - - - 13,339 32		
	25,948	64
By amount for clothing, &c. furnished lunatic hospital at Williamsburg	1,166	72
By - ditto - - - ditto - ditto - at Taunton -	1,065	06
By amount for clothing furnished prisoners from Ward No. 1. 316 84		
Ditto - furnished discharged convicts - ditto - 135 33		
Ditto - for cloth &c. furnished prisoners from Ward No. 3 348 02		
	800	19
By amount for materials furnished, repairs, improvements, &c. Ward No. 2 - - - - - - - - 745 09		
Ditto, - - Ward No. 4, including coffins for deceased convicts - - - - - - - - 761 82*		
	1,506	91
By amount for contingencies, Ward No. 1 - - - 11 06		
Ditto - - ditto - „ - 2 - - - - 9 68		
Ditto - - ditto - „ - 3 - - - - 47 90		
Ditto - - ditto - „ - 4 - - - - 75 53		
	144	17
By amount for permanent improvements paid by the general agent -	206	85
By amount of raw materials as per inventory - - 8,402 10		
Ditto machinery, fixtures, &c. - - - - 5,046 55		
Ditto raw materials on which labour has been expended 2,492 77		
Articles of contingency - - - - - - 1,777 04		
	17,718 46	
Amount of manufactured articles - - - - 5,033 78		
	22,752	24
TOTAL - - - $.	53,590	78

October 1st:—Balance in favour of manufacturing operations, $. 1,967. 86.

VIRGINIA.

STATEMENT showing the Number of PRISONERS in confinement on the 30th September 1832, the Number received, pardoned, discharged and who died from that day until the 30th September 1833.

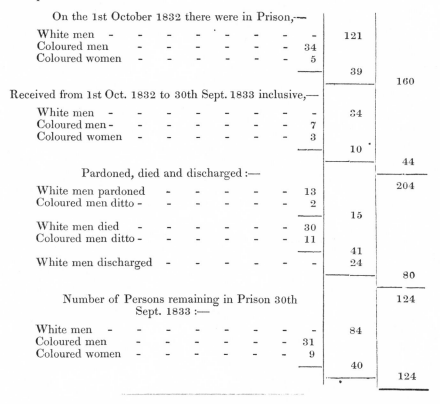

On the 1st October 1832 there were in Prison,—

White men - - - - - - - -		121		
Coloured men - - - - - -	34			
Coloured women - - - - - -	5			
		39		
				160

Received from 1st Oct. 1832 to 30th Sept. 1833 inclusive,—

White men - - - - - - - -		34		
Coloured men - - - - - - -	7			
Coloured women - - - - - -	3			
		10		
				44
				204

Pardoned, died and discharged :—

White men pardoned - - - - -	13		
Coloured men ditto - - - - - -	2		
		15	
White men died - - - - - -	30		
Coloured men ditto - - - - - -	11		
		41	
White men discharged - - - - - -		24	
			80
			124

Number of Persons remaining in Prison 30th Sept. 1833 :—

White men - - - - - - - -		84	
Coloured men - - - - - -	31		
Coloured women - - - - - -	9		
		40	
			124

CRIMES of PRISONERS received into the PENITENTIARY from 1st October 1832 to 30th September 1833 :—

For murder, second degree - -	4	Brought forward - -	16
Voluntary manslaughter - -	5	Horse stealing - - - -	6
Unlawful stabbing - - -	2	Grand larceny - - - -	10
Stealing from Negroes - -	1	Forgery - - - - -	2
Arson - - - - -	2	Passing counterfeit bank notes -	3
Robbery - - - -	1	Bigamy - - - - -	1
Stealing Slaves - - -	1	Felony - - - - -	6
Carried forward - -	16	TOTAL - -	44

STATEMENT showing the Ages of the CONVICTS now in the PENITENTIARY at the time they came in (except two, who are for life, whose ages are given at present, one being 33, and the other 50 years old).

15 were - - - 16 years and under - - - 20 years.
31 „ - - - 20 „ „ - - - 25 „
24 „ - - - 25 „ „ - - - 30 „
13 „ - - - 30 „ „ - - - 35 „
12 „ - - - 35 „ „ - - - 40 „
4 „ - - - 40 „ „ - - - 45 „
5 „ - - - 45 „; „ - - - 50 „
7 „ - - - 50 „ „ - - - 60 „
1 „ - - - 60 „ „ - - - 70 „
1 „ - - - 70 „ „ - - - 73 „

113 males

FEMALES, all of whom were coloured persons :

6 were - - - 16 years and under - - - 20 years.
3 „ - - - 20 „ „ - - - 28 „

Total - 122

VIRGINIA.

NUMBER of Convicts committed to the Virginia Penitentiary at Richmond, from its commencement to September 1833.

CRIMES.	1800	1801	1802	1803	1804	1805	1806	1807	1808	1809	1810	1811	1812	1813	1814	1815	1816	1817	1818	1819	1820	1821	1822	1823	1824	1825	1826	1827	1828	1829	1830	1831	1832	1833 to Sept.
Murder, second degree	2	3	2	3	4	4	2	8	3	4	2	2	2	6	2	4	7	8	1	4	5	12	8	9	5	4	2	5	5	4	3	4	2	3
Stealing Slaves	—	—	—	—	—	—	—	—	—	2	—	1	—	1	2	—	—	1	2	—	—	—	—	2	1	2	2	1	—	6	1	1	—	2
Horse Stealing	6	7	11	11	12	11	6	9	7	15	3	5	5	7	3	11	5	10	14	10	12	7	3	2	8	4	7	9	8	7	7	6	3	3
Petit Larceny	4	11	9	15	2	10	6	10	1	1	5	1	8	7	10	7	15	11	6	15	18	21	17	13	6	1	3	7	11	1	10	14	18	3
Grand Larceny	3	6	10	12	8	12	7	11	12	8	9	11	20	16	10	13	28	22	22	20	33	18	33	31	24	11	16	7	11	16	10	14	18	3
Highway Robbery	1	—	—	—	—	—	—	2	2	—	—	—	—	—	—	—	—	—	—	—	—	—	—	—	—	—	—	—	—	—	—	—	—	—
Passing Counterfeit Money	—	—	—	1	2	—	—	—	—	1	2	3	1	—	5	—	—	—	1	2	—	1	1	2	—	1	—	2	1	1	5	2	2	1
Forgery	1	—	1	2	—	2	5	2	4	1	1	3	1	3	4	3	3	4	1	3	6	3	10	5	8	—	3	3	4	6	5	1	3	1
Felony	—	3	6	7	6	8	1	5	1	1	—	3	—	2	9	—	2	2	1	4	1	1	—	7	4	1	3	1	3	3	5	3	3	1
Maiming	1	1	—	—	—	1	—	—	—	—	—	—	1	3	1	—	1	1	1	1	—	—	3	—	—	—	3	—	—	—	5	4	—	—
Voluntary Manslaughter	—	—	1	1	—	—	—	—	—	—	1	1	1	—	4	1	—	—	1	—	6	3	3	—	2	2	—	4	2	3	7	3	3	2
Burglary	1	1	2	2	1	—	3	2	1	2	—	—	2	1	—	1	3	2	1	2	1	1	3	2	2	1	1	1	—	1	5	4	—	1
Manslaughter	—	—	1	—	—	—	—	—	—	—	—	—	1	—	1	1	—	—	1	4	—	3	3	1	1	—	1	4	2	6	5	3	3	3
Biting off the Ear	2	—	1	—	1	—	—	1	—	—	—	1	—	—	—	—	1	—	1	2	—	1	3	—	—	2	—	1	—	—	7	3	—	—
Insurrection	—	—	—	—	—	—	—	—	—	—	—	—	—	—	—	—	—	—	—	—	—	—	—	—	—	—	—	1	—	1	—	—	—	—
Rape	—	—	—	—	—	—	—	1	1	1	1	1	—	1	—	—	—	3	—	4	1	2	1	—	1	—	1	2	—	2	1	—	—	—
Stabbing	—	—	—	—	—	—	—	—	—	—	1	—	1	1	1	2	1	2	2	2	4	2	2	2	2	2	1	1	1	—	2	2	3	—
Arson	—	—	—	—	—	—	—	1	—	2	—	4	—	—	1	—	—	1	—	1	1	—	2	1	1	1	—	2	—	1	—	2	—	1
Misdemeanor	—	—	—	—	—	—	2	—	—	—	—	—	—	—	1	—	—	—	—	—	—	3	—	—	—	—	1	—	—	—	1	1	—	—
Stealing	—	—	—	—	—	—	4	—	1	2	—	1	1	1	—	—	1	5	2	2	2	1	1	1	1	—	—	2	1	—	—	—	—	1
Slitting the Ear	—	—	—	—	—	—	1	—	1	2	—	—	2	—	—	—	1	—	—	1	2	2	2	—	—	—	1	—	—	1	—	—	—	—
Breach of the Peace	—	—	—	—	—	—	—	1	—	—	—	—	—	—	1	1	—	—	1	—	1	—	—	1	—	—	—	2	1	—	2	—	—	—
Sodomy	—	—	—	—	—	—	—	—	—	—	—	—	—	—	—	—	—	—	—	1	—	—	1	—	—	—	1	1	1	—	—	—	—	—
Shooting	—	—	—	—	—	—	—	—	—	—	—	—	—	1	—	—	—	—	1	—	2	—	2	1	—	—	—	—	—	—	—	2	—	1
Hog Stealing	—	—	—	—	—	1	—	—	—	—	—	—	—	—	1	—	—	1	—	1	—	—	1	1	—	—	1	—	2	—	—	—	3	—
Embezzlement	—	—	—	—	—	—	—	—	—	—	—	—	—	—	—	—	—	1	—	—	1	1	—	—	—	—	—	—	1	—	—	—	—	—
Bigamy	—	—	—	—	—	—	—	—	—	—	—	—	—	—	—	—	—	1	—	1	2	—	—	—	—	—	—	—	—	—	—	—	—	—
Robbing the Mail	—	—	—	—	—	—	—	—	—	—	—	—	—	—	—	—	—	1	1	1	1	—	—	—	—	—	—	—	—	—	—	—	—	—
Breaking Gaol	—	—	—	—	—	—	—	—	—	—	—	—	—	1	—	—	—	—	—	—	1	—	—	—	—	—	—	—	—	—	—	—	—	—
Robbery	—	—	—	—	—	—	—	—	—	—	—	—	—	—	—	—	1	3	—	1	—	—	—	—	—	—	—	2	—	2	2	1	1	—
TOTAL	21	33	44	55	41	51	39	54	37	41	25	34	49	52	34	45	74	78	61	80	93	80	104	83	62	34	44	43	40	53	51	61	36	21
Pardoned, white persons	—	—	4	4	1	1	—	14	12	9	11	10	28	17	18	6	7	10	11	9	18	13	18	12	15	2	3	4	5	3	4	5	12	7
Ditto, black and coloured	—	—	—	—	—	—	2	4	—	—	—	5	5	6	2	2	2	4	—	1	—	2	13	14	16	19	17	15	17	21	15	21	51	6
Deaths	—	1	2	2	1	1	7	2	—	—	3	—	—	2	3	6	4	9	4	12	10	14	13	14	16	—	—	15	—	21	15	21	—	—
Second and Third Convictions	1	1	1	1	1	1	1	3	1	4	1	1	5	1	3	6	6	4	6	5	5	4	5	9	4	3	2	2	1	—	—	4	1	—

STATEMENT, showing the Number of CONVICTS received in the PENITENTIARY, with the Pardons, Deaths, Escapes and Discharges in each Year, until the 30th of November 1833.

VIRGINIA.

YEARS.	Number received.	Number pardoned each Year.	Number died each Year.	Number escaped each Year.	Number discharged each Year.	Number in the Prison on the 1st January each Year.	Number received for second, third and fourth Offences, and included in the whole Number received.
1800	21	-	1	1			
1801	33	-	1	-	10	19	
1802	44	-	1	-	16	41	No account.
1803	55	3	2	-	31	68	
1804	41	1	1	3	33	87	
1805	50	-	1	-	21	90	
1806	40	5	5	1	34	118	
1807	54	18	3	-	22	113	3
1808	37	11	-	-	29	124	1
1809	40	8	1	-	31	121	4
1810	25	11	3	-	20	121	1
1811	33	10	5	-	18	112	1
1812	50	34	-	-	11	112	5
1813	52	17	5	-	33	117	
1814	33	23	3	-	15	114	3
1815	45	9	6	-	14	106	6
1816	74	9	3	-	26	122	6
1817	77	16	9	-	39	158	4
1818	60	9	7	-	47	171	6
1819	80	12	11	-	34	168	5
1820	93	20	9	-	44	191	5
1821	81	13	15	-	55	211	4
1822	103	20	12	-	60	209	5
1823	83	12	14	-	66	220	9
1824	62	15	16	6	45	211	4
1825	34	1	23	-	47	191	3
1826	52	6	18	-	33	154	2
1827	43	4	17	-	28	149	2
1828	50	6	17	-	21	143	1
1829	55	4	21	-	24	149	
1830	57	4	15	-	25	155	
1831	49	5	25	-	22	168	4
1832	43	13	51	-	20	165	1
1833	37	11	9	-	19	124	1
TOTAL	1,786	330	330	11	993	137 average number.	86*

* For second, third and fourth Offences, on 30th November 1833.

Of 164 Prisoners in confinement in 1832, there were natives of Virginia, 115; of the United States, 35; of England, 1; of Ireland, 5; of France, 1; of Holland, 4; of Germany, 1; Switzerland, 1; and of the Isle Gaulet, 1.

NUMBER of PRISONERS admitted into the HOSPITAL of the PENITENTIARY.

MONTHS.	1824.	1825.	1826.	1827.	1828.	1829.	1830.	1831.	1832.	1833.
January	33	55	27	54	13	33	28	19	26	8
February	20	22	73	37	45	39	27	16	10	20
March	38	29	21	36	13	32	18	10	24	25
April	70	29	23	39	30	25	25	26	22	22
May	53	60	27	52	39	23	53	22	25	29
June	103	35	46	36	76	32	32	25	33	46
July	61	46	30	45	78	50	33	23	43	30
August	97	72	40	55	40	22	25	30	62	45
September	47	42	27	34	52	30	13	71	†23	15
October	46	39	45	19	49	34	10	50	†	20
November	53	39	23	–	31	18	11	29	†	12
December	28	27	27	18	38	53	31	34	†	–
TOTALS	649	495	409	425	504	391	306	355	268	272

† These Returns are incomplete from September 1832 until January 1833. The cholera commenced 27 September 1832, and continued until late in October: 147 persons were attacked with that disease, and 28 convicts and one transport died. All business was suspended from 1st to 19th October. Other diseases were also very severe during the time.

VIRGINIA.   PREAMBLE TO THE ACT PASSED IN 1798 FOR THE AMENDMENT OF THE PENAL LAWS.

"WHEREAS it frequently happens that wicked and dissolute men, resigning themselves to the dominion of inordinate passions, commit violations on the lives, liberties and property of others; and the secure enjoyment of these having principally induced men to enter into society, Government would be defective in its principal purpose were it not to restrain such criminal acts by inflicting due punishment on those who perpetrate them: but it appears at the same time equally desirable, from the purposes of society, that a member thereof committing an inferior injury does not wholly forfeit the protection of his fellow citizens, but after suffering punishment in proportion to his offence, is entitled to protection from all greater suffering; so that it becomes a duty in the legislature to arrange in a proper scale the crimes which it may be necessary for them to repress, and to adjust thereto a corresponding gradation of punishment: And whereas the reformation of offenders, an object highly meriting the attention of the laws, is not affected at all by capital punishments which exterminate instead of reforming, and should be the last melancholy resource against those whose existence is become inconsistent with the safety of their fellow-citizens, which also weaken the state by cutting off so many who if reformed might be restored sound members to society, who even under a course of labour might be rendered useful to the community, and who would be living and long continued examples to deter others from committing the like offences: And forasmuch as experience in all ages and countries has shown that cruel and sanguinary laws defeat their own purpose by engaging the benevolence of mankind to withhold prosecutions, to smother testimony, or to listen to it with bias, and by producing in many instances a total dispensation and impunity under the names of pardon and benefit of clergy; when, if the punishment were only proportioned to the injury, men would feel it their inclination as well as their duty to see the laws observed: For rendering crimes and punishments therefore more proportionate to each other, Be it enacted," &c.

PUNISHMENTS for the principal Offences in this STATE.

OFFENCES.		PUNISHMENTS.
Abduction, &c.	Forcible abduction and marriage	Imprisonment in the penitentiary from two to ten years.
	Unlawfully taking away from parent or guardian any female under 10 years of age.	Imprisonment not exceeding two years.
	Taking away and deflowering such maid or woman child.	Imprisonment not exceeding five years.
Arson, &c.	Wilfully setting fire to any house in a town by night or day.	Death.
	Accessaries to arson	Imprisonment in the penitentiary from ten to twenty-one years.
	Maliciously by night or day setting fire to any barn, shop, stable, stack of wheat, house for tobacco or corn, &c. or aiding or abetting.	- - Payment of damages; and confinement in the penitentiary or gaol from two to five years.
	Wilfully burning any house or houses other than those before enumerated, either by night or by day.	Imprisonment in the penitentiary from one to ten years.
	Wilfully setting fire to or burning bridge of the value of $100.	Imprisonment in the penitentiary from two to ten years.
Bribery and Embracery.	Juror accepting a bribe	- - Fine not less than ten times the amount or value of the bribe taken; imprisoned six months, and the same disabilities as in the case of perjury.
	Procuring a juror to accept a bribe	Fine and disabilities as before, and imprisonment for twelve months.
Burglary, &c.	- - - - - - -	- - Restoration or payment of value taken; and confinement in the penitentiary from five to ten years.
	Feloniously breaking into any warehouse or storehouse, and taking money, goods, chattels, &c., or aiding and abetting.	Imprisonment in the penitentiary from one to ten years.
Duelling	Killing a person in a duel	Death.
	Challenging or accepting a challenge	For ever disqualified from office.
Embezzlement. See Officer.		

PUNISHMENTS for the principal Offences in this State—*continued*.

VIRGINIA.

OFFENCES.		PUNISHMENTS.
Forgery - - -	- - Forgery of current coin, or bank notes, or aiding with intent to defraud, or passing or offering to pass such coin or bank notes with intent to defraud.	Imprisonment in the penitentiary from ten to twenty years.
	Forging or procuring to be forged, or keeping and concealing any instrument for the purpose of forging coin, bank notes, &c., or the seal of any banking company, or any public official seal.	- - When against a banking company, imprisonment in the penitentiary from five to fifteen years; when in relation to any other public seal, imprisonment in the penitentiary from one to ten years.
	Forgery of any check, note or order on any bank, &c., or obtaining or attempting to obtain money, &c. by means of such check, &c., or aiding therein.	Imprisonment in the penitentiary from two to ten years.
	Forgery of any land warrant, or other warrant issued by this State or the United States, or any bill of credit, record, deed, will; or destroying or concealing any will, &c., or aiding therein.	Imprisonment in the penitentiary from one to ten years.
	Forging or counterfeiting the brand or mark of any inspector of tobacco, or exporting tobacco with such forged brand or mark, with intent to defraud.	Imprisonment in the penitentiary from one to ten years.
Fraud - - -	Obtaining money or goods by false tokens.	Imprisonment not exceeding one year, and the pillory.
Gaming - - -	- - Keeping a faro bank, E O table, &c., or suffering them to be used on the premises of any inn-holder, &c.	- - Imprisonment in the penitentiary from one to two years, and fine not exceeding $500.
Horse stealing -	Or accessary - - - -	Imprisonment in the penitentiary from five to ten years, and restitution.
	Buyers or receivers of stolen horses knowing them to be such, and harbourers of the thieves.	Imprisonment in the penitentiary from six months to four years.
Kidnapping - -	Stealing or selling a free person for a slave.	Imprisonment in the penitentiary from one to ten years.
	Surrendering persons to be transported out of the United States.	Imprisonment in the penitentiary from one to ten years.
	If person so transported be executed	Death.
Larceny - - - *See* also Horse stealing, Robbery, Burglary, Slaves.	- - Stealing or taking away any record, writ, return, process, warrant, &c. of any court.	Imprisonment in the penitentiary from one to ten years.
	Stealing to the value of $10 or upwards, and accessaries before the fact.	- - Restitution of goods or payment of the value, and imprisonment in the penitentiary from one to three years.
	Under $10; first offence - -	- - Restitution or payment, and imprisonment in the county gaol from one to six months, and kept on penitentiary diet, and punished by stripes at the discretion of the court, to be inflicted at one or different times, provided that no more than thirty-nine stripes be inflicted at one time.
	Second offence - -	Imprisonment in the penitentiary from five to ten years.
Maiming - -	- - Cutting out the tongue, putting out the eye, wounding, shooting, &c., and aiding therein maliciously and on purpose, with intention to maim, disfigure, disable or kill.	- - Imprisonment in the penitentiary from two to ten years, and fine not exceeding $1,000, and liable in damages to party injured.
	When not done maliciously and with such purpose.	Imprisonment in penitentiary from one to seven years, and liable to action.
Malicious Mischief -	Destruction or wilful injury of a canal and its appurtenances.	Imprisonment in penitentiary from two to ten years.

(*continued.*)

593.

p 2

Punishments for the principal Offences in this State—*continued*.

OFFENCES.		PUNISHMENTS.
Manslaughter -	Voluntary * - - - - -	- - Imprisonment in penitentiary from two to ten years, and security for good behaviour for such time as the court may order.
Murder - - -	Of first degree - - - -	Death.
	Of second degree - - - -	Imprisonment in the penitentiary from five to eighteen years.
Officer - - -	Taking fees not appointed by law for discharging his duty.	- - Fine and imprisonment at the discretion of the jury, and afterwards dismissed.
	Embezzlement or connivance thereat by an officer of the bank.	Imprisonment in the penitentiary from three to ten years.
Perjury - - -	And subornation of - - -	- - Fine not exceeding $ 1,000; imprisonment not exceeding one year; forfeiture of any office of honour or profit which he might hold; and to be for ever incapable of holding any office in the State.
Rape - - -	Or accessary - - - -	Imprisonment in the penitentiary from ten to twenty-one years.
	Carnally knowing or abusing female child under 10 years of age, or accessary before the fact.	Imprisonment in the penitentiary from one to ten years.
Riot - - -	- - - - - - -	-- Imprisonment and fine, as determined by a jury before whom trial may be had.
Robbery - -	Or accessary before the fact - -	- - Restitution or payment, and imprisonment in the penitentiary from five to ten years.
Second offence -	- - Persons having been once sentenced to the penitentiary for an offence, if afterwards convicted of any other offence, which on the first conviction would subject them to confinement in the penitentiary for a term not less than five years,	Death.
	Less than for five years - - -	Imprisonment in penitentiary from ten to twenty years.
	Any person after having been twice before convicted and sentenced to the penitentiary who shall a third time be convicted.	Death.
Slaves - - - *See* also Kidnapping.	- - Free persons joining slaves in conspiracy to rebel or murder any free person.	Death.
	Stealing a slave - - - -	Imprisonment in the penitentiary from three to eight years.
Sodomy and Bestiality	- - - - - - -	Imprisonment in the penitentiary from one to ten years.
Treason - -	- - - - - - -	Death.

* In case of involuntary manslaughter perpetrated in the commission of an unlawful act, the prisoner may be tried for misdemeanor.

The punishments inflicted on slaves are omitted; but they consist principally, though not entirely, of death and flogging. Of the offences mentioned above, besides those which are capital in other cases, the following, when committed by slaves, are punished with death; viz. burning barns, bridges, &c., housebreaking, forgery, horse-stealing, grand larceny, malicious mischief, rape and sodomy.

Any free negro or mulatto convicted of an offence by law punishable with imprisonment in the gaol and penitentiary for more than two years, is to be punished, instead of such confinement, by stripes at the discretion of the jury, sold as a slave, and transported as a slave beyond the limits of the United States.

Receivers of stolen goods may in the first instance be prosecuted for a misdemeanor, in which case they will not be liable as accessaries on conviction of the principal.

The jury determine the exact punishment within the limits prescribed by law.

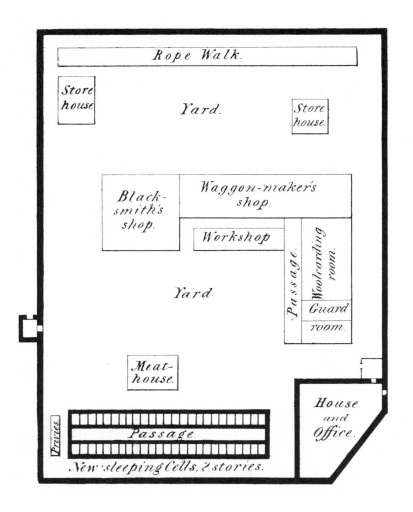

PLAN
of the
STATE PRISON
at
FRANKFORT, KENTUCKY.

KENTUCKY.

STATE PRISON AT FRANKFORD.

THE erection of this Penitentiary was authorized by a law passed in the year 1798; the object, as expressed in the preamble to the Act, being " to render crimes and their punishments proportionate to each other, and to reform instead of to exterminate offenders."

The prison has been built in the north-east corner of the town of Frankford, about half a mile distant from the Kentucky River. The exterior wall is of rough stone, 26 feet in height, and incloses about two acres of ground in the form of a parallelogram. The principal building, which has been recently erected for the separate confinement of the convicts at night, is of stone, 140 feet long, and two stories high. It is divided in the centre by a passage from end to end, above and below, on the sides of which are placed 100 dormitories, each seven feet long, four feet wide, and seven feet high. They are lighted and ventilated by means of grated windows, but are not warmed. The buildings of the old part of the prison consist of a dwelling-house for the keeper, three stories high, with the office and store-rooms; also a building about 80 feet long, and three stories high, having nine work-rooms. There is another building 120 feet long, two stories high, open from end to end, used as workshops. Several smaller buildings are placed irregularly in the yards, and there is a long inclosure on one side, used as a rope-walk. Many of the partitions in the work-rooms have been recently removed, in order to afford increased space for labour, and to place the prisoners as much as possible within the view of the officers.

This Penitentiary is managed in a peculiar manner. The officers are, a keeper appointed by the governor of the State, and two assistant keepers, a clerk, and four guards. The labour of the prisoners was farmed out to the present keeper in 1825. He guarantees a certain annual profit to the State of at least 1,000 dollars, or one half the profits of the labour of the prisoners. This, under his skilful management, has amounted on an average to about 3,000 dollars annually: the other half he was allowed to reserve for his remuneration. There are no females in confinement. None of the prisoners are under 16 years of age.

The following were the occupations of the prisoners when I visited the prison. Stone-cutters, 6; blacksmiths, 16; waggon and plough-makers, 12; chair-makers, 5; coopers, 2; brush-maker, 1; sleigh-maker, 1; wool-spinners, 2; wool-carders, 4; cloth-dressers, 2; weaving broadcloth, jean, carpeting and flannel, 6; spinning twine for bagging, 10; weaving bagging, 3; hatters, 10; shoemakers, 6; engineer and fireman, 2; miller, 1; cooks, 3. Total 92.

The prisoners are not so strictly prevented from exchanging words as in some other Penitentiaries, although the rules prohibit all conversation. The punishment for offences in the prison is whipping: the number of stripes must not exceed ten for the same offence at any one time. The daily ration is not limited, but consists of a plentiful supply of wholesome bread, bacon, beef, soup, rye, coffee and vegetables, according to the season of the year. The average cost of food per head is six cents daily (threepence). When a prisoner is first committed, his head is shaved close, and after being thoroughly cleansed he is clothed in a prison uniform.

There is no place set apart for the sick, the number of whom does not average more than one per diem. Except during the prevalence of the cholera, only one prisoner has died of disease (under which he had long laboured) in the last five years. During the same period one prisoner has been shot by the guard, one was stabbed by a fellow prisoner, and one hung himself.

About two-thirds of the prisoners can read when they enter the Penitentiary. Religious service is not performed on Sundays. The friends of the prisoners are allowed to visit them in the presence of the keeper. The " rules" to be observed are printed, and a copy is fixed in every cell. The following regulations exhibit the daily routine of the discipline.

At daybreak in the morning the guard on duty rings the alarm-bell. The convicts must then dress, make their beds and sweep their rooms, when the assistant keeper proceeds with the guard to open the cell doors. The prisoners step out of their cells, form into single file, and march in silence to their respective workshops. The foreman of each shop marches behind his division, and if any of the prisoners are disorderly he is required to report the circumstance to the keeper. When arrived at their respective places of labour, the prisoners wash themselves, and proceed directly to work. Each man has a place assigned to him, which he must not quit without obtaining leave. He is to be careful that nothing committed to him is wasted, and is responsible for the quality of his work. The prisoners must not turn their eyes from their employment to look at any person passing, nor speak to any without permission. Each shop has a separate privy. At meal-times the prisoners quit their work, form into single file, march to their respective places in the eating-room, and there take their seats in silence. During meals a convict is to hold up his hand if he wants bread, his spoon for soup, his knife for meat, his fork for vegetables, and his cup for coffee or drink. When the meal is finished, the prisoners wait until a bell rings,

KENTUCKY.

when they rise from their seats and march back to the workshops in single file, the foreman of each shop always marching in the rear of his division. On quitting labour at night, the men in each of the divisions form in single file, and march to their respective cells, taking with them, as they pass along, their water and night buckets. After entering the cells, each man hands the hasp of his door to the guard, to be locked up.

On Sunday the bell rings as on other mornings, and the prisoners march to their workshops, when they wash themselves, and are marched back to breakfast as usual. After breakfast those who are to be locked up return to their cells, and the others proceed for a short time to a school-room, from whence they return to their cells. Whenever Divine Service is performed all the prisoners are required to attend in the chapel.

The convicts are at all times not only forbidden to speak to each other, but also to the guard, unless on business; and if they wish to speak to the keeper or assistant keeper, on any subject, they must first ask permission.

In order that the nature of the offence, and the former character and conduct of the convicts, may be known, the law directs that the court before whom any conviction takes place shall furnish the keeper of the Penitentiary with a brief statement of the circumstances connected with the crime committed by each prisoner: such reports are required to be inserted in the prison register.

The wife of a convict may apply to the Court of Chancery, who can direct the payment of alimony during her husband's confinement in the Penitentiary. The infant children of convicts are to be regarded as orphans, and may have guardians appointed by the court, and be bound as apprentices, &c.

By an Act passed in 1810, it is decreed that the convicts shall be subsisted from the profits of their labour arising from the sale of articles manufactured in the prison, or by the exchange of such articles for others necessary for their subsistence; and that no money shall be drawn from the treasury to be applied to the purposes of the gaol and Penitentiary.

The simple fact that 90 prisoners are employed at no less than 18 different profitable occupations in which the labourers are instructed and superintended principally by the keeper, shows that he must possess a practical and extensive acquaintance with trades and manufactures. The Kentucky State Prison is in fact a successful manufactory, rather than a Penitentiary to deter from the commission of crime by operating on the fears and better feelings of the convicts. The keeper had no hesitation in admitting to me that the imprisonment had no beneficial effect upon them. The absence of stated moral and religious service is a serious evil. It is probable that any material improvement will take place in the Penitentiary, either in this or any other respect, so long as the productive labour of the prisoners continues to be regarded as the first consideration. The spirit of the contract with the keeper (who is a highly respectable and intelligent man) shows that the main object of the Legislature is the profitable employment of the prisoners, and not the prevention of crime, either by the correction or reformation of the offender.

NUMBER of Convicts committed to the Kentucky State Prison at Frankford, in each of the Years 1828, 1829, 1830, 1831 and 1832, distinguishing the nature of their Offences.

C R I M E S.	1828.	1829.	1830.	1831.	1832.
Manslaughter - - - - -	3	4	3	2	3
Burglary - - - - - -	2	3	5	1	—
Forgery or Counterfeiting - - -	1	7	2	1	3
Highway Robbery - - - -	1	—	3	1	—
Horse-stealing - - - - -	10	4	8	6	4
Larceny - - - - - -	8	10	10	14	7
Perjury - - - - - -	1	1	—	—	1
Bigamy - - - - - -	1	1	—	—	—
Kidnapping - - - - -	1	1	—	—	—
Felony - - - - - -	5	7	11	16	7
Maiming - - - - - -	4	—	1	1	—
	37	38	43	42	25
Pardoned - -	4	5	2	6	7

PARTICULARS respecting the CONVICTS Committed to the STATE PRISON of KENTUCKY, in 1828, 1829 and 1830.

Age.	OFFENCE.	Sentence.	Place of Nativity.	OCCUPATION.	Degree of Instruction.	Conduct before Committal, as far as can be ascertained.	Conduct since Imprisonment.
		Yrs. Mos.					
34	Stealing Linen - -	2 —	Kentucky -	Cooper - -	Can Read -	Bad, 2d Conv^n	Good.
23	Stealing Gun - -	2 —	Kentucky -	Idler - -	Cannot Read	Idler, bad -	Good.
25	Stealing Linen -	4 —	Kentucky -	None - -	Read & Write	2d Conviction	Good.
20	Stealing Money -	2 —	Tennessee -	None - -	Unlearned -	Idler - -	Good.
28	Stealing Goods -	2 —	Pennsylvania	None - -	Can Read -	2d Conviction	Good.
53	Passing Counterfeit Money.	4 —	Virginia -	Farmer - -	Learned -	Good - -	Tolerably good.
29	Felony - - -	2 —	Philadelphia -	Sailor - -	Learned -	Dissipated -	Tolerably good.
23	Stealing Canoe -	1 —	Kentucky -	Farmer - -	Can Read -	Dissipated -	Pardoned.
40	Stealing Coat - -	2 —	Ireland - -	Farmer - -	Unlearned -	Dissipated -	Trifling.
26	Stealing Money -	1 —	Kenucky -	Idler - -	Unlearned -	Dissipated -	Trifling.
26	Stealing Money -	1 —	Kentucky -	Farmer - -	Unlearned -	Dissipated -	Good.
28	Killing his wife -	3 —	Tennessee -	Brickmaker -	Can Read -	Rambler -	Good.
27	Stealing Coffee -	1 —	Pennsylvania	Boatman -	Read & Write	Rambler -	Good.
26	Stealing Money -	2 —	Kentucky -	Farmer - -	Learned -	Bad - -	Good.
24	Stealing Negro -	2 —	Kentucky -	Stonemason -	Can Read -	Good - -	Good.
28	Swindling - -	2 —	Kentucky -	Farmer - -	Can Read -	Good - -	Good, pardoned.
32	Stabbing - -	2 —	Kentucky -	Farmer - -	Unlearned -	Dissipated -	Good.
26	Bigamy - - -	2 —	Kentucky -	Shoemaker -	Unlearned -	Dissipated -	Good, dead.
23	Stealing - - -	1 —	Ireland - -	Labourer -	Learned -	Dissipated -	Good.
17	Felony - - -	1 —	Cincinnati -	None - -	Unlearned -	Very bad -	Good.
29	Felony - - -	2 —	Virginia -	None - -	Unlearned -	Very bad -	Good.
24	Horse-stealing -	4 —	Tennessee -	None - -	Unlearned -	Very bad -	Good.
24	Felony - - -	2 —	Kentucky -	Blacksmith -	Read & Write	Good - -	Good.
23	Manslaughter -	3 —	Kentucky -	Farmer - -	Read & Write	Dissipated -	Good.
17	Felony - - -	1 —	Kentucky -	None - -	Read & Write	Bad - -	Pardoned.
18	Felony - - -	2 —	Kentucky -	None - -	Read & Write	Bad, 2d Conv^n	Bad.
46	Horse-stealing -	4 —	North Carolina	Farmer - -	Can Read -	Good - -	Good.
30	Stealing Cloth -	2 —	Baltimore -	Stealing -	Learned -	Stealing -	Bad.
22	Horse-stealing -	4 —	Kentucky -	Farmer - -	Unlearned -	Good -	Dead.
25	Felony - - -	4 —	Virginia -	Idler - -	Learned -	Rambler -	Not very good.
33	Passing Counterfeit Money.	1 —	Virginia -	Cabinet-maker	Learned -	Suspicious -	Not very
26	Stealing Money -	1 —	Kentucky -	Labourer -	Unlearned -	Idler.	—
34	Manslaughter -	6 —	Virginia -	Farmer - -	Learned -	Not good -	Good.
46	Felony - - -	2 —	Germany -	None - -	Can Read -	Idler - -	Good.
39	House-breaking -	Life	Virginia -	Blacksmith -	Can Read -	Bad - -	Good.
34	House-burning -	1 year	Kentucky -	Farmer - -	Can Read -	Good - -	Good.
23	Stealing Money -	1 —	Kentucky -	Farmer - -	Can Read -	Not good -	Good.
23	Stealing Watch -	2 —	New York -	Stealing -	Learned -	Very bad.	—
29	Felony - - -	1 9	Kentucky -	None - -	Unlearned -	Idler - -	Good.
38	Felony - - -	1 —	Philadelphia -	Ropemaker -	Learned -	Dissipated -	Tolerably good.
20	Horse-stealing -	4 —	North Carolina	Idler - -	Unlearned -	Dissipated -	Tolerably good.
63	Horse-stealing -	4 —	Virginia -	Horse-racer -	Learned -	Racer - -	Tolerably good.
19	Stealing Watch -	1 —	Kentucky -	Horse-racer -	Learned -	Racer - -	Tolerably good.
21	Stealing Watch -	3 —	Kentucky -	Horse-racer -	Learned -	Racer - -	Tolerably good.
29	House-burning -	1 —	Virginia -	Not known -	Learned -	Stealing.	—
35	Forgery - - -	2 —	Ireland - -	Grocer - -	Learned -	Good - -	Good.
23	Felony - - -	1½ —	New York -	Rambler -	Learned -	Bad - -	Good.
35	Felony - - -	2 —	Pennsylvania -	Boatman -	Learned -	- - -	Good.
17	Stealing - - -	2 —	Kentucky -	Idler - -	Learned -	Idler, 2d Conv^n	Bad.
46	Highway Robbery -	3 —	Tennessee -	Blacksmith -	Learned -	Not good -	Good.
29	Highway Robbery -	3 —	Tennessee -	Farmer - -	Learned -	Good - -	Tolerably good; dead.
23	Highway Robbery -	3 —	Tennessee -	Farmer - -	Learned -	Good - -	Tolerably good.
53	Manslaughter -	10 —	Virginia -	Farmer - -	Learned -	Dissipated -	Good; dead.
30	Forgery - - -	1 —	Ireland - -	Stonemason -	Learned -	Dissipated -	Good.
26	Stabbing - -	1 —	Kentucky -	Farmer - -	Unlearned -	Dissipated -	Good.
30	Felony - - -	1 —	Virginia -	Not known -	Can Read -	Very bad -	Good.
19	Felony - - -	1½ —	Kentucky -	Not known -	Unlearned -	Very bad -	Not good.
25	Horse-stealing -	4 —	Tennessee -	Idler - -	Read & Write	Very bad -	Not good.
20	Horse-stealing -	4 —	Kentucky -	Farmer - -	Read & Write	Good - -	Not good.
26	House-breaking -	1 —	Kentucky -	Farmer - -	Can Read -	Good - -	Not good.
27	Maiming - -	1 —	Kentucky -	Labourer -	Can Read -	Good - -	Not good.
27	Burglary - -	3 —	Kentucky -	Labourer -	Can Read -	Good - -	Not good.
21	Stealing Saddle -	1½ —	Kentucky -	Farmer - -	Can Read -	Bad - -	Not good.
17	Felony - - -	1 —	Ohio - -	Farmer - -	Can Read -	Good - -	Bad.
53	Felony - - -	3 —	Germany -	Baker - -	Unlearned -	Dissipated -	Good.
20	House-breaking -	1 —	Ohio - -	Carpenter -	Learned -	Good - -	Good.
26	Horse-stealing -	5 —	Ohio - -	Labourer -	Can Read -	Idler - -	Good.
46	Manslaughter -	2 —	Ireland - -	Weaver -	Learned -	Dissipated -	Good, pardoned.

Age.	OFFENCE.	Sentence.		Place of Nativity.	OCCUPATION.	Degree of Instruction.	Conduct before Committal, as far as can be ascertained.	Conduct since Imprisonment.
		Yrs.	Mos.					
17	Felony - - -	1	—	Ohio - -	Idler - -	Learned -	Idler - -	Good.
22	Felony - - -	1	—	Kentucky -	Idler - -	Learned -	Idler - -	Good.
42	Stealing Cloth - -	2	—	New York -	Shoemaker -	Learned -	Bad - -	Good.
53	Passing Counterfeit Money.	4	—	Virginia -	Farmer - -	Learned -	Good - -	Good.
39	Passing Counterfeit Money.	4	—	Virginia -	Blacksmith -	Learned -	Suspicious -	Good.
44	Passing Counterfeit Money.	4	—	Virginia -	Gentleman -	Learned -	Suspicious -	Good.
70	Stealing - - -	1	—	Virginia -	Farmer - -	Learned -	Suspicious -	Good.
20	Horse-stealing - -	4	—	Kentucky -	Skinner -	Learned -	Idler - -	Good.
20	Dropping Pigeons -	4	—	Ohio - -	Swindler -	Learned -	Bad - -	Bad.
23	Stealing Clothes -	1½	—	Kentucky -	Blacksmith -	Unlearned -	Good - -	Good.
26	Felony - - -	2	—	Pennsylvannia	Carpenter -	Learned -	Good - -	Good.
36	Horse-stealing - -	8	—	Virginia -	Shoemaker -	Learned -	Good - -	Good.
28	Felony - - -	1	—	Virginia -	Shoemaker -	Learned -	Good - -	Good.
22	Felony - - -	1	—	Kentucky -	Farmer - -	Learned -	Good - -	Good.
23	Felony - - -	3	7	Kentucky -	Farmer - -	Unlearned -	Good - -	Good.
33	Horse-stealing - -	5	—	Kentucky -	Rambler -	Unlearned -	Bad - -	2d Conviction.
22	Stealing Money -	6	—	Pennsylvannia	Rambler -	Unlearned -	Bad - -	2d Conviction.
21	Stealing Money -	3	—	Ohio - -	Rambler -	Unlearned -	Bad - -	Good.
22	Stealing Cloth - -	2	—	New York -	Shoemaker -	Learned -	Bad - -	Good.

PUNISHMENTS for the principal OFFENCES in this STATE.

OFFENCES.	PUNISHMENTS.
Abduction, aiding or abetting therein - - - - -	- - Imprisonment in the Penitentiary from two to seven years.
Adultery - - {Of children under 14 years of age -	Penitentiary from six months to five years.
- - - - - - - -	Fine, 5 l. for each offence.
Arson, &c. - {- - Burning dwelling-house, court-house, public office, prison, &c.	- - Penitentiary from seven to twenty-one years.
{Tobacco or store-house, stacks, timber,&c.	Penitentiary from one to six years.
{Burning Penitentiary house - -	Death.
Assault - - {With intent to rob - - - -	Penitentiary from one to two years.
Bastardy - - {- - Mother concealing the death of bas-tard child.	Penitentiary from two to seven years.
Bigamy - - - - - - - - -	Penitentiary from three to nine years.
Bribery, Embra-cery, &c. {- - Selling vote for office; or concern-ing administration of office, executive government, or revenue.	- - Amerced and imprisoned at discretion of jury, and if a member of Assembly, expelled.
{Corrupting a juror; or juror being so corrupted.	- - Penitentiary from one to six years, in-capable of serving on a jury.
{Attempt to corrupt - - - -	- - Fine and imprisonment at discretion of jury.
Burglary, &c. (See also Rob-bery.) {And accessaries before the fact - -	- - Penitentiary from three to ten years, and restitution of property.
{Breaking dwelling or out-house by day, and taking to the value of 5 s., or aiding therein.	Penitentiary from one to five years.
{Breaking warehouse by day or night, and taking to the amount of $3, or aiding therein.	Penitentiary from one to seven years.
Cattle - - {Fraudulent alteration of marks - -	Fine 50 l., imprisonment six months.
Coin. (See Forgery.)	
Compounding Felony - - - - - - -	Pillory two hours, fine 5 l.
Embezzlement - {- - By shippers, or non delivery at the proper public warehouse.	Penitentiary from one to five years.
{Of public documents, records, &c. -	Penitentiary from two to ten years.
Escape - - {Convict escaping from penitentiary -	Additional two years.
Extortion - {By threats of violence or accusation -	Penitentiary from one to two years.
Forgery, &c. - {- - Forging or uttering forged instru-ments to defraud, aiding and abetting.	Penitentiary from two to six years.
{Manufacturing United States bank-note paper, and possessing instruments for so doing, without authority.	Penitentiary from two to ten years.
{Engraving plates for United States bank-notes, or possessing same without authority.	Penitentiary from one to four years.

OFFENCES.		PUNISHMENTS.
Forgery, &c. - (*continued*.)	Counterfeiting or uttering coin, or aiding	- - Penitentiary from four to fifteen years, and fine not exceeding $ 1,000.
	Making, mending, selling or keeping instruments or metals for coining, without authority ; aiding and abetting.	Penitentiary from one to four years.
Fornication -	- - - - - - - -	Fine 2 *l.* 10 *s.* for each offence.
Fraud. (*See* also Embezzlement.)	- - Fraudulently removing or defacing a corner tree to any survey of the commonwealth, or being accessary before the fact.	Penitentiary from four to eight years.
Gaming - -	Keeping tables - - - -	Penitentiary from three to twelve months.
Hog-stealing -	First offence - - - -	- - Imprisonment not exceeding twelve months, and fine not exceeding 10 *l.*
	Second offence - - - - -	From six to ten years.
Horse-stealing -	Or accessary before the fact - -	- - Penitentiary from two to seven years, and restitution.
Kidnapping -	Stealing and selling free person as slave	Penitentiary from five to ten years.
Larceny.(*See* also Horse-stealing, Burglary, Hog-stealing.)	Stealing upwards of the value of $ 4 -	- - Penitentiary from two to four years, and restitution.
	Under $ 4 - - - -	Penitentiary from one to two years.
	Stealing land warrant, altering or passing one stolen.	Penitentiary from two to ten years.
	Stealing a slave - - -	Imprisonment from two to nine years.
	Stealing from a church, vessel, &c. -	Penitentiary from one to seven years.
	Receiving stolen goods - -	- - Penitentiary from six months to three years, and restitution.
Maiming and disfiguring - - - - -		Penitentiary from six months to five years.
Malicious mischief.	Stopping water or well in salt works -	Penitentiary from one to three years.
Manslaughter (Voluntary *).	First offence - - - -	- - Imprisonment at hard labour and solitude from two to ten years, and security for life or less time.
	Second offence - - - -	- - Imprisonment as before, from six to fourteen years.
	By stabbing, shooting, striking, &c. without malice aforethought (not accidental or in self-defence.)	Penitentiary from six months to six years.
Murder. (*See* also Stabbing, Poison.)	First degree - - - -	Death.
	Second degree - - - -	- - Imprisonment at hard labour and solitude from five to eighteen years.
Officer - -	Inspector giving false receipt -	Penitentiary from one to seven years.
	Arresting minister of religion in performance of service.	- - Fine and imprisonment at discretion of jury, and satisfaction to the party injured.
	Refusing to assist sheriff in his office -	Fine, $ 15.
Perjury - -	And subornation thereof - -	- - Penitentiary from two to six years, and oath not admissible.
Poison - -	Administering when death does not ensue	Penitentiary from one to five years.
Rape - -	- - Including abuse of child under 12 years, and accessaries before the fact.	Penitentiary from ten to twenty-one years.
Receiving stolen goods. (*See* Larceny.)		
Robbery. (*See* also Assault.)	And being accessary before the fact -	Penitentiary from three to ten years.
	When committed in a house or booth -	Penitentiary from one to six years.
Ship. (*See* also Embezzlement.)	- - Occasioning loss of ship in distress, or stealing from her.	Penitentiary from one to seven years.
Sodomy - -	- - - - - - -	Penitentiary from two to five years.
Stabbing - -	- - Shooting, &c. with intent to kill, when death does not ensue.	Penitentiary from one to five years.
	When death ensues within 6 months -	Penitentiary from six months to two years.
Treason - -	High - - - - - -	- - Imprisonment at hard labour or in solitude from six to twelve years.
	Petit - - - - - -	Like murder, according to degree.

N. B.—The precise degree of punishment, within the limits prescribed by law, is determined by the jury. The laws relating to imprisonment in Kentucky do not apply to slaves. Every slave committing murder, arson.or rape, is to suffer death; and for all other offences to be flogged at the whipping-post, to the extent of 39 lashes.

* Involuntary manslaughter, arising from the party being engaged in an unlawful act, is treated as a misdemeanor, according to the nature of such act.

TENNESSEE.

STATE PRISON AT NASHVILLE.

TENNESSEE.   THIS Penitentiary is on a level plain, about half a mile westward of the city of Nashville, and covers nearly three acres of ground. The plot of ground in the rear of the main building is 310 feet by 300 feet, and inclosed with a stone-wall 30 feet high. The front building and wings occupy a length of 310 feet by 58 feet in depth, and are intended to be three stories high. A number of the prisoners have daily been employed in assisting in the erection of the buildings. During the last year (1833) a range of workshops, two stories high, upwards of 200 feet in length and 30 feet in width, was entirely built by the convicts. These shops will admit of the employment of 200 workmen. The prisoners are also occupied in various other ways for the benefit of the State. The rocky surface of the yards has been lowered and made level, and a large reservoir excavated. A number of the cell-doors have been made in the prison. The convicts are regularly employed as stone-cutters, blacksmiths, carpenters, bricklayers, waggon-makers, coopers, chain-makers, tailors, shoemakers and hatters. Notwithstanding the amount of labour performed by the convicts in the buildings and works of the prison, the Institution would, at the end of the year 1833, have exhibited a considerable profit in other departments, but for the fatal ravages of the cholera which made its appearance in the beginning of June, and spread so rapidly that in a few days labour of all kinds was necessarily suspended. For three months from the commencement of this dreadful scourge, scarcely any work could be performed, not a single convict having escaped an attack. Additional expenditure has been likewise occasioned in providing for the sick.

Each convict is lodged at night in a separate dormitory. At day-light in the morning the guard on duty knocks at the door of each cell, at which signal the prisoner repeats his name aloud. He then dresses, washes, and stands in readiness to repair to the workshop immediately on the unlocking of the cell-door. During the day the convicts are kept closely employed. The regulations require that they should be " brisk and lively in their motions throughout the working hours." The prisoners are not allowed to speak to each other unless by permission, and in the presence of the keeper, nor are they permitted to hold any conversation with the guards or assistant-keepers, nor to speak to or look at any person visiting the Penitentiary.

In case of misbehaviour, or refusal to obey the order of the keeper or guards, the convict is punished by solitary confinement for a period not exceeding 30 days, five days being added to his sentence for every day thus spent; and also by a restricted diet of bread and water. The law prohibits the use of the whip; but the warden has requested to be allowed to inflict corporal punishment, from a conviction that strict discipline cannot be maintained without it. My impressions of the moral benefits to be derived from this prison are very unfavourable. The mental and religious improvement of the prisoners appears to be greatly neglected, the main object being to establish a profitable manufactury. In this design the State will probably succeed, as no prisoner is committed for a shorter period than two years, and as the warden of the prison possesses an extensive knowledge of mechanical employments. There are no females in this Penitentiary.

The following is the AMOUNT of the INCOME and EXPENDITURE of the PRISON for Two Years, from 30th September 1831 to 30th September 1833.

INCOME.	Dollars.	Cents.
Shoe department - - - - - - - - -	2,562	55
Coopers' ditto - - - - - - - -	478	91
Stone ditto - - - - - - - - -	2,443	38
Tailors' ditto - - - - - - - -	1,727	32
Hatters' ditto - - - - - - - -	2,277	32
Blacksmiths' ditto - - - - - - -	3,203	21
Waggon-makers' ditto - - - - - - -	1,879	46
Carpenters' ditto - - - - - - - -	2,780	33
Chair and Turning ditto - - - - - -	677	71
Labourers' ditto - - - - - - - -	715	3
Bricklayers' ditto - - - - - - -	1,013	63
Property on hand - - - - - - -	1,057	50
Debts due to the prison - - - - - - -	2,407	18
Total Income - - -	23,223	53

EXPENDITURE.	Dollars.	Cents.
Expenses - - - - - - - - -	3,153	50
Balance due to keeper - - - - - - -	4,607	58
Amount received from treasurer - - - - -	8,909	97
Balance, being profits of Labour - - -	6,552	48
Total - -	23,223	53

TENNESSEE.

Number of convicts in confinemeut, 30th September 1830 -   -   - 21

Received since: White males   -   -   - 75 }

           Coloured ditto   -   - 2 }   -   -   -   - 77

                                  Total   -   -   98

Discharged by expiration of sentence   -   -   -   -   -   - 9

Pardoned -   -   -   -   -   -   -   -   -   - 2

Died -   -   -   -   -   -   -   -   -   -   - 20

Number in confinement, 30th September 1833 -   -   -   - 67

                                  Total   -   -   98

EMPLOYMENT of Convicts, September 30, 1833.

Shoemakers -   -   -   -   -   -   -   -   -   - 6

Coopers -   -   -   -   -   -   -   -   -   - 2

Stonecutters -   -   -   -   -   -   -   -   - 8

Tailors -   -   -   -   -   -   -   -   -   - 2

Hatters -   -   -   -   -   -   -   -   -   - 8

Blacksmiths -   -   -   -   -   -   -   -   - 7

Waggon-makers -   -   -   -   -   -   -   -   - 6

Carpenters -   -   -   -   -   -   -   -   - 5

Turners -   -   -   -   -   -   -   -   -   - 1

Bricklayers -   -   -   -   -   -   -   -   - 7

Labourers -   -   -   -   -   -   -   -   - 4

Water-carriers and attending shops -   -   -   -   - 3

Cooking and washing -   -   -   -   -   -   - 2

Attending hospital -   -   -   -   -   -   -   - 1

Sick, in hospital -   -   -   -   -   -   -   - 5

                                  Total   -   -   - 67

NUMBER of Convicts committed to the TENNESSEE State Prison at *Nashville*, from its Commencement to 1833.

	1831.	1832.	1833.
Stealing - - - - - - - - - - -	2	1	1
Manslaughter - - - - - - - - - -	1	2	1
Grand larceny - - - - - - - - -	4	9	2
Petit larceny - - - - - - - - -	9	14	7
Shooting - - - - - - - - - - -	1	—	—
Horse-stealing - - - - - - - - -	9	5	2
Passing counterfeit money - - - - - - -	2	3	2
Murder, 2d degree - - - - - - - -	1	—	1
Forgery - - - - - - - - - - -	3	1	2
Assault with intent to kill - - - - - - -	1	1	3
Perjury - - - - - - - - - -	2	—	—
Aiding the escape of prisoners - - - - - -	1	—	—
Burglary - - - - - - - - - -	—	4	1
Maiming - - - - - - - - - -	—	1	—
Murder, 1st degree, commuted - - - - - -	—	—	1
Totals - - -	36	41	23
Discharged by expiration of sentence - - - - - -	—	4	8
Pardons - - - - - - - - - -	—	1	1
Deaths by cholera, out of 83 prisoners attacked - - - -	—	—	21

Ages   -   -   15   to   20   -   -   -   -   -   8

     —   -   -   20   to   30   -   -   -   -   -   42

     —   -   -   30   to   40   -   -   -   -   -   24

     —   -   -   40   to   50   -   -   -   -   -   14

     --   -   -   50   to   60   -   -   -   -   -   4

TENNESSEE.

PUNISHMENTS for the principal OFFENCES in this State.

OFFENCES.		PUNISHMENTS.
Accessaries -	- - After the fact, in case of murder of first degree.	Punished as murderers of second degree.
	All others, except near relations, which exception does not extend to the offence of resisting officers.	As principals.
Arson - -	- - Setting fire to house or outhouse of another, or any house in a city.	- - Imprisonment in the Penitentiary from five to twenty-one years *.
	Setting fire to any house, barn, store-house, haystack, &c. or building containing valuable property.	- - Penitentiary from two to twenty-one years *.
Assault - -	- - With intent to commit murder of first degree.	- - Penitentiary from three to twenty-one years.
	With intent to commit rape - -	Penitentiary from two to ten years.
	With intent to commit robbery - -	Penitentiary from two to six years.
Bigamy - -	- - - - - - -	Penitentiary from two to twenty-one years*.
Bribery and Embracery.	- - Officer in administration of justice taking bribe.	- - Penitentiary from three to twenty-one years *.
	Giving bribe to such officer or juror -	Penitentiary from two to ten years.
Burglary, &c. -	- - - - - - -	Penitentiary from five to fifteen years *.
	Housebreaking by day with felonious intent	Penitentiary from three to ten years *.
Coin. (*See* Forgery.)		
Conspiracy to indict	- - - - - - -	Penitentiary from two to ten years.
Duelling - -	- - Fighting, challenging or bearing a challenge.	Penitentiary from three to ten years.
	Posting for not fighting, and publisher refusing to give up author answerable.	Penitentiary for two years.
Escape, &c. -	- - Forcibly or by menaces liberating prisoner in custody or charge, or after conviction of felony; or aiding and abetting.	Penitentiary from two to ten years.
	Officer voluntarily allowing escape -	Penitentiary from two to ten years.
Forgery, Coining, &c.	- - Counterfeiting coin, bank-notes, bills, cheques, &c., or passing them or having them in possession, altering or filling up. Making instruments or plates, or concealing, keeping them for counterfeiting, or making or keeping bank-note paper or instruments for making it. Any forgery to the prejudice of another's right, or passing any forged paper. Destroying or concealing wills - -	Penitentiary from three to fifteen years.
Fraud - -	- - Obtaining money or goods by false tokens, letters.	Penitentiary from three to fifteen years.
Gaming - -	- - Playing and exhibiting certain games (faro, thimble, and the grandmother's trick).	Penitentiary from two to five years.
Horse-stealing, or receiving stolen horses	- - -	Penitentiary from three to ten years*.
Incest - -	- - - - - - -	Penitentiary from five to twenty-one years*.
Kidnapping and selling as slaves - - - -		Penitentiary from five to fifteen years *.
Larceny - - (*See* also Robbery, Horse-stealing, Slaves.)	- - Stealing to the value of upwards of $10, or knowingly receiving to that amount (grand larceny).	Penitentiary from three to ten years *.
	$10 or under, or knowingly receiving (petit larceny).	- - Penitentiary from one to five years, or fine and imprisonment, at discretion of court, on recommendation of jury *.
	Stealing public records or papers from public offices, to the injury of any one.	Penitentiary from three to fifteen years.
	Stealing or receiving notes, bills of exchange, &c.	Penitentiary from three to fifteen years *
Maiming, disfiguring, &c. - - - - -		Penitentiary from two to ten years.
Malicious Mischief.	Destroying corner trees - - -	Penitentiary from two to five years.
Manslaughter -	Voluntary - - - - -	Penitentiary from two to ten years *.
	Involuntary - - - - -	Penitentiary from one to five years *.
Murder - -	- - First degree,—by poison, lying in wait, or any other kind of wilful, deliberate, malicious and premeditated killing, or in an attempt at arson, rape, robbery, burglary or larceny.	Death.
	Second degree,—all other kinds of killing with malice aforethought, either express or implied.	Penitentiary from ten to twenty-one years.

⊙

OFFENCES.		PUNISHMENTS.
Officer - - (*See* also Bribery, Escape.)	- - Having care of public books, and refusing to give them up to the proper authorities of state, or obliterating or defacing them.	Penitentiary from five to ten years.
Perjury, or subornation of perjury - - - -		Penitentiary from three to fifteen years *.
Poison - -	- - Administering when death does not ensue.	- - Penitentiary from three to twenty-one years.
Rape - -	- - Including abuse of child under ten years of age.	- - Penitentiary from ten to twenty-one years *.
Receiving stolen goods. (*See* Larceny.)		
Rescue. (*See* Escape.)		
Robbery - -	- - - - - - -	Penitentiary from five to fifteen years *.
Slaves - - (*See* also Note 4.)	Stealing a slave - - - -	Penitentiary from five to fifteen years *.
Sodomy - -	- - - - - - -	Penitentiary from five to fifteen years *.

N. B.—All persons convicted of any of the above offences are disqualified from holding any office under the State.

Property stolen to be restored; if not, execution for the value, or damages for fraud or injury, to be determined by jury, to issue against the convict.

The above punishments, with the exception of that inflicted on officers detaining public books, are imposed by an Act of 9th December 1829, the 67th clause of which is as follows: "Whoever shall be convicted, either as principal or accessary, of any felony or other offence not otherwise provided for by this Act, which is now punishable by death or stripes, shall undergo confinement in the said Gaol and Penitentiary-house for a period not less than two or more than 10 years."

The above Act does not apply in any way to offences committed by slaves.

By a subsequent Act, a convict sentenced to a shorter term of imprisonment than two years is not to be confined in the Penitentiary; where, therefore, the punishment awarded to any of the offences above mentioned falls short of this time, it is to be carried into execution in the County Gaol.

The precise degree of punishment, within the limits prescribed by law, is determined by the jury.

* This mark signifies that the convict to whose punishment it is affixed is also rendered infamous, and incapable of being examined as a witness.

O H I O.

STATE PRISON AT COLUMBUS.

THE Penitentiary for Ohio was erected in 1816, and is situated at Columbus, the capital of the State. It is an ill-constructed and very insecure building, and was originally calculated for only 30 prisoners. It stands on elevated ground, at the back of the Scioto river; but the surface is so uneven as to enable the convicts in certain positions to evade the observation of the guards. The wall which incloses the ground is 400 feet long, 150 feet wide, and 14 feet high. The keeper's house, on the east side, is a brick building two stories high. The cell-buildings are on the north side of the wall, 150 feet long and 30 feet wide, of brick, two stories high. A passage, eight feet wide, runs through the centre, and the sleeping cells are ranged on each side. The doors have gratings in them, and being placed opposite to each other the prisoners can communicate throughout the building when locked up at night. There are 50 cells now occupied, the dimensions of each being nine feet by seven feet. At one end of the cell-building is the kitchen and dining-hall. Over the kitchen is the hospital, a room 30 feet by 16 feet, which is also used as a work-room for shoemakers and tailors. In the basement story, below the surface of the ground, are several cells for solitary confinement, each eight feet by six feet. The walls are of stone, lined with plank. These cells are quite dark, the entrance to them being from a trap door in the ground-floor above. Convicts are confined in these dungeons for short periods, according to the sentence of the court.

In the rear of the keeper's house are the workshops which are small and badly arranged, enabling the prisoners to be in close association with each other without any system of inspection. They were employed as waggon-makers, wheelwrights, blacksmiths, locksmiths, coopers, cabinet-makers, shoemakers and tailors, also in grinding corn and baking bread for the prison. The women were occupied in making and mending the linen, &c. Owing to the want of room, 75 prisoners only could be employed in the workshops, the remainder were shut up in the cells. It is probably owing to this cause that the labour of the prisoners has not hitherto been productive. The yearly reports of the keeper show a considerable excess of expenditure over the receipts and earnings. The cost to the State of the Penitentiary, containing on an average 165 convicts, during the year 1831, was $12,655, including the charges of conviction and transport, which amounted to $6,509, and after deducting the earnings of the prisoners.

At the period of my first visit to this Penitentiary there were 190 convicts in confinement, viz. 163 white men, 20 coloured persons, four white women, and three coloured women. On a subsequent visit the number in confinement was 203, of whom 114 were employed on the works of a new Penitentiary now erecting. Several are also engaged in making bricks, at the distance of half a mile from the prison. Whenever the convicts exceed in number 120, the governor of the State is driven to the necessity of granting pardons, in order to make room for new prisoners. From this circumstance, the sentence of commitment to this Penitentiary (the shortest term of which by law is for three years) has not lately on an average exceeded 21 months. Several of the prisoners are sentenced for life. There were four lunatics in confinement. The prisoners are not restricted to any particular quantity of food. The usual daily allowance is one pound of bread and one pound of beef. During the year the cost of food varies from $37 to $42 per head. The prisoners associate together at meal times. There are no inspectors. The moral and religious welfare of the prisoners is entirely neglected. There was no service performed on the Sunday at the period of my visit.

During the prevalence of cholera, 127 prisoners were attacked by the premonitory symptoms, and 27 with the disease in a malignant form. Of these, 11 cases only proved fatal. The convicts in this prison, in common with all others, are on their committal placed at those trades at which they can be most profitably employed. The consequence is that prisoners of every variety of character become indiscriminately associated; and as strictness of discipline is impracticable, conversation during the day must take place. The defective construction of this prison is such as to render it impossible to prevent intercourse between the prisoners, during the hours of labour, notwithstanding the greatest exertions on the part of the officers; and even did they succeed, the most favourable opportunities are in this respect afforded to the convicts after they leave work and retire to their night cells, as they usually sleep not less than four in one room. The women are crowded together in one apartment.

The consequence is, as might naturally be expected, that much of the time of the prisoners, on retiring to their cells, is spent in mutual contamination and in devising plans of escape. Shortly after my visit, a scheme of this kind was arranged, and had nearly been put into execution. It was discovered that a box of tools to be used in housebreaking had actually
been

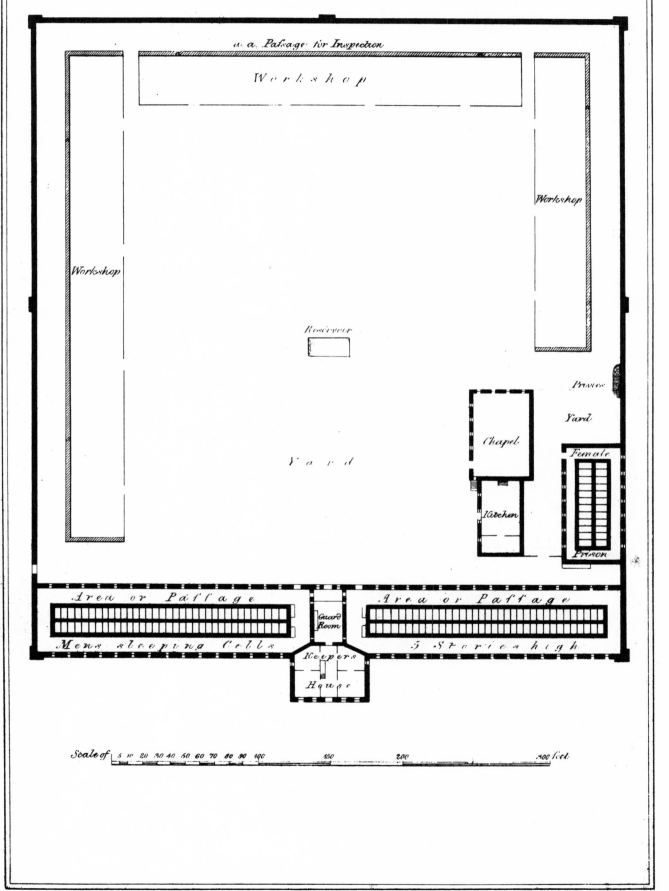

Plan of the *NEW PENITENTIARY* at Columbus, Ohio.

a. a. Passage for Inspection

Workshop

Workshop

Workshop

Reservoir

Prison

Yard

Chapel

Yard

Female

Kitchen

Prison

Area or Passage

Area or Passage

Guard Room

Mens sleeping Cells

5 Stories high

Keepers House

Scale of 5 10 20 30 40 50 60 70 80 90 100   150   200   300 feet

J. Basire lithog.

been made in the prison during the ordinary hours of labour. Such is the insecurity of the building that the officers can be seldom sure of the safety of their lives, although there are ten guards stationed in various parts armed with rifles. In the year 1831 no less than 25 escapes took place. The law allows one guard to every fifteen prisoners. This Penitentiary cannot in fact be more correctly described than in the language of a report made to the Legislature, in 1831 : " A more perfect system for the dissemination of vice could not be devised than is to be found within the walls of the Ohio prison."

In consequence of these defects and of the very unproductive results of the labour of the prisoners, the State has purchased a plot of land, about eight acres, in Franklinton, not far distant from the old prison, and contiguous to extensive beds of limestone. The building of a new Penitentiary, according to the annexed plan, is now in progress. The prison, when completed, is to contain 700 cells : about half that number, together with the keeper's house, will probably be finished this summer.

The whole of the south front of the ground, 400 feet in extent, is to be occupied by the prison buildings, the keeper's house being placed in the centre and forming the general entrance by a hall or passage 12 feet wide which leads to the guard-room. Beyond is another passage, having on each side the entrances to the wing buildings which contain the sleeping cells. In the guard-room there are to be inspection-apertures, to command a view of the long passages or areas in front of the cells. The buildings on each side of the keeper's house are intended to be alike, and to contain the dormitories (arranged on the Auburn plan), with a double range of cells back to back, and an area around, 11 feet wide, inclosed with walls and roofed over. Each wing will contain 70 cells on each story. The whole is to be five stories high. Each cell is to be seven feet long, three feet six inches wide, and seven feet high. The cells, however, are deficient in a most material point—the means of ventilation. The prison for the females will form a detached building in the rear, with a double range of cells, 24 in number. The upper floor of this building is to form an hospital, having a distinct entrance from a staircase on the outside. An airing-yard is attached to the women's prison, adjoining to which is the general kitchen. Beyond, is a building for the chapel, 60 feet by 40 feet.

The prison yard in the rear is 400 feet square, inclosed with a boundary wall 25 feet high and three feet thick, having a small guard-tower at each angle, and also in the centre of each side. The workshops will form a long range of buildings, occupying three sides of the spacious yard in the rear, detached about 25 feet from the boundary wall. It is intended to have a secret passage at the back of the range of workshops, as at Auburn, from which the prisoners may be inspected without their knowledge. A large tank, or reservoir of water, is to be formed in the centre of the yard. It is proposed in the first instance to erect the prison with only 500 cells, and to add the remaining 200, as occasion may require.

The following is the estimate of the expense of building and completing the prison :—

	Dollars.
Cost of land	6,180
Building the prison with 500 cells	58,261
Ditto - - - with 200 additional cells	13,986
Total Cost - - - -	78,427

Deduct estimated amount of convicts' labour :—

In Prison building with 500 cells - - - *Dollars* 16,020		
Additional ditto - - 200 cells - - - - - 3,663		19,683
Cost, exclusive of Labour of Convicts - - -		58,744

NUMBER of Convicts committed to the Ohio State Prison, at *Columbus*, from its Commencement in 1815 to 1832.

	1815.	1816.	1817.	1818.	1819.	1820.	1821.	1822.	1823.	1824.	1825.	1826.	1827.	1828.	1829.	1830.	1831.	1832.
Number annually rec'd	7	29	33	35	54	61	53	40	127	No Return	69	60	No Return	58	65	76	93	114
Pardoned	–	–	–	–	–	–	–	20	–		9	40		16	27	25	59	32
Escaped	–	–	–	–	–	–	–	4	–		2	1		14	7	4	25	18
Died	–	–	–	–	–	–	–	5	5		2	2		4	–	–	2	1
In Prison at the end of the Year	–	–	–	–	–	–	123	114	111		153	160		107	132	165	166	215
Crimes:																		
Murder (1st degree)	–	–	–	–	–	–	–	–	–	–	–	–	–	1	3	3	–	1
— (2d degree)	–	1	–	1	–	–	–	3	5	–	9	10	–	6	9	12	10	9
Manslaughter	–	–	1	–	–	–	–	–	–	–	6	7	–	6	4	–	3	5
Assault and Battery, with intent to kill	2	1	–	–	–	–	–	–	1	–	2	2	–	4	8	13	8	12
Stabbing	–	–	–	–	–	–	–	–	–	–	5	5	–	2	4	–	8	7
Rape	–	–	–	1	–	–	–	3	2	–	8	9	–	5	5	5	5	6
Assault with intent to commit rape	–	–	–	–	–	–	–	–	–	–	–	–	–	–	1	4	–	7
Horse-stealing	1	6	4	3	–	–	–	26	30	–	55	41	–	29	32	42	42	54
Burglary	–	–	–	1	–	–	–	7	11	–	26	35	–	19	25	28	33	39
Larceny	4	13	17	13	–	–	–	22	30	–	19	18	–	18	27	36	19	32
Robbery	1	–	–	–	–	–	–	–	–	–	–	–	–	1	1	2	1	2
Passing counterfeit money and counterfeiting	–	1	8	5	–	–	–	18	17	–	12	12	–	6	4	12	12	22
Forgery	–	3	1	3	No Return			7	8	No Return	4	1	–	1	4	–	3	12
Arson	–	–	1	–	–	–	–	4	5	–	5	5	–	1	1	1	4	3
Perjury	–	1	–	1	–	–	–	–	–	–	1	6	–	5	3	2	3	3
Incest	–	–	–	–	–	–	–	–	–	–	–	–	–	1	1	3	2	1
Mail robbery	–	–	–	–	–	–	–	–	1	–	–	1	–	1	1	1	1	–
Maiming	–	–	–	1	–	–	–	–	–	–	2	1	–	–	1	3	–	–
Stealing	–	–	–	2	–	–	–	–	–	–	–	–	–	–	–	–	–	–
Rape on Daughter	–	–	–	–	–	–	–	–	–	–	–	–	–	–	–	2	–	–
Breaking Canal Banks	–	–	–	–	–	–	–	–	–	–	–	–	–	1	1	1	–	–
Receiving stolen Goods	–	–	–	–	–	–	–	–	–	–	–	–	–	–	1	1	–	–
Bigamy	–	1	–	–	–	–	–	–	–	–	1	1	–	–	–	1	–	–
Shooting with intent to kill	–	–	–	–	–	–	–	–	–	–	3	2	1	–	–	–	–	–
Housebreaking	–	–	–	–	–	–	–	–	–	–	2	–	–	–	–	–	–	–
Felony	1	1	3	1	–	–	–	–	–	–	–	–	–	–	–	–	–	–
Sheep-stealing	–	–	–	–	–	–	–	1	–	–	–	–	–	–	–	–	–	–
Total	9	28	35	32	–	–	–	91	110	–	–	160	156	107	132	165	166	215

SENTENCES.

	1831.	1832.
For Life	15	12
30 years	–	1
20 –	1	1
16 –	1	1
15 –	1	1
14 –	2	1
13 –	–	1
12 –	–	2
10 –	4	3
8 –	1	–
7 –	19	21
9 –	1	–
6 –	19	21
5 –	38	45
4 –	11	28
3 –	53	77
1 –	–	–
	166	215

PUNISHMENTS for the Principal Offences in this State.

OFFENCES.		PUNISHMENTS.
Accessaries	- - Before the fact, in capital felonies, or those punished by imprisonment for life.	The same as the principals.
	In other felonies	- - Imprisonment in penitentiary at hard labour, for any time within the limits prescribed to the punishment of the principals.
Adultery	Living in a state of; woman	- - Dungeon of county gaol, on bread and water, not exceeding thirty days.
	Ditto ; man	- - The same, and fine not exceeding $ 200.
Arson, &c.	- - Burning dwelling-house, outhouse, barn, building, warehouse, &c. of another, church, bridge, worth $ 50.	- - Penitentiary, at hard labour, from three to twenty years.
	Setting fire to the same with intent to burn.	- - Penitentiary, at hard labour, from three to seven years.
Assault	- - With intent to commit murder, rape or robbery.	- - Penitentiary, at hard labour, from three to seven years.
	Assault and battery	- - Dungeon of county gaol, on bread and water, not exceeding ten days, or fine not exceeding $ 150, or both, and liable to an action by party injured.
Bigamy	- - Where wife or husband not wilfully absent for three successive years next preceding.	- - Penitentiary, at hard labour, from three to seven years.

OHIO.

OFFENCES.	PUNISHMENTS.
Bribery, Embracery, &c. - - Juror or witness receiving a bribe, or person attempting to corrupt them by promises, &c.	- - Dungeon of county gaol, on bread and water, not exceeding thirty days, and fine not exceeding $500.
Bribing, or attempting to bribe a judge or arbitrator.	Fine from $50 to $1,000.
Bribery of officer to procure an escape	Fine from $25 to $200.
Bribery at an election - -	Fine not exceeding $500.
Burglary, &c. - - Breaking and entering house, warehouse, factory, church, &c., with intent to commit * certain offences by night.	- - Penitentiary, at hard labour, from three to ten years.
Entering without breaking by day or night, and attempting to kill, disfigure, maim, rob, stab, or commit rape or arson.	- - Penitentiary, at hard labour, from three to seven years.
Entering a house where a person is dwelling, and using, or being armed for, violence, by night.	- - Dungeon of county gaol, on bread and water, not exceeding thirty days, or fine not exceeding $500, or both.
The same by day - - - -	- - Dungeon of county gaol, on bread and water, not exceeding twenty days, or fine not exceeding $100, or both.
Coining - - *See* Forgery.	
Dead Bodies - - - Disinterring, or removing or attempting it, or being concerned therein.	- - Dungeon of county gaol, not exceeding thirty days, or fine not exceeding $1,000, or both.
Duelling - - - Giving, accepting, or bearing a challenge, or being concerned in a duel as principal, or second when death ensues.	- - The same as murder of the first or second degree, as the case may be.
When death does not ensue - -	- - Penitentiary, at hard labour, from three to ten years, and disqualified from holding office.
Escape - - Sheriff or jailor voluntarily allowing it (*See also* Bribery.)	- - Close confinement not exceeding ten days, or fine of $500, or both.
Refusing to assist sheriff in securing a prisoner.	Fine not exceeding $50.
Assisting prisoner in an escape, or attempt at escape.	- - Dungeon of county gaol, not exceeding thirty days, or fine from $50 to $500, or both.
Forcible rescue from gaol or custody of officer.	- - Dungeon of county gaol on bread and water, not exceeding thirty days, and fine not exceeding $500.
Extortion - *See* Officer, *and* Threats.	
False personation - - Personating another before a court **Pretences, &c.** of justice, &c., or officer empowered to (*See also* Fraud grant marriage licences. *and* Swindling.)	- - Penitentiary, at hard labour, from three to six years.
Obtaining money or goods by false tokens, or under false pretences.	- - Dungeon of county gaol, on bread and water, not exceeding ten days, or fine not exceeding $500, or both.
Forgery, &c. - - - Of will, deed, record, check, note, receipt, warrant, &c., to defraud, or uttering the same.	- - Penitentiary, at hard labour from three to twenty years.
Counterfeiting, or uttering counterfeit current coin, making instruments for coining, or plates for forging, or altering bank notes, or having them in possession.	- - Penitentiary, at hard labour, from three to ten years.
Selling counterfeit notes, &c., not filled up, or having some in possession, or uttering notes, &c., purporting to be by a company not in existence.	- - Penitentiary, at hard labour, from three to seven years.
Attempting to pass counterfeit notes or coin.	- - Penitentiary, at hard labour, from three to six years.
Fornication - Living in a state of - - - -	- - Dungeon of county gaol, not exceeding ten days, and fine not exceeding $100.
Fraud, &c. - *See also* False Pretences. Fraudulent sale of lands without title -	- - Penitentiary, at hard labour, from three to seven years.

* " Any deed by this act declared criminal." The best general description appears to be, " offences punishable by death or penitentiary imprisonment," though this is not exact.

OHIO.

OFFENCES.		PUNISHMENTS.
Fraud, &c., *cont*ᵈ	Conveyance to defraud creditors -	- - Dungeon of county gaol, on bread and water, not exceeding ten days, and fine not exceeding $500, or both.
Horse stealing -	- - Or knowingly receiving or concealing stolen horses, or harbouring the thief.	- - Penitentiary, at hard labour, from three to fifteen years.
Incest - -	- - - - - - -	- - Penitentiary, at hard labour, from three to ten years.
Kidnapping -	A free black or mulatto - - -	- - Penitentiary, at hard labour, from three to seven years.
Larceny - -	*See also* Robbery *and* Horse Stealing.	
	Stealing personal property to the amount of $50, or receiving the same, or harbouring the thieves.	- - Penitentiary, at hard labour, from three to seven years.
	Stealing under $50 - - -	- - Restore twofold, and dungeon of county gaol, on bread and water, not exceeding thirty days, or fine not exceeding $200, or both.
	Receiving the same - - - -	- - Fine and imprisonment, or either, as for stealing.
Maiming, disfiguring, &c.	- - With express purpose, or with intent to kill.	- - Penitentiary, at hard labour, from three to twenty years.
	Stabbing or shooting at, with intent to kill or wound.	- - Penitentiary, at hard labour, from three to five years.
Malicious Mischief.	- - To bridges, land-marks, &c. - -	- - Dungeon of county gaol, on bread and water, not exceeding thirty days, or fine $500, or both.
	To monuments, tombstones, &c. -	- - Solitary imprisonment in dungeon in county gaol not exceeding thirty days, or fine not exceeding $200, or both.
	Altering marks on cattle - -	- - Fine $50, and liable to treble damages to party injured.
	Setting fire to hay or corn stacks, &c., fences, timbers, &c.	- - Dungeon of county gaol, not exceeding thirty days, or fine from $10 to $500, or both, and answerable to party injured in double damages.
	Setting fire to woods, prairies, &c. -	- - Fine $50, to stand committed till sentence complied with, and liable to party injured.
	Killing horses, sheep, cattle, swine (not trespassing.)	- - Dungeon of county gaol, on bread and water, not exceeding twenty days, and fine from $5 to $100, and liable to owner for double the value.
	Destroying fruit or other garden trees	- - Fine from $5 to $500, and liable to owner for double value.
	Cutting or injuring other trees -	- - Fine from $5 to $100, and liable for double value to the owner.
	- - Ornamental trees in public walk, common, &c.	- - Fine from $5 to $100; liable to party injured in double damages.
	Destroying or disfiguring mile-stones, or guide posts.	- - Imprisoned not exceeding ten days, or fined not exceeding $50, or both.
Manslaughter -	- - Killing without malice, or in a sudden quarrel, or unintentionally in the commission of an unlawful act.	- - Penitentiary, at hard labour, from three to ten years.
Murder - -	- - 1st* degree. Killing purposely with deliberate malice, or in the perpetration of, or attempt at rape, arson, robbery or burglary.	Death.
	2d Degree. Killing purposely, but without deliberate malice.	Penitentiary at hard labour for life.
Officer, &c. - (*See* also Escape and Bribery.)	- - Usurpation of office, or oppression under colour thereof, by an usurper.	- - Dungeon of county gaol not exceeding ten days, or fine not exceeding $250, or both.
	Extortion by officer - - -	- - Dungeon of county gaol, on bread and water ten days, or fine of $200, or both; disqualified for office for seven years.
	Officers stirring up suits - -	- - Fine $500; answerable to party injured in treble damages.
	Corrupt injury by, under colour of office	- - Fine $200; and answerable to party injured in treble damages.

* The jury who find a prisoner guilty determine the degree of punishment. When convicted on his own confession in court, the court determines the degree on an examination of witnesses.

OHIO.

OFFENCES.		PUNISHMENTS.
Officer—*cont*^d.	- - Officer having care of gaol, suffering it to be foul, so as to endanger health of prisoners.	Fine not exceeding $ 100.
	Constable neglecting to serve warrant where offence is capital, or punished by penitentiary imprisonment.	- - Imprisonment in county gaol not exceeding ten days, or fine not exceeding $ 500, or both, and forfeiture of office.
	Where offence is of a minor nature -	- - Imprisonment not exceeding ten days, or fine not exceeding $ 100, or both, and forfeiture of office.
	Officer suffering person sentenced to solitary confinement, or to be fed on bread and watèr, to be dealt with less severely.	Fine not exceeding $ 100.
	Resisting any officer of justice, or abusing a judge or justice of peace, in the execution of his office.	- - Dungeon of county gaol, on bread and water, not exceeding twenty days; or fine not exceeding $ 200; or both.
Perjury, or subornation of perjury - - - -		- - Penitentiary, at hard labour, from three to seven years.
Poison - -	- - When death ensues - - -	*See* Murder.
	Administering or preparing poison with intent to kill, or assisting therein.	- - Penitentiary, at hard labour, from three to fifteen years.
Rape, &c. -	- - Of daughter or sister - - -	Penitentiary, at hard labour, for life.
	Of other woman, including abuse of child under 10 years by male upwards of 17 years.	- - Penitentiary, at hard labour, from ten to twenty years.
	Carnal knowledge of an insane woman (not wife) by male upwards of 18 years.	- - Penitentiary, at hard labour, from three to ten years.
Rescue - -	*See* Escape.	
Receiving Stolen Goods, &c. *See* Larceny.		
Riot, Affray, &c.	- - Assembling to the number of three or more with intent to commit violence, or agreeing so to do when assembled.	- - Dungeon of county gaol, on bread and water, not exceeding ten days, and fine not exceeding $ 200.
	Refusing to assist justices in dispersing rioters.	Fine not exceeding $ 25.
	Obstructing anthorities in dispersing rioters, or committing any violent act.	- - Dungeon of county gaol, on bread and water, not exceeding thirty days, and fine not exceeding $ 500, and security for not exceeding one year.
	Boxing by agreement - - -	- - Close confinement in county gaol for not exceeding ten days; or fine not exceeding $ 50; or both.
Robbery -	- - Taking property from the person by violence or fear.	- - Penitentiary, at hard labour, from three to twenty years.
Swindling -	*See* False Pretences and Fraud.	—
Threats - -	- - Attempt to extort money by threatening letters.	- - Dungeon of county gaol, on bread and water, not exceeding ten days; or fine from $ 50 to $ 500; or both.

N.B.—The Court determines the precise degree of punishment within the limits prescribed by law, and also if the convict* shall be imprisoned in solitude in the penitentiary cell for any, and if so for what, period of his imprisonment.

The property of a convict is liable for the costs of his prosecution.

* This is confined to offences specified in a certain Act. *See* note, p. 129.

INDIANA.

STATE PRISON AT JEFFERSONVILLE.

ON approaching this prison, I found the gates wide open, and several of the prisoners working in the yard at stone-masonry. At a short distance was a man sitting on a gate, who immediately came towards me, armed with a pair of rifle-barrelled pistols. He informed me that the keeper of the penitentiary lived at about a quarter of a mile distance. I went thither, and he accompanied me back. There were at this time 55 convicts in the prison, who were employed as blacksmiths (4), carpenters (4), wheelwrights (4), coopers (6), bedstead-makers (8), and the remainder as masons, brickmakers, &c. Of the whole number, eight were coloured people. There were no females. The State farms the convicts to the keeper for a certain sum per annum; and he appears to have the uncontrolled management of them. He employs the convicts outside the walls in the service of individuals whenever he can do so advantageously: as many as 15 convicts have been thus let on hire at a time. Upon such occasions a guard is placed over the men. Fire-arms, indeed, appeared to form the principal security of the prison.

This penitentiary was erected in 1820. The dormitories, thirteen in number, are on the upper story. Their dimensions are about 6 feet by 9, and 8 feet high. From the number of persons usually in confinement, at least four or five men were necessarily placed in each of these small cells at night. Here also the prisoners were shut up during the whole of the Sunday. The coloured men sleep apart from the other prisoners, but there is no further classification. The misdemeanant and the murderer may be confined in the same cell. At sun-rise, the prisoners are required to leave their cells, and are locked up at sun-set. During the night, an armed guard is on duty in the passage to prevent conversation, as well as to detect attempts at escape. I was told that each prisoner is allowed to have a Bible in the cell, the darkness of which, however, would prevent the possibility of reading, if any one of the four prisoners confined in it were so inclined. There is no moral instruction nor religious service.

There is no limitation in the quantity of bread furnished: the quality however was not good. Each man receives daily one pound of pork and a quantity of milk. The friends of the prisoners are permitted to visit them, and to bring them various articles of provisions. They may also receive letters, which have been inspected by the keeper. Shoes and stockings are not provided, and only such other articles of clothing as may be absolutely necessary.

The keeper makes a report once a year on the state of the penitentiary. Two inspectors are appointed by the legislature: they are required to visit the prison only twice a year, and reside at a distance. The penitentiary is 30 miles from the capital. The establishment consists of the keeper, two assistants, and two trade superintendents. About half the prisoners are in irons which are placed on them according to their supposed disposition and character. The "cow-hide" whip is freely used. The imprisonment does not operate in deterring from the commission of further offences, a fact which the keeper admitted: "The prisoners," he said, "commit new crimes, although scarcely out of the shade of the penitentiary."

There is sufficient space to admit of the buildings being enlarged, and it was in contemplation to erect 20 additional cells.

PUNISHMENTS for the principal OFFENCES in this State.

OFFENCES.		PUNISHMENTS.
Adultery -	If a male - - - - -	Fine not exceeding $ 300.
	If a female - - - -	- - Imprisonment not exceeding three months.
Arson - -	- - - - - - -	- - Imprisonment and hard labour in State prison from one to ten years.
Assault	and battery - -	- - Fine not exceeding $ 1,000; or imprisonment not exceeding six months; or both*.
	With intent to commit rape - -	- - Imprisonment and hard labour from two to fourteen years, and fine not exceeding $ 1,000.
Barratry, &c. -	- - - - - - -	- - Imprisonment not exceeding six months, and fine not exceeding $ 500.
Bigamy -	- - - - - - -	- - Imprisonment and hard labour in State prison from two to five years, and fine not exceeding $ 1,000.

* A magistrate may impose a fine to the amount of $ 3.

OFFENCES.		PUNISHMENTS.	INDIANA.
Bribery - -	Bribing a judge - - - -	- - Imprisonment and hard labour in State prison from two to ten years.	
Burglary -	- - - - - - -	- - Imprisonment and hard labour in State prison from one to fourteen years, and a fine not exceeding $1,000.	
Compounding Felony (where goods are stolen) - -		Fine double the value of goods stolen.	
Dead bodies -	Removing, &c. - - - -	Fine not exceeding $1,000.	
Duelling - -	If death does not ensue - -	- - Fine not exceeding $5,000, and imprisonment not exceeding one year.	
	If death ensues - - - -	Death.	
	Bearing a challenge - - -	Imprisonment not exceeding one year.	
Forgery, &c. -	In general - - - -	- - Imprisonment and hard labour in State prison from two to fourteen years, and fine not exceeding $1,000.	
	Possessing apparatus for forgery -	- - Fine as before; imprisonment and hard labour in State prison from two to five years.	
Fraud - -	- - Obtaining goods, &c. under false pretences.	- - Imprisonment from one to seven years, and fine not exceeding double the value obtained.	
Kidnapping -	- - - - - -	- - Imprisonment and hard labour in State prison from two to fourteen years.	
Larceny - -	- - Stealing to the value of $5 or upwards, (grand larceny.)	- - Fine double the value of the property stolen, and imprisonment at hard labour in State prison from two to fourteen years.	
	Under $5, (petit larceny) - -	- - Imprisonment at hard labour in State prison for one year, if a male, and fine not exceeding $100; if a female, imprisonment at hard labour not exceeding sixty days.	
	Second offence - - -	The same as grand larceny.	
	Receiving stolen goods - - -	The same as stealing.	
Maiming, &c. -	- - Cutting on purpose to disfigure, cutting out tongue, or otherwise maiming with malice aforethought.	- - Imprisonment and hard labour in State prison from two to fourteen years, and fine of $1,000.	
	Otherwise maiming without malice aforethought.	- - Fine from $5 to $2,000; imprisonment in common gaol from twenty days to six months.	
Manslaughter -	- - - - - - -	- - Imprisonment at hard labour from one to twenty-one years, and fine not exceeding $1,000.	
Murder - -	- - - - - - -	Death.	
Officer - -	- - Obstructing in the execution of legal process.	Fine not exceeding $10,000.	
Perjury - -	- - - - - - -	- - Imprisonment and hard labour in State prison from two to twenty-one years, fine not exceeding $1,000, and to be deemed infamous and incompetent as a witness.	
Rape - -	- - - - - - -	- - Imprisonment and hard labour in State prison from five to twenty-one years.	
Receiving stolen goods. See Larceny.			
Riot, &c. -	- - - - - - -	Fine not exceeding $500.	
	Unlawful assemblage of three or more persons.	Fine not exceeding $100.	
Robbery - -	- - - - - - -	- - Imprisonment and hard labour in State prison from one to fourteen years, and fine not exceeding $1,000.	
Slaves - -	Harbouring slaves - - - -	- - Fine not exceeding $500. and liable in damages to the party injured.	
Treason - -	- - - - - - -	Death.	

N.B.—Murder, rape, treason, kidnapping and perjury, are declared infamous, and the convict is incapable of serving public offices.

The punishment of female convicts sentenced to hard labour may be limited to such periods, less than three months, as the court or jury may think proper, and it is to be carried into execution in the county gaol, by confinement there to such hard labour as may be suitable.

If a convict at the expiration of his sentence cannot pay the sum which he has been fined, he may be detained at hard labour until he has worked out the amount, receiving credit for 20 cents. a day. In all cases the costs incurred in sending the guilty party to prison are to be repaid by him to the county in like manner, unless they shall have been discharged before the expiration of his sentence.

RHODE
ISLAND.

PUNISHMENTS FOR THE PRINCIPAL OFFENCES IN THE
STATE OF RHODE ISLAND.

OFFENCES.		PUNISHMENTS.
Adultery -	- - - - - - - -	- - Fine, not exceeding $200, and imprisonment not exceeding six months.
Arson, &c. -	Or accessary before the fact - -	Death.
	Burning houses, barns, outhouses, or any other building, the burning of which would not amount to arson at common law.	- - Fine not exceeding $5,000, and imprisonment not exceeding five years, pillory, and to be cropped on both ears while in pillory, and be branded with the letter B.
	Burning stacks of corn, hay, grain, &c.	- - Fine not exceeding $1,000, and imprisonment not exceeding one year.
Assault and Battery -	- - - - - -	- - Fine not exceeding $100, and imprisonment not exceeding six months, or either.
	With intent to commit murder, rape, robbery, sodomy or burglary.	- - Fine not exceeding $1,000, and imprisonment not exceeding two years.
Bastardy -	- - Concealing death of bastard child, where evidence of murder does not exist.	- - Fine not exceeding $300, or imprisonment not exceeding one year, or both.
Bigamy - -	- - - - - - -	- - To be set on the gallows one hour, with rope round the neck ; fine not exceeding $1,000, and imprisonment not exceeding two years.
Blasphemy -	- - - - - - -	- - Fine not exceeding $100, and imprisonment not exceeding two months.
Bribery, Embracery, &c.	- - Giving or receiving bribes to or by judge, justice or juror.	- - Fine not exceeding $2,000, and imprisonment not exceeding two years, and disqualified for office.
	Embracery, conspiracy or common barratry.	- - Fine not exceeding $500, and imprisonment not exceeding six months.
Burglary -	- - Or being accessary before the fact	Death.
Coin - -	See Forgery.	
Duelling - -	Though death does not ensue - -	- - To be carried publicly in a cart to gallows, and set thereon with a rope about neck, for one hour, and imprisonment not exceeding one year, or both.
	Challenging or accepting a challenge, or aiding therein, though no duel be fought.	- - Fine not exceeding $500, and imprisonment not exceeding six months.
Escape, &c. -	- - Rescuing prisoners convicted of or charged with murder.	- - Fine not exceeding $2,000, or imprisonment not exceeding five years.
	With any other crime - - -	- - Fine not exceeding $1,000, and imprisonment not exceeding two years.
	Conveying instruments to prisoners to enable them to escape, when no escape is effected.	- - Fine not exceeding $500, and imprisonment not exceeding one year.
	If prisoner escapes thereby - -	- - The same punishment as the prisoner, unless the offence be capital, in which case fine not exceeding $3,000, and imprisonment not exceeding five years.
	Convict escaping, if retaken - -	- - Imprisonment not exceeding six months after completion of sentence.
	Officer suffering a voluntary escape by a prisoner charged with or convicted of a capital offence.	- - Fine not exceeding $3,000, and imprisonment not exceeding six years.
	If offence not capital - - -	The same as for prisoner's offence.
	Suffering a negligent escape . - -	- - Fine not exceeding $1,000, and imprisonment not exceeding two years.
Extortion -	See Officer.	
Forgery, Coining, &c.	- - Of notes, bills, certificates or other securities, wills or records, or uttering the same, or bringing into the State, or having in possession, forged bank notes, with intent to pass, or making, or having in possession, plates for forging.	- - To be placed in pillory, and to have his ears cropped, and to be branded with the letter C.; imprisonment not exceeding six years, and fine not exceeding $4,000 ; all or any of the above.
	Counterfeiting coin, or having base coin in possession with intent to pass, or making or having tools in possession for forging coins.	

RHODE
ISLAND.

OFFENCES.		*PUNISHMENTS.
Fornication -	- - - - - -	- - Fine not exceeding $ 5, and imprisonment not exceeding five days.
Horse-stealing -	Or accessary before fact - - -	- - To return horse to owner, and to pay value thereof, or if not returned to pay double value, fine not exceeding $ 1,000, imprisonment not exceeding three years, and whipping not exceeding one hundred stripes.
	Accessaries after the fact - - -	- - Fine not exceeding $ 500, and imprisonment not exceeding two years.
Kidnapping, &c.	- - Transporting any free person unlawfully out of the State.	- - Fine not exceeding $ 1,000, and imprisonment not exceeding two years.
Larceny - -	- - Stealing to any amount, or accessary before fact.	- - To restore property, and pay full value to owner, if not restored to pay double value; fine not exceeding $ 1,000, imprisonment not exceeding two years, and whipping not exceeding fifty stripes, or any of the above.
	Stealing fruit - - - -	- - Fine not exceeding $ 50, or if convicted before a justice of the peace not exceeding $ 10, or imprisonment not exceeding one month, or both, and pay treble damages to owner.
	Receiving stolen goods - - -	The same as stealing.
Maiming, disfiguring, &c.	- - With intent to do so, or being accessary before the fact.	- - Fine from $ 50 to $ 2,000, (three-parts of which go to the party injured); and imprisonment not exceeding two years.
Malicious Mischief.	- - Killing, cutting or dismembering beasts of another.	- - Fine not exceeding $ 100, and imprisonment not exceeding two months, or either, and pay the owner treble damages.
Manslaughter *	- - - - - - -	- - Fine not exceeding $ 1,000, and imprisonment from six months to two years, and to find security for good behaviour.
Murder - -	- - - - - -	Death.
Officers,&c. (See also Escape, Bribery.)	Obstructing officers in their duty -	- - Fine not exceeding $ 200, and imprisonment not exceeding one year, or either.
	Usurping office - - -	- - Fine not exceeding $ 200, imprisonment not exceeding one year.
	Extortion by an officer - -	- - Fine not exceeding $ 500, imprisonment not exceeding two years, and to pay to the party aggrieved two-fold damages.
Perjury - -	Or subornation of perjury - - -	- - Fine not exceeding $ 1,000, to be placed in the pillory not exceeding four hours, and cropped and branded as in casr of forgery, and imprisonment not exceeding three years; all or any of the above.
	Inciting to perjury, when not committed.	- - Fine not exceeding $ 500, and imprisonment not exceeding one year.
Rape - -	Or accessary before fact - - -	Death.
Receiving Stolen Goods.	See Larceny.	
Rescue - -	See Escape.	
Robbery -	Or accessary before fact - - -	Death.
Sodomy - -	Or accessary before fact—first offence	- - To be set on a gallows not exceeding four hours, and imprisonment in common gaol not exceeding three years, and fine not exceeding $ 1,000.
	Second offence - - -	Death.
Treason - -	- - - - - - -	Death.

* In case of involuntary Manslaughter, committed in the perpetration of an unlawful act, the prisoner may be convicted of the unlawful act only.

N. B.—The Court determines the precise amount of punishment within the prescribed limits.
A prisoner indicted for a greater may be convicted of any less offence of the same kind.

DELAWARE.
————

PUNISHMENTS FOR THE PRINCIPAL OFFENCES IN THE
STATE OF DELAWARE.

OFFENCES.	PUNISHMENTS.
Adultery - - - - - - - -	Fine $ 100.
Arson, &c. - - - Burning any dwelling-house, court-house, or any office in which public records are kept.	Death.
Burning other buildings, vessels, &c. -	- - Fine from $ 500 to $ 6,000, to pay the owner fourfold the value of property destroyed. Pillory, one-hour; whipping, not exceeding sixty lashes; imprisonment not exceeding two years, and afterwards to be sold to service from four to fourteen years.
Burning building by the owner to defraud insurers.	- - Fine four times the amount of insurance; and to be sold as a servant from three to seven years.
Burning grain, hay, boards, &c. -	- - Fine not exceeding $ 3,000; whipping not exceeding thirty-nine lashes, and to be sold as servant for a term not exceeding four years.
Attempting to burn any building, grain, hay, lumber, &c.	- - Fine not exceeding $ 3,000; whipping not exceeding thirty-nine lashes, and to be sold as servant for a term not exceeding four years.
Assault - - With intent to murder - - -	- - Fine from $ 500 to to $ 6,000; pillory for one hour; imprisonment, not exceeding two years, and at the expiration of such imprisonment, to be sold as a servant for a term from one to seven years.
With intent to ravish - - -	- - Fine from $ 400 to $ 5,000, pillory one hour, sixty lashes, and imprisonment not exceeding two years, and afterwards to be sold as a servant not exceeding fourteen years.
With intent to rob - - - -	- - Fine from $ 200 to $ 1,000; thirty-nine lashes, imprisonment not exceeding two years, and afterwards to be sold to service for four years.
Bigamy - - - - - - - - -	- - Fine from $ 400 to $ 2,000, and imprisonment from five months to one year.
Burglary, &c. - - - Breaking dwelling-house by night with felonious intent.	Death.
Breaking in to any office where records are kept, in the night time, to purloin, alter, injure, &c.	- - Fine from $ 500 to $ 5,000, thirty-nine lashes, imprisonment not exceeding one year, and afterwards to be sold to service not exceeding seven years.
Breaking house, &c. in day-time, or entering without breaking, either by day or night; breaking and entering by night any shop, warehouse, &c. to commit any felony.	- - Pillory for one hour; thirty nine lashes, imprisonment not exceeding one year, and afterwards to be sold to service from two to seven years, and if goods, &c. were taken, pay fourfold their value, unless such goods are returned.
Duelling - - - - Giving, accepting, or bearing a challenge, engaging in a duel, or being a second, whether the duel take place or not, or being in any way concerned in aiding or encouraging.	- - Fine $ 1,000, imprisonment for three months, and to be for ever disqualified from holding office.
Forgery - - - - Forging bank notes or other instruments affecting banks, or passing or attempting to pass the same.	- - Fine from $ 500 to $ 2,000, pillory one hour, solitary imprisonment not exceeding three months, and to wear on the outside garment, between the shoulders, from two to five years, the letter F, not less than six inches long and two inches wide; the F to be of a scarlet colour.

OFFENCES.		PUNISHMENTS.
Forgery—cont.	- - Making plates or instruments for counterfeiting bank bills, or possessing such plates, &c. with intent to use, or having in possession any unfinished bills with intent to finish or fill up.	- - Fine from $ 500 to $ 4,000, pillory one hour, 39 lashes, imprisonment not exceeding two years, and to wear the letter F (mentioned above) not less than five years afterwards.
	Forging promissory note, bill, order, receipt, will, deed, &c., or uttering, passing, or attempting to pass such.	- - Fine from $ 500 to $ 2,000; pillory one hour; solitary imprisonment for three months, and wear the letter F (as above) from two to five years afterwards.
	Counterfeiting public seals, or having them in possession with intent to use, and concealing them, or unlawfully and corruptly affixing a true seal to any instrument or writing.	- - Fine not exceeding $ 1,000, and imprisonment from six months to two years.
	Forging, altering, embezzling or destroying public records.	- - Fine from $ 500 to $ 4,000, solitary imprisonment for three months, and to wear the letter F (as before) not less than five years after.
Fraud - -	- - Imposture, &c., pretending to exercise witchcraft, conjuration, fortune-telling, &c.	- - To be publicly whipped, 21 lashes, and fined not exceeding $ 100.
Horse-stealing -	See Larceny.	
Kidnapping, or assisting to Kidnap.	First offence - - - - -	- - Fine from $ 1,000 to $ 2,000, pillory one hour, 60 lashes, solitary confinement from three to seven years, and afterwards to be sold as a servant to the highest bidder for seven years.
	Second offence - - - -	Death.
Larceny - -	Stealing goods, bank-notes, &c. &c.*	- - Payment to the owner of fourfold the value of goods not restored; if restored, twofold the value; 21 lashes, and to wear for six months afterwards a Roman T, of a scarlet colour, on the back of the outside garment, between the shoulders, the said T to be not less than four inches long and one inch wide.
	Second offence - - - -	- - Payment to the owner, as on first offence, 39 lashes, pillory one hour, and to be sold to service for any time from one to seven years.
	Receiving stolen goods - - -	- - Payment to the owner as before, 21 lashes, and to wear for six months the Roman letter R, as directed in regard to T for stealing.
	Second offence - - - -	- - Payment to the owner as before; 39 lashes, pillory one hour, and sold to service from one to seven years.
	Stealing slave, horse, ass or mule, breaking or picking any lock, and feloniously stealing goods, money or effects, &c.	- - Payment to the owner as before. Pillory for one hour, 39 lashes, and to be sold to service for seven years.
	Disposing, or offering to dispose, of any horse, ass or mule, stolen in another State.	- - Imprisonment not exceeding two years, and 39 lashes, and if the sale be effected, to forfeit 4 times the price to the purchaser.
	Buying or receiving, knowing them to be stolen, any slave, horse, ass, &c.	- - Fine and payment to the owner, when property is not restored, fourfold the value, and when the property is restored, twofold the value; 39 lashes, and to be sold to service for seven years.
Maiming -	Maliciously maiming by lying in wait	- - Fine from $ 400 to $ 2,000; 60 lashes, imprisonment not exceeding two years, and afterwards to be sold as a servant from four to seven years.

(*continued*)

* Free negroes or mulattoes convicted of this offence are liable to be sold as slaves, and that in such a way that the purchaser may convey them out of the State.

OFFENCES.		PUNISHMENTS.
Maiming—*contd*.	Without lying in wait - - -	- - Fine from $ 200 to $ 2,000, and imprisonment from three months to one year.
	By the loss of a genital member -	Death.
Manslaughter -	First degree, first offence - - -	- - Fine from $ 200 to $ 3,000, and imprisonment not exceeding two years.
	second offence - -	- - Fine from $ 400 to $ 6,000, and imprisonment not exceeding four years.
	Second degree - - - -	- - Fine from $ 100 to $ 1,000, and imprisonment not exceeding one year.
Murder. (*See* also Assault.)	- - - - - - -	Death.
Perjury, or Subornation of Perjury - - - -		- - Fine from $ 500 to $ 2,000, pillory for one hour, and to be sold to service from four to seven years.
Poison - -	Wilfully administering - - -	- - Fine from $ 500 to $ 10,000, pillory for one hour, 60 lashes, imprisonment not exceeding four years, and afterwards sold as a servant, not exceeding fourteen years.
Rape. (*See* also Assault.)	- - - - - - -	Death.
	Carnal abuse of a female child under 10 years of age.	- - Fine from $ 400 to $ 5,000, pillory one hour, 60 lashes, imprisonment not exceeding two years, and to be sold as a servant not exceeding fourteen years.
Riot - -	- - - - - - -	- - Fine from $ 20 to $ 200, and imprisonment not exceeding six months.
Robbery. (*See* also Assault.)	- - On or near the highway, or in a dwelling-house.	- - Fine from $ 1,000 to $ 5,000, pillory for one hour, 60 lashes, imprisonment not exceeding four years, and afterwards to be sold as a servant for fifteen years.
	Committed in any other place - -	- - Fine from $ 500 to $ 2,000, pillory one hour, 39 lashes, imprisonment not more than two years, and afterwards to be sold as a servant for ten years.
Sodomy - -	- - - - - - -	- - Fine $ 1,000, solitary imprisonment not exceeding three years, and 60 lashes.
Treason - -	- - - - - - -	Death.

PUNISHMENTS FOR THE PRINCIPAL OFFENCES IN THE

STATE OF ILLINOIS.

OFFENCES.		PUNISHMENTS.
Abduction -	Forcible - - - - .. -	Imprisonment not exceeding two years.
	Deflowering a child under 16, without parents' consent.	Imprisonment five years.
	Forcible and stolen marriage -	Same as bigamy.
Assault and Battery - - - - - - -		- - Fine not exceeding $100; to enter into recognizances for good behaviour for not exceeding one year.
Arson - - - - - - - - -		Death.
Bigamy - - - - - - - - - -		- - Whipping from 100 to 300 lashes, fine from $100 to $500, and imprisonment from six to twelve months.
Compounding Felony, in cases of theft - - -		Fine to the value of the article stolen.
Forgery - -	In general - - - - -	- - Fined double amount forged, half to party injured, pillory not exceeding three hours. Accessaries deemed principals.
	Counterfeiting - - - -	- - Fine not exceeding $500, and 75 lashes, and disqualified as witness or juror.
Fraud - -	- - - - - - -	- - Fine not exceeding $300; and payment of double value to injured party.
	Obtaining goods under false pretences -	Same as larceny.
Hog-stealing -	- - - - - - -	- - Fine from $50 to $100, and whipping from 25 to 30 lashes.
Larceny - -	To any amount, first offence -	- - To restore property or double its value, fine not exceeding double value, and whipping not exceeding 31 lashes *.
	Second offence - - - -	- - Restitution and payment as before, and fine not exceeding fourfold the value, and whipping not exceeding 39 lashes.
Maiming, &c. -	- - - - - - -	- - Imprisonment from one to six months, fine, from $50 to $1,000.
Manslaughter -	- - - - - - -	Imprisonment not exceeding two years.
Murder - -	- - - - - - -	Death.
Perjury - -	- - - - - - -	- - Fine not exceeding $1,000, whipping not exceeding 39 lashes, and disqualified as witness, juror, &c.
Rape -	- - - - - - -	Death.
Riot - -	Of three or more persons - -	- - Fine not exceeding $300, whipping not exceeding 39 stripes, and to find security for not exceeding one year, if the first, and ten years if the second offence.
Sodomy - -	- - - - - - -	- - Fine not exceeding $500, imprisonment from one to five years, and whipping from 100 to 500 stripes.
Treason - -	- - - - - - -	Death.

N. B.—When the convict cannot pay the costs and fines, the Court may sell or let him on hire for such time as the judge may think reasonable, to any person who will pay the fine and costs; and if a servant so hired abscond, he shall, on conviction, receive 39 stripes, and serve two days for every one lost.

---

* If the convict is unable to pay the sum required, he may be bound to any suitable person to labour for seven years.

PUNISHMENTS FOR THE PRINCIPAL OFFENCES, IN THE

STATE OF MISSOURI.

OFFENCES.		PUNISHMENTS.
Accessaries -	Before the fact in all cases - - -	To be punished the same as principals.
	Harbouring felons (not near relatives) -	- - Fine not exceeding $ 500, or imprisonment not exceeding three years.
Adultery -	- - Living in an open state of adultery or fornication.	- - Fine not exceeding $ 200, or imprisonment not exceeding one year, or both.
Arson, &c. (See also Malicious Mischief.)	- - Burning house, storehouse, building, vessel of another, or of the State, or with intent to defraud insurers.	- - Imprisonment not exceeding seven years, and fine not exceeding $ 10,000.
Assault - -	And Battery - - - - -	- - Fine (assessed by jury before justice of peace) from $ 1 to $ 80.
	With intent to commit rape or murder	- - Fine not exceeding $ 3,000, and imprisonment not exceeding seven years.
	With intent to rob - - - -	- - Fine not exceeding $ 500, and imprisonment not exceeding seven years.
Bigamy - -	- - - - - - - -	- - Fine from $ 100 to $ 500. Imprisonment from six to twelve months, whipping not exceeding 39 stripes, to be rendered infamous, and incapable of giving evidence, or holding office.
Bribery, Embracery, &c.	- - Bribing a judge, or justice, or other officer, or member of the General Assembly; or such persons being bribed.	- - Fine not exceeding $ 1,000, imprisonment not exceeding one year, and disqualified for being witness, juror, holding office, or voting.
	Attempt to bribe - - - -	- - Fine not exceeding $ 500, and imprisonment not exceeding one year.
	Influencing, or attempting to influence, votes at elections by bribes or threats.	- - Fine from $ 100 to $ 1,250, and disqualified as before.
	Elector receiving bribe - - -	- - Fine not exceeding $ 500, and disqualified for voting at State elections for ten years.
	Buying or selling offices or votes -	- - Fine not exceeding $ 5,000, imprisonment not exceeding five years, and disqualified from holding office and voting.
	Corrupting, or attempting to corrupt a juror.	- - Fine not exceeding $ 300, and imprisonment net exceeding one year.
	Juror corrupted - - - -	- - Fine not exceeding $ 600; imprisonment not exceeding two years, and disqualified as a juror.
Burglary, &c.	- - Breaking into dwelling-house by night, with felonious intent.	- - Fine not exceeding $ 500, and imprisonment not exceeding seven years.
	So breaking, and stealing from the house broken into.	- - Fine, in addition, treble the value of thing stolen, (of which one-third shall go to the injured party,) and whipping not exceeding 39 stripes.
	So breaking, and committing or attempting, or being armed for, acts of violence.	- - Pillory for three hours; imprisonment not exceeding seven years, in addition to the above punishment.
	Housebreaking by day with intent to steal.	Whipping not exceeding 39 stripes.
Coining - -	See Forgery.	
Compounding Offences - - - - -		Fine double the sum compounded for.
Conspiracy to Indict - - - - - - -		- - Fine not exceeding $ 2,000, or imprisonment not exceeding two years, or both.
Dead Bodies -	- - Disinterring and removing dead bodies, or assisting thereat, or knowingly being concerned in dissecting, &c. bodies illegally removed.	- - Fine from $ 100 to $ 500, and imprisonment from three to twelve months.
Duelling -	Killing in a duel - - - -	Death.
Escape, &c. -	- - Rescuing person convicted of capital offence, or officer voluntarily permitting such an one to escape.	Death.
	The same in the case of any other prisoner, or officer negligently permitting any escape.	- - Fine not exceeding $ 1,000, and imprisonment not exceeding three years, or both; and officer removed from office.

OFFENCES.		PUNISHMENTS.
Escape, &c.— *continued.*	Furnishing means of, or aiding in, an escape, or attempt to escape.	- - Fine not exceeding $ 500, or imprisonment not exceeding two years, or both.
Extortion -	By public officer - - - -	Fine not exceeding $ 500.
	By threats of violence or criminal accusation.	- - Fine not exceeding $ 300, or imprisonment not exceeding one year, or both.
False Personation, &c.	In courts of law - - - -	- - Fine not exceeding $ 5,000, or imprisonment not exceeding seven years, or both.
	Falsifying, altering or stealing records	- - Fine and imprisonment as before, and not exceeding 39 stripes.
	Obtaining money or goods under false pretences.	As theft to same amount.
Fornication -	*See* Adultery.	
Forgery, Coining, &c.	- - Counterfeiting or altering seal of State or court, or unlawfully affixing the same.	- - Fine not exceeding $ 5,000, and imprisonment not exceeding five years.
	Counterfeiting or knowingly passing a counterfeit warrant or public security; altering, defacing or concealing deeds for fraudulent purpose.	- - Fine double the amount of fraud, imprisonment not exceeding five years, 39 stripes, pillory two hours, and to be rendered incapable of being witness, juror, voting or holding office.
	Counterfeiting bank-notes, bills, &c. or altering them, or aiding therein, or knowingly passing or uttering.	- - Fine not exceeding $ 1,000, pillory two hours, not exceeding 39 stripes, imprisonment not exceeding five years, and disqualified as above.
	Selling paper for counterfeiting, or possessing frame or mould for making such.	- - Fine not exceeding $ 1,000, whipping not exceeding 39 stripes, pillory two hours, and disqualified as before.
	Counterfeiting or attempting to pass current coin.	- - Fine not exceeding $ 1,000, imprisonment not exceeding ten years, 39 lashes, pillory two hours, and incapacitated from being witness, juror, or holding office.
	Possessing counterfeit or unfinished notes or coin; making, mending, buying, selling or concealing instruments for coining, clipping, &c.	- - Fine not exceeding $ 500, imprisonment not exceeding three years, 39 stripes, pillory two hours, and disqualified as before.
	Destroying notes, bills, securities, wills, documents, &c. to injure or defraud.	- - Fine not exceeding $ 500, and imprisonment not exceeding three years, or either.
Fraud. (*See* also False Personation.	- - Fraudulent conveyance of property, or being privy thereto.	- - Fine not exceeding $ 1,000, and liable in damages to party injured.
	Making a second conveyance without reciting the former one.	- - Fine not exceeding $ 5,000, and imprisonment not exceeding five years, and liable in double damages to party injured.
Gaming - -	Setting up tables - - - -	- - Fine from $ 50 to $ 500, and imprisonment not exceeding one year.
	Suffering tables to be set up in one's house.	Fine from $ 50 to $ 500.
Hog-stealing -	Or altering mark with intent to steal	- - Fine not exceeding $ 100, and 39 stripes.
Horse-stealing	- - - - - - -	- - Double damages, fine not exceeding $ 500, whipping not exceeding 39 stripes, and disqualified from voting, giving evidence, serving on jury, or holding office.
Kidnapping -	To make slaves of free men - -	- - Whipping not exceeding 39 stripes, and imprisonment not exceeding ten years, unless the party stolen is restored within the time, in which case the punishment will be fine not exceeding $ 1,000
Larceny. (*See* also Horse-stealing, Burglary and Hog-stealing.	- - Stealing or embezzling money, goods, &c.	- - Fine double value, restitution, whipping not exceeding 39 stripes, and pillory not exceeding two hours.
	Second offence - - - -	- - As before, except the fine being fourfold the value.
	In cases of deeds or documents - -	- - Imprisonment not exceeding one year, 39 stripes, and fine, determined by the value of property to which the document refers, not exceeding $ 500.

(continued)

MISSOURI.

OFFENCES.		PUNISHMENTS.
Larceny— *continued.*	Stealing slaves - - - - -	- - Fine double the value, to restore slave and pay his value to party injured, and in default of restitution, pay double damages, to be whipped not exceeding 39 stripes, and disqualified from voting, giving evidence, serving as juror and holding office; unless restitution, imprisonment not exceeding ten years.
	Receivers generally, or harbourers of the thieves.	Same as thieves.
Maiming, &c. -	- - - - - - - -	- - Fine not exceeding $ 3,000, and imprisonment not exceeding three years.
Malicious Mischief.	- - Burning stacks of hay, corn, &c.; destroying, damaging houses, bridges, banks, trees, fences, or burning carts, letting loose canoes, &c.; killing or wounding cattle.	- - Fine not exceeding $ 100; imprisonment not exceeding one year, or both.
Manslaughter -	Voluntary - - - - -	- - Fine not exceeding $ 3,000, and imprisonment not exceeding three years.
	Involuntary, in commission of unlawful act not likely to lead to death, (except robbery, or burglary, in which cases it is murder).	- - Fine not exceeding $ 1,000, and imprisonment not exceeding one year.
Murder. (*See* also Assault) - - - -		Death.
	Administering poison with intent to murder, or produce miscarriage.	- - Fine not exceeding $ 3,000, and imprisonment not exceeding seven years.
Officer - - (*See* also Bribery, Escape, Extortion.)	Obstructing officer in his duty - -	- - Fine not exceeding $ 300, and imprisonment not exceeding one year.
Perjury or Subornation.	By woman charging a rape - -	Imprisonment for life.
	In other cases on trials for felony -	Punishment inflicted for the felony.
	In other matters - - - -	- - Fine not exceeding $ 1,000, imprisonment not exceeding three years, pillory one hour, and rendered incapable of being witness, juror, holding office, or voting.
Poison. (*See* Murder.)		
Rape - - (*See* also Assault.)	- - Including abuse of children under 10 years of age.	Castration.
Rescue. (*See* Escape.)		
Receiving stolen Goods. (*See* Larceny.)		
Riot - -	- - - - - - - -	- - (To be tried by jury before justice of the peace,) fine from $ 1 to $ 80.
Robbery. (*See* also Assault) - - - -		- - Imprisonment not exceeding seven years, fine not exceeding $ 500, and treble the value of property taken (of which one-third is to go to the party robbed), and whipping not exceeding 39 stripes.
	Attempting, or armed for, or committing, any acts of violence.	- - As before, with the addition of the pillory for not exceeding three hours, and further imprisonment not exceeding seven years.
Ships - -	- - Burning, destroying or casting away to defraud underwriters.	- - Fine not exceeding $ 10,000, and imprisonment not exceeding seven years.
Slaves. (*See* Larceny. *See* also Note.)		
Treason - -	- - - - - - - -	Death.
	Misprision of - - - - -	Fine not exceeding $ 1,000, or imprisonment not exceeding seven years.

Note.—The punishment for the second offence is double, and for the third treble that for the first, when the punishment is imprisonment or whipping.

White females are not to be whipped or stand in the pillory, but to be imprisoned in lieu thereof, at the discretion of the court.

The above punishments do not generally apply to slaves, with respect to whom the punishment for murder or arson is death; for rape, or attempt to commit a rape on a white woman, castration; for most other offences they are to be punished, at the discretion of the court, by stripes instead of fine and imprisonment. If they commit an offence for which restitution is required, this shall be made by the master, and in the event of his refusing, the slave shall be sold to raise the requisite sum.

When the degree of punishment is uncertain, or any discretion is left to the court by statute, the jury determine it, if they can agree; if not, the court. This is by a law passed in 1831, previously to which all such discretion was exercised by the court. This law also enacts, that the court shall in no instance on the trial of any indictment, sum up or comment upon the evidence given in the cause, unless at the request of both parties or their counsel, but may instruct the jury as to the law of the case.

PUNISHMENTS FOR THE PRINCIPAL OFFENCES IN THE

STATE OF GEORGIA.

OFFENCES.	PUNISHMENTS.
Abduction. (*See* Kidnapping.)	
Accessaries - (where no other punishment is specified.) - - Before the fact, as well as those aiding and abetting (who are principals in the second degree.)	- - The same as the actual perpetrators of the crime.
After the fact, if the crime of the principal is punishable by death, or labour in Penitentiary.	- - Labour in the Penitentiary from one to three years.
If not so punishable - - - -	- - Fine or imprisonment in common gaol, or both.
Adultery - - - - - - - -	- - Fine not exceeding $500, or imprisonment in common gaol not exceeding sixty days, or both.
Arson, &c. (*See* also Malicious Mischief.) - - Wilfully and maliciously burning, or setting fire to any house or outhouse, if life is lost thereby, or if the house or outhouse is in a town or village - - -	} Death.
Wilfully and maliciously burning the dwelling-house of another, not in a town or village.	- - Labour in the Penitentiary from five to twenty years.
Setting fire to the same, with intent to burn.	- - Labour in the Penitentiary from three to seven years.
Burning outhouse, barn, stable, &c. not in a town or village.	- - Labour in the Penitentiary from two to seven years.
Setting fire to the same, with intent to burn.	- - Labour in the Penitentiary from one to three years.
Assault - - And Battery - - - - -	- - Fine, or imprisonment in common gaol, or both.
With intent, &c. (*See* Murder, Rape, Robbery, Attempt.)	
With intent to spoil clothes - -	- - Fine not exceeding $200, and imprisonment in common gaol from three months to a year.
Attempt * - - - At any crime, when some act is done towards its commission, and when no other punishment is specified,	
If the crime attempted is punishable by death.	- - Labour in Penitentiary from two to seven years.
If by labour in Penitentiary for a term not less than four years.	- - Labour in Penitentiary from one to four years.
If by labour in Penitentiary for a term not less than two years.	Labour in Penitentiary for one year.
If by labour in Penitentiary or for a term not exceeding one year.	- - Fine not exceeding $500, or imprisonment in common gaol, or both.
If by fine not exceeding $500, or imprisonment in common gaol, or both.	Fine, or imprisonment in common gaol.
Bastardy - - - Mother concealing the death of a bastard child.	- - Fine, or imprisonment in common gaol, or both.
(*See* also Murder) Putative father refusing to give security for the maintenance and education of a bastard child.	- - Fine of $700 for each child, to be improved and applied to the education and maintenance of the child; if unable to pay, three months' imprisonment in common gaol.
Bigamy † - The person marrying a second time -	- - Labour in Penitentiary from two to four years.
The second husband or wife, if aware of the previous marriage.	- - Labour in Penitentiary from one to three years.
Bribery, Embracery, &c. (*See* also Election.) - - Bribing or attempting to bribe judicial or any public officers, to obtain their vote, influence, or favour, in their official capacity.	- - Labour in the Penitentiary from one to five years.
Officer taking a bribe - - -	- - Labour in the Penitentiary from two to ten years, and the loss of his office.
Corruptly influencing a juror - -	- - Labour in the Penitentiary from one to four years.
Juror so influenced - - - -	- - Labour in the Penitentiary from two to five years, and disqualified as a juror.
	(*continued*)

* A person may, on an indictment for any crime, be found guilty of the attempt, if the evidence fails to prove the actual perpetration.

† Although the second marriage is void, yet the children begotten before prosecution are legitimate.

GEORGIA.

OFFENCES.		PUNISHMENTS.
Burglary, &c. - (See also Larceny, under which title the law of this State classes some kinds of housebreaking.)	- - Breaking and entering the dwelling-house of another, or outhouse within its curtilage, with intent to commit a felony; by night.	- - Labour in the Penitentiary from four to seven years.
	By day - - - - - -	- - Labour in the Penitentiary from three to five years.
Coining, &c. (See Forgery.)		
Compounding Offence.	- - Punishable by death or labour in Penitentiary.	- - Labour in the Penitentiary from one to five years.
	By informer under a penal statute -	- - Fine, to the amount receivable in case of conviction.
Conspiracy to indict falsely - - - - - -		- - Labour in the Penitentiary from one to five years.
Dead Bodies -	- - Disinterring without permission, or receiving or purchasing bodies so disinterred.	- - Fine, or imprisonment in common gaol, or both.
Duelling -	- - Fighting, or being second in a duel, if death ensues.	Death.
	If death does not ensue - - ` -	- - Labour in the Penitentiary from four to eight years.
	Giving or accepting, or knowingly bearing a challenge.	- - Fine not less than $ 500, and imprisonment in common gaol not exceeding six months; or if the jury so recommend, labour in the Penitentiary from one to two years, in addition to the fine.
	Posting, &c. for refusing to fight -	- - Fine not exceeding $ 500, and imprisonment in common gaol not exceeding sixty days.
Election - -	- - Voting more than once at any election, or out of the county where a person resides, for members of the legislature, or for county officers.	- - Labour in the Penitentiary from one to two years.
	Being concerned in buying or selling a vote, or unlawfully voting at any election.	- - Labour in the Penitentiary from one to four years.
Embezzlement -	- - Of any books, documents or property of the State, or any bank or corporate body, by any servants or officers thereof; of goods, property or documents intrusted to their care, by factors, carriers or other bailies, or the fraudulent conversion of the same, or of the price thereof.	- - Labour in the Penitentiary from two to seven years.
	The fraudulent conversion of property trusted to him in the way of business, by a clerk, agent or servant.	- - Labour in the Penitentiary from one to five years.
Escape. (See Rescue. Officer.)		
Extortion -	By officer - - - - - -	Fine, and dismissal.
	By threatening letters, or so attempting to extort.	- - Labour in the Penitentiary from two to four years.
False Personation, Pretences, &c. (See also Swindling, Forgery.)	- - Acknowledging judgment, &c. in the name of a party not assenting, except in the case of attorney on the record.	- - Labour in the Penitentiary from one to four years.
	Answering as witness in an assumed character, or falsely personating another to his damage, in any judicial proceeding.	- - Labour in the Penitentiary from one to five years.
	Fraudulently personating another to obtain money, goods, &c.	- - The same; or in trivial cases, fine and imprisonment in common gaol.
Forgery - -	- - Fraudulently forging, making or altering any State certificate, warrant or order for public money; or any bond, will, or receipt; or knowingly uttering the same when forged; or so making or signing bank-notes or bills; or counterfeiting gold, silver or copper coin; or passing the same knowing it to be counterfeit; or possessing, for the purpose of forgery, bank-note paper, types, &c.	- - Labour in the Penitentiary from two to ten years.
	Making, printing, or signing, a check or draft upon any incorporated bank.	- - Labour in the Penitentiary from three to seven years.
	Altering a genuine note, bill, or check, of or on any such bank.	- - Labour in the Penitentiary from three to ten years.
	Fraudulently uttering, or tendering in payment a forged or altered note, bill, or check, of or on such bank; or having the same in possession with intent so to do; or forging or altering a note, bill, or check, of or on any other body corporate, individual, or firm; or fraudulently uttering or tendering the same.	- - Labour in the Penitentiary from two to ten years.

OFFENCES.	PUNISHMENTS.
Forgery - - (*continued*)	Forging or altering any other writing -	- - Labour in the Penitentiary from two to five years.
	Counterfeiting the seal of state, or of any court, office, or corporation, or fraudulently making use of such when counterfeited.	- - Labour in the Penitentiary from two to ten years.
	Drawing, indorsing, or accepting a bill or note in a fictitious name; or a person putting his own name to any instrument falsely representing himself; or obtaining money or goods by means of a counterfeit letter, or one made in a fictitious name.	- - Labour in the Penitentiary from two to seven years.
Fornication -	- - - - - - - - -	- - Fine not exceeding $ 500, or imprisonment in common gaol not exceeding sixty days, or both; but the punishment may be prevented by the intermarriage of the parties.
Gaming, &c. -	Keeping a gaming-house - -	- - Fine not exceeding $ 500, and imprisonment in common gaol not exceeding six months.
	Keeping certain tables, and presiding at them.	- - Fine and imprisonment as before, or either.
	Playing or betting at such tables -	Fine from $ 20 to $ 100.
	Cheating at play - - -	- - Fine to the amount of five times the value won, and imprisonment.
Horse-stealing, &c. (*See* Larceny.)		
Incest - -	- - Or intermarriage within the Levitical degrees.	- - Labour in the Penitentiary from one to three years.
Kidnapping, &c.	- - Conveying out of the State, against his will, any white person or free person of colour; or forcibly or fraudulently carrying or enticing away from a parent or guardian any free white child under 12 years.	- - Labour in the Penitentiary from four to seven years.
Larceny - - (*See* also Slave).	- - Simple theft, not exceeding the value of $20.	- - Imprisonment in common gaol not exceeding one year.
	Exceeding $ 20 - - - - -	- - Labour in the Penitentiary from one to five years.
	Stealing or destroying document to affect the title to any property.	- - Labour in the Penitentiary from one to three years.
	Stealing instrument for securing the payment of money, or operating as a receipt or discharge.	- - Labour in the Penitentiary from one to four years.
	Stealing any article of value from any vessel, wreck or water-craft.	- - Labour in the Penitentiary from one to five years.
	Stealing a horse, mule or ass -	- - Labour in the Penitentiary from two to five years.
	If more than one at the same time -	- - Labour in the Penitentiary from six to fourteen years.
	Stealing, or fraudently branding or altering the mark of cattle, (*i. e.* animals horned, or having the hoof cloven, other than hogs,) or hogs, not exceeding the value of $ 20.	- - Imprisonment in the common gaol not exceeding six months.
	Cattle, exceeding the value of $ 20 -	- - Labour in the Penitentiary from one to four years.
	Hogs, exceeding the value of $ 20 -	- - Labour in the Penitentiary from one to three years.
	Stealing other domestic animals fit for food.	- - Fine, or imprisonment in common gaol, or both.
	Stealing from the person - - -	- - Labour in the Penitentiary from two to five years, the greater punishment being inflicted for the offence more publicly committed.
	Stealing from a house, shop or warehouse.	- - Labour in the Penitentiary from two to five years.
	Breaking or entering the same, with intent to steal.	- - Labour in the Penitentiary from one to three years.
	If by such breaking any person in the house is put in fear.	- - Labour in the Penitentiary from two to five years.
	Breaking and entering any house or building, other than a dwelling-house or its appurtenances, with intent to steal.	- - Labour in the Penitentiary from two to four years.
	The same, and actually stealing -	- - Labour in the Penitentiary from three to five years.
	If violence or menaces are used, or any person be put in fear.	- - Labour in the Penitentiary not less than four years.

(*continued*)

GEORGIA.

OFFENCES.	PUNISHMENTS.
Larceny - (*continued*) - - Entering and stealing from a hut, booth, &c.	- - Labour in the Penitentiary from one to four years.
Receiving stolen goods - - -	The same as stealing.
Libel - - - - - - - - -	- - Fine not exceeding $1,000, and imprisonment in common gaol not exceeding one year.
Maiming, Disfiguring, &c. - - Cutting out the tongue, or injuring or wounding the private parts of another, with intent to maim and disfigure, maliciously and on purpose, whilst fighting or otherwise.	- - Labour in the Penitentiary from five to fifteen years.
Putting out an eye, or cutting or biting off the nose, ear or lip, under the same circumstances.	- - Labour in the Penitentiary from two to five years.
Putting out both eyes, or one, if the party injured has but one eye, under the same circumstances.	- - Labour in the Penitentiary for life.
Castrating another, under the same circumstances.	Death.
Slitting or biting the nose, ear or lip, under the same circumstances.	- - Labour in the Penitentiary from one to three years, or fine and imprisonment in common gaol.
Cutting or biting off, or disabling any limb or member not mentioned above, under the same circumstances.	- - Labour in the Penitentiary from one to five years, or fine and imprisonment in common gaol.
Malicious Mischief, &c. - - Tearing, burning, or destroying documents, letters, instruments, account-books, &c., with intent either of injuring or defrauding.	- - Labour in the Penitentiary from one to four years; in trivial cases, fine or imprisonment in common gaol, or both.
Setting fire to, or making holes in, or doing any act tending to the loss, or destruction of, a vessel of above $200 value.	- - Labour in the Penitentiary from three to seven years.
If of the value of $200, or less - -	- - Fine and imprisonment in common gaol, or both.
Injuring, or destroying, turnpike houses, gates, &c., or locks, or navigation works.	- - Labour in the Penitentiary from one to four years.
Breaking down, injuring, or destroying, a bridge, bank or dam.	- - Labour in the Penitentiary from one to three years, or fine and imprisonment in common gaol.
Removing or destroying beacons or buoys placed by authority.	- - Labour in the Penitentiary from two to five years.
Setting fire to stacks of hay, corn, &c. -	- - Labour in the Penitentiary from one to three years.
Setting fire to woods, lands or marshes, to the injury of another.	- - Imprisonment in common gaol not exceeding six months.
Cutting down boundary tree or landmark, fraudulently or maliciously.	- - Fine not exceeding $500, and imprisonment in common gaol not exceeding one year.
Cutting down, or destroying, trees growing for shelter, ornament, shade or profit.	- - Fine, or imprisonment in common gaol, or both.
Defacing, altering, or removing, milestones or guide-posts.	- - Fine not exceeding $50, and imprisonment in common gaol not exceeding thirty days.
Killing or maiming any horses, mules, cattle or hogs.	Fine or imprisonment in common gaol.
Manslaughter - - - Voluntary, (as in a passion, without deliberation.)	- - Labour in the Penitentiary from two to four years.
Involuntary, in the commission of an unlawful act, other than will make the crime amount to murder.	- - Labour in the Penitentiary from one to three years.
Involuntary, in doing a lawful act without due discretion or caution.	- - Fine, or imprisonment in common gaol, or both.
Murder - - - - Killing a human being with malice aforethought; or in the commission of an unlawful act which naturally tends to the loss of life; or of a crime punishable by death or confinement in the Penitentiary; or in the prosecution of a riotous intent.	} Death.
A person advising a pregnant woman to kill her child, if she does so after its birth.	As an accessary before the fact.
Assault with intent to murder, by using a weapon likely to produce death.	- - Labour in the Penitentiary from two to four years.
Officer - - - - Public officer falsifying, withdrawing, (*See* also Bribery, embezzling, or destroying, official documents. Extortion.)	- - Labour in the Penitentiary from two to ten years.

OFFENCES.	PUNISHMENTS.
Officer - - *(continued)* - - At expiration of office, withholding official documents from his successor.	- - Fine, or imprisonment in common gaol, or both.
False imprisonment by a magistrate's warrant or process, manifestly illegal, and showing malice.	- - Magistrate removed from office, and all persons maliciously concerned fined or imprisoned in common gaol, or confined to labour in Penitentiary from one to two years.
Justice of peace guilty of oppression under colour of his office, or of any tyrannical partiality.	- - Fine, or imprisonment in common gaol, or both, and removal from office.
Officer assaulting under colour of office	- - Fine, and imprisonment in common gaol not exceeding one year.
Gaoler guilty of cruelty or oppression -	- - Labour in the Penitentiary from one to three years, and removal from office.
Keeper of a prison refusing to receive convicts.	- - Labour in the Penitentiary not exceeding ten years.
Officer refusing to receive persons charged with an indictable offence, or voluntarily permitting the escape of a prisoner in his custody, charged with or convicted of any crime.	- - Labour in the Penitentiary from two to seven years, and dismissal.
President, director, or officer violating the charter of any chartered bank; or any president or director being present and not dissenting from an act of violation, or continuing director for 3 months after the facts of such violation appear on the books; or president and directors paying dividends out of the capital or other source than the net profits of a bank, or purchasing shares with the capital; or any person being president or director of any chartered bank, when it becomes insolvent or stops payment, unless able to show that the affairs of the bank have been fairly and legally administered -	- - Labour in the Penitentiary from one to ten years.
Being president or director of a bank, making an assignment in contemplation of or after insolvency (except for the benefit of creditors); or officer or agent purchasing the bills or notes of a bank below their expressed value - - -	- - Labour in the Penitentiary from four to ten years.
Perjury, &c. - - - In a judicial proceeding, if any one is thereby convicted of an offence punishable by death, or imprisonment for life.	Death, or imprisonment for life.
If not - - - - - -	- - Labour in the Penitentiary from four to ten years, and disqualified as a witness.
False swearing, not in a judicial proceeding, or subornation of perjury or false swearing.	- - Labour in the Penitentiary from three to ten years, and disqualified as a witness.
Rape - - - - - - - - -	- - Labour in the Penitentiary from two to twenty years.
Assault, with intent to commit - -	- - Labour in the Penitentiary from one to five years.
Rescue, Escape, &c. (*See* also **Officer.**) - - Rescuing prisoner in custody on civil process.	- - Fine to the amount of prisoner's debt, and imprisonment in common gaol not exceeding six months.
In custody on criminal process, unless prisoner is acquitted.	- - The same as prisoner would be liable to if convicted.
If prisoner be acquitted - - -	- - Imprisonment in common gaol not exceeding one year.
Attempt to rescue prisoner in custody on criminal process.	- - Labour in the Penitentiary from one to two years, or imprisonment in common gaol not exceeding six months.
Assisting prisoner in escaping, or in attempting to escape, from sheriff or other officer.	- - Labour in the Penitentiary from one to five years.
- - Assisting prisoner in escaping, or in attempting to escape, from gaol, or conveying tools for such purpose.	- - Labour in the Penitentiary from one to four years.
Assisting prisoner in escaping, or in attempting to escape from the Penitentiary, or prisoner so escaping.	Labour in the Penitentiary for four years.
Prisoner assaulting an officer of Penitentiary with any weapon calculated to do serious bodily harm; or any person persuading or advising such assault.	- - Labour in the Penitentiary from two to five years, in addition to the sentence then in force.
Obstructing sheriffs or other officers in the execution of their duty.	- - Fine, and imprisonment in common gaol not exceeding one year.
Receiving Stolen Goods. (*See* Larceny.)	

(*continued*)

OFFENCES.	PUNISHMENTS.
Riot - - Under aggravated circumstances - -	- - Labour in the Penitentiary from one to three years.
Persons assembling to disturb the peace, or acting tumultuously, or fighting in a public place.	- - Fine, or imprisonment in common gaol, or both.
Robbery - By means of actual violence - - -	- - Labour in the Penitentiary from four to seven years.
By intimidation, without violence -	- - Labour in the Penitentiary from two to five years.
Assault, with intent to rob - - -	- - Labour in the Penitentiary from two to four years.
Slaves and Persons of Colour. - - Exciting, or attempting to excite insurrection among slaves, or introducing, or being instrumental in introducing, or circulating written or printed papers to excite insurrection, conspiracy, or resistance on the part of slaves, negroes or free people of colour - - - - -	Death.
Stealing a slave, or inducing him to run away, with the intention of selling or appropriating him.	- - Labour in Penitentiary from four to ten years.
Removing the slave of another without the consent of his owner, but without an intent of depriving him of his property in the slave.	- - Fine, or imprisonment in common gaol not exceeding six months, or both.
Harbouring or concealing a slave, to the injury of the owner.	- - Fine not exceeding the value of the slave, and imprisonment in common gaol not exceeding six months, and liable to the owner for the value of the slave's services whilst concealed.
Introducing slaves into the State, except by citizens for their own service, under certain restrictions.	- - Fine not exceeding $500 for each slave, and labour in Penitentiary from one to four years.
Purchasing or receiving slaves illegally introduced, knowing them to be so.	Fine $500 for each slave.
Any person, other than the owner, overseer, or employer, beating or wounding a slave; or any person beating or wounding a free person of colour, without sufficient provocation.	- - Fine, or imprisonment in common gaol not exceeding six months, or both; and liable to owner for damage done to the slave.
Cruelty to slaves by owner or employer, whereby their health is injured.	- - Fine, or imprisonment in common gaol not exceeding six months, or both.
Dealing with slaves in other than certain commodities, without authority from their owners.	The same.
Itinerant traders dealing with slaves, except in the presence of their masters.	- - Fine not exceeding $1,000 (half to the prosecutor), and committed until payment.
Supplying slaves or free persons of colour with spirits, wine, cider, or any intoxicating liquors, except such as the owner may supply for their own use and benefit,—first offence - - - -	Fine from $10 to $50.
Second offence - - - - -	- - Fine not exceeding $500, and imprisonment in common gaol not exceeding sixty days.
Any person teaching, a slave, negro, or free person of colour to read or write either written or printed characters, or procuring, suffering or permitting a slave, negro or person of colour to transact business for him in writing.	- - Fine, or imprisonment in common gaol not exceeding six months, or both.
Any person owning, or having in his possession, and under his control, any printing press or types, and using or employing, or permitting to be used or employed, any slave or free person of colour in setting up of types or other labour about the office, requiring in said slave or free person of colour a knowledge of reading or writing.	Fine not exceeding $100.
Any person of colour, whether free or slave, preaching, exhorting or joining in any religious exercise with any person of colour, free or slave, in the presence of more than 7 persons of colour, and neglecting to obtain a certain certificate or licence.	- - Fine not exceeding $500, and imprisonment. If property insufficient to pay the fine, imprisonment not exceeding six months, and whipping not exceeding 39 lashes.

OFFENCES.		PUNISHMENTS.
Slaves, &c. - *(continued)*	- - Any free person of colour owning, using or carrying fire-arms.	- - Whipping, 39 lashes, and arms sold; price, after paying costs, given to informer.
Sodomy and Bestiality - - - - - - -		Labour in the Penitentiary for life.
	Attempt to commit - - - -	- - Labour in the Penitentiary from two to four years.
Stabbing - -	- - Not in self-defence, when death does not ensue.	- - Fine not exceeding $1,000, and labour in the Penitentiary from one to two years.
Swindling - *(See also False Pretences).*	- - By false representations of solvency, respectability, &c.	- - Fine, and imprisonment in common gaol, or both.
	Putting dirt or rubbish into bales of goods, for the purpose of increasing their bulk or weight.	- - Labour in the Penitentiary from one to five years.
Threatening Letters. *(See Extortion.)*		
Treason - -	- - 1st degree.—Levying war against the State, or adhering to or aiding its enemies.	Death.
	2d degree.— Knowledge and concealment of treason, without participation.	- - Hard labour in the Penitentiary for four years.
Vagrancy -	- - Any persons wandering about, leading an idle life, without property to support them, and able to work and to support themselves in a respectable way, on failure or refusal to give security for good behaviour and industry for a year.	- - Labour in the Penitentiary from two to four years.
	Persons found with instruments about them for the purpose of thieving or housebreaking, or found about houses or outhouses, with the intent of stealing, &c.	- - Labour in the Penitentiary from one to five years, or imprisonment in common gaol.

N. B.—Any person counselling, advising or encouraging an infant under 10 years of age, an idiot or a lunatic, to commit any crime, shall suffer the punishment appointed for such crime.

A person making another drunk by fraud, artifice or contrivance, for the purpose of having a crime committed, shall, if the crime be committed, suffer the punishment awarded for its commission.

If a married woman or slave commits any crime not punishable by death, under the threats or coercion of the husband or master, the husband or master shall suffer the punishment awarded for the crime.

A person committing an offence punishable by imprisonment in the Penitentiary, after conviction of a similar or any other offence so punished, shall suffer the longest period of imprisonment prescribed as the punishment for the offence.

In other cases the court determines the precise amount of punishment within the prescribed limits, regard being paid to any recommendation of the jury.

A prisoner convicted on more than one indictment shall suffer the punishment for both his offences, one after the expiration of the other.

A person sentenced to labour in the Penitentiary is rendered incapable of holding any public office or trust.

HOUSE OF REFUGE, PHILADELPHIA.

ARTICLES OF ASSOCIATION.

PHILADELPHIA.

" Refuge."

THE undersigned citizens of the Commonwealth of Pennsylvania associate for the purpose of establishing and conducting an institution for the confinement and reform of youthful delinquents, to be denominated " The House of Refuge."

Every citizen subscribing these articles of association, and paying 50 dollars, or 10 dollars annually for six years, shall be a member for life ; and every citizen subscribing these articles, and paying two dollars annually, shall be a member while he continues to contribute.

On the first Monday of May next, and annually thereafter on that day, and at such place as may be designated by notice in at least two of the daily newspapers published in the city of Philadelphia, the members of the association shall assemble and elect the following officers :

1st. A president, two vice-presidents, a treasurer, and a secretary of the association.

2d. A Board of 21 Managers, of whom five shall constitute a quorum, for the transaction of business, who shall appoint from their own number a chairman and a secretary, and prescribe the respective duties of each.

This Board shall also appoint a committee of 12 judicious females, to assist in the management of the House of Refuge, by imparting advice to the youth confined therein, and by bestowing their attention and care upon the domestic economy of the establishment.

This Board shall employ a superintendent and a matron, with such other assistants as they may deem necessary, and fix the compensations for their services ; and they shall select two physicians and two solicitors, who may consent to act gratuitously.

This Board shall provide a suitable building as a House of Refuge in the city or county of Philadelphia, and establish such regulations respecting the religious and moral education, training, employment, discipline and safe-keeping of its inhabitants as may be deemed expedient and proper.

This Board shall make a written report of its proceedings, and the treasurer shall furnish a full exhibition of his accounts at every annual meeting of the association ; and the president, or either of the vice-presidents, at the written request of 10 members, shall call special meetings of the association.

These articles may be altered and additions made thereto at any annual or special meeting of the association, provided notice in writing of the proposed alteration or additions shall have been furnished to the Board of Managers at least one month before they are considered ; and of any such notice it shall be the duty of the Board of Managers to give due and public information.

AN ACT to Incorporate the Subscribers to the Articles of Association, for the purposes of establishing and conducting an Institution for the Confinement and Reformation of Youthful Delinquents, under the title of " The HOUSE OF REFUGE."

WHEREAS an association of citizens of this Commonwealth hath been formed in the city and county of Philadelphia, for the humane and laudable purpose of reforming juvenile delinquents, and separating them from the society and intercourse of old and experienced offenders, with whom within the prisons of the said city they have been heretofore associated, and thereby exposed to the contamination of every species of vice and crime ; and the members of the said association having prayed to be incorporated, therefore,

Sect. 1. Be it enacted by the Senate and House of Representatives of the Commonwealth of Pennsylvania, in General Assembly met, and it is hereby enacted by the authority of the same, that all such persons as now are or shall hereafter become subscribers to the said association in the manner hereinafter provided be, and they are hereby incorporated and made a body politic in law, by the name, style and title of " The House of Refuge," and by that name, style and title shall have perpetual succession, with the power to have a common seal and to change the same at pleasure, to make contracts relative to the institution, to sue and be sued, and by that name and style be capable in law of purchasing, taking, holding and conveying any estate, real or personal, for the use of said corporation ; provided that the annual income of such estate shall not exceed in value 5,000 dollars, nor be applied to any other purpose than those for which this incorporation is formed, and also to establish bye-laws and orders for the regulation of the said society, and the preservation and application of the funds thereof, provided the same be not repugnant to the constitution and laws of the United States, or of this Commonwealth.

Sect. 2. And be it further enacted, by the authority aforesaid, that every person who hath subscribed the said articles of association, or who shall hereafter subscribe the same, and

pay

pay to the funds of the institution the sum of 50 dollars, or 10 dollars annually for the term of six years, shall be a member for life; and every person paying the sum of two dollars annually shall be a member, while he continues to contribute the said sum, such payment to be made at the time and in the manner to be prescribed by the bye-laws of the said association.

Sect. 3. And be it further enacted by the authority aforesaid, that the estate and concerns of the said corporation shall be conducted by the following officers: A president, two vice-presidents, a treasurer and a secretary, and 21 managers, of whom five shall constitute a quorum for the transaction of business, who shall appoint from their own body a chairman and a secretary, and prescribe the duties of each. That the members of the said association shall assemble on the first Monday of May annually, at such place in the said city as the Board of Managers may from time to time appoint, and of which the president, or in case of his absence or refusal to give the same, the secretary or any member of the said association, shall give notice in at least two of the daily papers of the city of Philadelphia, and elect by a plurality of ballots the aforesaid officers; and whenever any vacancy shall occur by death, removal from the city or county, or otherwise, the same shall be filled for the remainder of the year by such person, being a subscriber to the said articles of association, as the Board of Managers for the time being, or a major part of them, shall appoint, provided that the notice of the election to be held in May next may be given by the committee appointed for that purpose, by a meeting of citizens held on the 1st day of March instant.

Sect. 4. And be it further enacted, by the authority aforesaid, that if the annual election shall not take place on the day appointed for that purpose, the said corporation shall not therefore be dissolved, but the members of the said Board shall continue in office until a new election, which shall be had at such time and place, and after such notice as the said Board shall prescribe; and in case of an equality of votes for any one or more persons as a member or members of the said Board of Managers, the said Board shall determine which of such persons shall be considered as elected; and such person or persons shall take his or their seats, and act accordingly.

Sect. 5. And be it further enacted, by the authority aforesaid, that the Board of Managers shall provide a suitable building as a house of refuge in the city or county of Philadelphia, and establish such regulations respecting the religious and moral education, training, employment, discipline and safe-keeping of its inhabitants, as may be deemed expedient and proper.

Sect. 6. And be it further enacted, by the authority aforesaid, that the said managers shall, at their discretion, receive into the said House of Refuge such children who shall be taken up or committed as vagrants, or upon any criminal charge, or duly convicted of criminal offences, as may in the judgment of the Court of Oyer and Terminer, or of the Court of Quarter Sessions of the peace of the county, or of the Mayor's Court of the city of Philadelphia, or of any alderman or justice of the peace, or of the managers of the almshouse and house of employment, be deemed proper objects; and the said managers of the House of Refuge shall have power to place the said children committed to their care, during the minority of the said children, at such employments, and cause them to be instructed in such branches of useful knowledge as may be suitable to their years and capacities; and they shall have power, in 'heir discretion, to bind out the said children, with their consent, as apprentices during their m iority, to such persons and at such places, to learn such proper trades and employments as in their judgment will be most conducive to the reformation and amendment, and will tend to the future benefit and advantage of such children; provided that the charge and power of the said managers upon and over the said children shall not extend, in the case of females, beyond the age of 18 years.

Sect. 7. And be it further enacted, by the authority aforesaid, that the said managers of the House of Refuge under this Act may from time to time make bye-laws, ordinances and regulations relative to the management, government, instruction, discipline, employment and disposition of the said children while in the said House of Refuge, not contrary to law, as they may deem proper, and may appoint such officers, agents and servants as they may deem necessary to transact the business of the said corporation, and may designate their duties. And further, that the said managers shall make annual report to the Legislature of this Commonwealth of the number of children received by them into the said House of Refuge; the disposition which shall be made of the said children, by instructing or employing them in the said House of Refuge, or by binding them out as apprentices; the receipts and expenditures of the said managers, and generally all such facts and particulars as may tend to exhibit the effects, whether beneficial or otherwise, of the said association, and the right to alter, amend or repeal this Act, is hereby reserved on the part of the Commonwealth.

Sect. 8. And be it further enacted, by the authority aforesaid, that the lot of ground, and the buildings which may be erected thereon for the use and objects of the said association, shall be free of tax.

Approved March 23d, 1826.

————————

The fourth section of the " Act to endow the House of Refuge," and for other purposes therein mentioned, passed the 2d of March 1827, directs, that the managers of the House of Refuge shall receive into the same such children who shall be convicted in the Court of Oyer and Terminer or Quarter Sessions of any county except the county of Philadelphia, or Mayor's Court of any city except the city of Philadelphia, of any offence which, under the existing laws, would be punished by imprisonment in the Penitentiary, as may be, in the judgment of the said courts, deemed proper objects for the House of Refuge; and the children so received shall be clothed, maintained and instructed by the said managers at the public expense of the proper county; and the accounts of the said children shall be kept by the managers, in the same manner that the accounts of convicts in the Penitentiary are now directed to be kept by the inspectors thereof; and the said managers of the House of Refuge shall have power to place the said children committed to their care, during the minority of the said children, at such employments, and cause them to be instructed in such branches of useful knowledge, as may be suitable to their years and capacities; and they shall have power, in their discretion, to bind out the said children, with their consent, as apprentices during their minority, to such persons and at such places, to learn such proper trades and employments, as in their judgment will be most conducive to the reformation and amendment, and will tend to the future benefit and advantage of such children; provided that the charge and power of the said managers upon and over the said children shall not extend, in the case of females, beyond the age of 18 years; and provided that this section shall not be construed to apply to children received into the said House of Refuge from the city and county of Philadelphia, or to repeal or affect the the sixth section of the Act intituled, " An Act to Incorporate the Subscribers to the Articles of Association, for the purpose of establishing and conducting an Institution for the Confinement and Reformation of Youthful Delinquents, under the Title of ' The House of Refuge,'" passed the 23d day of March 1826.

A SUPPLEMENT to the Act intituled, " An Act to Endow the House of Refuge, and for other Purposes ;" passed the 2d day of March 1827.

Sect. 1. Be it enacted by the Senate and House of Representatives of the Commonwealth of Pennsylvania in General Assembly met, and it is hereby enacted by the authority of the same, that the commissioners of the county of Philadelphia are hereby authorized and required to pay over to the treasurer of the House of Refuge, out of the county funds, in lieu of the annual payment of 5,000 dollars authorized and required to be paid by them in pursuance of the provisions of the third section of the Act to which this is a Supplement, the annual sum of 10,000 dollars, until the 2d day of March 1832, for the purposes mentioned and prescribed in and by the third section of the said Act; the first payment for the year ending on the 10th day of April 1830, to be made at any time during said month, and each of the two succeeding payments to be made during the month of March, in the years 1831 and 1832 respectively.

Approved March 27th, 1830.

RULES OF THE HOUSE OF REFUGE IN PHILADELPHIA.

Means by which the House of Refuge proposes to effect the Reformation of Juvenile Delinquents.

First, security of their persons; second, inspection; third, classification; fourth, constant employment; fifth, education, combined with moral and religious instruction; sixth, coarse but suitable food and clothing; seventh, space for exercise conducive to health; eighth, separation of the sexes; ninth, accommodation for and attendance on the sick.

Sect. 1. The following standing committees shall be annually appointed by the Board of Managers; viz.

An Executive Committee, an Indenturing Committee, a Finance Committee, a Chapel Committeee, a Ladies' Committee.

There shall be the following officers; viz., two physicians and surgeons, whose services shall be gratuitous, both married men and experienced in their profession; two solicitors, whose services shall be gratuitous; a superintendent; an assistant superintendent; a matron; an assistant matron; teachers and such other officers as the Board of Managers shall from time to time find necessary. All the officers of the house shall hold their appointments during the pleasure of the Board of Managers.

Sect. 2. *The Executive Committee.*

The Executive Committee shall consist of the Indenturing Committee, a secretary, who shall be appointed by the Board, and who shall be a permanant member of the committee, and six other members, who shall be elected by the Board, the term of service of one of whom shall expire monthly, and a new election take place to fill the vacancy· The Executive Committee shall, under the direction of the Board of Managers, have the charge and management of the House of Refuge. The duties of this committee are comprised in the following articles; viz.

First. The committee shall appoint by ballot a chairman, who shall preside at the meetings of the committee.

Second. The secretary shall keep regular minutes of all their proceedings, which minutes shall be submitted to the Board of Managers at each stated meeting. He shall notify, in writing, all sub-committees of their appointment.

Third. The committee shall meet at least once in each week for the transaction of business. Five members shall form a quorum.

Fourth.

Fourth. A sub-committee of two shall be appointed to visit the House of Refuge weekly, or oftener if necessary, to confer with the superintendent and matron, in conformity with the regulations of the Executive Committee.   One of this sub-committee shall retire monthly and another member be appointed.   In case either of the committees should be prevented from attending at the house, he shall procure another member of the Executive Committee to attend in his place.   This committee shall record in a book, to be read at the meetings of the Executive Committee, such observations as the committee may deem proper.

Fifth. All purchases and contracts for supplies of the House of Refuge shall be made by, or under the direction of, the Executive Committee.   They shall keep the house in repair, and make payments to all the officers at the rate of salary fixed by the managers.

Sixth. All bills, after having been examined and approved by the committee, and noted on the minutes, shall be paid by drafts on the treasurer, signed by the chairman and secretary of the Executive Committee.

Seventh. They shall be authorized to enter into such contracts as they may from time to time think proper with any person or persons for the employment of the inmates in any work, manufacture or trade, and to appoint such assistants as they may think necessary for the purpose of instructing them in any work or manufacture which may be introduced into the institution.

Eighth. The committee may suspend any of the officers in the employ of, or appointed by, the Board of Managers for neglect of duty, or disobedience of orders, until the pleasure of the Board of Managers shall be known.

Ninth. When vacancies occur in the offices of superintendent or assistant, matron or assistant, or teachers, it shall be the duty of the Executive Committee to nominate suitable persons to the Board of Managers to fill such vacancies.

Tenth. All reports of sub-committees shall be in writing, and signed by a majority of the committee.

Eleventh. The committee shall have charge of the Sunday-schools, and it shall be their duty to procure suitable instructors, and to make a quarterly report, in writing, to the Board of Managers on the state of the said schools.

Twelfth. At the request of the Executive Committee, the chairman of the Board of Managers shall call special meetings of the Board.

Sect. 3. *Finance Committee.*

The treasurer, together with two members of the Board, annually to be elected for that purpose, shall form a Committee of Finance.

Sect. 4. *The Indenturing or Apprenticing Committee.*

The Board of Managers shall elect, by ballot, an Indenturing Committee of five members, whose duty it shall be to decide upon all applications from persons who wish to have such children as have become sufficiently reformed apprenticed to them.   The inmates shall be bound only to persons of good moral character, who, in the opinion of the committee, will feel a deep interest in the reformation of the children placed under their care.

No inmate shall be apprenticed to a tavern-keeper or distiller of spirituous liquors; and girls shall not be apprenticed to unmarried men, or placed in boarding-houses, or in public academies.

No child shall be put to service out of the House of Refuge, unless under regular indentures from the Board of Managers; and none shall be apprenticed to any person or persons residing in the city of Philadelphia, or within 20 miles thereof, unless with the consent of the Executive Committee, and in all cases preference shall be given to applications from persons who do not reside in towns, but in the most distant parts of the country.

A Bible and printed paper of advice and instruction, relative to his or her future conduct, shall be given to each inmate when apprenticed; a printed letter shall also be given with the indenture to those under whose control the children are placed, recommending them particularly to their parental care and affection.

No child shall be apprenticed until he or she shall have resided at least one year in the house, given satisfactory evidence of reformation, and learned to read and write; except in special cases, and then only with the consent of the Executive Committee.

The committee shall keep regular minutes of their proceedings, which shall be laid before the Board of Managers at each stated meeting.

Sect. 5. *The Chapel Committee.*

The Chapel Committee shall consist of five members, and shall be appointed annually by the Board of Managers.   It shall be the duty of this committee to procure clergymen to officiate at the house on Sundays, both morning and afternoon; and at least one of the committee shall attend at those times, or procure a manager to attend in his place.   The service shall commence at such time as the committee may direct.

No religious meetings shall be held at any other times, except on special occasions, and then only with the permission of the Executive Committee.

Persons may be admitted to attend divine worship at the chapel by the permission of a member of the Board of Managers, and those residing in the immediate neighbourhood may obtain permanent tickets from any member of the Chapel Committee or from the superintendent.   Visitors will not be permitted to remain on the premises after divine service.

PHILADELPHIA.

" Refuge."

Sect. 6. The Ladies' Committee.

A Committee consisting of 12 ladies shall be annually elected by the Board of Managers.

It shall be the duty of the committee monthly to visit the female department, and to advise and confer with the matron relative to the management thereof. They shall also appoint a sub-committee to visit the House of Refuge weekly, to inspect the female apartments, to excite in the girls a sense of virtue and piety, to inculcate habits of cleanliness, industry and strict attention to the directions of the matron and the rules of the house, and to make such suggestions to her as they may think likely to be useful. The committee will report quarterly to the Board of Managers on the state of the female department, and offer such remarks as they may from time to time deem advisable. They shall supply all vacancies that may occur in the committee.

Sect. 7. The Authority and Duties of the Superintendent.

First. He shall have the superintendence of the male and female departments of the House of Refuge, and shall cause to be enforced all the rules and regulations adopted for their government, subject at all times to the consent of the Board of Managers and the Executive Committee.

Second. He shall, with the advice and consent of the Executive Committee, appoint all the sub-officers of the house, and, if necessary, he may suspend any officer of the house for gross neglect of duty, until the pleasure of the Board of Managers or Executive Committee shall be known.

Third. He shall, under the direction of the Indenturing Committee, correspond with the individuals to whom the inmates are apprenticed.

Fourth. He shall keep a register of the name and age, a sketch of the life and description of the person of every inmate placed under his care, when received, by whom committed, on what charge, and any other remarks that may be useful. He shall be authorized to inflict such punishment on the inmates as may be necessary to preserve order and discipline in the institution, reporting the same in special cases to the Executive Committee. He shall keep an alphabetical record of the names of the parents, guardians or near relations of inmates admitted to visit them, with the date of the visits, and such remarks as he may think proper.

Fifth. He shall be careful to have a regular account kept of the expenses of the institution, with every item properly designated, also an inventory of the whole personal property under his care belonging to the House of Refuge, and the manner in which the same may have been disposed of, and shall, in December, March, June and September in each year, make a full and detailed report to the Board on the state of the institution.

Sixth. He shall keep a record of events worthy of note, the number of inmates in the house, how employed, the number discharged and under what circumstances, and a statement of the supplies necessary to be purchased, and submit the same, and any other matter he may deem necessary, to the Executive Committee at every stated meeting.

Seventh. He shall keep a list of those inmates who have been the longest in the house, designating such of them as in his opinion have become sufficiently reformed to be indentured, which list shall be delivered to the Indenturing Committee.

Eighth. In case of the indisposition, absence or death of the superintendent, his duty shall be performed by the assistant superintendent, under the direction of the Executive Committee.

Sect. 8. The Matron and Assistant.

The matron shall have the immediate care and superintendence of the females placed in the House of Refuge. She shall reside in the house, and shall not absent herself from the premises without the knowledge of the superintendent, or, in his absence, without the consent of the Visiting Committee.

Second. She shall superintend the work and take charge of the clothes and bedding of the female department, and shall accompany the superintendent or other officer whenever it may be necessary for them to visit the apartments of the females.

Third. She shall endeavour to unfold to those under her charge the advantage of a moral and religious life, and impress upon them a conviction of the evils and miseries that attend the wicked and profligate; she shall be authorized to punish them for misconduct. She shall keep a record of all events worthy of notice, which shall be submitted to the inspection of the Ladies' Committee.

Fourth. The assistant matron and all other females employed shall receive their orders from the matron.

Fifth. In case of the indisposition, absence or death of the matron, her duties shall be performed by the assistant matron.

Sect. 9. The Assistant Keepers.

The officers and persons employed shall conduct themselves in strict conformity with the rules of the establishment. They shall receive their orders from and obey the directions of the superintendent, and shall not absent themselves from the premises without his permission. The sub-officers shall perform such duties as the superintendent may require.

Sect. 10. Labour and Instruction.

The inmates shall be employed on an average four hours in school and eight hours at some mechanical or other labour, every day in the year except Sundays and Christmas-day, agreeably to a scale to be adopted by the Executive Committee.

The

The schools shall be provided with the necessary apparatus to instruct the children in spelling, reading, writing, arithmetic, geography and book-keeping.

The inmates shall have the use of the library, under the direction of the superintendent, and new books shall, before they are placed in the library, be approved by the Executive Committee; and all pamphlets and newspapers shall be submitted to this committee before they are received into the house.

Sect. 11. *Employment.*

The inmates shall be employed in such occupations as the Executive Committee may designate.

The introduction of labour into the House of Refuge will be regarded principally with reference to the moral benefits rather than to the profits to be derived from it. If the employment shall not be productive of much pecuniary advantage, still the gain to this city and State will eventually prove very considerable from the reformation, and consequently reduced number, of offenders. Preference will always be given to those trades, the knowledge of which will enable the children to earn their subsistence on their discharge from the House of Refuge.

Sect. 12. *Arrangement of Time.*

A bell shall be rung every morning a quarter of an hour before the unlocking of the lodging rooms, and also at the hour of unlocking, when the children shall be prepared to leave their rooms in order to wash, &c. previous to going to work or school.

The hours for beginning and leaving off work, taking breakfast, dinner and supper, attending school, and rising and retiring to sleep, shall be in conformity with a table prepared by the Executive Committee, and each hour shall be designated by the ringing of a bell, as the superintendent may direct.

On Sundays and Christmas-day the children, after washing, dressing, &c. shall proceed to the school or lecture-room, and shall be employed as in Sunday-schools until the hour of breakfast, after which they shall be occupied in the same manner until the hour of religious services, and so throughout the day, with such relaxation as the superintendent may direct.

Sect. 13. *Food.*

The children shall be supplied with a sufficient quantity of coarse but wholesome food, according to a dietary established by the Executive Committee.

Sect. 14. *Clothing.*

The inmates shall be clothed in coarse but comfortable apparel of a cheap and durable kind. All the clothes shall, if practicable, be made up by the inmates.

Sect. 15. *Separation and Classification.*

The female shall have no communication with the male inmates of the house.

Each inmate shall be lodged in a separate dormitory properly ventilated, but so as to preclude any conversation or intercourse.

The inmates shall be classed according to their moral conduct.

The classes shall be distinguished in such manner as the superintendent and Executive Committee may direct.

Such inmates as behave well, are orderly in their conduct, and attentive to their studies, shall be rewarded monthly by the superintendent and matron, in the presence of the Visiting Committee and inmates; and those who have behaved well for three months in succession shall form a class of honour and wear a badge of distinction.

Sect. 16. *General Regulations.*

No spirituous liquors or tobacco shall, under any pretence whatever, be introduced into any part of the premises, except by order of the physicians.

No games or plays having a tendency to gambling shall be permitted.

In case of sickness the patient shall be removed to the infirmary.

The inmates shall not be permitted to leave the house except in case of the illness of their parents or near relations, and then only by the permission of the superintendent, and accompanied by one of the officers of the house.

Visiters will be admitted on the first and third Wednesdays of each month, by a permit, signed by any member of the Board of Managers. Strangers may, by the written permission of a member of the Board, be admitted at any time. No visiter can be allowed to converse with the inmates without the consent of the superintendent, or of a manager when present.

The parents, guardians or near relations of the inmates may be permitted to visit them once in three months, under such regulations as the Executive Committee may make.

No inmate shall be allowed to receive presents of any kind except as rewards for good conduct, and then only through the superintendent or matron, and with the consent and approbation of the Visiting Committee.

N.B.—The " Rules " for the government of the " Refuge " at *New York* are not reprinted, being similar in their general tendency to the foregoing.

ENGLAND
AND WALES.

MISCELLANEOUS.

ENGLAND AND WALES.

GENERAL ESTIMATE of the EXPENSE of ALTERING or ENLARGING the COUNTY PRISONS, &c. in *England* and *Wales*, (included in the Act 4 Geo. 4, c. 64,) with a view of providing separate SLEEPING CELLS for the greatest number of Prisoners confined at one time during the Year 1832.

[Framed from Parliamentary Return, (No. 484,) Ordered, by The House of Commons, to be printed, 5th July 1833.*]

COUNTIES and PRISONS.	Greatest Number of Prisoners at one time.	Number of Sleeping Cells.	Number of Day Rooms or Wards.	Additional Cells may be made by dividing large Rooms.	New Cells wanting.	Estimated Expense of providing separate Cells.	REMARKS.
ENGLAND.						£.	
BEDFORD:							
County Gaol and House of Correction.	78	41	7	12	25	1,240*	- - Erected in 1800. Central building, with three wings attached.
New House of Correction.	51	50	4	–	–	–	- - Erected in 1820. The cell buildings are round the airing courts. Cost about 6,000 *l.*
BERKS:							
Reading County Gaol and House of Correction.	155	22	16	61	72	2,196	- - Erected in 1780. Additions are now being made.
Abingdon House of Correction.	57	32	5	23	2	330	- - Erected in 1810. Central building, with three wings.
BUCKS:							
Aylesbury County Gaol and House of Correction.	237	140	20	76	21	1,341	- - An old gaol, built at various times: many of the cells are very small and badly constructed.
CAMBRIDGE:							
County Gaol and House of Correction.	84	70	10	14	–	130	- - Erected in 1805. Radiating plan. Central building, and four detached wings.
Wisbeach House of Correction.	56	21	1	–	35	1,400*	- - Built in 1821, with Sessions house adjoining.
Ely - - ditto - -	30	16	4	8	6	322	- - ditto - - -ditto.
CHESTER:							
County Gaol - -	148	105	8	32	11	780	- - Erected in 1790. Polygonal building round the airing courts. The debtors have a separate prison in front.
City Gaol and House of Correction.	36	27	12	12	–	–	- - Erected in 1805.
Knutsford County House of Correction.	287	162	8	66	59	3,680*	- - Erected in 1820. Radiating plan. Central building, and four large detached wings. Cost about 50,000 *l.*
CORNWALL:							
Bodmin County Gaol and House of Correction.	164	176	14	–	–	–	- - Built in 1778. Recently enlarged. Some of the dormitories are only 2 ft. 6 in. wide.
Launceston County House of Correction.	(No return.)						

* *Note.*—Some of the Returns do not contain any statement of the expense. In these cases the new cells have been estimated at 40 *l.* each; and the additional cells, from dividing the day-rooms, &c., at 20 *l.* each. Such estimates are marked against thus *.

⊙

COUNTIES and PRISONS.	Greatest Number of Prisoners at one time.	Number of Sleeping Cells.	Number of Day Rooms, or Wards.	Additional Cells may be made by dividing large Rooms.	New Cells wanting.	Estimated Expense of providing separate Cells.	REMARKS.
						£.	
CUMBERLAND:							
Carlisle County Gaol and House of Correction.	116	124	13	–	–	–	- - Erected in 1825. Radiating plan. Central building and six detached wings. Cost about 40,000 l.
Whitehaven House of Correction.	8	10	4	–	–	–	
DERBY:							
County Gaol and House of Correction.	180	151	22	29	–	506	- - Erected in 1824. Radiating plan. Central building and seven detached wings (25 debtors' rooms). Cost about 50,000 l., including purchase of ground.
DEVON:							
Exeter County Gaol -	139	132	14	22	–	–	- - Erected in 1790. Quadrangular plan. Recently much enlarged. The debtors occupy a separate prison.
					30	3,034	
Exeter House of Correction.	184	100	12	54	–	–	- - Erected in 1807, adjoining the gaol. Central building, and three wings detached.
Exeter City Gaol and House of Correction.	33	22	8	12	–	260	Erected in 1818.
DORSET:							
Dorchester County Gaol and House of Correction.	173	72	13	76	25	2,520*	- - Erected in 1790. Quadrangular plan. Four detached buildings.
DURHAM:							
County Gaol and House of Correction.	194	48	21	68	126	4,350	- - Erected in 1810. Polygonal building round the airing courts. A new range of cells is about to be erected. Debtors rooms are not included.
ESSEX:							
Chelmsford County Gaol and House of Correction (females.)	43	58	12	–	–	–	- - Erected in 1776. Plan irregular and defective. The male debtors have about 28 separate rooms.
Springfield County Gaol and House of Correction (for males only)	323	243	14	47	33	5,050	- - Erected in 1826. Radiating plan; seven detached wings. Cost about 52,000 l.
Ilford County House of Correction.	50	48	5	–	2	60	- - Erected in 1830. Radiating plan. Cost about 6,500 l.
Halstead - - ditto -	57	40	5	–	17	700	
Newport - - ditto -	12	9	2	7	–	140*	
Colchester - ditto -	–	–	2	–	–	–	A new prison is building.
GLOUCESTER:							Erected in 1790. Quadrangular plan. The penitentiary occupies one wing of the gaol: it contains the same number of day or work-cells as sleeping cells.
County Gaol - -	217	111	10	–	106	4,240*	
Penitentiary - -	124	78	–	–	46	1,840*	
City Gaol and House of Correction.	39	8	4	21	10	800	Erected in 1784.
Horsley County House of Correction.	80	90	3	–	–	–	- - Erected in 1788. Quadrangular plan.
Northleach - ditto -	60	77	2	–	–	–	- - Erected in 1790. Polygonal building round airing courts: 25 of the cells are used as work cells.
Littledean - ditto -	32	23	4	12	–	240*	- - Erected in 1788. There are also 10 work rooms.
Lawford's Gate ditto -	26	38	–	–	–	–	- - Erected in 1788. There are also sixteen work cells.

ENGLAND
AND WALES.

COUNTIES and PRISONS.	Greatest Number of Prisoners at one time.	Number of Sleeping Cells.	Number of Day Rooms or Wards.	Additional Cells may be made by dividing large Rooms.	New Cells wanting.	Estimated Expense of providing separate Cells.	REMARKS.
HANTS:						£.	
Winchester County Gaol	144	98	10	–	46	1,840*	- - Erected in 1790 : the debtors' prison (separate) in 1805. Quadrangular plan.
Winchester County House of Correction.	225	61	9	88	76	1,500	- - Erected in 1805. Plan similar to the gaol.
Gosport - ditto - -	45	20	4	18	7	640*	
Newport (Isle of Wight) ditto	21	22	6	–	–	–	
Portsmouth Borough Prison.	73	50	9	11	12	700*	- - Erected in 1806. Quadrangular plan. Is now enlarging.
HEREFORD :							
County Gaol and House of Correction.	114	80	10	–	34	2,040	- - Erected in 1790. Central building, and four wings attached; (29 debtors' cells).
HERTS:							
County Gaol - -	83	34	8	25	24	1,300	- - Erected in 1780. Quadrangular plan.
County House of Correction - - -	96	49	4	20	27	1,250	- - This prison adjoins the gaol.
HUNTINGDON:							
County Gaol and House of Correction.	45	46	8	–	–	–	- - Erected in 1829. Central building, with three detached wings, at right angles. Cost about 21,000 l.
KENT:							
Maidstone County Gaol and House of Correction.	486	389	36	97	–	1,940*	- - Erected in 1816. Radiating plan. Four central stations : 15 detached wing buildings. Cost 192,000 l.
Canterbury - ditto -	77	48	8	16	13	840*	- - Radiating plan. Three detached wing buildings.
LANCASTER:							
County Gaol (exclusive of debtors).	299	131	35	60	108	4,356	- - Plan irregular. The additions in 1821 cost about 30,000 l. The new part surrounds the airing courts. There are also 72 work-cells.
Liverpool, Kirkdale House of Correction.	704	370	21	92	242	20,000	- - Erected in 1820. Cost 40,000 l. Circular plan : the cell buildings surround the courts.
Manchester, Salford House of Correction.	637	440	24	197	–	2,331	- - The old part built in 1788. Enlarged in 1816 and 1827. There are also 150 work rooms.
Preston County House of Correction.	283	160	11	12	111	11,130	- - The old part built in 1790. Much enlarged in 1828. There are also 67 work rooms.
Liverpool Borough Prison.	228	326	14	–	–	–	- - Erected in 1788. Radiating plan : six detached wings ; (176 debtors' rooms.)
LEICESTER :							
County Gaol - -	92	116	17	–	–	--	- - Erected in 1827. Radiating plan : six wings. Cost about 40,000 l.; (35 debtors' rooms.)
Ditto House of Correction.	113	46	13	29	38	4,966	- - Enlarged in 1816. Three wing buildings at right angles.
Borough Gaol - -	48	37	4	14	–	400 ⎫	- - Altered and enlarged in 1830 from the old county gaol. Cost about 13,000 l.
Ditto House of Correction - - -	44	30	3	14	–	600 ⎭	
LINCOLN :							
County Gaol (exclusive of debtors).	49	21	12	4	24	2,200	- - Erected in 1790. Quadrangular plan.
Louth County House of Correction.	76	60	10	36	–	290	- - Enlarged in 1827. Cost about 11,000 l.

ENGLAND
AND WALES.

COUNTIES and PRISONS.	Greatest Number of Prisoners at one time.	Number of Sleeping Cells.	Number of Day Rooms or Wards.	Additional Cells may be made by dividing large Rooms.	New Cells wanting.	Estimated Expense of providing separate Cells.	REMARKS.
						£.	
LINCOLN—(continued)							
Kirton County House of Correction.	74	26	8	29	19	390	- - Erected in 1809. Quadrangular plan.
Folkingham ditto -	37	30	10	13	–	40	- - Erected in 1808. Polygonal building round airing courts.
Skirbeck - ditto -	20	11	–	–	9	360*	Erected in 1809.
Spalding - ditto -	63	45	7	32	–	416	- - Erected in 1826. Cost about 16,000 l.
Spilsby - ditto -	51	63	13	–	–	–	- - Erected in 1826. Three radiating wing buildings. Cost about 14,000 l.
MIDDLESEX:							
Clerkenwell County Gaol.	407	20	10	132	266	12,200	- - Rebuilt and enlarged in 1818. Quadrangular plan.
Cold Bath Fields House of Correction.	1,340	404	34	324	612	23,438	- - Erected in 1790. Recently much enlarged. A new prison for vagrants, and also one for females; both on the radiating plan.
Newgate, London City Gaol.	610	33	10	129	462	21,060*	- - Built in 1780. Quadrangular plan. No space for additional cells.
Giltspur-street, House of Correction.	160	22	10	28	110	4,960*	Ditto - - ditto.
London Bridewell -	108	46	–	23	39	1,750	- - Lately erected in St. George's Fields, Southwark.
Westminster City Gaol and House of Correction.	–	–	–	–	–	–	- - A new prison just completed, on the radiating plan, containing about 500 cells, with 48 day-rooms: each of the latter may be divided into 3 cells. Cost about 130,000 l.
MONMOUTH:							
County Gaol and House of Correction.	70	36	10	34	–	612	Erected in 1788.
Usk County House of Correction.	35	18	4	17	–	306	Erected in 1821.
NORFOLK:							
Norwich County Gaol and House of Correction.	216	229	18	–	–	–	- - Rebuilt and enlarged in 1824. Part polygonal, and three radiating wings. Cost about 50,000 l.
Norwich City Gaol -	55	59	8	–	–	–	⎫ - - Erected in 1826. Radiating plan: four detached ⎬ wings. Cost about 20,000 l.
Norwich City House of Correction - -	51	39	6	–	12	600	⎭
Walsingham County House of Correction.	97	32	6	33	32	1,535	- - Erected in 1790. Enlarged in 1821.
Swaffham - ditto -	60	40	3	30	–	300	Ditto - - ditto.
Wymondham ditto -	–	22	3	–	–	–	- - No return of prisoners, the building having been shut up. It is now reoccupied.
NORTHAMPTON:							
County Gaol and House of Correction.	139	80	12	20	39	1,500	- - Enlarged in 1829. Quadrangular plan.
NORTHUMBERLAND:							
Morpeth County Gaol -	57	44	14	18	–	992	- - Erected in 1824. Polygonal buildings round the airing courts. Cost about 35,000 l.
Tynemouth House of Correction.	18	14	2	–	4	160*	
Alnwick - ditto -	20	8	2	6	6	360*	
Hexham - ditto -	14	6	6	8	–	250	
Newcastle Town Gaol and House of Correction.	127	47	13	48	32	3,510	- Erected in 1824. Radiating plan: six detached wings; (18 debtors' rooms). Cost about 40,000 l.
							(continued)

ENGLAND
AND WALES.

COUNTIES and PRISONS.	Greatest Number of Prisoners at one time.	Number of Sleeping Cells.	Number of Day Rooms or Wards.	Additional Cells may be made by dividing large Rooms.	New Cells wanting.	Estimated Expense of providing separate Cells.	REMARKS.
NOTTINGHAM:						£.	
County Gaol - -	53	17	3	–	36	4,520	- - A defective prison; the site, being very limited, and in the rear of the court-house. Eighteen cells are now building.
Town Gaol - -	52	16	3	6	30	1,320*	- - A new gaol is about to be erected.
Ditto House of Correction.	108	102	11	–	6	50	Enlarged in 1829.
Southwell County House of Correction.	160	129	11	61	–	587	- - Erected in 1808, and enlarged in 1829. Polygonal building; part radiating with three wings. Cost about 14,000 l.
OXFORD:							
County Gaol and House of Correction.	207	136	11	35	36	2,140*	- - Partly rebuilt in 1788, on the site of the ancient castle. Four wings: plan irregular.
RUTLAND:							
Oakham County Gaol & House of Correction.	17	31	7	–	–	–	- - Erected in 1806. Central building, and three detached wings.
SHROPSHIRE:							
Shrewsbury County Gaol and House of Correction.	261	156	26	87	18	900	- - Erected in 1790. Quadrangular plan.
SOMERSET:							
Ilchester County Gaol	176	30	12	124	22	1,200	- - Plan irregular: erected at different periods.
Shepton Mallett House of Correction.	300	45	19	172	83	5,537	- - Enlarged in 1823. Quadrangular plan.
Wilton House of Correction.	152	12	14	121	19	3,840	Ditto - - ditto.
Bristol City Gaol and House of Correction.	242	195	10	42	5	1,040*	- - Erected in 1820. Radiating plan. Central building and four detached wings. Cost about 56,000 l.
Ditto, Old House of Correction.	–	–	–	–	–	–	- - Unoccupied, having been partly destroyed by fire.
STAFFORD:							
County Gaol and House of Correction.	388	333	19	40	15	1,400	- - Erected in 1793. Quadrangular plan. A new house of correction recently built, containing 114 cells. The latter cost about 6,000 l.
SUFFOLK:							
Bury County Gaol and House of Correction.	210	140	14	28	42	7,000	- - Erected in 1802. Radiating plan. Four detached wings. Enlarged in 1820.
Ipswich, ditto - -	160	143	11	–	17	680*	- - Erected in 1790. Central building, with four wings attached.
Beccles House of Correction.	39	24	8	16	–	76	Enlarged in 1823.
Woodbridge, ditto -	27	16	2	–	11	300	Erected in 1804.
SURREY:							
Horsemonger Lane County Gaol.	210	169	10	76	–	1,270	- - Erected in 1790. Quadrangular plan. There are also 57 rooms for debtors.

COUNTIES and PRISONS.	Greatest Number of Prisoners at one time.	Number of Sleeping Cells.	Number of Day Rooms or Wards.	Additional Cells may be made by dividing large Rooms.	New Cells wanting.	Estimated Expense of providing separate Cells.	REMARKS.
SURREY—*continued.*						£.	
Brixton House of Correction.	285	112	10	80	93	4,750	- - Erected in 1821. Polygonal buildings round the airing courts. Cost (including site) 35,000 *l.*
Guildford - ditto -	128	89	7	4	35	2,500	- - The same. Plan similar. Cost (including site) 24,000 *l.*
Kingston House of Correction.	43	10	2	–	33	1,320*	
Southwark, Borough Gaol.	101	8	5	19	74	3,340*	- - Enlarged in 1822.
SUSSEX:							
Horsham County Gaol	67	35	8	14	18	2,400	- - Erected in 1780. Quadrangular plan. There are also 23 debtors' rooms.
Lewes' County House of Correction.	158	75	9	26	57	7,140	- - Erected in 1788. Quadrangular plan. Fifty-two cells are now building : these will cost about 5,000 *l.*
Petworth ditto - -	83	32	7	14	37	5,600	
Battle ditto - -	12	8	–	–	4	160*	Built in 1821.
WARWICK:							
County Gaol - -	260	92	9	53	115	8,069	- - Defective plan. Site limited, and fronting two streets ; (exclusive of debtors' rooms for about 50.)
Ditto, House of Correction.	254	64	9	92	98	5,577	- - Plan irregular and defective.
Coventry City Prison -	58	84	10	–	–	–	- - Erected in 1830. Radiating plan : three wings. Cost about 14,000 *l.*
WESTMORLAND:							
Appleby County Gaol and House of Correction.	19	25	10	–	–	–	Enlarged in 1826.
Kendal County House of Correction.	35	33	–	12	–	150	
WILTS:							
Salisbury County Gaol (exclusive of debtors.)	133	73	10	17	43	2,059	- - Erected in 1821. Quadrangular plan : four detached buildings. Cost, including site, 25,000 *l.*
Devizes County House of Correction.	183	210	–	–	–	–	- - Erected in 1816. Circular building round airing courts. Cost about 40,000 *l.*
Ditto, Old Bridewell -	63	12	4	40	11	480	
Marlborough ditto -	28	4	4	24	–	294	
WORCESTER:							
County Gaol and House of Correction.	200	79	11	102	19	2,518	- - Erected in 1812. Radiating plan : six detached wings.
City Gaol and House of Correction.	43	51	8	–	–	–	- - Erected in 1824. Semicircular building round airing courts. Cost about 10,000 *l.*

(continued)

x

ENGLAND
AND WALES.

COUNTIES and PRISONS.	Greatest Number of Prisoners at one time.	Number of Sleeping Cells.	Number of Day Rooms or Wards.	Additional Cells may be made by dividing large Rooms.	New Cells wanting.	Estimated Expense of providing separate Cells.	REMARKS.
YORK :						£.	
County Gaol - -	346	185	17	161	–	3,220*	- - A new prison nearly completed : 112 cells unfinished. Has cost about 60,000 l. Erected in 1802.
City Gaol - - -	37	36	7	–	–	–	- - Erected in 1815. Three detached wings.
Ditto, House of Correction.	45	21	6	24	–	480*	
North Allerton, North Riding House of Correction.	87	32	7	86	–	562	Enlarged in 1828.
Beverley, East Riding ditto.	102	61	14	42	–	790	- - Enlarged in 1821. Central building and four detached wings. Cost about 20,000 l.
Wakefield, West Riding ditto.	562	329	19	62	171	9,840	- - Enlarged in 1821. Polygonal cell buildings round the courts : work rooms radiating. Cost about 40,000 l.
Kingston-upon-Hull Town Prison	130	68	21	28	34	1,732	- - Erected in 1830. Radiating plan ; four wings, (22 debtors' rooms). Cost about 30,000 l.
TOTAL, ENGLAND -	17,508	9,874	1,159	4,017	4,212	263,062	
WALES.							
ANGLESEY :							
Beaumaris County Gaol and House of Correction.	24	25	6	–	–	–	- - Erected in 1828. Central building, and three small wings attached. Cost about 7,500 l.
BRECON :							
County Gaol and House of Correction.	33	9	5	20	4	280	Erected in 1782.
CARDIGAN :							
County Gaol and House of Correction.	16	28	6	–	–	–	- - Erected in 1796. Central building, and three small wings.
CARMARTHEN :							
County Gaol - -	26	20	2	–	6 }	500	- - Enlarged in 1825. Plan irregular : buildings round the courts.
Ditto House of Correction.	20	24	3	–	– }		
CARNARVON :							
County Gaol and House of Correction.	32	13	3	10	9	439	
DENBIGH :							
Ruthen County Gaol and House of Correction.	39	12	6	29	–	580*	- - Rebuilt in 1825. Cost about 7,000 l.
FLINT :							
County Gaol and House of Correction.	34	10	4	8	16	1,450	Enlarged in 1818.
GLAMORGAN :							
Cardiff County Gaol -	61	30	10	27	4	291	- - A new prison just finished. Cost about 10,000 l.
Swansea House of Correction.	49	53	4	–	–	–	- - Erected in 1828. Polygonal building round the courts. Cost about 4,500 l.

COUNTIES and PRISONS.	Greatest Number of Prisoners at one time.	Number of Sleeping Cells.	Number of Day Rooms or Wards.	Additional Cells may be made by dividing large Rooms	New Cells wanting.	Estimated Expense of providing separate Cells.	REMARKS.
MERIONETH:						£.	
Dolgelly County Gaol and House of Correction.	24	–	3	30	–	600*	- - Erected in 1828. Cost about 2,500 l.
MONTGOMERY:							
County Gaol - -	18	17	8	17	–	82 }	- - A new prison is just finish-
Ditto House of Correction.	18	9	–	10	–	92 }	ed, to contain about 50 cells.
PEMBROKE:							
Haverfordwest County Gaol and House of Correction.	62	44	8	12	6	385	- - Enlarged in 1820. Cost about 3,500 l.
RADNOR:							
Presteign County Gaol and House of Correction.	18	32	3	–	–	–	- - Erected in 1822. Four wing buildings attached. Cost about 3,500 l.
WALES - - -	474	326	71	163	45	4,699	
ENGLAND - -	17,508	9,874	1,159	4,017	4,212	263,062	
TOTAL - -	17,982	10,200	1,230	4,180	4,257	267,761	

It appears from the preceding statement, that of 136 prisons included in the Gaol Act, 36 only have a sufficient number of cells to admit of each person being confined separately at night. The total number of offenders in these prisons at one time in the year was 17,982, but the number of sleeping-rooms and cells was only 10,200; leaving a deficiency of 7,782 cells. In several gaols of the largest description, which were originally constructed without sleeping-cells, (as Newgate, Clerkenwell, &c.) the number of persons in each night-room varies from 15 to 30; while in many prisons which contain separate cells, the increase of offenders has of late years rendered it necessary to place three or more together at night.

There are altogether in the county prisons, &c. about 1,200 day-rooms,* for the different classes of criminals, most of which, together with the large sleeping-rooms, may be divided into cells. But even with this subdivision, it appears that there would still be a deficiency of about 4,000 cells. The space usually allotted for each individual in the present large sleeping-rooms does not exceed 2 feet 6 inches, which is scarcely half the width requisite for a single cell. The dimensions of each sleeping-cell should be at least 8 feet by 6 feet, and 10 feet high, if arched; but if the ceiling is flat, 9 feet will be a sufficient height. As a security against prisoners communicating together from adjoining cells, the division-walls should be two bricks thick. Those cells in which prisoners are intended to be employed in solitude, for a lengthened period, should not be less than 10 feet by 8 feet, and 10 feet high. Scarcely any of the present gaols contain cells of sufficient capacity for this purpose, with the exception of those rooms which are appropriated for debtors.

The prisons which are included in the Gaol Act may be classed as follows, in regard to their particular form of construction :

Radiating plans, having the means of central inspection - - -	15
Ditto, but in which the inspection is incomplete - - - -	18
Ditto, ditto, buildings attached to centre - - - - -	10
Circular or polygonal plan, with buildings round airing courts - -	13
Quadrangular plan, or parallel buildings - - - - -	41
Irregular plans, (chiefly old prisons) - - - - - -	28
Ditto, with modern additions - - - - - - -	11
TOTAL - - - -	136

* This number does not include the rooms appropriated for debtors, which are generally larger than the ordinary prison cells. It is calculated that about 2,000 additional cells may be formed from the apartments now occupied by debtors. But the expense of such alterations is not included in the above statement.

ENGLAND
AND WALES.

GENERAL ESTIMATE of the EXPENSE of ALTERING or ENLARGING the PRISONS belonging to CORPORATE and other Local Jurisdictions, (not included in the Act 4 Geo. 4, c. 64,) for the purpose of providing SEPARATE CELLS for the greatest Number of Prisoners confined at one time during the Year 1832.

[Framed from Parliamentary Returns, (Nos. 484 & 485) Ordered, by The House of Commons, to be printed, 5 July 1833.*]

PRISONS.	Greatest Number of Prisoners at one time.	Number of Rooms and Cells.	Additional Cells to be made by dividing large Rooms.	New Cells wanting.	Estimated Expenses.	REMARKS.
					£.	
Abingdon Borough Gaol -	2	2	-	–	–	- - For temporary confinement and debtors.
Andover - ditto -	5	3	2	–	42	- - Rebuilt in 1814. Cost about 700 l.
Axbridge - ditto -	5	2	1	2	100 *	Lock-up house.
Banbury Borough Gaol and House of Correction.	15	5	-	10	400 *	
Barnstaple - ditto - ditto	9	22	-	–	–	- - Rebuilt in 1828. Cost about 1,600 l.
Basingstoke Town Gaol -	6	3	2	1	80 *	Built in 1816.
Bath City Gaol - -	6	6	-	–	-	For temporary confinement only.
Ditto Debtors' Prison -	28	13	16	–	320 *	
Berwick-on-Tweed Borough Gaol and House of Correction.	33	12	30	–	600 *	
Beverley Town Gaol -	9	13	–	–	–	
Bewdley Borough Gaol -	no return	-	–	–	–	Lock-up house. Rebuilt.
Bideford Borough Gaol -	6	6	–	–	–	Rebuilt in 1831. Cost 260 l.
Birmingham Town Gaol, for debtors.	42	4	12	26	1,280 *	
Bishop's Castle Borough Gaol.	-	2	–	–	–	Lock-up house, and for debtors.
Boston Borough Gaol and House of Correction.	31	22	5	4	210	Erected in 1818. Cost 4,600 l.
Bradford Town Gaol, for debtors.	26	9	20	–	400 *	
Bradninch Borough Gaol -	2	5	–	–	–	
Bridgnorth Town Gaol -	10	7	5	–	100 *	- - For temporary confinement, and debtors.
Bridgwater Borough Gaol -	11	6	6	–	120 *	Enlarged in 1822.
Bridport - - ditto -	-	2	–	–	–	Lock-up house.
Buckingham - ditto -	6	4	2	–	16	The assizes are held here yearly.
Cambridge Town Gaol and House of Correction.	47	52	–	–	–	- - A new prison built in 1828, on the radiating plan, for eight classes. Cost 12,000 l.
Canterbury City Gaol and House of Correction.	28	26	6	–	120 *	- - Enlarged in 1830. Cost about 4,000 l.
Chesterfield Town Gaol, for debtors.	no return	-	–	–	–	
Chichester City Gaol -	13	6	1	6	260 *	
Chipping-Norton Borough Gaol.	-	2	–	–	–	Lock-up house.
Clithero Borough Gaol -	-	-	–	–	–	Ditto. Recently built.
Cockermouth Ditto - -	8	3	–	5	200 *	For temporary confinement.
Colchester Borough Gaol and House of Correction.	28	8	16	4	500	
Congleton Borough Gaol -	2	4	–	–	–	Lock-up house.
Dartmouth Borough Gaol	3	2	–	1	40 *	- - Erected in 1813. Cost about 300 l.
Daventry - ditto -	2	4	–	–	–	Erected in 1826. Cost 420 l.
Deal Town Gaol - -	7	4	7	–	50	
Derby Borough Gaol and House of Correction.	41	26	22	–	187	- - Since 1830, the old County Gaol has been occupied by the borough prisoners.

* *Note.*—At those prisons where no statement of the expense has been returned, the new cells are estimated at 40 l. each; and the additional cells, from dividing the day-rooms, &c., at 20 l. each. No estimates were received from the places marked against thus *.

ENGLAND
AND WALES.

PRISONS.	Greatest Number of Prisoners at one Time.	Number of Rooms and Cells.	Additional Cells to be made by dividing large Rooms.	New Cells wanting.	Estimated Expenses.	REMARKS.
					£.	
Doncaster Borough Gaol -	12	8	8	–	160 *	- - Rebuilt in 1829. Cost about 3,000 l.
Dover Town Gaol & House of Correction.	33	10	23	–	460 *	- - Erected in 1823. Cost about 6,000 l.
Dover Castle Debtors Gaol	30	8	10	12	680 *	
Droitwich Borough Gaol -	no return	-	–	–	–	Lock-up house.
Dymchurch Town Gaol -	2	4	–	–	–	
Ecclesall Debtors' Gaol -	28	5	10	13	720 *	
Ely Franchise Gaol - -	17	7	8	2	240 *	
Evesham Borough Gaol -	8	4	2	2	110	
Eye - - ditto - -	3	2	–	1	25	Built in 1817.
Falmouth Town Gaol and House of Correction.	12	7	–	5	200 *	Built in 1830. Cost 410 l.
Faversham Town Gaol -	5	4	1	–	20 *	Built in 1815. Cost about 1,200 l.
Folkstone - ditto - -	3	3	–	–	–	
Fordwich - ditto - -	no return	-	–	–	–	Lock-up house.
Grantham Borough Gaol and House of Correction.	21	16	–	5	200 *	- - Erected in 1823. Cost about 1,200 l.
Gravesend Town Gaol -	6	2	2	2	230	Lock-up house, and for debtors.
Greenwich Debtors' Gaol -	15	4	–	11	300	
Great Grimsby Borough Gaol	5	3	–	2	80 *	
Halifax Town Gaol, debtors	16	7	10	–	200 *	
Harwich Borough Gaol -	11	6	–	5	200 *	
Hastings Town Gaol -	9	5	4	–	60	- - Erected in 1821. Cost about 800 l.
Hedon Borough Gaol -	no return.	1	–	–	–	Lock-up house.
Helleston - ditto - -	ditto	1	–	–	–	- Ditto.
Henley-upon-Thames Town Gaol.	ditto	2	–	–	–	- Ditto.
Hereford City Gaol and House of Correction.	18	9	–	9	360 *	Enlarged in 1825.
Hertford Borough Gaol -	3	4	–	–	–	Contracted with county.
Hexham Town Gaol, debtors	3	6	–	–	–	
Hythe Town Gaol - -	4	3	1	–	25	
Ipswich Borough Gaol -	41	31	–	10	500 ⎫	Recently enlarged.
Ditto - ditto - Bridewell	8	10	–	–	– ⎭	
Kingston-upon-Thames Town Gaol, for debtors.	10	no return.	–	–	–	United with county.
Knaresborough Gaol -	3	5	–	–	–	Lock-up house.
Ditto - Castle Gaol, debtors	8	2	2	4	200 *	
Lancaster Borough Gaol -	12	2	3	7	340 *	
Launceston Town Gaol -	1	3	–	–	–	Contracted with county.
Leeds Borough Gaol -	86	12	4	70	7,000	- - Erected in 1813, for temporary confinement and prisoners during the sessions. The estimate includes the purchase of ground necessary for additions.
Lenton Debtors' Gaol -	13	5	4	4	200	
Leominster Borough Gaol -	2	3	–	–	–	Lock-up house, and for debtors.
Lichfield City Gaol and House of Correction.	16	20	–	–	–	Recently enlarged.
Lincoln City Gaol & House of Correction.	23	19	8	–	150	- - Erected in 1807. Cost about 7,000 l.
Liskeard Borough Gaol -	no return.	2	–	–	–	Lock-up house.
Looe, East - ditto - -	2	3	–	–	–	- Ditto.
Looe, West - ditto - -	1	2	–	–	–	- Ditto.
Ludlow Town Gaol - -	4	9	–	–	–	Enlarged in 1821.
Lydd Town Gaol - -	no return.	2	–	–	–	Lock-up house.
Lyme Regis Borough Gaol	ditto	2	–	–	–	- Ditto.
Lynn Borough Gaol and House of Correction.	18	26	–	–	–	- - Enlarged in 1830. Cost about 1,100 l.
Macclesfield Town Gaol -	no return	2	–	–	–	Lock-up house.
Ditto - Debtors' Gaol	6	5	3	–	100	Rebuilt in 1826.
Maidenhead Town Gaol -	no return.	2	–	–	–	Lock-up house.
Marlborough Town Gaol -	ditto	–	–	–	–	Ditto - part of Guildhall.

(continued)

ENGLAND
AND WALES.

PRISONS.	Greatest Number of Prisoners at one time.	Number of Rooms and Cells.	Additional Cells to be made by dividing large Rooms.	New Cells wanting.	Estimated Expenses.	REMARKS.
					£.	
Newark Borough Gaol -	13	5	11	–	150	
Newbury - ditto - -	12	8	4	–	80*	
Newcastle-under-Lyme Town Gaol.	21	5	4	12	800	
Northampton Town Gaol and House of Correction.	32	17	4	11	600	- - Enlarged in 1823. Cost about 900 l.
Okehampton Borough Gaol	3	2	↘	1	320	- - Estimate for a new prison, to contain 4 rooms.
Oswestry Borough Gaol -	4	4	–	–	–	Erected in 1828. Cost about 500 l.
Oxford City Gaol and House of Correction.	35	38	–	–	–	Erected about 1790.
Penrith Town Gaol - -	no return		–	–	–	Lock-up house.
Penryn Borough Gaol -	3	2	–	1	40*	
Penzance Town Gaol and House of Correction.	15	8	8	–	160*	Erected in 1825. Cost 675 l.
Peterborough City Gaol -	16	4	3	9	420*	} - - These prisons are detached from each other.
Ditto - House of Correction.	28	11	2	15	640*	
Plymouth Borough Gaol and House of Correction.	32	17	–	15	210	Recently enlarged.
Plympton-earle Borough Gaol.	2	2	–	–	–	Lock-up house.
Pontefract Borough Gaol -	7	5	–	2	150	- Ditto - - and for debtors.
Poole Town Gaol and House of Correction.	6	8	–	–	–	
Queenborough Borough Gaol.	1	2	–	–	–	Lock-up house.
Reading Borough Gaol -	10	11	–	–	–	
Richmond - ditto - -	4	2	–	2	100	
Ditto - Liberty Gaol, for debtors.	5	5	–	–	–	
Ripon Liberty Gaol, debtors	2	5	–	–	–	} These are separate prisons.
Ditto Borough Gaol and House of Correction.	17	17	–	–	–	
Rochester City Gaol and House of Correction.	9	9	–	–	–	
Romford Liberty Gaol -	7	3	3	1	100*	
Romney New Town Gaol -	1	6	–	–	–	Lock-up house. Enlarged in 1824.
Romsey Town Gaol -	no return	2	–	–	–	- Ditto - - Rebuilt in 1821.
Rothwell Town Gaol, debtors.	18	12	–	6	200	
Rye Town Gaol - -	4	6	∓	–	–	Contracted with county.
Saffron-Walden Town Gaol	4	4	–	–	–	Erected in 1820. Cost 500 l.
St. Alban's Liberty Gaol -	29	11	18	–	360*	} - - Enlarged in 1826, at the expense of 1,400 l.
Ditto - House of Correction.	42	7	18	17	1,040*	
St. Briavel's Liberty Gaol, for debtors.	5	1	–	4	160	
St. Ive's Borough Gaol -	1	2	–	–	–	For temporary confinement.
Saltash - - ditto - -	2	4	–	–	–	- - - Ditto.
Sandwich Town Gaol and House of Correction.	21	26	–	–	–	- - Erected in 1830. Cost about 4,500 l.
Scarborough Town Gaol, for debtors.	4	4	–	–	–	
Scarborough House of Correction.	6	3	3	–	60*	
Seaford Town Gaol - -	1	2	–	–	–	Lock-up house.
Shaftesbury Borough Gaol	no return	2	–	–	–	- Ditto.
Sheffield Town Gaol, debtors	85	11	44	30	2,080*	
Southampton Town Gaol -	11	5	2	4	200*	
Ditto - - House of Correction.	25	9	5	11	540*	
Ditto - - Debtors' Gaol	9	6	3	–	60*	
South-Molton Borough Gaol	4	6	–	–	–	- - Rebuilt in 1828. Cost about 1,500 l.
Southwold - - ditto -	2	4	–	–	–	
Stamford Borough Gaol and House of Correction.	10	16	–	–	–	
Stockport Town Gaol -	no return	–	–	–	–	Lock-up house, and for debtors.
Sudbury Borough Gaol -	ditto	4	–	–	–	- - Lock-up house. Rebuilt in 1830. Cost 580 l.
Sutton-Coldfield Town Gaol	ditto	–	–	–	–	Lock-up house. Built in 1830.

PRISONS.	Greatest Number of Prisoners at one time.	Number of Rooms and Cells.	Additional Cells to be made by dividing large Rooms.	New Cells wanting.	Estimated Expenses.	REMARKS.
					£.	
Tenterden Town Gaol -	3	4	—	—	—	Contracted with county.
Tewkesbury Borough Gaol and House of Correction.	12	10	2	—	40*	- - Erected in 1816. Cost about 3,000 l.
Thetford Borough Gaol -	8	11	—	—	—	
Tiverton Liberty Gaol, for debtors.	2	1	—	1	37	
Tiverton House of Correction	10	8	2	—	50	
Torrington Borough Gaol -	4	5	—	—	—	
Totness - - ditto -	no return	2	—	—	—	Lock-up house.
Tregony - - ditto -	—	1	—	—	—	- Ditto.
Truro - - - ditto -	9	6	3	—	60*	Contracted with county.
Wallingford - ditto -	3	2	—	1	40*	
Walsall - - ditto -	9	8	1	—	20*	
Wareham - - ditto -	no return	1	—	—	—	Lock-up house.
Wellington Liberty Gaol, debtors.	9	6	4	—	49	
Wells City Gaol - -	no return	—	—	—	—	- Erected in 1805. Cost 575 l. For temporary confinement, and at the assizes.
Weymouth Borough Gaol -	2	2	—	—	—	Lock-up house.
Wigan - - ditto - -	no return	5	—	—	—	- Ditto.
Wilton - - ditto - -	ditto	—	—	—	—	- Ditto.
Winchelsea Town Gaol -	—	3	—	—	—	- Ditto.
Winchester City Gaol -	8	7	—	1	127	- - Erected in 1801. Cost about 3,000 l.
Windsor Borough Gaol -	20	10	2	8	30*	
Wokingham Town Gaol -	no return	—	—	—	—	Lock-up house.
Wycombe (Chipping) Borough Gaol.	8	4	2	2	120*	- - For temporary confinement. Built in 1818.
Yarmouth Town Gaol -	27	26	1	—	20*	⎫ - - Enlarged in 1824. Cost about
Ditto - Ho. of Correction	25	16	4	5	280*	⎭ 4,000 l.
York, St. Peter's, Liberty Gaol	3	6	—	—	—	
TOTAL, ENGLAND - -	1,679	1,070	409	382	27,458	
WALES.						
Aberystwith Town Gaol -	7	2	—	5	200*	
Bala - - - ditto - -	2	4	—	—	—	
Brecknock Borough Gaol -	3	4	—	—	—	
Carmarthen ditto -	26	14	—	12	150	Erected in 1809. Cost 2,100 l.
Corwen - - ditto - -	3	5	—	—	—	
Kidwelly - ditto - -	2	4	—	—	—	Lock-up house.
Newport - - ditto - -	no return	—	—	—	—	- Ditto.
Pembroke - ditto - -	2	2	—	—	—	- Ditto.
Radnor - - ditto - -	3	2	1	—	20*	- Ditto.
Swansea Debtors' Gaol -	10	4	8	—	160	
Tenby Borough Gaol -	no return	2	—	—	—	
Welsh-pool ditto - -	ditto	—	—	—	—	Lock-up house.
Wrexham - ditto - -	9	6	—	3	120*	For temporary confinement.
TOTAL, WALES - -	67	49	9	20	650	
TOTAL ENGLAND ⎱ - - and WALES ⎰	1,746	1,119	418	402	28,108	

TREAD-WHEEL LABOUR.

Variations in the Number of Hours of Labour, and Feet Ascent per Day, on the TREAD-WHEELS at the following Prisons, (from Parliamentary Returns inserted in Report of Select Committee on Secondary Punishments, 1832.)

PRISONS.	Hours of Labour.		Feet Ascent per Day.	
	Summer.	Winter.	Summer.	Winter.
Bedford Gaol - - - - - -	10	7	5,000	3,600
— House of Correction - - - -	10	6	9,333	—
Durham Gaol - - - - -	9	6	10,867	7,560
Exeter House of Correction - - - -	8	7	9,860	8,612
Knutsford Ditto - - - - -	10	7	14,000	9,800
Reading Gaol - - - - -	8	8	12,564	12,564
Worcester Gaol - - - - -	10	8	13,600	10,880

No. 2.—ENGLAND AND WALES (COUNTY PRISONS, &c.)

STATEMENT showing the want of uniformity in the management of the several PRISONS included in the Gaol Act; the average Number in confinement at one time; the whole Number committed during the Year; the proportion of Prisoners at Hard Labour or other Employments; the Amount of Earnings; Cost of Food, Clothing and Bedding; annual Expense for Maintenance; Salaries of Officers; Cost of Buildings and Repairs;* Number of Sick and Deaths; Punishments by Solitary Confinement, &c.

* The annual expense of Prison buildings and repairs is taken from the average cost of the last thirty years, during which period many of the Gaols have been rebuilt or enlarged; and on this account the sum appears high. In estimating, however, the cost per head, the average number of prisoners is taken for the last year, although in former years the number was considerably less.

[Compiled from the "Gaol Returns" for 1832, Ordered by the House of Commons to be printed, 18 February 1833; and also from Parliamentary Returns of "Prison Expenses," "Gaolers' Salaries," &c. for 1832.]

COUNTY PRISONS, &c.	Average Number of Prisoners at one time.	Proportion of Prisoners at Hard Labour, or other Employments — Tread-wheel, &c.	Other Employments.	Prisoners' Earnings during the Year. (£. s. d.)	Weekly Cost of Food per Head. (s. d.)	Annual Cost of Clothing and Bedding per Head — Males. (£. s. d.)	Females. (£. s. d.)	Maintenance of Prisoners. (£.)	Salaries of Officers. (£.)	Annual Expense for each Prisoner. (£. s.)	Average Annual Expenses of Buildings and Repairs. (for 30 years) (£.)	Total Annual Expense of each Prisoner. (£. s.)	Solitary Confinement.	Whipping.	Irons.	Greatest Number of Sick at one time.	Deaths during the Year.	Total Number of Prisoners during the Year.
ENGLAND.																		
BEDFORD: County Gaol and House of Correction.	53	27 p' cent.	-	no account -	2/6 ; 3/- if at hard labour.	3 10 -	- - -	472	436	17 -	435	25 -	18	-	8	10	-	171
BERKS: New House of Correction.	38	84 p' cent.	-	52 18 3	3/3	3 7 6	- - -	370	358	19 -	275 new prison.	26 -	15	-	-	7	-	229
BERKS: Reading County Gaol and House of Correction.	126	53 p' cent.	4 p' cent.	no account -	before trial 3/2 ; 2/7 after trial ; if at hard labour 3/7¾.	3 13 8	3 3 9	2,766	757	28 -	530 new prison.	32 -	30	2	-	12	-	495
BUCKS: Abingdon House of Correction (tried and untried.)	38	[no tread-wheel,] 68 p' cent. various.	-	48 16 10	3/2 ; 2/6 for short periods (one month and under,)	2 7 9	2 6 -	903	350	33 -	616 new prison.	49 -	7	1	1	6	-	220
BUCKS: Aylesbury County Gaol and House of Correction.	177	36 p' cent.	14 p' cent.	no account -	3/6 if at hard labour.	no account	no account	2,038	856	16 -	1,114	22 15 -	10	-	-	21	14 (9 of cholera.)	668
CAMBRIDGE: County Gaol and House of Correction.	72	47 p' cent.	14 p' cent.	61 15 5	1/10 ; 2/7 if at hard labour.	2 - -	- - -	697	630	18 -	737 new prison.	28 -	6	-	2	3	-	344
CHESTER: County Gaol	119	[no tread-wheel,] 42 p' cent. various.	-	615 16 9	2/1	1 17 6	- - -	2,143	1,103	27 -	2,765 including new county courts.	50 -	54	-	4	16	4	157

Prison	No.	%	%	Earnings £ s. d.	Cost	£ s. d.	£ s. d.	£ s. d.	Total				(new)									Greatest no.
Knutsford House of Correction (tried and untried.)	265	46 p'cent.	7 p'cent.	1,032 5 1	2/4	2 5	—	—	3,419	999	17	—	3,113 new prison.	28	—	22	—	—	24	2		1,109
CORNWALL: Bodmin County Gaol and House of Correction.	152	57 p'cent.	8 p'cent.	no account	2/6	— 18 9	16	—	1,731	985	18	—	461	21	—	44	—	20	5	1		684
CUMBERLAND: Carlisle County Gaol and House of Correction.	97	50 p'cent.	4 p'cent.	no account	2/1 (3/3 if at hard labour.)	2 4 6	—	—	1,197	786	20 10	—	1,440 new prison.	35	—	16	—	—	15	6 (all of cholera.)		390
DERBY: County Gaol and House of Correction.	149	47 p'cent.	5 p'cent.	no account	2/9	2 3 3	1 15 10	—	1,547	959	16 16	—	2,450 new prison.	33	—	111	—	—	14	—		644
DEVON: Exeter County Gaol and House of Correction. (Separate prisons, but adjoining.)	253	56 p'cent.	5 p'cent.	192 8 10	2/10	no account	—	—	3,033	960	15 15	—	2,633 chiefly new.	26	—	143	53	3	9 / 34	4 (3 of cholera) / 4 (1 of cholera)		460 / 758
DORSET: Dorchester County Gaol and House of Correction.	142	54 p'cent.	20 p'cent.	no account	2/6	2 10	—	—	1,661	774	17	—	664	21 16	—	188	1	2	6	2		563
DURHAM: County Gaol and House of Correction.	235	60 p'cent. various.	—	no account	2/9	4 1 8	3 13 9	—	2,996	1,107	17 10	—	5,052 new prison and county courts.	39	—	65	—	3	12	2		1,024
ESSEX: Chelmsford County Gaol and House of Correction.	77	—	30 p'cent. (females.)	no account	2/11	3 10	—	—	651	892	20	—	921	32	—	7	—	—	11	1		377
Springfield ditto	302	36 p'cent.	22 p'cent.	225 6 2	2/11 (3/9 if at hard labour.)	2 6	—	—	3,458	1,230	15 10	—	1,738 new prison.	21	—	139	1	4	33	1		1,400
Ilford House of Correction (tried and untried.)	43	32 p'cent.	—	none	2/2	2 6	—	—	843	433	29	10	212 new prison.	34 10	—	6	—	—	5	—		377
Halstead ditto	40	80 p'cent.	—	none	3/4½ no account	1 1	—	—	776	272	26	—	110	28 19	—	—	—	—	5	—		404
Newport ditto (untried)	8	—	—	none	3/6 no account	—	—	—	166	50	27	—	37	31	—	—	—	—	2	—		41
Colchester ditto	5	—	—	none	none	—	—	—	151	93	48	—	24	53 10	—	—	—	—	—	—		61
GLOUCESTER: County Gaol (Penitentiary not included.)	161	—	14 p'cent.	no account	2/-½	3 16	—	—	2,165	1,298	21 10	—	590	25	—	71	—	6	4	3		722
Horsley House of Correction (tried and untried.)	79	68 p'cent.	6 p'cent.	no account	no account	—	—	—	549	268	10 7	—	64	11 3	—	—	—	—	2	—		377
Northleach House of Correction (tried and untried.)	52	90 p'cent.	—	46 13 11	2/6	3 16	—	—	317	267	11 5	—	48	12 3	—	—	—	—	2	1		412
Little Dean ditto (tried and untried.)	28	no tread-wheel, 86 p'cent. various.	—	4 18 7	2/	3 16	—	—	202	180	13 13	—	32	14	—	4	—	—	—	—		130
Lawford's Gate ditto	18	85 p'cent.	—	none	no account	7	—	—	370	187	30 18	—	40	33	—	—	—	—	;	—		393
Carried forward	2,729	—	—	2,280 19 10	—	—	—	—	34,621	16,230	—	—	26,101	—	—	956	58	53	258	45		12,610

593.   y

ENGLAND and WALES (County Prisons, &c.)—*continued.*

COUNTY PRISONS, &c.	Average Number of Prisoners at one time.	Proportion at Hard Labour — Tread-wheel, &c.	Proportion — Other Employments.	Prisoners' Earnings during the Year.	Weekly Cost of Food per Head.	Clothing & Bedding per Head — Males	Clothing & Bedding per Head — Females	Maintenance of Prisoners.	Salaries of Officers.	Annual Expense for each Prisoner.	Average Annual Expenses of Buildings and Repairs.	Total Annual Expense for each Prisoner.	Punishments — Solitary Confinement.	Punishments — Whipping.	Punishments — Irons.	Greatest Number of Sick at one time.	Deaths during the Year.	Total Number of Prisoners during the Year.
				£ s. d.	s. d.	£ s. d.	£ s. d.	£	£	£ s. d.	£	£ s.						
Brought forward	2,729	-	-	2,280 19 10	-	-	-	34,621	16,230	- - -	26,101	- -	956	58	53	258	45	12,610
HANTS: Winchester County Gaol	109	-	-	no account	Criminals 2/1 Debtors, 3/2	Criminals 1 19 – Debtors 3 6 –	-	675	785	13 8	102	14 7	-	-	2	1	-	454
Ditto House of Correction	180	91 p' cent.	-	no account	2/4¼ 3/1½ if at hard labour.	2 14	-	1,929	635	14 4	635 new prison.	17 15	11	-	-	4	-	710
Gosport ditto (tried and untried).	36	No Tread-wheel. 38 per cent. various.	-	none	2/4	no account		173	270	12 6	120	15 12	32	-	1	3	-	372
HEREFORD: County Gaol and House of Correction.	108	No Tread-wheel. 84 per cent. various.	-	102 1 10	3/8	1 19 –	-	1,419	864	21 -	344	24 -	69	-	2	9	1	406
HERTFORD: County Gaol and House of Correction (separate Prisons, but adjoining.)	165	38 p' cent.	4 p' cent.	no account	1/9 3/6 if at hard labour.	no account		1,933	994	17 15	331	20 -	40	-	10	3 / 5	- / 1	305 / 380
HUNTINGDON: County Gaol and House of Correction.	34	20 p' cent.	-	6 5 8	1/9 3/6 if at hard labour.	2 - -	-	444	322	22 10	709 new prison.	43 6	27	3	1	3	-	159
KENT: Maidstone County Gaol & House of Correction.	430	46 p' cent.	11 p' cent.	no account	2/3½	Clothing, - 10 7	- 5 7	3,661	1,767	12 12	7,817 new prison.	30 16	550	-	1	20	7	2,060
Canterbury ditto	75	66 p' cent.	9 p' cent.	25 6 11	2/4½	2 9 9	1 19 6	662	600	17 -	301	20 16	65	-	-	7	1	425
LANCASTER: County Gaol	470	11 p' cent.	43 p' cent.	399 5 9	Criminals 2/2½ Debtors 1/5	1 13 9	-	2,856	2,184	10 14	2,080 part new.	15 2	178	-	-	16	10	999
Liverpool, Kirkdale House of Correction (tried and untried.)	682	56 p' cent.	4 p' cent.	about 800 - -	1/6½	Clothing, - 14 6	- 12 -	6,843	1,907	12 16	3,108 new prison.	17 7	52	1	27	57	35 (34 of cholera.)	3,052
Manchester, Salford House of Correction (tried and untried.)	563	53 p' cent.	21 p' cent.	772 1 6	Males, 1/7 Females, 1/1¼	2 12 -	-	6,881	2,279	16 5	3,153 chiefly new.	21 17	70	-	-	30	22 (19 of cholera.)	3,800
Preston ditto (tried and untried.)	274	45 p' cent.	28 p' cent.	284 10 10 exclusive of repairs, &c. about £.400	1/8¼	2 4 -	-	3,185	978	15 4	862 part new.	18 -	274	-	-	11	2 (1 of cholera.)	1,223

Institution	No.	%	%	Expenditure £ s. d.	Allowance / rate	Daily allowance	In prison	Committed	days	days	Cost of building, &c.	Cost per prisoner £ s.					Deaths (of cholera)	Total
LEICESTER: County Gaol	79	-	-	no account	Before trial, Males, 2/2 Females, 1/10	1 3 7½	862	633	19	-	2,265 new prison.	47 10	81	-	1	6	1	409
House of Correction	101	80 p'cent.	3 p'cent.	114 5 4	2/5 3/1¼ at hard labour.	1 7 1	1,331	521	18	-	709 part new.	25	142	-	-	5	-	532
LINCOLN: County Gaol	61	-	-	none	2/8½ 3/6	2 13 -	990	1,010	32	15	no account	27 10	1	-	1	7	5	197
Louth House of Correction (tried and untried.)	66	58 p'cent.	55 p'cent. / 23 p'cent.	41 13 7	3/6 (each committal.)	- 13 -	927	488	21	8	401 chiefly new.	32 6	6	-	1	5	3	374
Spalding ditto (tried and untried.)	52	30 p'cent.	60 p'cent.	no account	3/7½	1 10 -	741	232	19	-	707 new prison.	-	10	-	1	7	-	248
Kirton ditto (tried and untried.)	65	44 p'cent.	8 p'cent.	24 16 10	no account	-	697	403	17	14	no account new prison.	34 14	47	-	2	10	2	425
Folkingham ditto (tried and untried.)	30	45 p'cent.	16 p'cent	9 10 8	2/7	no settled allowance	386	260	21	10	395 new prison.	42 10	1	-	1	6	2	178
Spilsby ditto (tried and untried.)	39	57 p'cent. (various.)	-	none	3/6	1 10 10	769	382	29	10	511 new prison.	24 13	4	-	-	7	-	191
Skirbeck ditto (tried and untried.)	17	30 p'cent.	-	none	3/6	no account	271	63	19	13	85 new prison.	-	-	-	-	-	-	113
MIDDLESEX: Clerkenwell County Gaol	336	-	13 p'cent.	no account	2/-	1 11 6	2,956	2,306	15	13	1,801 chiefly new.	21	149	-	-	9	5 (2 of cholera.)	7,782
Coldbath-fields House of Correction (tried and untried.)	1,254	85 p'cent. (various.)	-	228 6 10	3/1	2 5 2	20,545	4,863	20	5	Included in prisoners' expenses.	20 5	1,374	2	1	97	64 (36 of cholera.)	12,543
MONMOUTH: County Gaol and House of Correction.	52	20 p'cent.	3 p'cent.	31 7 6	2/3½ after 3 months.	2 8	1,001	261	24	5	144	27	14	-	2	1	-	118
Usk House of Correction (tried and untried.)	30	46 p'cent.	-	none	2/6	3 5 -	383	144	17	10	51 new prison.	19	20	-	-	2	1	169
NORFOLK: Norwich County Gaol and House of Correction.	170	60 p'cent. (various.)	-	no account	3/3 if at hard labour. Debtors, 1/6.	2 - 6	2,077	1,302	19	15	2,290 rebuilt and enlarged.	33 6	64	-	-	2	3	761
Walsingham House of Correction (tried and untried.)	78	48 p'cent.	12 p'cent.	92 1 4	2/8	2 - -	776	628	18	-	211 enlarged.	20 15	35	2	-	3	2	450
Swaffham ditto (tried and untried.)	51	63 p'cent.	-	no account	no account	no account	395	625	20	-	295 enlarged.	25 15	1	1	1	no acct	-	250
Wymondham ditto (tried and untried; females.)	24	-	80 p'cent.	no account	3/-	no account	355	245	25	-	159	31 12	2	-	-	3	-	72
NORTHAMPTON: County Gaol and House of Correction.	106	30 p'cent.	11 p'cent.	no account	2/9	3 6 -	1,847	480	21	18	405 enlarged.	25 15	28	-	-	7	2	409
Carried forward	8,466	-	-	5,612 14 5	-	-	102,591	44,661	-	-	56,092	-	4,303	67	105	604	214	52,176

593.

y 2

ENGLAND and WALES (COUNTY PRISONS, &c.)—continued.

COUNTY PRISONS, &c.	Average number of Prisoners at one time.	Proportion at Hard Labour — Tread-wheel, &c.	Proportion — Other Employments.	Prisoners' Earnings during the Year.	Weekly Cost of Food per Head.	Clothing & Bedding per Head — Males.	Clothing & Bedding — Females.	Maintenance of Prisoners.	Salaries of Officers.	Annual Expense for each Prisoner.	Average Annual Expenses of Buildings and Repairs.	Total Annual Expense for each Prisoner.	Punishments — Solitary Confinement.	Punishments — Whipping.	Punishments — Irons.	Greatest Number of Sick at one time.	Deaths during the Year.	Total Number of Prisoners during the Year.
				£ s. d.	s. d.	£ s. d.	£ s. d.	£	£	£ s.	£	£ s.						
Brought forward	8,466	-	-	5,612 14 5	-	- - -	- - -	102,591	44,661	- -	56,092	- -	4,303	67	105	604	214	52,176
NORTHUMBERLAND: Morpeth County Gaol and House of Correction.	54	60 p'cent.	8 p'cent.	no account	paid in money. 2/4	no account		602	503	20 10	2,380 new prison and county courts.	64 10	-	-	-	2	1	163
Tynemouth House of Correction (tried and untried.)	15	-	70 p'cent.	no account	ditto	no account		156	75	15 8	21	16 15	-	-	-	3	-	137
Alnwick ditto (tried and untried.)	14	-	42 p'cent.	no account	ditto	no account		154	54	15 -	52	18 -	-	-	-	4	-	173
Hexham ditto (tried and untried.)	9	-	44 p'cent.	no account	ditto	- 10 6		92	40	14 15	1½	16 -	-	-	-	2	1	61
NOTTINGHAM: County Gaol -	46	none	-	- none	3/6	1 5 -		453	430	19 -	260	24 15	10	-	1	10	-	159
Southwell House of Correction (tried and untried.)	154	52 p'cent.	14 p'cent	no account	2/11			1,500	655	14 -	490	17 -	140	-	1	39	-	864
OXFORD: County Gaol and House of Correction.	145	64 p'cent.	10 p'cent.	16 5 2	2/8	3 9 -		2,263	827	21 6	442	24 7	no account		-	18	5 3 from cholera	635
RUTLAND: Oakham County Gaol and House of Correction.	16	-	12 p'cent.	no account	3/6	3 18 -		170	260	26 15	369 new prison.	49 18	-	-	1	1	-	44
SALOP: Shrewsbury County Gaol and House of Correction.	176	No tread-wheel. 56 p'cent.	33 p'cent.	780 1 2	2/- ¼	1 1 -		2,220	937	18 -	680	21 16	77	1	3	9	5 2 from cholera	927
SOMERSET: Ilchester County Gaol -	137	-	54 p'cent.	none -	2/9	3 6 -		6,561	890	17 5	452 enlarged	-	131	-	2	6	4	432
Shepton Mallet House of Correction (tried and untried.)	250	56 p'cent.	10 p'cent.	339 17 1	2/1	3 10 6			826		462 (much enlarged)	19 13	31	1	2	8	2	1,179
Wilton ditto (tried and untried.)	128	52 p'cent.	8 p'cent.	288 4 5	2/9	3 10 6			600	-	341 (much enlarged)	-	61	-	3	4	-	580
STAFFORD: County Gaol and House of Correction.	363	50 p'cent.	13 p'cent.	576 13 11	1/11¾	3 1 -		5,552	1,372	19 -	705 enlarged	21 -	69	-	10	10	4	1,783

Establishment	No.	Employment A	Employment B	Earnings (£ s. d.)	Weekly cost	Allowance	Greatest no.	No.	(pair)	Capacity	(ages)	Col	Col	Col	Col	Col	Col
SUFFOLK: Bury County Gaol and House of Correction.	164		54 p' cent · 12 p' cent	186 13 2	1/10; 3/2 if at hard labour.	2 13 - · 2 5 6	1,869	1,043	18 -	1,530 new prison.	27	30	-	3	6	1	775
Ipswich ditto	125		all after trial.	no account	no account	no account	1,009	643	13 5	735 ditto.	19	31	-	1	1	-	518
Beccles House of Correction (tried and untried.)	39		53 p' cent · 15 p' cent	no account	2/1; 2/8 if at hard labour.	6 12 -	227	308	13 15	427 chiefly new.	24 15	13	-	-	5	-	154
Woodbridge House of Correction (tried and untried.)	25			none	3/	no account	306	150	18 -	252 new prison.	28	3	-	-	5	-	125
SURREY: Newington County Gaol	304			none	2/; 2/2 after trial.	1 19 8 · 2 3 8	2,092	1,798	12 16	750	15 5	189	-	2	12	10 (4 from cholera)	3,146
Brixton House of Correction.	236	all convicted.		no account	2/4	18/	2,011	1,369	14 6	1,832 new prison.	22	503	-	-	25	2	2,378
Guildford ditto	112	ditto	women	109 2 3	2/9	clothing, 15/	1,222	604	16 6	842	23 16	147	-	1	7	1 of cholera	485
Kingston ditto (tried and untried.)	31		labour voluntary.	no account	2/7½	2 5 0	383	353	23 15	173 enlarged.	29 6	12	-	-	4	-	288
SUSSEX: Horsham County Gaol	74		no regular employment	no account	2/7½	no account	958	616	21 5	274	24 19	11	-	-	9	1	232
Lewes House of Correction (tried and untried.)	128		78 p' cent · 8 p' cent.	70 18 8	2/10	2 2 6 · 1 18 10	1,386	801	17 -	362 enlarged.	20	79	-	-	6	3	922
Petworth ditto (tried and untried.)	62		65 p' cent · 16 p' cent.	71 1 2	2/6½	bedding, 6/6	535	548	17 10	83	18 16	3	-	-	6	-	296
Battel ditto (tried and untried.)	8		none	none	2/8	3 - -	58	60	14 15	63 new prison.	22 12	-	-	-	1	-	79
WARWICK: County Gaol - House of Correction (tried and untried.)	218 / 229	12 p' cent. · 82 p' cent	12 p' cent. · 6 p' cent.	33 15 2 / no account	2/8 / 2/8½	4 4 - / 18/each committal.	2,532 / 2,216	1,068 / 822	16 10 / 13 6	617 / 664	19 5 / 16 3	51 / 48	-	2 / 2	5 / 6	5 / 4	771 / 967
WESTMORELAND: Appleby County Gaol and House of Correction. Kendal House of Correction (tried and untried.)	18 / 18	- / no account	58 p' cent / -	no account / no account	2/4 / no account	no account / ditto	327	165 / 152	18	426 enlarged. / 94	32 6	-	-	-	3	-	59
WILTSHIRE: Salisbury County Gaol	109		20 p: cent.	none	2/5	no account	1,154	678	17 -	1,206 new prison.	28	4	-	20	5	-	255
Devizes House of Correction.	169	98 p' cent.		no account	2/6	2 6 6	2,448	767	19 -	1,748 new prison.	29	184	-	-	9	5	681
Carried forward	12,042			8,085 6 7			143,047	64,075		74,836		6,130	70	158	835	268	71,444

593.　　　　y 3

ENGLAND AND WALES (COUNTY PRISONS, &c.)—continued.

COUNTY PRISONS, &c.	Average Number of Prisoners at one time.	Proportion of Prisoners at Hard Labour, or other Employments. — Tread-wheel, &c.	Other Employments.	Prisoners' Earnings during the Year. (£ s. d.)	Weekly Cost of Food per Head. (s. d.)	Annual Cost of Clothing and Bedding per Head — Males. (£ s. d.)	Females. (£ s. d.)	Maintenance of Prisoners. (£)	Salaries of Officers. (£)	Annual Expense for each Prisoner. (£ s.)	Average Annual Expenses of Buildings and Repairs. (£)	Total Annual Expense for each Prisoner.	Punishments — Solitary Confinement.	Whipping.	Irons.	Greatest Number of Sick at one time.	Deaths during the Year.	Total Number of Prisoners during the Year.
Brought forward	12,042	-	-	8,085 6 7	-	-	-	143,047	64,075	-	74,836	-	6,130	70	158	835	268	71,444
WILTSHIRE—cont^d. Devizes old House of Correction (untried.)	40	-	none	none	2/1	no clothing bedding 15/		384	175	14 -	no account	-	7	-	-	2	-	211
Marlborough ditto (tried and untried).	19	-	none	none	2/0½	no account		129	140	14 -	27	15 12	-	1	1	2	-	95
WORCESTER: County Gaol and House of Correction.	181	40 p' cent.	6 p' cent.	164 12 9	1/9 3/8 if at hard labour.	3 1 -	2 16 -	1,796	1,131	16 4	1,128 new prison.	22 8	88	4	17	12	2	754
YORK: County Gaol	249	-	No regular employment.	no account	criminals 2/3 debtors 1/1¼	no account		1,989	1,943	15 16	1,011	20 -	9	-	-	18	4	773
North Allerton, North Riding, House of Correction (tried & untried.)	68	54 p' cent.	18 p' cent.	57 - 6	5/	- 7 6 each committal.	-	760	610	20 3	619 enlarged.	29 5	32	-	-	12	-	334
Beverley, East Riding, ditto (tried and untried.)	80	60 p' cent.	13 p' cent.	no account	2/6	4 11 -	-	1,071	563	20 10	1,378 part new.	37 14	39	-	-	10	-	459
Wakefield, West Riding, ditto (tried and untried.)	463	22 p' cent.	72 p' cent.	no account	2/3	6 10 -	-	4,079	1,346	11 15	2,046 part new.	16 -	250	-	-	56	28 (20 of cholera.)	2,662
TOTAL	13,142	-	-	8,306 19 10	-	-	-	153,255	69,983	-	81,045	-	6,555	75	176	947	302	76,732
WALES.																	
ANGLESEY: Beaumaris County Gaol and House of Correction.	22	no tread-wheel, 32 p' cent. various.	-	no account	2/4 in money.	no regular allowance		129	115	11 -	296 new prison.	24 10	7	-	-	2	-	63
BRECON: County Gaol and House of Correction.	26	42 p' cent. various.	-	none	1/7	3 4 9	-	250	290	20 15	111	25 -	3	-	2	-	-	74

Prison	No.	Nature of hard labour	Earnings	Cost per prisoner	(small)											Total
CARDIGAN: County Gaol and House of Correction.	15	41 p' cent. various. (10 p' cent.)	no account	2/2; 2/8½ if at hard labour.	2 2	126	180	20 8	44	23 6	4	–	–	2	–	51
CARMARTHEN: County Gaol and House of Correction (separate prisons).	25	no tread-wheel, 46 p' cent. various.	no account	from 2/ to 4/	no account	340	240	23 4	214	31 15	3	–	5	2	–	{62 53}
CARNARVON: County Gaol and House of Correction.	28	35 p' cent. various.	no account	2/4	no account	301	159	16 8	78	19 –	–	–	–	3	1	78
DENBIGH: Ruthin County Gaol and House of Correction.	30	42 p' cent. various.	no account	2/6 in money.	1 –	275	261	17 17	504 rebuilt.	34 13	–	3	3	3	1	108
FLINT: County Gaol and House of Correction.	33	no tread-wheel, 30 p' cent. various.	no account	3/	no account	425	180	18 6	201 enlarged.	24 8	–	–	–	1	–	82
GLAMORGAN: Cardiff County Gaol	48	18 p' cent. 30 p' cent.	none	2/4½	2 10 –	702	460	24 5	97	26 5	5	–	8 –	9	2	181
Swansea House of Correction (tried and untried.)	39	42 p' cent. 50 p' cent.	no account	2/9	2 9 6	413	215	16 –	183 new prison.	21 –	13	–	–	9	–	197
MERIONETH: Dolgelly County Gaol and House of Correction.	17	no tread-wheel, 17 p' cent. various.	no account	2/6 in money.	no account	152	114	15 15	105 new prison.	21 16	–	–	–	–	–	35
MONTGOMERY: County Gaol	20	–	none	2/	no account	325	90	18 8	214 a new Prison is building.	24 15	–	–	–	{4	–	53
House of Correction	14	–	none	2/	no account	182	30								–	102
PEMBROKE: Haverfordwest, County Gaol and House of Correction.	40	55 p' cent. 32 p' cent.	no account	2/9	– 10 1	456	201	16 8	279 enlarged.	23 8	4	–	2	7	2	263
RADNOR: Presteign County Gaol and House of Correction.	15	no tread-wheel, 17 p' ceat. various.	no account	3/	no account	152	125	18 10	123	26 13	–	–	–	–	–	49
TOTAL, WALES	372		– –			4,228	2,660		2,449		39	3	20	42	6	1,451
TOTAL, ENGLAND	13,142		8,306 19 10			153,255	69,983		81,045		6,555	75	176	947	302	76,732
ENGLAND & WALES	13,514		8,306 19 10			157,483	72,643		83,494		6,594	78	196	989	308	78,183
Corporate Prisons in England included in Act [vide p. 177.]	2,123		236 17 –			no account	no acc.t		16,136		354	10	18	189	37	22,889

593.

y 4

ENGLAND.—(Prisons of Corporate Jurisdictions, &c.)

Prisons of Corporate Jurisdictions included in the GAOL ACT.	Average Number of Prisoners at one time.	Proportion of Prisoners at Hard Labour, or other Employments. — Tread-wheel, &c.	Proportion — Other Employments.	Prisoners' Earnings during the Year.	Weekly Cost of Food per Head.	Annual Cost of Clothing and Bedding per Head — Males.	Clothing — Females.	Maintenance of Prisoners.	Salaries of Officers.	Annual Expense for each Prisoner.	Average Annual Expenses of Buildings and Repairs.	Total Annual Expense for each Prisoner.	Solitary Confinement.	Whipping.	Irons.	Greatest Number of Sick at one time.	Deaths during the Year.	Total Number of Prisoners during the Year.
				£. s. d.	s. d.	£. s. d.	£. s. d.				£.							
CITY OF LONDON: Newgate Gaol	490	none	5 p'cent.	no account	2/3	no account	no account	no account	—	—	1,670	—	20	—	2	29	4 (2 of chol.)	3,217
House of Correction, Giltspur-street.	142	no tread-wheel, 50 p'cent. various.	—	77 10 6	2/3	2 1 9	1 16 9	no account	—	—	660	—	26	—	1	10	5 (2 of cholera.)	5,920
Southwark Borough Gaol	94	none	none	none	1/8	- 18 9	—	no account	—	—	551	—	—	—	—	no account	2 of cholera	1,553
CITY OF WESTMINSTER. Tothill-fields House of Correction.	167	none	—	no account	no account	no account	—	no account	—	—	no account	—	62	—	—	5	3	3,857
CITY OF BRISTOL: New Gaol and House of Correction.	210	24 p'cent	36 p'cent.	no account	no account	no account	—	no account	—	—	2,326	—	15	—	—	30	14 (9 of cholera.)	610
Old Prison	28	—	33 p'cent.	none	no account	no account	—	no account	—	—	109	—	—	—	—	1	—	190
CITY OF CHESTER: Gaol and House of Correction.	27	—	80 p'cent.	no account	2/6	no account	—	no account	—	—	557 (new.)	—	2	—	—	2	—	55
CITY OF COVENTRY: Gaol and House of Correction.	51	34 p'cent.	—	no account	1/2	- 3 each committal.	—	no account	—	—	545 (new.)	—	1	—	—	2	—	304
CITY OF EXETER: Gaol and House of Correction.	35	27 p'cent.	21 p'cent.	no account	3/6 if at hard labour.	3 19 7	—	no account	—	—	372 (new.)	—	6	—	1	—	1	233
CITY OF GLOUCESTER: Gaol and House of Correction.	31	36 p'cent.	—	no account	2/11	no account	—	no account	—	—	285 (enlarged.)	—	—	—	—	5	—	90
CITY OF NORWICH: Gaol and House of Correction.	78	18 p'cent.	7 p'cent.	none	1/5½ debtors; 2/7¼ criminals; 3/1 if at hard labour.	3 1 6	—	no account	—	—	757 (new.)	—	92	1	1	8	—	900

Location	No.	Per cent.	Per cent.	£ s. d.	Ratio	£ s. d.	£ s. d.	Account	Capacity						No. committed
CITY OF WORCESTER: Gaol and House of Correction.	34	19 p'cent.	9 p'cent.	no account	2/10	3 - -	-	no account	427 (new.)	14	-	1	2	-	308
CITY OF YORK: Gaol	27	-	5 p'cent.	no account	2/10	1 5 6	-	no account	1,048 (new.)	-	-	-	7	-	91
House of Correction	50	31 p'cent.	26 p'cent.	no account	3/	1 5 6	-	no account	540 (new.)	9	3	4	10	-	447
TOWN OF KINGSTON-UPON-HULL: Gaol and House of Correction.	94	38 p'cent.	-	104 5 6	2/10	- 3 10 each committal.	-	on account	1,198 (new.)	-	-	-	28	2	756
BOROUGH OF LEICESTER: Gaol and House of Correction.	72	39 p'cent.	-	none	2/4	2 9 -	-	no account	606 (enlarged.)	24	-	3	8	-	829
BOROUGH OF LIVERPOOL: Gaol	173	none	none	none	2/11	- 10 10 each committal.	-	no account	1,172 (enlarged.)	4	6	1	4	3	1,655
TOWN OF NEWCASTLE-UPON-TYNE: Gaol and House of Correction.	100	46 p'cent.	5 p'cent.	55 1 -	2/4	2 1 6	1 19 -	no account	1,698 (new.)	48	-	-	38	1	691
TOWN OF NOTTINGHAM: Gaol	50	none	4 p'cent.	none	3/	1 15 -	-	no account	223	-	-	1	7	-	133
House of Correction	108	15 p'cent.	13 p'cent.	no account	3/7	1 13 6	-	no account	762 (rebuilt.)	20	-	4	7	1	1,045
BOROUGH OF PORTSMOUTH: Gaol and House of Correction:	62	-	15 p'cent.	no account	2/6	1 16 -	-	no account	630 (new.)	21	-	-	7	1	405
TOTAL	2,123	-	-	236 17	-	-	-	-	16,136	354	10	18	189	37	22,889

The total number of Prisoners (including Debtors and Vagrants) committed to the several Gaols and Houses of Correction in England and Wales (included in the Act) during the year 1832, was 101,072. This statement, however, includes all such prisoners as were again committed for further offences.* Many persons also, who, after conviction, pass from the Gaol to the House of Correction, where these are separate establishments, are returned at each prison, and consequently the aggregate amount is increased beyond the actual number of Criminal Offenders.

The general proportions of prisoners included in the Gaol Returns, are as follows :—Felons, 39¾ per cent.——Misdemeanants, &c. 49½ per cent.——Debtors, 10¾ per cent.

Of the criminal prisoners, the proportion of those convicted was 46 per cent, and of those for trial 54 per cent (the numbers being taken immediately preceding the Michaelmas Sessions.)

The proportion of Female Criminals to Males, was one in five. Of Male Criminals under 17 years of age, one in eleven. Of Females under 17 years of age, one in thirteen.

* During the year the number of prisoners who were ascertained to have been previously in confinement was (according to the Gaol Returns) 7,575. The number who had been confined twice, 2,718. Ditto thrice, 1,284. Ditto four times or oftener, 1,695. The re-committals appear to be heaviest at Houses of Correction. This arises from the great proportion of summary convictions for minor offences, vagrants, &c. which are sentenced to short terms of confinement; and it is generally found that offenders of this description return to prison more frequently than any others, in consequence of their destitute and friendless state when discharged.

In 1832 the number of Vagrants, &c. committed to the Houses of Correction in England and Wales, under the Act 5 Geo. IV. c. 83, amounted to 15,624, according to Returns published in the Report of the Poor Law Commissioners. Vide page 192 of this Appendix.

The total number of persons confined for Debt in the several Gaols during the year 1832, amounted to 16,661. This number embraces those confined in prisons exclusively for Debtors, as the King's Bench, Fleet, Marshalsea, &c. These prisons are not included in the Gaol Returns.

SCOTLAND.

STATEMENT of the Number of PRISONERS committed to the several Gaols, &c. during the Year; the greatest Number in confinement at one time, and the Number of Rooms and Cells in each Prison, &c.

COUNTIES, &c.	Number of Prisoners committed during the Year.	Greatest Number of Prisoners at one time.	Number of Rooms and Cells.	REMARKS.
ABERDEEN: County and Burgh Gaol - -	801	Debtors 65 Criminals 64 ——— 129	day rooms - 8 } sick rooms - 2 } sleeping rooms 60 }	A new prison built in 1830. Quadrangular form: six airing courts.
Ditto - Bridewell - -	no account	60	- - - 101	- - Erected in 1818. Parallelogram: four stories high. Each prisoner has a working-cell and also a sleeping-cell. Airing court round the building.
Old. Aberdeen Burgh Gaol - -	no account	no account	- - - 1 }	
Old Meldrum - ditto - -	- -	- -	- - - 2 }	
Fraserburgh - ditto - -	- -	- -	- - - 2 }	Lock-up houses for temporary confinement.
Inverary - - ditto - -	- -	- -	- - - 2 }	
Kintore - - ditto - -	- -	- -	- - - 1 }	
Peterhead - - ditto - -	- -	- -	- - - 1 }	
ARGYLE: Inverary County and Burgh Gaol -	87	36	day room - 1 } sleeping rooms 13 }	Erected about 1820. One airing court.
Campbell-town Burgh Gaol - - Isle of Mull Lock-up House.	41	17	- - - 6	Erected in 1747. No airing court.
AYR: County and Burgh Gaol - -	188	38	day rooms - 5 } cells - - 44 }	Erected in 1818. Four airing courts.
Irvine Burgh Gaol - - - (There are also fourteen lock up houses in different Burghs.)	40	10	rooms - 4	Erected in 1745. No airing courts. No resident keeper.
BANFF: County and Burgh Gaol - -	61	20	rooms - 5	Erected in 1798. No airing court. No resident keeper.
Cullen Burgh Gaol - - -	- -	- -	cells - - 3	Built in 1823. For temporary confinement only. No yard.
BERWICK: Greenlaw Connty and Burgh Gaol -	36	14	day rooms - 3 } cells - - 18 }	Erected in 1824. Three airing yards.
Lauder Burgh Gaol - - - (There are also four lock-up houses in different Burghs.)	10	2	rooms - 3	No airing yard. No resident keeper.
BUTE: Rothesay County and Burgh Gaol -	29	8	rooms - 4	Only one court. No resident keeper.
CAITHNESS: Wick County and Burgh Gaol -	no account	no account	rooms - 4	Erected in 1750.
CLACKMANNAN: The old Gaol having been in a ruinous state since the year 1815, the prisoners are committed to the adjoining county, Stirling. Alloa Lock-up House - - -	- -	- -	- - - 3	
CROMARTY: County and Burgh Gaol - -	- -	no account	rooms - 3	Erected in 1774.
DUMBARTON: County and Burgh Gaol - -	70	15	day rooms - 3 } cells - - 12 }	Erected in 1826. One large court round the prison.
Kirkintilloch Burgh Gaol - -	no account	- -	rooms - 2	Erected in 1813. No yard.
DUMFRIES: County and Burgh Gaol and House of Correction.	179	28	day rooms - 2 } cells - - 28 }	Erected in 1806. Two airing courts.
Annan Burgh Gaol - - -	24	4	rooms - 4	Erected about 1722. No airing court. No resident keeper.
Sanquhar - ditto - - -	26	3	rooms - 3	No airing yard. No resident keeper.
Lochmaben ditto - - - -	no account	- -	rooms - 2	No airing yard.
Carried forward - - -	1,592	384	- - - 355	

SCOTLAND (GAOLS, &c.)—*continued.*

COUNTIES, &c.	Number of Prisoners committed during the Year.	Greatest Number of Prisoners at one time.	Number of Rooms and Cells.	REMARKS.
Brought forward - - -	1,592	384	- - - 355	
EDINBURGH:				
County and City Gaol - - -	1,142	143	day rooms - 8 ⎫ sick ditto - 2 ⎬ cells - - 58 ⎭	Erected in 1816. Seven airing yards.
Ditto - - Bridewell - -	1,103	205	working cells 52 ⎱ sleeping d° 132 ⎰	Semicircular plan; four stories high. Tread-wheel labour and other employments.
Ditto - - Lock-up House -	1,192	50	rooms - 8	No airing yard.
Canongate (Debtors') Gaol - -	330	39	rooms - 9	No airing yard.
Leith Town Gaol - - - -	no account	- -	day rooms - 2 ⎱ cells - - 12 ⎰	Erected in 1828. No airing court.
Musselburgh ditto - - -	35	7	rooms - 4	No airing yard. No resident keeper.
Dalkeith - ditto - - -	29	5	rooms - 2	For temporary confinement. No airing yard. No resident keeper.
ELGIN:				
County and Burgh Gaol - -	32	- -	cells - - 2 rooms - 4	No yard. No resident keeper. This prison is about to be rebuilt.
Forres Burgh Gaol - - -	9	4	rooms - 2	No yard. No resident keeper.
FIFE:				
Cupar County and Burgh Gaol -	92	21	rooms - 10	Erected in 1813. One airing court.
Dunfermline Burgh Gaol - -	41	- -	rooms - 5	Erected in 1769. No airing yard.
Kirkaldy - - ditto - - -	90	18	rooms - 12	Erected in 1826. One airing court. No resident keeper.
Inverkeithing - ditto - - -	9	2	rooms - 3	Built in 1770. No airing yard.
Kinghorn - - ditto - - -	no account	- -	rooms - 2	Erected in 1827. One airing yard.
Dysart - - - ditto - - -	15	4	rooms - 4	An ancient building. No yard.
Auchtermuchty ditto - - -	10	2	rooms - 4	Built in 1728. One yard. No resident keeper.
Falkland - - ditto - - -	17	4	rooms - 2	Built in 1801. No yard. No resident keeper.
St. Andrew's - ditto - - -	13	- -	rooms - 4	No yard.
Pittenweem - ditto - - -	8	2	rooms - 3	No yard: no apartments for keeper.
Newburgh - - ditto - - -	no account	- -	rooms - 2	No residence for keeper.
Burnt-island - ditto - - -	3	1	rooms - 3	No yard. No resident keeper.
Earls-ferry - ditto - - -	- -	- -	rooms - 3	Erected in 1785. No airing yard. No re- [sident keeper.
Crail - - - ditto - - -	- -	2	rooms - 2	No yard.
Kilrenny - - ditto - - -	- -	- -	rooms - 2	No yard. No keeper's residence.
Anstruther, West - - -	- -	- -	rooms - 2	No yard.
Anstruther, East - - - -	5	2	rooms - 2	No yard.
FORFAR:				
County and Burgh Gaol - -	52	21	rooms - 5	Erected in 1788. No airing yard. No residence for keeper.
Dundee Burgh Gaol - - -	388	52	rooms - 10	Erected in 1734. No yard. No resident keeper. This prison is about to be rebuilt.
Aberbrothock ditto - - -	32	7	rooms - 7	No yard. No resident keeper.
Brechin - ditto - - -	33	8	rooms - 3	No yard. No resident keeper.
Montrose - ditto - - -	21	8	rooms - 3	No yard. No resident keeper.
HADDINGTON:				
County and Burgh Gaol - -	155	13	rooms - 9	No yard.
Dunbar Burgh Gaol - - -	12	3	rooms - 3	No yard.
North Berwick ditto - - -	- -	1	rooms - 2	No yard. No apartment for keeper.
INVERNESS:				
County and Burgh Gaol - -	120	37	rooms - 13	Assize town for seven counties. No court. [No resident keeper.
Portree (Isle of Sky) Lock-up House	- -	- -	cells - - 4	No yard.
Grantown Lock-up House - -	- -	- -	rooms - 2	
Kingussie ditto - - - -	- -	- -	rooms - 2	
KINCARDINE:				
Stone-haven County and Burgh Gaol	26	10	rooms - 5	No yard nor court.
Inverbervie Burgh Gaol - -	- -	- -	rooms - 2	For temporary confinement. No yard.
KINROSS:				
County Gaol - - - -	20	4	rooms - 4 ⎱ cells - - 2 ⎰	Erected in 1826. One airing court. No resident keeper.
KIRKCUDBRIGHT:				
County and Burgh Gaol - -	40	10	day rooms - 4 ⎫ sick rooms - 2 ⎬ cells - - 12 ⎭	Erected in 1816. Two airing yards.
New Galloway Burgh Gaol - -	9	5	rooms - 4	No yard.
Maxwell-town - ditto - -	- -	- -	rooms - 4	No yard.
Castle-Douglas ditto - -	- -	- -	rooms - 2	No yard.
Carried forward - - -	6,675	1,074	- - - 821	

SCOTLAND (GAOLS, &c.)—*continued.*

COUNTIES, &c.	Number of Prisoners committed during the Year.	Greatest Number of Prisoners at one time.	Number of Rooms and Cells.		REMARKS.
Brought forward - - -	6,675	1,074	- - - 821		
LANARK:					
Glasgow County and City Gaol -	1,202	185	day rooms - 10 cells - - 88	}	Erected in 1813. Quadrangular form. Two airing courts.
Ditto Bridewell - - -	1,389	275	cells - - 285		New part erected in 1826. Radiating plan: four detached wings.
Lanark Burgh Gaol - - -	26	8	rooms - 4		No yard. No resident keeper.
Catton - ditto - - -	153	8	rooms - 12		Erected in 1820. One yard. No residence for keeper.
Rutherglen ditto - - -	14	5	rooms - 6		No yard.
Hamilton ditto - - -	68	18	rooms - 5		No resident keeper.
Gorbals - ditto - - -	-	-	cells - 9 day rooms - 3	}	Erected in 1826. One airing ground.
Anderston ditto - - - (There are also five lock-up houses in other Burghs.)	35	3	day rooms - 2 cells - 6	}	Erected in 1826. No airing yard.
LINLITHGOW:					
County and Burgh Gaol - -	45	12	rooms - 6		No airing court.
Queensferry Burgh Gaol - -	- -	- -	room - 1		Lock-up house.
NAIRN:					
County and Burgh Gaol - -	22	7	rooms - 4		Erected in 1818. No yard. No residence for keeper.
ORKNEY:					
County and Burgh Gaol - -	14	3	rooms - 6		Built in 1744. No airing yard. No keeper resident.
PEEBLES:					
County and Burgh Gaol - -	24	11	rooms - 3		Erected in 1798. No airing ground.
PERTH:					
County and City Gaol - -	288	47	rooms and cells 31		Erected in 1815. Four airing courts. No [chapel.
Culross Burgh Gaol - -	23	3	rooms - 2		No yard.
Dunblane Lock-up House - -	- -	- -	rooms - 4		
Dunkeld - ditto - -	- -	- -	room - 1		
RENFREW:					
Paisley County Gaol and House of Correction.	436	37	rooms and cells 78		Erected in 1820. Two airing courts.
Greenock Burgh Gaol - - -	296	59	rooms - 6 cells - 30	}	Erected in 1810. One court yard.
Port Glasgow Gaol - - -	17	4	rooms - 2 cells - 5	}	Erected in 1815. No yard.
Renfrew Burgh Gaol - - -	- -	1	rooms - 3		Erected in 1690. No yard. No residence for keeper.
ROSS:					
Tain County and Burgh Gaol -	36	13	rooms - 10		Enlarged in 1826.
Dingwall Burgh Gaol - - -	58	19	- - -		A new prison is in progress.
Fortrose - ditto - - -	15	6	rooms - 2		No yard.
Stornoway ditto - - -	- -	- -	room - 1		A new prison is to be built.
ROXBURGH:					
Jedburgh County Gaol and House of Correction. (Lock-up houses at Melrose, Kelso, Hawick, and New Castleton.)	54	14	day rooms - 6 cells - 19 ditto in Bridewell - 16	}	Erected in 1822. Six airing yards.
SELKIRK:					
County and Burgh Gaol - -	13	4	day rooms - 2 cells - 9	}	Erected in 1804. One airing ground.
STIRLING:					
County and Burgh Gaol - -	213	42	rooms - 16		- - This prison is also used for the adjoining county, Clackmannan. It was erected in 1807. No airing ground. No resident [keeper.
Falkirk Burgh Gaol - - -	- -	- -	- - 2		For temporary confinement.
Kilsyth - ditto - - -	8	- -	- - 2		- - ditto.
SUTHERLAND:					
Dornoch County and Burgh Gaol -	40	18	day rooms - 2 cells - 4	}	No yard No residence for keeper.
WIGTOWN:					
County and Burgh Gaol - -	28	10	rooms - 6		Erected in 1777. No yard. No keepers' rooms.
Stranraer Burgh Gaol - -	43	9	rooms and cells 6		No yard. No resident keeper.
Whithorn ditto - - -	10	3	rooms and cells 5		Erected in 1814. No yard. No resident keeper.
ZETLAND:					
Lerwick Burgh Gaol - - -	8	4	rooms - 4		No keeper's residence. No yard.
TOTAL - - -	11,253	1,902	- - 1,545		

IRELAND; COUNTY GAOLS, &c.

STATEMENT of the Number of PRISONERS committed to the several GAOLS, &c. during the Year 1833; the average Number, and also the greatest Number in confinement at one time; the Number of separate Sleeping Rooms and Cells; description of Employment and Amount of Earnings; weekly Cost of Diet, Salaries of Officers; Total Annual Expenses of each Prison, and the average Cost per Head for each Prisoner.

COUNTIES AND PRISONS.	Total Number of Prisoners committed during the Year.	Average Number at one time.	Greatest Number at one time.	Number of Sleeping Cells.	Other Sleeping Rooms.	DESCRIPTION of EMPLOYMENT.	AMOUNT of EARNINGS. (£. s.)	SCHOOLS.	Weekly Cost of Diet per Head. (s. d.)	Officers' Salaries yearly. (£.)	Total Annual Expenses of Prison. (£.)	Average Cost per Head for each Prisoner. (£. s.)	REMARKS.
ANTRIM: Carrickfergus County Gaol	680	120	182	50	10	Stone breaking	Males 20 -, Females 5 -	Male and Female.	1 10½	965	2,159	18 -	To be a new gaol.
Belfast House of Correction	No account.												To be enlarged.
ARMAGH: County Gaol	663	107	158		30	Tread-wheel and stone breaking,	Males 18 10, Females 24 18	Female	1 4	666	1,976	18 10	
CARLOW: County Gaol	428	46	72	62	10	Tread-wheel and stone breaking.	Males 85 7, Females 66 2	Male and Female.	1 10½	572	1,106	24 -	Additions, in 1830, on radiating plan.
CAVAN: County Gaol	499	111	161	74	19	Tread-wheel and various trades.	Males 235 14, Females 66 6	ditto	1 5½	597	1,566	14 2	Additions, on radiating plan.
CLARE: Ennis County Gaol	623	121	194	65	8	Tread-wheel, stone breaking, &c.	Males 43 17, Females 5 11	ditto	1 11	848	2,009	16 12	Erected in 1818: semicircular plan.
CORK: County Gaol	1,176	188	333	171	84	ditto - ditto -	No account	ditto	1 9	1,583	3,566	19 -	Erected in 1824, on radiating plan.
City Gaol	895	150	191	108	14	Tread-wheel	Females 87 12	ditto	1 10½	1,325	2,751	18 7	Erected in 1824: radiating plan.
DONEGAL: Lifford County Gaol	578	100	146	85	15	Various trades	Males 43 2, Females 44 4	ditto	1 5½	568	1,676	16 15	Additions in 1824, on semicircular plan.
DOWN: Downpatrick County Gaol	540	135	163	200	16	Tread-wheel and trades	Males 59 3, Females 39 1	ditto	1 7¼	1,024	2,077	15 8	Erected in 1827: radiating plan.
DUBLIN: Kilmainham County Gaol	486	90	148	74	15	Tread-wheel, making clothing, &c.	Males 23 11, Females 17 1	ditto	2 5¾	1,208	2,607	28 19	A very defective prison.
Newgate City Gaol			350	52			692 11						
Richmond Bridewell			274	84									
Smithfield Penitentiary													
FERMANAGH: Enniskillen County Gaol	458	71	97	36	10	Tread-wheel, stone breaking, &c.	Males 76 5, Females 17 10	ditto		488	1,385	19 10	Built about 20 years.
GALWAY: County Gaol	469	130	209	83	15	Stone breaking	None -	ditto	3 7¼	765	2,505	19 5	Erected in 1811: semicircular plan.
Town Gaol	320	26	44	15	7	None	None	None -	2 7½	362	633	24 6	New gaol building, on semicircular plan.
KERRY: Tralee County Gaol	666	123	187	79	6	Tread-wheel and stone breaking.	Males 46 17, Females 31 16	Male and Female.	1 10	981	2,052	16 14	Part new in 1829.
KILDARE: Naas County Gaol	350	60	84	62	13	Trades, &c.	Males 2 10, Females 40 12	ditto	3 4¼	480	1,428	23 16	Erected in 1830: radiating plan.
Athy ditto				32	6								
KILKENNY: County Gaol	746	118	200	48	12	Tread-wheel, &c.		ditto	2 1½	715	1,935	16 8	New prison wanting.
City Gaol	209	40	58	15	3	Stone breaking -		Female	3 2½	288	583	14 12	
Carried forward	9,786	1,736	3,251	1,395	293		1,793			13,435	32,017		

IRELAND (COUNTY GAOLS, &c.)—continued.

COUNTIES AND PRISONS.	Total Number of Prisoners committed during the Year.	Average Number at one time.	Greatest Number at one time.	Number of Sleeping Cells.	Other Sleeping Rooms.	DESCRIPTION of EMPLOYMENT.	AMOUNT of EARNINGS.	SCHOOLS.	Weekly Cost of Diet per Head. (s. d.)	Officers' Salaries yearly. (£)	Total Annual Expenses of Prison. (£)	Average Cost per Head for each Prisoner. (£ s)	REMARKS.
Brought forward -	9,786	1,736	3,261	1,395	293	-	1,793 -	-	-	13,435	32,017	-	
KING'S COUNTY:													
Tullamore County Gaol	690	116	152	112	12	Stone breaking, &c.	Females - 8 10	Male and Female	1 7¼	706	1,976	17 -	Erected in 1829 : radiating plan.
LEITRIM:													
Carrick on Shannon County Gaol	476	103	128	81	18	Stone breaking and tread-wheel.	Males - 112 8 / Females - 32 -	Male and Female.	1 3¾	645	1,463	14 4	Part new : semicircular plan.
LIMERICK:													
County Gaol -	640	113	159	111	14	Tread-wheel, &c.	-	- ditto	1 9	892	1,763	15 12	Erected in 1822 : radiating plan.
City Gaol -	420	67	87	84	15	- ditto -	-	Males	1 9	624	1,110	16 11	Enlarged in 1826.
LONDONDERRY:													
County Gaol -	616	105	153	179	19	Stone breaking and trades.	Males - 144 5 / Females - 38 9	Males	1 3¾	733	2,149	20 9	Part new in 1824 : semicircular plan.
LONGFORD:													
County Gaol -	488	73	115	73	13	Tread-wheel and trades	Females - 3 16	Male and Female.	1 5½	504	1,255	17 4	Erected in 1825 : semicircular plan.
LOUTH:													
Dundalk County Gaol -	348	65	82	31	10	Tread-wheel, &c. -	-	- ditto	1 9	635	1,240	19 -	Part new - - ditto.
Drogheda Town Gaol -	285	27	40	16	3	Stone breaking -	-	None	1 7¼	201	448	16 12	Erected about 20 years.
MAYO:													
Castlebar County Gaol	1,396	195	246	16	11	None -	-	-	1 5½	1,160	No account.	-	New gaol, just finished.
MEATH:													
Trim County Gaol -	370	82	120	29	12	Tread-wheel, stone breaking, &c.	Males - 1 3 / Females - 17 13	Male and Female.	1 5½	912	1,465	18 -	Erected in 1832 : radiating plan.
MONAGHAN:													
County Gaol -	377	92	127	75	11	Tread-wheel, &c.	-	- ditto	1 3¾	552	1,374	15 -	Ditto - 1823 : semicircular plan.
QUEEN'S COUNTY:													
Maryborough County Gaol	755	145	219	75	36	Tread-wheel and trades	Males - 488 1 / Females - 56 9	- ditto	1 2½	847	1,904	13 2	New : radiating plan.
ROSCOMMON:													
County Gaol -	571	143	196	64	19	Tread-wheel, &c. -	-	- ditto	3 6	811	2,902	20 5	Erected in 1819 : semicircular plan.
SLIGO:													
County Gaol -	785	138	177	84	17	Tread-wheel and trades	Males - 250 7 / Females - 15 10	- ditto	1 5	722	1,629	11 16	Ditto in 1823 : ditto.
TIPPERARY:													
Clonmel County Gaol -	1,472	248	343	79	18	Tread-wheel, &c. -	-	- ditto	2 1½	1,423	3,656	14 14	House of Correction building.
TYRONE:													
Omagh County Gaol -	747	128	185	67	24	Tread-wheel and trades	Males - 54 6 / Females - 22 10	- ditto	1 10¾	757	2,373	18 11	Additions in 1826 : semicircular plan.
WATERFORD:													
County Gaol -	215	51	89	54	10	Tread-wheel -	Females - 40 19	Females -	2 5¾	500	998	19 11	Part erected in 1824 : radiating plan.
City Gaol -	157	19	55	14	6	- ditto -	Females - 48 3	- ditto -	2 5¾	455	689	36 -	
WESTMEATH:													
Mullingar County Gaol	530	106	150	100	15	- ditto -		Male and Female.	2 4	837	1,654	15 12	Erected in 1828.
WEXFORD:													
County Gaol -	233	60	85	42	16	- ditto -		- ditto -	2 9	664	1,814	30 4	Additions made in 1823, on radiating plan.
WICKLOW:													
County Gaol -	141	36	58	32	3	- ditto -	Females - 8 4	- ditto -	1 10¾	435	933	26 -	Additions in 1823, on semicircular plan.
	21,498	3,848	6,217	2,813	595		3,135 13			28,450	64,812		

IRELAND—*continued.*

STATEMENT of the Expenses incurred by the support of the BRIDEWELLS and other small Local PRISONS, during the year 1833.

COUNTIES AND PRISONS.	YEARLY EXPENSES.					
	£.	s.	d.	£.	s.	d.
ANTRIM:						
Antrim Bridewell: 2 rooms	24	15	11			
Ballymena ditto	31	6	5			
Ballymoney ditto	24	17	7			
				80	19	11
ARMAGH:						
Ballybolt Bridewell	35	14	6			
Lurgan ditto	12	11	11			
Market-hill ditto	10	17	2			
				59	3	7
CARLOW:						
Moneybeg Bridewell.						
Tullow ditto.						
CAVAN:						
Bailieborough Bridewell (new) 2 day-rooms, 5 cells, 2 yards	6	–	3			
Bally-connell ditto (new) 2 day-rooms, 3 cells, 2 yards.						
Coote-hill ditto (new) 2 day-rooms, 3 cells, 2 yards	16	9	6			
				22	9	9
CLARE:						
Ennistymond Bridewell	9	10	10			
Kilrush ditto	10	18	10			
Six-mile-Bridge ditto	7	15	3			
Tulla ditto	15	10	7½			
				43	15	6½
CORK:						
Bandon Bridewell	42	2	11½			
Bantry ditto	31	17	4½			
Castletown ditto	8	19	2			
Clonakilty ditto	13	8	8			
Cove ditto	12	17	11½			
Dunmanway ditto	18	–	–			
Fermoy ditto	43	7	4			
Kanturk ditto	21	4	–			
Kinsale Corporation Prison.						
Macroom Bridewell	23	14	2½			
Mallow ditto	44	16	3			
Middleton ditto	14	3	11½			
Mill-street ditto	5	18	7			
Mitchelstown ditto	29	19	3			
Roscarberry ditto	14	10	11			
Skibbereen ditto	21	2	8½			
Youghall Corporation Prison.						
				346	3	4
DONEGAL:						
Donegal Bridewell	4	2	–¼			
Letterkenny ditto	12	13	7½			
				16	15	8
DOWN:						
Newry Bridewell	–	–	–	60	6	5½
DUBLIN:						
Sheriff's Prison, City Marshalsea, Four Court's ditto, and St. Sepulchre's Manor Prison: (four distinct prisons)	no account.					
Carried forward £.	–	–	–	629	14	3

IRELAND.

STATEMENT of the Expenses incurred by the support of the BRIDEWELLS, &c.—*continued.*

COUNTIES AND PRISONS.	£.	s.	d.	.	s.	d.
Brought forward - - -	-	-	-	629	14	3
FERMANAGH :						
Newtown-Butler Bridewell.						
GALWAY :						
Ballinasloe Bridewell - - - - - - -	30	19	5			
Clifden ditto (temporary) - - - - -	59	2	4			
Eyrecourt ditto - - - - - - -	24	—	—			
Gort ditto - - - - - - -	73	15	7½			
Loughrea ditto (temporary) - - - - -	97	19	—			
Tuam ditto - - - - - - -	22	1	5			
Woodford ditto - - - - - - -	10	17	—			
				318	14	9½
KERRY :						
Cahirseveen Bridewell (new) - - - - - -	16	3	2			
Castle Island ditto (new) - - - - -	11	—	6			
Dingle ditto (new) - - - - - -	13	17	9			
Kenmare ditto - - - - - - -	15	1	6			
Killarney ditto (new) - - - - - -	19	1	—			
Listowell ditto (new) - - - - - -	16	15	11			
Mill-town ditto (new) - - - - - -	5	16	9½			
Tarbert ditto - - - - - - -	9	18	10			
KILKENNY :				107	15	5½
Thomas-town Bridewell : 2 cells - - - - - -	-	-	-	5	2	3
KING'S COUNTY :						
Parson's-town district Bridewell : 2 day-rooms, 10 cells, 2 yards.						
Philips-town Gaol.						
LEITRIM :						
Manor-Hamilton Bridewell - - - - - - -	-	-	-	7	5	10
LIMERICK :						
Bruff Bridewell - - - - - - - -	16	5	7			
Croom ditto - - - - - - - -	9	19	2			
Glynn ditto (new) - - - - - -	5	4	8			
Kilfinnan ditto (new) - - - - - -	10	4	—			
Newcastle ditto - - - - - - -	15	5	—			
Rathkeale ditto - - - - - - -	24	2	11			
				81	1	4
LONDONDERRY :						
Coleraine Bridewell, (to be rebuilt) - - - - -	21	1	5			
Magherafelt ditto, no room for keeper - - - -	24	15	10			
Newtown-Limavady ditto (new), 2 rooms - - - -	7	18	5			
				53	15	8
LOUTH :						
Ardee Bridewell - - - - - - - -	-	-	-	3	8	3½
MAYO :						
Ballinrobe Bridewell : 3 day-rooms, 4 large cells, 4 yards -	-	-	-	7	12	1
MEATH :						
Kells Bridewell : 2 day-rooms, 7 cells, 2 yards - - -	-	-	-	14	17	5
Navan ditto.						
MONAGHAN :						
Carrickmacross Bridewell, (new) - - - - -	16	18	8			
Castle-blayney ditto - - - - - -	48	16	3			
				65	14	11
Carried forward - - - £.	-	-	-	1,295	2	3½

STATEMENT of the Expenses incurred by the support of the BRIDEWELLS, &c.—*continued.*   IRELAND.

COUNTIES AND PRISONS.	YEARLY EXPENSES.					
	£.	s.	d.	£.	s.	d.
Brought forward - - -	-	-	-	1,295	2	3½
QUEEN'S COUNTY:						
Abbey-leix Bridewell, (new) - - - - - -	10	13	6			
Borris-in-Ossory ditto - - - - - - -	5	8	7			
Stradbally ditto - - - - - - -	5	18	–			
				22	–	1
ROSCOMMON:						
Athlone Bridewell - - - - - - - -	24	3	11			
Royle ditto - 2 day-rooms, 10 cells, 2 yards - -	29	1	–			
Castle-rea ditto - - - - - - - -	15	1	2½			
Strokes-town ditto - - - - - - - -	24	4	4½			
				92	10	6
SLIGO:						
Ballymott Bridewell - - - - - - -	–	–	–	13	11	6½
TIPPERARY:						
Borrisikane Bridewell : 5 cells, 1 yard - - - - -	23	3	9			
Cahir ditto 1 day-room, 4 cells - - - -	17	18	10½			
Cashel ditto 3 day-rooms, 8 cells, 2 yards - -	69	12	6			
Clogheen ditto (new) - - - - - -	13	4	3½			
Nenagh ditto 3 day-rooms, 9 cells, 2 yards - -	117	14	–			
New Birmingham ditto - - - - - - -	9	16	–			
Newport - ditto 2 cells - - - - -	8	1	5			
Roscrea - ditto 4 day-rooms, 12 cells, 2 yards -	38	11	–			
Templemore ditto - - - - - - -	53	13	–			
Thurles - ditto 4 day-rooms, 22 cells, 2 yards -	95	8	6			
Tipperary - ditto 2 day-rooms, 4 cells - - -	18	19	10			
				466	3	2
TYRONE:						
Clogher Bridewell, (new) - - - - - -	12	19	2			
Dungannon ditto.						
Strabane ditto - - - - - - - -	7	8	10½			
				20	8	–½
WATERFORD:						
Dungarvon Bridewell : 10 cells - - - - - -	43	–	4			
Lismore Lock-up-house : 2 cells - - - - -	5	13	1½			
				48	13	5½
WESTMEATH:						
Moate Bridewell, (new) - - - - - - -	–	–	–	53	19	6
WEXFORD:						
Enniscorthy Bridewell - - - - - - -	9	9	9			
Gorey - ditto - - - - - - -	12	13	11			
New Ross ditto - - - - - - -	8	5	7			
				30	9	3
WICKLOW:						
Baltinglass District Bridewell : 4 day-rooms, 10 cells, 4 yards						
TOTAL - - - - - -	–	–	–	2,042	17	10

ENGLAND
and
WALES.

STATEMENT of the Number of CRIMINAL OFFENDERS Committed for Trial at the Assizes and Sessions in *England* and *Wales*, during each of the last Seven Years. Also the Numbers Convicted, Acquitted and not Prosecuted; with the Sentences of the Convicted.

This Statement does not include a large number of persons who are committed to prison for such offences as are not brought under the cognizance of the Courts of Assize and Quarter Sessions;—comprising Summary Convictions before Police Magistrates and Justices at Petty Sessions, Vagrants, Offenders against the Revenue and Martial Laws, Debtors, and Prisoners committed for re-examination, &c. [The aggregate number committed to the several Prisons during the year will be seen by reference to the Tables at p. 175 and 177.]

In the YEARS COUNTIES.	1827. Number of Persons.	1828. Number of Persons.	1829. Number of Persons.	1830. Number of Persons.	1831. Number of Persons.	1832. Number of Persons.	1833. Number of Persons.
ANGLESEY	16	7	12	14	8	23	10
BEDFORD	108	109	134	134	103	100	112
BERKS	208	190	212	170	291	193	209
BRECON	16	21	17	20	14	30	33
BUCKS	182	153	188	151	311	188	187
CAMBRIDGE	152	159	194	147	165	201	171
CARDIGAN	9	9	3	12	11	16	7
CARMARTHEN	17	40	23	42	51	42	31
CARNARVON	22	18	15	19	36	22	18
CHESTER	497	466	542	534	513	572	589
CORNWALL	150	126	122	193	145	195	180
CUMBERLAND	79	53	47	74	74	75	87
DENBIGH	26	34	35	28	32	32	54
DERBY	160	171	175	194	202	218	179
DEVON	432	425	430	494	399	481	405
DORSET	167	144	141	205	177	166	133
DURHAM	175	123	139	103	133	158	183
ESSEX	451	363	587	491	607	683	590
FLINT	22	22	20	31	27	20	30
GLAMORGAN	54	49	54	89	132	78	81
GLOUCESTER	415	389	449	535	636	609	509
(BRISTOL)	139	177	171	174	188	273	213
HANTS	341	354	396	424	567	464	484
HEREFORD	150	127	155	145	166	147	152
HERTS	205	199	235	274	194	293	307
HUNTINGDON	31	19	44	36	85	34	50
KENT	632	604	665	649	640	773	677
LANCASTER	2,459	2,011	2,226	2,028	2,352	2,624	2,305
LEICESTER	260	247	249	196	181	248	268
LINCOLN	329	302	337	258	307	299	389
MERIONETH	6	7	3	12	3	9	13
MIDDLESEX	3,381	3,516	3,567	3,390	3,514	3,739	3,692
MONMOUTH	95	55	109	126	129	110	104
MONTGOMERY	22	17	32	40	30	25	44
NORFOLK	486	421	536	429	549	532	539
NORTHAMPTON	176	122	183	152	168	195	179
NORTHUMBERLAND	96	122	116	82	108	80	93
NOTTINGHAM	298	289	358	300	316	343	314
OXFORD	210	141	167	193	270	217	216
PEMBROKE	42	18	21	24	19	32	34
RADNOR	15	15	8	17	15	14	12
RUTLAND	14	16	20	15	11	10	16
SALOP	178	168	165	225	228	261	284
SOMERSET	646	495	674	643	616	696	597
STAFFORD	569	575	613	563	644	698	753
SUFFOLK	351	283	357	362	371	453	454
SURREY	663	680	716	708	733	943	850
SUSSEX	309	308	378	360	314	283	396
WARWICK	605	608	705	691	665	705	671
WESTMORLAND	20	19	11	22	17	28	21
WILTS	365	281	346	418	568	346	301
WORCESTER	250	203	282	264	342	316	337
YORK	1,223	1,094	1,291	1,207	1,270	1,537	1,509
TOTAL	17,924	16,564	18,675	18,107	19,647	20,829	20,072

NUMBER OF PERSONS

COMMITTED, CONVICTED, SENTENCED, ACQUITTED, &c. &c.

In the YEARS - -	1827.	1828.	1829.	1830.	1831.	1832.	1833.	Total Number in the Seven Years.
	Number of Persons.	Number of Persons.	Number of Persons.	Number of Persons.	Number of Persons.	Number of Persons	Number of Persons.	
COMMITTED for Trial:								
Viz. MALES - - -	15,154	13,832	15,556	15,135	16,600	17,486	16,804	110,567
FEMALES - - -	2,770	2,732	3,119	2,972	3,047	3,343	3,268	21,251
TOTAL - - -	17,924	16,564	18,675	18,107	19,647	20,829	20,072	131,818
CONVICTED and SENTENCED:								
To DEATH * - - -	1,529	1,165	1,385	1,397	1,601	1,449	931	9,457
TRANSPORTATION, for Life -	198	317	396	405	334	546	783	2,979
Ditto - 35 Years - -	- -	- -	1	- -	- -	- -	- -	1
Ditto - 28 Years - -	1	1	- -	2	1	1	- -	6
Ditto - 21 Years - -	1	- -	2	- -	1	- -	2	6
Ditto - 14 Years - -	293	508	691	659	638	764	734	4,287
Ditto - 10 Years - -	- -	1	- -	- -	1	1	4	7
Ditto - 9 Years - -	- -	- -	- -	1	- -	- -	- -	1
Ditto - 7 Years - -	2,232	2,046	2,285	2,169	2,340	2,603	2,546	16,221
IMPRISONMENT, and severally to be whipped, fined, kept to hard labour, &c. ⎡5 Years - - -	1	- -	- -	- -	- -	- -	- -	1
4 Years - - -	- -	1	- -	- -	- -	- -	1	2
3 Years - - -	11	11	7	1	5	3	5	43
2 Years, and above 1 Year - -	296	243	235	209	226	230	234	1,673
1 Year, and above 6 Months -	1,433	1,117	1,277	1,220	1,311	1,304	1,388	9,050
⎣6 Months, and under	6,251	5,991	6,646	6,458	7,012	7,644	7,618	47,620
WHIPPING,—and FINE -	321	322	336	284	360	402	200	2,225
TOTAL CONVICTED - -	12,567	11,723	13,261	12,805	13,830	14,947	14,446	93,579
ACQUITTED - - -	3,407	3,169	3,614	3,470	3,723	3,716	3,793	24,892
No BILLS FOUND, and NOT PROSECUTED	1,950	1,672	1,800	1,832	2,094	2,166	1,833	13,347
TOTAL - - -	17,924	16,564	18,675	18,107	19,647	20,829	20,072	131,818
* Of whom were EXECUTED -	73	59	74	46	52	54	33	391

a a 2

ENGLAND and WALES.

ANALYSIS of Criminal Offences during the last Three Years.

	In the Year 1831.	In the Year 1832.	In the Year 1833.
Number of Persons committed for trial at the Assizes and Sessions in England and Wales	19,647	20,829	20,072
Proportion for crimes against the person -	5½ per cent.	4¾ per cent.	5 per cent.
Ditto for crimes against property - - -	94 "	94¾ "	94¼ "
Ditto for other crimes* - - - - -	½ "	½ "	¾ "
Number of convictions - - - - - -	13,830	14,947	14,446
Proportion for crimes against the person -	3¾ per cent.	3¼ per cent.	3½ per cent.
Ditto for crimes against property - - -	95¾ "	96¼ "	95¾ "
Ditto for other crimes - - - - - -	½ "	½ "	¾ "
Proportion of convictions to commitments -	70¼ per cent.	71½ per cent.	72 per cent.
Ditto of acquittals to commitments - -	19 "	18 "	18¾ "
Ditto not prosecuted, or no bills found - -	10¾ "	10½ "	9¼ "
Proportion of Sentences.†			
Death, executed - - - - - -	0.37 p' cent.	0.37 p' cent.	0.25 p' cent.
Ditto, not executed‡ - - - - - -	11.2 "	9.33 "	6.25 "
Transportation for life - - - - - -	2.4 "	3.6 "	5.4 "
Ditto for 14 years - - - - - -	4.63 "	5.2 "	5.2 "
Ditto for 7 years - - - - -	17. "	17.5 "	17.6 "
Imprisonment for above one year - - -	1.65 "	1.6 "	1.7 "
Ditto from 6 to 12 months - - - - -	9.55 "	8.7 "	9.6 "
Ditto for six months and under - - -	50.6 "	51. "	52.6 "
Whipping, fine, &c. - - - - - -	2.6 "	2.7 "	1.4 "
Number sentenced to death - - - - -	1,601	1,449	931
Proportion for crimes against the person - -	23 per cent.	21½ per cent.	32½ per cent.
Ditto for crimes against property - - -	76¼ "	78 "	66 "
Ditto for other crimes - - - - - -	¾ "	½ "	1½ "
Number Executed:			
For crimes against the person § - - -	26	28	20
For crimes against property ‖ - - -	25	26	10
For other crimes ¶ - - - - -	1	–	3
Total executed - - -	52 or one in 31 sentenced.	54 or one in 27 sentenced.	33 or one in 28 sentenced.

* The crimes included under this head are bigamy, perjury, sodomy or other unnatural offence, transport being at large, and treason.

† For the respective numbers sentenced, *see* the preceding Table, page 187.

‡ The ultimate punishment inflicted on this large proportion of criminals (on whom sentence of death was recorded) is not stated in the Official Returns. In most instances the sentences are commuted for transportation. Some few of the best cases are admitted into the Milbank Penitentiary.

§ The crimes in these cases were murder, or intent to kill or poison, rape, and highway-robbery. The number of executions for murder decreased from 15 in the year 1832 to six in the year 1833.

‖ The crimes in these cases were arson, burglary and larceny, piracy, riot and felony, sheep-stealing, and stealing letter inclosing bank notes. During the three years under notice there were as many as 41 executions for the crime of arson, but in the preceding year [1830], there were only six.

¶ In all these cases the crime was sodomy.

STATEMENT of the NUMBER of CRIMINAL OFFENDERS committed for Trial in the several Counties in *Scotland*, during the year 1833; also the Numbers convicted, acquitted, &c., with the Sentences of the convicted.

These numbers are exclusive of summary convictions before magistrates, vagrants, prisoners committed for re-examination and debtors.

COUNTIES.	Males.	Females.	TOTAL.
ABERDEEN	208	55	263
ARGYLE	56	5	61
AYR	81	8	89
BANFF	10	1	11
BERWICK	14	2	16
BUTE	7	2	9
CAITHNESS	25	8	33
CLACKMANNAN	16	14	30
CROMARTY (included in Ross)	—	—	—
DUMBARTON	29	5	34
DUMFRIES	66	9	75
EDINBURGH	410	175	585
ELGIN	22	1	23
FIFE	102	12	114
FORFAR	177	49	226
HADDINGTON	52	4	56
INVERNESS	33	4	37
KINCARDINE	20	3	23
KINROSS	20	–	20
KIRKCUDBRIGHT	23	3	26
LANARK	397	145	542
LINLITHGOW	33	4	37
NAIRN	5	1	6
ORKNEY	3	1	4
PEEBLES	8	6	14
PERTH	175	31	206
RENFREW	198	37	235
ROSS	11	2	13
ROXBURGH	67	7	74
SELKIRK	–	2	2
STIRLING	68	16	84
SUTHERLAND	1	–	1
WIGTOWN	24	11	35
ZETLAND	—	—	—
Total convicted	**2,361**	**623**	**2,984**
Liberated without trial	486	119	605
Convicted*	1,417	380	1,797
Outlawed	27	4	31
Acquitted (Insane, 6.)	174	44	218
Remaining in Gaol for trial	147	57	204
On Bail for trial	110	19	129
Total	**2,361**	**623**	**2,984**

* SENTENCES of the Convicted:

	Males.	Females.	TOTAL.
Death (executed, 3 males)	9	1	10
Ditto, Sentence commuted	5	1	6
Transportation for Life	46	–	46
Ditto for 14 years	85	23	108
Ditto for 7 years	165	74	239
Imprisonment above one year	21	8	29
Ditto for 12 months and above six	138	28	166
Ditto for six months and above three	252	83	335
Ditto for three months and under	646	157	803
Fined	46	4	50
To find caution	4	1	5
Total convicted	**1,417**	**380**	**1,797**

IRELAND.

IRELAND.

STATEMENT of the Number of PERSONS charged with CRIMINAL OFFENCES, who were committed to the different GAOLS in *Ireland*, for Trial at the Assizes and Sessions, during the last Seven Years; distinguishing the Number Convicted, Acquitted, and against whom no Bills were found, and who were not prosecuted;—also the Sentences of those Convicted; and the Number Executed.

These Numbers are exclusive of summary Convictions before Police Magistrates and Justices at Petty Sessions, Prisoners committed for re-examination, and Debtors.

NUMBER of PERSONS charged with CRIMINAL OFFENCES, and Committed for Trial, in each County.

In the YEARS COUNTIES.	1827. Number of Persons.	1828. Number of Persons.	1829. Number of Persons.	1830. Number of Persons.	1831. Number of Persons.	1832. Number of Persons.	1833. Number of Persons.
ANTRIM	427	454	338	533	528	373	450
ARMAGH	578	549	490	301	403	397	404
CARLOW	273	228	158	220	195	236	351
CAVAN	461	301	280	304	306	202	236
CLARE	344	215	215	370	598	578	349
CORK	1,488	976	969	1,021	859	861	1,098
CORK CITY	490	483	423	502	534	529	611
DONEGAL	542	472	527	487	445	353	472
DOWN	446	270	346	358	355	350	364
DUBLIN	506	393	366	450	413	410	456
DUBLIN CITY	2,122	1,982	2,096	2,128	2,312	2,384	2,005
FERMANAGH	278	277	357	294	283	328	340
GALWAY	451	458	394	483	529	489	481
GALWAY TOWN	73	136	337	127	141	107	113
KERRY	1,099	944	639	389	468	431	467
KILDARE	138	78	325	135	174	277	490
KILKENNY	364	221	174	221	171	199	367
KILKENNY CITY	137	115	109	153	116	127	151
KING'S COUNTY	543	563	576	313	273	271	428
LEITRIM	391	380	372	282	209	293	389
LIMERICK	526	337	255	441	431	272	640
LIMERICK CITY	345	255	346	365	326	336	420
LONDONDERRY	405	237	292	260	268	217	351
LONGFORD	389	330	404	429	300	391	409
LOUTH	300	218	147	164	166	199	183
DROGHEDA TOWN	61	66	34	48	43	34	80
MAYO	319	346	387	829	1,235	705	973
MEATH	320	212	243	247	288	240	284
MONAGHAN	447	352	321	310	361	279	386
QUEEN'S COUNTY	373	189	388	454	456	582	528
ROSCOMMON	424	456	455	438	528	470	544
SLIGO	427	402	559	532	505	360	423
TIPPERARY	755	519	581	700	720	1,414	1,005
TYRONE	410	330	289	394	226	228	309
WATERFORD	366	224	210	196	226	177	218
WATERFORD CITY	160	145	133	228	151	180	157
WESTMEATH	342	288	336	347	320	404	543
WEXFORD	287	179	224	208	192	245	233
WICKLOW	214	103	156	133	138	128	111
TOTAL	18,031	14,683	15,271	15,794	16,192	16,056	17,819

IRELAND.

NUMBER OF PERSONS

COMMITTED, CONVICTED, SENTENCED, ACQUITTED, &c. &c.

In the YEARS - -	1827. Number of Persons.	1828. Number of Persons.	1829. Number of Persons.	1830. Number of Persons.	1831. Number of Persons.	1832. Number of Persons.	1833. Number of Persons.	Total Number in the Seven Years.
COMMITTED for Trial:								
Viz. MALES - - -	14,598	11,919	12,471	12,709	13,148	13,160	14,923	92,928
FEMALES - -	3,433	2,764	2,800	3,085	3,044	2,896	2,896	20,918
TOTAL - - -	18,031	14,683	15,271	15,794	16,192	16,056	17,819	113,846
CONVICTED and SENTENCED:								
To DEATH * - - -	346	211	224	262	307	319	237	1,906
TRANSPORTATION, for Life	118	66	51	93	178	162	224	892
14 Years	44	20	15	25	26	29	21	180
7 Years	985	665	746	839	872	956	711	5,774
Imprisonment 3 Years - -	1	3	2	- -	1	1	10	17
2 Years, and above 1 Year	69	75	90	55	120	102	199	710
1 Year, and above 6 Months	947	880	919	563	844	914	924	5,991
6 Months, and under -	6,846	6,449	6,526	7,506	6,840	6,905	8,836	49,908
FINE - - - -	851	900	876	559	417	372	282	4,257
TOTAL CONVICTED - -	10,207	9,269	9,449	9,902	9,605	9,759	11,444	69,635
ACQUITTED - -	3,059	2,245	2,622	2,429	2,893	2,449	2,405	18,102
No BILLS FOUND -	4,461	3,078	3,200	3,463	3,694	3,848	3,970	25,714
BAILED, and NOT PROSECUTED -	304	91	- -	- -	- -	- -	- -	395
TOTAL - - -	18,031	14,683	15,271	15,794	16,192	16,056	17,819	113,846
* Of whom were EXECUTED -	37	21	38	39	37	39	39	250

MASSACHUSETTS.   The school committee in the city of Boston, and the respective committees of the several towns throughout the State, are required to make a report annually to the secretary of the Commonwealth, of the amount collected during the year, the number of school districts into which the respective towns are divided, the aggregate number of months during which the several schools were kept, the proportion kept by male and by female teachers, the whole number of pupils who have attended any of the schools, and the number of individuals between 14 and 21 years of age who are unable to read and write. Every town is furnished annually by the Secretary of State with a blank return, agreeably to the following form :—

RETURN of the SCHOOL COMMITTEE of ————————, concerning SCHOOLS, for the Year ending May   , A. D.

Amount paid for Public Instruction during the Year.	Number of Public School Districts.	Aggregate Time of keeping Schools in the Year estimated in Months, and what portion was kept by Male, and what by Female Teachers.	Whole Number of Pupils attending the Schools kept by Town in the course of the Year.	Number of Academies and Private Schools.	Number of Pupils in Academies and Private Schools, not attending Public Schools.	Estimated Amount of Compensation of Instruction of Academies and Private Schools.	Number of Persons between 14 & 21 unable to Read and Write.

Attest   }School Committee.

When a meeting of the inhabitants of any school district is called for the purpose of raising money for the erection of a school, and a majority of the voters present are opposed to the measure, any five or more of the freeholders, who are inhabitants of the school district, or if there be not so many freeholders, any five of the inhabitants paying taxes, may apply to the " select men" of the town, requesting them to insert in their warrant for calling the next town meeting, an article requiring the opinion of the inhabitants relative to the expediency of raising money for the purpose, and if the majority present shall agree to support a school, they shall vote such a sum as they shall think necessary.

Every school district is incorporated so as to be enabled to bring or defend any Action.

If the inhabitants of any town refuse or neglect, at the annual meeting for the choice of town officers, to vote money for the support of schools as provided by law, and to choose a committee to superintend the schools, or, if the town be divided into school districts, " prudential committees" in the several districts, every such town shall forfeit a sum equal to twice the highest sum which the town had ever voted for the support of schools, and for refusing or neglecting to choose either of the committees aforesaid, a further penalty shall be incurred of not more than 200, nor less than 100 dollars. The money so recovered to be applied, one-fourth to the use of the county and three-fourths to that of the school committee, if any such body exist; if not, to the select men for the support of schools therein.

The results of this law will appear from the following abstract of the school returns made to the General Court in January 1833, from 99 towns in this State. At this period, the number of school districts was 791, and the amount paid for public instruction 98,086 dollars. The aggregate time of keeping schools in the year estimated in months, 2,586 by male teachers, and 3,725 by female teachers.

The whole number of pupils attending the schools kept by the towns in the course of the year, was 49,582.

The towns from which the returns are made are distributed in about equal proportions in the various counties of the State. The population of those towns in 1830, was 201,681. The whole number of towns in Massachusetts was 305. Returns were transmitted from 99, so that information was received from one-third, and nearly the same proportion of the population. The extent of elementary instruction throughout the State may therefore be thus estimated :

Towns - - - - - - - - -	305
Cost of public instruction - - - - - - -	$ 294,259
Number of school districts - - - - - -	2,273
Months by male teachers· - - - - - 7,758	
Months by female teachers - - - - 11,175	
Total months - - - - - -	18,933
Pupils in public schools - - - - - - -	148,656
Academies and private schools - - - - - -	1,185
Pupils in academies and private schools - - - - -	24,852
Pay of teachers in academies and private schools - - -	$ 243,883
Number between 14 and 21, who cannot read - - - -	30

The

The male teachers are allowed a salary of from 10 to 25 dollars per month. The average is probably about 15 dollars. Females are generally paid by the week, from 75 cents to three dollars; the average being about one dollar and 25 cents. There is no school fund in this State. The number of public schools of various descriptions in Boston, in January 1830, was as follows : nine grammar schools, nine writing schools, one Latin and one English high school for boys; fifty-seven primary schools for children between four and seven years of age; two schools in the house of industry, and one school denominated " the house of reformation ;" making together 80 public schools, the pupils in attendance at which amounted to 7,430. The expense incurred for the support of these schools in 1829, was $ 65,500. The whole number of schools in the city, public and private, was 235, and the number of pupils in attendance 11,448. The expense of tuition, fuel, books, &c. was $ 196,829.

MAINE.

Population under 15 years of age   -   -   -   -   172,431.
Ditto - - from 5 to 15   -   -   -   -   -   106,007.

WHEN Maine became a separate state, one of the earliest measures of the Legislature was an improvement of the system then in operation for the support of common schools. By that system, a town could not be required to establish a school until 60 families had become resident in it. The present law removed this limitation by enacting that every town should raise annually for the maintenance of common schools, a sum, including the income of any incorporated school fund, at least equal to 40 cents for each inhabitant, a part not exceeding one-third to be applied to the instruction of females. It is the duty of the assessor to assign to each school district a proportion of the money annually raised in each year for the support of common schools, according to the number of children therein between the ages of four and twenty-one. A committee of superintendence is chosen by ballot annually in each town, consisting of not less than three nor more than seven persons, whose business it shall be to examine schoolmasters and mistresses, to visit and inspect schools, and inquire into their regulation and discipline. The committee have power to dismiss incompetent teachers and select school-books. An agent for each school district is appointed at the annual meeting for the choice of town officers, whose duty it is to engage the schoolmasters or mistresses, and to make the necessary arrangements for the management of the school.

School-books are required to be furnished by the parents, but if they are unable to do so, the books are provided at the public expense.

No alien is eligible as a master. He is required previously to his appointment to produce a certificate from the superintending school committee of the town where the school is kept, and also from some person of liberal education, literary pursuits, and good moral character, residing within the county, that he is well qualified to instruct youth in reading, writing, the English grammar, arithmetic, and other branches of learning usually taught in common schools ; and also a certificate from the select men of the town, or assessors of the place to which he belongs, " that he is a person of sober life and conversation, and sustains a good moral character." Certificates as to character, and qualifications, are also required of all candidates for the office of schoolmistress.

If any town neglect to raise the required funds annually for the support of schools, the inhabitants forfeit a sum not less than twice, nor more than four times the amount of such failure or deficiency.

The respective towns determine the number and define the limits of the school districts.

In the year 1825, the Legislature required a report from each town, respecting the number of school districts and of children ordinarily in attendance, the period allotted to their instruction, and the funds by which they were supported. These returns were made in the year 1826 from the ten counties of the State, and the following was the result :

Number of school districts - - - - - - -	2,499
Number of persons between 4 and 21 - - - - -	137,831
Number who usually attend school - - - - -	101,325
Money required to be raised annually - - - - -	$ 119,334
Amount actually raised from taxes - - - - -	$ 132,263
Total expenditure, taxes and permanent funds - - -	$ 137,878
Average monthly wages for teachers - - - - -	$ 12,024
Average annual expense of each scholar - - - - -	$ 1,35

The whole amount of income from permanent funds was $ 5,614. 65. The aggregate number of months in which the schools were open under male instructors, was 5,161, and under female teachers, 6,285. The probable increase of scholars annually is 6,035, and the whole number of scholars in the State in 1833 has been estimated at 140,000. The number of pupils annually attending each school district averaged 40, and the monthly expense of the instruction of each scholar was 30 cents. The proportion of pupils to the whole population was 30 per cent.

It appears that on an average the respective counties raised more than the proportion

b b 2 required

MAINE.

required by law, and some from one-fourth more to nearly double; yet even this on the whole has been but sufficient to support the schools on an average of about four months in the year; two months under male, and for about the same term under female teachers. It does not appear that before the passing of the law, schools were generally maintained throughout the State for any less number of months annually than they have been since, and the annual amount then actually raised proves that the new law has done little more to extend the means of education than as it affected towns having less than 50 families, and which were not affected by the former law. The free grammar-schools are said to have been superseded both in this State and in Massachusetts by the establishment of private academies founded by individual exertion in many parts of the country, and frequently aided by special grants of land from the Legislature. The academies, however, not being entirely free schools, do not supply instruction for all classes of the community.

NEW
HAMPSHIRE.

NEW HAMPSHIRE.

Population under 15 years of age - - - - - 104,539.
Ditto - - from 5 to 15 - - - - - - - 70,228.

COMMON schools are established throughout this State, and for their support a sum amounting since the year 1818 to $90,000, is annually raised by a separate tax. The laws now in force afford the means of education to every child. The State has a literary fund amounting to $64,000, formed by a tax of one-half per cent. on the capital of the banks. The proceeds of this fund, with the addition of an annual income of $9,000, derived from a tax on banks, are appropriated to the support of schools. The sum annually collected gives an average of $455 to each town, or about one dollar to each individual in the State of suitable age to attend school. In addition to this grant, a large number of the towns have property in school lands, or funds formed from the sale of them, the interest of which is devoted to education. Moreover, the literary fund collected by a tax on the several banks in the State, and originally designed for the " endowment or support of a college for instruction in the higher branches of science and literature," was " by a law passed in 1829, distributed among the several towns, according to the proportion paid by them of the public taxes, to be applied to the support and maintenance of common free schools, or to other purposes of education." The whole amount of the fund actually distributed since the passing of the law, is $95,582, and the amount annually accruing from the tax on banks, to be hereafter distributed, is about $10,000. The division of towns into school districts, renders it practicable for all children in the State to attend school either in summer or winter. In 1823, the number of school districts was 1,698, and of school-houses, 1,560. Of the former, there are at present at least 1,732, and of the latter, 1,601. Judging from returns received from a number of towns in Merrimack county, it is concluded that one in 46 of the whole population annually attends the free schools, including those who attend private schools and also academies; one in 30 of the entire population of the State attends school during some portion of the year. Besides the elementary branches of education, viz. reading, spelling, writing, arithmetic, grammar, and geography, the elder scholars, in many of the schools, are instructed in history, astronomy, natural philosophy, and chemistry, as well as in book-keeping and surveying. They are thus qualified to become teachers.

VERMONT.

VERMONT.

Population under 15 years of age - - - - - 115,639.
Ditto - - from 5 to 15 - - - - - - - 67,505.

SEVERAL laws have been passed in this State for the support of public education since the year 1797. In 1824, the select men in the several towns were authorized to assess a tax of two cents in the dollar, in lieu of one cent, as heretofore, on the rateable estate of the inhabitants. No district, however, can receive any benefit from the money unless it shall have kept a school, from other resources, for the term of two months immediately before the distribution of the school fund.* The amount raised by the general law for the support of schools, at three per cent. on the valuation of taxes, is between $50,000 and $60,000, and about as much more is supposed to be derived from the school district taxes. The State has a literary fund from a tax of six per cent. on the annual profits of the banks.

Each

---

* At any meeting legally convened for that purpose, the inhabitants may, by vote, direct the collection of the school-tax in such articles of produce, at the market price, as may be most advantageous to the town.

⊙

Each organized town shall support a school for the instruction of youth in English reading, writing, and arithmetic, and the inhabitants are required, when one school is insufficient for the purpose, to divide the town into as many school districts as may be judged most convenient. A committee is appointed in each district who in conjunction with the select men of the town are the trustees of the schools.

This State has a literary fund, derived principally from a tax of six per cent. on the annual profits of the banks. The amount on loan in September 1829, was $23,763.

The number of district schools in 1831, was about 2,400. Taking the whole number of persons between the ages of five and 20, inclusive, this estimate would show about 43 scholars to each school district. It is supposed, however, that the average number who attend school in each district, is less than 30. The Legislature, in 1832, applied to the school fund, $9,586.*

---

* In November 1800, the following general law was passed for the encouragement of libraries in this State.

" Whereas a number of petitions have been presented to this Legislature from various library societies in this State, praying to be incorporated into bodies corporate and politic for ever, with such powers, privileges and immunities as will best answer the laudable purposes for which they are associated: therefore, to assist and encourage the said societies in the prosecution and advancement of useful knowledge and rational entertainment, and to establish an uniformity through the various societies of the same kind in the State :

" Sect. 1.—It is hereby enacted, by the General Assembly of the State of Vermont, that whenever any number of persons shall associate together with a view of promoting literary knowledge and information, by purchasing a library and forming themselves into a society, the members of each and every society so formed be, and they are and shall be, a body corporate and politic in deed and in name, by such name and style as a majority of the members of said society may agree upon ; and by such name, they and their successors are hereby constituted and confirmed a body corporate and politic in law, to have perpetual succession :

" Sect. 2.—That each and every corporation formed as aforesaid are and shall for ever hereafter be able and capable in law to sue and be sued, plead and be impleaded, answer and be answered unto, defend and be defended, in all and any courts of justice and other places, in all manner of suits, actions, complaints, pleas, causes and matters, of what nature or kind soever :

" Sect. 3.—That each and every corporation so formed as aforesaid shall have full power to make their own bye-laws and regulations, such as appointing the time and place of holding their meetings, drawing books out of such library and returning them to the same, regulating the mode of electing their officers, determining the authority and duty of each officer, establishing the mode of admitting members into said society, and regulating all other interests and concerns of said corporation ; provided such bye-laws and regulations shall not be repugnant to the constitution and laws of this State :

" Sect. 4.—That each and every society formed and incorporated as aforesaid shall have full power and authority to levy, assess and collect any tax on the members of such society, which the said society, at a meeting previously warned for that purpose, shall agree upon ; provided, that no tax shall be laid on the members of any such society, unless at least two-thirds of the members present at such meeting vote in favour of such tax : provided also, that no taxes granted or assessed by any society as aforesaid shall be levied on or collected out of the estate of any member of such society, other than such estate he, she or they hold in common with such society :

" Sect. 5.—That each and every society incorporated as aforesaid shall have full power and authority to lay any fine or forfeiture on any member of such society, for damaging books or neglect of any other duty imposed on such member by the bye-laws and regulations of such society : provided, that in no case the fine or forfeiture amount to a greater sum than the confiscation or forfeiture of such member's share or interest in such society. And it is further provided, that no fine or forfeiture shall be laid upon or collected from any member, unless for some breach of duty for which the fine and forfeiture has previously been defined and ascertained by the bye-laws of such society :

" Sect. 6.—Provided nevertheless, and it is hereby further enacted, that no bye-laws or regulations of any or either of the corporations formed agreeably to this Act shall be binding upon officers or members, unless the same shall have been proposed at one regular meeting of such society, and received and enacted at another, after the intervention of at least thirty days :

" Sect. 7.—Provided also, and it is hereby further enacted, that none of the bye-laws or regulations of any such society shall be repealed or set aside at a meeting of such society, except it be at an annual meeting :

" Sect. 8.—That when any number of persons shall associate and meet for the purposes contemplated in the first section of this Act, they shall have power to choose a moderator and clerk, which clerk so chosen is hereby empowered to warn a meeting of such associates, notifying the time and place of holding such meeting by giving personal notice, or such other notice as the society shall direct."

CONNECTICUT.

CONNECTICUT.
—————

Population under 15 years of age	-	-	-	-	-	106,500.
Ditto - - from 5 to 15	-	-	-	-	-	69,197.

THIS State was at a very early period of its history divided into parochial societies, which in 1717 were empowered by the Legislature to levy a tax on the inhabitants, and frame regulations for the support of schools. In 1795, the proceeds of certain lands (now forming part of the State of Ohio) amounting to $1,200,000, were voted for this purpose. This fund now amounts to no less a sum than $1,700,000; about $70,000 are divided annually among the schools. The Act of 1795 directed that school districts should be formed in almost every part of the State.

Every school society is required to hold an annual meeting, appoint a committee for the management of its affairs, a committee for each school district, and a number of persons, not exceeding nine, to be overseers or visitors of the several schools. The districts are legal corporations, with power to levy a tax for the erection and repair of a school-house, furnishing it with all proper accommodation, and supplying the house with fuel. The teacher is selected by the committee of the school district, and appointed, with their assent, by the society; but he is not allowed to commence his duties until he has been examined and approved by the visitors. The visitors have a general discretionary power to prescribe regulations, and may at any time displace the teacher. It is their duty to visit the schools at certain periods, to exact such exercises as may enable them to judge of the proficiency of the pupils, and to superintend and direct the general course of instruction. Each society may institute within its limits a school for instruction in the higher branches of literature. This school belongs exclusively to no district, but its privileges are common to the whole society, and it derives a proportionate share (according to its number of pupils) of the school fund. The school fund is managed by a single commissioner, who pays to the treasurer of the State its annual net proceeds. The treasurer remits twice in each year, to the several societies which have conformed to the requisitions of the law, the sums then in the treasury, proportioned to the number of children in each society between the ages of four and 16, as ascertained by actual enumeration, but not until the committee of each society have certified that the monies previously received from the treasury for the like purpose have been wholly expended in paying and boarding teachers duly examined and approved, and that their schools have in all respects been kept according to law. The funds are also distributed among the several districts in each society in a similar proportion.

A system, sustained by funds so ample, might be expected to produce extensive results. It is however remarkable, that the state of education in Connecticut is not superior to what it was before the creation of this fund. The means of instruction had previously been so excellent, that for 60 years not an instance had been known of an individual appearing before a court of justice who could not write his name; but of late years there have been cases of gross ignorance, even among members of the school committees, and the effect of the fund seems to have been to render parents indifferent to the education of their children. The State having by its bounty virtually declared that parents need no longer pay for the instruction of their children, the interest of the former has been materially diminished, and the sense of obligation connected with this subject has in a great degree been destroyed. Schools are kept open about eight months in the year upon an average, or about three to four months in the winter and four to five in the summer. Summer schools are usually opened in May, those for the winter in November; but in many parts of the State the winter schools do not commence before the 1st of December, and the summer schools are often suspended because the public money is exhausted on the previous winter school, or established by a feeble contribution for a short time only. Much indifference is said to prevail both as to setting up schools and the qualifications of teachers; and it is generally considered, that in selecting a teacher the committee keep principally in view the amount of money likely to be received from the State treasury and society fund, and employ an instructor for such length of time and on such terms as will just absorb that sum and no more. The average compensation, in addition to board, is about $11 per month for male teachers, and a dollar per week for females. It seems scarcely understood by parents, or even by some teachers, that duty requires them to devote any greater part of their time to school than the six hours usually allotted to this purpose. The whole number of pupils who attend each of the winter schools is upon the average about 40; the number in attendance in summer is much less. The size of school-houses is generally much too small. They are badly built and lighted*.

_____

* There are but few school libraries in Connecticut. There are about 200 school societies, embracing from 1,500 to 1,800 districts; and there is only one library furnished by the proprietors of the school out of the whole number.

RHODE ISLAND.

Population under 15 - - - - - - - - 35,397.
Ditto - - from 5 to 15 . - - - - - - - 22,041.

In 1828 the Legislature appropriated $10,000 annually for the support of public schools, with authority to each town to raise by tax double the amount of its proportion of that sum. The inhabitants of all the towns availed themselves of this law, and the whole number of schools now probably exceeds 700. There are no official returns from which correct information on this point can be derived.

Every child of a suitable age is freely admitted into the schools. All who attend are taught reading, writing, and the elements of arithmetic; and the elder scholars, grammar and geography. In large towns there are also primary schools for children between four and seven years of age, who are instructed by females. It is not compulsory on parents to send their children. The schools are inspected by a committee appointed at town meetings, and a public examination takes place quarterly. In towns sufficiently large, there are schools especially appropriated to coloured children. Owing to the want of room, boys and girls are generally taught in the same room. The parents, except in a few cases of extreme distress, are able to furnish books, and when they cannot do so, they receive assistance for the purpose. The teachers, who are usually under-graduates of colleges, receive from $15 to $30 per month, and their board. The masters of the common schools in Providence receive $500 without any additional allowance, and the ushers $250 per annum. The salary of the mistresses is about $200 per annum. The absence of returns prevents my giving any accurate statement of the actual numbers who derive the benefits of education from this system, the success of which is said to be most gratifying and complete.

In the six New England States, taken together, there are not less than 500,000 children educated in the common schools. The aggregate population of these six States was, according to the census of 1830, 1,944,688. It is computed that the number of children between the ages of five and fifteen, being the most usual ages of the pupils in the common schools in these and other old settled States, bears a proportion but little short of one-fourth to the whole population. In 1830, therefore, the number of children between five and fifteen in the New England States, including those of colour, might be taken at 488,672. In that year the white population, between five and fifteen, was 473,508, which is in the ratio of 24–9 to the whole. Making due allowance for the increase of population since the year 1830, it will be found that the benefits of elementary education in New England are universally diffused.

NEW YORK.

Population under 15 years of age - - - - - 813,789.
Ditto - - from 5 to 15 - - - - - - 503,884.

The laws for the support of public instruction in this State have been framed with much care, and attended with great success. The following is an abridgment of the principal clauses:

The proceeds of all lands which belonged to the State on the 1st day of January 1823, (except such parts thereof as may be reserved or appropriated to public use, or ceded to the United States) together with "the Common-school Fund," are to form a perpetual capital, the interest of which is to be appropriated to the support of common schools throughout the State. There shall be annually distributed from the revenue of the common-school fund, at the discretion of the superintendent of common schools, the sum of 100,000 dollars for their support, to be designated "School Monies;" and as often as such revenue shall be increased by the sum of 10,000 dollars, this sum shall be added for distribution.

The founders and benefactors of any school on the system of Bell or Lancaster, or any other approved by the board of regents*, may be incorporated. The trustees of any common school districts, within which any Lancasterian or other select school is established, with the consent of the majority of the inhabitants, may agree to make the same a district school. Every school thus incorporated shall be subject to the control of the "regents," and shall make such returns respecting the state of its funds, and the system of instruction and discipline, as they may from time to time require.

There shall be a superintendent of common schools whose duty it shall be to prepare and submit an annual report to the Legislature, containing a statement of their condition throughout the State, estimates and accounts of the expenditure of schools, plans for the improvement and management of the school fund, and for the organization of schools, and such other matters relating to his office in regard to common schools as he shall deem it expedient to communicate.

In

---

* This board consists of twenty-one members, in whom the government of the New York University is vested.

NEW YORK.

In every year in which a census of the population shall have been taken, the superintendent shall apportion the "school monies" to he annually distributed among the several counties of the State, and the share of each county among the respective towns and cities. It is the duty of the board of supervisors of each county, by the declaration of a rate at a public meeting, to add to the sums of money to be raised in each of the towns, a sum equal to the monies which have been apportioned to such town by the superintendent. It is the duty of the commissioners of common schools in each town to divide the same into a convenient number of school districts, to distribute the school grants in proportion to the number of children residing in each, between the ages of five and fifteen, and to transmit annually to the county clerk a report, stating the number of districts which they have formed, the length of time a school shall have been kept in each, distinguishing what portion of that time the school shall have been kept by qualified teachers, the amount of public money received in each district, the number of children taught in each, and the number of children between five and sixteen years of age residing in each ; the amount received from the county treasurer, from the town collector, and from any other source, the manner in which such monies have been expended, and if any and what part remain unspent, and for what cause. The commissioners neglecting to make such report within the period prescribed by law shall severally forfeit to their town, for the use of the common schools, the sum of ten dollars ; and the share of "school monies" apportioned to such town for the ensuing year may, in the discretion of the superintendant of common schools, be withheld, and distributed among other towns in the same county from which the necessary reports shall have been received. When the share of "school monies" is thus lost to a town, the commissioners guilty of such neglect shall forfeit to the town the full amount, with interest; for the payment of which they shall be jointly and separately liable.

The commissioners, together with certain others elected in each town, form the inspectors of the common schools in such town. The inspectors, or any three of them, are to examine the qualifications of all persons offering themselves as candidates for the office of teacher, as to character, learning, and ability. If the result of this inquiry be satisfactory to the inspectors, they shall deliver to the candidate a certificate to that effect. This certificate they can at any time annul, giving at least ten days previous notice, in writing, to the teacher and the trustees of the district in which he may be employed. It is the duty of the inspectors to visit all common schools within their town as shall be organized according to law, at least once a year, and oftener if they shall deem it necessary ; on which occasions they shall examine into the state and condition of the schools, both in respect to their good order and the progress of the pupils, and may give advice and direction to the trustees and teachers, as to the government of the school, and the course of studies to be pursued.

On the formation of a school district, a public meeting is required to be held within twenty days. Every person shall be entitled to vote at this meeting who shall be a freeholder, or shall have been assessed to pay taxes in the year in which he votes, or the preceding year, or shall possess clear personal property to the amount of fifty dollars, liable to taxation in the district. The inhabitants at this meeting may designate a site for the school-house, appoint trustees, and levy such tax as may be sufficient for the purchase or lease, as well as for the support of the schools ; but no tax for this purpose shall exceed the sum of 400 dollars, unless the commissioners of the town shall certify that a larger sum is required to be raised. The trustees appointed at this meeting have power to call special meetings of the taxable inhabitants to carry the resolutions of the general meeting into effect as to the purchase or building of a school-house, and to employ and remunerate the teachers. They are required annually to make a report to the school commissioners, stating the whole time any school has been kept in the district during the year, the amount of monies received from the commissioners, and the manner in which the same has been expended, the number of children taught, as well as the number resident in the district. No teacher shall be deemed qualified who has not received a certificate to that effect from the inspectors.

Whenever the clerk of the corporation of the city of New York shall receive notice from the superintendent of common schools, of the amount apportioned to the city for the encouragement of schools therein, he shall lay the same before the corporation, who shall annually raise from the inhabitants a sum equal to the sum specified in such notice. The corporation shall at least once in three years designate the schools which shall be entitled to receive a share of the school monies, and prescribe the rules under which the same shall be received. The trustees of every such school shall annually make a report to the commissioners of school money, stating, 1st. The average number of scholars, between four and sixteen years of age, which shall have been taught free of expense. 2d. The average number that has actually attended such schools during the year. This is to be ascertained by the teachers keeping an exact account of the number of scholars present every school-time or half-day, which being added together, and divided by the whole number of school times in the year, shall be considered the average. 3d. The times during which such schools have been kept open during the year. 4th. The amount of monies last received from the commissioners, and the purposes for and the manner in which the same shall have been expended. 5th. A particular account of the state of the schools under their care, and of the property and affairs of such school or society.

It shall be the duty of the commissioners of school money to call for such reports by advertisements in two or more of the public newspapers; to apportion annually the amount deposited for the several schools; to visit those receiving such monies, at least twice in the year, to examine their registers and other books, and require such other proof, on oath

or

or otherwise, as they shall see fit, relating to matters connected with the interests of the schools; to make a report annually to the corporation, and to the superintendent. The apportionment of school monies shall be made according to the average number of children between four and sixteen who shall have actually attended such school during the preceding year; but no school shall be entitled to a portion of such money that has not been kept open at least nine months during the year. The common council of the city have power to raise by tax a sum not exceeding 500 dollars annually, on the inhabitants of such district, for repairing the school-house therein, and defraying the expense of the school. The trustees of each school have power to exempt from the payment of all charges those scholars whose parents are unable to bear the expense.

The annual report of the superintendent of common schools of this State, made to the Legislature in January 1834, contains much valuable information. From this document it appears that there are 9,690 school districts in the State, and that reports have been received from 9,107. There were at the close of the year 1832, 522,618 children between five and sixteen years of age residing in the several school districts from which reports had been received, and 512,475 children were taught in those districts during that year. The latter number attended school for an average period of eight months. There was an increase of 17,516 over the number who received instruction in the year, while the actual increase in the whole number enumerated, between five and sixteen years of age, was 13,756. The number of children taught, however, are not to be considered as having received instruction during the whole average period of eight months for which the schools have been kept open, but as having at some period in the year been in attendance. In the counties which have been long settled, the proportion of children who attend the common schools to the whole number enumerated is usually much smaller than in other counties more recently settled, and in which the population is rapidly on the increase. This circumstance is to be accounted for in a great degree by the fact that the former counties abound in private schools, of which there are of course but very few in young States. Comparing the number of children taught with the whole number enumerated in the first six towns noticed in the reports of the several counties of Allegany, Orleans and Wayne (comparatively new), and of Albany, King's and Ulster, which have been long settled (excluding the city of Albany and the principal school districts in Brooklyn), this disparity will appear very striking.

	Number of Children Taught.	Number of Children Enumerated.	Excess of Numbers Taught over those Enumerated.
Allegany - - - -	2,346	2,060	286
Orleans - - - -	3,977	3,459	518
Wayne - - - -	4,207	3,970	237
	10,530	9,489	1,041

			Excess of Numbers Enumerated over those Taught.
Albany - - - -	4,312	5,464	1,152
King's - - - -	600	1,504	904
Ulster - - - -	3,240	4,567	1,327
	8,152	11,535	3,383

These results may be taken as a fair criterion of the extent of common school instruction in the State of New York, and with the exception of cities and large villages, in which there is always a considerable number of children who from the neglect or inability of their parents are deprived of the benefits of instruction, it is probable that the several parts of the State would be found to participate with great equality in the advantages of education, if the number of pupils in private schools could be ascertained.

In each of 22 out of the 55 counties in the State there are upwards of 200 organized school districts. In 11 counties the number exceeds 250; in Oneida, 354; in Genessee, 320; and in Otsego, 310. The number of towns and wards in the State is 820. In 113 towns, about 1,000 children are instructed; in 17 towns, 1,500; and in four towns about 2,000. In 76 towns there are about 20 organized school districts; in 24, about 25; and in 11, 30. The average number of organized districts to each town in the State is nearly 12 ½, and the number of scholars instructed, compared with the whole number of districts from which reports were received, gives an average of 56 and a fraction to each.

The following is a Summary of the Abstract from the Returns of Common Schools in the several towns and counties of this State for the year 1833 *.

* Report of the Superintendent of Common Schools, 1834.

SUMMARY of ABSTRACT, made from the RETURNS of COMMON SCHOOLS in the Year 1833.

COUNTIES.	Number of Towns and Wards in each County.	Whole Number of School Districts in the Towns which have made Returns.	Whole Number of School Districts which have made Reports.	Average Number of Months in which Schools have been taught in the Counties.	Amount of Public Money received and expended in the Districts, (as stated in the Returns) during the Year 1832.	Amount paid for Teachers' Wages, besides Public Money.	Number of Children taught in the School Districts which have made Returns.	Number of Children between the ages of 5 and 16 years residing therein, as stated in said Returns.	Amount of Public Money distributed to the Districts by the Commissioners in April 1833.
Albany	14	155	155	9	$ 6,849 11	$10,088 03	10,624	15,107	$ 6,926 67
Allegany	26	251	224	6	3,390 79	5,381 20	10,276	9,684	3,704 85
Broome	11	143	126	7	1,948 05	3,183 39	5,739	5,214	2,159 02
Cattaraugus	21	184	149	7	1,999 55	3,569 87	6,761	6,090	2,721 92
Cayuga	22	257	255	9	6,895 25	9,528 29	15,216	14,202	7,408 17
Chautauque	24	279	250	6	3,540 36	7,953 61	13,188	11,937	5,308 94
Chenango	19	274	265	7	6,131 56	6,782 35	13,452	11,410	5,984 07
Clinton	8	111	97	7	3,071 11	2,657 93	5,115	6,055	3,149 95
Columbia	18	187	185	9	4,152 59	11,134 81	10,297	11,465	3,831 58
Cortland	11	161	161	7	3,588 39	4,048 05	8,478	7,398	3,483 01
Delaware	18	238	225	7	3,615 98	6,284 67	10,887	9,977	3,520 25
Dutchess	18	206	195	9	5,179 99	14,021 62	9,563	12,997	5,409 45
Erie	21	231	200	7	4,436 38	6,878 12	11,895	12,345	5,330 16
Essex	15	139	122	6	2,346 02	3,384 00	6,199	5,639	2,259 99
Franklin	12	88	84	6	1,923 08	1,634 55	3,781	3,714	2,126 97
Genessee	24	320	313	8	6,025 23	13,711 41	20,452	17,524	6,230 66
Greene	11	148	142	8	3,374 70	6,202 79	8,100	8,485	3,394 91
Herkimer	18	192	185	8	4,041 12	8,522 33	11,113	10,809	3,929 81
Jefferson	19	289	276	7	5,835 53	11,327 43	16,724	15,754	5,911 98
Kings	6	20	19	11	1,861 56	3,633 33	1,730	5,260	2,085 00
Lewis	11	114	103	6	1,750 09	3,056 11	4,756	4,764	1,841 31
Livingston	12	161	155	8	3,922 99	7,233 97	9,429	9,075	3,764 72
Madison	13	218	214	7	5,570 25	6,397 45	13,264	11,440	5,128 44
Monroe	16	232	224	8	6,386 45	13,630 16	15,139	15,275	6,549 71
Montgomery	19	223	213	7	4,568 71	11,071 19	11,462	13,860	4,671 15
New York	15	28	28	12	94,311 69	- -	5,523	- -	84,311 69
Niagara	11	124	117	6	2,227 73	3,662 29	6,006	6,383	2,358 54
Oneida	29	354	336	8	8,082 51	11,552 07	19,143	20,377	8,072 49
Onondaga	17	284	263	8	9,572 17	8,241 54	17,444	17,744	10,047 04
Ontario	14	212	197	8	4,680 58	10,301 55	12,158	11,870	4,848 26
Orange	14	189	175	9	5,069 96	14,267 11	10,538	12,635	4,875 79
Orleans	8	124	115	8	2,653 51	4,425 91	7,092	6,208	2,749 60
Oswego	20	213	185	6	3,301 08	4,832 01	9,671	9,509	3,842 43
Otsego	22	310	301	8	5,820 10	9,705 52	16,770	15,425	5,639 86
Putnam	5	68	66	8	1,408 87	3,079 60	2,925	3,745	1,422 72
Queens	6	76	65	9	2,310 78	5,978 47	3,025	5,737	2,473 65
Rensselaer	19	190	181	8	5,608 49	9,759 46	11,638	14,462	5,239 76
Richmond	4	20	20	10	843 56	2,552 48	1,310	2,397	843 56
Rockland	4	33	32	10	963 23	4,123 42	1,646	2,684	971 32
Saratoga	20	211	200	8	4,289 75	9,123 15	10,952	10,824	4,137 47
Schenectady	7	59	57	8	913 29	1,578 89	2,510	3,130	913 15
Schoharie	10	160	152	8	2,962 72	5,936 52	7,579	8,626	2,915 37
Seneca	10	113	108	9	4,176 74	6,229 14	7,001	6,908	4,061 87
St. Lawrence	24	295	269	6	6,191 19	6,065 75	12,298	12,867	6,615 26
Steuben	24	264	247	6	4,094 13	5,929 05	12,164	11,782	4,265 96
Suffolk	9	128	117	9	2,800 70	7,407 70	7,216	7,422	2,882 73
Sullivan	9	89	74	6	1,776 96	1,297 97	3,349	3,577	2,018 73
Tioga	18	190	163	6	3,348 41	4,861 14	8,625	8,563	3,603 94
Tompkins	10	202	199	8	7,836 89	5,608 68	12,352	11,897	7,856 99
Ulster	14	155	147	8	3,824 59	7,828 40	7,599	10,907	3,910 75
Warren	9	99	95	6	1,378 81	2,199 78	4,189	3,605	1,368 62
Washington	17	253	242	7	4,832 37	9,122 89	12,974	11,600	4,371 50
Wayne	15	190	185	7	4,136 20	6,683 70	11,438	10,901	4,191 17
Westchester	21	134	134	10	3,879 47	11,744 27	7,185	9,140	3,879 47
Yates	8	102	100	8	2,031 76	4,281 24	6,515	6,213	2,215 91
Total	820	9,690	9,107	8	307,733 08	369,696 36	512,475	522,618	313,938 29

THE following Comparative View of the RETURNS OF COMMON SCHOOLS from 1816 to 1834, (from the Appendix to the Official Reports,) will show the progress of Public Instruction in the State.

The Year in which the Report was made to the Legislature.	Number of Towns from which the Returns were made.	Whole Number of School Districts in the said Towns.	Number of School Districts from which Returns were received.	Amount of Public Money received in said Towns.	Amount paid for Teachers' Wages in the Districts, over and above Public Money.	Number of Children taught in the School Districts making Returns.	Number of Children between 5 and 15 or 16 Years of Age, residing in those Districts.	Proportion of the Number of Children taught to the Number of Children reported between the ages of 5 and 15 or 16 Years.
1816 - -	338	2,755	2,631	$ 55,720 98	- - -	140,106	176,449	14 to 15
1817 - -	355	3,713	2,873	64,834 88	- - -	170,385	198,440	6 to 7
1818 - -	374	3,264	3,228	73,235 42	- - -	183,253	218,969	5 to 6
1819 - -	402	4,614	3,844	93,010 54	- - -	210,316	235,871	8 to 9
1820 - -	515	5,763	5,118	117,151 07	- - -	271,877	302,703	9 to 10
1821 - -	545	6,332	5,489	146,418 08	- - -	304,559	317,633	24 to 25
1822 - -	611	6,659	5,882	157,195 04	- - -	332,979	339,258	42 to 43
1823 - -	649	7,051	6,255	173,420 60	- - -	351,173	357,029	44 to 45
1824 - -	656	7,382	6,705	182,820 25	- - -	377,034	373,208	94 to 93
1825 - -	698	7,642	6,876	182,741 61	- - -	402,940	383,500	101 to 96
1826 - -	700	7,773	7,117	182,790 09	- - -	425,586	395,586	100 to 93
1827 - -	721	8,114	7,550	185,720 46	- - -	431,601	411,256	21 to 20
1828 - -	742	8,298	7,806	222,995 77	- - -	441,856	419,216	96 to 91
1829 - -	757	8,609	8,164	232,343 21	- - -	468,205	449,113	25 to 24
1830 - -	773	8,872	8,292	214,840 14	$ 297,048 44	480,041	468,257	40 to 41
1831 - -	785	9,063	8,631	238,641 36	346,807 20	499,424	497,503	250 to 249
1832 - -	703	9,339	8,841	244,998 85	374,001 54	507,105	509,967	165 to 166
1833 - -	811	9,600	8,941	305,582 78	358,320 17	494,959	508,878	36 to 37
1834 - -	820	9,690	9,107	307,733 08	369,696 36	512,475	522,618	50 to 51

It appears, by the reports of the commissioners of common schools, that the sum of 313,938 dollars was paid by them to the trustees of the several school districts in April 1833. The amount expended by the trustees in 1832, was 307,733 dollars ; of which the sum of $100,000 was received from the common-school fund, $189,139 levied by taxation in the State, and $18,593 derived from local funds. The amount paid for the wages of teachers, in addition to the public money, in 1833, was 369,696 dollars ; the amount of salaries being 677,429 dollars, from which sum, however, should be deducted about $50,000, expended for school-houses, &c. in the city of New York. The capital of the common-school fund, from 1806 to the present time, is shown by the following Table *:

---

* Report of the Superintendent of Common Schools.

NEW YORK.

COMMON SCHOOL FUND, from 1806 to 1834.

The following Table exhibits the Capital of the School Fund, according to the Annual Reports of the Comptroller, from the foundation of the Fund in 1805-6 to 1834 ; also the Annual Interest or Revenue derived from the Fund ; the Amount annually apportioned from the State Treasury, and the Increase and Decrease of the Capital each Year.

YEARS.	CAPITAL.	Annual Revenue or Interest.	Sum annually paid from State Treasury.	Increase of Capital from Year to Year.
1806 - -	58,757 24	Not stated -	[No distribu-	—
1807 - -	183,162 96	- - ditto -	tion to be made	124,405 72
1808 - -	307,164 56	- - ditto -	until the reve-	124,001 60
1809 - -	390,637 15	24,115 46	nue amounted to	83,472 59
1810 - -	428,177 91	26,480 77	$50,000.]	37,540 76
1811 - -	483,326 29	36,427 64	- - -	55,148 38
1812 - -	558,464 69	45,216 95	- - -	75,138 40
1813 - -	636,758 07	47,612 16	- - -	78,293 38
1814 - -	822,064 94	57,248 39	- - -	185,306 87
1815 - -	861,457 89	57,539 88	- - -	39,392 95
1816 - -	934,015 13	64,053 01	60,000 00	72,557 24
1817 - -	982,242 26	69,555 29	60,000 00	48,227 13
1818 - -	971,361 31	68,770 00	60,000 00	*
1819 - -	1,103,949 09	70,556 04	60,000 00	132,587 78
1820 - -	1,229,076 00	78,944 56	70,000 00	125,126 91
1821 - -	1,215,526 00	77,144 56	80,000 00	†
1822 - -	1,152,630 57	77,417 86	80,000 00	‡
1823 - -	1,155,827 40	72,515 09	80,000 00	3,196 83
1824 - -	1,172,913 28	75,315 05	80,000 00	17,085 88
1825 - -	1,288,309 47	81,815 41	80,000 00	115,396 19
1826 - -	1,319,886 46	86,429 93	80,000 00	31,576 99
1827 - -	1,353,477 64	81,381 90	100,000 00	33,591 18
1828 - -	1,611,096 80	89,034 96	100,000 00	257,619 16
1829 - -	1,684,628 80	94,626 25	100,000 00	73,532 00
1830 - -	1,661,081 24	100,678 60	100,000 00	§
1831 - -	1,696,743 66	80,043 86	100,000 00	35,662 42
1832 - -	1,704,159 40	93,755 31	100,000 00	7,415 74
1833 - -	1,735,175 28	109,117 77	100,000 00	31,015 88
1834 - -	1,754,046 84	- - -	- - -	18,871 56

| | | | $1,490,000 00 | 1,806,163 54 |

* Loss - - - - - -	$10,880 95	
† - - - - - -	13,550 00	
‡ - - - - - -	62,895 43	
§ - - - - - -	23,547 56	
Deduct - - -		110,873 94

Total Increase - - - $ | 1,695,289 60

The sums placed in the column of "revenue or interest," in the foregoing Table, are generally estimates, prior to the year 1825 ; from 1825 to 1833, inclusive, the sums actually received into the treasury on account of revenue are given.   The deficiencies in the annual revenue of the school fund to meet the apportionment have been paid from the general fund, and are as follows :

1819 - - - - - - - - -	$13,500 00
1820 - - - - - - - - - -	7,000 00
1822 - - - - - - - - -	9,309 81
1823 - - - - - - - - -	8,000 00
1824 - - - - - - - - -	9,000 00
1825 - - - - - - - - -	2,630 26
1827 - - - - - - - - -	18,618 10
1828 - - - - - - - - -	10,965 04
1829 - - - - - - - - -	5,373 75
1830 - - - - - - - - -	19,956 14
	$104,353 10

The total amount paid from the general fund to make up deficiencies in the revenue of the school fund for the annual distribution to the schools is $104,353. 10 cents.   Of this sum, $22,000 has been refunded, in compliance with the laws of 1820 and 1823. The loss to

the

the general fund by contributions to the school fund revenue, after deducting the latter sum, is $81,853. 10.

The unproductive capital of the school fund consists of lands of the estimated value of 173,664 dollars. This sum added to the productive capital, amounts to 1,927,711 dollars. It is computed that the productive capital is likely in a few years to reach 2,000,000 of dollars. The principle on which the apportionment of the public money for the support of common schools proceeds, is to allow a sum which shall furnish an inducement to the inhabitants to raise, by voluntary contributions, such an additional sum as will, when combined, be adequate to the object. Of the whole amount (exceeding 1,000,000 of dollars for the present year) expended upon the system of public instruction in this State, *the common school fund pays less than one-eleventh.* The superintendent reports his opinion, that this proportion of the expenses is fully adequate to the end in view. It would appear that the proportion of the common school fund to the whole number of children has diminished, as, in 1827, the sum of 100,000 dollars was first distributed among the common schools, and the number of children taught was 431,601, giving 23 cents and a fraction to each scholar; whereas the same amount distributed in 1833, among 512,475 children, gives but 19¾ cents to each. It is, however, believed that the income of the fund will soon be increased by augmentations of its productive capital, so as to admit of a distribution of 110,000 dollars per annum, which will again raise the amount apportioned to 20 cents per scholar. "Experience in other States," says the superintendent, "has proved what has been abundantly confirmed by our own, that too large a sum of public money distributed among the common schools has no salutary effect. Beyond a certain point, the voluntary contributions of the inhabitants decline in amount with almost uniform regularity, as the contributions from a public fund increase. In almost every case in which a town possesses a local fund, the amount paid for teachers' wages above the public money is about as much less, compared with other towns having no local fund, as the amount received from that source. The sum now distributed from the common school fund is as great as is necessary to accomplish every object of such a distribution; and it is not probable that any augmentations of the productive capital, from any other source than the sales of the lands now unproductive, which are appropriated to the uses of the fund, will be necessary for many years to come. Neither is it probable that any deficiencies of revenue will occur to render necessary a resort to the general fund, as authorized by the revised statutes. Should the general fund at any future day be recruited, so as to admit of an augmentation of the capital or revenue of the common school fund, or both, the policy of increasing the sum annually distributed to the common schools, beyond an amount which shall, when taken in connexion with the number of children annually taught in them, exceed the present rate of apportionment, would be in the highest degree questionable."

Although the organization of the "common schools," in all that relates to their external concerns, is susceptible of but little improvement, their internal condition is far from being free from objection. The standard of education is lower than might be expected, considering the liberal provision made for their support. This is in a great measure attributable to the want of a sufficient number of well-trained and qualified teachers. It has been a favourite opinion in the state of New York, that seminaries should be created at the public expense, for the education of teachers, on the plan of the Normal Schools of Prussia, France and the German States. But the intelligent superintendent, from whose report I have quoted, is opposed to this plan, on the ground that the adoption of *a part* only of the system of public instruction in those European States would not be successful, *unless other parts also of that system were also adopted,* to which the prevailing opinions and state of society in the United States would present insuperable objections. His observations upon this subject I give at length, as, although by no means unanswerable, they apply with some force to the projected establishment of Normal Schools in Great Britain.

"The system of popular instruction in Prussia is essentially compulsory. The teachers are educated at public institutions prepared for the purpose. Their vocation is chosen for life. They are appointed under the authority of the government, without the agency or consent, direct or indirect, of the inhabitants. Their salaries are also fixed by the authority of the government, and a retiring allowance or pension is secured to them when they have become unable to discharge their duties. It is hardly necessary to say that the leading features of such a system are wholly incompatible with the genius of our institutions. Yet, in order to give effect to the plan which contemplates the education of teachers at the public expense we must go a step farther, and make the employment of them, when educated, obligatory on the school districts; and even this would be of no avail, if the regulation of their wages were left to the districts; for unless an adequate compensation were provided for them, they would naturally seek more profitable pursuits, and the object of the State in educating them would be wholly defeated. It is well known that the standard of compensation for teachers is very low, and it would hardly be expected that the State should create expensive establishments for their education, without adopting such ulterior arrangements as to insure their employment by the school districts. The system must of necessity, therefore, become compulsory at the outset to secure its own execution; the districts must be compelled to employ the teachers, and pay them competent wages. It was probably in view of the difficulty of providing for the successful operation of such a system that the plan of establishing seminaries for their education was abandoned by the Legislature after full consideration, and the encouragement of the incorporated academies, by pecuniary aid, as nurseries of teachers for the common schools, was deemed more practicable and promising in its results. Accordingly, the Legislature,

NEW YORK.

by the Act of April 13th, 1827, added $150,000 to the " Literature Fund," the revenue of which amounting to $10,000 is annually apportioned to the academies, with a view, in the language of the Act referred to, to ' promote the education of the teachers.' That the academies, now 65 in number, are fully adequate to the object contemplated by the Legislature, hardly admits of doubt. In the year 1831, the St. Lawrence academy at Potsdam, St. Lawrence county, sent out 80 teachers of common schools, having previously established a separate department of instruction for their education*. In the year 1832, the Lowville academy in Lewis county furnished 20 teachers; and in the years 1831 and 1832, the Canandaigua academy in Ontario county furnished 50. The Oxford academy, in Chenango county, has also established a department of instruction for common school teachers, and others will follow the example as the necessity for it becomes manifest. By an understanding among themselves, or by means of directions from the regents of the university, to whose visitation the academies are subject, a perfect uniformity in the methods of instruction may be attained. The same uniformity will gradually extend to the common schools, and remedy the inconvenience arising from the frequent changes of system, which must result from a change of teachers, so long as they are not prepared according to any uniform plan. If the academies are relied on for common school teachers, the demand will always precede the supply, and those which shall have established departments of instruction will maintain them or not, as occasion may require. There is clearly no alternative but to rely on such a system, or to adopt one which shall make the employment of teachers obligatory on the districts. All that is necessary to give full effect to the first is that the academies should have an adequate inducement to introduce proper branches of instruction, and this must be found in the willingness of the inhabitants of school districts to pay teachers such wages as will present to persons of competent abilities, a motive to prepare themselves for the business of teaching, and to pursue it as a permanent vocation. The difficulty to be surmounted, therefore, is not so much to provide for the education of teachers, as to make the school districts appreciate the advantage and the necessity of employing them. The demand is not, as a general rule, for competent teachers at any price, but for cheap teachers of any qualifications. So long as this evil exists, the responsible and delicate task of training the mind to habits of correct reflection, thus giving to the future character a moral impulse, which no subsequent counteraction may be able to resist, will in many cases devolve on those who resort to the business of teaching as a temporary expedient, in the absence of less profitable occupation, and who are frequently as deficient in capacity as they are in experience. In some parts of the State more liberal views are entertained, but they are by no means general, and the danger is that the evil adverted to, if continued, may bring a degree of disrepute upon the whole system.

" It becomes of the highest importance, therefore, to provide, if possible, a remedy for it, by convincing the inhabitants of school districts that their true interests consist in paying such a compensation as will secure teachers of proper qualifications. This change can only be wrought by the gradual influence of opinion. But opinion itself may be influenced, and the progress of more just and liberal sentiments aided, by the teachers instructed at the academies, who will go forth among the people, and bring under their observation the more uniform and successful methods of communicating knowledge which they will have acquired. Something may also be done in furtherance of the same object, by correcting some existing defects in the course of instruction in the common schools. Indeed, until this great change can be effected, it is of the utmost importance that the

course

---

* " The regents of the university, in their annual report to the Legislature for the year 1832, after referring to the education of teachers in the St. Lawrence and Canandaigua academies, make the following observations :

" There is no doubt that a thousand instructors might readily be prepared annually for the common schools, a number exceeding by nearly 200 the average number supplied by the seminaries of Prussia. It only remains for the school districts to furnish the inducement, by offering wages which shall be equal to the average profits of other occupations. The advantages of a regular system of instruction in the principles of teaching need no illustration. Experience is constantly suggesting improved methods for the communication of knowledge, and for the discipline of youthful minds ; and works have recently been published embodying the results of observation and practice. With the aid of these, and with such a course of instruction as has been adopted at the St. Lawrence academy, teachers attain, in a very short time, to qualifications which would otherwise be the fruit of long and painful experience, equally embarrassing to themselves, and fatal to the progress of their pupils. The regents are decidedly of opinion that the academies are the proper instruments for accomplishing the great object of supplying the common schools with teachers. These institutions have already the advantages of convenient edifices, in some cases of large permanent funds, valuable libraries, and philosophical apparatus, amounting in all to an investment of about half a million of dollars, as will be seen by the abstract. By engrafting upon the course of studies a department of instruction in the principles of teaching, the respectability and capacity of the institution will be increased, and those who are qualifying themselves for the business of instruction may enjoy the benefits of all the other branches which enter into the ordinary academic course. In every point of view, it is conceived that this is the most advisable method of preparing instructors. Under this impression, the regents take the liberty of remarking that in case the condition of the public finances shall, at a future day, admit of an additional appropriation to the object of promoting the education of teachers, the end may be much more advantageously attained by connecting it with the academies, than by creating a separate establishment for the purpose."

course of instruction should be so judicious in its subjects, and so simple and orderly in its arrangements, as to require comparatively less of those who superintend its execution. Although no system can be made so perfect as to be carried into execution without some experience in those to whose charge it is committed, it is nevertheless true, that the inconveniences to be apprehended from a want of experience and capacity, may be in a great degree mitigated by a plan of instruction containing within itself a series of subjects judiciously chosen, with a view to their practical utility and moral influence, and arranged in the order best calculated to make a lasting impression on the mind.

" In speaking of the prevailing incompetency of teachers, it is not to be understood that the evil is of recent origin, or that it has grown out of an increasing indifference on the part of the people to the subject of common school education. The teachers now are probably as competent, in all respects, as they have been at any previous period of time. But the progress of society in general knowledge has, during the last few years, been rapid beyond all former example, while with few exceptions, the same branches of instruction and the same methods have maintained their ground in the common schools. The standard of education has not kept pace with the progress of intelligence, and the result has been to lay bare existing defects, which in less enlightened periods might have escaped observation."

Complaint has been made that the system of instruction in these schools is not sufficiently practical in its tendencies; that the children are not instructed in the knowledge of the nature of the government under which they live, and of the obligations of those who administer it; that they are not made acquainted with the duties of the various district officers, so as to fit them afterwards for such trusts, and that they are not made familiar with the main principles of constitutional and criminal law. At present the usual course of instruction is confined to the acquirement of reading and writing, the study of grammar, geography and arithmetic. The prevailing opinion seems to be, that it would be impolitic to prescribe class-books by public authority for the use of common schools, and that the choice is better left to the inhabitants of the school districts, the State guiding the course of instruction, so far as the subjects of study are concerned. Voluntary associations of teachers and others have already been formed with a view to improve the schools, by suggestions with regard to books and methods of instruction.*

In the city of New York, the " Public School Society" is gradually adding to the facilities which already exist for public instruction. During the last year seven primary schools were established, having each an average of 128 pupils. The object of these institutions is to teach the first rudiments preparatory to the admission of the child into a public school. The public schools are not altogether inattentive to this object, five of the thirteen having already established primary departments. It would however appear, that notwithstanding the efforts of the Public School Society, the extension of education does little more than keep pace with the increase of population. The population of this city between five and 15, is said to be 52,000. In the public schools nearly 11,000 children receive instruction annually, and in the private schools (the number of which is about 500) about 22,000, leaving 19,000 who attend no school. If even 50 per cent. be deducted for errors and every other imaginable cause, there will still remain about 10,000 wholly destitute of instruction. The annual expenditure on the public schools amounts to $94,311, being equal to $17 and seven cents for each scholar during the whole year.

At the commencement of the year 1832, there were annually instructed in private schools, including colleges and academies, in various parts of the state of New York, about 43,000 scholars.

---

* The establishment of district libraries is thus suggested by the superintendent, in his Report:

" If the inhabitants of school districts were authorized to lay a tax upon their property, for the purpose of purchasing libraries for the use of the districts, such a power might, with proper restrictions, become a most efficient instrument in diffusing useful knowledge and in elevating the intellectual character of the people. By means of the improvements which have been made in the art of printing, a volume bound in boards, containing as much matter as the New Testament, can be sold at a profit for 10 cents. The sum of 10 dollars would therefore furnish a school district with 100 volumes, which might be kept under such regulations as the inhabitants should adopt for their common use. A vast amount of useful information might in this manner be collected where it would be easily accessible, and its influence could hardly fail to be in the highest degree salutary, by furnishing the means of improvement to those who have finished their common school education, as well as to those who have not. The demand for books would ensure extensive editions of works containing matter judiciously selected, at prices which competition would soon reduce to the lowest rate at which they could be furnished. By making the imposition of the tax wholly discretionary with the inhabitants of each district, and leaving the selection of the works under their entire control, the danger of rendering such a provision subservient to the propagation of particular doctrines or opinions would be effectually guarded against by their watchfulness and intelligence. The power of the inhabitants to levy taxes is restricted to specific objects, and a legislative Act would be necessary to enlarge it. Should the Legislature deem it expedient to pass such an Act, and thus make the taxable property of each school district contribute to its intellectual improvement, in a still higher degree than it does already, it would be proper to limit the amount authorized to be raised annually to such a sum as would not be burthensome to the districts of the lowest pecuniary ability. Thus the amount authorized to be raised to make a beginning might be limited to 15 or 20 dollars, and to five dollars annually for such subsequent additions as it might be desirable to make. So small a tax could hardly be felt in any case by those on whom it would devolve to contribute it; and as its imposition would be voluntary, it would be made only where its tendency would be to produce salutary effects."

NEW YORK.
scholars. Taking this number, even without assuming any increase, there will be an aggregate of more than 555,000 as the very least number of persons actually receiving instruction in the State.

The superintendent thus concludes his highly valuable report :

" Upon a careful examination of the system of common school instruction in this State, there will be found great reason to rejoice that results so satisfactory have been obtained, that its benefits are so widely diffused, and that the standard of education is gradually, though slowly, rising. If much remains to be done, it is little in comparison with the difficulties which have already been surmounted. The organization of the system is complete, the public fund secures to it annually a sum entirely adequate to call forth the necessary exertions from those on whose voluntary contributions its support mainly depends ; and with proper zeal and attention (to the creation of which it is the duty of all classes to contribute), on the part of those most deeply interested in its prosperity, the field of instruction cannot fail to be speedily enlarged so as to be commensurate with the progress of the age in useful knowledge, and with the high responsibilities of those who are restricted to it in preparing themselves for the active business of life."

The public School Society of New York, already mentioned, was incorporated on the 9th of April 1805, by the name of " The Society for establishing a Free School in the City of New York, for the Education of such poor Children as do not belong to, or are not provided for by, any religious Society." On the 1st April 1808, its powers were extended to the instruction of any children who are proper objects of a gratuitous education, and its name changed to that of " The Free School Society of New York." By an Act passed in January 1826, the title was again altered to that of " The Public School Society of New York," and its powers further extended, so as to embrace children of all descriptions, whether the objects of gratuitous education or not. It is the aim of this society to instruct, as far as its means extend, all children in the city of New York, not otherwise provided for. It has already been stated that this object is yet very far from being attained, the society being encumbered with a large debt, and having to sustain considerable expense for the erection of school-houses, &c. The yearly income of the society is limited to $10,000. The society is governed by a president, vice-president, and 50 trustees. Any person contributing $10 becomes a member. The trustees may require of the pupils a moderate compensation, which however is occasionally remitted, no child being denied the benefits of the institution on account of the poverty of its parents.

In addition to the laws which relate to public instruction throughout the State there is also a special Act for the city of New York, which, as a county, receives its proportion of the State Fund, according to its comparative population, and is required to raise by tax on the assessed property of the citizens an equal amount. The societies and schools allowed to receive the common school monies are the Public School Society, the trustees of the African Free School, two orphan asylums, the Mechanics' Society, the School for the Blind, and four small schools beyond the thickly settled part of the city. The Public School Society receives from eight to nine-tenths of the whole amount, and is the only one not restricted to the payment of teachers only out of the school monies. The amount received by the city from the State Fund, in 1832, was about 10,000 dollars. A similar sum was raised under the general law, and 70,000 dollars by virtue of the special Acts levied by tax upon the citizens for the exclusive purpose of common school instruction, making 90,000 dollars.

The schools established by law, and participating in the common school fund, are exclusively day schools. Infant schools and Sunday schools are supported by private contributions, and conducted frequently by gratuitous teachers. The district schools, as well as the city public schools, are open to all without distinction. In the city of New York, part of the " school monies " is appropriated towards the support of free schools exclusively, for coloured children ; but in the country, owing to the scattered nature of the population, especially of the coloured children, their education is much neglected, the parents of the white children objecting to the attendance of a coloured child at a district school. The district schools are generally small, varying from 30 to 70 children. They are not conducted as those in the city, on the monitorial system. Very little, if any, religious instruction is communicated, in order to avoid giving offence to the members of any particular sect or denomination. If the Bible be read, it is seldom explained or commented upon. Many of the scholars, however, especially in the city, attend the Sunday schools in which religious instruction is imparted. None of the schools which participate in the public funds are confined to any particular religious sect, with the single exception of an orphan asylum in the city, under the control of the Roman Catholics. There are sectarian schools incorporated by law, but they do not draw upon the common school fund. Manual labour has not hitherto been introduced into the schools. A society has, however, been lately formed in New York, for the purpose of promoting that object, the state of the country being in many parts highly favourable to the introduction of labour into public establishments. In the district schools the boys and girls are taught together ; but they are instructed in separate apartments in the city public schools. In the district schools, the average expense of education for each child is estimated at about two dollars and a quarter per annum ; in the city, at from four to five dollars. The master receives in the country from 10 to 12 dollars per month, and generally his board alternately in the families of the parents. When a female is employed, the compensation is usually about half that
allowed

allowed to a male teacher. In the city the male teachers are paid 800 dollars per annum, and the female instructors 350. It has been proposed to raise the salaries of the former to 1,000 and of the latter to 400 dollars. The ordinary expense of a district school, besides salaries, may be estimated at from 75 to 100 dollars.*

In numerous instances, the district schools are badly organized, and placed under the charge of improper and incompetent persons, owing to the prevailing disposition of parents to employ cheap teachers. The evil is not of a character to be remedied by legal provisions.

NEW JERSEY.

Population, under 15 years old - - - - - - 128,703
Ditto - - from 5 to 15 ditto - - - - - 79,695

THE legislature of New Jersey has not until lately bestowed any attention on the establishment of a system of common schools. The consequence has been, that great ignorance has prevailed among the people. In 1828 many friends to education in this State formed themselves into a society, and procured information respecting the moral condition of the lower classes. From these inquiries it appeared that in the whole state 11,742 children were entirely destitute of elementary instruction, and that about 15,000 adults were unable to read. In many towns more than half the children never attended school, and in 40 districts no school whatever existed. Among the different causes adduced to explain this low condition in the instruction of the people, one of the most effective was the small allowance to teachers, which rarely exceeded a dollar and a half to two dollars per quarter. In several of the summer schools, taught by females, spelling and reading, and some easy lessons, were the only branches of instruction; and in but few of the public schools was anything taught but spelling, reading, writing and arithmetic. Few schools were continued for more than nine months in the year; and by far the greater part were kept only from three to six months. Thus, in addition to those who were destitute of instruction, thousands of children in the State received only a partial and very imperfect education, and in many places not only from disqualified, but also, it is stated, from immoral teachers.

These and other facts, published in the reports of the " Society of the Friends of Education," have had the gratifying effect of awakening throughout the State considerable attention to the cause of popular instruction; and measures are in progress which promise important and happy results. A school fund, now exceeding 250,000 dollars, invested by the legislature, is managed by trustees, and is steadily increasing; while a large portion of its annual income (20,000 dollars annually) is distributed to such townships, for the support of common schools, as will voluntarily raise an equal sum by taxation: this money is also intended to be applied to the purposes of education throughout the community. For want, however, of an efficient agent to attend to the subject, the fund still remains dormant; and no efforts appear to be made by the public to avail themselves of the grant of the legislature.

PENNSYLVANIA.

White Population, under 15 years of age - - - - 581,180
Ditto - - from 5 to 15 ditto - - - - - 351,380

WILLIAM PENN, in his Introduction to " The Frame of Government," which he published and proposed for adoption in 1682, observes, " That which makes a good constitution must keep it, namely, men of wisdom and virtue; qualities that, because they descend not with worldly inheritance, must be carefully propagated by a virtuous education of youth." In the " Frame" itself he provides, that the governor and provincial council shall erect and order all public schools; yet this important object, as far at least as concerns the lower classes, seems to have been greatly neglected by the legislature. Although it was determined at the Revolution that " the legislature, as soon as conveniently may be, shall provide by law for the establishment of schools throughout the State, in such a manner that the poor may be taught gratis," the first step for the accomplishment of this measure was not taken until the year 1809, when it was enacted that those parents who
were

---

* In the large houses in the city, with three schools, primary, girls and boys in separate rooms, and containing together from 600 to 900 children, the annual expense may be stated, exclusive of teachers' salaries, but including interest on the house, pay of monitors, &c. at 2,000 dollars.

PENNSYLVANIA. were unable to pay the expense incurred in sending their children to school, should inform the magistrates, and that the cost should be defrayed from the county fund. But even in 1830 this law still remained a dead letter. The "Pennsylvania Society for the promotion of Public Schools" did not then hesitate to say, "that they regarded the invidious distinction of rich and poor, which that law involved, as the great and radical defect inherent in the school system of Pennsylvania, because it is in opposition to the most sensitive and strongest feelings of the citizens. The feelings of the poorer classes will not permit them to enrol themselves as *paupers*, in order that their children may receive their education from the charity of the State." To support this assertion, the Society stated that there were at least 400,000 children in Pennsylvania, between the ages of 5 and 15; and of these there were not 150,000 in all the schools of the State. The average proportion of children educated in any one year, compared with the entire number, appeared to be about one to three.

To remedy such glaring defects, the committee of the society proposed a draught of an Education Bill, the first principle of which was, to render it entirely optional with each district to adopt the plan proposed; the second, that the schools should be "*Common Schools*," in which every inhabitant who paid taxes should have a right to send his children to be instructed by teachers whose qualifications should be ascertained. The last and most important was that the expense of the schools should be defrayed in part by a tax on the inhabitants, and partly by a fund to be created for the purpose. Unfortunately, however, only that part of the Bill was adopted which provides for the establishment of the latter object. An Act was passed appropriating certain monies arising from land, sales, &c. to be placed at interest, as soon as collected, for a school fund, until the interest should amount to 100,000 dollars, after which time the amount was to be appropriated to the support of common schools, in such a manner as might thereafter be provided by law.

It was not expected that the interest of the school fund would amount to the sum of 100,000 dollars before the year 1840. In the meantime the public opinion in favour of an entire change in the system, induced the legislature to appoint in the last year (1833) a joint committee of the two houses to determine on a system of general education. This committee proposed a Bill which has since passed into a law. In the report which accompanied the draught of the Bill, the committee stated that the number of voters in the State unable to read have been computed at 100,000, and that about 2,500 persons become voters annually who are equally ignorant. Assuming the last census as a basis, they say, "We have 635,849 children under 20 years of age; between 400,000 and 500,000 of these are by the constitution placed under the guardianship of the legislature. Of these, by official returns made last year to the secretary of the commonwealth, only 17,462 are now receiving (and that nominally perhaps) instruction *gratis*."

By the new Act the city of Philadelphia, the county of Philadelphia, and every other county of the State, are each to constitute a school division, and every ward, borough, or township, is to constitute a school district. In each school district six persons are to be elected by the inhabitants, who are to be called school directors, whose duty it will be to determine the number of schools to be opened in their respective districts, to cause suitable buildings to be erected, purchased, or hired for schools; to appoint capable teachers, at liberal salaries; to have the general superintendence of the schools in their respective districts; to pay the necessary expenses incurred thereby; to decide whether manual labour shall be connected with the schools or not, and to visit every school within their school district by two or more of their members, at least once in every month, and cause the result of the said visit to be entered on the minutes of the board of directors. They are also to make an annual and full report of the condition of each school in their district to the inspectors of divisions. The inspectors of divisions, two in number, are to be appointed in the school division, composed of the county and city of Philadelphia, by the district court of the city and county, and in the other counties by the several courts of common pleas in the commonwealth, and their duty will be to visit every school in their respective districts, at least once in every three months, to inquire into the moral character, learning, and ability of the several teachers employed therein; to examine every person employed as a teacher, and if found qualified and of good moral character, to give him a certificate to that effect, which shall be valid for a year from the date thereof, and no longer. The school inspectors are further required minutely to examine into the state and condition of the schools, both in regard to the progress of the scholars in learning, and to the good order of the schools, and make an annual report to the superintendent of the public schools. The secretary of the commonwealth is appointed superintendent of all public schools, and it is his duty to prepare and submit an annual report to the legislature, containing a statement of the condition of the common schools, estimates, and accounts of expenditures of the school funds, plans for the improvements of the common-school system, and whatever else he may deem it expedient to communicate.

In each school division, a joint meeting of the county commissioners and one delegate from each board of school directors is annually to be held, for the purpose of deciding whether or not a tax shall be raised for the expenditure of each district, and if decided in the affirmative, the tax is not to be less in amount than double the funds which are furnished from the treasury of the commonwealth in aid of the schools of the district. If it be determined by such delegate meeting that no appropriation for common schools shall be made by a tax on the school districts of the division or county for the current year, the said division or county is to receive no proportion of the school fund from the State for that year. The proportion of such school fund which would have gone to such division or county,

if

if the appropriation had been made, is then to be given to other divisions in which it may have been determined to make such appropriation.

The want of competent teachers is every where felt. It is not proposed to adopt the practice which prevails in Prussia of training masters in separate seminaries, because the committee consider that the existing colleges might be able to furnish a model school as a suitable course of instruction for teachers, and the superintendent is therefore instructed to examine, with this view, the colleges and academies of the commonwealth, and to take the necessary measures for training a sufficient number of qualified masters.

As country schools may be benefited by the union of literary instruction and manual labour, it is intended to attach a small plot of land to the schoolhouses, which are also to be arranged for use as workshops. This connexion, however, is left to the discretion of the inhabitants of the district.

The most striking feature in this plan is doubtless the appointment of a general superintendent, a measure which had previously been adopted in the State of New York. To this appointment the great improvement which it is universally admitted has taken place in the condition of the common schools, is principally, and I think with great reason, ascribed. This plan resembles the system enforced some years since in Prussia, and at present in France. In Prussia the striking amendment which has taken place in the education of the lower classes is in a great measure to be attributed to the vigilance of the general superintendent. The only difference existing in this respect between the system pursued in the State of New York and that of Prussia and France, is that in the former the care of the schools is delegated to persons who have already much other business of importance on their hands; while in the latter countries the population and number of the schools are so extensive as to render a separate appointment absolutely indispensable. It is to be apprehended that the secretaries of the larger States, when pressed by other public duties, will not have sufficient leisure to give that attention to the improvement of the common schools which the great importance of these institutions demands.

Notwithstanding the absence of legal provisions, the lower classes of the city of Philadelphia have not been left entirely destitute of mental education, a small number of children having received instruction in the " Charity and Lancasterian schools." The whole number of children educated gratuitously in that city, in the year 1832, amounted however but to 6,237, which forms but a small proportion to the whole of the population, which in 1830 was computed at 160,000 *.

---

* An excellent institution was formed in Philadelphia, in the year 1831, with a view to promote the moral and religious welfare of young mechanics. It is computed that there are in the city of Philadelphia not less than from 10,000 to 12,000 of this valuable class of young persons, many of whom are in a great measure destitute of the means of self-improvement. Evening lectures on natural philosophy, astronomy, geography, &c. are delivered, and are attended by several hundreds. A large reading-room, furnished with a valuable collection of useful books, pamphlets and newspapers, is open several evenings in each week. A place of worship is open for them on Sundays, and is attended by considerable numbers.

There exists in Philadelphia another institution of a highly interesting character, supported and managed by an Association, called the "Apprentices' Library Company." Its object is to encourage a habit of useful reading among young people after they have quitted school. The large number of lads who procure books from the library, and the eagerness with which they avail themselves of the benefits which it imparts, are extremely creditable to the youth of Philadelphia. This body was incorporated in 1820, and the collection, in 1832, amounted to not less than 8,000 volumes. The books are chosen by the managers with great judgment, and a conscientious regard to the best interests of the rising generation; embracing works of a religious tendency, and in almost every department of science, literature, and the useful arts. All works having a tendency to vitiate the mind, or to unsettle or weaken religious principles and feelings, are of course carefully excluded. Four evenings in each week the library is opened for the distribution of books. In 1832, the number of lads having books from the institution was 921. No one is eligible as a member under seven or above 20 years of age. It is estimated that about 6,000 young persons have enjoyed the benefits of this library since its establishment.

This institution has very essentially contributed to the promotion of orderly and virtuous habits, and given a great impulse in favour of the intellectual and moral cultivation of the youthful mind. It has been followed by other institutions of a literary and scientific character, which are now actively employed in the dissemination of useful knowledge. The institution may be said to occupy a middle and very important rank in the business of education, " sweetening the toils of apprenticeship by the rich repast furnished in the works of the wise and good, and removing the tendency to vicious indulgence which idleness too frequently induces.†"

† Report of the " Apprentices' Library Company," for 1833.

MARYLAND.

White Population, under 15 years old - - - -	119,437
Ditto - - from 5 to 15 years old - - - -	73,344
Slave Population - - - - - - - -	102,878

THE amount of the public funds for the support of common schools, at the close of the year 1831, was 142,063 dollars. This sum, however, includes 47,293 dollars, belonging to different counties, for the education of indigent children, and is usually known by the name of the Free-school Fund.

In 1825 a law was passed in relation to primary schools. A superintendent of common schools was appointed. The counties were divided into school districts, and a tax on the banks, amounting to about 12,000 dollars, was appropriated to their support. The law empowered each county and city to tax its whole wealth in support of such schools, and each section of a county to do the same, independently of the other parts, at the option of the electors. The practical result has been that the largest portions of the State have not acted under the law, and have no public schools; whilst a few counties, perhaps three or four, are making encouraging progress, and providing for the expense by a general tax. In the cities where education is sustained by public opinion, schools have been erected; but even here, their number falls far short of what is required by the extent of the youthful population.

The money arising from the tax on the banks is divided equally among the several counties, and expended by them at their discretion.

In those counties where common schools have been established according to law, every citizen can claim, as a right, instruction for his children, without any further contribution than his proportion of the general tax, if he has contributed thereto; if not, the instruction is entirely gratuitous. In the cities, the schools of which are governed by local legislation, each pupil must pay one dollar per quarter for tuition and books. The remainder of the sums necessary for the support of the schools is raised by a tax on property.

Candidates as teachers of the public schools are examined by a board of commissioners, entrusted by law with the general management of the schools in their respective districts. The applicants for such situations are only required by law to be duly qualified in reading, writing and arithmetic.

The monitorial system is generally adopted, but variously modified, especially in the larger schools. Religious instruction is not communicated.

The school-houses are situated with a view to the convenience of the greatest number, but in many places the children have to travel a considerable distance to attend a school.

In the country, boys and girls are taught in the same apartment, from the want of suitable accommodation; but in the cities they attend separate schools.

The teachers receive a salary, which is paid by the commissioners; but no provision is made for them except when engaged in actual service.

The number of coloured children under 10 years of age amounts, in Maryland, to 51,103. Some provision, it might be expected, would be made for their education; but such is not the case. A portion of the coloured population provide for the instruction of their children.

There are no means of ascertaining the number of scholars attending the schools, nor the proportion which they bear to the whole population: the result, however, would not be favourable to the present system. It was ascertained in 1830, that in the city of Baltimore there were 14,279 children, from five to 15 years of age. The number of schools was 175, which were attended by 5,250 scholars. To this number must be added that of the children receiving instruction in charity schools, and who were estimated to amount to 1,000. The number of charity schools is not known. The mode and terms of admission to these schools are regulated by their respective trustees.

OHIO.

White Population, under 15 years of age - - - -	445,282
Ditto - - from 5 to 15 - - - - - -	258,998.

THE first attempt in this State to establish a system of elementary education for all classes was made by the legislature in 1827; but it was only in 1831 that any decisive steps were taken on the subject. According to an Act dated 17th February 1831, all fines levied on persons committing immoral practices are to be paid to the township treasury, for the use of common schools in the township in which the offence is committed. By another Act, passed in the following month, the formation of a fund was ordained by the sale of lands appropriated by Congress for the use and support of common schools, and by donations and bequests. This fund is to be allowed to accumulate until the year 1835, when the interest

arising

ar sing from it is to be distributed to the several counties in proportion to the number of white male inhabitants above the age of twenty-one. The lands granted by the United States government to the State of Ohio for school purposes, to which this law refers, is a section, or 640 acres in every township or town of six square miles. This is called "School Section, No. 16," and belongs to the township. In many instances, however, these lands have been sold, the proceeds paid into the State treasury, and the interest arising from this fund is applicable in the township for school purposes.

By an Act passed about the same period, the system of education now established by law was completed. A fund is to be raised by the several townships for the use of common schools, for the instruction of white youth of every class and description without distinction, in reading, writing and arithmetic, and other necessary branches of education. The tax is to be levied upon the *ad valorem* amount of the general list of taxable property, the property of blacks and mulattoes excepted, at the rate of three-fourths of a mill on the dollar, and if it be deemed expedient, the county commissioner may order the addition of one-fourth of a mill. According to the same law the townships are to be divided into school districts, and in every district a commission is to be appointed by the householders, consisting of three directors, a clerk and a treasurer. It is the duty of the clerk to record the proceedings of the board of directors, and to make a return annually to the county auditor of the number of white youth in the district between 4 and 21 years of age. The treasurer disburses the funds of the district. The tax imposed for school purposes is collected by the county collector, paid into the county treasury, and afterwards apportioned to the districts in proportion to the number of the scholars in each, between the ages of 4 and 21 years. School examiners, not more than ten nor less than five, are appointed every two years by the county courts, who investigate the qualifications of the candidates for situations as teachers within the county. If the applicant be qualified, a certificate, which serves as a recommendation to the directors, is granted to him. If no school district be found in a township within three years after the passing of the Act, the money levied for the purposes of schools is to be paid to the townships in which those districts have been organized.

This system, established by law, has been generally introduced, but it has not been followed by those effects which were expected from it. This is partly ascribed to the neglect of some of its provisions, and also to an unwillingness to give an adequate compensation to qualified instructors. Teachers are usually employed by the month or quarter, at the rate of $ 12 to $ 20 per month, a paltry allowance in a State where wages of every description are remarkably high. It is said that improvements in the management of the schools are not attended to, because the inhabitants generally, and especially the more influential classes, are prejudiced against public instruction. Although, according to law, every citizen can claim as a right, instruction for his children in any common school situated within his district, the more wealthy seldom avail themselves of this privilege, being desirous of having their children educated at private schools.

The school fund amounted, in 1833, to $ 550,000.

Nothing is taught in the common schools but reading, writing, and arithmetic. The principles of morality and virtue are inculcated as far as that can be done without the communication of religious instruction.

As it is presumed that every parent can, without inconvenience, furnish books for his children, the poorer classes are not supplied with any from the school fund.

In some of the private schools manual labour has been connected with study; and as this union has produced good effects the object has become popular among the inhabitants, and will probably be imitated in the common schools. It has not, however, been yet introduced.

There is no law which provides for the education of the coloured people. They may establish schools for their own children. Prejudice on the part of the parents of white children universally excludes any coloured child from a common or private school.

Hitherto, education has not so far advanced as to render it possible to ascertain the number of scholars in attendance at the common schools, nor to calculate the cost per head for each scholar. The latter depends, of course, on the number, and this varies greatly: in some schools there are 25, in others 60 pupils. In every township or district, the juvenile population during the winter season has the opportunity of attending a common school, and a large majority avails itself of this advantage. In the adult population of this State, about one-twentieth are unable to read, and about one-tenth cannot write. Among the rising generation, very few will be found who have not had the benefit of some degree of education; and the number deficient in the first rudiments of school-instruction is stated to be not one in 30.

In Cincinnati the common schools are much better conducted than in the rural districts, the instructors being better paid*. The principal teachers receive a salary of $ 400, and an assistant teacher of $ 250 per annum. A mistress has generally $ 210 per annum. This salary is paid out of the school fund; but in Cincinnati the law authorizes a tax of two mills on the dollar of the *ad valorem* amount of taxable property. In 17 free schools in this city there are about 2,500 children.

---

* In the village schools, boys and girls are taught in the same apartment, and by teachers of either sex, as most convenient; but in Cincinnati and other large towns, the common schools, male and female, are kept in distinct rooms.

ILLINOIS.

White Population, under 15 years of age - - - - 79,286.
Ditto - - from 5 to 15 - - - - - 44,023.

A THIRTY-SIXTH part of each township is granted by the United States' government for the support of schools in this State, and a fund arising out of 3 per cent. on the net proceeds of the United States' lands sold within the State, is appropriated to the encouragement of learning, of which a sixth part is required to be bestowed on a college.

The State of Illinois contained in 1831 about 61,000 inhabitants, of whom 47,895 were from 4 to 16 years of age. It was then ascertained that the whole number of children who attended school for one quarter or a less portion of the year, was only 12,000, or about one-fourth of those who were of a suitable age to be at school. There existed then 560 schools, and the average number in each amounted therefore to about twenty-two.

In 1832 the school fund which was annually accumulating by the sale of the lands granted by the United States' government, amounted to $ 82,000, but it was found that if the interest of this capital at 10 per cent. was to be divided for the instruction of children of a suitable age, the number of which was calculated to amount to 64,000, the fund would only allow an eighth of a dollar per annum for the education of each scholar.

In 1833 the legislature of Illinois passed a law according to which school districts are to be established; and it was ordered that the interest derived from the sale of the school lands in each township should be divided annually among the respective teachers, according to the number of the scholars residing in the township possessing the fund, and the number of days they had attended during the preceding twelve months, in the following manner:

"The teacher shall make a schedule of the names of all scholars attending his school, who reside within the township to which the school fund belongs, from the interest of which he wishes to obtain a part of his compensation; and on every day on which a school shall be kept by him, he shall set down, under the proper date, and opposite to the name of each scholar, the attendance or absence of such scholar. Immediately after the month of October, or sooner, if his school shall come to a close, the said teacher shall add together the number of days which each scholar residing in the proper township shall have attended his school, and set down the total number of days opposite the name of such scholar. He shall then add together their several amounts, and set down the total number at the bottom of the schedule, and this total number, after the schedule shall have been examined, and, if necessary, corrected by the school commissioner, shall be the criterion by which he shall be governed in making the appointment aforesaid; but no such schedule shall be taken into consideration unless it shall be accompanied by a certificate from a majority of the trustees of the school, or from five of the employers of the teacher, setting forth that they believe the schedule to be correct, and that the said teacher has, to the best of their knowledge and belief, given gratuitous instruction in the said school to all such orphans and children of indigent parents, residing in the vicinity, as have been presented for that purpose by the trustees of the said school." Sec. 4.

The objections which may be raised against a system like that which is thus adopted by law in the State of Illinois must be obvious to every reader who has given his attention to the subject, but the principle on which the plan has been founded is new, and its operations therefore deserve attention.

DELAWARE.

White Population, under 15 years old - - - - 25,073.
Ditto - - from 5 to 15 years - - - - 15,683.
Slave Population - - - - - - - - 3,305.

BUT little information has been obtained concerning the state of popular instruction in Delaware. There exists a school fund, the amount of which is $ 170,000. A tax is also levied for the support of schools on the New York plan. It is proposed to appoint a superintendent to attend to the distribution of the fund.

INDIANA.

White Population under 15 years of age - - - - 177,234.
Ditto - - from 5 to 15 years - - - - 99,949.

To every township of six square miles, one section, consisting of 640 acres, was granted by the United States' government for school purposes, and by the sale of these lands the State is now collecting a school fund. But it does not appear that any steps have been taken by the legislature to establish a general system of education for the lower classes. As, however, such a system has been introduced in the neighbouring State of Ohio, it is supposed that Indiana will, at no great distance of time, follow the example; the more so, as it is computed that about one eighth of the population, viz. 22,000 children and 18,000 adults, cannot read. It is stated that not more than one child in five enjoys the benefits of education.

KENTUCKY.

White Population under 15 years of age - - - -	251,882.
Ditto - - from 5 to 15 - - - - - -	143,738.
Slave Population - - - - - - - -	165,350.

In this State as in all those situated on the west of the Alleghany Mountains, a thirty-sixth part of each township has been granted for school purposes by the United States' government, and by the sale of these lands a fund is accumulating which in 1832 amounted to $ 140,917. It does not appear that any part of this capital or the interest thereof has hitherto been applied to the education of the poor, nor that any measure has been adopted by the Legislature for that purpose. The consequences may be easily imagined. In the returns made by the deputy marshals of each county to the marshal of the State, in connexion with the census of 1830, it was stated that in that year, of the whole number of children between five and fifteen (143,738) 103,337, or upwards of five-sevenths, attended no school. The following Tables, formed by President Peers, of Lexington, show the proportion of children between the ages of five and fifteen years of age who receive no instruction in twenty of the counties of this State.

1.—Ten Counties showing the least proportion of Children at School.

COUNTIES.	No. of Schools.	No. of Children from 5 to 15 years.	Proportion at School.
Morgan - - -	- none -	893	none in 893
Russel - - -	28	926	10 - 300
Clay - - -	51	959	10 - 180
Perry - - -	52	992	10 - 180
Pike - - -	53	785	10 - 140
Laurel - - -	41	582	10 - 140
Harlam - - -	64	841	10 - 130
Knox - - -	113	1,104	10 - 100
Cumberland - -	241	2,005	10 - 90
Carey - -	126	1,154	10 - 95

2.—Ten Counties showing the greatest proportion of Children at School.

COUNTIES.	No. of Schools.	No. of Children from 5 to 15 years.	Proportion at School.
Bourbon - .. -	1,246	3,019	10 in 23
Fayette* - -	1,122	3,870	10 - 36
Mason - -	1,180	3,080	10 - 26
Woodford - -	666	1,812	10 - 28
Mercer - -	1,043	3,441	10 - 34
Scott - -	690	2,525	10 - 36
Pulaski - -	599	2,438	10 - 40
Washington - -	907	4,119	10 - 42
Madison - -	1,054	3,446	10 - 34
Nelson - · -	957	957	10 - 30

As most of the States bordering on Kentucky have lately made an effort to procure some kind of instruction for the poorer classes, it is possible that the Legislature of this State may take some effective steps towards this object.

* Exclusive of Lexington, where about 500 of 1,000 children are at School.

VIRGINIA.

White Population under 15 years of age   -   -   -   - 315,196.
Ditto - - from 5 to 15 years -   -   -   -   - 186,992.
Slave Population   -   -   -   -   -   -   -   - 469,724.

THE first attempt to establish a general system of education was made in 1796, when a law was adopted providing elementary schools for all the children in the State.   But this law was never enforced, and its failure is chiefly to be attributed to its inherent defects. By this statute, the court of each county was required to determine for itself when this Act should be carried into execution.   By another provision, the expense of these schools was to be borne by the inhabitants of the county, every one contributing in the proportion of his general tax-rate.   The education of the poor was thus thrown on the rich, and as the magistrates, who were of the more wealthy class, were unwilling to incur their share of the burthen, they refused to execute the provisions of the law.   The schools were therefore not established.

No other legislative measure was adopted on the subject of education until the year 1809, when an Act was passed creating " a literary fund" for the encouragement of education, and to which all fines, escheats, and forfeitures of every description were to be appropriated, leaving the mode of applying it to future legislatures.   It was expected that in this manner a considerable capital would shortly accumulate ; the sum, however, in 1816 proved but inconsiderable, and the Legislature at that period transferred to the " fund" the principal part of a large claim due to the state of Virginia by the general government.   By this accession, the amount had so much increased that in 1818 it amounted to upwards of 900,000 dollars, and yielded an annual income of more than 50,000 dollars, exclusive of accessions occasionally made to it from fines and forfeitures.

The Legislature determined on applying this revenue to the education of the highest as well as of the lowest classes.

A permanent appropriation of 45,000 dollars per annum was made for the education of the poor, and 15,000 dollars per annum for the erection and support of a university.

The first sum was distributed among the several counties and corporate towns of the State, according to the number of the free white population, and placed under the management and control of school commissioners, there being not less than five nor more than fifteen for each county and town, who are to be annually appointed by their respective courts. These commissioners have the sole power of determining the number to be instructed, as well as the sum to be paid for their education, and of selecting the children to be sent to the school with the assent of their parents or guardians.   The commissioners are required to make annual reports of their proceedings to the president and directors of the literary fund, which reports by a subsequent law are ordered to be sent to the second auditor of the State.

This law, depending for its execution, first, on the county courts, and then on the zeal and activity of the school commissioners appointed by those courts, did not come into immediate operation in all the counties of the State.   In some, the plan was not regarded with favour from the belief that the money might be more beneficially applied in giving aid to schools of a higher class ; and in many, a difficulty in executing the law arose from the repugnance often felt even by the poorest individuals to have their children taught as " charity scholars," although at the public expense.   But gradually these difficulties disappeared, and now the system is almost generally introduced.   The following Table, extracted from the auditor's reports, shows the increase of instruction produced by the present system, with a continual decrease of expenditure.

YEARS.				Number of Counties.	Number of Poor Children instructed.	Average Cost of each Child.	
						dollars.	cents.
1822	-	-	-	48	3,298	7	03
1823	-	-	-	90	8,531	5	12 ½
1824	-	-	-	98	10,226	4	81
1825	-	-	-	99	9,679	4	90
1826	-	-	-	97	9,865	4	48
1827	-	-	-	102	11,007	4	34
1828	-	-	-	102	12,642	3	87
1829	-	-	-	101	11,799	3	33
1830	-	-	-	100	15,738	2	45

In the auditor's report of 1832, the number of poor white children in the State amounted, according to the returns of the school commissioners, to 31,231, being about one twenty-second part of the whole white population, and probably one-fifth of the number of children
between

between the ages of eight and fifteen. It is therefore evident that more than half of the white indigent children of the State received instruction at the public expense; but as, according to the same report, the average number of days in which each child actually attended these schools was only 62½ for the whole year (1832), it is not less certain that their acquirements must have been very partial and defective. This, however, is mostly to be attributed to the plan adopted by the school commissioners, according to which they consider it their duty to extend the benefits of instruction to as many of the children of the poor as possible; but as the means provided are not adequate to maintain all the children constantly at school, most of them are permitted to attend for a limited number of days only, so that the whole system is in some measure rendered nugatory.

As the instruction required by law in these schools, consisting only of reading, writing and arithmetic, can very well be acquired in the course of two years, it has been proposed to remedy the defect by confining the admission to children from 12 to 14 years of age, and requiring their attendance for the present average number of days. By this plan one-third only of the number of children now instructed will be taught, although they will be better educated. After remaining two years they would be followed by others, who again after the same period had elapsed would resign their places to an equal number. It cannot be doubted that by this method the children would be able to reap solid advantages, and after the lapse of six years it would be found that in this period the same number of children had been usefully instructed, as according to the present system are merely admitted into the schools, and but nominally taught.

The insufficiency of the " literary fund" to educate, according to the requirements of the law, all the poor children of the State, and still more the impossibility of exercising any control over the choice and conduct of the teachers, induced the Legislature in 1829 to endeavour to extend the system of primary schools for the children of the poor exclusively throughout the State, by the erection of district schools. According to the present practice, the number of " poor" children attending a school is very limited. It appears that in 1831 such children, amounting in number to 15,737, were sent to not less than 2,666 different schools, so that on an average but six attended each. The great body of the parents in general send their children to schools which are formed by the teachers on their own account, and as the number of " poor" children in attendance is very small in proportion to those who are paid for by their parents, the school commissioners have no control whatever over the choice of the instructors, nor any check on the mode in which these teachers find it convenient to conduct the business of instruction. Many of them are stated to be incompetent to impart the scanty instruction which is required by the law, viz. reading, writing and arithmetic.

To obtain a proper control over the teachers, the law of 1829 gave authority to the school commissioners of each county, whenever they thought that the purposes of education would be thereby promoted, to divide the county into districts of from three to seven miles square; and as soon as the inhabitants shall have raised three-fifths of the sum required to build a school-house in the district, the commissioners were authorized to contribute the other two-fifths, and to pay a sum not exceeding 100 dollars towards the salary of a teacher, provided the inhabitants of the district contribute an equal or greater amount. At the school thus provided, every white child in the district may be taught gratis. Each school is to be placed under the control of three trustees, of whom one is appointed by the school commissioners and the remainder by the private contributors.

Had the results corresponded to the good intentions of the Legislature, the system of education in Virginia would ere now have been brought much nearer to the plan adopted for this purpose in the northern States; but it does not appear that the new law was supported by public opinion. Of the 105 counties in the State, the school commissioners in 12 only had in the year after the law passed either proceeded to divide their respective counties into districts, or expressed a decided approbation of the law, whilst nearly an equal number in their annual report to the auditor seemed to prefer the old system. In three counties only has an attempt to establish such district schools been made: they are apparently obtaining the favour of the public, as may be seen from the subjoined Table, extracted from the second auditor's reports for the years 1831 and 1832.

COUNTIES.		Number of Districts.	Number of Districts in which Schools have been Established.		Annual Compensation allowed Teachers by School Commissioners.		Annual Compensation allowed Teachers by Inhabitants.		Whole Number of Children at School.		Number of Poor Children at School.	
			1830:	1831:	1830:	1831:	1830:	1831:	1830:	1831:	1830:	1831:
Franklin	-	34	1	6	70	396	150	828	55	299	17	98
Monroe -	-	31	1	2	66	146	120	240	40	107	9	26
Washington	-	49	10	28	400	1,076	1,500	4,497	339	1,069	70	238
			12	36	536	1,618	1,770	5,565	434	1,475	96	362

VIRGINIA.

The second auditor, in his report, observes, that the annual cost of each child in the common schools averages 2 dollars and 45 cents, and at the district schools 3 dollars and 9 cents. He declares his opinion in favour of the former system, but appears to forget that the average number of days in which the children were in attendance in the common schools was only 62, and although he is unable to ascertain the average number of " attendance days" in the district schools, it may be reasonably expected to amount at least to double that number : in this case, the district schools would no doubt appear the much cheaper system of instruction.

But the slow progress of the district schools may in part be attributed to the existence of the domestic schools, in which the largest part of the youth of both sexes in Virginia receive their elementary instruction. Domestic instruction is very commonly thus conducted : An individual in the country engages a teacher at a moderate salary, viz. from 200 to 300 dollars per annum, exclusive of his board. He then receives the children of his neighbours as scholars, and some of them also as boarders ; and thus a school is established. But the teachers to be met with in these domestic schools are represented to be very inferior.

If the number of " poor" children sent in 1831 to the district schools, amounting to 362, be added to those instructed in the common school, it will be found that not less than 16,000 children of this description have received instruction at the expense of " the literary fund." Considering that the system is but of recent date, it cannot be denied that the results are satisfactory, and give rise to the expectation that in the course of another period of 15 or 20 years all the " poor" children in Virginia will enjoy the benefit of instruction. For that purpose, indeed, it would be necessary that a larger sum than 45,000 dollars should be appropriated from the "literary fund." That this will shortly take place may be expected with certainty, as this fund, by an economical management, has increased from 900,000 to 1,550,000 dollars, and produces an annual revenue of between 70,000 and 80,000 dollars.

The coloured population, both slave and free, amounted, according to the census of 1830, to 517,105 individuals, or to about 35 per cent. of the whole population. The number of coloured children under 10 years of age was 183,445, of which 16,221 were born of free parents. It is supposed that the number of such children between five and fifteen was one fourth less, or about 136,584. The laws so far from providing any kind of education for the rising generation of the coloured citizens and slaves of the State, expressly prohibit them from receiving any instruction.

TENNESSEE.

TENNESSEE.

White Population, under 15 years of age	- - - -	272,916.
Ditto - - from 5 to 15 -	- - - - -	157,941.
Slave Population	- - - - - - -	142,382.

It is but lately that the attention of this State has been drawn to the subject of education. Within the last three years, a small sum has been applied to the instruction of youth between the ages of six and eighteen. This appropriation however is so limited, that it can produce no sensible effects, if it be true, as was stated in 1830, that about 160,000 youth were still quite destitute of any kind of means of education. The sum raised was given to a committee, whose duty it is to procure and pay a teacher. The Legislature has lately reduced the licences on liquor-shops from 15 or 20 dollars to 5 dollars, the funds arising from which tax are to be applied to the support of public instruction. About the same time a system of common schools, not unlike that of Connecticut, was determined upon, and some attempts have been made by the Legislature to appropriate funds adequate to carry the plan into operation.

The coloured population, both slave and free, amounts to 146,208, and their children under 10 years of age to 55,895 ; namely, 54,281 slaves and 1,614 the children of free parents. All are quite destitute of instruction, the laws not permitting them to partake of its advantages.

NORTH CAROLINA.

NORTH CAROLINA.

White Population, under 15 years of age	- - - -	220,107.
Ditto - - from 5 to 15 years -	- - - -	129,583.
Slave Population	- - - - - -	246,462.

This State has " a literary fund," arising from bank-dividends, of 70,000 dollars, and it has been enacted by the Legislature that when this sum has reached a sufficient amount, the interest is to be divided among the several counties, according to the amount of their free white population, for the instruction of the poorer classes. No other step has been taken for that purpose by the Legislature. Recently, some efforts have been made to arouse the public attention to the subject of education.

Here too, as in Virginia, the coloured people, whose children between five and fifteen amounted in 1830 to not less than 75,000, (the number of those under ten years being 97,563,) are excluded by the laws from deriving any moral or religious instruction.

SOUTH CAROLINA.

White Population under 15 years of age	-	-	-	120,254.
Ditto - - from 5 to 15 -	-	-	-	71,431.
Slave Population - - -	-	-	-	315,665.

It does not appear that any provision for the education of the poorer classes was made in this State before the year 1821, when a free-school system was adopted on the plan of that in Virginia; and in October 1824 there had been appropriated on account of free-schools 441,176 dollars. About that period, an annual appropriation, from 37,000 to 38,000 dollars, was made for that purpose by the Legislature; but there are no data on which to form a more precise idea of the effects of this measure. About 8,000 or 9,000 children are stated to receive instruction.

The coloured population of South Carolina amounted, according to the census of 1830, to 265,784, of which the number of children under 10 years was 106,036; namely, 103,344 slaves, and 2,692 born of free parents. These children are entirely destitute of education, the law excluding them from participating in the benefits of instruction.

GEORGIA.

White Population under 15 years of age	-	-	-	146,856.
Ditto - - from 5 to 15 -	-	-	-	82,871.
Slave Population - - -	-	-	-	217,470.

There is " a poor school fund" amounting to 250,000 dollars, the interest of which is divided among the several counties of this State, according to their proportion of white population, and applied to the education of the poor. Hitherto, however, no definite plan has been devised to render this money available to that class for which it was designed.

The coloured population in Georgia amounts, by the census of 1830, to 220,017, and their children under 10 years of age to 77,184; namely, 76,469 slaves, and 715 children of free negroes. They are prohibited by law from receiving any degree of education.

Much had at one time been effected in ameliorating the condition of the Indians in this State by the exertions of the missionaries. The moral and religious condition of this interesting people had become materially improved, and their manners civilized. Spirit drinking was greatly on the decrease, and an anxiety highly creditable to their parental feelings was evinced for the education of their children. But the labours of the missionaries were arrested. A law was passed for the purpose of prohibiting them from imparting religious instruction to the Indians, and a few clergymen who were engaged in this benevolent work, and who disregarded the injunction, were for this offence committed to the Penitentiary. It is difficult to conceive any treatment more deeply fraught with cruelty and oppression than that to which the Indians have been subjected.

FLORIDA.

Population by census of 1830	-	-	-	34,722.
Slave Population - - -	-	-	-	15,510.

In 1831 an education society was formed in Florida. One of its reports contains some interesting accounts of the state of education in this territory. In the counties of St. John and Mosquito, there were 579 white children, of both sexes, under fifteen years of age, 238 of whom were under five. The number of children in St. Augustin, the only place where a school is to be found, was 463, and of these 137 children of both sexes attended school daily. Of nine schools there were three, containing 57 children, conducted by teachers qualified to impart elementary instruction in the respective branches of education. Thus, out of a number of 341 children between the ages of 5 and 15, there are but 57 who are likely to obtain elementary education; 80 receive but precarious instruction, and 204 are left to grow up in entire ignorance.

The Congress of the United States had set apart for the establishment of common schools a large tract of land, valued at 10,000 dollars; but it seems that these lands have been lost to the schools by certain prior claims, arising out of former grants.

ALABAMA.

White Population under 15 years of age   -   -   -   -   97,608.
Ditto -   -   from 5 to 15 -   -   -   -   -   -   53,504.
Slave Population   -   -   -   -   -   -   -   -   117,294.

By an Act of Congress, dated in March 1819, 640 acres of land were granted to the inhabitants of each township in this State for the use of schools, and two entire townships for a seminary for the higher branches of learning.

It does not appear that as yet any fund has been created by the sale of the lands granted for general education; or if that has been done, that any system of instruction has yet been adopted for the lower classes.

MISSISSIPPI.

White Population under 15 years of age   -   -   -   -   34,734.
Ditto -   -   from 5 to 15 years -   -   -   -   -   19,497.
Slave Population   -   -   -   -   -   -   -   65,659.

The lands granted by the Congress of the United States, for the purpose of education, in the State of Mississippi consist of 640 acres in each township of six square miles, and amount to 800,000 acres. They have been valued at 2,000,000 dollars. By the sale of some of these lands a " Literary Fund" has been formed, which in 1832 amounted to 30,000 or 40,000 dollars; but no portion of it is available until it shall amount to 500,000 dollars. Not having at present sufficient funds for appropriation, the Legislature has not yet adopted any system in regard to primary schools; and it has been estimated that at least 8,000 or 9,000 children of a suitable age receive no instruction.

LOUISIANA.

White Population under 15 years of age   -   -   -   -   38,637.
Ditto -   -   from 5 to 15 -   -   -   -   -   -   22,869.
Slave Population   -   -   -   -   -   -   -   109,631.

The United States' Government has granted to this State 873,000 acres for the support of schools. From the sale of the latter, a school fund has been formed, but its amount is not publicly known. The Legislature, however, has appropriated about 40,000 dollars per annum for the education of the poorer classes, which sum is divided among the counties, according to the amount of their white population: but little is known as to the manner in which this money is appropriated, or the effects which it has produced.

The coloured population, consisting of 126,298 individuals, with 32,457 children, of whom 5,143 were of free parents, are not allowed to be instructed.

TERRITORY OF ARKANSAS.

Population by census of 1830   -   -   -   -   -   -   30,380.
Slave Population   -   -   -   -   -   -   -   -   4,578.

The Creek Indians who, driven from the States of Georgia and Alabama, have emigrated beyond the Mississippi, are settled on the banks of the Arkansas and Verdigris rivers, on the west of the Ozark mountains. They are represented to amount to 2,500 or 3,000. They are described as being strictly agricultural, and as having settled as near to each other as their farms will admit. In almost any part of the settlement 50 children can be collected within a circle of two miles It is highly creditable to these oppressed and interesting people to learn that they are desirous of giving an education to their children, and have made repeated applications to have their children taken from home to be instructed. The progress of the children of the Creek Indians, when they are instructed properly, is stated to be very rapid, and equal to that of any nation.

MISSOURI.

White Population under 15 years   -   -   -   -   -   59,049.
Ditto -   -   from 5 to 15 -   -   -   -   -   -   32,957.
Slave Population   -   -   -   -   -   -   -   24,996.

By the laws of this State, the lands granted by Congress to each township of six square miles, and consisting of 640 acres, are to be placed under the care of three commissioners in every county, to be chosen by the courts; and the proceeds from these lands are to be paid into the county treasury, until at least two thirds of the inhabitants of a township apply to the court, petitioning that their township may be erected into a school district. The inhabitants of the school district so formed, are required to elect five trustees, together with a clerk and a treasurer; and the money collected from the lands situated in their township, and previously deposited in the county treasury, is to be paid to the board of trustees for the erection of a schoolhouse, and other necessary expenses. To the trustees also the management of the school lands is entrusted. If the expense attending the school shall exceed the proceeds from the school lands, they are empowered, upon petition of two thirds of the householders, to levy taxes to supply the deficiency, but only on the property of those who have children to send to school, and according to the number of scholars each individual shall send. The householders elect from the trustees school visitors. They are to examine, choose, and appoint the teachers, and watch over their moral conduct, and the performance of their duties. The board of trustees shall annually determine what number of children are to be educated during the current year at any of the common schools, free of expense, and allow to the instructor such compensation from the school funds as they shall deem reasonable; and they shall in this choice proceed in such a manner as in their opinion is best calculated to extend the benefits of education equally to all poor children. How far these laws have been effective in spreading education and instruction among its inhabitants, cannot with any accuracy be ascertained.

From the foregoing statements it will appear that there are three distinct kinds of legislative provision for the support of common schools in the United States: 1st, by taxation; 2dly, by appropriation; and 3dly, by the combination of both these resources.

The experience derived in the several States from these measures has very strikingly evinced their comparative efficacy. The plan of taxation has been adopted from the commencement by the Legislatures of New Hampshire, Massachusetts, and Vermont. In New Hampshire, the Governor states that " the effect has been very salutary. Scarcely a single native citizen under 40 years of age, of either sex, can be found who has not been taught to read and write his native language." " It has," he says, " elevated the character of our population in point of intelligence and moral habits." These remarks equally apply to the State of Vermont. Of the common schools in Massachusetts, Governor Lincoln reports, " that the practical operation of the laws has been to secure, in every district and village of the commonwealth, the means of regular instruction to children in the elementary branches of learning; and where there was wealth and population to justify the occasion, the establishment and support of schools of competent character to prepare youth for admission to college, or to enter upon the active business of life. Certain it is," he adds, " that there has never been any want of interest manifested here, either in raising a sufficient amount of money, or in attending to its most useful application."

Connecticut and Rhode Island present illustrations of the second plan, the effect of which has been thus described by Dr. Wayland, the respected president of " Brown University," Providence: " It is generally supposed that legislative effort should be directed to the accumulation and distribution of large funds to be appropriated to this object. I am disposed to believe that this opinion is erroneous. Funds are valuable in this case as a *condiment*, not as an *aliment*. They should never be so large as to render a considerable degree of personal effort on the part of the parent unnecessary. The universal law of Divine Providence in the distribution of its favours is the *quid pro quo*. The adoption of any other, except in the case of absolute helplessness, is, so far as I have observed, pernicious. A fund is only useful in this sort of case, in so far as it induces men to help themselves. If they will help themselves without it, so much the better. As soon as they are aware of the value of education, and it has elevated them to a certain point of moral acquisition, they will not want it; nay, if it be continued after they have arrived at this point, I think it may be injurious in its effects." This view of the effect produced by the establishment of permanent funds for the support of schools is also confirmed by the experience derived in Connecticut. " A public fund," observes a distinguished member of the Legislature*, " for the instruction of youth in common schools, is of no comparative worth as a means of relieving want. A higher value would consist in its being made an instrument for exciting general exertion for the attainment of that important end. In proportion as it excites and fosters a salutary zeal, it is a public blessing. It may have, on any other principle of application, a contrary tendency, and become worse than useless. It may be justly questioned whether the school fund has been of any use in Connecticut. It has furnished a supply where there was no deficiency. Content with the ancient standard of school instruction, the people have permitted the expense of sustaining it to be taken off their hands, and have aimed at nothing higher. They expended about an equal sum before the school fund existed."

New York, by the combination of both plans, has advanced more rapidly in education than any other State in the Union. This system aids those who tax themselves, exactly in proportion to their contributions.

The plan of providing for education by means of funds or annual grants from the Treasury

---

* Hon. R. M. Sherman, of Connecticut.

e e 3

MISSOURI.

sury has been adopted by several States. In the west, a section of land in each township is appropriated to the support of schools, either by the State or by the United States.

Pennsylvania, Virginia, South Carolina and Louisiana have made annual grants for the support of free schools for the instruction of the " Poor." This distinction in favour of " the poor " has been considered invidious and fatal to the success of the system. On this point the superintendent of common schools in the State of New York, observes, " The radical difference between our school system and the provision for instruction in Pennsylvania and Virginia is, that ours embraces the whole population, and theirs only the 'poor.' To this, more than to any single cause, may be ascribed the success of our plan and the failure of theirs."

Mr. Mercer, of Virginia, in a discourse on Popular Education, delivered at Princeton, New Jersey, states, that Virginia and New York almost at the same moment provided and set apart a permanent fund for primary or common schools. In Virginia, a sum of 45,000 dollars is annually appropriated to the counties, and a portion for each county is placed at the disposal of the commissioners, annually appointed by the respective courts, and charged with the application of the sum received by each to the education, by such schools as may be found to exist, of the children of those parents who are unable to pay for their instruction. The entire number of children benefited by " the fund, during certain portions of the last year, is but about 10,000, being less than a moiety of the total number reported to be in a condition to require, for their education, public aid." In New York, with only double this sum, education is provided for 500,000 children.

The success of the New York system is in no small degree to be attributed to the appointment by the Government of an officer to attend to the management and distribution of the fund. The example of New York has in this respect been followed by the State of Maryland, with every prospect of success.

For the information contained in these Notes I have been especially indebted to " The Annals of Education," (edited by Mr. Woodbridge, of Boston,) a work which has essentially contributed to the progress of knowledge by the diffusion of sound views and approved methods of communicating instruction. The statistical facts are principally derived from official Returns, inserted in the pages of that valuable and interesting publication. Although in every State some legislative provision exists for elementary instruction, its extent is, with the exception of New England and New York, far from being adequate to the wants of the population, and even where schools abound, their usefulness is not unfrequently impaired by defective management and the incompetency of teachers. Some interesting information on this head has lately been collected by the " American School Agents' Society ;" a valuable institution recently established, from whose inquiries it appears that in five States only, viz. Pennsylvania, Kentucky, Tennessee, Indiana and Illinois, it is ascertained that there are at least 600,000 children who have no ordinary means of elementary instruction, making on the average nearly one-fifth of the whole population of these States. The juvenile population of Maryland, Virginia, North and South Carolina and Ohio, amounts to 803,219. It appears probable that the numbers instructed in these States do not exceed the average proportion of those in Pennsylvania and Kentucky ; and this would leave two-thirds, or 462,000 children, without schools. How far the employment of private instructors among the higher classes of some of these States may vary this estimate, it is impossible to judge.

The remainder of the western States and territories cannot be supposed to be better supplied than Tennessee and Indiana : of 190,000 children in these States, about 150,000 are stated to be destitute of elementary instruction. According to this principle of calculation, there is reason to believe that there were in 1830, in the States south and west of New York, 1,210,000 children without the benefits of education. With the rapid increase of those States, amounting to 45 or 50 per cent. in 10 years, the amount cannot be correctly estimated at less than 1,400,000 in the whole United States.

This estimate, however, does not include the children of the coloured population. If the number of these children, which probably does not fall short of half a million, be added, it will be found that the youth entirely destitute of instruction in the States south and west of New York do not amount to less than 1,900,000. In those parts of the Union scarcely more than one-fifth of the rising generation, of a suitable age, have the opportunity of attending schools.

POPULATION

POPULATION of the *United States.*

	Population in 1830.	Number of Slaves, 1830.
Maine - - - - - . - -	399,462	—
New Hampshire - - - - -	269,533	—
Vermont - - - - - -	280,679	—
Massachusetts - - - . -	610,014	—
Rhode Island - - . - -	97,210	14
Connecticut - - - - -	297,711	23
New York - - - - - -	1,913,508	46
New Jersey - - - - -	320,779	2,246
Pennsylvania - - - - -	1,347,672	386
Delaware - - - - -	76,739	3,305
Maryland - - - - -	446,913	102,878
Virginia - - - - -	1,211,272	469,724
N. Carolina - - - - -	738,470	246,462
S. Carolina - - - - -	581,458	315,665
Georgia - - - - -	516,567	217,470
Alabama - - - - -	308,997	117,294
Mississippi - - - - -	136,806	65,659
Louisiana - - - - -	215,575	109,631
Tennessee - - - - -	684,822	142,382
Kentucky - - - - -	688,844	165,350
Ohio - - - - - -	937,679	—
Indiana - - - - -	341,582	—
Illinois - - - - -	157,575	746
Missouri - - - - -	140,074	24,990
D. of Columbia - - - -	39,858	6,050
Michigan Territory - - -	31,260	27
Arkansas Territory - - -	30,383	4,578
Florida Territory - - - -	34,723	15,510
TOTAL - - -	12,856,165	2,010,436

INDEX.

INDEX.

A.

B.

C.

D.

M.

Maine, description of the State Prison at Thomaston, *Rep.* 22 ; with plan, *App.* 88.
———— Number of convicts committed, &c. *App.* 89.
———— Punishments for the principal offences in the State of, *App.* 90.
———— Common schools in, *App.* 195.
———— Population in the State of, *App.* 195 ; 223.
Maryland, description of the State prison at Baltimore, *Rep.* 22 ; with plan, *App.* 94.
———— Number of convicts committed, &c. *App.* 98.
———— Punishments for the principal offences in the State of, *App.* 100.
———— Common schools in, *App.* 212.
———— Population in the State of, *App.* 212 ; 223.
Massachusetts, description of State Prison at Charlestown, *Rep.* 22 ; with plan, *App.* 57.
———— Number of convicts committed, &c. *App.* 62.
———— Punishments for the principal offences in the State of, *App.* 64.
———— Common schools in, *App.* 193.
———— Population in the State of, *App.* 193 ; 223.
Michigan, Territory of, population in, *App.* 223.
Milbank Penitentiary, *Rep.* 29.
Missouri, punishments for the principal offences in the State of, *App.* 140.
———— Common schools in, *App.* 220.
———— Population in the State of, *App.* 220 ; 223.
Mississippi, Common schools in, *App.* 220.
———— Population in the State of, *App.* 220 ; 223.

N.

New England, population of, superior in morals and intelligence, *Rep.* 25.
Newgate, London, disgraceful state of, *Rep.* 30.
New Hampshire, description of the State Prison at Concord, with plan, *App.* 78.
———— Number of convicts committed, &c. *App.* 81.
———— Punishments for the principal offences in the State of, *App.* 82.
———— Common schools in, *App.* 196.
———— Population in the State of, *App.* 196 : 223.
New Jersey, description of the State Prison at Trenton, *Rep.* 22 ; with plan, *App.* 49.
———— Number of convicts committed, &c., *App.* 52.
———— Punishments for the principal offences in the State of, *App.* 54.
———— Common schools in, *App.* 209.
———— Population in the State of, *App.* 209 ; 223.
New York, State Prison at Greenwich, *Rep.* 16.
———————— at Auburn, description of, *Rep.* 16 ; with plan, *App.* 23.
———— Occupations of convicts, *Rep.* 27.
———— Number of commitments, &c., *Rep.* 28.
———— Defective state of discipline of female prisoners in the State of, *Rep.* 21.
———— State Prison at Sing-Sing, description of, *Rep.* 19 ; with plan, *App.* 29.
———— Number of convicts committed, &c. *App.* 34.
———— Punishments for the principal offences in the State of, *App.* 40.
———— Crimes and convictions in the several counties of the State of, *App.* 45.
———— Common schools in, *App.* 199.
———— Population in the State of, *App.* 199 ; 223.
North Carolina, common schools in, *App.* 218.
———— Population in the State of, *App.* 218 ; 223.

O.

Ohio. Description of the State Prison at Columbus, *Rep.* 23 ; with plan, *App.* 126.
———— Number of convicts committed, &c. *App.* 128.
———— Punishments for the principal offences in the State of, *App.* 128.
———— Common schools in, *App.* 212.
———— Population in the State of, *App.* 212 ; 223.
Officers of Prisons, subordinate. Increased attention to character and qualifications desirable, *Rep.* 41.